THE CONSCIENCE OF THE PARTY

THE CONSCIENCE OF THE PARTY

Hu Yaobang, China's Communist Reformer

ROBERT L. SUETTINGER

HARVARD UNIVERSITY PRESS
Cambridge, Massachusetts
London, England
2024

All statements of fact, opinion, or analysis expressed are those of the author and do not reflect the official positions or views of the U.S. Government. Nothing in the contents should be construed as asserting or implying U.S. Government authentication of information or endorsement of the author's views.

Library of Congress Cataloging-in-Publication Data

Names: Suettinger, Robert, author.
Title: The conscience of the Party : Hu Yaobang, China's communist reformer /
    Robert L. Suettinger.
Description: Cambridge, Massachusetts : Harvard University Press, 2024. |
    Includes bibliographical references and index.
Identifiers: LCCN 2024003391 | ISBN 9780674272804 (cloth)
Subjects: LCSH: Hu, Yaobang. | Zhongguo gong chan dang—History. | China—
    Politics and government—1976–2002. | China—Politics and government—1949–1976.
Classification: LCC DS779.26 .S83 2024 | DDC 320.95109/04—dc23/eng/20240212
LC record available at https://lccn.loc.gov/2024003391

CONTENTS

THE CONSCIENCE OF THE PARTY

INTRODUCTION "Soul of the Nation"

The name Hu Yaobang is not familiar to most Americans, even those who pay attention to events and personalities in the People's Republic of China (PRC). But Hu Yaobang is not just well-known to most Chinese of a certain age and education but is also still highly esteemed and fondly remembered. He is the subject of numerous laudatory books and articles in Chinese. Unlike most previous leaders of the Chinese Communist Party (CCP), including Mao Zedong and Deng Xiaoping, Hu Yaobang has a reputation that remains bright and unsullied. "Soul of China," "conscience of the Communists," "pioneer of reform," "voice of the people," "humanistic leader," "great democrat"—all are terms that were used to describe him after his unexpected death on April 15, 1989.

Within two days of his passing, students and ordinary people began streaming to Beijing's Tiananmen Square to place flowers, wreaths, banners, and slogans commemorating Hu Yaobang's virtue as a contrast to the CCP leaders who succeeded him, who had brought about his downfall two years earlier. They defied police blockades and orders from city and national officials. They came in the thousands and hundreds of thousands, blocking off the center of the capital, demanding the kinds of changes—honesty and integrity, political accountability—they associated with Hu Yaobang. They stood in silent anger outside the Great Hall of the People while the CCP leadership went through the motions of honoring Hu's life on April 22.

After the memorial service, swelling crowds in Tiananmen Square shouted demands that their voices be heard, that their entreaties for better government, civic rights, and more democracy be granted. This was no longer about Hu Yaobang; it was about the party and the people. The protesters chanted and jeered, they fasted, they organized, they blocked traffic, they defied orders to leave. The party—badly divided, and dominated by elderly men—tried to ignore the commotion in the square while they vacillated and delayed, threatened and denounced, and plotted against each other. Finally they used the People's Liberation Army (PLA) to do what Hu Yaobang would never have done: They cleared Tiananmen Square by brute force on June 4, 1989, killing probably thousands of youthful demonstrators and ordinary citizens. Afterward, they arrested and incarcerated thousands more all over China, expelled the foreign journalists who had broadcast their humiliation, closed off avenues of communication with the outside world, and stilled the voices for reform of the CCP.[1] And in their efforts to restore the party's tattered reputation, they banned all mention of Hu Yaobang in the national media.

The basic premise of this book is that, for any country or political system, understanding its internal politics is a prerequisite for understanding that nation's foreign policies, goals, ambitions, and strategy. The People's Republic of China is distinguished by its determination to control information about its domestic politics—through tight security of its historical archives, carefully controlled research and publication of its own history, and officially approved CCP history "resolutions" that are altered and edited to reflect the preferences and perspectives of the current leadership. Hu Yaobang's life, which encompassed much of the CCP's existence, provides a useful lens through which to examine that history with greater detail and purpose, including many surprises and insights I hope readers will find noteworthy.

I begin and end this book with Hu Yaobang's death. On April 8, 1989, Hu, former general secretary and chairman of the CCP, suffered a severe heart attack during a party meeting in Beijing. Hu had attended few Politburo meetings since having been ousted as general secretary in January 1987; this was the first meeting he had intended to address since then, as it dealt with improving China's education system, a particular interest of his.[2] But he collapsed in pain halfway through the meeting. At the hospital he seemed to recover somewhat, and for the next few days he received visits from his family. But on April 15 he went into cardiac arrest and died at 7:53 a.m.

Hu's death precipitated intense activity by the leadership of the CCP, beginning with Politburo members meeting at noon to appoint a funeral committee.[3] For the public announcement, General Secretary Zhao Ziyang proposed a generous appraisal of Hu's service, suggesting he be honored as a "loyal, tried, and tested Communist fighter, a great proletarian revolutionary and politician, an outstanding political worker for our army and a prominent leader who held many important party posts over a long period of time." Zhao recommended funeral rites appropriate for a member of the Politburo Standing Committee, rather than for Hu's former rank as party chairman and general secretary. But because Zhao insisted that all decisions about the arrangements be approved by the party's ranking elders—Deng Xiaoping, Chen Yun, and Li Xiannian—the public announcement of Hu's death was not broadcast on China Central Television until the 6:30 p.m. news.[4]

Late on April 15 Zhao was advised that there might be demonstrations and rallies honoring Hu Yaobang, but he disregarded them. The Ministry of Public Security, however, warned that universities in Beijing should heighten their vigilance. Hu had been popular among students and ordinary citizens, and his death at the age of seventy-three was a profound shock. The ranking elders, by comparison, were all in their eighties. For the most part, public reaction to Hu's death was respectful sadness and heartfelt grief. Student responses were more spontaneous, with impromptu memorial halls established on Beijing campuses. Students and faculty began posting banners and wall posters expressing genuine sorrow and praising Hu's character and career.

Ordinary citizens, including many government workers, began converging spontaneously at the Martyrs Monument in Tiananmen Square, which was soon festooned with flowers, streamers, banners, and large memorial wreaths. In addition to messages of sorrow, there was praise for Hu as a "pioneer of democracy" and an "enlightened civil servant," whose reputation would be eternal. Some poetic couplets and banners were politically pointed, but most of the mourners were civil and subdued, saddened by the death of a man renowned for his good character. It did not take long, however, for the general mood to change, and for sociopolitical tensions that had been building for months to burst into the open.

By the time of the formal funeral on April 22, thousands of mourners filled Tiananmen Square outside the Great Hall, held back by police and People's Liberation Army soldiers. The crowd showed loyalty to and respect for an admired leader combined with a boiling rage at the party elders who had unseated him. They then lined and often blocked the streets from the Great Hall of the People to the Babaoshan Revolutionary Cemetery, causing Hu's funeral cortege to take more than an hour to complete what was ordinarily a twenty-minute trip. At the cemetery his body was cremated, but the ashes were not interred with the other heroes of the Revolution. At his family's request, a gravesite was constructed for him a year later in remote Jiangxi

Central Academy of Fine Art's impromptu memorial to Hu Yaobang, April 19, 1989. Inscriptions read (left) "Central Academy of Fine Arts with respect," and (right) "Whence can we call back his soul?" (Catherine Henriette / AFP)

Province, at a place named Gongqingcheng—Communist Youth City— where it remains a place of serene dignity, visited every year by thousands of ordinary people who honor his memory.

After Hu's memorial service, public rage only grew, exacerbated by the ineptitude and divisions within the CCP leadership. The reaction to Hu's passing was superseded by a dramatic confrontation between rulers and ruled that would paralyze Beijing for the next two months. It ended with the violent suppression of pro-democracy demonstrations in Tiananmen

Hu Yaobang's tomb at Fuhuashan, near Gongqingcheng in Jiangxi Province is distinctly modern and far removed from cemeteries for other Chinese Communist leaders. Situated in a large public park, the tomb is a unique monument to a well-respected leader, and is visited by thousands of people every year. (Author photo)

Square that would forever be known as the Tiananmen Massacre, or to most Chinese simply as *liu si* (六四—six-four, June 4). When the smoke had cleared and the blood was washed away, after the party leaders had purged Zhao Ziyang and appointed an unknown provincial leader, Jiang Zemin, to succeed him, the name of Hu Yaobang disappeared from nearly all PRC media, as if he had never existed.

But Hu was not forgotten. His family and former subordinates, who were the beneficiaries of his sophisticated mind, brilliant organizational skills, and courageous efforts to reform governance, wrote articles and garnered support for a rehabilitation of his reputation. The party ignored and blocked the issue for nearly sixteen years until General Secretary Hu Jintao (no relation) agreed to a partial restoration of Hu Yaobang's name in 2005. Hu Yaobang was immediately hailed by former vice-premier Tian Jiyun and others in *Yanhuang Chunqiu* magazine—an emerging voice for accurate historical research and reformist policies—as the "conscience of Communists" (共产党人的良心).[5]

As the CCP leadership struggled with policies, attitudes, and succession in the years that followed, Hu's name and his life and ideals became symbolic of the concepts for reform (*gaige*), including political structural reform, that the regime could not accomplish or even envision. Hu's personal honesty and humaneness were universally hailed, and articles in "liberal" media began advocating constitutional democracy, freedom of the press, and other reforms the CCP's new leader after 2012, Xi Jinping, would not tolerate.

On November 20, 2015, the centennial of Hu Yaobang's birth, Xi led the full CCP Politburo Standing Committee in a ceremony honoring Hu's life and career, in effect restoring him to the party's embrace. The meeting did not, however, erase the stain on his official record brought about by his illegal ouster and personal humiliation in January 1987; it did not revise the party's official judgment of his "errors" and did not allow the full story of his life to be told to the public. His *Selected Works* were carefully curated before they were published, and the last two volumes of his unofficial biography, held back from publication for five years, were redacted by official censors to remove any tangible hint of the ordeals he suffered in his last two years of life.

The following year Xi Jinping oversaw the shuttering of *Yanhuang Chunqiu* magazine and a further tightening of restrictions on freedom of the press. And by the time of the Twentieth Congress of the Chinese Communist Party in 2022, when Xi secured a third term as general secretary, the entire notion of "reform" had been hollowed out. Many of the shortcomings and abuses Hu Yaobang tried to correct—the cult of personality, lifetime tenure, ideological rigidity, and a lack of political accountability—have returned in force.

Hu Yaobang was a distinctive figure within the CCP leadership. He was even shorter than Deng Xiaoping—under five feet tall and weighing about a hundred pounds; Mao Zedong noted on first meeting him that he was "just a little guy." His physical stature directed his life choices from his earliest youth. He compensated by making friends with people larger than himself who could protect him, and by relying on his extraordinary intellectual gifts. Hu was chosen for special schooling in Hunan, but the Revolution intervened, particularly when active hostilities between the CCP and the Kuomintang (KMT) began in 1927. Unable to continue with middle school, at age fourteen Hu trekked off to join Mao Zedong's revolutionary base area in western Jiangxi. He was put to work in propaganda, publishing, and youth recruitment for the Red Army.

The Revolution was arduous. Hu barely survived the Long March; he overcame malaria, dysentery, shrapnel wounds, hepatitis, cerebral arachnoiditis, and other ailments caused by being poor, malnourished, and a heavy smoker. He was on the CCP committee of the military forces that won one of the bloodiest victories of the Chinese civil war, the Battle of Taiyuan, in early 1949. During the Cultural Revolution (1966–1976) he was repeatedly beaten with belts and wooden staves, then endured the brutal heat, humidity, and primitive conditions of a remote labor camp in Henan. He was tough, stubborn, resilient, self-confident, and tenacious under pressure.

A poor Hunan peasant by birth, Hu Yaobang knew the land and its people. He spoke with a heavy Hunan accent and sympathized with the overwhelming proportion of the Chinese population who worked the soil, the "old hundred names" (*laobaixing*). He worked for their benefit, not just because his ideology required it, but even when it was inconvenient to do so. During his CCP career, Hu visited two-thirds of the more than twenty-two hundred county-level administrative units in the PRC, and an even higher proportion of the ones designated poor. He liked to make unannounced visits to interact and eat meals with ordinary farmers. Although senior leaders lived in lavish splendor in Zhongnanhai, the former imperial palace the CCP uses as its headquarters, and in luxurious villas when they traveled, Hu lived in the same courtyard residence outside the official compound for more than thirty years, and often stayed in ordinary cadre dormitories and guesthouses when he traveled.

Hu was an avid reader, a self-taught writer and editor who spent much of his career in propaganda, but he was very conscious of its limitations and abuses. He was a poet and calligrapher, and enjoyed the company of accomplished writers and artists. He wrote his own and others' speeches and edited articles for national publications.

Hu Yaobang was a devoted acolyte of Mao Zedong, who advanced his early career appointments, especially to the Communist Youth League. But over time he grew disenchanted with Mao's intolerance, unrealistic policy choices, and personality cult. Hu worked often with Deng Xiaoping but never considered himself a protégé, and was disappointed by Deng's abuse of his powers and his willingness to accede to the demands of other elder CCP leaders, especially Mao. The Cultural Revolution (1966–1976) was a watershed event for Hu that led him to personally reevaluate his career and ideals. In its late stages Hu returned to assist Deng in restoring the party and government apparatus, but both of them angered a senescent Mao and were sidelined again.

In September 1976 Mao died, enabling Hua Guofeng and Ye Jianying to arrange a coup, arresting and imprisoning Mao's wife and her cohorts a few weeks later. A still-divided Politburo could not agree on the conditions for Deng's return, but Hua and Ye called on Hu Yaobang to return to the task of restoring the CCP to working order. Hu agreed in March 1977 to serve as executive chancellor of the Central Party School, which had suspended classes for several years.

With Deng still sidelined but a player-in-waiting, Hu came into his own, as both a gifted organizer and an ideological initiator. He cleared out leftist elements in the school's CCP committee, and reopened classes by late 1977. More importantly, he gathered a talented group of writers on ideological issues and circulated a twice-weekly magazine called *Theoretical Trends* to top Central Committee leaders. It focused frequently on Mao Zedong's ideological shortcomings, but without naming Mao.

Hu's next challenge was the party's Central Organization Department, which was mired in countless wrongful judgment cases dating from the Cultural Revolution, including many "special" cases involving charges of treason, which were still under the control of party vice-chairman Wang Dongxing. Hu reorganized the massive department, expanded its staff, organized meetings in regional areas to reverse verdicts on thousands of cadres, some of which dated to the 1950s and earlier, and personally worked on several hundred cases involving Mao's personal enemies. Ultimately he oversaw the reversal of more than half a million wrongful party judgments, affecting more than four million cadres and their families. Even Deng Xiaoping took notice, though not always favorably.

The meeting of the CCP's Eleventh Central Committee in December 1978 has long been considered a turning point in the party's ideological and political course, starting the era of reform under Deng Xiaoping. In this book I offer a slightly different perspective. The most important meeting at that time was a November Central Work Conference. That meeting was dominated by personnel issues, such as the restoration of several very senior leaders who had been disgraced or sidelined during the Cultural Revolution, including Chen Yun. Hu provided much of the evidence used to exonerate several old veterans. "Reform" was not yet a developed concept but more a set of attitudes supportive of Deng Xiaoping's drive to restore the Chinese economy and become the preeminent leader in the party. Power is the key goal for leaders at the top of the CCP, and the power to appoint one's own people to the key control bureaucracies—the military, the civil intelligence and security sector, the CCP central apparatus, and the propaganda organs—is the metric by which power can be evaluated.

Hu Yaobang's organizational achievements were rewarded with his election to the Politburo and his appointment as secretary general of the Central Committee and head of the Central Propaganda Department. Those two appointments owed as much to Hu's support from Hua Guofeng and Ye Jianying as to Deng's influence. But Hu did not have real power, and the new positions put him directly under Deng's thumb and, to a certain degree, directly in his way as Deng moved inexorably toward his goal of removing Hua Guofeng as CCP chairman.

Hu's support for ideological reform at a January 1979 Conference on Theoretical Work Principles infuriated many CCP elders who may have despised Mao but believed they needed his ideological weight and authority to maintain the party's rule. A furious Deng Xiaoping returned from a visit to the United States and brought the conference to a halt with a March 30 speech on the "Four Cardinal Principles." He insisted on loyalty to the Communist Party, socialism, one-party dictatorship, and Mao Zedong Thought. Hu beat a hasty retreat, but the damage was done, both to his relationship with Deng and to the dynamics of the CCP leadership in a reformist era.

Hu's organizational skills, ideological creativity, and growing popularity both within and outside the party kept his relationship with Deng from unraveling completely. At the meeting of the Twelfth Central Committee in 1982, Hu was formally chosen as general secretary, but his power was blunted by Hu's being under the direction of both Deng Xiaoping and Chen Yun, who in position and influence had grown to near parity with Deng. As historian Yang Jisheng put it, "Deng Xiaoping and Chen Yun were evenly matched, checked and balanced, neither could push the other out, neither could do without the other. On some major issues, they both had to agree before it would work."[6] Unfortunately for Hu, and for Premier Zhao Ziyang as well, Deng and Chen Yun seldom spoke to each other and refrained from attending Politburo Standing Committee meetings together. Their competition for power—while not widely recognized outside of China—was ultimately responsible not only for Hu's and Zhao's failures as general secretary, but also for the party's inability to deal with public discontent in the late 1980s.

As head of the Central Secretariat, Hu was able to push forward some of the regime's most far-reaching reforms, including the dissolution of the commune system and the opening up of special economic zones. Some of the reforms later attributed to Deng were actually Hu Yaobang's innovations that Deng adopted after Tiananmen.[7] Hu's relations with Chen Yun were frosty. Chen's supporters attacked Hu furiously on ideological issues for several years, while Chen criticized Deng indirectly by disparaging Hu, most notably in 1983 after Hu had given a speech advocating comprehensive reform. Hu's own relationship with Deng deteriorated under the hammer blows of increasingly open attacks by both Deng's and Chen's supporters and from Hu's own efforts to persuade the two to step down from the leadership in 1985–1986.

In the end, the October 1986 death of Hu's stalwart defender, Ye Jianying, may have impelled Deng and Chen (along with Li Xiannian) to agree that Hu had to go. Hu was overthrown in a "palace coup," planned and executed by these same elders, in a procedure that went directly against the CCP's own party charter. The proximate cause was student demonstrations on several campuses in December against the regime's failure to bring about the political and economic reforms it had been promising. Charges were laid against Hu that he "violated principles of the party's collective leadership and erred on issues of major political principles," although the details behind the accusations were never officially made public.[8] These charges were rejected by Hu after a long review of his own records and have been called into question by party historians through subsequent published research. The charges were very similar to the "miscarriage of justice" cases (*yuan jia cuo an*) Hu so successfully and massively reversed in 1977–1978. But Hu died before his own verdict could be reversed, and the CCP has refused to review it since that time.

Hu's actual ouster was contrived and ugly. Given the anxiety felt by party elders over the student demonstrations in Shanghai and Beijing critical of official corruption, Deng called the elders together at his home in late December and blamed the outbreaks on Hu Yaobang's "ineffective opposition to bourgeois liberalization [foreign influence]." He made the same charge in a subsequent meeting with some of Hu's younger colleagues. Hu was willing to sacrifice his own position to preserve changes already achieved, and he submitted his resignation personally to Deng in early January 1987. Deng ordered a party "life meeting" (*shenghuohui*)—usually a ritualized criticism and self-criticism session within one's peer group—to be convened by the Central Advisory Commission (CAC). For five consecutive days in January, nearly every member of the Politburo and Central Secretariat, together with selected CAC members, criticized Hu "until I stank," as

Hu described it, leaving him isolated, humiliated, and in tears.[9] On January 16, Deng and Chen Yun participated in an expanded Politburo meeting that recommended Hu be relieved as general secretary but allowed to remain on the Politburo. Just over two years later, Hu was dead.

Hu's life and career unfold in the pages to follow not as hagiography or an example of unrealistic virtue, but as the story of a capable and decent man operating in a system that did not always reward decency and innovation. In the end, it is a tragic story of one man's brave effort to bring about social, economic, and political improvement for the many, but losing out to the greed, envy, and hunger for power of the few. He was not a hero; he often knuckled under to men he believed wiser or more powerful than himself. But he had a strength, dignity, and integrity that inspired many of his subordinates and that still resonates today with people who believe the Communist Party can reform itself. His is a story that deserves to be told, as the world outside of the People's Republic of China struggles to understand Xi Jinping and what he has done, or undone.

Most of the documentary evidence used in this book is from Chinese-language articles written during 2006–2015 in historical periodical magazines, personal memoirs of senior party officials and military officers, and the pathbreaking books of historians like Gao Hua, Yang Jisheng, and many others who mostly published their works in Hong Kong. The internet made many of the history magazines that published short monographs of CCP history available to a wider audience outside of China. Magazines like *Yanhuang Chunqiu* and *Leader*, websites like Gongshiwang (Consensus Network) and Aisixiang (Love Thought) Network, and especially the Hu Yaobang Historical Materials Information Network (胡耀邦史料信息网 *Hu Yaobang shiliao xinxi wang*—hereafter abbreviated HYBSL) have been invaluable sources. Many of the articles cited in this book were on websites that subsequently have closed, or they have been taken down from other sites that remain open. Xi Jinping's clampdown on these magazines and websites and the 2019 suppression of dissent in Hong Kong have stilled most, but not all, of these voices.

Hu Yaobang was an honorable man, talented and optimistic and tolerant. His admirers and friends revere him to this day for his virtues and agree that he was the "conscience of the Communist Party" and the "soul of the nation." But Hu failed as a political reformer, and his successors have not learned, or been enabled, to do much better. Arguably, they are doing worse, and we should ask why.

1   Born to the Revolution

On November 20, 1915, Liu Minglun, wife of Hu Zulun, a poor peasant and part-time coal carrier of Cangfang, a village in Liuyang County, eastern Hunan Province, gave birth to a boy. The child lived, and his parents called him *jiu yazi,* or "ninth kid." Three days after the boy was born, a respected uncle was asked to give him a suitable name and suggested *yao-bang,* based on *yao* 耀, meaning glorious, and *bang* 帮, meaning nation or state. (The uncle's perusal of the Chinese classic *Book of Songs* had led him to believe the boy might become a worthy official.) Unlike many of his Communist Party colleagues, Hu Yaobang never changed his name.[1]

Peasant Origins

The Hu family dated their arrival in Cangfang, situated in a poor agricultural region in the rugged hills along the Hunan-Jiangxi border, to the mid-1600s, when their forebears had fled social instability in Jiangxi. Because of their Jiangxi origins, and probably because of their preservation of cultural and linguistic traditions of that region, the family was considered a "guest family" (*kejia,* or more commonly, Hakka). As such, they probably were subjected to some discrimination by local inhabitants who traced their roots back much further. The Hu family house, for example, was on inferior land—in an isolated valley about a mile from the main part of the village, backing up onto a low, steep hillside.

Being Hakka is a storied status in China, associated with a readiness to migrate en masse from troubled areas in the north to less populated regions in southern and central China. Versions of Hakka history trace three to five major migrations, dating back to the Qin Dynasty (221–206 BCE), but in larger numbers in the early Song Dynasty (960–1279 CE) and the Ming

Dynasty (1368–1644). The Hakka are a subgroup of the majority Han population and are not a recognized minority in China. But they have retained a separate identity in many areas, maintaining a distinct dialect of Chinese and various other Hakka cultural traditions. Today, being Hakka is more a matter of self-identification than of locality or language. Hu Yaobang was definitely Hakka, born into a Hakka family residing in an administrative district that was more than 60 percent Hakka in the early twentieth century.[2]

Hakka pride themselves on their independent spirit, boldness, and readiness to take action. They are considered tough, resilient, straightforward, and inured to hardship. They value education, fairness, and ethical behavior. Hakka families usually did not bind women's feet, and extended families often pooled resources to ensure that educational opportunities were made available without cost to young males.[3] One might also note that the Hakka have a history of rebellion against perceived oppression. For example, most of the leaders of the Taiping Rebellion, which nearly brought down the Qing Dynasty in the mid-nineteenth century, were Hakka. Two founding leaders of the Kuomintang, Sun Yat-sen and Liao Chung-kai, and several prominent Nationalist Army generals, were Hakka. And a significant number of Hakkas joined the Chinese Communist Party in its early revolutionary phase, becoming key leaders of the party, the Red Army, and subsequently the PRC government. In addition to Hu Yaobang, they included Zhu De and Ye Jianying, two of the CCP's most prominent military leaders; Li Lisan, one of the party's pioneers; and according to some accounts, Deng Xiaoping.[4]

Liuyang County was a center of revolutionary fervor in early twentieth-century China. Depopulated by famines, insurrections, and punitive taxes during the Qing Dynasty, Liuyang continued to be a locus of peasant unrest after the Taiping Rebellion was quelled in 1864. Later small-scale rebellions, though unsuccessful, helped bring about the fall of the Qing Dynasty and the establishment of the Republic of China in 1911. By the time of Hu's birth in 1915, however, the Republic was already dissolving as fractious local warlord armies contended for territorial hegemony and the right to establish a national government. Hunan was a central battleground, crisscrossed by feuding militias into the late 1920s. Absent a governing authority, local landlords and bandits made life miserable for most peasants, who began to organize in peasant associations to protect themselves and their interests. Mao Zedong would later do his best to stoke the antagonisms between Hunan peasants and landlords into a revolutionary movement.[5]

Hu Yaobang's father, Hu Zulun, was born in 1882 in the same house where he later raised his own family. His father, Hu Chenghan, had a rudimentary education and took steps to ensure that his sons were schooled. But Hu Chenghan died at age thirty-eight, six years after his wife had succumbed to illness. Fourteen-year-old Hu Zulun, his brother, and his sister passed into the care of their uncle, who provided as best he could, but the family fell on hard times. Within a short time Hu Zulun married Liu Minglun, daughter of a poor peasant and part-time fireworks maker from Wenjia City, about six miles from Cangfang. As with impoverished families all over China, endemic disease and poor sanitation caused the early death of several of the six sons and six (other sources say four) daughters born to the couple.

Hu Zulun had about an acre of land, on which he grew rice and vegetables, but it was not enough to provide for his family. So he gathered firewood and later took a daily round-trip walk of more than twelve miles to mining areas along the Hunan-Jiangxi border to buy coal for resale. It was grueling work; Hu Yaobang later recalled that his father's shoulders had swellings the size of small bags from carrying the heavy loads. He was so poor he resorted to smoking the leaves of local tong oil trees rather than regular tobacco.[6] His wife took up weaving at night, both to clothe her family and to supplement the family income by selling the simple material at the local market.[7]

The village government and CCP committee have endeavored to preserve Hu Yaobang's native village, even though he left it at a young age, rarely returned, and never supported projects to develop it economically. In 1995 the committee restored the house, which had fallen into disrepair after the departure of most of the family. It is now a nationally designated tourist attraction, with a museum of many photographs and artifacts and a commemorative hall displaying a statue of Hu Yaobang. The house stands as an example of the plain, hard life of Hunan peasants. Made of earthen brick and wood, with a blue-green ceramic tile roof, it has been painted with ocher inside and out, but is heavily stained and weathered by high humidity and frequent rainfall. The house is large—nineteen rooms and more than forty-eight hundred square feet—but it always held at least two families. Hu Zulun and his family occupied seven rooms, about twenty-one hundred square feet.[8] Inside, it is dark and austere, with little furniture, no artwork, and only the necessary items for a hand-to-mouth existence. Still, with a small brook running nearby and ample foliage providing shade, the house conveys tranquility.

Hu Yaobang's ancestral home, in Cangfang village, Hunan Province. A poor, remote Hakka settlement near Hunan's border with Jiangxi Province. As a boy, Hu walked more than 12 miles round-trip to elementary school. (Author photo)

"Ninth kid" was small and thin, but amiable and well-behaved. He took on the usual chores of a small child in a rural village, helping to gather firewood and tending livestock. His parents soon noted that he was intellectually curious and interested in reading, so the uncle who named him, Hu Zuyi, enrolled him in school at age five, with fees paid collectively by the Hu clan. Two years later the uncle took him to a larger elementary school about three miles from home, where Hu Yaobang started on a "classical" education, reading and reciting from books like the *Thousand Character Classic* and the Confucian *Three-Character Classic*. He surprised his teachers with his quick learning, prodigious memory, and flair for simple poetry.[9]

Hu Zuyi was so impressed by his nephew's academic ability that in 1925 he got the boy enrolled in the nearest government-sponsored upper elementary school, in Wenjia township. The Liren elementary school, a more modern school, taught a Westernized curriculum that included Chinese language, mathematics, geography, history, physical education, and, later, Sun Yat-sen's *Three People's Principles*.[10] The family could not afford to board the ten-year-old at the school, so Hu had to walk there and back every day, a total of about twelve and a half miles. Sometimes his father accompanied him, but more often he walked by himself, which made attending school a form of both physical and intellectual training. Later he credited his ability to survive the Long March in 1934 to four years of walking to a distant school.[11]

Hu Yaobang, recognized by his teachers as one of the brightest students in the school, was also one of the poorest and smallest. He not only was unable to board at the school but also was obliged to bring his own meals from home. That made him a target of some classmates' derision, but Hu later told his daughter that the bullying had only made him work harder. He had some protection from his cousin Yang Shijun, who recalled that, being older and stronger, he had kept the bullies at bay while Hu, being smarter, helped him with his homework. Hu later acknowledged his appreciation for the moral and financial support he received from some of his teachers.[12]

At the Liren school, Hu Yaobang's elementary education merged with the sociopolitical change going on in south-central China. The political situation had developed rapidly after the May Fourth movement of 1919. Thousands of youths organized themselves into political action groups, most prominently the Kuomintang (KMT) under Sun Yat-sen, and the Communist Party of China, founded in Shanghai in 1921. Both parties were supported financially and politically by the Communist International Movement (Comintern), headquartered in Moscow.

Despite Comintern orders for the two parties to cooperate, there was intense distrust and incessant maneuvering between them; the Communist Party was considered the more radical and dangerous to foreign interests and the sociopolitical status quo. In 1924 Sun set up the Whampoa Military Academy in Guangzhou and began training an army to unify China under the KMT. But he died in early 1925, and party leadership passed eventually to Chiang Kai-shek. Chiang, a military officer, was highly distrustful of the Communist Party, though he maintained the fragile "united front" the two parties had established in 1924. He began planning for what he would term the Northern Expedition, his campaign to topple the main warlords in central and eastern China. One of its principal routes was to go through Hunan.

At Hu Yaobang's school, the principal, Chen Shiqiao, and three other teachers had secretly joined the Communist Party. Chen was secretary of the regional branch and held meetings in the school. He actively indoctrinated students with Marxist-Leninist ideas and literature, and encouraged them with the kind of patriotic and antiforeign fervor that was increasingly common among China's young intellectuals. Hu and Yang Shijun learned a bit about social activism along with their mathematics and geography. Yang joined the Communist Youth League in 1925.

Party members at the school had begun to advocate for peasant activism and organization outside the school, in line with ideas developed in the Guangzhou Peasant Movement Training Institute by Peng Pai and Mao Zedong. In early 1926 Hunanese peasant organizers from the Institute fanned out across the province, encouraging poor farmers to form peasant associations to demand lower rents and lower interest rates from local landlords. The associations grew rapidly, with more than nine thousand peasants joining 586 village-level associations in Liuyang County alone.[13] According to Hu's biography, his father, mother, older brother, and other relatives became involved in peasant association work in their village.[14] Before long an element of "red terror" arose in parts of Hunan, and armed peasant bands killed a number of landlords.

By July 1926 Chiang Kai-shek had consolidated his control over the Kuomintang and, with a National Revolutionary Army (NRA) of more than one hundred thousand men funded and armed in part by the Soviet Union, he began the Northern Expedition against Wu Peifu and Sun Chuanfang, the two warlords who ruled central and eastern China, respectively. With enthusiastic support from local peasant associations, the army moved quickly through Hunan, occupying Changsha, the provincial capital, in July. By November the NRA had captured the Yangzi River port of Wuhan, where they established a temporary capital of the Republic of China. Chiang then led his army east, defeating the remaining forces of Sun Chuanfang and entering Shanghai in late March 1927.[15]

In Shanghai, Chiang decided to forcibly dissolve the united front with the Communist Party and purge the Kuomintang of all Communist influence. He ordered the arrest and killing of thousands of Communist Party members in Shanghai and elsewhere in southern China. He purged left-wing KMT members from the party's headquarters, which he moved from Wuhan to Nanjing. In a matter of weeks, membership in the Communist Party dropped from near sixty thousand nationally to less than ten thousand. Thousands of peasant association members were killed in the "white terror," when local landlord militias took revenge for the red terrors of the previous year.

In Liuyang, a ragtag peasant militia marched on Changsha in mid-May 1927, but they were easily defeated by KMT forces, and many were killed.[16] Subsequently the new KMT government in Liuyang began inquiries into earlier Communist activity in the county, and the Liren elementary school was closed for investigation. Chen Shiqiao and the other CCP members on the faculty fled, but most were subsequently captured and executed. Hu paid his respects at the homes of his absent teachers and heard rumors daily of arrests and summary executions. He had joined the Communist Children's Brigade at the school, but he was not held to account for it, and classes resumed by late summer.

Meanwhile, the Communist Party Central Committee attempted to regroup after the disasters in Shanghai and elsewhere, gathering in Wuhan in late April 1927 to reorganize and strike back against the KMT. It set plans for armed uprisings in various cities in southern China, in the hope that these would lead to widespread peasant revolts. The most important action was the Nanchang Uprising, essentially a mutiny inside a KMT army garrison in the Jiangxi provincial capital. Led by Zhou Enlai, Zhu De, and a few others, it began on August 1, 1927—a date commemorated to this day as the birth of the Chinese Red Army (which became the People's Liberation Army). Initially the twenty thousand Communist troops succeeded in seizing the garrison and capturing a large quantity of weapons and ammunition; but a strong KMT counterattack drove the rebels south, where they were harassed and decimated by other loyalist forces moving north from Guangdong. Due to high casualties and desertions, Zhu De led the surviving troops, fewer than two thousand, into the rugged Jinggangshan area of western Jiangxi, where they set up a base.[17]

A Central Committee meeting passed a resolution on August 7 setting the new direction of the CCP's revolutionary activities as leading an agrarian revolution and establishing a workers' and peasants' democratic republic. Mao Zedong had been assigned the task of attacking the Hunan provincial capital, Changsha. The so-called Autumn Harvest Uprising was scheduled to begin on September 7, 1927, but a postponement to September 11 allowed Mao a few more days to gather troops in the eastern Hunan-Jiangxi border region.

The three mixed regiments of about five thousand CCP soldiers and armed peasants were no match for the KMT troops stationed in Changsha, however, and by September 14 Mao gave the order to retreat and regroup in Wenjia, where Hu's school was still in session. On the evening of September 20, Mao addressed the remnants of his forces while awaiting the arrival of other units on the run after the Nanchang Uprising. He spoke in the exercise field of the Liren school, where Hu Yaobang and Yang Shijun, seeing Mao for the first time, listened intently. Sitting on a brick wall to get an unobstructed view, the two saw a tall, long-haired young man in a home-spun tunic speaking in a Hunan accent to a disparate but disciplined group of soldiers, armed peasants, and miners, telling them that they had lost some battles and needed to retreat.

That was no big deal, he said. It would be necessary for the success of the revolution to withdraw from active confrontation with KMT troops in urban areas and to seek sanctuary in isolated areas. The Red Army was just a small stone, he said, and Chiang Kai-shek was a large pot, but the day would come when the small stone would smash that pot, because the people were on the side of the Red Army. The young watchers on the wall were thrilled that they had seen such a splendid leader, and that night both set their lives on course for the revolution. Mao and his troops soon headed south, and life at the school returned to a degree of normalcy.[18]

In 1929 a young scholar from Liuyang County named Hu Jixian returned from study in Japan and persuaded the county government to establish the Liuyang County junior middle school. He recruited about twenty university-trained teachers and served as principal of the new, Western-style educational facility. As a boarding school, it was equipped with dormitories, athletic facilities, and a dining hall, in addition to its several classrooms. and its curriculum included English, mathematics, physics, history, geography, art, and music. Admission was based on competitive examinations, and Hu Yaobang and Yang Shijun both passed, with Hu's score putting him in the top ten of the fifty students enrolled in the first class. Hu's family managed to come up with tuition, room, and board—more than thirty silver dollars per year—and their talented young son headed off to Liuyang, about fifty miles from home, for the next phase in what they probably hoped would be a brilliant career as a scholar-official.[19]

Hu Yaobang thrived in this new environment, where his excellent memory, love of reading, writing skill, outgoing and disputatious temperament, and drive to excel all were brought to new heights. Classmates and teachers remembered him as one of the best students in the school; his work was often cited as a model for others to emulate.[20] Despite his short height, Hu played basketball, and he was a drummer in the school band. He was known for political activism and patriotic concern for the future of China, which was still beset with feuding warlords and foreign oppression.

Another political storm blew up in 1929, and again Hu Yaobang was right in its path. Local warlords had continued to battle each other for primacy in Hunan, with frequent small-scale skirmishes that disturbed the rhythms of commerce, agriculture, and education. The Communist Party had recovered and expanded its base areas in rural Hunan and Jiangxi, reestablishing party committees and guerrilla units in Liuyang. Hu went home for winter break in December 1929, and in early 1930 one of his friends recommended that he join the Communist Youth League. Hu quickly involved himself in propaganda activities, writing posters, songs, and other materials to get out the party's and the Red Army's messages.

When in February 1930 he returned to school, it was in chaos. Not only were CCP and KMT battles raging all around Liuyang, but the school itself was polarized between "red" (CCP) and "white" (KMT) sympathizers. Some students and several teachers fled the violence. Yang Shijun left to join the Chinese Worker-Peasant Red Army in Jiangxi that month. He changed his name to Yang Yong, and later would become one of the CCP's top generals. In April, the Fifth Red Army under the Hunanese general Peng Dehuai attacked eastern Liuyang County, including Wenjia, while the Sixth Red Army seized Liuyang municipality and occupied its government facilities. The Liuyang County junior middle school closed, and several faculty and students, including Hu Yaobang, fled to Changsha, where they continued classes in another school. But Peng's army, under orders from the new Central Committee, moved against Changsha as well and by July was fighting inside the city. Again Hu Yaobang's school closed, and Hu had no choice but to return to his home village. His school days were over.[21]

Going Up Jinggangshan

By late July 1930 Peng Dehuai's forces had seized much of Changsha and had established a temporary "soviet" government there, but in early August they retreated toward Liuyang under heavy attack from KMT forces.[22] They joined forces with Mao Zedong and Zhu De's Red First Brigade in Wenjia, forming the Red First Front Army. A soviet government established in Liuyang County in April was still operating in certain areas by the time Hu Yaobang returned home. Already a member of the Young Communist League, and literate, Hu was quickly put to work writing slogans, broadsheets, and educational materials. He wrote plays, organized a tuition-free school, and gave speeches on behalf of semiliterate guerrilla leaders. He and several children ran messages and delivered food from one area of CCP control to another, skirting villages controlled by KMT units. Hu progressed quickly within the local organization, and by October he was being recruited by the eastern Hunan CCP committee to become a *ganbu*—a cadre, or official.[23]

Hu then faced a personal dilemma. His father needed help in farming their meager fields. Yaobang was only fifteen years old, small and thin. But he had been active enough in the local Youth League to believe he might be subject to reprisal, perhaps even execution, if he stayed in Liuyang and the KMT moved back into that area. An honest appraisal of the Communist Party's prospects in the area would not have been encouraging. The uprisings in Hunan were failing, peasant troops were deserting, the Red Army was fading back into its Jiangxi redoubts, and KMT leaders were poised for revenge. Worse, although Hu would not have known, the CCP Central Committee was in disarray. On Comintern orders it abandoned attacks on urban centers like Changsha, then ousted one of young Hu Yaobang's heroes, Li Lisan, the general secretary responsible for having implemented the policy of attacking urban centers.

In the end it was Hu's own decision to leave home and take up the revolutionary cause. It was an ambitious decision for a young boy. He wanted the life of a hero, of a bold and independent soldier, challenging a political order he saw as weak and corrupt. According to Yang Zhongmei, Hu told his friends, "How can a boy take care of a few mu of fields and his home? I want to be like Li Lisan and take on the world. I must leave home and make revolution!"[24] So in late November 1930, seen off by his mother and older brother, Hu Yaobang walked out of Cangfang village, heading east toward the mountains of Jiangxi and the Communist Party base areas.

Details of Hu's activities after he arrived at the Jiangxi Soviet area (or Central Soviet area) are vague and somewhat contradictory. Recordkeeping was not well-developed, and the Central Soviet area was not a coherent and contiguous whole. Because of his previous experience in the Liuyang Children's Corps, in February 1931 Hu was attached to the Southeastern Hunan Communist Youth League Children's Bureau, in Yongxin, Jiangxi. There he was responsible for tasks that involved party agitation and propaganda, which included recruiting young peasants to the Youth League and the Red Army, educating them in the ways of the Communist Party, teaching them songs and slogans, publishing elementary Marxist theoretical tracts, and introducing the party's sociopolitical ideas to younger, less sophisticated audiences.[25]

Although the Jiangxi Soviet had been formed in 1928 when Mao Zedong and Zhu De joined up with several bandit leaders in Jinggangshan after the

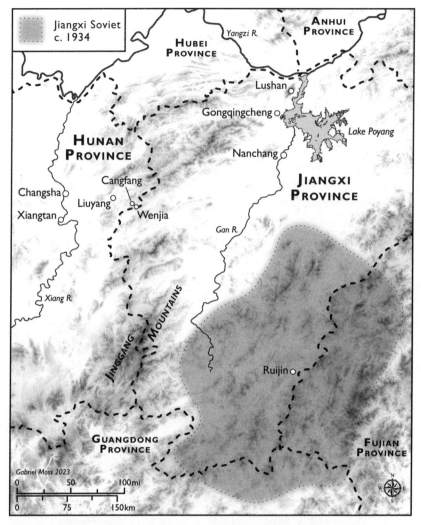

Map 1. The Hunan-Jiangxi region of central China, site of intense revolutionary activity in the 1920s and 1930s.

failure of the Nanchang and Changsha uprisings, the Chinese Soviet Republic was not formally established in Ruijin, Jiangxi, until November 7, 1931—the anniversary of the Bolshevik Revolution in Russia. Delegates at the Comintern-financed soviet delegates conference watched a military parade, celebrated the establishment of a new "country within a country," and elected Mao Zedong chairman of the Central Executive Committee and head of government, all with Moscow's approval.[26]

The Chinese Soviet Republic encompassed nine or ten smaller revolutionary bases in other south-central provinces, but they were semi-autonomous, separated from the Central Soviet by KMT armies. At its establishment, the Chinese Soviet Republic administered an area of approximately thirty thousand square kilometers in remote Hunan, Jiangxi, and Fujian Provinces, with a population of more than three million and a relatively stable economy. More importantly, it fielded an army of 140,000 to 150,000 soldiers who, although not as well-trained or as well-equipped as the KMT, were more than a match for local warlord militias. They could stand their ground against Chiang Kai-shek's efforts to encircle and annihilate the Communist strongholds. The Red Army was under very strict control, by the standards of the day, and soldiers were forbidden to steal from or mistreat the locals. Such constraints, along with a policy of redistributing land confiscated from wealthy landlords in the Soviet area, won the army popular support in remote Jiangxi. Mao developed a set of principles for guerrilla warfare that were well-suited to the rugged terrain. He described it in a letter to the Central Committee in January 1930: "The enemy advances, we retreat; the enemy camps, we harass; the enemy tires, we attack; the enemy retreats, we pursue."[27]

These tactics, carried out by resourceful military leaders, by late 1931 had enabled the Jiangxi Soviet to repel two annihilation campaigns mounted by the KMT army. A third such campaign was called off in September 1931 when the Japanese army invaded Manchuria with only token resistance from local warlords. The KMT government had to confront Japanese invasions not only in Manchuria, but also in Shanghai in early 1932, which required it to move many of its troops out of Jiangxi. Meanwhile, the Communist Party's new Soviet Republic continued to grow and stabilize as it established a working government apparatus, a military structure, and local party operations that helped build support among the poor peasants of the region.

In October the eastern Hunan party committee had reorganized itself into the Hunan-Jiangxi provincial committee, and Hu Yaobang was appointed secretary of its children's bureau. One of Hu's principal responsibilities was the publication of a newspaper for youth, for which he wrote articles, edited text, cut woodblock illustrations, and saw to distribution. This greatly impressed Feng Wenbin, who was then a Communist Youth League official assigned responsibility for recruitment in the Central Soviet.[28] Hu's position entailed travel and liaison with other Youth League personnel, and his personality, intelligence, and organizational talents soon won favorable notice.

Evading a Political Purge

Hu's first political crisis and threat to his life came in late 1932. Hu's biographers don't provide much detail on the events surrounding his experience at the time, but he and his friend Tan Qilong were arrested by Hunan-Jiangxi CCP authorities in December, on suspicion of being KMT agents, and sentenced to death. The background dates to late 1926, when Chiang Kai-shek secretly directed KMT right-wing leaders in Nanchang to organize an Anti-Bolshevik League (generally referred to by the English-language initials "AB" with the Chinese word for "league," *tuan*).

The AB League was intended to infiltrate Communist organizations and undermine them by taking them over and turning in key members to the police or military. Recent studies indicate that the AB League may have been dissolved by the left-wing KMT government in Nanjing by April 1927. Remaining remnants were driven out during the Nanchang Uprising of August 1927, when Communist forces occupied the provincial capital and destroyed its KMT infrastructure.[29] After their own rout from Nanchang, Mao's guerrilla troops retreated to Jinggangshan and fought numerous battles with KMT forces. In the autumn of 1930, when Mao's and Zhu De's troops captured the city of Ji'an, Jiangxi, they discovered documents in police headquarters indicating that the AB League still had more than two thousand members, including senior Red Army leaders and CCP members. Mao reported this information to the Central Committee Politburo and its Comintern advisers in Shanghai, demanding they investigate and take action.[30]

Mao's General Front Committee and the Southwest Jiangxi Soviet special committee, headed by Li Wenlin, agreed that swift and drastic action was necessary. They both established purge committees to discover AB League members. By late October the Southwest Jiangxi Soviet special committee reported to the Central Committee that it had executed more than one thousand AB League members, while Mao's General Front Committee reported it had rounded up forty-four hundred AB League members and other untrustworthy persons by early December and had executed more than two thousand. Mao also reported that the Southwest Jiangxi Soviet party committee itself had been infiltrated, and he ordered the arrest of most of its members.[31]

The brutality used to uncover "traitors" within Communist Party ranks was chilling—beatings, torture, forced confessions, and summary executions were all authorized by both the Central Committee in Shanghai and the

Jiangxi organizations. This reflected the ferocity of the political struggle between the KMT and the CCP, and the personalities of the revolutionary leaders. Mao Zedong, whose standing within the CCP had gone through ups and downs, began to show a vindictive and cruel streak that would be a hallmark of his leadership for the next several decades. Li Wenlin, with whom Mao had several disputes, was arrested in December 1930 for being an AB League member. Nanjing University historian Gao Hua examined the complex politics between Mao and Li Wenlin and concluded that a politically insecure Mao could not tolerate the challenge from Li and his colleagues, and preemptively purged them in 1930, and that the anti–AB League campaign that followed was a cover-up for an internal party struggle, which later went out of control.[32]

In December 1930 Mao's General Front Committee dispatched the head of its purge committee, with a Twelfth Army company, to the city of Futian, in southwestern Jiangxi, to deal with suspected AB League persons who had infiltrated the provincial party committee. They broke into party headquarters, and arrested 120 people, of whom twenty-four were summarily executed. All arrests were based upon oral confessions elicited by interrogations and torture. Prisoners were beaten until they gave up the names of their AB League superiors, subordinates, contacts, and targets. Given that the AB League by this point probably didn't really exist, these likely were false accusations, but no effort was made to investigate the veracity of the charges.[33]

In late December, Mao's purge committee began to arrest senior officers of the Twentieth Army, many of whom fled across the Gan River and set up positions in Hunan, where they called for Mao to be ousted and asked the Central Committee in Shanghai to hear their case.[34] Mao declared the "Futian incident" a "counterrevolutionary insurrection led by the class enemies in charge of the AB League," and called for the execution of the officers. In April 1931 the Politburo sent a delegation to Jiangxi to adjudicate, but they agreed with Mao that the Futian incident was an act of class warfare that needed to be punished at every level. The Twentieth Army leaders who came to the meeting were arrested and executed. Subsequently the Twentieth Army was disarmed, and nearly all its officers—perhaps as many as seven hundred men—were shot.[35]

Afterward the purge of the AB League within the party continued, and even expanded to areas not controlled by Mao. In three months, more than twenty-five hundred officers above brigade level in the Red Fourth Army—60 to 70 percent of its overall cadre strength—were executed, which "greatly

weakened the Red Army's fighting capability."[36] Noted party historian Yang
Kuisong estimated that 90 percent of the strength of the soviet areas was
sapped by the purges, citing twenty thousand to thirty thousand executed
in the Western Hubei-Henan Soviet, six thousand in the West Fujian Soviet,
and countless thousands in other areas. Some estimate that total casualties in the soviet areas during this period were as high as one hundred
thousand.[37]

Hu Yaobang was caught up in the AB League insanity in late 1932, by which
time it had nearly run its course. Hunan-Jiangxi provincial party secretary
Wang Shoudao had managed to keep the purges from getting out of hand,
despite orders from the Shanghai-based Central Committee to "ferret out"
AB League elements or risk being named a "rightist." According to Hu
Yaobang biographer Chen Liming, Hu and Tan Qilong were chatting quietly
one evening about how such a thing as the AB League could have happened,
and they were overheard by security personnel and reported to the provincial party committee. Given his past association with a teacher who had
been executed for being in the AB League, and his penchant for reading
and becoming an intellectual, Hu was accused of being a member of the
AB League.[38]

Tan Qilong remembered it differently: Instead, their names had been on
a list of AB League members compiled by the Hunan-Jiangxi provincial security bureau after torturing prisoners. Some members of the provincial
party committee were reluctant to execute them, finding it hard to believe
that two "little red devils" (boys who joined the revolution at a young age)
from poor peasant backgrounds could have joined a KMT spy organization.[39]
With the party secretary unable to decide, Central Soviet Youth League inspector Feng Wenbin, who was in the area to recruit Hu and Tan to do Youth
League work in Ruijin, suggested that the Central Youth League decide their
fates. Secretary Wang Shoudao agreed readily, and in early January 1933 the
three slipped through the KMT blockade and returned safely to Ruijin.[40]
There they were interrogated, but not tortured, by Youth League head Zhang
Aiping and Central Committee member Gu Zuolin. Gu dismissed the
charges against the youths and put Hu to work as a Communist Youth League
inspector. Tan Qilong served in top-level Youth League and CCP posts and
remained a close friend of Hu Yaobang.[41] Hu would tell the story all his life,
and some biographers claim it was the source of his lifelong opposition to
forced confessions and guilt by denunciation.

The Last Days of the Jiangxi Soviet

Hu threw himself enthusiastically into the work of the Youth League and the Children's Corps in the Jiangxi Soviet, as an inspector and probably a recruiter. Recruiting new members was one of the most important tasks of the Youth League, especially for the Red Army, which was taking significant casualties by late 1932. By mid-1933 the Youth League had "developed" nearly seventy-four thousand prospective members; more than fifteen thousand of the Red Army's total troops in September of that year had joined through the Youth League.[42] Hu himself was able to transfer directly from the Youth League to become a member of the Chinese Communist Party in September 1933, although he remained principally engaged in Youth League work. In recognition of his hard work and increasing value, Hu was chosen in early 1934 to replace Zhang Aiping as secretary general of the Central Bureau of the Communist Youth League. This made him responsible for all youth work in the area, including education, publications, supporting Red Army families, grain requisition, and providing sentries.[43]

Hu's promotion came at a time when overall conditions in the Jiangxi Soviet were deteriorating rapidly.[44] After the failure of the KMT's annihilation campaign in early 1933, Chiang Kai-shek moved to Nanchang to supervise yet another effort in September. He brought in a million more men, more aircraft and heavy armor, and a new military strategy—strings of fortified blockhouses to surround the soviet areas and gradually choke off access. Chiang had brought in German military advisers in the early 1930s, some of whom supervised the blockhouse construction. These fortifications were permanently occupied, connected by a network of paved roads, and virtually impossible for Red Army forces to get past. By late 1934 nearly fourteen thousand blockhouses surrounded the Central Soviet area. Red Army troops, advised by their Comintern military representative, Otto Braun, adopted trench warfare measures against them, with little success and many casualties.[45]

Compounding the Red Army's strategic woes were political-military shortcomings that had been building since the soviets were established in the late 1920s. The main problems were the disastrous agricultural and economic policies Mao and others instituted in the soviet areas, beginning with the violent expropriation of land from landlords and rich peasants, and the cascading effects of this on agriculture and commerce. As local markets dried up, the soviet areas became impoverished, and the Red Army had to expand into "white" (KMT) areas to find more resources. Worse still, by late 1933 people were physically fleeing the Central Soviet area for both economic and political reasons, finding the Communist Party to be just as oppressive as the landlords and warlords. When KMT forces were able to stabilize areas around the soviets, they began to strangle the CCP economically. By early 1934, food, cooking oil, and even salt began to be in short supply, and Hu and his Youth League colleagues found it increasingly difficult to recruit for the Red Army.[46]

The battle of Guangchang in April 1934 was probably the turning point for the Jiangxi Soviet. Red Army forces, seriously weakened by the execution of many military leaders in the anti–AB League purges, faced a larger, better-equipped, more mobile KMT force protected by the fortified blockhouses, moving steadily toward their capital at Ruijin. In a departure from the guerrilla strategy that had enabled them to stem earlier annihilation campaigns, the Red Army used mostly conventional mass attacks and World War I–style trench warfare in the three-week struggle for Guangchang. They lost badly, with six thousand killed and more than twenty thousand wounded.[47]

At this point the triumvirate that commanded the Central Committee and the Red Army—Zhou Enlai, Bo Gu (a returned student), and Otto Braun—informed Moscow that they saw two alternatives: staying in vulnerable soviet areas but shifting to smaller guerrilla operations; or moving all party, government, and military operations to another part of China, such as western Hunan. The Comintern dithered for five months, in part because CCP representatives in Moscow insisted the situation could not be that dire.[48] By the time evacuation plans were finally approved, the Red Army was already in staging positions for the Long March. The CCP Politburo had decided in September that most of the Red Army and all party and government functionaries should leave Jiangxi and retreat westward into Hunan, where they believed Chiang Kai-shek exercised little control.

Hu Yaobang's Long March

The Red Army's retreat from the forested mountains of Jiangxi to the bleak highlands of northern Shaanxi was an epic journey, across numerous rivers, mountain ranges, swamps, grasslands, and deserts, pursued by KMT armies and warlord forces. It was not very successful and hardly heroic. It started out with more than 120,000 personnel (86,000 in the Red Army) in mid-October 1934, moving south into Guangdong, west through Guangxi, Hunan, and Guizhou, then north through Sichuan into Shaanxi. When they arrived in October 1935, only about 8,000 remained, exhausted and dispirited. Objectively, it was disastrous, with several military defeats and mass desertions, compounded by internal CCP infighting and leadership indecision. Mao Zedong, through a deft use of foreign and domestic propaganda, was able to weave the story of the Long March into a semi-mythical tale of courage, fierce determination, and overcoming hardships. He so embellished and exaggerated Long March episodes that a few later historians have doubted some of the more dramatic tales.[49]

Hu Yaobang did not record his experiences on the Long March, and his biographers have collected only a few anecdotes, some of which are confused or contradictory. When the Long March began, Hu Yaobang was only eighteen and still had a youthful appearance, being under five feet tall and probably well under a hundred pounds—too small for combat duty. He was not told what was happening until just before the procession left, aware only that he needed to be prepared to move. He destroyed his papers and packed his few belongings, including treasured books like *Romance of the Three Kingdoms* and *Journey to the West*. He probably thought he was ready.

When the Red Army set out from Ruijin on October 10, Hu, as one of the leading Youth League secretaries, was assigned to the Central Column—made up of party and government staff. At least he was issued a rifle and ammunition.[50] As a party branch secretary, Hu was responsible for the political preparation of several young soldiers who were leaving home for the first time. He exhorted and reassured them, and helped them with preparations and good-byes.[51]

Crossing into Guangdong in late October, the Long March was large, noisy, and slow; one Red Army general compared it to an "emperor's sedan chair." The Central Column consisted of the "Jiangxi government, . . . [including] 7,000 reserves and porters carrying files and cupboards, the entire content of the Ruijin Library, the Red Army's reserves of silver and gold . . . , sewing machines, printing equipment," and much other extraneous material.[52] The early part of the march proceeded without serious KMT interference, thanks to timely bribes to Guangdong warlords. But by early November, Chiang Kai-shek's forces had begun to harass the slow-moving army. Desertions began to take a toll—porters abandoned their equipment, soldiers left in groups. Hu worked to prevent this, without much success. He led in the singing of

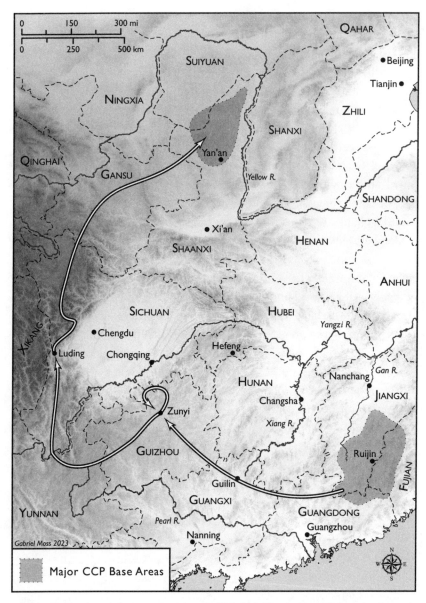

Map 2. The main route of the Red Army's "25,000 *li* Long March" from its Central Soviet base area in Jiangxi to northern Shaanxi, 1934–1935. Although the actual distance is still debated, the arduous trek through mountains and swampland of southwestern China, often under attack by KMT or local warlord forces, cost the Red Army nearly 90 percent of its troops.

"red songs" and helped his charges deal with blisters on their feet. But he soon contracted malaria. Unable to walk, he was carried on a stretcher for several days and received what medical attention was available.

Hu was barely recovered when the Red Army confronted blockading KMT troops at the Xiang River along the Hunan-Guangxi border in early December. Command hesitation left Red Army units stationary, open to attack by KMT aircraft and artillery, resulting in massive casualties and destruction of equipment. Further losses ensued when Communist forces tried crossing the river on flimsy pontoons while being bombed and strafed. Although CCP propaganda described it as a fierce battle, it was a catastrophic defeat, the scale of which has yet to be told. Years later participants described the river as having been like a "bath of blood," filled with corpses of men and horses, completely chaotic.

Of the 86,000 Red Army troops who left Jiangxi, only 30,000 showed up in Guizhou in early January. Why did the Red Army lose more than 50,000 soldiers in a two-day battle? Historians have disagreed. Some attribute the losses to the ineptitude of Red Army commanders, but it is more likely that many of the soldiers simply deserted or surrendered.[53] Hu Yaobang's chronology reveals only that he understood the gravity of the loss and was depressed and hard-pressed to help young soldiers recover from their grief at the deaths of so many friends.[54]

Central Committee and Red Army leaders, meeting in Guizhou in mid-December, initially blamed General Secretary Bo Gu and Comintern adviser Otto Braun for the Xiang River disaster. They decided to abandon the earlier plan to join an existing soviet in western Hunan, and instead to set up a new base area in the northern Guizhou / southern Sichuan region.[55] After taking the northern Guizhou city of Zunyi in January, with only token resistance from local warlords, the Politburo held an expanded meeting (including Red Army leaders), at which the errors of the past few months were critiqued in detail and a new leadership was chosen. Zhou Enlai remained the principal decision-maker, but Mao Zedong returned to the Politburo Standing Committee and was given authority over military affairs.[56] Having received information that Chiang Kai-shek had moved his headquarters and a large body of troops to Guiyang, the party decided to cross the Yangzi River and establish its base in western or northwestern Sichuan. After the meeting, the Red Army was reorganized, the Central Column was disbanded, and Hu was assigned as party branch secretary in a front-line military unit, the Thirteenth Regiment of the Red Third Corps.[57]

Despite having no combat experience or training, in February Hu participated in the Battle of Loushan Pass, an attack against a KMT outpost north of Zunyi that was the first important victory the Red Army had won since it left Jiangxi. Shortly afterward Hu was seriously wounded by bomb shrapnel; he lost a lot of blood and was rushed to a temporary hospital in Zunyi for treatment. The surgeon was not able to remove all the shrapnel, so Hu was carried on a stretcher when the Red Army moved to the border region to set up a soviet area. He was provided with a horse by his Youth League colleague Zhang Aiping, who had become a regimental political commissar.[58] Upon recovery, Hu was put in charge of a hospital unit, where he was responsible for many wounded soldiers. Hu was praised for his enthusiasm, good humor, and careful treatment of wounded and discouraged soldiers.[59]

By August the Red Army needed food supplies urgently and tried to secure grain from Tibetan minority inhabitants. They failed, and Hu was sent out with a group of grain requisition experts, a translator, and money to try another area. This time they succeeded in purchasing a supply of grain, for which Hu was given credit. At the northern Sichuan village of Mao-er-gai, the remaining Red Army forces split, with Mao and his forces moving toward the eastern side of the great grassland and other forces going to the western side.

Both sides suffered enormously in the weeklong trek across a seemingly boundless swamp with no habitation, no food, no roads, and no guides. The weather was hot and rainy, and the Red Army's numbers dwindled again as already weakened soldiers succumbed to disease and starvation. Hu's hospital unit was overwhelmed. At this point Hu Yaobang again developed malaria, and he collapsed in a ditch. His biography claims that he was rescued by his cousin, Yang Yong, whom he had not seen for several years. Yang, who was then a regimental political commissar, was wounded and had been given one of the few remaining horses to carry him while he recovered. Hu recognized him as he passed and called out to him, whereupon Yang dismounted, lifted his cousin onto the horse, and walked beside him for the rest of the slog through the marsh.[60]

After surviving the grasslands, Mao's troops arrived in southern Gansu and learned that a CCP base area, under its charismatic leader Liu Zhidan, was thriving in northern Shaanxi, some four hundred kilometers to the east. Mao ordered the march to continue. On October 19, 1935, the remaining eight thousand or so troops of the First Red Army arrived at the town of

Wuqi, in Shaanxi, and Mao declared the Long March finally over. Hu Yaobang had barely survived the 367-day trek through eleven provinces, numerous battles, life-threatening wounds, and constant illness.[61]

A Young Man Takes Stock

Hu Yaobang's birthplace, cultural heritage, and upbringing had put him in the path of China's political revolution in the early twentieth century and focused his choices early. His intelligence, diligence, and adaptability gave him the skills he needed to succeed in an ever-changing political environment. His literary interests and linguistic skills prepared him for propaganda work, and he excelled at it despite his abridged education. His short stature and youthful appearance typecast him for work with the Youth League and children's development, instead of combat roles. His sense of humor and natural empathy made him an effective political worker and an esteemed comrade. His modesty and honesty made him aware of his limitations, both physical and intellectual. His shrewdness enabled him to see the ebb and flow of interpersonal politics and to choose his allies and opponents carefully.

At the age of twenty, Hu Yaobang was tough—the Long March had proven that he was a survivor. He would look back on his experiences as a form of training and discipline—what could daunt him or defeat the Communist Party if the Long March could not? He was dedicated and loyal to the Communist Party and the Red Army, and particularly to its emergent leader, Mao Zedong, whom he had admired since he was a schoolboy. The Communist Party's future in northern Shaanxi in 1935, though, might not have filled Hu with optimism. The region was desperately poor, arid, and sunbaked, with people living in caves, eking out a meager existence on coarse grains and sheep products. Chiang Kai-shek had already begun harassing the newly arrived Red Army units. Meanwhile, Chiang had consolidated his control over much of China, and had stabilized the situation with respect to Japan so he could focus his attention on exterminating the CCP.

2 Basking in the Light of Mao Zedong

Although the Red Army's arrival in northern Shaanxi was the end of its Long March, it was hardly the end of its ordeals. Sick, malnourished, and dispirited, the troops could take little comfort from their surroundings in October 1935. Northern Shaanxi, situated on an arid loess plateau adjacent to the Yellow River, is dominated by mounds, plateaus, and cliffs caused by the easily eroded silt. With little forest or water resources, many inhabitants dug into the loess along rivers and cliffs to construct homes. The region was one of the earliest settled areas of China, and home to some of its greatest dynasties, such as the Qin, Han, and Tang. But its lack of water and fertile soil had left it isolated, sparsely populated, and poor.

After some rest and recuperation, Zhang Wentian—nominal general secretary of the CCP—convened a Politburo meeting in the town of Wayaobao on December 17, 1935. For more than a week, CCP and Red Army leaders discussed their future base area, military objectives, and strategic orientation. Mao Zedong called for stronger resistance against "the annexation of China by Japanese imperialism." He also called for a change in revolutionary tactics and the formation of a "broad revolutionary national united front," to include elements of some classes formerly considered class enemies by the party.[1] Although the CCP's relationship with the Communist International and its advisors in China was strained, Mao's speech was consistent with the position taken by the Comintern in July–August 1935, calling for a broad, international united front against fascism, including Japan's incursion into Manchuria.

Japanese expansion into the region had continued after the Russo-Japanese War (1904–1905), when Japan took over Russian interests in Manchuria, including the South Manchurian Railway, which connected the port of Dalian with Harbin. In 1928 the Japanese Kwantung army arranged for the assassination of the Chinese warlord of the region, Zhang Zuolin, and his replacement by his son, the "Young Marshal," Zhang Xueliang. In September 1931, it contrived the so-called Mukden incident—an explosion on the South Manchurian Railway, which brought the full force of the Japanese Imperial Army into Manchuria. It soon seized the major cities along the rail line, scattering Zhang's forces, which put up little or no resistance.[2]

Following the establishment in 1932 of the puppet state of Manchukuo, Japanese forces operated with impunity in Northeast China and expanded their operations westward. Zhang Xueliang's Northeastern Army of more than two hundred thousand fled west and did not engage with the Japanese army, which was better armed and better trained. Public Chinese outrage at the incursion, and at the slow response of the Chiang Kai-shek government in Nanjing, gave the CCP's change of direction added impetus.[3]

The Eastern Expedition

The CCP's new direction had more immediate objectives, which probably drove its actions more than the strategic shifts. As Yang Kuisong put it, the Red Army needed to "procure grain and recruit soldiers." Even with the addition of CCP forces that were already in northern Shaanxi, the Red Army numbered fewer than twenty thousand soldiers, and they were hungry. From their northern Shaanxi base, the easiest place to acquire both food and recruits was to cross the Yellow River into more fertile and populous Shanxi. The local warlord, Yan Xishan, was accused of cooperating with Japanese forces that were threatening North China. Therefore, despite their depleted ranks and near exhaustion, the Red Army was reorganized and ordered to undertake an Eastern Expedition. In February 1936, under Commander Peng Dehuai and Political Commissar Mao Zedong, the Chinese People's Red Army Anti-Japanese Vanguard Army set off eastward in two columns, crossing the Yellow River into Shanxi.[4]

Hu Yaobang had returned to Youth League work and was assigned as commander of a political work brigade, responsible for proselytizing, procuring grain, and recruiting for the Red Army in one of the first counties the army entered in Shanxi. The unit was under instructions to make a positive impression on the local populace—they were not to mistreat prisoners, expropriate land, shake down small business owners, or punish local officials.[5] Hu threw himself into the hard work with enthusiasm and optimism, despite opposition from Yan Xishan's political operatives. Hu's unit put up banners and posters in every village it passed through, advocating resistance against Japanese imperialism and patriotic cooperation among all parties and social classes. Although the team's achievements were probably meager, Hu's leadership was praised, and it was considered a positive experiment in "spreading Red" into Shanxi.[6]

Hu's success came at a heavy personal cost, however. Still recovering from his Long March illness, with food supplies short and working hours long, Hu began vomiting blood and fainted after a meeting in early March. For several days he could not take in food or water. Traditional medicines were of no use, and local doctors predicted his illness would be fatal. Hu's bodyguard sent word of his condition to the military unit to which they were attached. A military doctor was sent, administered some Western medicine, and Hu began to recover, although he could not walk and was carried on a stretcher.[7]

Meanwhile, the tide of battle on the Eastern Expedition turned decisively against the Red Army. In April, Yan Xishan appealed to Chiang Kai-shek for help. Despite a long-standing feud with Yan, Chiang agreed to set up a regional headquarters for annihilating Communists in Yan's capital of Taiyuan and sent ten Kuomintang (KMT) divisions toward Shanxi. Seeing that Red Army units were likely to be trapped, Peng and Mao ordered them back across the Yellow River in early May. Once in their redoubt, the CCP offered a cease-fire to "Mr. Chiang" so they could jointly resist the Japanese invaders.[8]

Safe and recovering in Shaanxi, Hu was introduced to Mao Zedong at a meeting in mid-May to summarize the seventy-five-day campaign. Mao had been briefed earlier on the work Hu had done in Shanxi, and called for Hu to "stand up and let everyone take a look at you." When the still youthful-looking Hu arose, Mao reportedly said, "Oh! It's a little guy," then asked for details on his work, which Hu delivered in his strong Hunan accent. It was Hu's first face-to-face meeting with the man who was to dominate his life for the next forty years.[9]

The Xi'an Incident

Shortly after the return from the Eastern Expedition, the situation for the CCP and the Red Army began to deteriorate again. Supplies gained in Shanxi did not last long, and the new recruits and prisoners were a drain on scarce resources. Food, clothing, medicine, weapons and ammunition, and money to buy them all were in extremely short supply. Secret negotiations had opened earlier in the year between CCP representatives and Zhang Xueliang's Northeast Army, then stationed around Xi'an, trading a cease-fire agreement for supplies and money. Zhang was willing to assist the Red Army because he was sympathetic to their cause, and, more importantly, because he saw them as way to get the Soviet Union more involved in fighting Japan in Asia.[10]

Secret talks also were going on between the CCP and the Nanjing government as to how the two sides could cease fighting each other and develop joint efforts against the Japanese threat, but in late 1936 they were still far apart. The Comintern was insisting that all efforts be devoted to developing a united front. Meanwhile, Chiang Kai-shek was preparing to move more troops into southern Shaanxi, where all three Red Front armies were concentrated and in weakened condition. In October 1936 Chiang formally established the Bandit Suppression General Headquarters in Xi'an, with himself as commander and Zhang Xueliang as deputy. He ordered the Northeastern Army to begin preparatory operations immediately, but Zhang took his time.[11] Zhang Xueliang was ready to break with Chiang completely; his deputy, Yang Hucheng, had earlier suggested capturing Chiang and controlling his military forces by threatening to kill him.[12] Both men had spoken with Communist Party contacts about seizing Chiang, but they were unable to get reassurances of Soviet assistance in fighting Japan and continued to temporize.

On December 4, 1936, Chiang Kai-shek flew to Xi'an to take personal command of the effort to eliminate the Communists. Although troops loyal to him were not present in force, many had been ordered to move toward Xi'an. On December 9, students demonstrated against a civil war, calling on Chiang to join a united front to resist Japan. Police dispersed them violently. When Zhang Xueliang went to Chiang's quarters outside Xi'an at the Huaqing Hot Springs to plead with him to listen to student demands, Chiang dismissed him rudely and ordered him to use machine guns against them.[13] After this, Zhang and Yang Hucheng decided to act quickly.

Early in the morning of December 12, elite units of Zhang Xueliang's Northeastern Army surrounded the Huaqing Hot Springs guesthouse, disarmed the external guards, and shot many of the sentries posted inside. Chiang Kai-shek was captured and brought into Xi'an with some of his aides. Zhang Xueliang immediately cabled Red Army headquarters: "For the sake of the Chinese people and in the interest of resisting Japan, we have detained Chiang and his important generals . . . in order to force the release of patriotic elements and to reorganize a coalition government. If elder brothers have any valued opinions, please reply soonest."[14]

The CCP leadership immediately transmitted the news to the Comintern and its own military units. But Politburo members were not in accord on how to respond and waited for the Comintern's response. On December 15, Mao and Zhou Enlai sent a cable to the Nanjing government demanding that it accept the proposal of Generals Zhang and Yang to form a united front government, remove Chiang from office, and cease preparations for civil war.[15] Positions shifted over the next few days, as divided and distrustful politicians in Nanjing, Xi'an, Yan'an, and Moscow all grappled with the implications of one of the world's most prominent leaders being taken hostage. The Comintern message to Yan'an—sent on December 16 but not decoded until the 20th—was blunt. It demanded the CCP publicly disavow the kidnapping, continue to press for a united front, and set Chiang Kai-shek free.[16]

On December 19, the CCP Politburo moderated their previous position, calling for a national salvation conference rather than a trial or execution of Chiang.[17] The cable from Moscow likely tipped the balance within the CCP leadership toward a peaceful resolution, but they only informed Zhang Xueliang of Moscow's attitude on December 21. Although Zhang was disheartened by the Soviet disapproval, he began looking for a way to free Chiang himself.[18] On December 22, Chiang's wife, Soong Mei-ling, and her brother, Song Ziwen (aka T. V. Soong), arrived in Xi'an, announcing their intent to seek a peaceful resolution on behalf of the Nanjing government. Chiang still refused to publicly sign any document, but told Song that, if released, he would convene a national salvation congress within three months, reorganize the government, and ally with the USSR and the Communist Party of China in resisting Japan.[19]

A meeting between Chiang Kai-shek and Zhou Enlai late that same evening produced the final outline of a settlement. Chiang agreed to cease efforts to exterminate the CCP, ally with the Red Army to resist Japan, and unite the country under his leadership. He also agreed to allow Soong Mei-ling and Song Ziwen to represent him with full powers in resolving all other problems pertaining to the incident and to permit Zhou Enlai to come to Nanjing to negotiate directly the details of the united front.[20]

Losers and Winners

On the afternoon of December 25, 1936, Chiang Kai-shek, Soong Mei-ling, and Song Ziwen, accompanied by Zhang Xueliang, boarded a plane and returned to Nanjing, ending two weeks of high drama, intrigue, and tension.[21] Zhang accompanied them for reasons that still are not clear. Upon arrival in Nanjing, Zhang accepted full responsibility for his actions, was arrested, tried in a military court, and sentenced to prison for ten years. Chiang commuted this to house arrest, but then extended it indefinitely. (Zhang was not released until 1975, after Chiang Kai-shek's death, and later emigrated to the United States, where he died in 1993.) Not long after the Xi'an Incident concluded, Chiang stripped Yang Hucheng of his Shaanxi command and ultimately arrested him. In 1949, when the Nationalists were defeated in the civil war and escaped to Taiwan, Yang and his family were secretly executed in Chongqing.[22]

Chiang Kai-shek returned to head a stronger government in Nanjing, having secured support from warlords in South China, isolated pro-Japanese elements within the KMT, and neutralized both the CCP and the northern warlords in Shaanxi and Shanxi. Chiang initially honored his agreements and continued negotiations on the shape of the government coalition and the details of military cooperation.

It seems likely that the formation of a united front caused the Japanese army to advance its plans for further incursions into Chinese territory. On July 7, 1937, the Marco Polo Bridge incident escalated into a full-scale Japanese attack on Nationalist forces and their local warlord allies in North and East China. Beijing fell within three weeks, the city of Tianjin in late July, and Shanghai in August. Nationalist armies resisted strongly, but they proved no match for the more mobile and better-trained Japanese troops, and suffered appalling losses. Thousands of Chinese civilians also were ruthlessly slaughtered by the invading Japanese armies. Chiang's decision to resist Japan in the wake of the Xi'an Incident proved disastrous to him, and to China, both in the short and the long term.[23]

Many historians claim that the Communist Party of China was the principal beneficiary of the changed politico-military situation that followed the Xi'an Incident.[24] Deft negotiations by Zhou Enlai, shrewd strategic calculations by Mao Zedong, support from the Soviet Union—which agreed in 1937 to provide much-needed arms and matériel to the Nanjing government—together with Japanese attacks to the south, away from CCP base areas, gave the Communists the space and time to recover. From a beaten-down and vulnerable collection of guerrilla bands in late 1936, the Second United Front with the Kuomintang enabled the CCP and the Red Army (soon renamed the Eighth Route Army) to recruit, organize, educate, and rebuild their forces for the inevitable showdown with Chiang Kai-shek. And not coincidentally, the CCP leader who led and benefited most from the Yan'an expansion was Mao Zedong.

Hu Goes Back to School

In November 1936, Hu Yaobang attended a Politburo-convened meeting with Youth League leaders to discuss how to respond to Chinese students' growing sympathy for calls to unite against Japan. The meeting called for the formation of a "democratic and free vast student movement" and directed Communist Youth League (CYL) members in KMT-dominated areas to disband and join legal and public youth organizations, even if they were still "under the influence of the Nationalist Party."[25] The Central Bureau of the CYL was abolished, although Hu and others continued doing youth organization work under different names. Hu's culminating achievement was participating as a delegate in the First Northwest Youth National Salvation Congress, in Yan'an in April 1937. Attended by three hundred delegates from various youth organizations, the congress was addressed by Mao Zedong, who explained the CCP's strategic decision to participate in an anti-Japanese united front. The congress elected an executive committee, of which Hu Yaobang was an alternate member.[26]

By this time, however, Hu had already moved on to the next phase of his career, continuing his education at the CCP's most prestigious training academy, the Chinese People's Resist Japan Military and Political University, usually referred to as Kang Da. Kang Da was the successor to the Chinese Worker-Peasant Red Army School established in the Jiangxi Soviet in 1933 and reestablished in 1936 in Wayaobao. When the CCP moved its headquarters to Yan'an in January 1937, the school also moved and was renamed a university.

In a speech to the first class of Kang Da students, Mao Zedong compared the school to the Whampoa Military Academy of Guangzhou, established in 1924, where many of the early military leaders of the Kuomintang and the CCP had studied. One of the Red Army's most illustrious leaders and a Whampoa graduate, Lin Biao, was named chancellor of Kang Da, Mao became political commissar, and another experienced political officer and security specialist, Luo Ruiqing, was named director of studies. The first class of 1,063 students, all senior army and party cadres, had begun study in June 1936, finishing in December.

Hu Yaobang was chosen for the second class, which began courses in March 1937. Its first two brigades were composed of battalion and company-grade officers and some civilian cadres. Hu, assigned to the First Brigade, was soon chosen secretary of its Communist Party branch.[27] Kang Da provided a very rudimentary education experience in its early days. There were no classrooms or lecture halls, no desks or chairs or chalkboards, and few books. Students sat on their packs or on triangular stools under canvas tarpaulins and took notes on their laps. Dormitories were in the numerous caves that surrounded Yan'an, some of them converted sheep pens, where the students slept on stone or clay beds. Millet and coarse vegetables made up most meals. Mao Zedong claimed the tough conditions were part of the revolutionary education process.

The curriculum included Marxism-Leninism, military tactics and strategy, politics, history, and remedial courses as needed. Many of the lectures on revolutionary history and practice were given by veteran CCP and Red Army leaders, especially Mao, Zhu De, Lin Biao, and Zhang Wentian. Mao would sometimes hold informal outdoor seminars on the day before his scheduled lectures.[28] Later, of course, Kang Da expanded, built classrooms and lecture halls, hired new faculty, opened local branches in CCP-controlled base areas, and ultimately trained more than twenty thousand army and party officials. But in its early years it was a small-scale operation, and those involved in it came to know each other well.

With a love of learning dating from childhood, Hu Yaobang soon came to the attention of his instructors, even though he was the youngest student in his class of mostly Red Army officers. He threw himself into study, reading the works of Marx and Lenin, and in his spare time Chinese history and literature. Hu always had a book in hand. Like his fellow students, he was enthralled by Mao's lectures, which combined explication of Marxist theory with war stories, peasant wisdom, humor, and powerful anti-Japanese and anti-imperialist rhetoric. Hu probably listened to over one hundred hours of Mao's lectures in his six-month course at Kang Da, absorbing ideas Mao would later incorporate into some of his most important theoretical treatises, such as "On Practice" and "On Contradictions."[29] Hu would sit at the front of the class to hear the soft-spoken Mao. Mao found Hu a conscientious

Mao Zedong lecturing in 1938 at the "Chinese People's Resist Japan Military and Political University," usually known as "Kang Da." Early conditions at the school were quite primitive, with few desks and chairs, no books, and many classes held outdoors. Hu Yaobang was a diligent student and a favorite of Mao's, doing political work among new recruits to the Communist Party from urban areas. (Wikimedia Commons)

student, and often called on him to give his views on the topics under discussion.[30]

The mutual regard between Mao and Hu deepened as Hu's study at Kang Da continued, and particularly once the Japanese invasion and the call to combat duty of many Red Army leaders depleted the university of administrators, instructors, and students. Chancellor Lin Biao was made commander of the Eighth Route Army's 115th Division, while Vice Chancellor Liu Bocheng assumed command of the 129th Division. Graduation for Kang Da Class 2 was moved from September to August to allow students to prepare for action against Japan in Shanxi. Hu Yaobang and twenty-seven other students from his brigade, however, were held over for advanced study at Kang Da, focusing on Mao's evolving theories about China's revolutionary experience and future direction. When that study concluded, Mao chose Hu to be deputy director of the university's Political Department, making him a key member of the school's leadership.[31]

Kang Da Class 3 started in August 1937 with 1,372 new students, most of whom were patriotic youth from KMT-controlled areas who had begun streaming into Yan'an, attracted by the idealism of the CCP. Hu explained to Mao that many of the new students were ill-disciplined and ideologically weak. Mao suggested that Hu establish a magazine to help educate and indoctrinate them. Hu was reluctant to take on the responsibility, and asked Mao to write the introductory article.

Mao's "Combat Liberalism" was published in the first issue of *Ideological Front* in September 1937. It was a hard-hitting article, deriding persons who lacked discipline, yearned for "unprincipled peace," and demonstrated "bourgeois selfishness" that "harmed the revolutionary collective."[32] Hu followed up in the next issue with his own article describing the struggle between liberalism and anti-liberalism, then threw himself into the editing, publication, and circulation of the magazine.

The flood of students arriving in Yan'an after the Japanese invasion required classes to be taught in different localities. Eight more branch universities were set up in other base areas controlled by the Communist Party, while more universities were established in Yan'an, including Women's University, the Lu Xun Institute of Art, Northern Shaanxi University, Yan'an University, and the Central Party School. The purpose was to train competent and committed cadres, including a significant number of female students, as soon as possible, a decision ratified by the Central Committee on March 5, 1938.

Section 1 of Class 4, for which Hu was appointed political commissar—responsible for all ideological and morale issues—moved to Wayaobao. Before they departed, Mao Zedong spoke to the section, reflecting the high esteem he had developed for Hu. Mao told the students he "wanted to recommend two people to you.... One is my respected old professor Zhang Ruxin, who ... could recite several of Marx's works fluently from memory, you can learn systematic Marxism-Leninism from him; one is the brigade's political commissar Hu Yaobang, his age is not much greater than yours, and I have watched this 'little red devil' growing up, studying enthusiastically and full of energy, and now he is ceaselessly writing articles for publication that are welcomed by readers. I hope you will take these two as your models and learn well from them."[33]

Promotion and Political Battles

In March 1939, Hu's career took an upward turn when Mao appointed him deputy director of the Organization Department of the General Political Department (GPD) of the Central Military Commission. Hu was then only twenty-three, still youthful looking, and his appointment was questioned by some military leaders. But Mao overruled them, even advancing Hu to be department director within a few months.[34] The organization department of any Communist Party unit is the personnel office—keeper of records, ranks, recommendations, appraisals, awards, demerits, and security clearances, and preparer of promotion lists and vacancy notices. Most of the Red Army's paper records had been lost on the Long March and had not been fully re-stored by the time Hu took over. His appointment was an indication of Mao's trust, but the job would be a bruising experience. Up until then, Hu had been a bystander to the political struggles that had so often roiled the Communist Party leadership. Now his actions would make a difference.

Chinese Communist Party history books generally portray Mao Zedong as the party's dominant leader from the Zunyi meeting of January 1935 on. But more recent scholarship, particularly work by Gao Hua, reveals the process to have been far more complex, requiring careful planning, political manipulation, and a fair measure of skullduggery for Mao to triumph over his adversaries and take full control by the Seventh Party Congress in 1945.[35] After the united front with the Kuomintang was established in late 1936, the responsibilities and territories of the Communist Party expanded, and even though his party no longer faced existential threats, Mao lost the ability to dominate its activities through personal interactions and regular party con-claves. By 1938, in fact, he had relatively few close allies in Yan'an.

A December 1937 Politburo meeting in Yan'an was the first major CCP meeting since Zunyi to readjust the leadership core, and Mao faced opposi-tion from Zhang Wentian and others he had outmaneuvered in earlier dis-putes. More troubling to Mao, perhaps, was the return of several senior leaders who had been studying in Moscow or working with the Comintern there. They included Wang Ming, Chen Yun, and a shadowy security specialist named Kang Sheng.

Although Mao retained his primary rank in the leadership, six of the Moscow-supported leaders joined him on the sixteen-member Politburo, with Wang Ming ranked second. The returnees carried with them both Moscow's imprimatur for leadership of the CCP and Moscow's doubts about whether Mao Zedong could carry out a "united front" policy that would tie down enough Japanese troops to keep them from attacking the Soviet Union.

Wang Ming used his two reports to the December meeting to indirectly attack Mao and others for not "putting the fight against Japan above all" and for insufficient attention to cooperation with the KMT. It was decided to send Wang Ming, Zhou Enlai, Bo Gu, and several others to Wuhan (where the Chiang Kai-shek government had retreated as the Japanese were preparing to assault Nanjing) to establish a CCP Yangzi Bureau responsible for negotiating with the Nationalist government on implementation of the united front. Wang's approach to joint political and military operations was more accommodating than Mao's, and although Wang was far less influential in the Central Committee and Politburo, Mao still considered him politically threatening. Wuhan thus was a convenient place both to get Wang out of Yan'an and to set him up for Mao's political/ideological trap.[36]

Liu Shaoqi, Peng Zhen, and other "underground" or "white area" Communist Party members were working primarily in North and Central China, organizing resistance to Japan. Liu and Mao had increased cooperation with each other in 1937, partly in opposition to Zhang Wentian.[37] Senior Eighth Route Army leaders, including Zhu De, Peng Dehuai, Nie Rongzhen, and others were in Shanxi, Chahar, and Hebei, establishing guerrilla units to attack Japanese rear areas. They had expanded the size of Communist forces from about 30,000 to 40,000 at the time of the Xi'an Incident to more than 160,000 by 1939.[38] They had cordial relations with Wang Ming and residual loyalty to Mao, but there was mutual suspicion and distrust among them.[39]

Mao moved quickly to strengthen his alliances within the readjusted leadership, mending fences temporarily with Zhang Wentian (still a member of the Central Secretariat), Ren Bishi, and Liu Shaoqi, and the recently returned Moscow trainees Chen Yun and Kang Sheng, who were responsible for the day-to-day business of the Politburo. By August 1938 another Long March veteran, Wang Jiaxiang, had returned to Yan'an from the USSR with assurances from the Comintern that Mao had its full support. Mao appointed his personal bodyguard to oversee security for all senior leaders in Yan'an.

Mao began urging senior Eighth Route Army commanders to focus their efforts, not on working with the National Revolutionary Army in engaging the Japanese in battle, but instead on building remote base areas behind Japanese lines and working to expand territory and personnel. He continued a steady volume of ideological writings that Sinicized the basic concepts of Marxism-Leninism, making them consistent with China's history and social conditions. Mao refined his own thoughts about military strategy and tactics in "On Protracted War." And he consolidated his position as the party's foremost theoretician by revising the understanding of its own history, depicting it as a series of "line struggles" between correct and incorrect ideas.[40]

Equally importantly, but perhaps less understood at the time, Mao issued a call for a study movement that would take senior cadres out of their everyday work positions and put them in classrooms to study Marxist-Leninist classics, along with Joseph Stalin's and Mao's own interpretations of their respective ideological movements. The failure of these classes to meet Mao's expectations in the early months led to even more intensive study and self-examination exercises that eventually became the Yan'an Rectification Movement (*Yan'an zhengfeng yundong*), which changed the Chinese Communist Party into Mao's personal political instrument.[41]

Kang Sheng's Role Expanded

Born in 1898 in Shandong, Kang Sheng joined the Communist Party in Shanghai in 1925 and was involved in violent uprisings and underground activities there. In 1928 he supported Wang Ming and the returned students (from Moscow) in their struggle for control of the party against Mao Zedong and the leadership of the Jiangxi Soviet. Wang Ming returned to the USSR in 1931 as principal delegate to the Comintern, and Kang, now a member of the CCP Central Committee in charge of intelligence collection, followed two years later, ostensibly as Wang's deputy. But he was also there to study the Soviet intelligence and security system, the People's Commissariat for Internal Affairs (NKVD).[42] Kang observed firsthand the "Great Purges" Stalin and Nikolai Yezhov undertook in 1936–1937 to rid the Soviet Communist Party of Stalin's political opponents. Kang is believed to have denounced several CCP-sponsored students in Moscow at the time as Trotskyites, resulting in several expulsions and even executions.[43]

Kang Sheng arrived in Yan'an in late 1937, and Mao Zedong may have had reason to believe that Kang was still a supporter of Wang Ming. But much of the CCP's intelligence apparatus had been lost during the Long March, and Mao needed to keep Zhou Enlai—who formerly controlled it—from re-establishing his influence. With the Japanese controlling a large swath of China's territory and with a very unsettled united front with the KMT, Mao wanted to restore the party's intelligence capabilities, and Kang Sheng probably appeared to be his best option for doing so.[44] Kang was intelligent enough to see that Mao had the real power in Yan'an and took early opportunities to side with him, deserting Wang Ming. Equally importantly, perhaps, Kang supported Mao by vouching for his mistress, Jiang Qing—a former Shanghai actress with a shady reputation—when other senior party leaders criticized the liaison and threatened to withhold permission for them to marry. In early 1938, Kang began taking positions of increasing influence and sensitivity that would have required Mao's explicit approval.[45]

In February 1939 Mao put Kang in charge of restructuring the CCP intelligence system, naming him to head the Central Social Department (CSD). At the same time, the Politburo approved the creation of a Central Intelligence Department within the Communist Party, which Kang Sheng controlled. Additionally, Kang was elevated to be deputy director of the Enemy Area Work Committee and director of the Political Security Agency, responsible for political security at the topmost level.[46]

The Central Social Department was Kang's main interest, given its focus on counterespionage work. Its declared purpose was "to prevent the enemies, traitors and spies from entering into our organization, ensure the success of our political tasks, and protect the organization from being damaged"; and to "collect all the proofs, documents and facts of the sabotages [*sic*] engaged in by enemy spies and traitors."[47] Kang moved quickly to recruit, train, indoctrinate, and deploy CSD agents and networks. He had already established his headquarters at Zaoyuan, a lush, green riverside area along in the northern part of Yan'an, which became a heavily guarded and restricted area, off-limits to ordinary cadres and students.[48] Kang cultivated a distinctive and sinister air, dressing in a black leather jacket, riding boots, and a Lenin-style cap, clutching a briefcase under his arm, and accompanied by four or more security men whenever he left his compound.[49]

Mao consults with his political security chief, Kang Sheng, just prior to the
Seventh CCP Congress in 1945. Kang, Moscow-trained in intelligence and
counterintelligence methods and organization, was chosen by Mao to head
the Central Social Department and other sensitive security organs in Yan'an.
Among those whose arrest Kang ordered was Hu Yaobang's new wife, Li Zhao.
(World History Archive—Alamy Stock Photo)

From Zaoyuan, Kang oversaw the manning of CCP United Front offices and covert networks in KMT-controlled areas and Japanese-occupied rural areas. Most importantly, he set up networks of informers in every party and military unit and university in CCP base areas, especially in Yan'an.[50] Kang's position in the CCP Secretariat and closeness to Mao meant that the weeding out of traitors would remain under the Center's control. But as Kang's networks and operations spread, they placed an increasingly powerful tool of intimidation in the hands of Kang and Mao—the Yan'an Rectification Campaign was coming, and Hu Yaobang would become personally involved.

Love Comes to Yan'an

The most important thing that happened to Hu Yaobang in 1939, notwithstanding his rapid promotion in the Central Military Commission, was the arrival in Yan'an of a petite, attractive, and intelligent young woman named Li Zhao. Born Li Shuxiu in Suxian, Anhui, on December 12, 1921, Li's background was very different from Hu's. Her father had been born into a wealthy family in Ningxiang, Hunan, and had studied military surveying, hoping to become an important military official. Her mother, Gao Huilan, was the daughter of a wealthy landowner. Li Shuxiu was still a toddler when her father left to work for a minor warlord in Hunan, never to return. In grief and sadness, Gao Huilan converted to Catholicism and lived a quiet but comfortable life in the family mansion with her mother, older sister, and daughter, whom they called "A-feng." A-feng avidly read the many books in the large residence and attended a Catholic school in Suxian, excelling in languages, history, and geography.[51]

After the Japanese invasion in 1937, Li Shuxiu and several schoolmates were caught up in the patriotic anger that swept the country. She joined a student volunteer service brigade that spread propaganda, trying to encourage local warlord soldiers to stand and fight rather than flee before the Japanese army. As the invasion progressed, Li and her fellow students were determined to take a more active role and looked for a way to go to Yan'an to join the Communist Party.

In January 1939, arrangements were made through underground CCP members for Li Shuxiu and her friends to meet up with a guerrilla unit in eastern Henan, and to travel on foot to Luoyang and by train to Xi'an and Yan'an.[52] Li and her companions changed their feminine-sounding names to something more revolutionary. Li Shuxiu—whose given name meant "virtuous and elegant"—changed her name to Li Zhao (李昭), meaning "bright and clear." When the guerrilla unit finally arrived, they agreed to help the upper-class teenage girls (Li Zhao was just eighteen) get to Yan'an to become revolutionary cadres, fighting for a new China. They set out in late February.[53]

The six-hundred-mile trek to Yan'an was arduous—they walked most of the way through rural Henan, suffering bad weather, checkpoints, bandits, bad food, grimy lodgings, and lice. By the time they reached Xi'an, Li Zhao was too ill to go on, and had to rest several days before taking a truck for the final leg to Yan'an. Once there, she underwent a political background check before being assigned to a school, and it wasn't until July that she entered the first class enrolled at China's Women's University. Li Zhao qualified to be in the advanced research class, studying Russian, natural sciences, and teaching methods. In less than a year she was eligible to join the Communist Party.[54]

Li Zhao met Hu Yaobang for the first time at a reception on October 10, the anniversary of the Soviet Union's "October Revolution," when she sat next to him in the only available empty chair. Although she had seen him several times and admired him as a senior official and reputed favorite of Mao Zedong, she had never spoken to him. On this occasion, they took to each other immediately, and friends soon afterward recognized they had a special attraction. They took long walks together, and sang revolutionary songs—Hu had a good singing voice. He spoke at length about his hopes for the revolution, his reading, his ideals. They called each other comrade. Accounts of his proposal include noble talk of working hand-in-hand for the revolution, mutual respect, and hope for the future.[55]

They married in November 1941, after Li had graduated from university and the party had given its approval. Their marriage contract had three clauses: (1) They would be fellow-comrades first, husband-and-wife second; (2) they would build a small family, but they would not forget they were struggling their whole lives for the Communist Party; and (3) in every situation and under all conditions, they would help and encourage each other, and go forward together.[56] These details don't have to be accurate to be true—the partnership of Hu Yaobang and Li Zhao would last for forty-eight years, a strong bond of affection and mutual respect that strengthened both of them through the trials and dangers that lay ahead. And those trials, at first, would come from Kang Sheng.

Yan'an Rectification

The term "rectification" in English draws its meaning from religious and civil law, meaning to make something right, to correct an error. The Chinese term used in Mao Zedong's 1942–1943 campaign was *zhengfeng* (整风), literally to "tidy up the wind," meaning to correct the work style of party members. The Chinese Communist Party's justification for the Yan'an Rectification Campaign asserts that the campaign was "of great significance in further correcting the Party's ideological line and strengthening the Party's own construction."[57] That meant that the political line of those who preceded Mao at the top of the CCP—Wang Ming in particular—was fundamentally erroneous and had to be corrected before the party could carry out the revolution.[58] Later scholars, such as Gao Hua, see the entire period from late 1938—when the Soviet-trained students returned from Moscow—to the Seventh CCP Congress in 1945 as a carefully orchestrated factional struggle, in which Mao used every tool he had to prevail over perceived adversaries. Those adversaries included not only Wang Ming and the returned students but some of Mao's own revolutionary comrades in the Eighth Route Army.[59]

Gao Hua details an evolving campaign that included both concerns about ideology, organization, and power struggles and Mao's and Kang's growing worry that the KMT was trying to undermine the Communist Party by subverting its young intellectual converts.[60] Other late arrivals in Yan'an included underground CCP members who had operated in the "white areas" under KMT control, some of whom had been arrested, many of whom had lost contact with their comrades far away. The CCP's first inclination was to educate and indoctrinate these young recruits and returnees with Marxist ideology from the classics. The problem was that such works seemed irrelevant to the Chinese revolutionary situation. Equally importantly, Mao was not sufficiently well-versed in them to instruct others. Instead, party members and even senior leaders looked to the returned students from Moscow for knowledge.[61]

The Yan'an Rectification Campaign proceeded in several phases. The first began in late August 1939 when the Central Committee issued a "decision on the consolidation of the party," which demanded that all party units review the credentials and histories of CCP members at all levels, beginning with the cadres. This initiated the "cadre examination" phase, to be done in cooperation with the Central Social Department. Kang Sheng dispatched secret "networkers" to every organization in Yan'an to collect information and report back to him. Because the CSD was short of staff, it probably coopted people in the CCP's and the CMC's organization departments to assist in the work of weeding out traitors. The first phase of Cadre Examination was relatively mild, so Mao and Kang moved on to the next phase in early 1941.

In May 1941 at a senior cadre conference, Mao delivered a speech titled "Reform Our Study," in which he criticized party members' general ignorance of their own Marxist-Leninist ideology and proposed a list of documents that all should study. Shortly afterward, he raised the stakes against the Russian-trained Politburo members by circulating materials about the CCP's history that criticized previous leaders from 1928 to 1935, charging them with fundamental errors in orientation and practice.[62] In September Mao made an important organizational adjustment, establishing a Central Advanced Study Group. Led by Mao, Kang Sheng, Ren Bishi, and Chen Yun, it would soon eclipse the Politburo and the Secretariat in political power.

By early 1942, Mao had changed the name of the Advanced Study Group to the Central General Study Committee, which was approved by the Politburo in June. For the next two years it would be the driving force in the Rectification Campaign. Mao was director, Kang Sheng was principal deputy director and secretary general. Liu Shaoqi and other leaders joined, but Mao and Kang made all the decisions on how *zhengfeng* was to be guided and oversaw the assignment of personnel to head subordinate study committees within both regional and functional CCP organs.[63]

In late 1942 the Rectification Campaign intensified. Party members were required repeatedly to write and publicize their class backgrounds and personal histories—not just for the organization and counterespionage departments, but for everyone. This kind of public self-examination—which became a hallmark of Mao's political campaigns—was referred to as "take off your pants and cut off your tails." It was not welcomed either by new CCP members with urban intellectual backgrounds or by older party cadres. It therefore required additional organizational and psychological pressure to gain full compliance. The goals were, first, to weed out those with questionable class backgrounds, KMT intelligence connections, or impure motives. Second, it imposed on every party member a sense of the party's domination of their lives and the requirement to put party goals and needs ahead of personal interests. The result was extreme organizational and psychological tension for every person in every organization in Yan'an.[64]

Collaboration with Kang Sheng

Hu's role in this escalating pressure project is not entirely clear. The most detailed account of his activities is by Taiwan scholar Chen Yong-fa, who used Hu's experience as one of several examples of how the Rectification worked, and how extreme it became in its later phases. Chen's book is based on KMT intelligence records from the period, which renders it somewhat questionable. But he found corroborating information, and the account, while not flattering to Hu, seems consistent with other available records and with his personality at the time.[65]

There was confusion in the early stages of the campaign, given its different goals—ideological indoctrination and trapping Mao's adversaries. Ultimately, Mao put Kang Sheng in charge of the Central Military Commission departments for rectification and cadre examination. He recommended that Kang turn to Hu Yaobang for help in weeding out the traitors that he and Kang both seemed certain were hiding everywhere.[66] Kang first put together a "leading small group" within the General Staff Department to oversee the process. It was headed by Ye Jianying and included Hu Yaobang.[67] Two sources—Hu's biographer Chen Liming and an account of Li Zhao's life—both assert that Hu was dual-hatted as a *chuzhang*, or section chief, in the Central Social Department, and thus doubly responsible to Kang Sheng.[68] Hu had already completed the rectification and cadre examination process in the Military Commission's Organization Department, where he was tasked with clearing out spies in the General Staff's Second Bureau, which was responsible for intelligence collection. In a department that had perhaps as many as two hundred personnel, most of them young, educated, and recently recruited, concerns about possible penetration by KMT special agents were not baseless, and Hu was expected to do the job with his usual enthusiasm.[69]

Kang Sheng, who was a key figure in Hu's life during this period, has become a classic villain in modern Chinese history. Even though he was in political favor when he died in 1975, he was discredited and vilified beginning in 1978, in part due to the efforts of Hu Yaobang. In 1980, after an extensive investigation, Kang was posthumously expelled from the CCP, his official eulogy rescinded and his cremated remains removed from the Babaoshan Revolutionary Cemetery. Subsequent accounts of Kang's role in CCP history were revised to reflect his "evil" influence. Kang thus became the default villain for everything that went wrong around him, exculpating others who may have been equally responsible. Gao Hua's *How the Red Sun Rose* makes it very clear, however, that Kang Sheng was doing exactly what Mao wanted him to do. Mao himself later allowed that he was in part responsible for the excesses of the Rectification Movement, in particular during its Rescue (*qiangjiu*) phase.[70]

Hu began the Rectification Campaign in full conformity with its goals and methods. He read the twenty-two articles prescribed by Mao, listened to speeches, and participated enthusiastically in group discussion sessions, including intense criticism of himself and his colleagues. At the same time, he participated in leadership small group sessions with Ye Jianying on how to bring the Rectification Campaign effectively to the various organs under the Central Military Commission. Then—and the exact timing is not clear—Hu was jarred by two events.

First, he was criticized by name in a large meeting of senior cadres by a military officer whose "inappropriate demand" Hu had refused to meet. The unnamed officer called out Hu for "bureaucratism, subjectivism, decentralism, by-the-bookism, and confusionism" (*hutu zhuyi*—a pun on Hu's surname). Mortified, Hu complained to the party's second-ranked leader, Liu Shaoqi. Liu's response was not recorded, but Hu vowed thereafter to become an even better revolutionary than his accuser.[71]

Second, and more ominous, Hu's wife, Li Zhao, was accused by Central Social Department informers of being a KMT spy. The exact timing of her ordeal is not known, but it probably was in late 1942. She was pregnant at the time, and her first son, Hu Deping, was born November 5.[72] The specific charges against her are uncertain, but Li Zhao was the daughter of a would-be warlord and a landed gentrywoman, and had been educated in a Catholic school—all things the Communist Party opposed. Moreover, the Rectification Campaign needed only oral charges—even those blurted out by people undergoing torture—for victims to be seized for interrogation. Accounts by those who fell under suspicion tell of intense psychological pressure, sensory and sleep deprivation, verbal abuse, public shaming, repeated demands for confessions, occasional physical beatings, and mock executions. Although the summary executions of the Jiangxi Soviet period did not appear to have been widely practiced during Yan'an Rectification, there are reports of perhaps thousands of deaths, many of them suicides by young people bereft of hope.[73]

Li Zhao and Hu Yaobang were not living together during this ordeal, but he was able to visit and reassure her of his belief in her innocence and his confidence that she had the strength to survive the experience. She was not sent to the cave prisons on the outskirts of Yan'an probably because she was caring for a newborn. But despite being an official in the CSD, Hu was not able to get his wife released from detention or have anyone intervene on her behalf. Li's ordeal was hardly surprising, given the level of paranoia that gripped Yan'an during this period and Kang Sheng's peculiar suspicion that any young, attractive, well-dressed woman was likely to be a special agent.[74] Li Zhao's life did not return to normal until sometime in 1943.

At a Politburo meeting in late April of that year, Mao again readjusted the top leadership, formally naming himself chairman (*zhuxi*) of the Politburo and of the three-member Secretariat (with Liu Shaoqi and Ren Bishi). According to Gao Hua, Mao at that point had attained his goal of having the "final decision power" for the party, with Liu as number two. At the same meeting, both Mao and Liu endorsed Kang Sheng's report on cadre examination as the party's principal task, primarily aimed at eliminating traitors.[75]

For his part, Hu Yaobang became more involved in the campaign, which was moving into a new phase involving more arrests and public confessions. With specific instruction from Kang Sheng, Hu stepped up the political pressure in the Second Bureau of the General Staff Department in late April / early May. Having already arrested two officers for corruption, he identified—with help from CSD "networkers"—some people with suspicious backgrounds and made it his goal to get them to confess. He organized large group meetings at which he harangued the young cadres about the prevalence of spies and the need to "watch for them, smell them, and arrest them." Hu boasted of having eight means of persuading people to confess, which he brought to bear both personally and through trusted proxies. In a matter of days, according to Chen Yong-fa, Hu had identified eighty-two suspects within the Second Bureau on whom he had collected thousands of pages of evidence—much of it hearsay or extracted by force. He pressured suspects to confess their errors publicly and to rely on the party for leniency and correction.[76]

Increasingly, Hu began to meet resistance, with young cadres accusing him of leftist errors, persecuting intellectuals, and forcing his views on others. Possibly in early May 1943, Hu's own doubts about the efficacy and propriety of the campaign led him to a turning point. Rather than follow Kang Sheng's latest orders to intensify the spy-hunting campaign, Hu issued guidelines to restrict it, limiting the excesses that had so shaken morale. Sources disagree on when he issued the orders but are consistent in describing their content:

(1) No beating or cursing of suspects; (2) no tying people up without prior approval from the party committee; (3) no forced confessions without sufficient evidence; and (4) strict prevention of suicides.[77] That such orders even had to be issued is evidence of how damaging the late phases of Yan'an Rectification had become.

When Kang Sheng learned of Hu's restrictions, he reportedly was not happy, and he sent his CSD deputy and experienced intelligence operative Li Kenong to remonstrate with Hu. According to Tang Fei, one of Hu's biographers, Kang had reported Hu's successes in the Second Bureau to Mao Zedong, who personally congratulated Hu. But the young man seems to have become thoroughly disillusioned with the Rectification Campaign by mid-1943. Hu not only resisted Li Kenong's efforts to get him to rescind his restrictions, but he added advice on what kinds of evidence should be acceptable and on how erroneous cases should be quickly reversed.[78] Hu told Mao that the claims he had dug out several spies in the General Staff Department were not true, and he described the damage being done by the efforts to expose nonexistent spies. He singled out forced confessions as the most harmful practice in the campaign.[79]

But the Rectification Campaign did not stop. With Mao's full blessing, in fact, the campaign went through one more paroxysm of persecution and violence in early July 1943, the "rescuing those who have slipped" phase. During a two-week period, perhaps as many as fourteen hundred people were arrested without evidence and underwent brutal interrogation at the hands of Central Social Department officials. In the last two weeks of July, several of Mao's colleagues, including Liu Shaoqi and Zhou Enlai, must have realized that this phase of rectification had done great damage to party morale while turning up very few actual spies. They were so intimidated by Mao at this point, however, that no one was willing to complain about rectification practices, although Mao may have recognized these problems on his own.[80] On July 30, Mao cabled a letter to senior party leaders outside Yan'an on the proper conduct of cadre examination, claiming that some "subjectivist practices" had emerged during rectification and implying that forced confessions needed to be curtailed.[81]

There was no criticism of Kang Sheng or immediate diminution of his authority, and no structural changes, just a gradual easing of the Rectification Campaign until it went into a screening phase in early 1944, when earlier errors were to be reviewed. Even what has been represented as Mao's apology for the excesses of rectification was quite ambiguous: "The campaign got a bit too hot," he said, "which made a few comrades feel wronged, and so on." And although some who had been designated as spies were exonerated, the number never constituted a majority, and at the end of the screening process in 1944, the Rectification Campaign was deemed to have been "completely correct."[82]

Hu Yaobang seems to have gone into eclipse following his efforts to moderate the rectification process. He clearly had no influence over decisions made by Mao or Kang Sheng in the final phases of the campaign. He may indeed have engendered their distrust or resentment. His biographers can find nothing of significance recorded about his activities from mid-1943 until the Seventh Congress of the Chinese Communist Party in April 1945. Presumably Hu returned to the Organization Department of the General Political Department and was involved in personnel work, such as the verification of credentials for delegates to the long-awaited Congress. Hu was identified as one of twenty-two members of the credentials verification committee, headed by Peng Zhen, and he did attend the congress as a delegate.[83]

The Chinese Communist Party and its leader had undergone enormous changes in the nine years since their arrival in northern Shaanxi. In late 1935 the CCP was a hungry and irresolute band of stragglers on the verge of starvation. By 1945 it had become a disciplined, trained, and confident political and military powerhouse, prepared to take on the KMT, its longtime foe, in a final battle for control of China. In 1935 the Communist Party had probably fewer than twenty thousand members. At the Seventh Congress, the 547 delegates represented more than 1.2 million members. After the Long March and the absorption of guerrillas in Shaanxi, the Red Army had numbered thirty thousand to forty thousand troops. The Eighth Route Army in 1945 numbered more than 1.5 million soldiers in several base areas, with ample small arms, machine guns, cavalry, and artillery, courtesy of the USSR. Although still smaller than Chiang Kai-shek's National Revolutionary Army, it had suffered far fewer casualties in battles against the Japanese invaders.

In 1936 the Communist Party was led by a feuding, disorganized group of peasant guerrillas, disaffected intellectuals, and Soviet-trained students. Now it was led by a single individual, Mao Zedong. At the beginning of the Yan'an period, Mao was a tough-minded but genial intellectual leader, first among equals, seeking to establish a political and ideological basis for China's revolutionary movement and a safe haven from its enemies. By 1945 Mao was an almost imperial figure—living in a well-guarded compound, served by a growing personal staff, unapproachable except by appointment. He was the undisputed arbiter of China's ideology, an autocrat who had humiliated and overwhelmed every other CCP leader, who had rewritten the party's history to match his version of events and reorganized its leadership to suit his needs.[84] Now he was Chairman Mao, his ideas enshrined in the newly adopted party constitution as Mao Zedong Thought, and he did not seem to object when people used the same cheer for him that had formerly been reserved for China's emperors, "May Chairman Mao live ten thousand years!" (*Mao zhuxi wansui!*)

Hu Yaobang, too, had changed. When he arrived at Yan'an, he had been a spindly, sickly "little red devil" who had barely survived the Long March. He had been a youth activist who was good at propaganda and organization, an enthusiastic and bright student of Mao Zedong, and a cheerleader for the revolution. Now he was a veteran party bureaucrat who had given orders to senior generals and persecuted as spies young cadres whom he did not believe actually were spies. He had cooperated with, then turned against, Kang Sheng, one of the party's most malevolent figures, and probably paid a price for it. He had married and started a family but could not protect his young wife from the psychological oppression of the political party they had joined.

Hu's biographers maintain that his attendance at the Seventh Congress as a delegate elevated his understanding of and respect for the Communist Party, its organizational strength and leadership.[85] While there is no reason to gainsay these judgments, one could portray Hu's ten years in Yan'an as a time of enveloping friendships and human relationships. He had stood in the light of Mao Zedong, but it grew increasingly harsh and injurious over time, and he may have felt the need to get away from it, however much he respected the Chairman. What would sustain Hu Yaobang in the difficult years to come were the friendships nurtured by close living and working quarters, intense but important work, mutual dedication and loyalties, and social bonding in a relatively relaxed and peaceful atmosphere. Some of Hu's most important friends during these years were Ye Jianying, with whom Hu worked in the General Staff Department; Wang Jiaxiang, his superior and mentor at the General Political Department and one of Mao's targets in the Rectification Campaign; Luo Ruiqing, one of his superiors at Kang Da, with whom he played *mahjongg;* and Tao Zhu and Wang Heshou, two friends in the GPD, with whom Hu swore a three-part covenant of loyalty after the Japanese surrender in August 1945.[86]

Once the Japanese surrendered, everyone in Yan'an knew that the real war—with the Kuomintang—would soon start. Troops and equipment needed to be deployed as quickly as possible. Bruised and embedded in a rectified CCP, Hu requested of Chairman Mao that he be sent to the front lines. Mao approved readily.

3 Winning the Wars, Securing Power

On the morning of August 6, 1945, an American B-29 Superfortress bomber, the Enola Gay, left Tinian airfield in the Marianas Islands and headed toward the Japanese industrial and port city of Hiroshima on the southern edge of the main island of Honshu. At about 8:15 a.m. local time, it released the first atomic bomb to be deployed in warfare from thirty-one thousand feet. It detonated at nineteen hundred feet with the strength of about 12,500 tons of TNT, destroying most of the city and killing more than a hundred thousand of its residents.[1]

The Soviet Union moved quickly after this, seeing an opportunity to seize valuable Japanese industrial assets in East Asia. Josef Stalin declared war on Japan on August 8 and ordered prepositioned Soviet armed forces to invade Manchuria the following day; they controlled most of it by the end of August.[2] On August 9 a plutonium bomb was dropped on the city of Nagasaki, causing appalling damage and killing at least 70,000 of the city's 178,000 people.[3] On August 10, Emperor Hirohito summoned the Supreme Council for the Direction of the War and ordered it to accept the Allied unconditional surrender terms, which had been set out by the Potsdam Declaration of July 26, 1945, signed by the governments of the United States, Great Britain and China, which had participated by radio. August 15 was the date agreed for hostilities to cease entirely.[4]

The War Ends, the War Begins

In China, both the Nationalist government of Chiang Kai-shek and the Communist Party of Mao Zedong were surprised by the rapid collapse of Japanese war efforts but moved to prepare for civil war. Chiang had not participated personally in the Potsdam Conference and had not been aware

of the US atomic weapons program. Prior to August, he apparently be-
lieved that the war with Japan would stretch on for another year or more.
After the Soviet invasion of Manchuria, he adjusted negotiations with
Moscow over a treaty of alliance, acceding to Soviet domination of Outer
Mongolia in exchange for what he thought would be limitations on its occupation of Manchuria and on its aid to the Chinese Communist Party.[5]
Chiang was uncertain of the support he could expect from the United
States, Nationalist China's principal ally and supporter. Relations had
soured in 1944, and although financial and materiel assistance was con-
tinuing, Chiang probably thought the United States would not have the
stomach for a lengthy civil war.[6]

Mao apparently thought that it would be mid-1946 before Japan's grip on
China could be broken.[7] He had husbanded his military resources since
1940, avoiding major engagements with Japanese forces and focusing on establishing personal control of the Communist Party and its military leadership. He had begun moving forces from northwest China base areas toward
the northeast, where the Kuomintang was weak and Soviet assistance would
be more readily available. But he was still far from ready to act in August 1945,
particularly in light of the Soviet Union's August 15 Treaty of Alliance with
the Chiang government, and the ensuing pressure from Moscow not to break
the United Front with the KMT.[8]

On August 16, Chiang sent a cable to Mao in Yan'an, inviting him to
Chongqing to begin negotiations on "big plans" for reunification. Mao demurred, unprepared to put his physical safety at risk in his enemy's capital
city. But Chiang persisted, and the United States offered to guarantee Mao's
safety. Moscow also cabled Yan'an, urging Mao to negotiate a coalition government.[9] Mao finally agreed, and arrived in Chongqing on August 28, accompanied on the flight from Yan'an by US ambassador Patrick Hurley. He
remained there until October 10, when the two sides signed the Double 10
Agreement, by which the CCP acknowledged the legitimacy of the KMT
government and was recognized in return as an opposition party. The two
sides agreed to use peaceful methods and negotiations to resolve disputes,
to establish a "peaceful, democratic, and unified" China based on Sun
Yat-sen's "three people's principles," and to participate in a constitutional
government after a national political consultative congress.[10] Mao left for
Yan'an the following day, telling his associates the agreement was just
"wastepaper." Chiang Kai-shek evidently felt the same way. Both sides began
concerted efforts to render the document meaningless.[11]

Hu Yaobang Volunteers

After Japan's formal surrender on September 2, 1945, all Japanese forces in Manchuria, South Sakhalin, and Korea north of the 38th Parallel were ordered to surrender to the Soviet Far East commander.[12] Manchuria and Japanese-occupied North China were the main prizes for both Chiang and Mao, both of whom had begun moving troops into position even while they were negotiating with each other. In late August, Eighth Route Army forces were ordered to begin moving from various guerrilla bases to areas in or close to Liaoning Province, the southernmost part of Manchuria. Mao's overall strategy was "develop to the north, defend to the south"—to secure territory in China's industrial heartland, seize weapons and equipment left by the Japanese, and link up with Soviet forces while preventing Nationalist Army units from moving into the region.[13] Chiang utilized US Marines in and around Tianjin to receive the surrender of Japanese troops. He began to use US Army Air Corps transports and US Navy ships to move Nationalist troops to urban areas of North China ahead of Chinese Communist ground forces. The stage was being set for a quick resumption of the Chinese civil war, and indeed there were numerous small-scale skirmishes, but larger geopolitical issues—namely, US relations with the Soviet Union and American unwillingness to be drawn into another war in Asia—kept the protagonists from taking precipitous actions or declaring that the cease-fire had collapsed.[14]

Hu Yaobang wanted badly to be part of the actual war against the KMT. He made a request to Mao through Ye Jianying to be relieved of his duties in the Central Military Commission, saying he had been in a headquarters role for too long.[15] Mao approved the request, and Lin Biao—who was preparing to leave Yan'an to head the Northeast People's Self-Defense Army— invited Hu to join him as a political officer.[16] Lin, scion of a wealthy Hubei family, had joined the Nanchang Uprising and fled to Jinggangshan with Mao and Zhu De. A daring combat commander, he became one of Mao's favorites, but was wounded in 1938 and evacuated to Moscow, where he stayed four years. On return, he was chancellor of Kang Da (where he worked with Hu Yaobang), commander of the Eighth Route Army's 115th Division, then in October 1945 was appointed commander of all CCP forces in the northeast, the most important command in the early civil war.

Before Hu left, he had to make difficult decisions about his family. His wife, Li Zhao, was prepared to follow him to the front, but they now had two children, Hu Deping, born in 1942, and a second son, born in February 1945. Not wishing to subject the boys to the perils of a war zone, they decided to leave Deping with a staffer in Yan'an but agonized over what to do with the second son. They finally arranged for a Shaanxi farm co-op leader named Liu Shichang to take the child. Hu suggested Liu raise the child as his own son, and they named him Liu Hu, using both family surnames. Biographic sketches of Li Zhao suggest she was very unhappy about leaving her children behind. They would not see the second child again for sixteen years.[17] Hu and Li set out in mid-October for the Northeast with a contingent of seven hundred to eight hundred CCP cadres, office workers, students, and assorted soldiers. By mid-November they had reached the headquarters of the *Jin-Cha-Ji* (Shanxi-Chahar-Hebei) Military District and party bureau, about two hundred kilometers northwest of Beijing in Zhangjiakou, a city that already had been "liberated."[18]

According to Xiaobing Li, in late 1945 the Nationalist government had "a total of 4.3 million troops, including 2 million regulars. Its forces were better equipped than the CCP forces, since they had received most of the weapons and equipment from surrendering Japanese troops in China and continued to receive U.S. military aid. . . . [They] controlled three-quarters of the country, and more than 300 million people. They occupied all of the large cities and controlled most of the railroads, highways, seaports, and transportation hubs."[19] The Nationalist Army was hampered, however, by the personnel losses it had suffered during the war against Japan; by the political feuding, corruption, and incompetence of senior officers; by the illiteracy and poor training of conscript soldiers; and by a lack of transport to move its armies to areas being left by Japanese forces.

In late 1945 the Eighth Route Army, New Fourth Army, and smaller units were scattered about in base areas of Northwest, North Central, and East China. Although the Eighth Route Army had been relatively stable in structure during the War of Resistance, in the civil war the CCP military structure would be constantly shifting, with units being moved and assigned to different commands. The Central Military Commission (CMC) ensured that the party, and especially Mao, had predominant influence on both the strategic direction of "Liberation Army" actions and its personnel deployments.[20]

The CMC divided its roughly 600,000 troops into 22 to 27 columns (*zongdui*), each consisting of three divisions of about 7,000 men. Adding in about 600,000 irregulars in smaller brigades and local militia units, the

Liberation Army totaled about 1.27 million men.[21] But with scattered guerrilla base areas and rudimentary communications, the focus of the military's capabilities, and ultimately the source of its success, lay in its seasoned regional combat commanders. These individuals, from a variety of family and educational backgrounds, knew little of Communist ideology, but knew the importance of loyalty to Mao Zedong from their experiences in the Yan'an Rectification Movement and before. More importantly, from 1945 onward they knew how to feed, move, fight, and maintain the loyalty of peasant armies in primitive conditions. Their command names, numbers, and regional assignments would change in the turbulent course of the next four years, and Mao would quarrel with most of them over strategy and personnel. But they were nearly always found near the top of the command structure: Zhu De was overall commander, and Lin Biao, Peng Dehuai, Nie Rongzhen, Chen Yi, Liu Bocheng, He Long, and Xu Xiangqian were the principal combat commanders.

Political Commissar Hu

Hu Yaobang ranked far below these Liberation Army leaders but would serve with several of them by the end of the civil war. His hopes to get in the thick of the fight in the Northeast were stymied in late 1945, however. The KMT Thirteenth Army, which the US Navy had transported to the port of Huludao in mid-October, raced westward and set up a blocking position along the main road into Liaoning near Pingquan. In early December Hu Yaobang and his assorted soldiers and students were unprepared to take on a well-equipped KMT army, so they encamped west of Pingquan to await orders.[22] In early January Xiao Ke, commander of the Hebei-Rehol-Liaoning Military District, requested that Hu be assigned as director of the district's political department. Yan'an approved and assigned him as the regional representative of the General Political Department.[23]

International political considerations also interrupted Hu's military career. In late November, US ambassador Patrick Hurley, on a home visit to Washington, resigned his post with a letter denouncing "professional foreign service men" in China, whom he charged had "sided with the Chinese Communist armed party" and deliberately sabotaged his efforts to avert the collapse of the Nationalist government.[24] Exasperated with Hurley's posturing, President Harry S. Truman nominated former chief of the combined staff and five-star general George C. Marshall to be "special representative to China." In view of the deteriorating situation on the ground in China, Marshall's instructions were to "bring to bear the influence of the United States to promote the unification of China by peaceful, democratic methods," and to "endeavor to effect a cessation of hostilities," particularly in North China.[25]

Marshall arrived in Chongqing in late December. Acting as intermediary between the KMT and the CCP, and by dint of his own formidable skills and reputation, he was able to arrange a cease-fire by January 10, 1946. Part of the cease-fire agreement was the establishment in Beijing of an executive headquarters (in Chinese, a "military reconciliation administrative bureau"), responsible for investigating and resolving cease-fire violations and competing territorial claims. The CCP's principal representative on that commission, located in the Beijing Hotel, was Ye Jianying.[26]

Son of a Guangdong Hakka merchant, Ye Jianying received some military education in Yunnan, then at Whampoa. He joined the Nanchang Uprising and the CCP in 1927, then fled to the USSR, returning to Jiangxi in 1930. A Long March survivor, Ye was a competent staff officer, and became a senior member of the CMC in Yan'an. There he worked closely with Hu Yaobang, and the two became close friends. Ye assisted Zhou Enlai doing Chongqing liaison work in 1937 and became a liaison officer for the Marshall mission. As such he was uniquely positioned to be helpful when Hu Yaobang's health failed him again in early 1946. Hu fell gravely ill with a high fever, debilitating abdominal pain, and diarrhea. His condition worsened, and Xiao Ke feared for his survival. Ye Jianying used his authority for on-site investigations to dispatch an aircraft to pick up Hu Yaobang and return him to Beijing, where he was sent to the Union Medical College Hospital and diagnosed with amoebic hepatitis. Ye arranged for Hu's bodyguard to be transferred to Beijing to supervise his care, and the local underground Communist Party brought in a traditional Chinese medicine doctor to treat him.

While recuperating, Hu did some administrative work for Ye and his chief of staff, Luo Ruiqing, another old friend from Kang Da, and was given the insignia of a major general to facilitate exchanges with KMT and American personnel in the executive office. In the tense and deteriorating situation in North China in the spring of 1946, those exchanges were unpleasant, and the still-unsophisticated thirty-year-old Hu is said to have found the KMT officers oily and officious, and the Americans arrogant and lacking in manners. By April, Hu's health had improved sufficiently that Ye Jianying agreed he should return to the headquarters in Zhangjiakou.[27]

In early June the Central Military Commission issued orders for the reorganization of Communist forces, forming the *Jin-Cha-Ji* Field Army, of which Nie Rongzhen was appointed commander and political commissar, with Xiao Ke as deputy commander and Luo Ruiqing as deputy political commissar. Four columns of more than twenty thousand men each were formed, and Hu Yaobang was appointed political commissar of the Fourth Column, commanded by Chen Zhengxiang. At the time of its formation, the *Jin-Cha-Ji* Military District was facing some 420,000 KMT and warlord troops.[28]

The political commissar system was intended to ensure Communist Party control of its military units. A party professional, not necessarily trained in military arts but responsible to the Central Committee, was placed in a position of authority in every military unit at every level. That individual was a key member—often the secretary in charge—of the party committee that made all military decisions for the unit. He usually held rank similar to the commander in the CCP cadre-rank system. Occasionally, when the commander was well-trusted, one individual might hold both positions, but that was the exception rather than the rule. The commander-commissar relationship was critically important.

In Liberation Army units, political commissars were responsible for maintaining the fighting morale, discipline, ideological commitment, loyalty, and security of young peasant recruits (or captured KMT prisoners). In many cases this was a matter of political and ideological education, delivered in field conditions. Commissars had several deputies, a political department, and subordinate officers down the chain of command. They were responsible for personnel issues, including promotions and demotions, assignments, and political security.[29]

Hu Yaobang was well-suited for this kind of position. Intelligent and affable, he was cooperative with both superiors and subordinates, and knew the fine points of ideology and how to do effective propaganda. His longstanding relationship with Mao Zedong put him in good stead with senior officers. His youthful appearance enabled him to interact with young soldiers without intimidating them, and he often chose to walk with the common fighters rather than ride on horseback with the officers.

Hu's literacy and love of poetry enabled him to put together a unique training manual for poorly educated soldiers. It was not only comprehensive but also memorable, because it was in the form of the *Three Character Classic*—every Chinese elementary schoolchild's primer, which Hu had studied years before. The illustrated *People's Army Three-Character Classic* (*renmin jundui sanzijing*) he supervised and helped edit had fifty-seven sections, all in three-character phrases, explaining the Communist Party, the Red Army, relations between army and people, the importance of study, and more.[30]

The Taste of Defeat

In July 1946 the Liberation Army's high command had decided to attack the Nationalist- held city of Datong, a key rail hub in northeastern Shanxi, to ease the pressure on the CCP's *Jin-Cha-Ji* headquarters at Zhangjiakou. The main fighting force was to be three columns from the *Jin-Cha-Ji* Field Army (including Hu Yaobang's Fourth Column), supplemented by several brigades of He Long's troops from the Shanxi-Suiyuan base area. They outnumbered the Nationalist defenders in and around Datong by about a five-to-one ratio and divided their forces between occupying outlying villages and laying siege to the city.[31]

Actual attacks on Datong began in early August and moved slowly, inflicting heavy casualties on local militia, forcing them back inside the city walls by early September. The airport south of the city remained in Nationalist hands, however, enabling supplies and reinforcements to be brought to the defenders. Chiang Kai-shek ordered KMT troops from west and east of Datong to move to the nearby city of Jining to break the blockade. On August 28 Mao Zedong cabled Nie Rongzhen and He Long, urging them to "annihilate" Beijing warlord Fu Zuoyi's arriving forces without compromising the siege of Datong. The on-scene commanders believed they could leave a portion of their troops in position around Datong and move a large force toward Jining to intercept Fu Zuoyi's Thirty-Fifth Army.[32]

On September 8 Fu Zuoyi's troops attacked Jining with air support, and were themselves assaulted two days later by Liberation Army forces from the south, including Hu Yaobang's Fourth Column. During two days of intense combat, in which Hu narrowly escaped being seriously wounded by air attacks, the Communist units inflicted heavy casualties, putting three of Fu Zuoyi's divisions out of action, killing as many as five thousand. Then Nie's troops paused to rest, allowing Fu time to reinforce his battered divisions and bring in three new divisions, including the US-equipped 101st Division. It was a significant mistake by the frontline CCP commanders, and they paid heavily for it.[33]

There is no way for one looking through historical articles and memoirs seventy years later to reconstruct accurately what happened next. Moreover, the normal fog of war has been thickened by recriminations and efforts to shift blame in ensuing investigations. But it appears that Fu Zuoyi's fresher, better-equipped troops moved faster than expected on September 12, out-flanked CCP forces, inflicted heavy casualties, and broke the blockade of Jining.[34] Poor communications and command inexperience made things worse, with various CCP units believing that other units had retreated, and consequently retreating themselves. As the day wore on, the retreats turned into a rout, and on September 13 the Military Commission agreed with Nie Rongzhen that his troops should withdraw from Jining. Having committed and lost so many troops at Jining, there was no way to renew the siege of Datong, and CCP troops withdrew from there as well on September 16.[35]

Although both sides claimed victory, both also suffered heavy casualties, more than ten thousand on each side.[36] But the initiative in the overall civil war situation appeared to swing toward the Nationalist side. Chiang Kai-shek said afterward that he thought the civil war could be over in a few months. Under growing pressure from Marshall to negotiate another cease-fire, Chiang Kai-shek and Zhou Enlai both continued talking with him and past each other, while preparations proceeded for a showdown at Zhangjiakou. Marshall threatened on October 1 to have himself recalled by President Truman unless both sides agreed to an immediate cease-fire. Both sides agreed in principle, but with conditions they knew the other side would reject.[37]

The Communist side probably had more reason to hope for a cease-fire as the extent of the debacle at Datong and Jining became clearer. Many of the thousands of soldiers lost by CCP units were seasoned veterans who could not be easily replaced by peasant recruits coming out of newly "liber-ated" areas. Nie Rongzhen informed Yan'an that his troops would try to ha-rass the KMT forces heading for Zhangjiakou, but they should be prepared to abandon it. The CMC and Mao agreed, but considering the city's strategic and psychological importance, implored him to undertake a vigorous defense.[38]

Hu Yaobang's Fourth Column, along with most of Nie's troops, raced to Zhangjiakou to take up blocking positions against an expected late-September assault by Nationalist forces coming from the west and east via the Beiping-Suiyuan railroad. CCP forces were concentrated east of the city and repulsed a KMT attack on September 29.[39] For the second time in a month, however, Nie and his commanders failed to consider Fu Zuoyi's skill as a tactician and the speed of his forces. Fu sent twenty thousand motorized infantry, cavalry, and armored troops north beyond the Great Wall. They then turned south and surprised the lightly defended northern part of Zhangjiakou. That attack quickly turned the tide of the battle.[40] Nie cobbled together a defense on October 10, but the Nationalist forces used captured Japanese tanks, American-supplied artillery, and air support to inflict heavy losses on the CCP troops, and Nie ordered them to withdraw at dusk.[41]

The following day Fu's commanders prepared for street-to-street fighting in their final assault on Zhangjiakou. But by early afternoon, they realized the city had been abandoned by the Red Army and the Communist Party infrastructure. All had all fled south and west, after destroying much of the "second Red capital." By evening, Fu's troops were in full control of the city, whose civilian residents welcomed them quietly.

Yan'an did not agree with Nie's (and Hu's private) assessment of the disaster that had befallen their forces in North China as "no big deal." Abandoning Zhangjiakou was indeed a big deal, and major changes followed it. The *Jin-Cha-Ji* Field Army was reorganized. Nie Rongzhen lost his positions as commander and political commissar to Xiao Ke and Luo Ruiqing, respectively.[42] Mao Zedong temporarily abandoned his strategic efforts to capture and hold cities and rail lines, and instead pressed Liberation Army units to establish absolute military superiority over individual KMT units, and to annihilate them, unit by unit.[43]

In mid-November, Chiang Kai-shek convened a meeting of the National Assembly without any CCP representation, confident that he would be able to defeat them in a matter of months. CCP negotiators assigned to the Marshall mediation mission asked to be returned to Yan'an and refused to participate in any further efforts to arrange a cease-fire or reduce tensions. For his part, Marshall became increasingly frustrated with both sides, and advanced his plans to terminate his mission. He would leave in early January 1947 to become Truman's secretary of state.[44]

Regaining Confidence and Momentum

Hu Yaobang's Fourth Column was not directly affected by command changes in the *Jin-Cha-Ji* Field Army and continued moving south in early 1947, engaging in small-scale battles in Hebei, mainly against warlord garrison troops, who often surrendered to the larger Communist forces. Hu was

Map 3. Major battles in which Hu Yaobang fought in North China, 1946–1949, under the command of Nie Rongzhen and Xu Xiangqian.

credited with both personal bravery and command resourcefulness in these engagements by his comrades-in-arms writing memoirs many years later.[45] The Zhengding-Taiyuan Campaign of April–May 1947 resulted in a series of Communist victories, strategically isolating Shijiazhuang, the capital of Hebei, and gaining control of rural areas from which new recruits could be drawn into Communist forces. Casualties were high, however, with more than six thousand dead or wounded.[46]

The *Jin-Cha-Ji* Field Army command was reorganized and enlarged in June 1947. Hu was assigned as political commissar of the Third Column, commanded by Zheng Weishan, which had about thirty thousand soldiers. In late September the army was able to trap an elite KMT force at Qingfengdian, capturing its commander, several senior officers, and eleven thousand prisoners after fierce fighting and more casualties.[47] That battle opened the possibility of capturing the key transportation hub of Shiji-azhuang, which had been isolated by Communist advances but was still heavily fortified and defended by more than twenty-four thousand KMT and local soldiers. The KMT commander boasted he had food and supplies sufficient for a three-year siege.[48]

In late October 1947 Mao Zedong ordered the *Jin-Cha-Ji* field command to rest for a few days, then to attack Shijiazhuang. He sent Zhu De to oversee the planning. After battle plans were fleshed out during a series of party committee meetings, Hu Yaobang gathered political officers of the Third Column for a morale-boosting talk before a battle that was expected to have heavy casualties. He tried to lighten spirits but told his subordinates it would be a hard battle requiring courage and bitter fighting.[49]

That prediction was fully realized beginning on November 6, 1947, when more than a hundred thousand *Jin-Cha-Ji* Field Army troops and militia began their attack on Shijiazhuang after heavy artillery bombardment had destroyed the city's power plant and weakened the city walls. Emerging from tunnels and scaling walls with siege ladders, Communist troops collapsed the outer defenses and moved quickly into the city center with disciplined and well-armed small units. But it still took six days of bloody hand-to-hand combat before the KMT commander surrendered the remains of his garrison on November 12. Twenty-one thousand defenders were taken prisoner and more than three thousand were killed, while the Communist armies suffered about six thousand dead and wounded.[50]

The capture of Shijiazhuang was a major strategic advance for the CCP, more than counterbalancing its loss of Yan'an in the spring of 1947. Mao and the rest of the leadership had already moved to Xibaipo, in northern Hebei, leaving the former capital open to an attack by Hu Zongnan, one of the KMT's foremost combat commanders. It began a period of serious losses for KMT forces across much of northern China, including in Manchuria, Shandong, and the Northwest. Nationalist morale began to crumble as Communist attacks chipped away at their troop strength, causing more and more units to surrender wholesale rather than fight. Of course, in the seesaw battles that took place often between various-sized KMT, warlord, and CCP units, many Communist prisoners were also taken. At Chiang Kai-shek's orders, however, captured Communist troops were not to be absorbed into Nationalist Army units. Probably recalling how Communist Party members had undermined Nationalist Army units in the 1920s, particularly before the

Nanchang Uprising of 1927, Chiang put most of his Communist prisoners into labor camps far from the front lines.[51]

In October 1947 Mao Zedong made a major announcement on behalf of what he called for the first time the Chinese People's Liberation Army (*Zhongguo renmin jiefangjun*). It marked a change in the CCP's policy on KMT personnel captured in battle. The new policy promised "those officers and soldiers who lay down their weapons, will without exception not be killed or disgraced, those who wish to remain will receive a pardon, those who want to go will be sent home."[52] Although this change in policy probably contributed to growth in the numbers of KMT soldiers willing to surrender, PRC scholars have acknowledged that few captives actually were given the option of returning home. Senior KMT officers were put into the labor camps far from front lines, while junior officers and ordinary soldiers were absorbed into People's Liberation Army units *in situ* after short periods of political indoctrination, sometimes on the same day.[53] But even though sources differ on details, the numbers are striking: by mid-1948 more than 1 million, and perhaps as many as 1.6 million, KMT soldiers had been taken prisoner by Communist forces. Most were absorbed immediately into PLA combat units. By the end of the mainland combat phase of the Chinese civil war (mid-1950), the number of KMT soldiers who had been captured, surrendered, mutinied, or "accepted conversion" (*jieshou gaibian*) to PLA troops was more than 6 million.[54]

PRC scholars with archival access quote official reports from some of Mao's leading generals that the addition of large numbers of captured prisoners, or "liberated fighters," resolved what had been an urgent shortage of replacements for PLA field army units in the first years of the civil war. Even units that suffered very high casualty rates grew in manpower by absorbing KMT prisoners. According to Peng Dehuai and Chen Yi, for example, the percentage of liberated fighters in PLA units in 1948–1949 was as high as 80 percent in some, and averaged 65 to 70 percent.[55] Several senior PLA commanders reported that they preferred KMT captives to the "emancipated peasants" conscripted out of the Communist base areas. The KMT troops, even though of poor peasant background and minimal education, at least had received some training, had combat experience, and obeyed orders.[56] Getting young peasant conscripts and captured KMT soldiers acclimated to PLA life, discipline, and ideology, then sending them into intense combat situations, was the responsibility of political officers like Hu Yaobang.

The Siege of Taiyuan

By December 1947 Mao Zedong told a Politburo meeting that the war had reached a turning point, with Communist forces no longer on the defensive and now carrying the battle to Nationalist-controlled areas.[57] This was certainly true in the North China Field Army operating area of Hebei and Shanxi Provinces. In late December and early 1948, Hu's Third Column was skirmishing with Nationalist troops under Fu Zuoyi and other local warlords south and west of Beijing. While inflicting moderate casualties, they succeeded in bottling up these government forces in their urban strongpoints, making them unable to aid the increasingly beleaguered Nationalist garrisons in the Northeast.[58]

The CMC reshuffled the North China commands again in May 1948, forming the North China Military District, commanded by Nie Rongzhen. The district had three corps, each of which had three columns of about twenty thousand men. Xu Xiangqian, despite being ill with pleurisy, was made commander and political commissar of the newly designated First Corps. Born into wealth in Shanxi, Xu had joined the KMT army in 1924 and studied at Whampoa. In 1927 he joined the CCP and became a guerrilla leader in western Hubei, eventually taking a separate route on the Long March. Xu arrived in Yan'an in 1937 and joined Liu Bocheng's 129th Division as deputy commander. In 1948 Hu Yaobang was promoted to head the Political Department of the Xu's First Corps, making him responsible for the conduct of political work for more than sixty thousand soldiers. The First Corps was given responsibility for operations in eastern and southern Shanxi Province, where the principal Nationalist leader was still Yan Xishan.

The Shanxi capital city of Taiyuan is in the valley of the Fen River, with low mountains to the east and west. Its walls, built during the Ming Dynasty, were in some places forty feet thick and sixty feet high. Yan Xishan had Chinese and Japanese engineers build a series of heavy fortresses, pillboxes, trenches, and barbed wire approximately thirty miles in all directions from the city, with special strongpoints in the mountainous areas. He built more fortifications inside the city, and mobilized thousands of the city's thirty thousand residents to assist in their supply and upkeep. His own army was estimated at around one hundred thousand men, with an additional thirty thousand from the Nationalist Army.[59]

On July 17, 1948, the CMC ordered the Taiyuan Front Committee to surround, undermine, and then attack the city. At first, Mao ordered the First

Corps to attack immediately and to complete the task in ten days. Xu Xiangqian requested a delay, explaining that his forces had suffered heavy casualties and were exhausted and short of experienced junior officers after recent battles. They needed time to organize and train the large numbers of liberated fighters and emancipated peasants that had recently joined the First Corps, and to accumulate the ordinance and materiel needed for a siege campaign. The CMC acceded to this request on July 23 and ordered Xu to rest and recuperate in Shijiazhuang while his troops tightened the noose around Taiyuan.[60] Hu Yaobang was a member of the Taiyuan Front CCP Committee.

In early September, Xu Xiangqian and Hu Yaobang both attended an expanded Politburo meeting in Xibaipo to discuss the strategic situation. Mao Zedong declared that the struggle against Chiang Kai-shek had moved into a new stage, from guerrilla to conventional war, and mandated the creation of a five-million-man army to bring down the Nationalist government within five years. He called for intensified military pressure on all fronts, particularly in Manchuria, around Beijing and Tianjin, in Central China above the Yangzi River, and in Shanxi.[61]

Xu being still too ill to resume command, he asked Hu Yaobang to return to First Corps headquarters southeast of Taiyuan to inform the troops of the "spirit" of the meeting. PLA forces outside Taiyuan numbered about eighty thousand, and included the three columns of Xu's First Corps and several independent brigades and an artillery battalion from other liberated areas. Contemporary military analysts point out that the ratio of Xu's to Yan's forces was at best 8:10, violating long-held norms that attacking forces need to outnumber defenders. PLA intelligence failed to take account of the quality of Yan's troops and their determination to hold out at all costs.[62] Yan boasted that he would die in the city and showed foreign reporters five hundred doses of cyanide he had prepared for his principal civil and military officials to take, should the city be captured by the Communist armies. He also had several hundred former Japanese soldiers who stayed in Shanxi as mercenaries instead of returning to Japan after the war.[63]

The focal point of Yan's defensive preparations was last-minute strengthening of his four fortresses in the Dongshan area. Located east of the city gates on a mountain ridge about a thousand feet above the Fen River plain, the forts were the key to the defense of the city, within easy artillery range of the city walls, the main airfield, and the northern industrial district with its munitions factories. The four main strongholds—Niutuosai, Shantou,

Xiaoyaotou, and Naoma—were each large, reinforced concrete and stone structures with heavy machine guns and artillery, connected by a network of three thousand additional pillboxes with overlapping fields of fire, underground tunnels, trenches, multiple-tier barbed wire fences, moats, and minefields. Yan boasted they were "fortresses within fortresses" that could withstand an attack by a hundred thousand troops, and that the Communists wouldn't dare to try.[64]

Xu returned to Taiyuan on October 10, but the actual attack order for the battle—drafted by Hu—was not issued until October 23, five days later than Xu's original battle plan. Hu himself went to the front lines at Naoma, where one column was preparing an uphill attack, and gave an inspirational speech.[65]

The ensuing seventeen days were a bloodbath, a deafening cacophony of artillery shells, bombs falling from aircraft, machine guns, and men screaming and shouting, charging wildly up hills and fleeing back down. At each of the four Dongshan strongholds, pillbox positions were taken and lost several times, and desperate hand-to-hand combat happened daily. Many died in collapsed tunnels, their bodies never recovered. Others died in poison gas attacks Yan used late in the campaign. Xiaoyaotou fell on October 31 to a desperate onslaught by Xu's Eighth Column. Shantou was captured and lost several times, but finally held by the Thirteenth Column on November 10. Naoma was taken by the Fifteenth Column on November 11, after fending off nineteen counterattacks by Yan's forces. Niutuoshan was the last bastion to fall, on November 13, after the PLA Seventh Column had taken devastating casualties, some battalions having only fifty surviving members.[66]

While precise casualty figures may not ever be known, PRC sources claim that Yan's forces suffered 20,000 casualties during this phase of the campaign. Peng Hai reported that the PLA First Corps had ordered, in advance, materials for 13,000 coffins, but it was not enough.[67] One writer, describing the seven monuments around Taiyuan that commemorate more than 7,300 "martyrs" (3,400 of them nameless), noted that more than 45,000 "fell in the liberation of Taiyuan," a number that probably includes losses in the final assault.[68] Xu's forces were victorious but shattered. With only four brigade-level units having been kept out of battle, Xu was in no position to press his attack on the city itself.

In other places around China, Communist forces were faring far better in large-scale battles against Nationalist armies. In Manchuria, Lin Biao's Northeast China Field Army completed its rout of Nationalist forces,

The battle for the strategically significant walled city of Taiyuan, in Shanxi Province, was fought in two phases, November 1948 and April 1949. Soldiers are shown crossing in front of Taiyuan's iconic Twin Pagoda Temple, where Red Army forces laid siege to the city and overwhelmed its defenses in one of the bloodiest battles of the civil war. (Top Photo Corporation / Alamy Stock Photo)

capturing Shenyang on November 2, 1948. The CMC ordered Lin not to rest, but to continue southward in pursuit of retreating KMT forces heading for Beijing and Tianjin, where decisive battles were expected to be fought before the end of the year. In Central China, several Nationalist armies surrendered to or were defeated by East China Field Army forces under Chen Yi and Central Plains Field Army troops under Liu Bocheng and his political commissar, Deng Xiaoping. The largest battle of the war was shaping up in the Huai-Hai region of Jiangsu and Henan.

On November 16 Mao telegraphed Xu Xiangqian, instructing him to pause in the campaign against Taiyuan so that Beijing warlord Fu Zuoyi would not lose hope, abandon the city, and take his army southward, thereby upsetting the balance of forces emerging in Central China. Exhausted by the battle, Xu readily obeyed. On November 29 the CMC ordered him to withdraw from the front line to recover his health, replacing him with a command triumvirate of Corps Deputy Commander Zhou Shidi, Hu Yaobang, and Deputy Political Commissar Chen Manyuan.[69]

The next few months were devoted to psychological warfare, although there were skirmishes north of Taiyuan to gain control of the airport, the chief point of supply for the city's defenders. Conditions of hunger among Yan's troops and civilians remaining in Taiyuan deteriorated into starvation. It is difficult to quantify the role hunger and malnourishment played in the fall of Taiyuan. Nationalist Chinese and Western accounts speak of "thousands" falling victim to starvation and some resorting to cannibalism, but provide few details or statistics.[70]

While Xu's combat units were recovering, Hu Yaobang was responsible for the political warfare waged by the CCP against the beleaguered city. This propaganda was directed at Yan's troops to undermine morale and loyalty, and to gain the sympathy and support of the civilian population inside Taiyuan. Methods included trying to persuade soldiers to defect, using friends and family letters or broadcasts on loudspeakers imploring them to give up. Wounded Yan army soldiers were sent back into the city to increase the strain on its scarce medical and food supplies. Propaganda flyers were fired into the city by artillery, and safe-conduct passes circulated inside the city.[71] These efforts were not notably successful.

The outcome of the Battle of Taiyuan would be decided by pure force, not political guile. On December 2, 1948, two corps of the North China Military District laid siege to Zhangjiakou, the city they had lost two years earlier, while eight hundred thousand soldiers of Lin Biao's victorious Northeast Field Army descended on Beijing from Manchuria. By January 1949 Fu Zuoyi was surrounded and unable to evacuate his forces because of artillery attacks on the Beijing and Tianjin airfields. When the Battle of Huai-Hai concluded on January 10 with another devastating defeat for Nationalist armies, Fu—who had been in negotiations with the CCP for several months—surrendered the city and half a million of his troops on January 22, 1949.

After this string of crushing defeats, Chiang Kai-shek surprised the world by stepping down as president of the Republic of China on January 21, 1949, ceding the position to his vice president, Li Zongren (Li Tsung-jen), warlord of Guangxi Province and a longtime adversary. Chiang moved to Guangzhou, along with a significant portion of the Republic of China's gold reserves, which he then moved to the island of Taiwan. Li Zongren, head of a badly divided KMT, its armies mostly defeated and its economy collapsing, made peace overtures toward the Communists in February.

At the end of December 1948, Mao had called for on the CCP to "carry the Revolution through to the end," by which he meant, "We must use the revolutionary method to wipe out all the forces of reaction resolutely, thoroughly, wholly and completely; . . . we must overthrow the reactionary rule of the Kuomintang on a country-wide scale and set up a republic that is a people's democratic dictatorship under the leadership of the proletariat and with the worker-peasant alliance as its main body."[72]

To facilitate moving armies from the North and Northwest into Sichuan Province, Yan Xishan's stronghold at Taiyuan and a smaller force at Datong had to be eliminated. In mid-March 1949, the Nineteenth and Twentieth Corps began transferring from the Beijing-Tianjin area west to Taiyuan, along with an artillery division from the Fourth Field Army, two of Fu Zuoyi's former divisions, and 15,000 soldiers from other CMC units. By the end of the month, the forces surrounding Taiyuan numbered over 250,000 with more than 1,300 artillery pieces. They were supported by an additional 250,000 to 300,000 local militia soldiers, porters, and logistics workers. Meanwhile, Yan's garrison forces had dwindled to 72,000 with about 900 howitzers.[73] After months of drastically reduced supplies, they were hungry and weak. Yan Xishan, citing the need to attend a meeting in Nanjing, fled Taiyuan on March 29, along with his family, aboard one of the last of his aircraft.

After the Second Plenum of the Seventh Central Committee met in Xibaipo to finalize war plans in early March, Mao sent PLA deputy commander and First Field Army commander Peng Dehuai to Taiyuan to assist Xu Xiangqian in the final offensive. In early April, Peng visited Xu at his recuperation quarters, where Xu asked him to oversee the operation, pleading his own debilitating illness. Peng agreed, although all battle orders would still be issued in Xu's name. Xu's command structure already had changed significantly, with the Nineteenth and Twentieth Corps commanders Yang Dezhi and Yang Chengwu holding equal command authority. The Taiyuan General Front Committee had been reorganized in late March, with a standing committee composed of four members of Xu's staff (including Hu Yaobang) and the additional commanders and commissars.[74] Hu spent most of his time for the next several weeks writing articles and briefing units on the importance of cooperating with other units and maintaining strict discipline. He accompanied Peng Dehuai on his inspections of various frontline units and positions.[75]

On April 21, after talks in Beijing failed to arrange a cease-fire between the KMT and the CCP, troops of the Twentieth Corps attacked the Wohushan fortress north of Taiyuan, easily capturing it. The following day the Taiyuan

General Front Committee issued a final ultimatum to the garrison, calling on it to lay down its arms and avoid needless damage to lives and property. There was no response. At 5:30 a.m. on April 24, thirteen hundred PLA artillery pieces opened fire on the walls, fortifications, and inner city of Taiyuan, with devastating effect. Within an hour, three PLA corps attacked simultaneously from north, east, and south, through and over the city's shattered walls. By 10:30 that morning, Yan Xishan's headquarters compound was secured, the subordinate officials he had left in charge were dead or captured, and thirty thousand troops were "completely annihilated." Taiyuan was finally "liberated."[76]

Taiyuan was a prostrate ruin, and political work was again essential in the wake of the PLA's victory. On April 24 Hu Yaobang was named the third-ranking member of the Taiyuan Military Control Commission. Xu Xiangqian was its nominal head, but Hu and Luo Ruiqing did most of the work as the ranking deputies. The commission took charge of finding the remaining members of Yan's military junta, some of whom had followed through on their pledge to commit suicide if the city fell to the Communists, although most had not.[77] It tried to put together a viable government, to clean up the devastation and restore the city's industrial production, and to feed the survivors of the siege and bombardment.[78]

The battle of Taiyuan was one of the longest and most costly engagements of the entire civil war, and the casualties were staggering: More than 45,000 PLA killed, many unidentified KMT prisoners; and over 130,000 Yan Army / KMT soldiers "annihilated." Some reports mention civilian casualties, using terms such as "impossible to count" or "innumerable," and imply they were comparable to the total numbers of military dead. Over a hundred of the PRC's "founding generals" took part in the six-month battle, but few memoirs cover Taiyuan in detail. It seems difficult to present the Battle of Taiyuan as anything other than tragic.

Carrying the Revolution through to the End

As the Eighteenth Corps prepared to move west to become part of Peng Dehuai's First Field Army in early May, Hu Yaobang wrote a series of morale-boosting articles in the corps newspaper, *The People's Soldiers*. Although the purpose was to improve political work in "moving forward" to new victories in Northwestern China, the articles and Hu's personal activities during this period speak to serious morale problems among the PLA soldiers after

Taiyuan. There was a general reluctance to continue a war that seemed basically over, and to fight it in an area so far from home and family. That led to some desertion and absenteeism, along with excessive requests for home leave. Hu made it clear that the assigned tasks were to liberate Xi'an, drive out the remaining KMT armies under Hu Zongnan, and to defeat the Moslem warlords who controlled much of Gansu and Qinghai.[79]

Xu Xiangqian was formally relieved of command and ordered to undergo a lengthy convalescence. Zhou Shidi took over as commander and commissar on May 25, and Hu retained his position as Political Department director, along with becoming a member of the First Field Army's CCP Committee. Over the next three months, the Eighteenth Corps was divided into smaller units that were deployed with elements of Peng Dehuai's troops in battles around Xi'an, Xianyang, Baoji, Lanzhou, and in Ningxia; some of the battles were intense and costly. Hu Zongnan and the Moslem warlords seldom were able to coordinate their plans or movements effectively, however. While they inflicted heavy casualties on several PLA units in July and August, they generally lost even larger numbers and continued retreating west into Qinghai and south into Sichuan. Hu Yaobang focused much of his attention during this period on writing propaganda articles for the corps newspaper, using the news of one unit's successes to inspire the others.[80]

Hu Yaobang and He Long were called back to Beijing in late July for ceremonies relating to the establishment of the People's Republic of China. It was a signal honor for both. Hu went as one of ten representatives of the Chinese New Democratic Youth League to attend the first meeting of the Chinese People's Political Consultative Conference (CPPCC). Hu had been elected to the Youth League leadership in late April 1949, even though he was not directly involved in its activities. He happily reestablished ties with his old colleagues and enjoyed the festive atmosphere that pervaded the city. On September 21, at the First Plenary session of the CPPCC in the former Imperial Palace in Zhongnanhai, Hu Yaobang stood with more than six hundred other delegates, wildly cheering, tears streaming down his face, when Mao Zedong intoned in a thick Hunan accent: "The Chinese people, who constitute one-fourth of humanity, now have stood up!"[81] And Hu proudly stood on the rostrum of Tiananmen on October 1, 1949, when the People's Republic of China was formally established and celebrated with a grand parade in its renamed capital of Beijing.

By the end of October both Hu and He Long had returned to Shaanxi with new orders. He Long was placed in charge of the final campaign of the civil war, the battle for the "Great Southwest." To prevent Sichuan from becoming a base area for prolonged anti-Communist operations, the CMC ordered the Second Field Army to accelerate its sweep west through Hunan / Hubei and up through Guizhou to attack Chongqing from the south, while He Long's forces were to attack from the north through Chengdu. Mao's strategic plan for the Eighteenth Corps was to have it keep Hu Zongnan's main forces in defensive mode along the mountainous Shaanxi-Sichuan border until late November–early December, by which time the Second Field Army would have closed off escape routes into Yunnan.[82]

On November 15 Chiang Kai-shek, recognizing that Mao had planned to trap him in Chongqing, hastily fled with a small staff to Chengdu, where he hoped that Hu Zongnan and his last few thousand loyal troops would help him establish an impregnable base area from which to make a comeback. It was a forlorn hope, but Hu Zongnan started withdrawing his dwindling forces from their defensive positions along Sichuan's northern border with Shaanxi and Gansu and headed for Chengdu.[83]

By December 3, with winter setting in, the Eighteenth Corps received word from Second Field Army headquarters that Chongqing was secure and progress was being made in closing off escape routes. He Long ordered his troops to march for Chengdu. It was a slow, cold, treacherous slog. Despite only token resistance, it took more than two weeks to go 350 kilometers from the border to the provincial capital. Hu Yaobang traveled with the Sixty-First Army (of which he was political commissar), on the easternmost of the three attack columns. By December 10, the Sixty-First Army had reached the city of Nanchong, in north-central Sichuan, and liberated it without resistance.[84]

Chiang Kai-shek exhorted Hu Zongnan to move his troops to Xichang, in southern Sichuan, and fight on. On December 10 he boarded an airplane and flew to Taiwan, where he presided over what remained of the government of the Republic of China. Not long afterward, Hu Zongnan held a senior officers meeting in Chengdu, exhorted his troops to fight on from Xichang, then boarded an airplane and flew to Hainan Island, which had not yet fallen under Communist control. Hu Zongnan, too, would end his days in Taiwan.[85] The commander of the KMT Seventh Army, Pei Changhui, had notified the PLA's Eighteenth Corps by messenger of his intention to "rebel" with most of the remaining KMT forces, and Hu Yaobang met with him on the evening of December 19, treating him with solicitude and courtesy. He arranged a meeting between Pei and He Long, which sealed the bargain and made possible the peaceful surrender of Chengdu on December 24.[86] On December 30 the Southwest Bureau and the Eighteenth Corps of the Northwest Field Army held a parade in Chengdu to celebrate the victory. Hu Yaobang joined in the celebration, probably knowing at that point that his military career was coming to an end.

Administering One-Fourth of a Large Province

Notwithstanding the relatively easy victories in the last major battles of the civil war, the PRC government faced a daunting task in bringing Sichuan under its control in 1949–1950. Sichuan's remoteness from the Chinese heartland—separated by mountains, rivers and non-Han minorities—had often meant it was not fully under central jurisdiction. And it had occasionally been an area where opponents of the ruling dynasty might foment rebellion. Even when the Nationalist government had moved its capital to Chongqing in 1937, several warlords had contended for different areas of Sichuan, and Chiang Kai-shek had little choice but to work with them.[87] In 1949 the new government in Beijing evidently was concerned that the province might not be controllable by a single provincial administration, given Chiang's retreat into the Southwest, the fact that there had been no significant Communist base operations in the region for more than ten years, and the presence there of hundreds of thousands of former KMT troops of unknown loyalty.

As an interim measure, the Central government decided to divide Sichuan into four administrative districts—namely, East Sichuan, South Sichuan, West Sichuan, and North Sichuan Districts—each equivalent to a province. All were under the overall political jurisdiction of the Southwest Bureau of the CCP, the administrative purview of the Southwest Military Control Commission, and the military command of the Southwest Military Region, respectively headed by Deng Xiaoping, Liu Bocheng, and He Long. Other units under the Southwest Bureau were Guizhou, Yunnan, and Xikang Provinces (Tibet had not yet been brought under PRC control), and the administrative capital of Chongqing Municipality.

Hu Yaobang, at the age of thirty-four, was named secretary of the North Sichuan Provisional Work Committee on December 10, 1949, the day Nanchong was taken, and his role as principal party secretary was confirmed eight days later in a joint announcement by the Central Committee and the Southwest Bureau.[88] The public announcement would not be made until February 1950, before which time Hu was phasing himself out of Eighteenth

Corps political work. How he came to be appointed to this new position is not clear. Probably he was informed of the impending assignment when he was in Beijing in September–October 1949, and possibly by Mao Zedong himself. Mao at least would have had to approve an appointment at this level. It was a significant promotion for Hu, given that the men assigned to the other three Sichuan districts were older than he and senior to him in military or party rank. Neither did Hu have any career associations with Deng Xiaoping, Liu Bocheng, or He Long prior to the invasion of the Southwest.

Hu's responsibilities were formidable. The North Sichuan Administrative District comprised an area about the size of the US state of New Jersey; roughly 1.6 million hectares (about 70 percent) of the district were arable land, and the population at that time was around 17.5 million. It had thirty-five predominantly rural counties (*xian*), four special districts (*zhuanqu*), and a regional capital at Nanchong, although most local governments were out of operation by the close of the civil war. Once a fertile agricultural region, North Sichuan's productivity had fallen off under weak KMT administration to about 80 percent of its prewar level. Most of its population— 98 percent—lived in rural villages, and most peasants subsisted on tiny plots of land, as Hu Yaobang himself had done in Hunan in his youth.

Transportation and communications were rudimentary, and many roads had fallen into disrepair during the war years. North Sichuan's minority population was not as large as in other areas in the Southwest, but its scattered *Hui* (Muslim), *Zang* (Tibetan), and *Qiang* villages were in poor and isolated areas of the northern part of the province, and tribal leaders were distrustful of the new Communist overlords.[89] In addition, Hu would be evaluated by how well he implemented the sweeping socioeconomic changes mandated by Mao Zedong's version of socialism, which had been implemented in many areas conquered earlier by the PLA, but not at all in the Southwest.

Killing Bandits and Counterrevolutionaries

But by far Hu's most challenging problem, initially, was what was called "bandit chaos" (*fei luan*) by CCP Southwest Bureau secretary Deng Xiaoping in 1950. In the first meeting with all his regional party and military chieftains in February, Deng made it clear that unless they were able to bring to an end the many violent attacks on newly established civil and military authorities by remaining KMT military units and bands of indigenous outlaws, the rest of their work would be wasted.[90] Estimates vary, but probably between four hundred thousand and five hundred thousand former KMT troops were still on the loose in the Southwest in early 1950. Moreover, hundreds of rural gangs (each numbering fifty to a thousand men), run by both genuine brigands and by anti-Communist local leaders, were active throughout the area. He Long, commander of the Southwest Military Region, was given principal responsibility for "bandit extermination" at the February meeting, and eventually threw most of his thirteen armies, thirty-seven divisions, and two corps into the battle, which lasted until late 1953.[91]

Hu Yaobang personally experienced the bandit problem while riding from Chengdu to Nanchong to take up his position officially on February 20, 1950. As he neared the outskirts of the capital city that evening, his convoy was ambushed by a small group of bandits, and Hu had to return fire from the front seat of his American-made Jeep before they were driven off. He convened his temporary administrative committee that same night, heard grim briefings on North Sichuan's overall conditions, and put improving security at the top of the list of things needing priority attention.[92] In the following week, Hu formally proclaimed the establishment of the North Sichuan CCP Committee (which he headed) and the North Sichuan Administrative Region, of which he was director. He was named political commissar of the North Sichuan Military District, while Wei Jie was made commander (concurrent with his Sixty-First Army command). Hu convened a large-scale "people's representatives" meeting in Nanchong, where he gave a spirit-boosting speech and mingled with delegates "from all walks of life," who received him courteously but guardedly.[93] Hu admitted that Communist Party members were going to be a minority of the administrators for a period of time, and exhorted all to have confidence, not to spread rumors, to guard against bandits, and to unite for a better North Sichuan.

In March the Southwest Bureau had sent a report to Beijing detailing its concerns about increasing violence and criminal activity, which included ambushes of Communist military units, executions of county and village officials, arson, kidnapping, rape, and interference with grain requisitions. The report caught the attention of Central authorities, who issued two important documents on March 18: "Instructions on Annihilating Bandits and Establishing a New Revolutionary Order" and "Instructions on Suppressing Counterrevolutionary Activities." Mao Zedong was visiting Moscow at the time, but Liu Shaoqi and other members of the Central leadership made clear that violent punishment was expected, and results were demanded "without hesitancy."[94]

On March 25 the Southwest Bureau held a meeting to transmit Central instructions on the Bandit Annihilation Campaign. Deng Xiaoping criticized local officials for being "afraid to kill," and while cautioning against excessive killing, he claimed that not killing enough people would isolate the party from the masses.[95] In April Hu Yaobang established a North Sichuan Bandit Suppression Committee with himself as head. By May he and Wei Jie had organized the Sixty-First Army into twenty-one operational units to attack bandit gangs, starting with the most seriously beset counties. On May 17, Hu—dressed in a military uniform and showing none of his usual good humor—held a senior cadre mobilization meeting to intensify the campaign. Hu demanded that bandit elimination be expanded and combined with the formation of peasant associations and self-defense groups in rural villages, which would later prove useful for land reform work. Finally, he called on all the soldiers and cadres to achieve the "target" (*mubiao*) of completely purging all North Sichuan's bandits and KMT special agents by September.[96]

What followed is not entirely clear, but it was bloody. By late August 1950, Hu Yaobang declared the goals of the campaign had been achieved early, with the "annihilation" of 73,000 bandits, of whom 24,000 were "only politically collapsed."[97] That likely means that military units and peasant self-defense forces killed at least 49,000 "bandits" in North Sichuan between mid-May and mid-August 1950.[98] The number is not inconsistent with the goals, quotas, and subsequent expansion of the Campaign to Suppress Counterrevolutionaries (*Zhenya fan'geming yundong*, the Zhenfan Campaign), that was still only at a low boil as far as Mao Zedong was concerned.

East China Normal University scholar Yang Kuisong began publishing articles on CCP history in about 2006 after extensive research in national and provincial archives. He focused on the 1950–1953 Zhenfan Campaign, in part because it had not received much scholarly attention, and in part because of its being one of the first of the national "political campaigns" directed by Mao Zedong. At first Yang only wanted to find out what had happened to several hundred thousand KMT military officers who had surrendered to Communist forces in the late stages of the civil war. What he discovered was that, of the former KMT soldiers and civilian officials rounded up during the Zhenfan Campaign, thousands were summarily executed across China, and many thousands more were sent off to labor camps and disappeared.[99]

Initially, the Bandit Annihilation and Zhenfan Campaigns were interconnected, both in political intent and in time. Both appear to have been a national response to the problems experienced in the Southwest, where hundreds of thousands of remaining KMT soldiers and former administrators, and almost a million PLA fighters and incoming CCP cadres, placed an enormous strain on the region's food reserves. Both campaigns were reflections of Mao Zedong's fixation on the continuing relevance of "class struggle" to the completion of China's revolution. More pragmatically, the regime was struggling with economic issues, including currency problems and grain shortages in the coastal areas. Mao's advice, as late as a Central Committee plenum in June 1950, was "don't attack on all fronts or make new enemies."[100]

Given Sichuan's role as one of China's largest grain-producing regions, Beijing had ordered in 1950 that the Southwest provide more than 2.5 million tons of grain to Shanghai. Deng Xiaoping was confronted with a problem: extracting that much grain tax while undertaking bandit suppression would engender resistance from landlords and ordinary peasants alike. But he pressed ahead aggressively—by August, in addition to North Sichuan's 73,000 bandits "destroyed," East Sichuan reported 95,000, South Sichuan 140,000, West Sichuan 50,000, Guizhou over 80,000, and Yunnan 62,000. Local peasant associations had been mobilized and energized, support for the regime had grown, and bandit activities had declined sharply, according to these preliminary reports.[101]

Were all those killed actually bandits? Early in the campaign, the regulations were blurry and were expanded to include ordinary criminals, prostitutes, drug users, small landlords, rich peasants, and low-level KMT military and civil officials. Legal authorities and procedures were vague, quick results were rewarded, delays were discouraged. Accusations were tantamount to arrest warrants. Local feuds were settled by one side arranging for the other side to be arrested as "counterrevolutionaries." A kind of killing frenzy existed within some of the military units.[102]

The role played by Mao Zedong was perplexing. By October 1950 he was demanding to know the details of arrests, prosecutions, and executions, badgering both Public Security Minister Luo Ruiqing and regional party bureau leaders for specific numbers, and criticizing excessive leniency toward class enemies. He personally participated in drafting the CCP resolution passed in October 1950 that energized and enabled the Ministry of Public Security and its local police departments to become more involved in the arrest and speedy punishment of counterrevolutionaries. Mao indicated that leniency, slow prosecution, and not killing "those that should be killed" would be considered an ideological error of a "rightist tendency." That started a wave of arrests and executions across the country that in many cases doubled the numbers of those previously arrested and executed by local authorities. Deng Xiaoping, for example, reported at the end of 1950 that 850,000 bandits and counterrevolutionaries had been "annihilated" in the Southwest region, nearly 70 percent more than he had reported in August. Mao Zedong cabled Deng his appreciation in late January 1951.[103]

Mao's personal telegrams to regional leaders went even farther in early 1951, stipulating quotas for counterrevolutionaries to be arrested and killed as a percentage of the district's overall population. For example, Mao advised Shanghai authorities in January they needed to execute publicly "in large batches" another two or three thousand people, Nanjing another thousand, suggesting they should be applying quotas of between 0.5 and 1.0 executions per thousand of total population. He acknowledged that some areas, such as Guizhou Province, had requested permission to kill as many as 3 per thousand, and he thought that was a bit too high, but that the numbers could vary, depending on circumstances.[104] This led to the Zhenfan Campaign going out of control. Within weeks provincial leaders from many areas, very likely including Hu Yaobang in North Sichuan, were complaining of excessive arrests and wanton killing they could not manage. Arrests were causing even temporary jails to be filled beyond capacity, and backlogs of counterrevolutionaries awaiting trial numbered in the hundreds of thousands. Local authorities were killing people almost whimsically, with little or no accountability.[105]

Hu Yaobang's biographers have reported little about Hu's response to the excesses brought about by the expansion of the campaign to exterminate bandits and its melding into the Zhenfan Campaign. Hu's son, Hu Deping, has said that his father was criticized for "killing few people" in Zhenfan, but does not substantiate the claim.[106] And given Hu Yaobang's unswerving loyalty to Mao Zedong and his need to go along with Deng Xiaoping's fierce demand to pacify the Southwest, it is unlikely he was eager to buck the tide of violence that was sweeping through the region.

Hu did try, however, to ensure that the forces under his command adhered to a semblance of order, however imperfect. He tried to get local officials to stay within the boundaries of policy from the Center. Near the end of the first phase of the Bandit Annihilation Campaign, Hu Yaobang sharply criticized his own military units for a lack of discipline, which he called "inexcusable."[107] But as the public security forces took over the enumeration, arrest, and punishment of "counterrevolutionary elements" in late 1950 and early 1951, and as personal telegrams from Mao superseded vague "regulations" from the PRC's Governing Council (issued too late in February), the problems only got worse.

According to a former Public Security Ministry official, Yin Shusheng, citing figures from a 1954 summary report on the Zhenfan Campaign, the period from January to May 1951 was the high-water mark for killing counterrevolutionaries. Of the 712,000 (probably a low estimate) killed in the entire 1950–1953 campaign, 543,000 died in the first year (beginning October 1950), and most of them in the five months from January to May 1951. The excesses included summary executions, mass executions in public squares, executions the day after arrest, executions to relieve overcrowding in jails, executions of entire families. Yin noted that the number executed in the three years of Zhenfan was greater than the total number of Nationalist and Communist soldiers killed in the four years of civil war.[108]

In early April 1951 Deng Xiaoping reported to the Center that proceeding to the next phase of executing some sixty thousand already in custody according to population quotas might exacerbate a "mood of killing quickly sprouting up in various localities." He recommended that the power to authorize executions be raised from county and village party committees to the administrative district level. Mao Zedong, probably having received similar messages from several places in China, circulated Deng's report nationwide. He then instructed the CCP Secretariat and the Ministry of Public Security to bring things under control. On April 20 he suggested the Southwest Bureau send half of the sixty thousand prisoners awaiting execution to work on road construction, land reclamation, and other large labor projects instead. On April 26 Deng transmitted instructions to Hu Yaobang that the party should exert leadership over Zhenfan, suspend killing in places where quotas had been exceeded, avoid killing when possible, send larger numbers to labor projects, and make efforts to clear up accumulated cases.[109]

Minister Luo Ruiqing convened a national conference of public security leaders on May 10–15. The conference passed a resolution, drafted by Mao Zedong himself, that reiterated a lower killing quota of 0.5 to 1.0 per thousand and ordered a temporary halt in places where that quota had been exceeded. It raised the authorization level for arrests to the administrative district level, and for executions to the provincial level to prevent "leftist" excesses. It ordered case backlogs to be cleared by September 1951, recommending that many currently in jail be sent to "labor reform" (laogai) to observe their behavior.[110] Mao told provincial leaders, "Generally, . . . if you kill too many, you lose public sympathy, and lose labor power."[111]

Doing Land Reform "Right"

But the next phase of the subjugation of the Southwest had already begun in January 1951, with the official start of the land reform (*tudi gaige*) campaign. Long the mainstay of the Chinese Communist Party's social programs, land reform had been postponed in North Sichuan and the rest of the region because of the late takeover of the Southwest and the gravity of bandit activities. That postponement gave the Southwest Bureau more time to organize and coordinate the land reform effort, although not long enough for the multiple campaigns—Zhenfan, bandit suppression, and land reform—to be differentiated. So violence continued to be a factor in the political life in North Sichuan until the land reform campaign was declared completed in the spring of 1952.[112]

According to a short study done by China West Normal University, located in Nanchong, Hu Yaobang had three main land reform problems in North Sichuan: unequal distribution of landholding (8.6 percent of the population owned nearly 40 percent of arable land), inefficient land utilization, and "deeply exploitative" rents for tenant farmers. Under strict guidelines from Deng Xiaoping and the Southwest Bureau, as well as Central directives, Hu displayed his organizational and propaganda skills in managing a socially disruptive and politically radical process of change. He began organizing his forces in mid-1950 and by November had transferred and trained more than 15,000 cadres and 330,000 civilian activists and volunteers to start on the first phase of land reform—the reduction of rents and returning of exorbitant deposits paid by tenant farmers. Earlier campaigns already had mobilized some 4.5 million peasants into local associations and self-defense forces.

Under Southwest Bureau guidance, Hu and his teams began a five-phase process in late 1950 with an extensive propaganda campaign to prepare rural villages, often in remote areas, for the changes that were coming. The second and most difficult phase began in January 1951, when Hu established the North Sichuan Land Reform General Work Brigade, with himself in charge. In March the serious work began in Bazhong County, with an experimental effort to enumerate and categorize village populations into five constituent classes—landlords (*dizhu*), rich peasants (*funong*), middle peasants (*zhongnong*), poor peasants (*pinnong*), and tenant farmers (*gunong*)—and to confiscate the assets of landlords.[113] This phase and the following one (expropriating the rental land and housing of rich peasants and struggling against landlords trying to sell or hide their belongings) involved mass meetings of poor peasants, the main force of land reform activism. At these village meetings, landlords were denounced in "speaking bitterness" (*suku*) sessions, which often became violent. Mobilizing poor peasants and raising their "class consciousness" were overriding goals of land reform, channeling peasant anger at perceived historical oppression into Communist Party–directed outcomes.[114]

Hu set three stages for the campaign in North Sichuan, each one involving about one- third of the land area of the province, with minority population districts being exempted from land reform until 1953. Deng and Hu agreed that there could not be "peaceful land reform," and criticized "rightist" land reform that did not turn public anger against once-privileged rural classes. At the same time, they sought to buffer from public humiliation wealthy individuals who had moved from rural areas into the cities to start small businesses and manufacturing plants. It was a delicate balance that was often lost when public anger overcame party discipline.[115] Although public security officials did not arrest and execute people as they did in earlier campaigns, mob violence was common during land reform. Most of the incidents documented by Yang Kuisong and others involved personal humiliation of landlords and rich peasants (of whom there were about 1.5 million in North Sichuan in 1950), to include beating them with sticks, stripping off their clothes, cutting their hair and beards, forcing confessions, destroying personal property, and so on. There were many suicides, plus reports of landlords and rich peasants having starved to death, deprived of all means of livelihood.[116]

Hu's biographers and other scholars insist that Hu maintained a disciplined approach to land reform, attaining results that transformed land ownership in North Sichuan while maintaining—even enhancing—economic production. As with earlier campaigns, Hu acknowledged that mistakes were made and excesses took place. But he was not called to account. Quite the opposite, in fact. His efforts were commended in 1952 by the Southwest Bureau, which observed, in response to his summary report, that land reform in North Sichuan had "progressed normally, which was very reassuring," and that his management of the campaign was "appropriate."[117] In the end, land ownership was significantly revamped, rural productivity increased, and the loyalty of most peasants was secured. Hu gained an enhanced reputation as one who implemented orders from above, organized and propagandized effectively, monitored and controlled his subordinates, and got results. Hu sent a commemorative book to all the cadres who took part in land reform, inscribed with the following quote from Chairman Mao:

"Fulfill your responsibility, uphold policy, investigate and study, seek truth from facts."[118]

Building Career Ties

Personal relationships (*guanxi*) are always the key factor in determining and analyzing the dynamics that drive politics and policies in China—not just who is in the same location or hierarchy as someone else, but the scope and content of their relationships. Hu Yaobang's subordinates in North Sichuan went on to mid-level careers in the CCP and the PLA, but none seemed to have much further contact with Hu. Of his Southwest Bureau provincial secretary-level peers, all remained in senior positions in the region or went on to higher positions in the party and army, some even becoming Politburo members. For Hu Yaobang, by far the most important relationship he developed during the two years and seven months he spent in North Sichuan was with Deng Xiaoping, secretary of the Southwest Bureau. Deng was the dominant figure in the region, and by virtue of his activist approach to the region's political, economic, and minorities issues, he was influential with Mao Zedong.

Hu Yaobang had known Deng's name and reputation for years, but he had never been assigned to the same region or military unit as Deng. Now working together regularly—Deng appears to have held Bureau meetings in Chongqing every few weeks—the two developed a working relationship that would continue the rest of Hu's life. Deng would usually be an overseer of Hu's work. Hu would be politically linked to Deng by his critics, and the two would rise and fall together twice. But Hu Yaobang claimed he was not a protégé of Deng Xiaoping; theirs was not a patron-client relationship, nor was Hu a member of a Deng faction. In a 2004 commemoration of Hu Yaobang, former vice-premier Tian Jiyun quoted Hu as saying: "Some people divide us into factions, saying Hu Yaobang is a disciple of Deng Xiaoping. That is complete nonsense. I joined the revolution in 1930 but didn't meet Deng Xiaoping until 1944."[119] Many of Hu's later career assignments were approved or affirmed by Deng, but they were not initiated by him. Hu would always insist that Mao Zedong was his main benefactor, not Deng.

Still, the two men developed a rapport that was congenial and respectful, characterized by political support and agreement on many issues and a degree of reciprocal trust. Observers would seldom refer to their relationship as a friendship, as it was bounded by their differences in age, rank, responsibilities, background, and temperament. Deng was a member of the Central Committee, a senior PLA officer, and the ranking leader of China's largest regional bureau, several cadre grades higher than Hu. Deng was thirteen years older, came from a small landholding family in Sichuan, and was well-educated. He went overseas to study in France, where he became a Communist Party member in association with Chen Yi and Nie Rongzhen. Hu was the son of a poor Hunan peasant, and although intellectually gifted, he left school at the age of fourteen to join the Communist rebels in Jinggangshan.

Both men became political commissars in the military, but Deng was a skilled strategist whose advice was sought by senior generals, Hu was valued for lecturing and inspiring troops before a battle. Both men were short, about five feet tall, with Hu a bit shorter. Deng was squat and round-faced, with a serious and phlegmatic demeanor; Hu was thin and wiry, bubbling with enthusiasm, affable and jocular. Hu was more intellectual than Deng, often reading Marxist-Leninist theoretical classics in addition to a broad array of other literary work. Deng was a man of action, not fond of books, known for his clever means or stratagems (*shouduan*) and for getting things done. Deng was a mediocre public speaker, plodding and monotonous, whereas Hu was fiery and animated, his high-pitched voice with its thick Hunan accent often accompanied by energetic gestures.

One thing the two men had in common, beginning from their days together in Chongqing, was an avid love for the game of contract bridge. Deng had only learned the game before his arrival in Chongqing, while Hu had acquired the rudiments in Yan'an, even though it was considered a game for Westernized intellectuals. He picked it up again at Deng's urging. The intellectual challenge, the complexity and the competitiveness appealed to both men, and they both excelled at it. They had very different styles, Deng being more deliberate and calculating in bidding and play, while Hu was more daring, not always sticking to bidding conventions. But they both enjoyed the intensity, and they both hated to lose. Throughout many years of their playing bridge in their spare time, their partners and observers considered Deng the better player, but Hu never gave up, and Deng appreciated his skill, though he preferred having Hu as an opponent rather than a partner. Most of all, they had a break from the daily grind, a chance to drink, smoke, snack, laugh, and play. The unwritten rule—because Deng chose his table partners by their skill, not their rank—was no talking politics at the table.[120]

"Three-Antis / Five-Antis"

Before Southwest districts had even completed the rural land reform campaign, the Center determined that the next step in the Chinese revolution would be bringing the "bourgeoisie" (*zichan jieji*) under better control. Just after liberation, CCP leaders wary of China's uncertain economic conditions had instructed local administrators to treat the owners of small businesses and manufacturing cautiously, not punishing them or expropriating their assets. Hu Yaobang went along with this, working with Nanchong's relatively few industrialists and its small business community to build trust and rebuild North Sichuan's nonagricultural economy.

In late 1951, however, several cases of embezzlement by party and local government leaders in North China convinced Mao Zedong that the CCP was in danger of losing its revolutionary élan, and that a mass campaign was necessary to clean out the rot that had begun to afflict it because of regular contact with "bourgeois" elements in society. The "Three Antis" (*sanfan yundong*) thus were born, the goals of which were to "oppose corruption, waste, and bureaucratism"—more a problem for officials than businessmen. The Center sent out formal notifications and instructions to all regional party organizations in December 1951 and January 1952 to organize the campaign, mobilize the masses, and start reporting their findings at once.[121]

Mao Zedong became involved early, ordering the execution of two officials, and calling for the "Three Antis" to become the centerpiece of a new party rectification campaign—similar to the Yan'an Rectification Campaign. He determined the phases of the campaign, set schedules, specified targets of investigation, and encouraged party committees to focus on punishing medium- and large-sized "tigers"—those who had embezzled between 1 and 10 million yuan. He insisted on involving the masses, which of course maximized the likelihood of errors (since ordinary citizens would have little way of determining what constituted waste or embezzlement), and violence.[122]

Deng Xiaoping wasted little time in bringing the campaign to the Southwest, convening a planning meeting on December 13 that produced a six-point plan, which included special investigation groups, mass mobilization, and full participation by senior party leaders at all levels. Mao approved the plan on December 17 and the Southwest Bureau held a meeting the following day to initiate the work.[123] The first phase of the campaign was collecting information and studying documents, with the sharpest focus being on those bureaucracies that handled large sums of money—banking, accounting,

construction, procurement, and transportation. Officials responsible for
these areas immediately came under suspicion of being "big tigers," and officials at all levels were pressured to "honestly confess" their corruption and
waste before the masses. According to Zhang Ming and other scholars,
270,000 officials in the Southwest region participated in the campaign, and
124,000 of them confessed to having been corrupt. Like the "AB League"
campaign in Jiangxi and the "Rescue" campaign in Yan'an, evidentiary
standards were lacking, unfounded accusations led to arrests, and physical
torture and forced confessions were common. Suicides followed as mob
pressures mounted.

Things got more difficult when Mao Zedong decided in late January 1952
to turn up the heat on "class struggle" and go after the source of the CCP's
corruption problem: China's capitalist class, the "bourgeoisie." The "Five
Antis" (*wu fan*) campaign was linked to the "Three Antis," but its target set
was more readily identifiable—any businessman, shop owner, industrialist,
factory owner, or goods-producer not already under the control of the state.
The goals of the "Five Antis" campaign were for everyone to oppose bribery,
theft of state property, tax evasion, cheating on government contracts, and
stealing state economic information on behalf of a foreign government. Party
investigation teams were authorized to enter any business establishment, review the books, interrogate the owners, seize assets, and levy fines. Many
businessmen fled, and some committed suicide to avoid being subjected to
harassment and indignity. In mid-February Mao continued to demand that
more "tigers" be exposed and criticized. Deng responded by setting quotas
for his provincial-level administrative units to accomplish before April.[124]

By mid-March, however, the economic effects of the two conjoined campaigns were becoming obvious nationwide: the urban economy nearly
ground to a halt. Factories and shops closed, inventories disappeared, food
supplies dwindled, laborers were dismissed, banks closed. Deng Xiaoping
sent Beijing a grim report that there were serious food shortages in
Chongqing, and that many citizens were "beginning to express their dissatisfaction with the Three Antis / Five Antis campaign." Reports like this from
Deng and other regional party leaders persuaded the Center to foreshorten
the campaign, according to Western and Chinese scholars.[125]

Hu Yaobang's role in "Five Antis" activity suggests that he was becoming
aware of the high costs of so-called "campaign" politics. He took charge of
the campaign in early 1952 to prevent it from going out of control.[126] He gathered materials, issued instructions, traveled to local districts, criticized

excesses, and resisted pressure from Chongqing to expand the campaign or set quotas for corrupt "tigers." North Sichuan initially reported netting 2,531 "tigers" of various sizes, but Hu Yaobang instituted a review and correction process for those who may have been coerced into admitting guilt, and 706 of these individuals were later declared to have been "false tigers."[127]

There is too little information to judge the level or sincerity of Hu Yao-bang's involvement in these kinds of political campaigns. Later in his life he would be critical of mass political campaigns for involving too many people against too many targets with too little information. But we have few retrospective glimpses by his admirers to evaluate what took place in North Sichuan during this period. Hu followed his orders, but tried not to exceed them, as so many others had done. Deng Xiaoping's evaluation of Hu—much quoted by his biographers but usually truncated—reflects Deng's thinking at the close of what was a somewhat troubling period for both men: Hu Yao-bang "did things well, had strong views, was not a blind follower, ran an industrious and honest administration, kept his hands clean."[128]

North Sichuan in 1952 was still an overwhelmingly agricultural region, with some sericulture and other light textile industries in Nanchong, and small agricultural products processing facilities in some of its district and county towns, so it is difficult to say whether the five phenomena to be opposed in the "Five Antis" campaign were very serious. There just weren't many capitalists. Hu Yaobang had been careful to reach out to and later shield some of the province's intellectuals—mostly from wealthy families, the natural targets of the "Three Antis–Five Antis" campaigns. In any case, when Deng Xiaoping reported to the Center in early May about the progress of the dual campaigns, North Sichuan was the only province in the Southwest Bureau that had already reported the work completed.[129]

Moving On

On June 7, 1952, the Southwest Bureau passed a brief message from the Central Organization Department to the North Sichuan Party Committee: "Hu Yaobang is being transferred to work at the Center. He is to arrive in Beijing by the end of July."[130] There was no indication of what position Hu was getting, but the move was part of a series of personnel changes that would bring to the capital people of proven administrative talent to take up new positions in the expanding government / party apparatus. Deng Xiaoping also would move to Beijing at the end of July. Their transfer was part of the process of reconstituting the five pieces of Sichuan into a single province. In less than three years Hu and his fellow regional administrators had transformed a hotbed of KMT leftover officials and abandoned soldiers, bandit gangs, secret society activists, and restive minorities into a mostly stable, productive, and coherent CCP-governed entity. Now they would turn administrative control of Sichuan, including the Tibetan region of Xikang, over to one of their fellows, Li Jingquan, who would run it with an iron hand.

Hu could not have been anything but thrilled to be moving from an isolated provincial backwater to the political center of the new China. He took his leave in Nanchong with little fanfare, enjoining friends and subordinates not to hold special farewell ceremonies or present gifts. On June 30 he left for Chongqing to pay his respects to Deng and others at the Southwest Bureau headquarters, accompanied only by one secretary, a security guard, and his ten-year-old son, Hu Deping. In early July they boarded a boat to cruise through the famous Three Gorges of the Yangzi River, debarked at Wuhan, and took a train to Beijing. The rest of his extended family—which included his third son, his parents, his mother-in-law, and a niece from his hometown—stayed with Li Zhao in Nanchong until the birth of a daughter three months later.[131]

Huang Tianxiang, one of Hu Yaobang's subordinates in North Sichuan, recalled one of Hu's speeches after he arrived in Nanchong in 1950. With characteristic self-deprecating humor, Hu asked rhetorically: "Yaobang is not five feet in stature, but will his coming to North Sichuan be advantageous for its people?" As Huang put it: "In the two years and eight months he was there, he exceeded expectations, led the cadres at all levels and the broad masses of people, established and consolidated a new democratic regime, completed a series of democratic reforms with land reform at its heart, restored and developed the economy and the educational / cultural system, raised a cadre corps, and completed the established goals."[132]

More importantly, he demonstrated his unswerving loyalty to the Communist Party and to Chairman Mao, even when he didn't completely agree with their policies. Hu had played an exemplary role in completing Mao's revolution, with all its accompanying violence, and as he headed to Beijing, his faith appeared to be intact. It would be sorely tested as that revolution continued.

4   Growing Doubts

Hu Yaobang and his son arrived in Beijing in mid-July 1952 and were put up in a senior cadre guesthouse not far from Zhongnanhai, the government and party headquarters located next to the Forbidden City. No one yet had told him why he had been transferred to Beijing; he had no job assignment. There had been rumors, of course. The one Hu found most attractive was that he had been summoned at the behest of Zhou Enlai, premier of the Government Administration Council, to be minister of construction. Hu looked forward to "building a new China" and particularly to helping ordinary people find good urban housing.[1] The fact that Deng Xiaoping had just been appointed Zhou's principal vice-premier probably reinforced Hu's expectations. But days went by without any word or message.

On August 1, An Ziwen, deputy director of the Central Organization Department, told Hu there had been a change in his assignment, and that he would be summoned for a talk soon.[2] Some days later, Hu was called into the presence of Liu Shaoqi, then second to Mao Zedong in the CCP hierarchy. Liu praised Hu for his youth, administrative and military experience, and skill in working with different people, and then informed him that he had been selected to be the leader of the party's Youth League.[3] It must have been clear to Hu that it was Mao Zedong who had made the decision, choosing his name from a list of three that Liu had provided.[4]

Despite the ostensible honor of being chosen to head the second-largest organization in the People's Republic of China—the China New Democratic Youth League then had more than six million members—Hu was crestfallen. He complained to his secretary that evening that he was thirty-seven years old and had a ten-year-old son but was being sent back to oversee the kind of work he had done as a teenager in Jiangxi.[5] But there was no way he could refuse. Hu himself had exhorted cadres in North Sichuan, "If the party orders you to go somewhere, you go there; if it orders you to do some work, you don't ask about wages, you just do your best."[6]

In 1952 the initial euphoria about the victory of the revolution and the establishment of a "People's Republic" had faded. The end of the civil war had brought thousands of party officials, military commanders, and commissars to Beijing to divide the spoils. New ministries and party organizations were established to deal with the complex and pressing problems of restoring China's economic and administrative structures. Some army commanders and commissars were given administrative and economic planning responsibilities for which they had no experience.

Although some observers consider the period from 1949 to 1953 to have been notable for the absence of sharp personal or policy-related leadership divisions, the growth of Central party and government bureaucracies and Mao's desire to accelerate the "socialist transformation" of Chinese society were causing increasing strains.[7] Mao was still nominally at the top of the Communist Party, the People's Liberation Army, and the government apparatus (as chairman of the Central People's Government Council), but his actual control of policy and personnel issues had diminished from its 1945 peak at the Seventh Party Congress. The five-member Central Secretariat he had formed to substitute for the Politburo during the civil war—Mao, Liu Shaoqi, Zhu De, Zhou Enlai, and Chen Yun (replacing Ren Bishi, who died in 1950)—remained intact in 1952, but power relationships had shifted.

Liu Shaoqi had grown stronger, in both his ideological authority and his day-to-day management of party affairs. Mao began grumbling about a "second headquarters," which may have been a warning, but he made it clear that Liu was his second-in-command.[8] Zhou Enlai gained significant power and patronage as premier and foreign minister, where he was the face of Chinese diplomacy. Gathering economic experts around himself, Zhou may have believed that China's overall economic development and planning were under his purview.

Zhu De remained commander in chief of the People's Liberation Army, under the Revolutionary Military Council, headed by Mao, with administrative details of running the PLA in the hands of chief of staff Nie Rongzhen. When the decision was made to send PLA troops into Korea in late October 1950, Peng Dehuai agreed to command the Chinese People's Volunteers, and thus became China's most important de facto military leader. Mao Zedong consented to his son Mao Anying joining the volunteers to serve at the front, and had him assigned to a seemingly safe position as a Russian translator in Peng's headquarters. On November 25, however, a US Air Force bombing raid on Peng's command post killed Mao Anying. Mao Zedong allegedly never forgave Peng for it.[9]

Taking Over the Youth League

Hu Yaobang knew little of this when he accepted the job of heading the Youth League. His immediate concern, upon reporting for duty on August 10, was that he was expected to organize and direct the League's main activity for the year, the annual meeting of its Central Committee, and had only two weeks to put it together. Hu held meetings with his principal subordinates in the Youth League secretariat and heard briefings on the existing plans for the congress and the reshuffle of the Youth League leadership. He consulted with Feng Wenbin—his old friend from the Jiangxi Soviet Youth League who had preceded him as head of the China New Democratic Youth League— on problems that had developed in relations between the League and the CCP Center, the top party leadership.[10]

On August 14 Hu presented a written briefing to Mao and Liu Shaoqi on the League's situation and asked for their advice and guidance. Once the League had the correct ideological guidance, he told them, its other problems would be easy to resolve. In the comments, or instructions (*pishi*), from the key party leaders that were required for any decision to be implemented, Mao Zedong wrote that he agreed with Hu's report, that there should be a party leadership meeting before the Youth League Congress to talk about its direction, and that he would meet personally with Hu before then to talk more about it.[11]

The Communist Youth League changed its name several times during the early years of the CCP-KMT cooperation and confrontation. Once the outcome of the civil war was clear, but youth activism was still needed to strengthen the legitimacy of the new regime, the CCP established the China New Democratic Youth League. Mao Zedong personally drafted its charter, exhorting the new organization to "unite with youth in every field of endeavor, lead them, strengthen study, and develop production."[12]

The transition from a revolutionary and wartime Youth League to a peacetime, postrevolutionary Youth League was difficult. The League had to change both its activities and its self-image. The League was to be one of the principal transmission systems for the party's policies and goals, a cheerleader for the leadership, and a specialized propagandist for whatever ideological line had been developed by Mao and the party Center. The Youth League was part of an important power system—propaganda and information are critical to any Leninist political party's maintenance of authority—but it was not a policy decision-making organization.

Hu Yaobang probably understood this point instinctively, both from his earlier Youth League experience and from his consultations in Beijing in August 1952. He worked day and night to craft a work report for the CYL Congress consistent with Marxist-Leninist principles and, more importantly, with Mao Zedong's thinking. On August 23, just prior to the opening of the congress, he met with Mao, Liu Shaoqi, other members of the Politburo Standing Committee, and Deng Xiaoping. Mao said that the principal characteristics of young people were boldness and enthusiasm, but they lacked knowledge. The Youth League, therefore, should emphasize learning (*xuexi*) of ideology, culture, science and technology, and physical education, so that youth could become better assistants to the party in developing the new China.[13]

Hu Yaobang incorporated Mao's instructions into his work report to the Third Plenum of the First Congress of the China New Democratic Youth League, held in Beijing from August 25 to September 4, 1952. It was attended by thirty-eight members and alternates of the League's Central Committee, representing more than six million Youth League members around the country.[14] Liu Shaoqi delivered a report on the work of the Central Committee, and the congress passed a "Resolution on Current Work Issues," which was slightly critical of errors in workstyle by previous unnamed CYL leaders. Mao did not meet with the delegates—which would have been a sign of full approval—but observed how the congress was managed, and after it concluded he approved the designation of Hu Yaobang as first secretary of the Youth League Central Committee.[15]

More than seventy years later, it is difficult to identify with the ideals or the enthusiasm of Communist Youth League congresses. They seem contrived and tedious, though it is doubtful the excitement was feigned. Hu's report was a collection of quotes from Chairman Mao, slogans, exhortations, instructions, and ideological boilerplate, the main messages of which were "Study, study and study again!" and put all youth work under the complete control of the Communist Party at every level.[16]

Although Mao had been concerned about an organization as large and potentially influential as the Youth League working independently from the party's leadership, he now suggested that it needed to develop its own agenda suitable to young people, not just act as an adjunct to the CCP. Hu would move in that direction, but he adhered closely to his position that the Youth League needed to follow party guidance and leadership above all, and that China's youth should be indoctrinated in party ideology and policies. As he put it in mid-1953, "propaganda and education work are the soul of the League's work."[17] Mao praised Hu's leadership and reassured him of his support, despite his relative youth, diminutive stature, and the doubts of some of his peers. "When a little guy mounts the stage," Hu later recalled Mao telling him, "maybe his stature is not so great, but don't worry, it's impossible to not be criticized and cursed a bit."[18]

Hu worked first on improving the League's flagship publications, especially the bimonthly *China Youth* and the daily newspaper, *Zhongguo Qingnian Bao* [*China Youth News*]. Prior to his appointment there had been a debate within the CYL leadership about the overall direction these publications should take. Some believed they should offer more practical advice to young people, including articles on food, fashion, travel, and photography. Hu quashed that idea, insisting that the Youth League's responsibility was to establish its "ideological prestige," and attend to the political, educational, and ideological health of China's youth.[19] In *China Youth* he regularly included articles on the Marxist-Leninist classics, and he invited some of China's revolutionary elders to write reminiscences, poems, and commentaries on current events and policy. Mao and Liu Shaoqi penned articles for the magazine on occasion, and Mao quipped that he liked *China Youth* better than *Renmin Ribao,* the official CCP newspaper.[20]

Hu's attention to the CYL's publications was hands-on. For several years he met regularly in his home with senior staff of *China Youth* to ensure they were aware of important political issues prior to publication deadlines, and he personally reviewed important articles before they went to press.[21] Staffers recalled these meetings as being informal, lively, interactive, and enjoyable, with Hu examining issues with acuity and wit. Due to his familiarity with Mao and other senior leaders, Hu occasionally was invited to expanded Politburo meetings, and was able to pass on to Youth League staff his understanding of contemporary policy issues.[22]

Hu eventually expanded the League's publications inventory, putting out two weekly supplement periodicals, Hot Pepper (*Lajiao*) and Sunday (*Xingqitian*), which contained popular news items, advice on growing up in the new China, guidance on proper behavior, clothing styles, hobbies, and occasionally pointed commentaries about unhealthy phenomena, like official corruption. According to the editor in charge of both supplements, they were popular with general audiences but not always with local officials. After Hu took over as chairman of the board of the China Youth Publishing House in April 1954, he expanded the scope of its publications still further, approving publications on science and stories about "socialist models" and heroes that appealed to young audiences.[23]

Aside from propaganda work, Hu expanded the League's role in social reforms, such as reducing illiteracy in rural China. He focused on promoting the 1950 Marriage Law, which espoused women's equality and abolished some traditional Chinese marriage practices, like arranged marriages and concubinage. It proved to be a hard sell with the general public, but Hu was an active supporter. He wrote articles for the *Renmin Ribao,* became a member of the State Council Committee on Thoroughly Implementing the Marriage Law, and held several CYL meetings in 1953 to publicize the statute. He also was active in the party's campaign to popularize the use of *putonghua* (standard Chinese—that is, Mandarin or northern Chinese dialect), even though he spoke with a heavy Hunan accent his entire life.

Hu was a strong supporter of the Youth League being active in China's economic reconstruction, which would help it increase membership. He gave a major speech to the national congress of China's labor unions in May 1953, pledging Youth League cooperation in efforts to reach and surpass national quotas in mining and other labor-intensive industries. For the next several years he encouraged the formation of small-scale youth work teams to be sent into difficult or time-sensitive construction projects, where their strength and enthusiasm could help complete high-priority tasks.[24]

The success of these endeavors led to larger-scale Youth League labor projects, such as sending groups of youth from urban areas and universities to do tree-planting and land reclamation work in remote areas of Heilongjiang, Jiangxi, and other provinces. In late 1955 Hu visited one of the land reclamation teams from Shanghai in a remote area of Jiangxi, near Poyang Lake. Conditions were cold and miserable, and Hu commended the young workers for their patriotism in reclaiming wasteland. They asked him to write an inscription for their project, but couldn't come up with a writing brush, so Hu improvised with bamboo sticks and cotton, writing the characters for "Communist Youth Commune" to everyone's delight. The experience touched Hu, and he kept in touch with the leaders of the small town of Gongqingcheng that eventually developed there. After his death in 1989, Hu's wife chose a site nearby for Hu's permanent burial site and memorial garden.[25]

Hu's energetic leadership brought both organizational and personal benefits. In late 1956 he reported to the Central Committee that the Youth League had grown from six million members to more than twenty million in four years, and had expanded into seven hundred thousand organizations in cities, villages, factories, schools, national government organs, and military units. It now had more than eighty thousand professional cadres, who supervised millions of young people in afforestation, land reclamation, construction, recycling scrap materials, mining, and agricultural and industrial work. Its publications circulated widely, and its books sold well as youth literacy grew in the mid-1950s. Both *China Youth* and *China Youth Daily* had circulations above one million by the end of the 1950s. The Central CYL Academy, which had been established in the late 1940s for training Youth League cadres, moved into new quarters in Beijing's Haidian District in 1954, and expanded its curriculum to include philosophy, political economics, and minority languages.[26]

Hu himself thrived. He was involved in drafting the 1954 state constitution and was elected to the Presidium of the Chinese People's Political Consultative Committee and the Standing Committee of the First National People's Congress in September 1954.[27] Hu was a member of the Sino-Soviet Friendship Association and held several honorary positions with other "mass organizations." He was given the rare perquisite of being allowed to travel to foreign countries, although these were limited to socialist bloc countries like Romania, the Soviet Union, and Albania.

In the Shadow of Mao Zedong

The five years after Hu Yaobang took over the Youth League were probably some of the happiest of his adult life. He was living in a comfortable courtyard-style house in the Dongcheng District of Beijing with his extended family. His wife was working as manager of the Beijing No. 2 Cotton Mill, a demanding position, so they saw little of each other during the week, although they seemed a solid and affectionate couple. Notwithstanding his earlier disappointment at being assigned to the Youth League, Hu seemed genuinely devoted to the youth of China, was developing his skills as an effective administrator of a large organization, and was cultivating a group of capable and trustworthy officials to assist in the work. China's economy was recovering, the Korean War had reached a truce in 1953, and relations with other members of the Communist bloc were cordial. Hu was well-regarded within the CCP bureaucracy and often included in senior-level party meetings. Liu Shaoqi and Zhu De were well-disposed toward him, as was his old Sichuan boss, Deng Xiaoping, who was rapidly rising within the CCP hierarchy.

But Mao Zedong was Hu's particular patron. Mao had selected him to head the Youth League, guided him to adopt the correct ideological and organizational orbits around the party, and was satisfied with the way Hu was managing an organization Mao considered important. Hu's respect for Mao had returned to near adulation, after some buffeting during the war years. At this point Hu Yaobang seemed an ardent Maoist, a true believer in Marxism-Leninism-Mao Zedong Thought, a tireless propagandist for all the party's policies, and a proponent of the notion that abiding by Chairman Mao and his ideas would guarantee the success of all of China's hopes for greatness.

At first the growing disputes within the top leadership of the CCP probably were of only passing interest to Hu. The purge of Gao Gang and Rao Shushi in early 1954—which remains controversial to this day—was a harbinger of things to come. Early twenty-first-century scholarship suggests Gao and Rao were victims of Mao's power struggle with Liu Shaoqi and Zhou Enlai. Gao Gang was brought to Beijing by Mao Zedong in late 1952 to head the State Planning Commission, but also to reduce some of Zhou Enlai's power in the Government Administration Council and to act as a counterbalance to Liu Shaoqi on the Politburo.[28] The plan failed when Gao was indiscreet with personnel information, alerting Zhou and Liu and drawing a counterattack. Mao warned the Politburo in December of the danger of "two headquarters" within the party, but apparently signaled his acquiescence in the takedown of Gao Gang and Central Organization Department director Rao Shushi.[29]

In February 1954, Gao and Rao were accused of "trying to seize power" in the party and of forming an "anti-party alliance." Zhou Enlai was Gao's principal accuser, while Deng Xiaoping, Chen Yun, and others provided detailed testimony of Rao Shushi's "crimes." Gao and Rao were charged with trying to damage the prestige of Zhou and Liu Shaoqi and of plotting to usurp their positions in the party. In the ten-point denunciation of Gao, it was alleged he tried to set up an "independent kingdom" in the Northeast, sowed discord between the party and the army, and caused problems in relations with the Soviet Union.[30]

There was probably fire behind the smoke of some of these charges, if not with the charge that the two men had established an "anti-party alliance."[31] But in inner-party power struggles, accuracy was not necessary. The accusation presupposed the verdict. Gao and Rao were subjected to endless interrogation and merciless criticism from erstwhile allies and were deserted by their supporters. Gao attempted suicide unsuccessfully but a few months later took an overdose of sleeping pills that was fatal. Rao Shushi maintained his innocence but was stripped of party membership and put in prison, where he went insane and was granted clemency, but was still in custody when he died in 1975. Mao had engineered the entire episode, but played no role in the actual criticisms.[32]

There were growing economic policy disputes between Mao and Zhou Enlai during this period, which both precipitated and were exacerbated by their interpersonal power competition. These policy differences were probably evident to Hu Yaobang, given that their arguments often were carried out in meetings of Zhou's State Council and Mao's Politburo and on the editorial pages of *Renmin Ribao*. The principal dispute was over the speed of China's transformation into a socialist state, but it extended to other areas of economic policy.

Andrew Walder points out that in the early 1950s, Mao was a strong proponent of Soviet-style central planning. This honeymoon period in bilateral relations brought significant Soviet investment in hundreds of industrial plants in China, along with thousands of Soviet and East European advisors to help build and operate them. The Soviet economic system appeared to be a successful growth model, and Chinese leaders, especially Mao, were eager to apply it in China, despite very different socioeconomic conditions.[33]

For the PRC, with its larger population, lower industrial capacity, and more intensive small-scale agriculture, the Soviet system was not a natural fit, so some officials wanted a longer and slower transition period to work out problems and achieve a more balanced socialist system. Zhou Enlai and Chen Yun, the emerging economic czar, favored careful growth plans with modest production quotas, funded by realistic budgets administered from the top down. Mao Zedong preferred a more rapid advance, relying on China's most abundant resource—its people, and particularly rural peasants—and the Communist Party's demonstrated ability to mobilize them.

In 1953, when initial plans were being drawn up, there was a consensus within the leadership, including Mao, that the socialist transformation of agriculture, industry, and commerce—that is, collectivization of agriculture and conversion of all industrial and commercial business to fully state-owned enterprises—would take at least fifteen years. But in 1955 Mao changed his mind, evidently because he believed that collectivization of Chinese agriculture was proceeding faster than expected and could move faster still, and that its lessons could be extended to the entire Chinese economy.[34]

Not long after the land reform process had been completed in the early 1950s, party cadres in some areas of China had begun promoting the formation of peasant mutual aid teams of six to eight households regularly sharing labor, tools, and draft animals to accomplish high-priority production tasks. By 1954, with the cooperation of CCP-controlled peasant associations, farmers were being combined into larger collectives, called primary agricultural producer cooperatives, usually numbering twenty to thirty households. In these more socialist collectives, tools and draft animals were held in common, but the land was not.

Encouraged by reports of successful cooperatives increasing production, in October 1954 Beijing called for speeding up the formation of agricultural producer cooperatives, setting a goal of six hundred thousand cooperatives to be set up by the following spring. Places where primary cooperatives had already formed were encouraged to combine them into larger "advanced producer cooperatives," in which peasants turned over their land to the collective and were compensated for their labor not with cash but with "work points."[35]

Problems began when village-level cadres, anxious for recognition from upper levels, forced the formation of advanced cooperatives over the objections of "middle peasants," who had more to lose and less to gain from sharing their resources. Rather than turn livestock over to their neighbors, many peasants slaughtered their cattle and pigs, and kept land out of production to avoid it being collectivized. The newly formed State Supply and Marketing system over-procured grain, creating shortages and angering peasants in several provinces. Arbitrary behavior by inexperienced lower-level cooperative officials included beatings, fines, and suspension of work points for noncompliant farmers. By March 1955 both government and party meetings at the Center were dominated by disputes over how to bring the situation under control—more than 670,000 cooperatives had been hastily organized in a few months, but increasing numbers of peasants were demanding to withdraw from them, and some were demonstrating violently.[36]

In July 1955 Mao doubled down on rapid expansion of agricultural producer cooperatives. When the Central Committee convened a meeting of provincial party secretaries to discuss agricultural work, Mao took the opportunity to criticize—without naming them—Rural Work Department director Deng Zihui and others in charge of economic work, principally Zhou Enlai and Chen Yun: "Some of our comrades, tottering along like a woman with bound feet, are complaining all the time, 'You're going too fast, much too fast.' Too much carping, unwarranted complaints, boundless anxiety and countless taboos—all this they take as the right policy to guide the socialist mass movement in the rural areas. No, this is not the right policy, it is the wrong one."[37] Mao called for a million cooperatives by the end of 1956, and for ensuring that rural cadres understood the need to increase production in order to provide both the food and the funds for urban industrialization. He directed skeptics and doubters to have faith that the peasant masses and the Communist Party could overcome difficulties and correct their mistakes.[38]

Politics Gets Personal

After the more formalized Soviet-style General Staff system was established in late 1954, Mao Zedong may have lost some of his ability to direct military affairs. He may have ceded a portion of his control over the growing CCP bureaucracy to Liu Shaoqi, who was organizing the upcoming Eighth Party Congress. Zhou Enlai exercised a prominent role in guiding economic and foreign policy. But Mao still held enormous power.

As CCP chairman, Mao could convene Politburo Standing Committee meetings, Politburo meetings, Secretariat meetings, and special conferences, setting their locales, participants and agendas. As the unchallenged master of Marxism-Leninism in China, Mao set the terms of the ideological debate, designated the study materials, and most importantly, refereed who was winning and losing. He reviewed the final drafts of party resolutions, directives, proclamations, and other documents. Mao even reviewed and edited the texts of speeches given by other leaders before they were delivered, and decided how documents would be distributed.[39] The official public voice of the Communist Party, *Renmin Ribao*, submitted all editorials or important policy articles for his approval prior to publication. Most importantly, all important personnel appointments to party or army positions required Mao's approval.

In late 1955 Mao used both his organizational powers and his propaganda predominance to raise the stakes in his economic policy battles. He attacked continuing "right deviationist conservative thinking" within the party as the principal cause of policy problems. In October he pressed forward his plans for speeding up the socialist transformation of agriculture, claiming that it could be accomplished in three to four years, rather than his earlier estimate of fifteen years.[40]

Zhou Enlai began to criticize (without naming Mao) tendencies toward "blind rash advance" (*mangmu maojin*), in particular the arbitrary raising of grain production targets, or quotas, at national and local levels.[41] Mao argued back that official skepticism about high quotas "poured cold water" on the enthusiasm of the peasant masses and made the achievement of the goals more difficult. In late 1955 Mao put forth a revised Twelve-Year Plan for Agricultural Development, which again advanced the timetable for China to catch up with Western economies, adding more areas of economic activity for high-quota development. Zhou instead advocated maintaining a steady, controlled pace of development. "It does not matter, if the conditions are not ripe, to wait a little," he said in an early 1956 speech. "What is wrong with announcing the completion of a socialist society a little later? It can still spur us on to better efforts."[42]

Throughout much of 1956 Zhou and Mao pushed back and forth, with Zhou supported by central budget planners and economic administrators and Mao drawing strength from provincial-level officials who expressed enthusiasm for his grandiose plans. Liu Shaoqi attempted to find a middle ground between the two increasingly antagonistic positions, managing to keep things in relative harmony as the CCP prepared to hold its first full party congress since 1945.

The Eighth Congress was scheduled to convene in the autumn of 1956. The party needed a structural overhaul, along with discussion of the current economic and political work reports, adoption of a new Communist Party charter, and approval of the five-year economic plan. As always, the most important item of business was approving the selection of new party leaders.

The Eighth Congress marked a significant upgrade in Hu Yaobang's political status. Not only was he chosen as a delegate and tasked with delivering an official report on Youth League work, but he was a member of the congress presidium, responsible for management of the meetings. Still, Hu was surprised to see his own name on the list of the ninety-seven full members to be elected to the Central Committee, especially because several other proposed alternate members were older than he, had more illustrious military careers, or held higher cadre rank. He wrote a letter in September 1956 to Deng Xiaoping and Chen Yun to forward to Mao requesting he be chosen only as an alternate member. Shortly afterward, Liu Lantao, a Central Secretariat member, explained to Hu that he had been selected because the Center believed that the Youth League should be represented on the Central Committee. Liu warned him not to raise the issue again.[43]

As the congress approached, international considerations played a role in the politics of the meetings. After Joseph Stalin's death in 1953, Sino-Soviet relations had stalled pending the outcome of the succession struggle in Moscow, which Nikita S. Khrushchev appeared to be winning. Khrushchev had visited China in late 1954 to bolster his prestige as the preeminent leader of the Communist Party of the Soviet Union (CPSU), but he had not impressed Mao or other Chinese leaders, even though he promised loans, economic aid, and training for Chinese nuclear engineers. Mao disliked the boisterous Khrushchev for both ideological and personal reasons, and Chinese leaders began hinting that Mao was the rightful heir to Stalin's position as leader of the international Communist movement.[44]

In late February 1956 Khrushchev had delivered a "secret speech" to the Twentieth Congress of the CPSU in Moscow entitled "On the Cult of Personality and Its Consequences." The speech was a startling denunciation of Stalin's political and personal excesses, his terror campaigns inside the Communist Party, and his strategic and economic failures. The Chinese delegation to the congress, headed by Zhu De and Deng Xiaoping, was briefed on the contents of the speech by Khrushchev himself, who visited them afterward to ask for their support. Deng returned immediately to Beijing to inform the CCP leadership.[45]

In mid-March, Mao convened four meetings of China's top leaders to discuss the speech and its implications. The obvious but unspoken counterparts for Stalin and the "cult of personality" in the Chinese system were Mao Zedong and his exalted status. Mao reportedly listened carefully to complaints about how Stalin had mishandled relations with the CCP over the years. In the next few months, as the Communist bloc struggled with the implications of de-Stalinization in the USSR, Mao acquiesced in proposed changes in the CCP structure, constitution, and focus that made him appear less like Stalin. For example, he agreed to take all references to Mao Zedong Thought out of the CCP charter, where it had been enshrined previously as "the guideline for all our work." He volunteered to step aside as state chairman, a ceremonial but powerless office. Most importantly, Mao agreed to some important changes in the party's ideological line and policy directions that would have momentous consequences.[46]

On September 15, 1956, the Eighth CCP Congress convened. After Mao's brief opening speech, Liu Shaoqi delivered the political report, which was always the centerpiece of any congress. Some changes of political / ideological line were significant. Liu announced that "a basic change in the alignment of class forces in our country" had taken place with the cooperativization of agriculture and the "conversion of capitalist industry and commerce . . . into joint state-private management. . . . [T]he extremely complex and arduous historical task of converting the system of private ownership of the means of production into the system of socialist public ownership has now been basically accomplished in our country. The question of who will win in the struggle between socialism and capitalism in our country has now been decided."[47]

Liu announced that "the task confronting the Party now is to build China into a great socialist country as quickly as possible . . . by uniting with all the forces at home and abroad that can be united. . . . Our principal ways of conducting such [class] struggles are education and persuasion. It is only for the few individuals who adopt a hostile attitude towards socialism and violate laws of the state that necessary compulsory methods of reform are adopted." Accordingly, Liu held out an olive branch to the non-Communist democratic parties of the PRC, declaring that "from now on, a policy of long-term coexistence of the Communist Party and the democratic parties and of mutual supervision between them should be adopted."[48] Party members and non-party leaders alike must have assumed that Mao approved these changes.

Within two years however, Mao would repudiate all of them. The First Plenum of the congress, held on September 28, changed the power structure within the party. Mao continued as chairman, with four vice-chairmen (Liu Shaoqi, Zhu De, Zhou Enlai, and Chen Yun) to assist him. The former five-man ruling Secretariat was replaced by a Politburo Standing Committee made up of six members—Mao, Liu, Zhu, Zhou, and Chen, plus Deng Xiaoping. The Politburo grew to seventeen full members and six alternate (candidate) members, with the addition of four of the ten PLA marshals who helped win the civil war (three others were held over from the Seventh Congress Politburo), and two economic specialists already in senior government positions.

The congress approved the establishment of an administrative unit below the Politburo—the Central Secretariat, headed by a general secretary, Deng Xiaoping—with authority to run day-to-day party affairs.[49] Notwithstanding the structural adjustments, the actual powerholders and their relationships did not change much. Despite a few minor changes in his own titles and perquisites, this appeared to be a leadership Mao Zedong could work with. Later he would change his mind.

However, within days of the close of the First Plenum, Mao was already having second thoughts about the new ideological line. According to Liu Shaoqi's wife, Mao told Liu at the October 1 National Day celebration in 1956 that he thought "the party's Eighth Congress formulation on the basic contradictions was incorrect." Liu was stunned but was unable to get Mao to elaborate.[50]

The Year Things Began to Fall Apart

Early in 1957 Mao followed through on the Eighth Congress pledge to promote "long-term coexistence and mutual supervision" with non-Communist party groups, and particularly intellectuals. In April 1956 Mao had coined the phrase "Let 100 flowers bloom, let 100 schools of thought contend" to refer to his proposal for easing ideological restrictions on the literary and scientific communities. Liu Shaoqi endorsed the idea, and *Renmin Ribao* published an editorial on it, but other leaders were not enthusiastic in light of the ongoing turmoil in Eastern Europe in the wake of the "secret speech."[51] Chinese intellectuals probably were wary of speaking their minds, having seen writer Hu Feng sentenced to twenty years in prison in 1955 for daring to criticize the party openly.[52]

What happened between April and June 1957 is still a source of dispute among Chinese historians. In February and March, another party rectification campaign appeared to be impending, as an effort to prevent the CCP from becoming a weak, complacent ruling party bereft of revolutionary fervor. Mao invited nonparty intellectuals to participate in criticizing the CCP's shortcomings. They did so with growing enthusiasm, particularly in urban areas, universities, and in the literary field. By early May a torrent of public criticism erupted about the Communist Party, its ideology, policies, and leaders, including Mao Zedong, who was likened to China's despotic first emperor, Qin Shi Huang. Initially, party media welcomed the criticism, urging greater publicity for critics to vent their dissatisfaction.

But it didn't last long. On May 15 Mao wrote an article for internal party distribution entitled "Things Are Beginning to Change," warning that there was a limit on how long the Center would tolerate criticism from rightist intellectuals.[53] In Politburo meetings Mao began referring to the disputes between the CCP and nonparty critics as "[not] a quarrel between a sister and her brother-in-law, but between the enemy and ourselves (di-wo)," and the attackers as "rightists," or class enemies. For most of the rest of the month the Politburo encouraged more open criticism while planning when and how to bring it to a close, an approach that was later called "luring the snakes from their holes." Mao said the campaign would only last another month or so, and not many party or Youth League members would be affected.[54]

But Mao put Deng Xiaoping in charge of the counterattack. The tough general secretary pursued it with ruthless efficiency, far exceeding the "few thousand" rightists Mao expected to seize and pushing individual bureaucracies hard to expand the campaign. Over the next two years, more than 550,000 people were labeled or officially declared rightists or "right-leaning"—or more colloquially, were made to wear a "rightist hat" (youpai de maozi). The grounds on which one could be labeled a rightist widened as the campaign intensified. The "errors" or "crimes" of those accused included being active in a non-Communist party, criticizing the CCP or its leaders, expressing admiration for democracy or any democratic country, reading foreign books, playing or listening to Western classical music, wearing stylish clothes, being a Christian or other religious believer, writing or speaking about heterodox ideas, listening to a speech by another declared rightist, or being a scientist, technology specialist, or teacher.

The process of being branded as a rightist was controlled by one's work unit, or danwei. Whether by public accusation—a "blooming and contending" meeting—or private denunciation, a list of suspected rightists was gathered by the work unit's CCP committee leaders. In some Central party units, Deng Xiaoping or other senior leaders demanded that more names be added to the list. There would often be discussions with the accused, but there was no formal trial, nor was confession necessary. The party committee had the final say.

Those formally labeled rightists could be suspended from any official positions, possibly denounced at a public meeting, and expelled from the Communist Party. Some rightists were permitted to remain in their units to be reeducated, but many were sent off to "reeducation through labor" (laodong jiaoyang) camps in remote parts of China.[55] Sentence durations were often unspecified, dependent upon judgments of the camp administrators at the Ministry of Public Security that the prisoner had been "reeducated" successfully. Many sent off in 1957–1958 were not allowed to return until 1977, when more than 99 percent of those labeled rightists were officially exonerated by the party through the efforts of Hu Yaobang.[56] How many died in the camps remains unpublicized.

But the number of victims of the anti-rightist campaign was much larger than 550,000. According to Guo Daohui, a law professor at Beijing University, more than 4.6 million people nationwide were officially labeled rightists during the late 1950s. Many were probably punished during the Great Leap Forward, when starving peasants and production brigade or other lower-level officials often were accused of being rightists simply for complaining about being hungry or reporting famine conditions to upper-level officials.

Chinese intellectuals and students were specifically targeted, which took a heavy toll on professors, scientists, researchers, doctors, even elementary and middle school teachers.[57] In some schools, laboratories, and units where China's estimated three million intellectuals were concentrated, 60 percent or more were labeled rightists and shipped off to education through labor. Writers, artists, musicians, and journalists were among those most likely to be imprisoned during this period by overeager bureaucrats seeking to impress their superiors or to meet arrest quotas.[58] From a political perspective, the anti-rightist persecution of both party members and nonparty persons set the stage for further political struggles, as Mao's indiscriminate use of the term "rightist" to threaten any who disagreed with him silenced reasonable opposition to his radical policies for years to come, transforming ordinary disputes into ideological warfare and "class struggle."

Mao declared at the Qingdao Conference in July 1957 that the struggle against "bourgeois rightism" was "an antagonistic, irreconcilable, life-and-death contradiction," subject to the harsh methods of class struggle with the enemy.[59] As Li Honglin put it, Mao's declaration broadened the concept of class struggle from being based on social class background to being based on a judgment of one's political thinking.[60] The consequences for both Chinese society and for the Chinese Communist Party would be disastrous.

Hu Yaobang and "Rightism" in the Youth League

On May 15, 1957, the China New Democratic Youth League convened its Third Congress in the Great Hall of the People in Beijing. It was to be a landmark congress, and most of the Politburo, including Mao Zedong, attended the ceremonial opening. Hu Yaobang announced that the congress would pass a resolution changing the name of the Youth League back to its original name of Communist Youth League (CYL). The reason it could do this, he said, was that the era of "large-scale class struggle" in China was over, the socialist revolution had been accomplished, the exploiting classes had "basically been eliminated," and the Communist Youth League could now devote itself to helping the party "struggle for the glorious ideals of communism."[61]

Hu may not have realized that Mao Zedong was already changing his mind about the tolerance for heterodox ideas and open political discourse. In his essay "Things Are Beginning to Change," which Mao wrote the day he attended the Youth League Congress but did not circulate until later, the chairman warned: "There are a great many new members in our Party (and even more in the Youth League) who are intellectuals, and it is true that a number of them are rather seriously afflicted with revisionist ideas."[62] More ominously, Mao told the closing ceremony of the CYL Congress on April 25, "All speech and actions that depart from socialism are wrong."

At the end of the congress, Hu was reelected first secretary of the CYL Central Committee, along with secretaries Liu Xiyuan, Luo Yi, Hu Keshi, Wang Wei, Liang Buting, and Xiang Nan.[63] Within two months they would be at each other's throats, some labeled as rightists. Hu was probably aware of problems of ideological heterodoxy within the CYL. In some ways he

Hu Yaobang welcomes Chairman Mao Zedong to a renamed Communist Youth League Congress in May 1957. Subsequently the CYL underwent a scorching "anti-rightist" purge.

encouraged it with his efforts to reach out to intellectuals, recruit members on university campuses, and foster independent thinking among his senior staff and in the League's publications. When he learned that *China Youth Daily* editor in chief Zhang Liqun and others were seeking more editorial independence, saying Youth League publications needed to be more than "megaphones for the Communist Party," Hu was probably concerned but didn't have time to do anything about it. Unfortunately for Zhang, Mao Zedong read about his remarks and was very angry.[64]

From mid-July to early September, while Hu was attending international Youth League congresses and celebrations in Moscow and Kiev, Deng Xiaoping unleashed the full force of the anti-rightist campaign on the Youth League Central Committee, with collaboration from some of Hu's deputies. Returning home through Xinjiang to inspect CYL work there, Hu made a long-distance telephone call to Beijing and was shocked to learn from Luo Yi, a member of the League secretariat, that "grievous damage" had been done to the League's central bureaucracy while he had been away. Luo (and Deng Xiaoping) had labeled many members of the League's central committee as rightists, including several editors or senior reporters of the *China Youth Daily*. Hu ordered Luo to cease further action against rightists and immediately flew back to Beijing.[65] He tried to get several of the denunciations rescinded but was unsuccessful. Remonstrating with Deng Xiaoping, Hu pleaded that *China Youth Daily* editor in chief Zhang Liqun's error in criticizing party publications was "confused and ironic," not evidence of rightist thinking. Deng replied, "That settles it, then. . . . But if he's confused, he cannot be editor in chief," and had Zhang sent down to a county-level committee for several years.[66]

Most of the first batch of CYL rightists were sent to "education through labor" camps in northwestern and northern China. The campaign dragged on for another year, and more CYL leaders were knocked down. At lower levels, the numbers punished were far higher and continued to be for several years. There is no record of Hu ever directly criticizing the larger movement at the time. In February 1958, seeing off senior CYL officials to their labor camp assignments, Hu tried to balance giving them comfort with justifying labor reform punishment for ideological errors.[67]

By contrast, Deng Xiaoping became increasingly determined to prosecute rightists both inside and outside the Communist Party, with a particular focus on intellectuals. In his report at the Central Committee meeting in September/October 1957, Deng promised that the campaign would "continue to deepen and expand. . . . We must win a complete victory." He warned "a few" party leaders against taking a "soft-hearted" approach to the issue and noted that the Youth League had displayed serious organizational and ideological problems while rooting out "rightism." He recommended that it "seriously carry out a reorganization" of its work.[68]

Hu Yaobang responded to Deng's and others' critiques of the League in his own address on October 10, promising to carry out a "political, organizational and ideological transformation of the cadre team" and "basically dig the rightists out" of all leadership positions.[69] At that point, however, little attention was paid to his viewpoint. With pressure at all levels to eliminate opposition to Mao's growing control over all policy areas, the League came under further scrutiny by Deng's Central Secretariat.

In June 1958 Liu Lantao singled out two senior CYL secretaries—Xiang Nan and Liang Buting—for criticism and punishment as "right opportunists." Hu telephoned Liu to discuss the situation but was cut off and warned that if he continued trying to defend his people, he risked being branded a "right deviationist" himself. Two more of Hu's key lieutenants then were summarily sacked, and one would spend twenty years in education through labor. Hu was filled with remorse, and with an even greater distaste for the politics of denunciation and accusation.[70] He reported to the Secretariat in July 1958 about the Youth League's efforts to correct its mistakes, drawing a warning from Deng that the League needed to be more modest about its achievements and remain in lockstep with the Communist Party's leadership.[71]

More than fifty members of the CYL Central Committee were declared to be rightists during the first year of the campaign, and several hundred more were labeled "middle rightists" and dismissed. Hu was at first contrite that he had failed to educate people around him to the ideological hazards they were facing, and even apologized to some of them. He would later recognize that the problems emanated from the top. According to one of his biographers, he began for the first time to have doubts about Mao and the cause he led.[72] But he kept those opinions to himself.

Mao Silences His Opposition

While Hu Yaobang was struggling to retain control of the fracturing Communist Youth League and restore its—and his own—standing with the party leadership, Mao Zedong was about to reinforce his domination and seize control of China's political and economic policies. In November 1957 Mao took his second trip to Moscow to celebrate the fortieth anniversary of the USSR's October Revolution. Deng was included in the delegation, and Mao singled him out as "the future leader of China and its Communist Party."[73] Mao was full of praise for the USSR's recent achievements, especially the two Sputnik satellites. When Khrushchev boasted that the USSR planned to surpass the United States within fifteen years, Mao responded that China would seek to overtake the United Kingdom within fifteen years.[74]

In late December, Mao urged economic planners to speed up the pace of economic growth. In *Renmin Ribao* editorials, Mao redirected the guiding slogan for all economic work to be "Go all out, aim higher, and achieve more, better, faster, and more economical results." He hailed provincial enthusiasm for a faster transition to socialism and reignited the 1956 controversy over "opposing rash advance" in setting targets for the planned economy.[75]

In early 1958 Mao convened a meeting of Central planners and selected provincial secretaries in Nanning, the capital of Guangxi, ostensibly to discuss the results of the just-concluded first five-year plan. But instead he used the meeting to attack those who had accused him of promoting "rash advance" two years earlier. In four speeches Mao told delegates not to use the term again, as it was a political statement that might discourage the enthusiasm of China's six hundred million people.[76]

Later, referring to a report he approved by Shanghai party first secretary Ke Qingshi on "braving wind and waves" to surpass the United Kingdom, Mao sarcastically asked Zhou Enlai if the premier could write such a report. Zhou said he could not, to which Mao responded, "Aren't you opposed to rash advance? I am one who is opposed to opposing rash advance." Zhou began composing his first of three *jiantao* [public confessions]. Mao then attacked several other senior economic officials, some by name, accusing them of "blockading" him. He began drafting guidelines for local cadres on how to carry out Beijing's economic directives in ways that later observers claimed would lead cadres to exaggerate their achievements.[77]

Mao used an "expanded" Politburo meeting in February 1958, a regional secretaries conference in Chengdu in March, and another in Wuhan in April to continue beating down those who disagreed with his economic plans. He insisted that "opposing rash advance" was non-Marxist and perhaps even rightist, a label that carried dire consequences. Zhou Enlai did a more detailed self-criticism at the Chengdu meeting, and China's principal economic officials—Chen Yun, Bo Yibo and Li Xiannian—hastened to follow suit. Even

Liu Shaoqi, who had only tried to ameliorate the disputes, acknowledged his error in not following Mao's guidance.[78]

Mao Zedong then undertook a "makeover" of the entire Eighth Party Congress, which had been held in 1956. The Second Meeting of the Eighth CCP Congress was convened in the Huairentang meeting hall in Zhong-nanhai, May 5–23, 1958. Like a standard CCP congress, it was preceded by a full Central Committee plenary meeting and followed by another one that announced personnel changes. Mao reviewed and edited its principal reports, invited several persons who were not members of the Central Committee to address the meeting, and gave four speeches. Under his close direction, the "2nd of the 8th" reversed many of the changes introduced at the 1956 congress.

It adopted "Go all out, aim high, and achieve greater, faster, better, and more economical results in socialist construction" as the "general line" (*zong luxian*) for the CCP's economic and political program. It amended the 1956 depiction of China's class struggle situation, saying that "the struggle between the bourgeoisie and the proletariat, between socialism and capitalism, is our main internal contradiction," and that it would be a "fierce, life-or-death contradiction." It affirmed the correctness of the anti-rightist campaigns of 1957, and approved Mao's position on the question of "opposing rash advance."[79]

The congress continued to strengthen Mao Zedong's organizational and ideological authority within the party, laying the political groundwork for the Great Leap Forward. The meeting silenced Mao's most important adversaries within the party. Chen Yun and Zhou Enlai read aloud formal, written self-criticisms at open meetings. Zhou then submitted his resignation as premier, asking the Politburo to decide if his continuing in that position was "appropriate or not." The Politburo took no formal action. Defense Minister Peng Dehuai asked to step down at the same time (June 1958), but his request was turned aside.[80]

The "2nd of the 8th" sessions had a great deal of inflated rhetoric about Mao Zedong and Mao Zedong Thought. Senior leaders seemed to vie with each other to flatter Mao, calling him an "enlightened man" and equating his ideas with "truth."[81] Mao earlier in 1958 had admitted this was a kind of "personality worship" that potentially could lead to tyranny, but now said that in his case, it was "correct personality worship," because, as he put it, quoting Lenin, "your dictatorship is not as good as my dictatorship."[82] The "makeover" Eighth Congress adopted Mao's challenge to surpass the United

Kingdom in steel production within fifteen years, and launched a Great Leap Forward campaign (*dayuejin yundong*) as China's overarching economic program. Provincial representatives vied with each other to promise high-speed economic growth in their regions.

Mao arranged several personnel changes that enhanced his personal power in important ways. First, he had Marshal Lin Biao—one of the most successful generals of the civil war—appointed vice chairman of the Central Committee. He established a monthly official publication devoted to ideology, *Hongqi* [Red Flag], under the direction of one of his secretaries, Chen Boda. Mao added to the Politburo two provincial leaders known for their enthusiastic support of his economic plans, Ke Qingshi from Shanghai and Li Jingquan from Sichuan.[83]

As for Hu Yaobang, he attended the "2nd of the 8th" Central Committee meetings, but he neither gave a speech nor recorded any impressions of the event.[84] He was still trying to recover his equilibrium within the CYL, holding a Youth League Central Committee plenum that lasted more than two months and ended up passing a resolution criticizing one of his closest associates. Hu may have been overcompensating for Central Secretariat criticisms by parroting the rapidly changing ideological line in speeches and Youth League publications. He even organized a three-hundred-member youth "tribute team" to visit Zhongnanhai on July 1 to pay respects to Mao Zedong and the CCP leadership.[85]

Having bent the Central Committee and State Council to his will and re-taken the initiative for personnel and policy in all areas, Mao now turned to the one institution he may have felt posed a threat to his power, the People's Liberation Army. He convened an "expanded" meeting of the Central Military Commission on May 27, 1958. Mao evidently believed the PLA was becoming too bureaucratic and "professional" in its approach to military affairs, too much like the USSR's Red Army. He called for an investigation into "dogmatism and sectarianism" in the army. His target was the Training Department of the Nanjing Military Academy, where two of the PLA's ten marshals and several senior generals were located.

Mao's methods at the month-long expanded CMC meeting were familiar. First, he inflamed interpersonal jealousies and rivalries that had afflicted the PLA for many years. Newly promoted CCP vice-chairman Lin Biao put Defense Minister Peng Dehuai on the spot with innuendo about Peng's relations with other generals. Mao specified several senior PLA leaders he thought deserved criticism, including Marshal Liu Bocheng, who had recently resigned as head of the Nanjing Military Academy; Xiao Ke, head of the academy's training department; and Su Yu, chief of the general staff.[86]

Mao brought in lower-ranking cadres to attack senior officials. Accused officials were expected to engage in a *jiantao* or "self-examination," which in practice usually connoted an involuntary self-confession. Delivered in a public setting, a *jiantao* often depended upon favorable audience reaction for the official to "pass the gate."[87] When Mao found the tenor of the CMC meeting too sedate, he privately called in other military officials to stir things up. One to whom he turned was Deng Xiaoping. According to Taiwan scholar Chung Yen-lin, Deng had been a member of the CMC since 1954, even though he was no longer a PLA officer, because his writ as general secretary extended to political-military affairs. Mao appointed Deng to head the Center's "anti-dogmatism leading small group." Deng saw to the implementation of Mao's strict measures against Su Yu, Xiao Ke, and several other senior officers—some of them his former subordinates. But he managed to divert any punishment away from Liu Bocheng, his old commander in the civil war. Liu was allowed to resign from the Nanjing Military Academy and then went into a long period of convalescence and political retirement, though he retained his positions as CMC vice-chairman and Politburo member.[88]

The expanded CMC meeting represented Mao's return to active engagement with the PLA, which he said he had not "grasped" for several years. It demonstrated his ability to take charge of its agenda and personnel issues at will. Mao's criticism of dogmatism was a reminder that his preference for "red" over "expert" held true for the army as well other fields. But the personnel issues were probably equally important. He turned Defense Minister Peng Dehuai against several other "old marshals," reinforced the prominence of Deng Xiaoping within the CMC, and struck down several senior generals on questionable charges. Most of the officers cashiered would not be rehabilitated until after Mao's death. In 1958 the PLA—like all other CCP bureaucracies—was firmly in Mao Zedong's grip, and it seemed clear he intended to keep it that way.[89]

The Devastation of the Great Leap Forward

The true scale of the human tragedy in the Great Leap Forward only began coming into focus some sixty years later. The number of people who starved to death, were worked or beaten to death, perished in labor camps, committed suicide, or otherwise died what were called "unnatural deaths" (*feizhengchang siwang*) from late 1958 through 1962 is "officially" listed as "more than 10 million."[90] According to the deputy director of the Central Party History Research Office, that figure came from the State Statistical Bureau, which was the "most authoritative department," but the archives on which it was based are still classified.[91] Later "official" accounts by other PRC bureaucracies raised estimated total deaths to sixteen to twenty million.[92]

Historian Yang Jisheng estimated the number who died outright of starvation during the Great Leap at about 34 to 36 million. But he also assessed the decline in China's total population during that period, including children that would have been born if normal population growth had taken place, was an additional 40 million, for a "total population loss" of 76 million.[93] Frank Dikötter estimated the number who starved or died as a result of the Great Leap at 45 million.[94]

The reasons the figures vary so greatly are twofold: the true number of deaths might not be known, given that many victims died away from their homes, searching for food, their bodies destroyed or buried in mass graves; and the Communist Party authorities have kept archives closed and do not want the number known.

For many years afterward, official PRC sources blamed "several years of natural calamities," such as flood and drought, often adding criticism of the Soviet Union, which suspended many important contracts as the Sino-Soviet ideological split worsened in 1959–1960.[95] But more recently Chinese scholars have concluded that drought conditions in some parts of China during those years were within normal parameters, and not the principal cause of the famine that accompanied the Great Leap. Yang Jisheng writes, "From 1958 to 1961, there were no large-scale droughts or floods within China, nor was there any large-scale occurrence of damagingly low temperatures. Conditions in those three years were normal."[96] Other scholars have discounted the effect of Soviet aid reductions, leaving the responsibility for the multiple tragedies of the Great Leap Forward largely in the domain of a "human disaster" (*renhuo*).[97]

The August 1958 Beidaihe Meeting

The problem, politically, was an overconcentration of power, demonstrated clearly in the "expanded Politburo meeting" Mao Zedong convened at the beachside resort of Beidaihe, August 17–30, 1958. The participants included provincial secretaries and leaders of the central ministries and departments that would oversee economic plans for the coming year. The agenda ranged from economic plans and targets to militia affairs to education. Mao set the ideological tone, which was hugely optimistic: China would surpass Great Britain and the United States in steel production in a short time on the strength of the enthusiasm of China's peasant masses, which would enable it to make the "transition to socialism" and soon after to communism, well ahead of previous expectations.[98]

Before the meeting, Mao had visited experimental "people's communes" (*renmin gongshe*) in Henan and Shandong and pronounced them "good," both as means of managing "production, livelihood, and political power," and as the "basic unit" of Chinese society that would enable it to make the transition to the utopian goals of socialism.[99] He therefore pressed hard at the Beidaihe meeting to advance the formation of people's communes throughout China before the end of October. This became a massive experiment in social engineering, transforming more than 740,000 of the agricultural producer cooperatives of 1954–1955 into some 26,000 people's communes in little more than a month. That number would grow to about 53,000 as communes were divided and merged. Each commune was further divided into "production brigades" and "production teams," for basic accounting and management purposes. Chinese media proudly announced that more than 99 percent of all rural households had been incorporated into communes by late October 1958.[100]

The transformation entailed the regimentation—even militarization—of rural society beneath a large system of CCP officials who had little alternative to using force to have their orders obeyed. And their orders were to "collectivize" (in effect, expropriate) all rural property, livestock, and equipment and put them under state management. In this instance, the expropriation included household cooking utensils and dining furniture. Mao had become enamored of the idea of communal dining halls (*gongshe shitang*) as a more efficient way to deliver more food to people and eliminate the family as the basic unit of socialist society. Peasant households were required to turn over pots and pans and other daily-use items to the communal dining halls and to take all their meals there. In some places, family residences were replaced by barracks-style communal housing, and work assignments were organized along quasi-military lines. As Yang Jisheng put it, "Control was virtually total. Political power extended into the most remote corners of China's map and allowed the dictatorship of the proletariat to invade every family, every brain, and every stomach."[101]

The Beidaihe meeting brought additional disaster to China's economy in the form of exaggerated production targets for the planned economy. The voices of restraint and realism having been silenced by the "2nd of the 8th" meeting, Mao and local leaders in August ratcheted up the production goals to be completed by the end of the year to levels many must have known were unachievable. Steel production was the most important example because it was Mao's benchmark. The PRC's 1957 steel production had been roughly 5.6 million metric tons, but Mao had prodded industrial leaders in late June to double the target for 1958 to 10.7 million tons, even though production was already running below 1957 levels. At the Beidaihe meeting he insisted that the target of 10.7 million tons must be met, to ensure that the (completely unrealistic) 1959 production goal of 18 to 20 million tons would be reached.[102] So began a national steelmaking frenzy in China, which, the official media proclaimed, exceeded the target for steel production in 1958, but which most experts regarded as a shocking waste of resources to produce mostly useless iron slag.[103]

Knowing that China's own steelmaking factories, even those provided by the USSR, did not have the capacity to produce that much steel, Mao and his economic planners organized a "mass campaign" to boost production. They mandated using agricultural labor to mine iron ore in remote mountain areas and to build wood-burning "soil blast furnaces" (*tu gaolu*) everywhere to smelt the ore. Such furnaces had been used in China for centuries but were not able to reach the higher temperatures required to make steel, and even knowledge of iron-smelting was not widespread. Thousands of small-scale, inefficient "backyard blast furnaces" were built all over China in late 1958, wasting enormous rural labor and denuding many forests for fuel. They produced low-grade, useless iron scoria (much of it from melting cooking utensils and tools) that the peasants called "iron turds." Meanwhile, crops already planted in 1958 rotted in the autumn ground with too few laborers to harvest them.[104]

The Beidaihe meeting also agreed to unrealistic agricultural production targets based upon exaggerated estimates of the productivity of communal farmland. In mid-1958 some of the "model" communes established in Henan and Shandong began boasting of astonishing increases in productivity per *mu* of land (one *mu* = about 1 / 6 acre), as much as twenty times greater than the previous year. These figures usually were reported on so-called satellite (*weixing*) fields, named in honor of Russian Sputnik satellites, and using experimental seeds and planting methods and large quantities of fertilizer. Central leaders, many of peasant origin who likely knew better, accepted that

Desperate to increase steel production to meet Mao Zedong's unrealistic
goals in 1958, thousands of wood-burning blast furnaces were built all over
China, resulting in a huge waste of resources and labor, and no usable steel.
(Wikimedia Commons)

higher yields could be achieved more broadly, and predicted that sharp increases in grain production would be achieved easily. Mao even mused about
what they would do with all the extra food.[105]

The worst problem, which had already begun with larger-scale collectivization in 1955–1956, was that the State Monopoly of Purchasing and Marketing (*Tonggou tongxiao*) was operating beyond its capacity to predict
supply and demand. Therefore, it over-procured grain from the farmers,
leaving them without enough to subsist on. Higher production quotas set

by the party meant the state would take more, leaving less for the farmers. Sales to the monopoly were mandatory, of course, and hoarding and hiding grain were severely punished by local authorities, often with beatings or imprisonment. These punishments grew heavier as supply problems worsened. Rural shortages were exacerbated in 1958 by the involuntary migration of tens of millions of peasants to iron ore mining and large-scale water conservancy projects (dams, reservoirs, and irrigation systems), where they had to be fed by the state.

Mao continued to conduct inspections of carefully selected communes, talking to commune leaders, giving instructions on-the-spot and circulating them to the rest of the country. He encouraged other leaders to do the same, which many did, including Hu Yaobang. The problem was that no one wanted to admit that they didn't understand or weren't enthusiastic about the party's plans. Lower-level officials were seldom honest with the visiting officials. They didn't talk about the food shortages, deteriorating conditions in communal dining halls, and peasant overwork. They talked instead about ideological questions, accounting and pay issues, and low-level cadre misbehavior.[106] So the problems persisted and worsened. Central authorities began responding in early 1959 with emergency food shipments to places where signs of malnutrition, particularly edema, were becoming unmistakable, and starvation deaths were beginning to be reported.

Another regional meeting in early 1959 and a Central Committee plenum in May brought further adjustments to the commune system in terms of structure, accounting, payment for work, and management.[107] By that time there were reports that twenty-five million people in central and eastern China had "no rice to eat." There were violent protests in the southwest. But other areas were falsely reporting bumper crops and peasant enthusiasm. Mao appears to have believed that, except for a few of the "leftist" errors and some residual ideological confusion about the nature of the communes, things were going quite well.[108]

Showdown at Lushan

In June 1959 Mao decided to hold another expanded Politburo meeting to address the increasingly obvious shortcomings of Great Leap policies. In order to give leaders a chance to rest, do some reading, and enjoy pleasant scenery, he arranged for the meeting to be held at Lushan, in Jiangxi.[109] A famous scenic spot much beloved by landscape artists for its steep, forested slopes and misty clouds, Lushan had been developed into a summer retreat, with several hundred villas, for Western businessmen and missionaries in the late nineteenth century. Chiang Kai-shek used the area as a refuge from sweltering Nanjing, and George Marshall had convened several meetings there during his efforts to mediate the civil war.

Mao envisioned the meeting as a working vacation, with structured discussions of his agenda in the morning and early afternoon, then movies, dances, and plays for evening entertainment. While it was understood that the primary purpose of the meeting was to "correct leftism" (*jiu zuo*), some referred to the conclave as a "fairy meeting" (*shenxian hui*) due to its light schedule. The meetings got underway on July 2 and were slated to go for two weeks or more. They were attended by most of the Politburo, along with provincial CCP secretaries eager to prove themselves to Mao.

The initial discussion sessions, divided into regional groupings, proceeded smoothly but were troubling to those who did not share Mao's view that everything was going well, most prominently Defense Minister Peng Dehuai. Peng and Mao were from the same region in Hunan, both had fled to the Jinggang mountains after the Nanchang Uprising, and they were once considered to be close friends, brothers in arms.[110] Their relationship had deteriorated during the civil war, and after 1949 it became coolly formal. Peng was celebrated as the successful commander of the Chinese People's Volunteers in the Korean War, but the issue of the death of Mao's son during that conflict still burdened their private relationship.

Crude and irreverent, Peng found offensive Mao's imperial airs after he became party chairman and didn't try to hide his views. When Mao forced Peng to purge his own officer corps in May 1958, the chill in their relationship turned to cold anger. Peng tried twice to resign as defense minister, but Mao wouldn't allow it. The personal animus probably was subsumed in Mao's growing concern that he did not have sufficient control over or loyalty from the People's Liberation Army.

After several days of feckless conversations about the accomplishments of the Great Leap Forward, Peng decided to take up his concerns directly with Mao. But when he called at the Chairman's villa on the afternoon of July 12, Mao was said to be sleeping, and Peng went back to his own villa and put his concerns in a letter delivered to Mao on July 14.[111] The letter was carefully written, starting with an acknowledgment of the successes of the Great Leap and how it had energized a great part of the Chinese population. But he said there were some problems that needed attention. First, a

Mao and "Chinese People's Volunteers" commander Peng Dehuai in 1953. Once considered "close comrades-in-arms" in Hunan, Mao and Peng's relationship deteriorated precipitously when Mao accused Peng of being the head of a "counter-revolutionary clique" in 1959. Peng died in prison during the Cultural Revolution. (CPA Media Pte Ltd / Alamy Stock Photo)

"boastful atmosphere" existed at every level and in every region, especially in the party media. Second, "bourgeois fanaticism makes us prone to make leftist mistakes." Third, putting "politics in command" (*zhengzhi guashuai*) could not replace economic laws.[112] All these critiques were aimed directly at Mao's belief that subjective will could bring miraculous results. Mao took Peng's letter badly, but he also saw it as an opportunity to strike at his opponents, and he took it.

Mao waited two days, then circulated Peng's letter to all the Lushan participants under the title: "Comrade Peng Dehuai's Book of Complaints" (*Peng Dehuai tongzhi de yijianshu*). Peng had neither titled the private letter nor expected it to be circulated. On July 17 Mao instructed the discussion groups to focus on the letter and to deliver daily reports of their meetings to him. It did not take long for him to discover that Peng's doubts were shared by many other senior party leaders, but he continued to bide his time, carefully reading the briefing reports. He began calling in reinforcements, party and military officials he could trust, including Lin Biao, Peng Zhen, Huang Kecheng, Yang Shangkun, and his old henchman from Yan'an days, Kang Sheng. "Come up the mountain," he implored, "speak out about this."

Huang Kecheng, Peng Dehuai's longtime subordinate and vice-minister of defense and chief of the General Staff, arrived at Lushan on July 17 and went to see his boss, who showed him the letter. Huang scolded Peng for his intemperate language, but said he supported him, and made a speech to that effect on July 19.[113] Zhang Wentian, the former party general secretary whom Mao had shoved aside at Yan'an, was already at Lushan. He had exchanged views with Peng Dehuai on the overall situation but had not read the letter before it was circulated. Nonetheless, he agreed with Peng and delivered a three-hour speech to his discussion group on July 21, setting out in detail both the achievements and the shortcomings of the Great Leap, and explicitly endorsing Peng's letter.[114]

On July 23 Mao Zedong counterattacked, completely changing the nature of the discussions at Lushan. In a rambling diatribe filled with historical references and ancient poems, bristling with defensiveness and animosity, he told a plenary session that party leaders needed to "toughen their scalps and stiffen their backbones." They should have more faith in the "General Line" and the ability of the peasants to understand "political economy," and have patience with things like communal dining halls that weren't working yet. In a direct challenge to Peng Dehuai, he threatened he would "go to the countryside to lead the peasants to overthrow the government. If those of you in the Liberation Army won't follow me, then I will go and find a Red Army and organize another Liberation Army. But I think the Liberation Army would follow me."[115]

Mao's speech turned the Lushan meeting from an effort to "correct leftism" into an all-out assault on "right-leaning opportunism," with Peng Dehuai its leading practitioner. As the week wore on, more party members came to Lushan, and criticism of Peng began to gain momentum. Impromptu expanded Politburo meetings and small group sessions began to malign the reputations of Peng Dehuai and others who criticized the Great Leap Forward.

Mao needed a bigger conspiracy, so he added Huang Kecheng to the mix and talked of a "military club" (*junshi julebu*) that included Zhang Wentian. Then he added in Zhou Xiaozhou, the Hunan party secretary who had accompanied Peng on his 1958 inspection and later was reluctant to denounce him—to have a four-member "anti-party clique" (*fandang jituan*) as the focus of attack. The four were obliged to perform *jiantao* but were never permitted to respond to the charges against them. The charges, of course, were exaggerated and false, but everyone had to play out the game under Mao's watchful eye.[116]

Hu Yaobang was inspecting Youth League work and performing ceremonial labor in Shandong when the Central Secretariat informed him his presence was required on Lushan by August 1. Despite being ill at the time, Hu took a special military flight to Jiangxi, then continued by car to Lushan, arriving on July 29. He may have had a general understanding of the original purposes of the Lushan meeting, but probably did not know until he arrived how tense the political situation had become. As a man of peasant origins, Hu had been skeptical of the production claims of "satellite" fields and had scolded some local leaders for exaggerating their production. But he could not argue the case with Mao and other senior leaders. In late 1958 Hu had increased his travels to local areas to inspect CYL work and encourage rebuilding after the "anti-rightist" campaign had decimated local ranks. In his travels to Henan in 1959, he learned for himself the difficulties peasants were beginning to face due to food shortages. But conditions were not yet extreme, and although he was uneasy, he was not alarmed.[117]

By the time Hu arrived at Lushan, the main issue at stake was purging "right deviationist" leaders at the heart of the Communist Party. Mao Zedong's speech to the Eighth Plenum on August 2 made it clear that the "Peng-Huang-Zhang-Zhou right-deviationist anti-party clique" was to be denounced and excised from the party. All of 149 members and alternate members of the Central Committee present were expected to "declare their opinion" (*biaotai*) about these four men and their perfidious behavior, and affirm their own loyalty to Mao's "Three Red Flags"—the party's General Line, the Great Leap Forward, and the people's communes.[118]

There is no formal record of Hu's thoughts, conversations, speeches, or notes from his time on Lushan. His biographers describe him as confused and worried. He knew all four "conspirators" well—all were from Hunan. He had served with Peng at the siege of Taiyuan and had been a neighbor and friend of Zhang Wentian at Yan'an. When told by a military colleague that several senior generals were finding the situation difficult to understand, Hu replied, "How could Peng *Laozong* ['Old Commander' Peng] oppose the Party and Chairman Mao? Chairman Mao, the old man, doesn't hear different opinions."[119]

At the small group sessions, he only mouthed a few platitudes supporting Chairman Mao's speech. He didn't even tell his *mishu* what he really thought when they were arranging his notes for the official record, which would go to Mao.[120] When the time came to vote on the "Resolution on the mistakes of the anti-party group headed by Comrade Peng Dehuai," Hu raised his hand to support the resolution, despite the its extreme language vilifying Peng and negating all his contributions to the revolution.[121] All four men were dismissed from their official positions, and although they retained their Communist Party membership, they became political outcasts and easy targets for persecution later.

It is difficult to overstate the impact of the Lushan meeting and Eighth Plenum. Mao Zedong proved yet again to be politically agile, dominating all opposition, and intolerant of opinions different from his own, to say nothing of direct criticism. He devised a new label with which to attack his political opponents in the party—"right-leaning opportunism"—that would be slapped on millions of party members in the coming years and would be used to intimidate countless others into remaining silent in the face of policy decisions they knew were wrong and harmful. Despite a brief acknowledgment that his own understanding of economics was limited, Mao was now fully in charge of China's economic policy. A few corrections were made by the Eighth Plenum—lowering some production quotas and changing target dates—but the fundamental flaws of the system were not addressed. And they would get far worse.

Perhaps most importantly, Mao again reconfigured the Central leadership. He completed his purge of the People's Liberation Army leadership at a Military Commission meeting in Beijing immediately following the Eighth Plenum. From August 18 to September 12 he convened an "expanded" CMC meeting, attended by more than twenty-eight thousand PLA officers. Mao, Liu Shaoqi, and Zhou Enlai all gave tough speeches, while Zhu De delivered a written confession of his failure to criticize Peng Dehuai sufficiently on Lushan. The meeting again pilloried Peng and Huang for opposing Mao and disparaged their previous military service. It then implicated four more senior PLA officers—all Peng subordinates—in the "military club" and launched an army-wide struggle against "right deviationist elements" in the PLA that brought down 1,848 officers before the end of the year.[122]

After the meeting confirmed the dismissal of Peng and Huang, Mao brought the more tractable Lin Biao to the top of the PLA hierarchy as minister of defense and ranking CMC vice-chairman. He appointed Luo Ruiqing, the tough-minded minister of public security and head of PLA security forces, to the position of chief of the General Staff. Both, of course, were completely willing to say or do anything to bring down their former "comrades in arms" and in the process improve their own positions of power.

As for Hu Yaobang, he soon realized that his lukewarm support for the attack on Peng Dehuai had come to Mao's attention, and he would pay a political price. As he later recounted to family and friends, Mao ignored him for the next two years, letting him "sit on the cold bench" (*zuo leng ban-deng*).[123] For several months after Lushan, Hu seemed to be trying to prove his loyalty and enthusiasm for the Three Red Flags by traveling, making speeches, writing articles, and otherwise cheerleading for policies he was beginning to doubt. Partly this was an effort to deflect the impact of the rolling investigation and purge of "right-deviationists" and "little Peng Dehuais" in the Youth League. It was only modestly successful, as CYL cadres again suffered heavily, especially those in educational and scientific institutions. But it might also have been an effort to recover his personal standing with the topmost leadership. Hu Yaobang, forty-five-year-old youth leader, facing a noxious political atmosphere in Beijing, probably saw little alternative but to continue to fight for the ideals he had espoused for more than thirty years and to follow the man who had been his idol and teacher for almost as long. Notwithstanding his own increasing ideological sophistication and education through voluminous reading, Hu Yaobang was still a loyal Maoist, a firm—but not unquestioning—believer in the chairman.

5   Into the Maelstrom

In the autumn of 1960, less than a year after the Lushan meeting, Hu Yaobang went on an inspection trip to North Sichuan, where he had headed the CCP committee a decade before. As he came south into Nanchong on a route he had traveled many times, he was shocked by the appearance of people walking alongside the road. They were dressed in rags, their faces pale and drawn, and some showed signs of malnutrition—puffy skin and bloated bellies. He reportedly said angrily, "They're not eating or dressed as well as when I was here after Liberation . . . and this is called a 'Great Leap Forward?!'" When told of unburied corpses of people who had starved to death, he was incensed: "He [Mao Zedong] has been surrounded and hoodwinked. He doesn't know the real situation!"[1] Two months later, at a Communist Youth League School forum, Hu was quoted saying that he did not believe the dire conditions he saw were caused by "natural disasters," the official explanation. Instead he faulted the "Communist wind" (excessive enthusiasm for the transition to socialism) for causing people to lose enthusiasm altogether for the Great Leap. He advised CYL publications to modulate propaganda for the Three Red Flags, aware that resentment over the Great Leap was growing in rural areas.[2]

Hu may or may not have said what is quoted above, but the sentiments seem plausible. After the Lushan meetings, he had worked to recover his standing with the Chairman. He had made speeches, attended rallies, and spoke at Youth League conclaves, extolling all the elements of the Great Leap Forward, including small-scale steel production. In March 1960 Hu had spoken at a national conference of the China Women's Federation, commending it for having adopted the slogan "Raising High the Banner of Mao Zedong Thought, Whip the Horse Even Harder, Leap Forward, Leap

Forward and Leap Forward Again!" In April 1960 he had told a meeting of the National People's Congress that the Great Leap Forward had given China's youth "the most valuable gift of spiritual wealth."[3] After all that, seeing the realities on the ground must have been a shock.

By late 1960 and early 1961, famine was devastating the countryside. Communal mess halls were running out of food, decisions made in late 1959 to permit private family plots were ignored at the local level, and many households had neither food nor pots to cook it in. Beefed-up local security forces established more local labor reform facilities to incarcerate people who had stolen food, raided granaries, beaten up commune or brigade officials, or tried to escape from starvation.[4] Desperate local cadres, unable to meet grain quotas and blaming "class enemies" for the shortages, began ransacking houses, beating, jailing, or killing those accused of hoarding. This intensified the resentment in the countryside over structural problems caused by the rapid communalization of farmland, the replacement of family-centered dining by communal mess halls, and the forced relocation of rural laborers to distant steel production and water conservancy projects.

What Hu Knew about the Great Leap Forward

While the country descended into famine and unrest in 1960–1961, Hu remained in Beijing, attending to Youth League business. The Hu family did experience some food shortages and reduced rations, but they were among the top-priority recipients of food procured by the state under a program referred to as "special needs," which provided grain, vegetables, meat, oil, sugar, cloth, and other rations for party, government, and foreign diplomatic personnel in Beijing according to a carefully regulated scale. Administered by the Ministry of Public Security, it was considered foolproof.[5] So Hu did not himself experience the privations of the rural areas, but he knew about them through official reports, backchannel communications from provincial Youth League leaders, and his own inspection tours.

Historian Gao Hua tried to discover what Mao and other senior officials understood about the situation in various parts of the country, and how they responded to it. By 1960 there had been several reports of edema epidemics and of large-scale "unnatural deaths," but Mao preferred to believe the reports from sycophants like Henan Province's first secretary, Wu Zhipu, who reported in March that 99 percent of the people in his province were using communal mess halls—even though he knew that hundreds of thousands of farmers were dying of starvation in Xinyang Prefecture because the mess halls had run out of food and closed.[6]

When large numbers of people continued to starve despite adjustments to party and government policies and emergency food shipments, the Center first blamed "counterrevolutionaries" and "landlords who had sneaked into the leadership" for hoarding grain and causing food shortages. In 1961, when Mao was informed that seven hundred thousand had died in Xinyang, he reportedly replied that the systemic failure was due to a "restoration of the landlord class and counterrevolutionary class retaliation." In the ensuing investigation in late 1961, hundreds of thousands of Xinyang cadres were investigated, and as many as ten thousand were purged. But the official view still was, as Yang Jisheng put it, that "the central government that formulated and promoted the fatal policies remained 'correct and glorious,' while the engenderer of the policies, Mao, was still 'sagacious and great,' and the system that had produced the famine was 'incomparably superior.'"[7]

Rather than revamping policies and allowing farmers to return to traditional agricultural patterns and practices, Beijing made provincial capitals responsible for providing emergency supplies to the worst-hit areas. Too often, however, the authorities were not aware of the scale of the shortages and starvation, because officials from the bottom up lied about the problems, falsified statistics, destroyed reports, silenced complaints, and confiscated letters pleading for help.[8]

Eventually, the party began to react, holding meetings to lower production quotas, increasing private agricultural plots, easing the requirement for large-scale steel production and massive dam and reservoir construction projects, and shifting grain transfers to areas of need. Authorities also recommended the consumption of "substitute food products" (*dai shipin*), such as straw, corn stalks, bird feces, vegetables, peanut buds, roots, tree bark, and cotton.[9] But Mao, aware of the growing problems, still refused to order corrective measures for the principal causes of starvation—the grain procurement system and the communal mess halls.[10]

Even when he did acknowledge the seriousness of the catastrophe gripping rural China, Mao kept insisting that the worst was over, and that things were getting better.[11] In a chilling article written in 2015, historical researcher Xiao Xiang (possibly a pseudonym) made the case that Mao was well-informed about starvation deaths as early as 1958, and reacted to the news with nonchalance or by passing the responsibility on to subordinates. Xiao concludes that Mao's attitude of "recklessness" and "contempt" for human life greatly amplified the cost of the policy mistakes made during the Great Leap Forward.[12]

Some farmers and frustrated local officials began taking matters into their own hands as early as 1959. They closed communal mess halls and began returning to their old ways of farming—with families tilling certain tracts of land, selling an agreed amount to the production brigade, and keeping excess produce for themselves. This practice was most commonly referred to as *bao chan dao hu* (包产到户), usually translated "household responsibility system," but more technically "contracting production to the household." It had been tried in 1956 in Zhejiang but was rejected and suppressed as heterodox. In light of the catastrophic failure of the commune system in 1958–1959, however, the practice sprang up again in Anhui, one of the provinces worst hit by starvation, and First Secretary Zeng Xisheng began recommending it to other areas. Its economic benefits in restoring production and reducing starvation were almost immediately evident.[13]

But senior leaders, uncertain, watched Mao for signs of approval. He had been resolutely against what he called "dividing the fields and going it alone" (*fen tian dan gan*) but seemed to vacillate in late 1960 and early 1961. At a March 1961 Central Committee work conference, it was agreed that the production team would act as the primary accounting unit for the rural economy (a production team was often about the same size as the former *nongcun,* or rural village), deemphasizing the communes. Mao told Zeng Xisheng that he could experiment with household farming for a year. In May it was agreed to disestablish the hated "unified supply and marketing system" that had so punished farmers with excessive quotas, and gradually to close communal mess halls.[14]

Leadership unity seemed to be fraying. Mao's relationship with Liu Shaoqi, always wary and formal, grew more distant as reports of calamitous policy failures mounted.[15] In April 1961 Liu spent several weeks in his home district in Hunan. There he saw hunger and deprivation, heard from villagers about how their plight was ignored, and clashed with provincial officials who were covering up the bad news. He came back angry and more convinced than ever that Great Leap Forward policies needed to retreat, but he could not sway Mao. The Chairman was morose and depressed, and probably also very angry.[16] Liu's replacement of Mao as state chairman in April 1959 probably exacerbated Mao's jealousy, but it had little effect on his power.[17] He was increasingly uncomfortable with other leaders at the Center and depended more on regional secretaries for political support.

Despite the disappointments of the Great Leap, Mao still dominated the political system. His old military comrades were no longer able to exchange candid views with him, and senior party leaders and government ministers remained silent on important policy issues. But ambitious toadies flattered Mao, and none more than Defense Minister Lin Biao. Lin began to expand the study of Mao Zedong Thought in the People's Liberation Army in 1959, and in May 1961 ordered the main PLA newspaper, *Jiefangjun Bao,* to publish a daily "Quotation from Chairman Mao" on the first page.[18]

Hu Yaobang had been attempting to get back into Mao's good graces after the Lushan meeting. Hu received permission to do an inspection tour of some of the worst-affected areas of China's heartland on September 4–29, 1961. With only three aides in tow, he traveled to Shandong, Jiangsu, Anhui, and Henan to survey conditions, talk to local leaders and farmers, and reassure them of Beijing's continuing concern. The conditions he discovered were appalling, and although local leaders tried to treat him hospitably, he refused special treatment and shared in the peasants' experiences, including eating "substitute food products."[19]

Among the places Hu visited was Fengyang County in Anhui, where the Youth League secretary told him that sixty thousand of the county's four hundred thousand residents had died of starvation since late 1958, and that more than 35 percent of those remaining suffered from malnutrition. He explained that Fengyang was experimenting with "responsibility fields," approved by Zeng Xisheng and Chairman Mao, and it was helping farmers restore grain production. Echoing Mao, Hu told the secretary not to use the *bao chan dao hu* (household responsibility) system, as it would lead to "dividing fields and going it alone," which he said was unacceptable. Elsewhere in Anhui, Hu saw similar scenes of starvation and misery (Anhui's death toll would top six million), and people seemed to look to him for guidance on whether they could adopt "responsibility fields." Hu held out the possibility of the communes "lending" fields to individual farm households (a Liu Shaoqi idea), but only to get through famine conditions.[20]

After completing his inspections, Hu stopped off in the city of Handan in Hebei to put his notes together for an official report. After consulting with his associates, he decided not to include in the report to Mao the conditions of starvation and destitution he had seen, but instead to focus on the good news and policy-relevant recommendations. He observed that "the situation really is better than last year," and praised Mao's recent policy initiatives for enabling the turnaround, especially easing confusion and competition between subordinate units of the commune system. Hu devoted substantial attention to the *bao chan dao hu* system promoted in Anhui, calling it "a method that has served a purpose but has a dangerous nature." Its utility was that it helped starving farmers recover from cadre malfeasance. The danger was that it could create "irreconcilable contradictions" between the unified management of the collective and household producers, resulting in an overall national reduction in grain production.[21]

When he got back to Beijing, Hu showed the report to a few Youth League Center colleagues, some of whom ridiculed it as superficial, "looking at the flowers from a galloping horse." Hu ignored them and submitted the report to the General Office, requesting that it be sent to Chairman Mao. Mao noted that it was well-written and "worth a look," and ordered it circulated to participants in an upcoming work conference.[22] Hu's report probably was not very consequential, but Mao no doubt appreciated the support.

Hu later regretted his failure to support the household responsibility system, which might have cost him his job. Mao and the Central Committee would ban the practice in 1962 and punish many of the Anhui officials who promoted it. Twenty years later, Hu returned to Anhui to apologize to some of the cadres he had met on his 1961 tour, acknowledging that they had been right, while he had helped lead rural policy down a dead-end road.[23]

The Seven-Thousand-Person Meeting in Beijing

In November 1961 the General Office sent out a notice to all CCP cadres at the county first-secretary level and above that they were to arrive in Beijing by January 8, 1962, to participate in an "expanded Central Committee work meeting." The meeting grew out of Deng Xiaoping's concern with China's grain situation in 1962 and uncertainty about whether quotas could be fulfilled. Mao suggested that a Central Committee work conference be held not only to unify thinking on grain production, but to do a preliminary evaluation of the Great Leap Forward. He recommended that it be expanded to include all Central party departments, State Council ministries, important factories, and mines. The result was the largest Central Committee meeting to date, attended by 7,118 cadres. With Mao on inspection and Liu Shaoqi convalescing in Guangzhou during December, Deng Xiaoping was responsible for most of the planning and logistics for the meeting, and he recommended that everyone bring their own rice and pork, given shortages in Beijing.[24]

The meeting ran from January 11 to February 7, with stringent guidelines on food and drink, but still with entertainment provided in the evening. Focused on finding ways to feed China's six hundred million people, it was at times solemn and at many times angry. The first phase was devoted to "unifying understanding" by preparing a report on the overall situation. Mao appointed the drafting team, headed by Liu Shaoqi, and instructed them to reach an agreement on the "principal contradictions" of the previous three years and to deliver an oral report to a plenary meeting at the conclusion of the drafting process.[25] On January 27, Liu Shaoqi presented his oral report. It is not clear if he vetted the draft with Mao beforehand. The three-hour speech had an electrifying impact on the delegates, and on Mao.

Turning to Mao's frequent use of the metaphor of one finger versus nine fingers to describe Great Leap shortcomings compared to its achievements, Liu said pointedly: "I'm afraid that it's the relationship between three fingers and seven fingers. And in some areas, shortcomings and mistakes are more than three fingers. . . . I went to a place in Hunan [his home village], the farmers said it was 'three parts natural disasters, seven parts man-made disasters.' If you do not admit this, people will not accept it." Liu concluded that the conference report affirmed the Three Red Flags—the general line, the Great Leap Forward, and the people's communes. But he added some caveats. There were "deviations in execution" of the general line; there was "one-sidedness" in the interpretation of the Great Leap Forward; and the people's communes were "promising" but done too quickly, without proper planning and testing.[26]

Liu's speech was greeted with sustained applause. Later Mao would tell people that he knew at the time that "revisionism wanted to overthrow us." The term "revisionism," in 1962, was the common name for the ideological approach of the Communist Party of the Soviet Union, and its leader, Nikita Khrushchev. Khrushchev's criticism of Mao, the CCP, and the Great Leap Forward had grown to the point where the two sides had formally broken party-to-party ties and Moscow had withdrawn its economic advisers from China. Mao was bitterly disparaging of Khrushchev's "revision" of Marxist theory. In time he would brand Liu Shaoqi "China's Khrushchev" and a "revisionist."[27]

Mao had scheduled Lin Biao to speak to the delegates in plenary session on January 29. Lin was an unimpressive figure, pale and gaunt, and an indifferent public speaker. He had spent much of the last two years out of Beijing, recovering from illness. On this occasion, however, he was just what Mao needed—an uncritical supporter with the authority of the PLA behind him. Lin got straight to the point of undoing the damage of Liu Shaoqi's speech. The Three Red Flags, he said, were completely correct—the creations of the revolution, the people, and the Communist Party. "In difficult times, we should rely on and believe more in the party's leadership, and Chairman Mao's leadership, so that we will more easily overcome the difficulties. And facts have proven that these difficulties . . . are precisely due to our not following the instructions of Chairman Mao or heeding Chairman Mao's warnings or doing things in line with Chairman Mao's thinking. If we listen to the words of Chairman Mao, understand Chairman Mao's spirit, then there will be far fewer detours on the march, and today's difficulties will be much smaller." Presiding over the meeting, Mao beamed and complimented Lin, and distributed the speech throughout the party.[28]

Mao himself came to the podium the following day, and delivered a surprisingly mild speech, rambling and jocular. He even included his version of a self-criticism, or *jiantao:* "Any mistakes that the Center has made ought to be my direct responsibility, and I also have an indirect share in the blame because I am the Chairman. . . . I don't want other people to shirk their responsibility . . . but the person primarily responsible should be me."[29]

After that brief self-criticism, Mao immediately turned to the first secretaries to take responsibility for their errors. He even called for the meeting to be extended beyond the Spring Festival so that all the delegates would be able to vent their anger. The anger-venting phase only lasted a few days, until Mao realized that many of the county secretaries were passing the blame on to higher-level authorities for irrational grain quotas, wasteful steelmaking and irrigation projects, and the communal mess halls, all ordered by Beijing.[30] Mao told his physician, Li Zhisui, the meetings had become a waste of time: "They complain all day and get to watch plays at night. They eat three full meals a day—and fart. That's what Marxism-Leninism means to them."[31] The day after the Spring Festival, February 7, the meeting was adjourned and the delegates sent home.

Hu Yaobang attended the seven-thousand-person meeting, but there is no detailed record of his activities or impressions. He invited several delegates to his home and inquired about the criticism of Zeng Xisheng—who had lied about death tolls and misinformed party leaders who visited Anhui. After the meeting concluded, the delegates were held over to criticize Zeng, who was sacked by Liu Shaoqi in early February. But Hu did not participate in those meetings.[32]

The Mao Zedong–Liu Shaoqi Feud

Notwithstanding good feelings about its "democratic" atmosphere, the seven-thousand-person meeting achieved little. No major policy or personnel changes were adopted, the Three Red Flags continued, no accountability was demanded for the "unnatural deaths," the self-criticisms were soon forgotten, and no one important was removed from office. Mao Zedong left Beijing for several months, putting Liu Shaoqi in charge of the daily work, although all major decisions still required Mao's approval.

With Mao aboard his special train traveling south, Liu Shaoqi exercised his political prerogative in calling meetings of the leadership. He convened a Politburo Standing Committee meeting on February 21–23 to discuss the state budget for 1962 and other economic policy issues. Neither Mao nor Lin Biao attended, but the other five members—Liu, Zhou Enlai, Zhu De, Deng Xiaoping, and Chen Yun—all participated. Chen Yun had been recuperating in Hangzhou, ostensibly from heart problems, but more likely out of dis-agreement with Great Leap Forward policies. Liu specifically asked him to give a report on China's economy.

Chen minced no words. "The present situation is difficult," he began, citing a five billion yuan budget deficit, reduced agricultural production, excessive investment in capital construction (such as water conservancy projects), se-rious inflation, a badly unbalanced economy, and poor living conditions in overcrowded cities.[33] Chen proposed a ten-year period of economic retreat and adjustment, reducing industrial production and capital construction, curbing inflation, increasing grain production, improving living standards, and restructuring the central planning apparatus. Liu endorsed Chen's report and faulted the seven-thousand-person meeting for not exposing problems thoroughly enough.[34]

Liu authorized Chen to deliver the report to the State Council, where its blunt pragmatism was well-received. But before circulating the speech to lower party levels, Liu, Zhou, and Deng Xiaoping traveled to Wuhan in mid-March to secure Mao's approval. Liu proposed that Chen Yun head up a restored State Finance and Economic Leading Small Group to coordinate economic recovery work. Mao was noncommittal. But Liu took advantage of Mao's absence from Beijing to circulate Chen's ideas and begin the retreat from Great Leap Forward policies. One of the policies he sought to change was the ban on household contracted farming. "We must retreat enough," Liu told his colleagues; "dividing the fields and going it alone isn't good to say, but *bao chan dao hu* is still all right."[35]

But the *bao chan dao hu* issue was not all right; it rankled Mao, because it was a rejection by millions of peasants of his plan for the collectivization of agriculture. In mid-March he sent his *mishu,* Tian Jiaying, and a team of rural work specialists to Hunan to see what was working and what was not in restoring agricultural productivity. They heard glowing reports about *bao chan dao hu* from farmers and low-level cadres. It was superior to communes and production brigades, the farmers insisted, and helped them recover from the bad policies of the Great Leap Forward.[36]

When the team reported this to Mao in Shanghai, he was furious. "We are taking the mass line," he told Tian. "But sometimes we cannot completely listen to the masses, such as in carrying out the household responsibility system, we cannot listen." After Mao returned to Beijing in early July, Chen Yun requested an audience to brief him on the economic readjustment program. Mao had long been critical of Chen for rightist tendencies, but recognized he was influential on economic issues. Chen told Mao that roughly 30 percent of China's rural areas were now practicing some form of household contracted production, which he supported. Mao grew even angrier.[37]

On July 8 Mao summoned Liu Shaoqi, Zhou Enlai, Deng Xiaoping, Tian Jiaying, and another *mishu,* Chen Boda, to an office in Zhongnanhai to make his views clear. He told them directly that he disapproved of *bao chan dao hu* and dividing communal fields among households. He gave instructions for a Central Committee work conference to be held on rural issues, beginning in mid-July.[38] Chen Yun, perhaps sensing the tide shifting, quietly returned to Hangzhou to resume his recuperation, sending a formal request for a leave of absence.

Mao's chronology indicates he had a meeting with Liu Shaoqi on July 10, but provides no details. Liu's wife recounted the substance of the meeting to her son some years later. The details may not be accurate, and the story is certainly not unbiased, but the account has a ring of truth, given subsequent events. When Liu arrived for the meeting, Mao was in the Zhongnanhai indoor swimming pool and he shouted angrily at Liu, "What was your hurry? Can't stand up to the pressure? Why didn't you push back?" Discomfited, Liu withdrew and waited in an anteroom for Mao to dress. When they reconvened, they quarreled. Mao vented his irritation with Tian Jiaying and

Chen Yun importuning him—with Liu's blessing—about *bao chan dao hu,* and with Liu's haste in rolling back failed Great Leap Forward policies. "You negate the Three Red Flags, the land is divided up, and you don't push back! What will happen after I die?" Mao bellowed. Liu also lost his temper, flaring back, "History will record the role you and I played in the starvation deaths of so many people, and the cannibalism must also be memorialized [officially explained]!" Eventually the two men regained their composure, and Mao agreed economic adjustments had to continue.[39] But now the breach was open. The feud was personal.

The following day the General Office announced that a work conference on agricultural issues would convene in Beidaihe on July 25. Mao prepared carefully, setting the agenda, stipulating invitees, getting briefings on agriculture, organizing group discussions, and requiring a core group to prepare documents for subsequent meetings. In his conference speech on August 6, Mao talked about class relations, continuing progress, agriculture, and the need for dictatorship, separating himself from the viewpoints that had dominated Liu Shaoqi's West Tower meeting in March.[40] Then he kept the meetings going for nearly two months, first at Beidaihe, then at a "preparatory conference" for the Tenth Plenum of the Eighth Central Committee in Beijing. Mao cajoled and prodded, insisting that others' viewpoints were too pessimistic, but that they needed to heed his warnings about the resurgence of class struggle.[41]

The culmination of the process was the Tenth Plenum, held September 24–27. The meeting was a major political triumph for Mao, the result of careful preparation. He led off with a strong speech, insisting that China's overall situation had not been good for several years but was now improving. He talked about the dissolution of the international Communist bloc, revisionism in Marxist-Leninist parties, and the principal CCP goal now being "the struggle between Marxism-Leninism and revisionism." "[In a socialist society] classes will continue to exist for a long time," he said. "We must acknowledge the existence of a struggle of class against class and admit the possibility of the restoration of reactionary classes. . . . From now on, we must talk about this every year, every month, every day. We will talk about it . . . at every meeting we hold."[42]

The Tenth Plenum approved resolutions charging those who spoke honestly about Great Leap Forward policies with "stirring up a darkness wind." Those who supported agricultural production responsibility systems were

Mao Zedong and Liu Shaoqi in 1964. Still cooperating, but by this time the relationship was irreconcilable, and would eventually shatter the CCP's collective leadership. Liu would die in prison during the Cultural Revolution. (Wikimedia Commons)

"taking the capitalist road." The overarching slogan of the plenum was "Never forget the class struggle," which Mao would use as the foundation for the next several political campaigns.[43]

In addition, Mao was able to make important personnel changes, adding three new members to Deng Xiaoping's Central Secretariat. Lu Dingyi would oversee propaganda work, Luo Ruiqing, then chief of the General Staff, would handle military affairs, and Kang Sheng, formerly head of the Central

Social Department in Yan'an, would do whatever Mao wanted him to do. Kang had returned to domestic political prominence in the summer of 1962 with a calculated attack on Vice-Premier Xi Zhongxun (father of Xi Jinping), for supporting the publication of a novel that glorified Liu Zhidan, whose Communist base area in Northern Shaanxi was the destination of the Long March. Kang accused Xi of being a member of an "anti-party clique" that included Gao Gang and Peng Dehuai.

At the close of the plenum, a resolution was passed setting up a "Xi Zhongxun special case investigation committee," with Kang Sheng at its head.[44] Similar committees were established for Peng Dehuai, who had requested reconsideration of his punishment, and for Deng Zihui, who had spearheaded efforts to adopt the household responsibility system. The precedent for establishing "special case investigations" with extralegal powers was now established.

The Tenth Plenum was a huge political victory for Mao and a setback for Liu Shaoqi. Liu suffered no loss of position or prestige, but the more pragmatic approach to economic recovery he had championed in February was discarded. The farmers' innovative means of correcting the errors of the Great Leap were anathematized, and those who promoted them would be punished. The spirit of the Tenth Plenum—"taking class struggle as the key link" (guiding principle)—would be applied harshly to resolving contradictions both inside and outside the party.

Going Home to Hunan

Hu Yaobang had left his Hunan village in November 1930, a young boy of fourteen setting out to become a revolutionary. Thirty-two years later, he went back as provisional first secretary of the Communist Party of Hunan's Xiangtan Prefecture. It was a temporary assignment, and in the CCP's grade structure it was a step or so below Hu's position as first secretary of the CYL. Official announcements indicated that he carried his CYL rank with him, remaining at its head for ceremonial and planning purposes, but leaving day-to-day management to his principal deputy, Hu Keshi, and other members of the CYL committee.[45]

In May 1962 the Central Secretariat had called for senior officials to volunteer to go to lower-level units to oversee economic recovery and strengthen the leadership of local party committees. Hu Yaobang was one of the first volunteers for the program, but it took six months for him to be finally ap-

proved for his new assignment. In the meantime, the political ground began
to shift under his feet as Mao and Liu jockeyed for power. In mid-July Liu
called a meeting of cadres awaiting temporary reassignments and repriori-
tized their responsibilities. He put increasing economic production as the
last of five tasks, after strengthening local party leadership, implementing
Central policies, reporting the local situation truthfully, and correcting mistaken work-styles of local cadres.[46] After attending increasingly strident
Tenth Plenum meetings through August and September, culminating in Mao
Zedong's clarion call to "never forget the class struggle," Hu Yaobang was
worried that the party's rural policies were veering even further off course.[47]

Xiangtan was not a random choice for Hu's local assignment. It included
not only Hu's home village but also the home villages of Mao, Peng Dehuai,
and many other prominent party and military leaders. Peng's inspection of
his hometown in 1959 and Liu Shaoqi's inspection of his nearby home
of Ningxiang had led to serious challenges to Mao's policies and authority.
While there is no evidence that Mao specifically chose Hu Yaobang to go to
Xiangtan, he had to approve the appointment, as did Liu Shaoqi. And both
would monitor the results of his work.

Xiangtan at that time was a geographically large prefecture, with ten counties, stretching from Dongting Lake—a flood basin of the Yangzi River—to
the southeastern part of Hunan abutting Jiangxi, where Hu had first joined
the revolution. About 70 percent of the land area was mountainous, and
only about 20 percent was arable, but it was still considered a "land of fish
and rice." During the Great Leap Forward, its agricultural production
dropped to pre-1949 levels. There had been widespread malnutrition, food
shortages, population flight, and death by starvation, although not at the
catastrophic levels experienced in Anhui and Sichuan. The region had begun
to recover in late 1962, but Hu would see plenty of misery—orphans, people
dressed in rags, ramshackle homes and buildings, unrepaired roads and
reservoirs—and other signs of poverty everywhere.

Hu arrived in November, accompanied by only one *mishu*, one guard, and
no family for what he expected would be a two-year tour. He struck up a
quick rapport with Hua Guofeng, the tall, phlegmatic, but genial man he was
replacing. Hua had been in Hunan since 1949 and had become a favorite
of Mao Zedong by capably administering the Chairman's hometown of
Shaoshan.

Hua had stepped back willingly to the position of second secretary of
Xiangtan, with the understanding that he would continue to handle routine

administrative work, while Hu focused on hands-on inspections, overseeing implementation of central policies, and reporting to Beijing on economic recovery and ideological work.[48] Hua gave Hu a candid briefing on Xiangtan. The Great Leap Forward had not only damaged grain production and decimated mountain forests but had seriously damaged relations between party cadres and ordinary peasants. Many officials had treated peasants cruelly, forcing them into communal mess halls, confiscating cooking implements, and refusing to give them permission to cultivate private plots, often resorting to violence and arbitrary disciplinary measures.

After Beijing revised its policies, the cadres became the objects of recriminations and dismissals. As a result, Hua said local party officials were angry and discouraged. Unable to reestablish their authority, they argued often with peasants, or had simply given in to demands that households be allowed to farm communal land under contracts. That had enabled agricultural production to recover somewhat, but many households still had no rice to eat.[49]

Hu and Hua set out on a whirlwind inspection of all the counties in Xiangtan. Hu threw himself into the work, reading about each county's history, productivity, public works, sideline industries, animal husbandry, fisheries, and more. He held detailed discussions with local officials, and often conversed directly with peasant farmers. His ability to speak the local dialect, together with his lack of official airs and his ready laugh made it possible for him to gather information easily. Hu often dismissed his official minders, and even sent his guards away so he could talk directly with grassroots cadres and peasants. He understood the need to focus everyone's attention on restoring grain production wherever feasible, but he also told people in mountainous areas to plant more suitable crops, like fir and tung trees, bamboo, tea, fruit, and camellia, and to open up unused waste land to contract production.[50]

In party headquarters towns, he would generally give a speech on the overall situation and what officials needed to do. His main message was optimism and encouragement. Hu was a dynamic speaker, his high-pitched voice strong and clear. Often he would interact with his audience, asking questions, reciting poetry, telling jokes. But he was serious about local cadres needing to pay attention to Central policy, to correct previous mistakes, and to study the Chairman's teachings. Years later, people still recalled listening to him with awe.[51]

In late January 1963 Hu finally got to Liuyang County, where he had grown up. He spent several days in Wenjia (where he went to school), met old friends and teachers, and observed the impoverished conditions. It was a dismaying experience. Hardly anything had changed for the better in thirty years, and many places seemed worse off. He walked to his old home in Cangfang (there was still no paved road) and left after two days, dissatisfied as ever with his older brother, Hu Yaofu, who had taken communal property for his own use (Hu forced him to return it), with his sister-in-law for constantly complaining about not having enough money, and with their children, who lounged around, smoking cigarettes and avoiding work.

While Hu Yaobang was visiting old haunts, Mao Zedong was holding a Central Committee work conference in Beijing to kick-start a political campaign to follow up on the Tenth Plenum. Liu Shaoqi delivered a work report devoted mostly to "opposing and preventing revisionism," but Mao frequently interrupted him, commenting that the party should pay more attention to its own revisionism problem, and that the only way to do so was by means of a Socialist Education campaign.[52]

Mao traveled to several southern provinces in March and April 1963 and was unhappy with the tepid response to his call for "socialist education." He convened another meeting in May, held in Hangzhou and called a "small-scale meeting attended by part of the Politburo Standing Committee and the regional secretaries."[53] Mao made several speeches, painting the domestic situation in dire terms. Without class struggle, he said, the "landlords, rich peasants, counterrevolutionaries and bad elements, all kinds of evil monsters will come out," undermining a weak Communist Party, and in a matter of a few years a "nationwide counterrevolutionary restoration will occur, the CCP will become a revisionist party . . . a fascist party, and the entire country will change color."[54]

Inexplicably, Hu Yaobang attended the Hangzhou meetings.[55] Neither his China Youth League nor Xiangtan positions would have authorized him to be included in such high-powered gatherings. It may have been an unplanned happenstance when Hu accompanied an Albanian youth delegation visiting Mao in early May, or he may have been invited by Mao because of his 1961 report criticizing *bao chan dao hu*.[56] But there is no record available of what Hu said at the conclave, or how he reacted to Mao's fiery language.

The Hangzhou meetings revised earlier party guidance on rural work, accentuating the class origins of ongoing problems and prescribing a peasant-led campaign to root out class enemies from corrupted grassroots production units. In other words, high-pressure struggle sessions against low-level cadres, arbitrary use of ideologically charged labels, forced confessions, trumped-up charges, and extralegal punishments were back. Hu had seen it before. When the Hangzhou meetings were over, Hu went to Wuhan, where he backed up his old Yan'an "sworn friend" Tao Zhu, then Central South Bureau first secretary, in conveying the spirit of the meeting to provincial party leaders from Guangdong, Guangxi, Henan, Hubei, Hunan, and Jiangxi. He then went back to Hunan to make similar presentations to provincial and Xiangtan district cadres.[57]

Hu was somewhat abashed to realize that his first few months of work in Xiangtan were contrary to what Chairman Mao wanted, and that his focus on restoring production was not appreciated. Others in the Hunan provincial CCP committee, especially First Secretary Zhang Pinghua and Second Secretary Wang Yanchun, had been advocating a more violent and confrontational approach to the problems of nonperforming cadres and the prevalence of household production contracts. Hu explained, "I did not remember the Chairman's instructions on class relations and class struggle made during the Tenth Plenary Session. . . . In order to do a good job, I would like not only to learn and appreciate the directives of the Center, but also to study Comrades Pinghua and Yanchun and other comrades."[58]

But Hu Yaobang was not in full agreement with them or with Mao on the conduct of the Socialist Education campaign. He was reluctant to inflict more punishment on already beleaguered grassroots cadres. He fully accepted the need for what were called the "Four Clean-Ups"—cleaning up corrupt practices by production team leaders in accounting, storehouses, financial affairs, and work points distribution. But he favored a more tolerant, educational approach, avoiding harsh tactics and language, calling it the "four investigations and four helps."

Still the pressure increased. Hu's first priority was no longer improving production but getting rid of the practice of bao chan dao hu, especially in his home county of Liuyang. Second, he had to make arrangements for the work assignments of some thirty-six hundred reporters and more than fifty-seven thousand propagandists Xiangtan sent out as work teams to publicize and observe how the Socialist Education campaign was going. Hu himself went to a remote area to help local officials understand the new policies.

Then he had to return to Liuyang to help deal with a serious drought. He drafted a preliminary report on the experience of one county implementing his more lenient approach to the Four Clean-Ups, but it was sharply criticized in Xiangtan and Changsha. Hu was exhausted and stressed; his health deteriorated in August, and the Xiangtan CCP committee recommended he take a rest. Hu thus became the first official guest at Mao's recently completed villa in Shaoshan, but he stayed in the luxurious mansion only a few days, spending much of his time rewriting his report on the Four Clean-Ups campaign in one county.[59]

For the next four months the record of Hu's activities is rather thin. He appeared to spend most of his time on grassroots-level investigations, and his principal message again was on restoring grain production and combating the drought. He may have spent more time in recuperation. The Hunan provincial committee was engrossed with the Four Clean-Ups campaign, but Hu seemed disengaged, not attending any of the numerous meetings.

In November Hu was drawn back into Youth League work, overseeing revisions of a draft work report being prepared for a national CYL congress to be held in June 1964. Hu was unhappy with the report, so several members of the drafting group came to Hunan in December to work on it with him. In February 1964 Hu returned to Beijing to present the draft to Deng Xiaoping's Central Secretariat for approval.[60] More revisions ensued, keeping Hu in Beijing.

Except for one more inspection trip to Xiangtan in April 1964, Hu's sojourn in his home province suddenly was over, several months short of its expected duration. None of the accounts of Hu's career provide any explanation for this change in plans, except to note that he felt some regret at not being able to complete his work in Xiangtan.[61]

Hu faced a welter of familiar CYL issues grown worse by the Mao-Liu feud. Although he joked about being nearly forty-nine years old and still in charge of youth and children's affairs, he was clearly frustrated. He sought a meeting with Mao Zedong prior to the CYL conference and asked to be replaced and reassigned, but Mao put him off. Hu, therefore, soldiered on, organizing the Ninth CYL Congress in June. All Politburo Standing Committee members except Lin Biao attended the opening ceremony, and the congress proceeded smoothly. In early July the CYL Central Committee reelected Hu as first secretary. Still, he made it known that he was looking for another position.[62]

Hu must have learned soon after his return to the capital how much the disagreements between Mao and Liu had escalated over the last two years. The Socialist Education campaign had vacillated since the Hangzhou meeting.[63] In the first few months, pilot projects had been established in many provinces, and work teams were sent out by provincial leaders to direct the restructuring of local commune and production brigade leadership. Violence often accompanied these efforts, and reports came in of thousands of beatings, forced confessions, and suicides in grassroots units. In September and October 1963, two separate sets of guidelines for the campaign were prepared, one from Mao, who was traveling, and another from Liu and Deng in Beijing. Instructions were finally circulated to lower levels under a new name, causing yet more confusion.[64]

In the winter of 1964 Liu took a more active role in directing the Four Clean-Ups, focusing on lower-level corruption in both rural areas and cities. It had become common parlance among regional party leaders, citing Mao, that "one-third of the leadership at the grass-roots level is not in our hands."[65] Liu's view was that the percentage was higher, and that urgent action was needed, including, in some places, a "seizure of power" from the "bourgeois elements" that had taken over the lower-level party committees. Ironically, Liu had become more leftist and impatient than Mao.[66] Liu wanted the target of the campaign to be county and commune-level party cadres, with investigatory work teams sent from upper levels, while Mao wanted to activate poor peasants to lead the campaign and aim their criticisms upward. He told regional bureau leaders in August 1964, after the Secretariat had appointed Liu to be in charge of the entire Socialist Education effort, "I hope that the localities will attack the Center. My method is to use the localities to isolate the Center."[67] Mao's principal target became "powerholders who have taken the capitalist road," later shortened to "capitalist roaders" (zou zi pai). He traveled extensively in south-central China, fostering support among regional bureau secretaries.[68]

Most importantly, Mao began to rely on support from Defense Minister Lin Biao, who was actively developing a cult of personality for Mao. Beginning in 1961 with daily "Quotations from Chairman Mao" in the PLA's daily newspaper, Lin used political training materials and military media to create an aura around Mao of unrivaled genius and absolute correctness that would reach its apogee in the Cultural Revolution. In May 1964 the PLA's General Political Department published two hundred quotations from the Chairman on thirty topics in a compact booklet. It distributed one copy to each PLA soldier, expecting the contents to be memorized for recitation in political study courses. Shortly afterward the PLA press began publishing more copies for local areas. Ultimately, over one billion copies of what came to be called the Little Red Book were printed and circulated, both inside China and worldwide.

Two Hundred Days in Shaanxi

On November 16, 1964, the first secretary of the Shaanxi CCP committee, Zhang Desheng, sent word to the Central Secretariat that illness prevented him from performing his duties and asked to be relieved. General Secretary Deng Xiaoping immediately suggested that Hu Yaobang be sent out as a replacement, and the Center approved.[69] For the next year and a half, even though Hu Yaobang was in remote Shaanxi, his health and career were primarily shaped by the escalating feud between Mao and Liu Shaoqi. His daughter wrote that Hu had "some misgivings" about accepting the posts of Shaanxi first secretary and third secretary of the Northwest Regional CCP Bureau, likely due to political and personal differences with Liu Lantao, first secretary of the Northwest Bureau, which controlled Shaanxi and four other provinces.[70] Liu had been the Central Secretariat member supervising the CYL in the mid-1950s and had overseen the anti-rightist purge of the Youth League leadership in 1957. He had chastised Hu in 1956 for being reluctant to accept full membership in the Central Committee. But more important, in 1964 they were on opposite sides of the rift between Mao and Liu Shaoqi. Liu Lantao was a longtime subordinate of Liu Shaoqi, whereas Hu's career had depended on Mao's favor.

Hu had done his homework on Shaanxi prior to going there, so he had a good idea of what a mess the province had become. It had been an isolated, poor, and dusty place when Hu first arrived there with the Long Marchers in 1935, and it had not improved much in the ensuing years. The Great Leap Forward, while not as catastrophic there as in other provinces, had still been a brutal blow to a place that often operated near subsistence levels. Its grain production between 1956 and 1964 had fallen by 23 percent, and its crop yields were below levels achieved in Tibet. Desertification had afflicted large areas of northern Shaanxi, and Beijing's policy of focusing almost exclusively on grain production resulted in widespread misuse of agricultural resources. Infrastructure had decayed, roads and bridges went unrepaired, and there was no major industry anywhere in the province. Education had suffered from a lack of teachers, and the illiteracy rate was estimated at over 43 percent.[71]

But the most serious problem was political. A combination of overzealous implementation of confusing Socialist Education policies and a witch hunt for supporters of an "anti-party clique" in Shaanxi had created a toxic political atmosphere. With Shaanxi party secretaries openly feuding among themselves and with the Northwest Bureau, Deng told Hu that his first task would be to unify the leadership. In 1964 Shaanxi led the nation in the numbers of party cadres under investigation (over fifteen thousand) or arrested and jailed (over eleven thousand) during the Four Clean-Ups campaign, averaging thirty-plus arrests per day. More than three thousand cadres had been expelled from the party, and more than six hundred had been killed, many of them having been forced to commit suicide.[72] Liu Lantao had been tasked to assist Kang Sheng in the investigation of the "Peng (Dehuai)-Gao (Gang)-Xi (Zhongxun) anti-party clique" and was seeking more victims to arrest.[73]

Yang Shangkun, director of the party's General Office, was investigating conditions in rural Shaanxi when Hu was appointed and advised Hu to say as little as possible the first year. When Hu reported for duty at Northwest Bureau headquarters in Xi'an on December 1, Liu Lantao suggested he stay in quarters provided by the Bureau rather than going to the Shaanxi CCP committee's guesthouse. The Shaanxi committee had a "factional problem," he explained.[74] But Hu responded that his principal responsibility was as Shaanxi first secretary, and it would be more convenient to reside near his work. Additionally, he asked to be excused from most Northwest Bureau responsibilities, except for attending important meetings. Liu Lantao agreed. It was a brusque start to what would become a difficult relationship.

Hu spent his first few days in Shaanxi in briefings with provincial party associates, then in lengthy Northwest Bureau meetings on the status of the Socialist Education campaign. Ordinarily he would have followed these with an introductory tour of the province, but he had been notified of a Central Committee work conference in Beijing on December 15, followed by a National People's Congress session, both of which he was obligated to attend. Hu did send the two CYL *mishu* he had brought with him to nearby rural areas to look around. As in Xiangtan, Hu brought his CYL position and cadre rank with him but had been instructed by Deng to spend 80 percent of his time on Shaanxi matters. Hu again was not accompanied by his family, who remained in his CYL housing in Beijing.

The Central Committee work conference was most noteworthy for bringing out into the open the dispute between Mao Zedong and Liu Shaoqi. At the opening session Mao repeatedly made querulous comments during Liu's introduction. They continued bickering at the work conference and expanded Politburo meetings, though their differences are usually portrayed by Chinese historians as ideological and procedural. Liu saw the "principal contradiction" as being between corrupt cadres and their landlord / rich peasant backers at grassroots levels, whereas Mao stepped up his attacks on the "capitalist roader faction." He did not name names, but the objects of his rage were becoming clearer: Liu, Deng, and senior economic officials, whom Mao claimed had shut him out.[75]

Mao's attitude toward Liu was increasingly bitter, tinged with jealousy. According to Central Party School historian Luo Pinghan, Mao had railed at Liu in a late November meeting that "It's still Shaoqi in command, the Four Clean-Ups and economic work are all controlled by you. They don't listen to me, but you are formidable, the big man in charge, and you grabbed [Deng] Xiaoping and the Premier."[76]

The dispute reached a turning point on Mao Zedong's seventy-first birthday, December 26, 1964. He previously had not permitted any commemoration of his birthday, but on this occasion, he allowed Jiang Qing and his bodyguard, Wang Dongxing, to organize a small party in a banquet room of the Great Hall of the People. Mao paid the bill and specified the guest list and seating arrangements for about forty people. At his table Mao seated several people who were not members of the Central Committee, some representatives of mass organizations, one of his favorite military leaders, and regional party secretary Tao Zhu and his wife, Zeng Zhi. Other key leaders, including Liu Shaoqi, Deng Xiaoping, Zhou Enlai, and the other regional bureau leaders, seated themselves at the other tables. Neither Zhu De nor Lin Biao was invited. Peng Zhen, the powerful head of the Beijing party committee, was not there. But Hu Yaobang was present, which was not warranted by anything but Mao's whim. Hu was the lowest-ranking party member invited.[77]

As described by Zeng Zhi, the banquet was surreal. Mao was garrulous, drinking freely while eating, calling out to guests with slights, historical allegories, or affronts aimed mostly at Liu Shaoqi, whom he did not name. He spoke forebodingly of people who "stick their tails in the air" (get conceited) with a few minor achievements, set up "independent kingdoms," or fail to report to him the way they once did. Shortly after the meal began, the room grew quiet, as people listened hard to try and decipher Mao's "words within words." Zeng wrote: "That night there was no birthday atmosphere, everyone was nervous and confused, what was going on with the Chairman? There was almost no sound in the room, just quiet, terrified people, listening to the Chairman sitting there laughing and scolding, we did not dare even to think."[78]

On December 28 the work conference concluded with the approval of a new set of instructions on the Socialist Education campaign, this one containing seventeen articles. Most were consistent with Liu Shaoqi's approach, including on the nature of the main problem, the targets, and the methods to be employed. Mao's insistence on attacking "powerholders taking the capitalist road" was the last of the articles. Notwithstanding the continuing disagreements, the General Office approved the revised "17 Articles" for circulation to lower levels of the party.

Three days later Mao ordered the circulation stopped and all copies destroyed. He and his secretary, Chen Boda, redrafted the entire document, repudiating the elements associated with Liu, and moving into first position the focus on the capitalist roaders and "socialism vs capitalism."[79] On January 3, 1965, the day when Liu Shaoqi was reelected state chairman by the National People's Congress, Mao convened an expanded Politburo Standing Committee meeting in Zhongnanhai, where he disparaged Liu's leadership of the Socialist Education campaign, calling Liu's proposal to dispatch large work teams "human wave tactics."[80] On January 14 the Party issued Mao's new guidelines, now called the "23 Articles." Mao was back in charge, and Liu was in his sights. The Chairman would tell visiting American journalist Edgar Snow in 1970 that he had decided during the "23 Articles" debate in January 1965 that he had to bring down Liu Shaoqi.[81]

Lost in the Mao-Liu contretemps was a significant difference of views expressed in the work conference by Hu Yaobang and Liu Lantao. In a speech on December 17, Liu Lantao said the main focus of the party in the Northwest's five provinces was "seizing power" in the nearly half of all counties where it had been lost. Liu claimed that the leadership of 149 of the region's 328 county-level party committees was "rotten, mostly rotten, or had serious problems."[82]

A week later Hu Yaobang presented a lengthy report on the situation in Shaanxi, in which he outlined important departures from Liu Lantao's hardline approach. On Socialist Education, Hu said, "The province has purged 660 full-time cadres. That's rather hasty. If we're impatient, then it's hard to avoid making mistakes." Denying errant cadres the opportunity to correct their mistakes, he added, "is also a negative policy error." Getting to the heart of his report, Hu said that he had been "scheming every day about how to get production up." He advocated boosting both farmer and cadre enthusiasm for production, and more importantly, bringing in chemical fertilizers and diversifying agriculture.[83]

Hu returned to Xi'an on January 17, 1965, energized to get down to work. In a retrospective interview, Yang Shangkun observed that Hu may have thought his views were in line with the "23 Articles," but he was insufficiently cautious in presenting them and didn't pay enough attention to the views of the Northwest Bureau.[84] Hu called a provincial party committee meeting where he delivered a summary of the "23 Articles" and presented his own prescriptions for correcting the leftist problems that had beset the party's work. He recommended beginning with "three suspends": suspend political arrests, suspend power seizures, and suspend double expulsions (from work and from the party). He insisted to his new committee that the purpose of the party was not to punish the people, but to educate and reform them. He counseled patient education and leniency rather than criticism and fines, firm ideological guidance but tolerance for different views. Support for Hu's views was "not unanimous" on the committee, his biographers admitted.[85]

After the Lunar New Year, Hu sent Shaanxi provincial committee secretaries out on inspections. He took a small staff in two jeeps to Ankang Prefecture, near the Sichuan border. From February 5 to 12, Hu visited seven counties, looking at agricultural conditions, chatting with cadres and ordinary farmers, and dispensing advice on solving various problems, all focused on the need for better agricultural production. He promoted diversified agriculture and recommended a "two-handed" focus on grain and forestry / animal husbandry in northern Shaanxi; grain and cotton in the central part of the province; grain and native products in southern Shaanxi.[86] Many grassroots cadres were hesitant to go along, having been whipsawed by changing political directives from Beijing and the vicious "you-die-I-live" competition among party cadres in Shaanxi.

Still in Ankang on February 14, Hu drafted a set of policy prescriptions on cadre development, which he sent by telephone to Xi'an at 2 a.m. with instructions that they be relayed to Northwest Bureau headquarters. This message—thereafter known as the "telephone communication"—offered a glimpse of the kinds of ideas Hu would espouse in later years. They were consistently against the kind of leftist extremism promoted by Liu Shaoqi nationally and Liu Lantao locally. Populist, production-focused, tolerant, and open-minded, Hu's proposals were not really consonant with Mao Zedong's thinking, but they were well ahead of their time. It didn't take long before Hu was reminded how heterodox they were.[87]

Hu's propositions on lenient treatment of cadres, known as the "four without exceptions," suggested that (1) all excessive punishments on cadres should be lightened; (2) those who had been expelled from office but not formally punished all should be put into work positions until their cases cleared; (3) cadres who had made mistakes but atoned and were promoting production should all be cleared; and (4) all those who continued to do bad things should be severely punished.[88]

Hu set out early on February 14 to continue his inspection, but provincial headquarters ordered several of his accompanying staff to return to Xi'an immediately to do research. Three days later Liu Lantao reached Hu by telephone, telling him, "I am informing you of the opinions of the Center and the Northwest Bureau. The four-article cadre policy you raised in your 'telephone communication' is not appropriate, it could cause a reversal of verdicts wind."[89] Hu denied the accusation, insisting his approach could be monitored. But his life-changing ordeal was already being plotted.

Liu Lantao had not acted without authorization. According to Lü Kejun, Liu had been in touch with both Yang Shangkun in Shaanxi and Peng Zhen in Beijing, reporting on Hu's controversial remarks.[90] Local leaders found threatening Hu's call for restoring leaders purged in the Socialist Education campaign if they "apologized and contributed to production"; what was involved was more than just correcting a mistaken judgment. Because these cases were not prosecuted through the courts or the law but were often based upon capricious power and party factions, overturning the final judgment implied rejecting the leaders who had made the charges. Not only did this diminish their authority, but it could also subject them to vengeance from those who had been (wrongfully) punished. So Hu's idea of correcting mistaken verdicts was the first of his heterodox "telephone communication" ideas rejected by Liu Lantao, who had ordered thousands of such arrests and punishments.

By the time Hu returned to Xi'an on February 25, Liu was ready with more. He had cabled Hu's proposals to Peng Zhen, who at that point was in charge of the Secretariat and reported to Mao and to Liu Shaoqi. Mao was not very interested, and simply responded, "Tell Yaobang to pay attention to this." Liu Shaoqi, however, added fuel to the fire. After reading Hu's telephone communication carefully, he reportedly said, "Isn't Hu Yaobang engaged in class struggle, so how can he ignore class struggle?"[91] Liu Lantao would elaborate on this, sarcastically asking Hu in a public meeting, "You only have two hands; if one hand is grasping grain production and one hand is grasping diversified [agricultural] operations, which hand will grasp class struggle?"[92]

Hu Yaobang submitted his first self-criticism on February 27 in the form of a *jiantao,* a written statement of faults. More would follow, as Liu Lantao increased the pressure. Typically the *jiantao* is intended to force people to abase themselves before their superiors, often in a large gathering. The offender must acknowledge mistakes, explain why they were made, apologize for them, and ask for forgiveness from the party and a chance to atone for the errors. This written statement is often rejected repeatedly by the people to whom it is addressed in order to reinforce the humiliation. As Sha Yexin put it: "When your spirit has been repeatedly tortured and completely destroyed by countless *jiantao,* then the ultimate purpose of the *jiantao* will have been achieved; that is, to make you give up self, give up thinking, give up testing, give up criticism, never allow the slightest heterodox ideas or have the slightest doubt; it is to make you a docile tool."[93]

As his ordeal continued and the stress mounted, Hu's health began to deteriorate. Meeting followed meeting in early March, and Hu was repeatedly called upon to explain not only his telephone communication proposals but other decisions he had made since arriving in Xi'an. Most of the accusations were exaggerations of his policy ideas, which were denounced as "bourgeois," "reactionary," and favoring "material incentives." Defenders and accusers squared off against each other, with the latter gaining and keeping their advantage.[94]

The Northwest Bureau convened a secretariat meeting on March 7 to which they did not invite Hu Yaobang but at which they examined his errors.[95] On March 10 the bureau called on Hu to answer the charges against him. Hu prepared another *jiantao,* and requested advice from Yang Shangkun, whom he probably believed could intervene on his behalf with help from the Center. Yang, who was aligned with Deng Xiaoping and Liu Shaoqi, suggested that Hu should not dispute Liu Lantao's criticisms and should try to calm his emotions.[96]

The following day the Bureau called another meeting to examine the Hu Yaobang situation. Liu Lantao's intent was not just to humiliate Hu, but to purge him. Hu put up a spirited, detailed defense of his actions, but he had come to Shaanxi with no support base and had not had time to build one. Liu Lantao packed the audience with his own minions, who accused Hu of a variety of errors, including opposing Liu Shaoqi.[97] As the shouting and sloganeering continued for five consecutive days, Hu began to suffer excruciating head and back pain and swelling, and his eyesight and hearing began to fail. On March 17 he was unable to get out of bed, and doctors insisted he be allowed to rest.[98]

Hu was diagnosed with cerebral arachnoiditis, a disorder characterized by acute inflammation of the membranes protecting the brain and spinal cord. It can cause severe, chronic neuropathic pain and, if untreated, damage to vision and hearing. Despite being confined to a hospital bed, Hu continued to try to find the right balance of regret and resistance in his *jiantao* to retain his position. A four-thousand-character letter to Liu Lantao took him five days to write and concluded: "With the urging and assistance of the Northwest Bureau, I am now determined to correct the mistakes with the high posture that a revolutionary should have."[99] While Hu was in the hospital, the Northwest Bureau continued to hold criticism meetings daily.

At a meeting on March 31 Yang Shangkun said that Hu had good intentions when he came to Shaanxi, but his thinking was "one-sided and vacillating," because he was eager to promote agricultural production in the province. He "mistakenly believed his original idea was correct and in line with the spirit of the '23 Articles,'" Yang insisted, but it was not an ideological "line error" in opposition to the party. He recommended that the meeting wrap up quickly, accept Hu's latest *jiantao,* and forego mentioning his name in critical summary material.[100]

Ignoring Yang's recommendations, the bureau authorized the Shaanxi Provincial CCP committee to distribute Hu's self-confession to all levels and begin collecting his speeches and other materials for further criticism. With Hu still in hospital in April, the dispute was referred to the Central Secretariat in Beijing. Peng Zhen appeared to support going forward with further investigation, but Deng may have been more reluctant. Yang Shangkun recommended the criticism sessions be postponed until the spring harvest could be gathered. Possibly unknown to the others, Mao had a medical specialist sent from Beijing to Xi'an to treat Hu.[101]

By May 19 Hu had recovered enough that he decided to leave the hospital, even though his doctors were not certain he was out of danger. The Northwest Bureau decided to convene another comprehensive criticism session on Hu, beginning on May 31, for which he was ordered to prepare yet another *jiantao.* In early June, Deng advised the Northwest Bureau not to rush to judgment or force Hu to attend a struggle session, and to allow the party to settle the issue in Beijing.[102] The Bureau disregarded Deng's advice and went ahead with a large-scale meeting on June 11. Hu delivered a lengthy defense on all the charges against him. Hu even rebutted Yang Shangkun's accusation that he had "vacillated": "I didn't waver on the Long March, how could I be wavering now?"[103] The meeting remained deadlocked for several more days and reached no conclusion. Hu Yaobang was exhausted.

At this point Beijing imposed a solution in the person of Marshal Ye Jianying—Hu's old superior officer and friend from Yan'an days. Ye flew to Xi'an on June 18 with no prior notification, ostensibly to inspect military education. He was accompanied by generals Zhang Zongxun and Zhang Aiping, who had rescued Hu in the purges of 1932. At the obligatory welcoming dinner by the Northwest Bureau party committee that evening, Zhang Aiping made a dramatic statement: "As we flew in . . . we saw the wheat crop growing quite satisfactorily, looks like a bumper harvest. Yaobang is thin, but Shaanxi is fat! Yaobang has been good for Shaanxi, ah!" The banquet hall was silent, probably realizing that the three senior PLA officers were there not on an inspection but on a rescue mission.[104]

After the banquet Ye Jianying took Hu aside and told him that Marshal He Long had told him Shaanxi was persecuting people, and that he had come to help. Hu was discouraged, telling Ye he had done six *jiantao*, but had still not passed. Ye advised, "Little brother, you missed too many meals in the old China, you cannot defeat these people in struggle. You can't talk clearly here, come back to Beijing to speak more about it."[105]

On June 20 Ye Jianying's special military aircraft left Xi'an with Hu Yaobang and his secretary aboard. Hu had requested leave from the Northwest Bureau to return to Beijing to recuperate, and Liu Lantao was in no position to deny it. Of his two-hundred-day sojourn in Xi'an, Hu had spent half of it under interrogation and political pressure. He was sick, angry, and no doubt dispirited. But he was out. The Northwest Bureau would hold another mass meeting in July to debate Hu's situation, which would continue to dominate the political discourse in Xi'an for the next several months. Other political battles, both ideological and personal, raged under the auspices of criticizing "the errors of Hu Yaobang."

In Beijing the embers that had fired the political flames in Xi'an continued to smolder. In the aftermath of the "23 Articles" fiasco, Liu Shaoqi had taken his colleagues' advice and tendered a self-criticism to Mao Zedong. He also invited other senior party leaders to his home for "party life meetings," with open discussions of his errors and shortcomings, and his merits. Notes of these meetings sent to Mao may have delayed further action against Liu. The Socialist Education campaign continued to be implemented unevenly around the country; by midyear only about a third of the nation's counties reported having completed it. According to Luo Pinghan, Mao lost interest in Socialist Education in the latter half of 1965, busying himself with other plans.[106]

Hu Yaobang was allowed to take leave in Beidaihe in July to recover his health. His wife and daughter accompanied him. Hu's daughter recalls the vacation with warm affection, seeing her father laugh, play games, and even sing songs.[107] But it couldn't last.

Political tensions in Beijing and Xi'an were rising through that summer. As the Northwest Bureau held more meetings to criticize Hu, the depth of invective and breadth of condemnation grew. Hu heard about it from visiting friends and wrote a letter to Beijing complaining about the treatment. In August, General Office director Yang Shangkun rejected Xi'an's efforts to declare Hu absent without permission in order to force his return.[108]

Finally Hu was notified that a special Secretariat meeting would be held to review his case on October 6, when a number of the Northwest Bureau and Shaanxi secretaries would be in Beijing for a Central Committee work conference. Arriving at the appointed Zhongnanhai meeting room, Hu was surprised to see Deng Xiaoping sitting by himself. Their conversation has been set down identically by several sources.

Deng: "Your argument is over, don't talk about it. You won't go back to Shaanxi, rest for a while and you will be assigned other work."

Hu: "Will the Center give me a verdict?"

Deng: "There is no need."

Hu: "They have already circulated [guidance] and they want to 'purge my remaining poison' from the cadre ranks . . ."

Deng: "What they say doesn't decide it, the Center has not given you a verdict."

Hu: "Will the points the General Secretary has spoken today be circulated as a document?"

Deng: "There is no need."[109]

Mao's role in Hu's ordeal remains opaque. Different sources have different versions of his brief involvement and obscure pronouncements. Even Man

Mei found the evidence of Mao's attitude toward her father "unclear."[110] The most credible overview is that Mao had sent Hu to Shaanxi in the first place, that Hu had comported himself in ways consistent with his longtime support of Mao, and that it was Mao who provided for his medical care and his evacuation. Mao implied as much in an October 1965 argument with Liu Lantao over continuing problems in Shaanxi. When Liu criticized Hu's work in the Northwest, Mao shot back, "If Hu was not revolutionary, how did he go back [to Beijing]? Who was the mastermind, who came up with the plans and advice?" Liu Lantao had sense enough not to answer.[111]

Preparing for the Cultural Revolution

Mao had bigger battles to fight, and the traps he had been preparing were now ready to be sprung. He appears to have concluded that the Communist Party was no longer under his control, nor was it moving in policy directions he favored. It had become ideologically impure, like the Communist Party of the Soviet Union, and more importantly, was being taken over by people he despised and distrusted. He would not allow that to happen. So he plotted what was, in effect, a palace coup from inside the palace.

The primary target was Liu Shaoqi and his supporters, including Deng Xiaoping, Peng Zhen, Bo Yibo, and others. But first Mao needed to ensure his own security and control of the most important power bureaucracies: the army, the internal security apparatus, the party's bureaucratic nerve centers, and the propaganda organs.[112] Mao's methods were straightforward: take out the top leaders of the relevant bureaucracies and replace them with people personally loyal to himself.

The first to fall was Yang Shangkun, deputy secretary of the Central Secretariat and director of the party's General Office, which oversaw the Central Security Bureau, responsible not only for guarding and protecting all party facilities but for providing personal security for every member of the top party leadership. Yang had held the position since 1945. Part of his remit was to keep accurate records of Mao's meetings, and the General Office had recording devices installed in Mao's offices, living quarters, and personal train cars, beginning in 1959.[113] Mao supposedly had approved this, but in 1965 he discovered the devices in his private train car, where he had sexual liaisons with an array of young females, and he demanded both an end to the practice and punishment of those responsible. Yang first was transferred to the Guangdong CCP committee, then sent to various health facilities, and in early 1966 was transferred to Shanxi, where he was arrested and jailed for the next twelve years. Mao replaced him as head of the General Office with Wang Dongxing, his personal bodyguard since the early 1940s. Unlike Yang, whose complicated history included study in the Soviet Union, underground party work under Peng Zhen, and a longtime association with Deng Xiaoping, Wang's personal loyalty to Mao was beyond doubt.[114]

Next Mao turned his attention to the People's Liberation Army. Although Defense Minister Lin Biao was fervently loyal, his health was bad, and he spent much of his time recuperating in the northeastern port city of Dalian. Still, he was the most influential leader in the PLA, and he advocated "giving prominence to politics" (*tuchu zhengzhi*), which emphasized political-ideological indoctrination over conventional military training. Lin left the day-to-day administration of the armed forces to Marshal He Long and the chief of General Staff, General Luo Ruiqing. By 1964 both Lin and Mao began to have concerns about Luo squeezing Lin out of all decision-making, and about his close cooperation with He Long, whom Mao perceived as being aligned with Liu Shaoqi and Deng. Luo had to go.[115]

On December 11, 1965, a special military transport aircraft was dispatched to Kunming to pick up Luo, who was on inspection, and bring him to Shanghai, where a secret Politburo Standing Committee meeting was underway. For the next several days Luo was subjected to unremitting criticism and damaging accusations about his "high-handedness," ambition, and disrespectful treatment of the old marshals. Luo was given no opportunity to defend himself.[116] He was then suspended from all his military positions and replaced as chief of General Staff by Yang Chengwu, a Mao favorite, while Ye Jianying took over Luo's secretary-general position on the Military Commission. Criticism of Luo continued into the following spring, and in Beijing in March 1966 Luo tried to commit suicide by jumping from a third-story window; he only broke his legs and was left crippled for life.[117]

What was noteworthy about the Luo case was that the evidence against him was so flimsy, he was never given a chance to rebut the charges, and erstwhile friends and associates turned on him instantly and viciously once it became clear Mao wanted him out. After his suicide attempt, Liu Shaoqi and Deng Xiaoping scoffed at Luo for not jumping headfirst; Ye Jianying even wrote a satirical poem about it.[118] Subsequently Luo was subjected to substandard medical treatment and unspeakable cruelty during the Cultural Revolution, when he was dragged out, unable to stand, for criticism sessions that included more physical abuse. All for no other reason, evidently, than that Lin Biao feared Luo would become too powerful and Mao wanted him out of the way.

Mao's third target on the way to dislodging Liu Shaoqi was Propaganda Department head and Central Secretariat member Lu Dingyi. Lu was a key figure in the development of all artistic, literary, and cultural products. As early as 1963 Mao had concluded that traditional art forms, especially the popular Peking Opera, were in need of revolutionary reform. In July 1964 he established a five-person group, of which Lu Dingyi and Beijing mayor Peng Zhen were members, to develop proposals for cultural reform. But the small group did little or nothing.

The proximate cause of Lu Dingyi's disgrace was a "discovery" that anonymous letters sent to Lin Biao over several years accusing Lin's wife, Ye Qun, of infidelity were written by Lu's wife, Yan Weibing. Yan was arrested in March 1966, and Lu was implicated. Lu claimed he knew nothing about the letters, but he faced an official reckoning in May.[119]

Like the brutal treatment meted out to Luo Ruiqing, the criticism of Lu Dingyi was surprisingly hostile and exaggerated. Lin Biao—who had placed a letter attesting to his wife's virtue on the chair of each attendee at the meeting—threatened to kill Lu on the spot. Yang Chengwu waved a fist in Lu's face, while the usually imperturbable Zhou Enlai hurled a teapot at him. Deng Xiaoping, in charge of the meeting while Mao was in Hangzhou, decided to bar Lu from attending further meetings, perhaps to prevent him from suffering bodily harm.[120] Lu would suffer plenty of harm during his interrogation and incarceration in the Cultural Revolution. But his fate would be linked with the fourth and most important piece of Mao's elaborate plot to set up Liu Shaoqi: bringing down Peng Zhen.

Peng Zhen was the Politburo member responsible for overseeing propaganda, the ranking secretary on the Central Secretariat, the principal secretary of the Beijing municipal CCP committee, and the mayor of the city. Tough-minded and outspoken, Peng was a longtime associate of Liu Shaoqi and not much trusted by Mao. Mao's appointment of Peng to head the cultural reform five-person small group in 1964 may have been a way of testing Peng's political loyalties.[121]

In November 1965 Mao sprang his trap. Mao had encouraged Yao Wenyuan, a secretary on the Shanghai municipal party committee, to write an article in a Shanghai newspaper attacking a play written by one of Peng Zhen's subordinates, Vice-Mayor Wu Han. The play told the story of a Ming Dynasty official, Hai Rui, who criticized the emperor and was fired and imprisoned.

The play was seen as an allegory for Mao's treatment of Defense Minister Peng Dehuai in 1959, and Yao Wenyuan condemned it as an attack on Chairman Mao. Mao had previewed and edited Yao's article.[122]

Beijing newspapers ignored the article for two weeks because Peng Zhen and Lu Dingyi had forbidden newspapers in the capital to republish it.[123] Finally Luo Ruiqing, in one of his last acts before his own humiliation at Mao's hands, ordered the PLA's *Jiefangjun Bao* to reprint the article on November 29, and *Renmin Ribao* did likewise the following day, with comments criticizing Yao.[124]

Peng Zhen at last called the five-person small group together in early February 1966 to prepare a response to the festering ideological dispute. On February 4, 1966, they completed an outline report that proposed limiting the discussion to academic circles and not allowing it to become political. Peng sent the draft report to Mao in Wuhan on February 7. Mao approved it with only minor changes, but that was only a delaying tactic. In mid-March he convened an expanded Politburo Standing Committee meeting in Hangzhou, at which he criticized intellectuals in the universities and the party media as "Communists in name only" and warned the Propaganda Department it was heading for abolition.[125]

On March 28–30, Mao met with Kang Sheng and Jiang Qing, and delivered instructions to the party Center in Beijing on several topics. He charged "university overlords" with suppressing leftist publications and protecting "anti-Communist intellectuals." He referred to the Central Propaganda Department as the "Palace of Hell" and said the "King of Hell" (that is, Lu Dingyi) should be overthrown. He exhorted local regions to gather a cohort of "rebellious spirits" and if the Center carried out "revisionism," these groups "must be prepared to attack the Center and carry out a 'Great Cultural Revolution.'"[126] The party Center was to criticize Peng Zhen, the Central Propaganda Department, the Beijing municipal committee, and the five-person small group, and if they continued protecting bad people and resisting the revolution, they "must be dissolved."[127]

Zhou Enlai approved Mao's instructions and Deng Xiaoping convened a Secretariat meeting, on April 9–12, that heard Kang Sheng and Chen Boda reiterate Mao's instructions and criticisms. Peng Zhen defended himself against the charges, but Deng and Zhou Enlai turned on him and declared that his errors amounted to opposing Mao Zedong and Mao Zedong Thought. The Secretariat recommended to the Politburo Standing Committee that the February outline be rescinded, and that a new report be written by a special "Cultural Revolution documents drafting group."[128]

Mao convened an expanded Politburo Standing Committee meeting in Hangzhou on April 19–26, while Liu Shaoqi was on an official visit to Southeast Asia. With Mao presiding, the Standing Committee annulled the February outline report, abolished Peng Zhen's five-person group, and denounced Peng Zhen. When Liu Shaoqi returned to China and was called to attend the last days of the Hangzhou meeting, he had to accept Mao's fait accompli. Peng Zhen was finished.

Peng returned to Beijing with some of his colleagues, but none of them spoke to him. Yang Jisheng has observed: "Within the Chinese Communist Party, the relations between people are political relations and class relations. Aside from this, there are no other relationships, one cannot have private friendships. Once Mao has lost political confidence in someone, others immediately draw a line with the person, keep their distance and even kick him while he is down."[129]

In May, still in Hangzhou, Mao pulled the levers of power in Beijing. He ordered an expanded Politburo meeting to be held, with Liu Shaoqi presiding. Prior to the meeting, the PLA daily newspaper published a strongly worded editorial, "Never Forget the Class Struggle," putting the Army's ideological weight squarely behind Mao Zedong. On May 8, Lu Dingyi was arrested. On May 10, the Beijing municipal party committee was reorganized, with Peng Zhen replaced as first secretary by a Mao favorite.

Also before the Standing Committee meeting, Mao ordered military security in Beijing to be beefed up. Zhou Enlai and CMC secretary general Ye Jianying had formed a "capital working group," which included both the chief of General Staff and the minister of public security, and which was responsible only to Zhou, who reported to Mao. The group implemented Mao's plan to bolster the PLA's presence, bringing in main force divisions from outside and putting them under the command of the Beijing Garrison. Yang Jisheng claims these steps were taken because Mao truly believed there were plans afoot for a coup d'état against him.[130]

Mao's expanded Standing Committee meeting convened on May 16, attended by more than seventy Central Committee members. Its initial focus was the final condemnation of Peng Zhen, Luo Ruiqing, Lu Dingyi, and Yang Shangkun, castigating them as an "anti–Mao Zedong, anti-party clique."[131] But Mao's deeper concerns were for his own security and the removal of Liu

Shaoqi. Taking down Peng Zhen and Yang Shangkun both strengthened Mao's security and gave him better control of party paperwork. Lu Dingyi's removal gave Mao more direct access to propaganda media and placated Jiang Qing, on whom Mao was increasingly reliant. Removing Luo Ruiqing strengthened Lin Biao's control of PLA operations. And removing at one swoop four critical members of Deng Xiaoping's Secretariat crippled that organization, rendering Liu Shaoqi more vulnerable.

The meeting passed what has become known as the "May 16 Circular," which historians agree was the programmatic document for the Cultural Revolution. The drafting group, chosen by Jiang Qing and headed by Chen Boda and Kang Sheng, began work in mid-April, but Mao Zedong wrote or rewrote large portions of every draft. The final version presented to the Beijing meeting highlighted Mao's personal contributions in boldface type, and no changes of any kind were permitted.

Substantively, the circular was pure Mao—vindictive, sarcastic, and unrelenting. And it was all about power and authority:

> The whole party must follow Comrade Mao Zedong's instructions, hold high the great banner of the proletarian Cultural Revolution, thoroughly expose the reactionary bourgeois stand of those . . . who oppose the party and socialism, thoroughly criticize and repudiate . . . those representatives of the bourgeoisie who have sneaked into the party, the government, the army, and all spheres of culture, to clear them out or transfer some of them to other positions. Above all, we must not entrust these people with the work of leading the Cultural Revolution. . . . Some of them we have already seen through, others we have not. Some are still trusted by us and are being trained as our successors, persons like Khrushchev, for example, who are still sleeping beside us.[132]

The resolution passed unanimously, under the direction of Liu Shaoqi, who even allowed those who were not Politburo members to vote. Some PRC historians assert that Liu did not realize the "Khrushchev sleeping beside us" was an oblique reference to himself. And Mao had been talking about opposing revisionism and the need for "class struggle" for so long that the language did not seem unduly provocative. The meeting continued, and on May 23 the "Peng-Luo-Lu-Yang anti-party clique" was formally removed from all official positions.[133]

The final business of the meeting was the establishment of a new Central Cultural Revolution small group. Again, this was directed by Mao from Hangzhou. No variations or disapprovals of his candidates were permitted. On May 28 the meeting approved the leadership slate Mao proposed: group leader—Chen Boda (Mao's *mishu*); adviser—Kang Sheng (former head of Mao's intelligence and security apparatus in Yan'an); deputy leaders—Jiang Qing (Mao's wife), Wang Renzhong (first secretary of the Central-South Bureau), Liu Zhijian (first deputy director of the PLA General Political Department), and Zhang Chunqiao (secretary of the Shanghai municipal party committee). There were seven other ordinary members: Xie Fuzhi, Yin Da, Wang Li, Guan Feng, Qi Benyu, Mu Xin, and Yao Wenyuan.[134]

Hu Yaobang on the Sidelines

Hu Yaobang's thoughts during this tumultuous period are unknown. He did not attend the critical meetings discussed above, probably citing health issues. But he might not even have been invited. He had left Xi'an under suspicion and criticism, which was continuing. He evidently made one last attempt, in December 1965, to get Mao to help resolve his situation. At Ye Jianying's suggestion, Hu's old friend and fellow "little red devil," Chen Pixian, invited him to Shanghai to get a medical examination. Chen had risen to the post of first secretary of the Shanghai committee in 1964 but had growing differences with his leftist subordinates, Zhang Chunqiao and Yao Wenyuan. Hu stayed in Shanghai for ten days and may have unsuccessfully sought an audience with Mao, who was there at the time. Chen promised to report his case to Mao, but to no avail.[135] Hu returned to Beijing with no resolution and no prospects for a next job.

Hu Yaobang was still titular head of the Communist Youth League, but he had turned over day-to-day management of the League to his deputy, Hu Keshi. He attended at least some of the sessions of the CYL plenum in Beijing in April 1966 but did not make a speech or play a leading role.[136] At fifty-one, Hu probably had no desire to return to full-time work at Youth League headquarters. He had taken an important career step forward with the assignments to Hunan and Shaanxi, but both had turned to ashes. Intense factional political pressure at both the national and the provincial level had brought about a collapse of his health. Still recuperating, Hu was no doubt disquieted to learn in February 1966 that he had been named the key member of a "right opportunist anti-party clique" in Shaanxi, along with two former subordinates. While there was little danger he would be sent back to Shaanxi to face these charges, Hu opted to continue recuperating in his home in Beijing.

Hu was probably very satisfied with the work the CYL had done under his guidance. It had become a loyal, diligent auxiliary of the Party, recruiting, educating, and indoctrinating millions of future party members. Its Central Committee had been honed by Hu into an efficient management team, with a stable core and steady turnover as youth leaders moved off to other positions. He could hardly have foreseen, in May 1966, that the Youth League he had worked so hard to nurture for so many years would be torn apart within three months by his venerated Chairman Mao Zedong, using the very middle school and college youth Hu had sought to train.

6 Cultural Revolutions

A great deal has been written about the "Great Proletarian Cultural Revolution," its causes, tragic and evil figures, atrocities and cruelty, unexpected twists and turns, and ultimate failure and abandonment. Hundreds of books and countless articles in many languages have tried to explain the inexplicable, fathom the unfathomable, and make sense of the senseless. But much is still locked away in party archives, many exculpatory lies have been told, and many memories are still too painful for the Cultural Revolution's many victims. The CCP has decided it is no longer convenient to explore the topic or understand it in depth. At the time, Hu Yaobang was nominal head of the Communist Youth League in 1966, recovering his health from factional infighting that paralyzed two provinces where he had temporary assignments, Hunan and Shaanxi. Hu still identified himself as a supporter of Mao Zedong, but also had ties to others who were caught up in the political strife of the early 1960s. The complex relationships that convulsed the Communist Party during the Cultural Revolution would take Hu Yaobang from loyal Maoist to victim of that revolution's excesses. For Hu, the Cultural Revolution was a watershed in his career, leading him almost unwittingly to being an agent of change.

Above all, the Cultural Revolution is about Mao Zedong. He is the central figure who plotted the initial moves, guided by the muddled memories and chaotic theories of a seventy-one-year-old revolutionary who perhaps had seen many of his ideas go wrong but could not admit it. He was pampered, jealous, and spiteful, narcissistic yet insecure, fearful that those he had groomed to succeed him were too eager to take power from him. Ever mindful of his enormous personal authority and the ways he could use it against others, he plotted the downfall of former comrades, connived at their mistreatment, and withheld medical care that could have saved some from death. Isolated and lonely, long out of touch with the Chinese people, Mao continued for ten long years to wield his power without concern for its consequences; and in the end, his health and judgment ravaged by illness, he became a pliant tool in the hands of those who translated his incomprehensible grunts into political commands of their own.

But equally important, both for Mao's colleagues in the 1960s and his successors today, was the implacable efficiency of the system, the structure of power that the Communist Party of China put in place. That system was Mao's creation. Combining the credulousness of ordinary party members, for whom Marxism was a foreign dogma full of difficult-to-pronounce names and peculiar concepts, with the cynical manipulation of high priests in a theocracy, along with the ruthless discipline of a criminal gang, the CCP had become the dominant force in Chinese society by 1965, when Mao set out to destroy and remake it.

That is the main story of the Cultural Revolution—Mao had become disenchanted with his creation and set about constructing it anew. But the principal components of the party's control mechanism—the military, the security apparatus, the propaganda organs, and the Central bureaucracy—remained. Even when Mao turned his wrath on each of them individually, manipulating and even disbanding some, he was able to manipulate them, with the help of key supporters, to come away victorious. But they would eventually return.

The distinguishing characteristic of the Cultural Revolution, at least in its early phase, was Mao's use of the revolutionary fervor of the nation's youth to batter down resistance within the party to his ideas and programs. Some of the most vivid images of the period are the films of mass demonstrations in Tiananmen Square, with one to two million youth in military formations, waving copies from *Quotations of Chairman Mao,* rhythmically chanting "Long live Chairman Mao," Mao waving benignly, basking in the adulation of the innocents. Ultimately, acting at his behest, those youth would become an instrument of mob rule.

In this chapter I will not focus on Mao's goals, much less his thoughts, but will try to summarize the principal phases of the Cultural Revolution, relying primarily on a small number of classic studies. Then I will concentrate on Hu Yaobang's experience of the Cultural Revolution and the impact it had on his life and thinking.[1]

The Cultural Revolution and the Youth League

After the May 16 Circular had called on the whole party to criticize and repudiate "reactionary bourgeois ideas" in academic work, education, journalism, literature and art, and publishing, it was only a matter of time before tensions in Beijing universities broke out into the open. Mao, still in Hangzhou, had secretly dispatched a small team to investigate / instigate the situation at Beijing University (Beida) in mid-May. They encouraged a junior faculty member to go public over her feud with the university administration. This self-avowed leftist faculty member, Nie Yuanzi, and several colleagues pasted up "the country's first Marxist big-character poster" (*dazibao*) on May 25, denouncing several administrators for trying to lead the nascent Cultural Revolution onto a "revisionist" path. It quickly generated hundreds of other *dazibao* on campus, some critical of Nie. The minister of education and the new first secretary of Beijing visited the campus and authorized a critical discussion of the poster, probably in the hope that the situation could be controlled.[2]

But a copy of the poster was sent to Mao Zedong, who approved of its tone and content and on May 31 ordered it to be publicized nationwide. The Cultural Revolution Group (CRG), which that same day had "seized power" at the offices of *Renmin Ribao,* ordered the text to be broadcast. It was republished on June 1, along with a front-page editorial entitled "Sweep Away All Monsters." Written by Chen Boda and coordinated with Kang Sheng, the editorial called for a nationwide Cultural Revolution to "completely destroy the old ideology, old culture, old customs, and old habits caused by all the exploiting classes that poisoned the people for thousands of years."[3] The Cultural Revolution would soon be sweeping the entire country.

Liu Shaoqi had received no advance notice of the editorial's publication, although he had approved the CRG takeover of *Renmin Ribao* and a work team's takeover of the Central Propaganda Department.[4] On June 3 Liu convened an expanded meeting of the Politburo to decide what to do about growing turmoil in Beijing's school system. The meeting issued an "eight-point regulation" to restrict student activities within school compounds, and to send work teams of senior cadres from party departments and State Council ministries to university campuses to bring the situation under control. And because student unruliness was spreading to Beijing's middle and even elementary schools, the Politburo assigned to the Communist Youth

League (CYL) leadership the task of organizing work teams for secondary schools.[5]

With Hu Yaobang still recuperating at home, Executive Secretary Hu Keshi called an emergency meeting of the CYL Secretariat on the evening of June 3 and began organizing cadres to dispatch to schools in Beijing. When the decisions were reported to Hu Yaobang, he was uncomfortable with the work teams idea, but did not countermand the decision, since it was mandated by the Politburo.[6] Starting with sixteen work teams made up of CYL and Beijing municipal committee cadres, eventually more than eighteen hundred CYL officials were participating in more than three hundred work teams all over the city's eight school districts.[7] Their instructions were to "digest and dissolve the newly organized Red Guards [*hongweibing*]" in the middle schools attached to Beijing and Qinghua Universities, and bring them under more effective control.[8]

But the work teams were encountering resistance at universities. Liu had directed the work groups to attack university administrators, which further divided the already factionalized protestors. Student groups were based in part on class background and family lineage. The children of many of the top CCP leaders were soon drawn into the turmoil. Members of the CRG also became directly involved in supporting different student groups. Soon thousands of big-character posters festooned every bit of available wall space at Beida and Qinghua, denouncing or defending administrators, teachers, and other students.[9]

CYL work groups were having comparable problems controlling younger activists. Notwithstanding Politburo orders that Cultural Revolution activities should not disrupt normal activities, by mid-June secondary schools were immobilized by feuds between competing student groups. Centrally dispatched work groups began detaining some of the more prominent leftist students. In response, on June 18 radical students began physically abusing administrators, teachers, and work team members.[10] In Politburo meetings chaired by Liu Shaoqi in July, disagreements between Liu and Deng and CRG members became acrimonious, with Chen Boda charging that students were being "suppressed" by work groups.

On July 16 the Chairman went swimming in the Yangzi River near Wuhan. Photos of a grinning seventy-one-year-old Mao Zedong, accompanied in the water by PLA soldiers, soon appeared in every newspaper nationwide. The message was clear: Mao was healthy, he was afloat, he was supported by the army, and he was coming back. The next day Mao notified Deng Xiaoping he was returning to Beijing and that no Politburo meetings were to be held before he got there.[11]

Mao Zedong's Cultural Revolution: Red Terror

Upon arriving in Beijing on July 17, Mao went straight to the Diaoyutai guesthouse, where the CRG had set up its headquarters. In a series of Politburo meetings over the next several days, Mao made it very clear that he disliked the work teams' being sent into the schools and was determined to have them withdrawn. Angry and imperious, Mao set August 1–5 as the date for the Eleventh Plenum of the Eighth Central Committee, giving his Politburo colleagues little time to prepare reports for it. Unbeknownst to them, Mao also had sent a letter to Beijing middle school Red Guards expressing his "enthusiastic support" for their opposition to "landlords, the bourgeoisie, imperialists, revisionists and their running dogs." He coined a phrase that would resound loudly throughout China for the next decade: "It is right to rebel!" (*zaofan you li!*).[12]

Even before the plenum, the abolition of the work teams sent to schools and universities was publicly announced at a July 29 mass rally at the Great Hall of the People. That same evening, Red Guards from eight middle schools marched into Communist Youth League headquarters, shouted slogans, put up posters, and denounced the CYL leadership by name. Hu Yaobang told Hu Keshi that the Cultural Revolution Group was behind it, and that Deng Xiaoping should be warned about such "abnormal" practices.[13]

Hu attended the Eleventh Plenum, which began on schedule on August 1 but soon veered off into a degree of abnormality that must have shocked him. After Mao's introductory speech, Liu Shaoqi began a brief report on the Center's work since the Tenth Plenum, talking about the Cultural Revolution and the work group issue. At this point Mao began to interrupt Liu with angry and derisive criticism, accusing the Center of repressing students in the same way the Qing Dynasty and Chiang Kai-shek had done. Liu was contrite, but Mao kept up the attack for two hours in front of the entire Central Committee.[14]

That same evening, the Cultural Revolution Group summoned Hu Keshi and members of the CYL Secretariat to Diaoyutai to report on the CYL's work. Hu Yaobang accompanied them voluntarily, even though he technically had not overseen the Youth League while recuperating. Kang Sheng, Chen Boda, and Jiang Qing took turns berating them all for following orders from Liu and Deng to pressure Red Guards into accepting discipline from CYL work groups. Kang accused them of serious ideological errors, Chen Boda claimed their minds were corrupted and they had turned the Youth League into an "old person's league." But Jiang Qing made it personal, first telling Hu Yaobang he was ill and didn't need to be there, then saying, "[Your] fear of a mass movement changed you, Hu Yaobang, from a 'little red devil' (*hong xiao gui*) into a 'cowardly spirit' (*dan xiao gui*)."[15] Jiang would later say with pride, "I was Chairman Mao's dog. Whomever he let me bite, I bit that person."[16] Hu Yaobang probably understood on that August evening in Diaoyutai that Jiang Qing's insult meant he had fallen out of favor with Mao Zedong.

In the small group meetings on the second day of the plenum, the CYL and Hu Yaobang himself came under heavy attack. Mao Zedong led the charge, repeating Kang Sheng's criticism that Hu Yaobang and Hu Keshi had committed "errors of direction and errors of line" by sending work groups into schools to control student protestors. And the errors were done deliberately. "Not only did they not support the young students' movement," Mao charged, "they actually suppressed the student movement, which should be strictly punished."[17]

On August 5 Mao declared that the plenary meeting would be extended for another week. More importantly, he wrote and immediately publicized a big-character poster of his own, which he called, "Bombard the Headquarters—My First Big Character Poster." Short but direct, Mao's poster attacked "leading comrades" who had "enforced a bourgeois dictatorship and struck down the surging movement of the Great Cultural Revolution of the proletariat. They have . . . encircled and suppressed revolutionaries, stifled opinions differing from their own, [and] imposed a white terror."[18] His poster was meant not simply to demonstrate his solidarity with the Red Guards and demonstrating students, but to deploy them as a weapon against his opponents. Fanatically loyal to him, noisy and fearless, the masses of Red Guards were Mao's chosen tool for the next phase in his struggle for power against the "capitalist roaders."

Mao had sent word to Lin Biao in Dalian on August 4 that he should come to Beijing to attend the plenum. Lin and his wife arrived on August 8. After meeting with Mao, Lin met with the Cultural Revolution Group that evening and pledged to bring down the "reactionary authorities" in a "tumultuous, earth-shaking, stormy and vigorous" manner.[19] On August 8 the Central Committee Plenum approved a sixteen-clause decision on the future direction of the Cultural Revolution, including criticism of the way it had gone before. After a couple days of timid discussions, Mao closed the plenum by "bombarding his own headquarters," instituting a Central Committee election on August 12 that dramatically altered both the Politburo and its Standing Committee. He added six members to the Politburo (three of them "old marshals" of the PLA), increased the number of Standing Committee members from seven to eleven, and made major changes in their rank order. Liu Shaoqi and Deng Xiaoping were demoted, while three members of the CRG (Tao Zhu, Chen Boda, and Kang Sheng) were added to the Standing Committee. Lin Biao was the only person nominated to be a party vice-chairman, replacing Liu Shaoqi as the number two leader and becoming Mao's heir apparent.[20] The new Standing Committee would meet only once, and would appear in public only once, when Mao reviewed more than one million Red Guards assembled in Tiananmen Square. Then Mao began dismantling the committee.

Hu Yaobang's Cultural Revolution—Pain and Humiliation

On August 13, the day after the plenum concluded, the Red Guards came for Hu Yaobang. That evening, the CRG held a rally of several thousand Red Guards in Beijing's Workers Stadium. Newly chosen Standing Committee member Li Fuchun, speaking on behalf of Mao, declared that the Youth League leadership was to be reorganized. After the rally, thousands of chanting demonstrators converged on the CYL headquarters building at No. 3 Zhengyi Road, while smaller squads of Red Guards made their way to Hu Yaobang's (and Hu Keshi's) home in Fuqiang Hutong. Forcing their way in, they seized the two men, and other members of the CYL Secretariat, and took them back to CYL headquarters to be "dragged out for struggle." Hu Yaobang was one of the first Central Committee members to be publicly subjected to struggle by Red Guards, and the first to be physically harmed.[21]

Hu's first struggle session went on until 3 a.m. the following morning, after which he was forbidden to return home. He tried to calm angry demonstrators—who had covered the CYL courtyard with posters and banners—by agreeing to meet in an auditorium to answer questions. He was asked why he protected "rightists" in the 1950s, how he had "disappeared" on the Long March, what were his relations with Liu and Deng, and whether he opposed Chairman Mao. At the end, he was ordered to stay in the building to write a *jiantao* of his errors. Many of these Red Guards were children of

Public shaming and criticism were near-universal phenomena in the Cultural Revolution, to which Hu Yaobang was repeatedly subjected. Here three obscure officials are forced to bow before their accusers, with placards listing their "crimes" and crossing out their names, denoting their tormentors' belief they should be executed. (CPA Media Pte Ltd / Alamy Stock Photo)

senior cadres, some of whom he knew. At the end of their interrogation, however, Hu Yaobang was still not certain who had orchestrated the attack on CYL headquarters.

Li Fuchun returned with another large Red Guard contingent on August 15 to announce a simplified set of charges against the CYL leaders. The "three Hu's and one Wang"—Hu Yaobang, Hu Keshi, Hu Qili, and Wang Wei—had not raised the red flag of Mao Zedong Thought high enough, had not followed the mass line well enough, and had blocked the Red Guards from exposing their mistakes. They were therefore suspended from duty to examine their errors, the CYL Central Secretariat was dissolved, and a new provisional Secretariat was established. There were no documents, simply verbal accusations with no detailed evidence. Li instructed the Red Guards to treat all members of the Secretariat with dignity and respect.[22]

In the following days Hu Yaobang's degradation began in earnest. First, all the bureaus and departments of the CYL were taken over by "revolutionary" youth with no idea what to do. All CYL publications ceased, and all organizational activity was suspended.[23] The principal activity of the new provisional leadership was denunciation of the "three Hu's and one Wang."

They typically began with mass demonstration meetings, usually at the CYL headquarters building, where the four men were paraded before several hundred demonstrators who chanted slogans, shouted insults, and waved banners. Often the four were led onto a stage or a courtyard balcony by young toughs who held their arms straight back and forced them to bend over at the waist in a painful, deep bowing posture called the "jet plane position," after the swept-back wings of a MiG-15 fighter. The victims would remain in this position for up to an hour. Sometimes they were forced to kneel, would have tall dunce caps placed on their heads and demeaning placards hung around their necks. Hu Yaobang's *mishu* later praised him as an "iron man" who instructed his younger colleagues on how to endure pain despite suffering from neurological disease and other disorders.[24]

On August 18 Mao Zedong met with more than a million Red Guards who had gathered in Tiananmen Square to pay homage to their deity. Man Mei claims her father began to be physically beaten by Red Guards that same day while the Red Guards responsible for the security of CYL headquarters went to attend the rally. When those responsible for security returned, they found that all the Secretariat members had been beaten—their clothing was tattered and bloody, their faces were bruised and swollen, placards were hung around their necks, and the hair of some had been shaved off.[25]

In late August and early September, the security situation continued to deteriorate as members of the CRG exhorted a growing "rebel faction" (*zaofan pai*) within the Red Guard movement to do more to punish the capitalist roaders. Liu Shaoqi and Deng Xiaoping had been suspended from their duties but had not been further punished, so the crowds directed their anger at the Youth League. CYL leaders began to be transported to local schools and factories for struggle sessions, where the sessions were harder to control. While at CYL headquarters, the "three Hu's and one Wang" could be separated from the crowds by being on a balcony or stage. But in other places it became difficult to prevent rowdy students from demonstrating their hatred for people they believed to be "against Chairman Mao." On one occasion, when Hu Yaobang refused to admit he was a "three-anti criminal" (anti-party, anti-socialism, and anti-Mao), he was attacked by a seventeen-year-old girl who slashed at his head and face with a leather belt, drawing blood. On another occasion during this period, Hu was beaten with wooden poles, and for several days he could not stand straight or walk without crutches.[26]

Hu Keshi recalled December 1966 as one of the worst times. He recounted an episode when Hu Yaobang, thrown to the floor and thrashed with belts by several Red Guards, was rolling around screaming in pain. He believed that Hu Yaobang was probably beaten ten to twenty times during this period; Hu Keshi himself and Hu Qili were beaten far more often.[27] This phase of the Cultural Revolution coincided with a change in the composition of Red Guard activists, from "old Red Guards"—children of senior cadres—to the Rebel Faction, who were from more varied social backgrounds and more fanatically loyal to Chairman Mao.[28]

When he wasn't being paraded in front of screaming youth, Hu Yaobang was confined to what was called a "cowshed" (*niu peng*). The name derived not from being a cattle enclosure, but from being the place where the "cow ghosts and snake spirits" (*niugui sheshen*), the designated enemies, were confined during the early phase of the Cultural Revolution. In the case of the Communist Youth League, these were storage huts in a courtyard of CYL headquarters. Each hut held twenty to thirty detainees, who slept on mats on the floor, guarded by Red Guards or low-level CYL staffers. Senior CYL Secretariat members were each kept in separate "cowsheds," but occasionally could speak briefly with each other during toilet breaks. None were allowed to return home, except in case of family emergencies.[29]

While Hu was sequestered in CYL headquarters and not allowed to see his family, his wife, Li Zhao, also was isolated at her workplace and could not return home. Hu's oldest son, Hu Deping, was "making revolution" at Beida, his second son was at Qinghua, and his youngest son and daughter were in secondary schools. All were impacted by the Cultural Revolution's slide into anarchy. Li Zhao's mother, who had lived with the family for years, was sent back to her home in Anhui for investigation, and Hu's mother fell gravely ill. Hu's official salary had been suspended since August, and it was often difficult to maintain sufficient supplies of food and fuel as winter set in. The family home often was nearly vacant, with drivers, secretaries, and other staff having been sent away. In these circumstances, Man Mei returned home one morning in late 1966 to find that Red Guards had ransacked their compound. While the family did not have a lot of valuables or money, the young vandals destroyed many of Hu's beloved books, scattering torn pages all over the courtyard.[30]

On January 6, 1967, the so-called January Storm took place in Shanghai, during which revolutionary rebels and students seized power, declaring they no longer accepted the authority of the Shanghai CCP committee. Mao approved the seizure of power but did not like them calling themselves a "People's Commune," and their label was eventually changed to "Revolutionary Committee of Shanghai Municipality." The Revolutionary Committee was headed by Zhang Chunqiao and Yao Wenyuan; a young factory labor leader named Wang Hongwen was principal deputy. Most of the members of the previous CCP committee and the municipal government were dismissed or jailed, many were beaten, and some were killed.[31]

As the power seizure phase of the Cultural Revolution proceeded with Mao's approval, factional infighting increased nationwide. At CYL headquarters it became impossible to ascertain who was in charge. Li Fuchun visited again in early February, telling the "rebel faction" Red Guards who had replaced the "old Red Guards" that Hu Yaobang had "opposed Chairman Mao for many years," which set off an intense new round of criticism. Hu apparently decided to rebuff all further efforts to get him to admit his "crimes" or atone for his mistakes, which brought him even more abuse.[32]

The violent factional infighting during the formation of "revolutionary committees" dissolved social order in many cities, so Mao decided in late January that People's Liberation Army units should "support the broad masses of the left." This order was subsequently refined into orders to the PLA "to support the left, the peasants and the workers and to carry out military training and military control" in areas or institutions that had fallen into disorder. This directive became known as the Three Supports and Two Militaries (*san zhi liang jun*).[33] But without clear guidelines on how to determine which of the feuding rebel groups were satisfactorily leftist, PLA unit commanders and commissars themselves often were drawn into local political disputes. Some members of the Cultural Revolution Group then began to favor seizures of power within military units, which brought Ye Jianying and other PLA veterans to the point of open defiance.[34]

That defiance, expressed at a raucous February 1967 Politburo meeting attended by members of the CRG and PLA veterans, further divided the leadership. Mao was enraged when he heard of it, denounced what he called the February Countercurrent by the old soldiers, and threatened to start a new armed uprising against them. In the end he fired the impromptu Politburo leadership group that had been running day-to-day affairs, turning those responsibilities over to the CRG, with Zhou Enlai in charge. In February and March the veterans were required to do humiliating *jiantao* and were subsequently sidelined.[35]

The Cultural Revolution Group took over most of the functions of the Politburo and its Standing Committee by August 1966. Here ranking members Jiang Qing, Zhou Enlai, and Kang Sheng review Red Guards from a jeep at a stadium rally in late 1966. (Wikimedia Commons)

It is unlikely that Hu Yaobang knew about much about this leadership infighting, although he probably heard rumors in the CYL cowshed. His life continued to be an interminable routine of daily criticism, which often included being spat upon, cursed at, showered with garbage and personal insults, forced to kneel or assume the jet plane position, and physical beatings.

Adding to his torment, Hu's eighty-six-year-old mother, Liu Minglun, died suddenly of a cerebral hemorrhage in the spring of 1967, while Hu was still incarcerated. Hu Deping, his eldest son, was allowed to escort his father to the hospital morgue, where for the first time he saw his father weeping inconsolably, having been unable to look after his mother in her illness. Only a few weeks later one of his closest associates on the CYL Secretariat committed suicide rather than face more Red Guard persecution.[36]

Hu Yaobang was a small man, suffering from poor health, but he was mentally tough, strong-willed, and stubborn. He consistently resisted his tormentors' demands that he confess to being a "three anti element." But he may have been approaching a breaking point. What he was undergoing was torture, and he may have believed it was sanctioned by Mao. Hu's biographers cautiously suggest that Hu was "conflicted" in his feelings for Mao during this period. Having observed the changes in the Chairman's personal and official behavior, his intolerance for others' opinions, and the ideologically untenable campaigns, Hu began during this period to examine rigorously but privately his own feelings about the revolution he had served so faithfully.[37]

In July 1967 Hu was taken to an automobile factory in southwestern Beijing for another struggle session. Infuriated by his stubbornness, "rebel faction" workers there beat him senseless, to the point that he could not walk without assistance and was in constant pain. Hu family complaints to Zhou Enlai finally were heard, and they were allowed to take food to their father in the CYL cowshed, and to escort him to a local hospital for examinations and treatment.[38] In early 1968, as part of the "three supports and two militaries," a military control group was sent to CYL headquarters to bring order to the situation. This eased the conditions for the prisoners by limiting struggle sessions, but it also added an additional layer of punishment—namely, being assigned demeaning tasks like cleaning latrines and being hauled off to rural areas to do manual labor. And in Hu's case, the military control group assigned to the CYL was ordered to investigate his political history, particularly his relationships with Deng Xiaoping and Liu Shaoqi.[39]

Kang Sheng's Cultural Revolution: The Special Case Investigations

Kang Sheng—once Mao's trusted intelligence chief at Yan'an—was no longer needed after 1945 and was quietly exiled to Shandong. From there he slowly worked his way back into Mao's graces, with the help of Jiang Qing. As Mao's paranoia and alienation from the party bureaucracy grew in the wake of the Great Leap Forward, Kang slowly returned to the inner circle. He flattered the Chairman and helped him see veiled attacks in novels and plays, and by the time Mao was ready to move against his opponents in 1966, Kang had become an "adviser" to the Central Cultural Revolution Group. Kang used early Red Guard rallies to bring down several key members of the Central Investigation Department, recover his influence over the foreign and domestic intelligence collection organs, and gain access to their files.[40]

The Central Case Examination Committee was initially set up at the same May 1966 expanded Politburo meeting that launched the Cultural Revolution. It was directed first against the "Peng-Luo-Lu-Yang anti-party clique," who had been ousted at that meeting. Zhou Enlai was in charge and reported directly to Mao. As more veteran cadres came under scrutiny, its name changed to Central Case Examination Group (CCEG) and it grew in size and outreach. Nominally under the Politburo Standing Committee, it was controlled by the CRG. Kang Sheng personally oversaw many cases, particularly those involving accusations of treason or espionage dating back to the Yan'an era.[41]

The CCEG's activities were run through three numbered offices. Office 1—headed by Wang Dongxing and housed in the General Office—was responsible for investigating officials in the CCP and State Council. Office 2—headed by the chief of the PLA General Staff and headquartered in the administrative office of the Central Military Commission—was to investigate political enemies among senior PLA officers. Office 3—headed by Minister of Public Security Xie Fuzhi—was responsible for finding political disloyalty within the security apparatus and for special, large investigations.[42]

Each office ran several high-profile investigations focused on individuals considered to be Mao's main enemies. The goal of each investigation was to discover materials (*cailiao*) to prove the person under investigation was an enemy of Chairman Mao, the CCP, socialism, or the revolution—and had been for years. Special case workers mostly were military or security officials with experience in political investigations. They were authorized to travel anywhere, review any records, interrogate any person, and use any method to obtain incriminating material.

Those methods included beatings, torture, imprisonment, pressure on family members, even forced suicides. The CCEG collected evidence to support whatever accusations had already been made against an individual by Mao or others on the CRG. The investigations didn't need to have standing in a court, as no trials were ever held. They just needed to support the label or charge. PLA Air Force commander and CCEG Office 2 chief Wu Faxian wrote later that he believed most of the evidence gathered by the special case groups was false.[43]

Available statistics vary, and investigative material has disappeared into official archives, but the CCEG and its local counterparts may have investigated more than two million cadres between 1967 and 1979, when they were abolished by dint of Hu Yaobang's efforts. Almost seven hundred of those investigated were above vice-ministerial rank, and included ten Politburo or Secretariat members, numerous general-grade officers in the PLA, and more than half the members of the Central Committee.[44] How many of the

CCEG's suspects died during their ordeals is still a state secret, but large-scale investigations carried out by Office 3 reportedly caused the deaths of thousands. Liu Shaoqi, He Long, Tao Zhu, and Peng Dehuai all died of medical malfeasance by doctors under the orders of special case groups.[45]

Hu's biographers have little to report about him in the last half of 1967 and most of 1968. He remained in the cowshed, unable to go home. His family and some friends were able to visit him at the CYL headquarters, although he was shackled when meeting them and had to report on who they were.[46] After the CYL military control group took charge in March 1968, he was less frequently besieged by mobs, but his health probably worsened as he was more often given difficult labor assignments and his living conditions deteriorated. He was on a list Kang Sheng prepared for Jiang Qing of members of the Eighth Central Committee who had been sidelined but not yet included in special cases. That meant that he was still suspected of being disloyal, but Mao had not yet authorized an investigation.[47]

Hu was repeatedly interrogated by the military representatives about his personal history and especially about relationships with other leaders. Many of the people he had worked with were by mid-1968 objects of scrutiny by special case groups, and Hu was kept busy writing voluminous "materials" about them.[48] He filled several hundred pages with testimony. Hu's biographers maintain that he did not try to blacken anyone's reputation, did not attach labels or denounce anyone in these writings. They were objective, fair, and honest, and thus made the "rebel faction" unhappy. They were also literate and generally free of writing errors or erasures.[49]

False Reprieve?

On October 12, 1968, the military representatives at CYL headquarters were instructed to bring Hu Yaobang at once to the Jingxi Hotel. The Jingxi was run by the PLA for senior military and CCP guests, and for large party or military meetings. In this case, Hu was told he was going there to be interrogated but actually he was brought to attend the Twelfth Plenum of the Eighth Central Committee. Unkempt and in cowshed clothes, Hu was allowed into Beijing's most exclusive guesthouse; his military escorts were denied entry.[50]

Hu's release was the result of several political conundrums. First, the Central Special Case Group on Liu Shaoqi had completed its work, and Mao wanted what remained of the Central Committee to hear the evidence and vote Liu out of the party. Second, preparations were being made to hold the long-delayed Ninth Congress of the CCP, and the selection process for the new leadership was underway. The CCEG, in some ways, had done its jobs too well: Only 40 of the 97 full members and 19 of 96 alternate members of the Eighth Central Committee were deemed eligible to attend the plenum. The rest had either died or had been declared guilty of "crimes" by Kang Sheng and the CCEG. Mao did not have a quorum for his meeting.[51]

There were plenty of alternates to fill the vacancies, even a few delegates who had been "liberated" from detention. Mao specifically asked for Hu Yaobang to be added to the delegate list. In preparatory meetings, Mao reportedly said, "Hu Yaobang grew up as a poor child, I understand him. What problems does he have? Count him in."[52] So Hu was allowed to attend the plenum, held October 13 to October 31, 1968. Additional benefits, of far greater importance to Hu, were that he was allowed to return home for the first time in two years and his cadre rank and salary were restored.

Hu probably was aware of the price of his freedom: a vote in favor of all the resolutions proposed for Central Committee approval. As had been done with numerous important party work meetings, the Twelfth Plenum itself was "expanded," meaning that Mao could pack it with people who would not otherwise have been allowed to cast a vote. Even with ten new alternate members to replace those who had died, the plenum was attended by more nonmembers than members of the Central Committee.[53]

The work report, speeches by Mao, Lin Biao, Zhou Enlai, and others, and the draft party constitution made clear how much the party's structure of power had changed. Mao was fully in charge, and every document and speech included exaggerated praise of his person, leadership, or thoughts. The Cultural Revolution was the centerpiece of the achievements praised in the work report. The Central Cultural Revolution Group was now ranked ahead of both the State Council and the Military Commission in the party's protocol list, and the CRG was Mao's "inner circle," consisting of his wife, *mishu,* and most trusted advisors.[54]

The capstone of the plenum was the approval of the CCEG report on the investigation of Liu Shaoqi. It was a scurrilous document, distorting Liu's activities in the CCP from its earliest days in the 1920s, accusing him of being a "traitor, renegade, scab and running dog of evil imperialists, modern revisionists and Kuomintang reactionaries."[55] But everyone attending knew on the final day of the plenum, Liu's seventieth birthday, when a resolution was introduced to "forever expel Liu Shaoqi from the party and revoke all of his positions inside and outside the party," that they would have to raise a hand in support. Hu Yaobang did so, but was sitting next to a woman named Chen Shaomin, who refused to raise her hand, resting it instead on the table and pretending to be asleep. The vote was announced as unanimous, but some noticed Chen's gesture, and queried her about it. "It's my right," she insisted, earning the admiration of Hu Yaobang and others who regretted being forced to vote against their consciences.

Hu's situation after the Twelfth Plenum was anomalous. He might have expected to be reelected as a member of the Ninth Central Committee at the upcoming congress. But he was told he first had to ingratiate himself with Jiang Qing by making a full confession of his errors, which he was unwilling to do. He had avoided shaking Kang Sheng's hand during a break at the plenum and knew that had been noticed. He was probably grateful to Chairman Mao for continuing to trust him, but was uncertain whether he fully trusted Mao, and was disturbed by the trappings of his personality cult. Hu was allowed to live at his home with his family, but the military representatives still came every day, demanding he write self-examinations, ideological declarations, and evidentiary materials for other investigations.[56]

But Hu Yaobang was not reelected to the Central Committee at the CCP's Ninth National Congress, which met April 1–24, 1969. Lin Biao, Kang Sheng, and Jiang Qing are all cited as having "blocked" Hu from membership. The unspoken truth, however, was that Mao Zedong probably decided against putting Hu on the Central Committee. His reasons are unknown. Mao was the final arbiter on most of the decisions of the Ninth Congress, as in previous Central Committee meetings. He acceded to Lin Biao's nomination of his own cronies to Central Committee and Politburo positions because he needed the army to maintain order in this turbulent phase of the Cultural Revolution. Mao also brought in several of his own supporters to the topmost leadership, including some military region commanders not beholden to Lin. Hu Yaobang was broken and the Communist Youth League was under military control. Mao did not need Hu.

Hu's children have spoken about—but not released the full content of—a letter that Hu Yaobang wrote to Mao in March 1969. The family has chosen to publicize only a few words of this ten-thousand-character memorial (*wanyanshu*). As Hu Deping describes it, his father talked about the inappropriateness of the "Stalinist era planned economy" that China had long copied, particularly its failure to promote agricultural growth or use resources effectively. If Mao read the letter (and it is not certain that he did), he would not have missed the analogy to the Great Leap Forward. More directly, Hu referred to Mao's core teaching—"Never forget the class struggle"—which Hu said he had studied repeatedly but "stubbornly cannot understand."[57] Hu probably knew that such sentiments could cost him a Central Committee position and perhaps his salary and rank as well. He told his family during the party congress, "If you sell your soul for a salary, what is the meaning of living? . . . I can still work, I can feed myself. If I don't have a salary, that is a good thing for my children, they can work hard on their own."[58] So Hu attended the Ninth Congress as a delegate but was dropped from the Central Committee. A few days after the conclave closed, he was sent to a labor camp. And Kang Sheng formally opened a special case file on him.

Lin Biao's Cultural Revolution: Triumph, Failure and Flight

The story of the Cultural Revolution cannot be told fully without factoring in the rise to power, abuse of power, failure, and fall of Lin Biao. But the story of Lin Biao cannot be told in the context of what is publicly known about the Cultural Revolution. The truth of Lin Biao remains in archives that will probably remain sealed as long as the Communist Party of China is in power. His story has been so plastered over with judgments, inaccuracies, and lies designed to blame Lin and exculpate Mao Zedong from the excesses of the Cultural Revolution that it is impossible to say with any certainty who he was, what he accomplished, or even how he died. Lin is frozen in the CCP's dark mirror of its own history, damned as a "conspirator, careerist, counter-revolutionary, and criminal," who "rigged up a counter-revolutionary clique in an attempt to seize supreme power and, taking advantage of Comrade Mao Zedong's errors, committed many crimes behind his back, bringing disaster to the country and the people."[59]

Hu Yaobang witnessed the apogee of Lin Biao's career at the Ninth Congress, when Lin was named in the CCP Constitution as the only vice-chairman of the party and Mao Zedong's legitimate successor. Lin Biao was a natural choice for the seventy-seven-year-old Chairman. Lin had been Mao's principal advocate within the armed forces since replacing Peng Dehuai in 1959. He had come to Mao's defense in 1962, when Liu Shaoqi had sought to reverse Mao's disastrous economic policies. He had built Mao's personality cult within the PLA, ordering millions of copies of the *Little Red Book* of Mao's quotations to be distributed all over China, and pledging that the army would become a "great school for studying Mao Zedong Thought."

Ill and in seclusion for many years, a reluctant participant or nonparticipant in Politburo Standing Committee meetings, Lin came to Mao's aid again in 1966, actively participating in both the May and August party meetings that set the Cultural Revolution in motion.

By early 1967 Mao's Cultural Revolution had plunged the country into chaos. Red Guard and "revolutionary rebel" disputes erupted into armed conflicts all over China after Mao and the CRG called for "seizing power" at all levels. Both in Beijing bureaucracies and in the provinces, party and government leadership dissolved into warring factions, prompting both Mao and Premier Zhou Enlai to call on the only organization that remained able to restore order and provide leadership, the People's Liberation Army. By late 1968 virtually all remaining Central bureaucracies were headed by military control groups, and most of the "revolutionary committees" being formed to replace regional CCP and government organizations were dominated by commanders and political commissars of local PLA units.[60]

The PLA itself was highly factionalized and regionalized, its main armies being divided among eleven large military regions, which Mao sometimes referred to as "independent kingdoms." Its senior officer corps was divided by complex webs of interpersonal relations and local unit loyalties dating back to the civil war and before. Lin Biao made use of his close ties to Mao to sideline several rival "old marshals" who had participated in the "February Countercurrent," even though he shared their revulsion at CRG efforts to promote power seizures in military academies and regional commands. He also used the Special Case Group investigations against his most serious rival, Marshal He Long, and to root out any remaining sympathy for purged Chief of Staff Luo Ruiqing. The CMC Standing Committee had been suspended in mid-1967, replaced by a CMC Administrative Group (*junwei banshi zu*), which Lin staffed with his wife and several cronies.[61]

The period of PLA dominance over Cultural Revolution decisions and actions—from mid-1967 to the Ninth Congress in April 1969—was perhaps the darkest and most violent phase of the Cultural Revolution. The principal targets of the PLA's efforts to "support the left" actually turned out to be the leftist elements that Mao wanted to support. Recent studies of the Cultural Revolution conclude that PLA officers were basically conservative in their outlook, defending order and discipline, and they focused their attacks on those trying to overthrow the status quo, causing thousands of casualties.[62] After the "three supports and two militaries" campaign was started in early 1967, more than 2.8 million PLA officers and fighters were sent out to various localities, ministries, and party departments to form military control groups. They replaced decimated bureaucracies, built workable leadership groups in factionalized units, controlled Red Guard violence, supplemented beleaguered public security forces, and managed the growing number of labor reform camps being established all over China. Their work created resentment and anger everywhere.[63]

During the Cultural Revolution, two new forms of labor reform were devised to deal with those who had fallen from favor: The "up to the mountains and down to the villages" (*shangshan xiaxiang*) or "Rustication of Educated Youth" campaign in late 1968 and the "May 7 Cadre Schools" campaign in early 1969 began to receive large numbers of people displaced by the Cultural Revolution. PLA soldiers played key roles in rounding up, transporting, and enforcing the displacement of as many as seventeen million educated youth, and in transporting and guarding more than one hundred thousand Central CCP and State Council officials who lost their positions in 1968–1969.[64]

The directive creating the cadre schools originated in a letter Mao sent to Lin Biao on May 7, 1966, in response to Lin's plans to make the PLA a "great school for learning Mao Zedong Thought." Mao suggested that the students should also learn politics, military affairs, and culture, and set up small factories and productive enterprises on the side.[65] The idea came to be viewed as a solution to a growing political and logistical problem: the large number of displaced cadres housed in cowsheds in various ministries and departments. They no longer had prospects for employment, as Mao had decided in October 1968 to streamline the party and government, and pressure grew to take decisive action. Mao reportedly believed that 80 to 90 percent of central staffers could be released with no loss of efficiency, and because most of them were intellectuals, and hard labor would do them good.[66]

Many rural areas already were swamped with rusticated youth, and few localities had anything other than undeveloped wasteland on which to build a labor reform facility. But from late 1968 to late 1969, the Center established 106 May 7 Cadre Schools in eighteen provinces, mostly in Henan, Hubei, and Jiangxi. An estimated 100,000 to 135,000 officials, including some family members, were sent to them. By late 1971, after Lin Biao's death, they began to be disestablished, but that process stretched out over several years. Henan Province had the most May 7 facilities, with twenty camps, eight of them in Xinyang Prefecture.[67] Xinyang was still suffering from the catastrophic loss of more than a million of its original eight million residents who starved to death during the Great Leap Forward. There was unutilized land available for labor camps.

On April 15, 1969, some two thousand cadres from the Central Committee of the Communist Youth League began their transport by train and truck to the CYL's May 7 Cadre School at the Huanghu Farm in Huangchuan County, Xinyang Prefecture, Henan. After two or three days of travel, they arrived at what must have seemed like hell on earth. Huanghu Farm had already been a prison labor facility, but it was mostly deserted in 1969. There were no buildings to house the newly arrived cadres, no wells or drinkable water, no sanitary facilities, no hospitals or clinics, no roads or transport, no electricity. Huangchuan is located in the southeast part of Henan, a steam-bath area of high temperatures, high humidity, heavy rainfall, and thick cloud cover. A land of mud and mosquitoes in summer, cold and damp in winter.[68]

Huanghu Farm was run by PLA officers and soldiers as a military facility, with military discipline and order, organized in companies and platoons. Its deputy chief military representative, Zhang Lishun, told his charges the facility had been chosen for its hostile environment and challenging conditions, so they would know that they were no longer "cadres" but "labor reform prisoners," and that they would be there as peasants for the rest of their lives. They were not even permitted to call each other "comrade."[69]

When Hu Yaobang arrived at Huanghu Farm in mid-May, he found his colleagues dispirited and angry. But the military representatives informed him he would not enjoy any privileges of rank or respect for the elderly (Hu was fifty-four). He had no authority in Huanghu. He was there to be investigated and incarcerated. That meant the resumption of his regular routine of writing *jiantao* and "materials." He was there to be reeducated. At first the only books allowed were the *Selected Works* of Marx and Engels, Lenin, and Mao Zedong, each in four volumes. Hu read them by kerosene lamp, late into the evening, taking copious notes. He treated his notebooks like prized possessions, refusing to let anyone else even carry them.[70]

Mostly Hu Yaobang was at Huanghu Farm to do manual labor, which he did with enthusiasm and little complaint. Digging wells, enlarging ponds, building dormitories, hauling stones, transplanting rice, threshing grain, digging irrigation ditches—all the tasks that were required to get a primitive farm into operation, Hu did willingly. He had been a Hunan farm boy once and knew how to work. He even was voted a model laborer by his fellows, but the military representatives refused to allow him to accept the award, due to his status as a capitalist roader. They sometimes gave him extra work or withheld work-saving tools to pressure him to be more cooperative. Hu received thirty yuan per month (about twelve US dollars, at the exchange rate for that era), from which he bought his meals at the cafeteria and his ever-present cigarettes.[71]

Hu Yaobang was older than most of the other prisoners and tired easily. On several occasions he collapsed from exhaustion or heat prostration. Sometimes his labor group overrode military representative objections and gave him lighter work to do. But Hu usually volunteered to do heavier tasks, which made a favorable impression on his CYL colleagues. That impression was magnified by Hu's sense of humor and overall positive outlook. Accounts of his life during this period are replete with anecdotes about how he enjoyed making people laugh, easing their anxieties. And it served to remind them of his leadership, even though he held no formal position.

Hu had learned since the earliest days of the Cultural Revolution that admitting any of the charges leveled against him would not bring relief from the political pressure but simply more bullying and new accusations. So he refused to play the game. He would admit that he had made some mistakes in the course of his seventeen years as head of the Communist Youth League. Earlier he had admitted being a capitalist roader, guilty by association with Deng Xiaoping. After reading through the Marxist canons about capitalism, he decided that charge was spurious and withdrew his earlier statements. The PLA special case group officers wrote a confession for him; all he had to do was to sign it. He refused, offering instead to write his own statement that could be appended to the phony confession and sent forward to the Center for adjudication. No deal.[72] The exhausting labor, the miserable conditions, and his accumulated ailments began to take a toll. He suffered from a prolapsed rectum and painful hemorrhoids. He had a shoulder ailment and serious back pain from transplanting rice. He suffered occasional fainting spells. His malaria returned in the rain and heat, and he lost weight. He contracted hepatitis from the squalid conditions and exhaustion, and there was no medical facility near Huanghu Farm where he could get proper treatment.[73] In the spring of 1971 Hu finally agreed to efforts by friends in Beijing to have him brought back for medical consultations. The deciding factor was a mole on his eyebrow that had become infected and was suppurating. The military representatives at first refused the request, but ultimately allowed him to take family visitation leave.

The trip to Beijing was only a short respite, and he was not able to see any of his children, who could not return home from their own work assignments. By midsummer, he returned to Huanghu Farm.[74] Before his return he managed to make contact by letter with the wife of Premier Zhou Enlai, Deng Yingchao, but was unable to meet with her. After he had returned to Huanghu, she telephoned to speak with him, but the military representatives intercepted the call and passed on her message that she would try to see him the next time he was in Beijing. The military representatives were furious, and probably a bit alarmed, accusing Hu of "indiscipline" for trying to get senior officials to intervene in his case.[75]

There is no record of what else Hu Yaobang may have learned on his brief sojourn in Beijing, but the summer of 1971 was a tense and very strange period of CCP politics, and people must have been talking. While Hu had been sweltering and suffering in southern Henan, elite politics in Beijing also were heating up. Relations between Mao and Lin Biao, the designated successor, his "closest comrade-in-arms," had gone from mutual dependency in 1969 to tense antagonism by 1970.

Mao's relationship with Lin deteriorated further in the lead-up to the Second Plenum of the Ninth Central Committee, which met August 23 to September 6, 1970, at Lushan—where Mao had humiliated Peng Dehuai in 1959. The meeting quickly turned into a power struggle between what remained of Mao's Central CRG and Lin's CMC administrative group. The substantive disagreements involved whether to reestablish the post of state chairman (formerly held by Liu Shaoqi) at the next National People's Congress meeting. Neither Mao nor Lin wanted the job, but also neither wanted the other to have it, despite its being only a ceremonial post. The proxy battle heated up, with Lin's generals supporting the reestablishment of the position, while Zhang Chunqiao and his Shanghai supporters criticized the idea.[76]

Mao also broke with Lin and Chen Boda over the excesses of the personality cult at the Lushan meeting. Mao apparently had begun to feel the constant adulation was unnecessary and theoretically embarrassing. But Lin and Chen had developed a new theory of Mao's "genius" that they wanted the plenum to approve. Lin raised the idea in his opening address, and when Zhang Chunqiao opposed it, Lin's CMC administrative group rose in righteous wrath. But Mao had begun to see the army as too powerful, and at a hastily convened expanded Politburo Standing Committee meeting on August 25 he launched into a tirade against Chen Boda, who had broken with the CRG and openly supported Lin Biao.[77] At the meeting Mao ordered that Chen be "suspended for introspection," while several members of Lin's

CMC administrative group were directed to prepare *jiantao*.[78] Chastened and humiliated, Lin Biao returned with his wife to his Dalian retreat, where he was later reported to be lethargic and unwilling to leave his quarters.[79]

In mid-August 1971 Mao Zedong left Beijing by train on a secret "southern tour" to Wuhan, Changsha, Nanchang, and other places. His purpose was to meet with political allies and military leaders not closely tied to Lin Biao, warn them of likely trouble ahead, and solicit their support. He accused Lin and his CMC administrative group of carrying out secret attacks on the party and of committing "line errors" as serious as those of Liu Shaoqi. Lin heard the news through his own network. Mao returned secretly to Beijing on September 12, evidently concerned about his security.[80]

What happened next remains a series of mysteries, even fifty years later. They began in the early morning of September 13, with the crash of a PRC Air Force Trident transport aircraft near the city of Öndörkhaan in the Mongolian People's Republic. Mongolian government investigators visited the site later that day, ascertained it was a PRC military aircraft, and discovered nine bodies in the wreckage, all burned beyond recognition, some wearing PLA uniforms. They invited officials from the Soviet embassy to view the site, then summoned the PRC ambassador to protest the violation of Mongolian airspace by an unidentified PRC military aircraft. Chinese officials later were allowed to investigate the crash scene, where they took photographs but did not remove any of the bodies. If there was a "black box" flight data recorder on the aircraft, its disposition remains one of the many mysteries about Trident aircraft No. 256. There was no news coverage of the crash for several weeks afterward.[81]

PRC government, party, and military officials had been monitoring the flight since its takeoff from Shanhaiguan Airfield, near Beidaihe, at about 12:30 a.m. Even before they learned the plane had crashed, they began to gather details of what had happened on the ground and wrap them in tight layers of security. They followed up with investigations, arrests, and the crafting of a cover story. Despite the lack of a forensic investigation of the crash site or the victims, the CCP General Office on September 18 issued a highly classified and restricted distribution Central Document, *Zhongfa* [1971] No. 57, titled "Central Committee Notice concerning the Defection and Flight of Lin Biao." The document had few details of the events of September 13. It disclosed that a military helicopter was brought down north of Beijing with conspirators and classified documents aboard, and the fact that Lin Biao's daughter had reported his treachery. The rest was boilerplate praise of Mao and condemnation of Chen Boda and the losers of previous "line struggles."[82]

As a Lin Biao special case group began work in mid-September, more details emerged to build a conspiracy tale about Lin and his family. The principal evidence was a purported plot by Lin Biao's son, Lin Liguo, to assassinate Mao and end the Cultural Revolution. The document "Minutes of the 571 Project," by Lin Liguo, was disclosed to senior party leaders in November 1971, and to a larger audience in early 1972. Lin Liguo's "571 Project" document contained barbed references to Mao as "B-52" and Qin Shi Huang, and speculated about methods to kill him, but the "Minutes" were not a coherent plan, nor was there ever much evidence of it having been put into effect.[83]

Telling an accurate story was hardly the point of what happened after Lin's death, however. Mao's main goal was to recover the political power Lin and his cronies had gained in the chaos of the Cultural Revolution. Decisions happened quickly. On the same morning as Lin's flight, the entire PLA Air Force was grounded, and several of its senior officers were arrested. On September 24, Lin Biao's "four guardian generals" on the CMC administrative group—Huang Yongsheng, Wu Faxian, Li Zuopeng, and Qiu Huizuo—were reported to be "suspended for investigation" and probably were in jail shortly thereafter.[84] Ye Jianying was put in charge of the Central Military Commission's daily work, heading up a CMC office meeting that superseded Lin's CMC administrative office.[85]

What, after all, had happened to Lin Biao? Theories and explanations abound, all based on conflicting evidence, some of it manufactured ex post facto to make Lin's conspiracy look deeper or make Mao look more clear-sighted. After the Ninth Congress the Mao-Lin relationship had deteriorated rapidly into what noted historian Gao Hua described as "completely a contest for power."[86] Mao had given Lin a ceremonial title as successor, but little real power, and by late 1969 Mao began planning to bring him down. Lin Biao and his wife feared and despised Mao, but seemed prepared to wait the old man out. When Mao's plans to oust and humiliate Lin became clear at the Second Plenum, Lin retreated but rebuffed Mao's demand that he confess his errors.

Ill and depressed, Lin may indeed have decided to flee. Yet there is no compelling reason to believe the official account of Lin Biao's last hours— that he hastily boarded the Trident aircraft along with his wife and son and other staffers after a dramatic shootout with PLA troops on the drive from

Beidaihe to Shanhaiguan; that the aircraft did not have enough fuel to reach its destination in the Soviet Union and crashed in the Mongolian desert trying to make an emergency landing. That account is contradicted by the Mongolian government's forensic report, which concluded that the crash probably was caused by "pilot error," given that the aircraft hit the ground traveling at six hundred kilometers per hour with landing gear up and engines at full speed. Moreover, the explosion following impact was substantial and long in duration, indicating the plane was not short of fuel.[87]

It is difficult to discount the suspicions of several prominent contemporary PRC historians, such as Han Gang, Wang Haiguang, Yang Jisheng, and others that the full story has not yet been told and might never be. That leads to the possibility that Mao Zedong and Zhou Enlai may have been complicit in the death of Lin Biao, if not directly responsible. Several historians and conspiracy theorists have speculated on scenarios, but none are verifiable in the present circumstances.

Jiang Qing and Deng Xiaoping's Cultural Revolution: Dyslexic Politics

Lin Biao's prominent role in supporting Mao's Cultural Revolution came to a fiery end in the Mongolian desert, and so did the Cultural Revolution itself as a viable mass movement. Much of the content of Mao's personality cult was tied to Lin: The *Little Red Book,* the theory of Mao's genius, Lin as the "closest comrade-in-arms" and successor, and so on. It all disappeared as the regime began to cleanse Mao and the Cultural Revolution of any association with Lin Biao. Some Chinese hoped that the country could now begin returning to some semblance of normal life: factories and schools opening, government offices functioning, transportation running, leisure activities returning, political campaigns abating.[88]

Zhou Enlai was in the unenviable position of having to put together a recovery plan for the wobbling economy, restore a workable coalition within the divided CCP leadership, and create a credible public account of Lin Biao's perfidy. He also had to manage a high-stakes visit from US president Richard M. Nixon. Zhou handled these tasks deftly, but at great personal cost. First, he again incurred the attention and jealousy of Mao. Second, he was diagnosed in May 1972 with bladder cancer, which was in an early stage that doctors thought curable.

However, any medical report on a Politburo leader required Mao's approval—the obligatory *pishi*—even before it could be delivered to the patient. Mao instructed the doctors not to tell Zhou or his wife about his condition, to make no further examinations, and to avoid surgery in favor of improved nutrition.[89]

In late 1971, Mao himself was in very poor health, according to his doctor, Li Zhisui. At seventy-eight he had aged visibly; he stooped over and walked with a shuffle. Pneumonia, high blood pressure, and depression had combined to keep him bedridden for several weeks following the Lin Biao affair. He began rousing himself only when the impending Nixon visit in early 1972 induced a change in his attitude toward foreign and domestic policy, and toward his health.[90] In early January Mao attended the funeral of Chen Yi, one of the "old marshals" he had sidelined in 1967, making a show of mourning. He hinted that Deng Xiaoping, Chen's civil war comrade-in-arms, might be exonerated from his disgrace, a message Zhou Enlai reportedly welcomed.[91]

Although branded early in the Cultural Revolution as the "number 2 capitalist roader in the party" after Liu Shaoqi, Deng Xiaoping had been protected by Mao from the kinds of physical abuse Liu suffered. He had been publicly humiliated, dragged out for struggle with his wife, and his house had been invaded by Red Guards. Far worse, one of his sons had been crippled in 1968 after he jumped (or was pushed) from a fourth-floor window at Beijing University to escape Red Guard interrogation, breaking his spine. Mao refused to allow Deng to be "forever expelled from the party" in 1968, as Liu Shaoqi had been. After the Ninth Congress, Deng was sent to rural Jiangxi for labor reform, but in conditions far more comfortable than Hu Yaobang's. Deng lived in a two-story courtyard home with his wife, and his children were allowed to visit for extended periods.[92]

After word reached him of Lin Biao's death, Deng wrote a letter to Mao through Wang Dongxing, praising the Chairman's "wisdom" in unmasking Lin's betrayal. He thanked Mao for the opportunity to "reform himself" through labor and study and hoped he could have a chance to "do a little work for the party" at some future date. But it was not until Deng wrote an even more self-abasing letter in August, admitting he had "put forward a counterrevolutionary reactionary bourgeois line together with Liu Shaoqi" and that he had been "saved" by the Cultural Revolution, that the Chairman considered bringing him back to Beijing.[93]

Mao needed Deng more than he would have admitted. In late 1971 and early 1972 Mao's political position was the worst it had been in several years. The CCP was nearly an empty shell, noisy and incompetent. Lin Biao had died a disloyal traitor; Zhou Enlai was old, sick, and distrusted. Two of the five members of the Standing Committee were dead or disgraced, and eight of twenty-five members or alternate members of the Politburo had been removed. The PLA was carrying out yet another sweeping purge of its senior officers under Ye Jianying, arresting or suspending hundreds of officers who were implicated in Lin Liguo's plot or who, for other reasons, had stood on Lin Biao's side politically.[94]

The security apparatus was in tattered condition. Minister of Public Security Xie Fuzhi had gone along with the Cultural Revolution Group's late 1966 call to "smash" the Public Security Ministry and the public prosecutorial and court systems, arresting or suspending thousands of national and provincial-level police officers, an action that Mao said made him "happy."[95] Military control groups stepped in to replace them in 1968, but public order continued to deteriorate. Xie Fuzhi was sidelined by cancer in 1970 and died in early 1972, precipitating further shakeups in the public security system. Kang Sheng, who oversaw the security apparatus for the Politburo Standing Committee, also fell ill with cancer in 1970 and made few public appearances.

The CRG was rendered irrelevant when Mao turned against Chen Boda at the Second Plenum. He ordered the establishment in October 1970 of a Central Organization and Propaganda Group, headed by Kang Sheng, with principal members being Jiang Qing, Zhang Chunqiao, and Yao Wenyuan. In addition to what remained of the Central Organization Department, all the major CCP media outlets were put under the new group's supervision. With Kang Sheng's serious illness, the new group was under Jiang Qing's control, meaning under Mao's unsteady direction.[96]

In some ways the political struggles of the post–Lin Biao period resolved themselves into a line struggle for two sides of Chairman Mao's personality: pragmatic realist and leader of his country versus vengeful revolutionary and destroyer of conventions. These two contrasting visions were reflected in the factional alignments that divided the CCP in the last five years of Mao's life: Zhou Enlai and Deng Xiaoping, supported by PLA veterans and party stalwarts, versus Jiang Qing and what would be called the Gang of Four, supported by those who had benefited from the Cultural Revolution. In the early 1970s Mao may have been able to manipulate and balance these two factions within the CCP leadership, but that facility declined with his health as the decade wore on.

Central politics after the Lin Biao incident shrank down to personal struggles within the confines of Zhongnanhai and Diaoyutai, the principal residential and office complexes for the senior leadership. Larger issues of policy and performance—especially conditions in the countryside and economic issues—got lost in the noise of left versus right ideological battles. Mostly, it was pure power politics, zero-sum, malicious, and usually decided by Mao. The first of the showdowns began with deciding on how to carry out the required mass campaign to criticize Lin Biao—Was he a leftist or a rightist? The answer had little to do with Lin Biao or his actions and attitudes, and much to do with the factional alignments after his death.

During this period of rising factional tensions Hu Yaobang had quietly returned home to recuperate, per Zhou Enlai's instructions. He returned to his home at No. 6 Fuqiang Hutong in October 1972 to find it nearly empty, the only resident being his mother-in-law, who was in failing health. His wife had returned from her own ministry's May 7 Cadre School but was not living at home, and his three sons and his daughter were scattered around to different schools and military units. Hu checked into the Peace Hospital for surgery to remove the infected mole, losing half his right eyebrow in the process, then returned home.

Hu was "liberated" from the cadre school, but far from free. He was still in the hands of a Central special case group, which seemed prepared to offer him a low-level position in Ningxia in exchange for him either writing a *jiantao* or signing the one they had prepared for him. Hu refused to sign it and attached his own statement to include with the report. In Beijing he was called to CYL headquarters—which was firmly under leftist control—and pressured again about the statement. Special case investigators came to his house to demand that he expose former colleagues and provide evidence against others. He refused, at times with great anger. The Ningxia offer disappeared.

But Hu kept himself busy. He went out walking, but hesitated to call on old friends, knowing he was an object of suspicion. He didn't invite them to his home, but when they came anyway, he welcomed them, and they talked at length about politics.[97] Before the Cultural Revolution, Hu had been well-known for inviting colleagues to his home for meals and talk, but now the foot traffic to his door aroused suspicion. Politburo member Ji Dengkui came to visit Hu and warned him there were "too many people" visiting his house.[98]

The new CYL leaders charged that he was organizing a "dark society" in his home, implying he was plotting against the party Center.[99]

Mostly Hu spent his time reading. "Reading is what I spend most of my money on, it is my greatest desire and pleasure," he told friends and family.[100] No longer in a world devoid of books, Hu read everything he could lay his hands on: Marxist classics, Chinese dynastic histories, ancient and modern literature, translated works of Shakespeare and Tolstoy, philosophy and ethics, and science and technology. He even studied English. Hu's tastes were eclectic, but his appetite for knowledge was voracious and his reading habits were disciplined—he kept a daily count of the number of characters he read.[101] Many of these he discussed with Hu Deping, who had studied history and literature at Beida.

But often Hu Yaobang would sit alone on a sofa, smoking one cigarette after another, trying to sort through his experiences and what he was reading. There are no diaries or notebooks or letters to help understand Hu's thoughts or conclusions during this period, although a few reactions to conversations with old friends or the children of old friends have been published. His biographers—some of whom had been with him for many years—maintain that Hu began to reach conclusions during this period that he subsequently would put into practice. Their observations are subjective, but probably accurate.

Hu's personal experience from Xiangtan in 1962 to his release from labor camp in 1972 was of being under near-constant political attack and criticism. His work focus had been on restoring production and improving the livelihood of the common people. The Center's constant concentration on class struggle and political campaigns one after another had not improved the lot of Chinese people, or the PRC's position in the world. Hu seems to have concluded that the party was at fault for this—that "inner party struggle" and the absence of "normal democratic life" had facilitated toadyism, personal dictatorship, and wrong-headed policies that failed. Countless party cadres had been punished, jailed, disabled, and killed, their families scattered, because of the distortion of proper party norms and procedures.[102]

Hu also began to manifest a sense of ambivalence about Mao during this period. He found the personality cult that had built up around Mao to be repugnant and misguided. But he was still under Mao's spell. He still wanted to see the Chairman. He told Ji Dengkui in 1972 that he was prepared to take any position the party offered, but that he wanted to see Chairman Mao before he accepted the transfer. As Hu Deping related his father's request, Hu

Yaobang seemed to have thought that he could reason with Mao, talk him out of some of the Cultural Revolution policies that had been so damaging. But he also feared that if he accepted a position far from Beijing, he might never see the Chairman again.[103] In any case, he was not allowed to see Mao. Ji Dengkui probably saw to that. Mao did not need to see Hu Yaobang.

Meanwhile, Deng Xiaoping had languished, waiting for Mao to make a decision on his petition to return. Finally, in March 1973, Mao approved Zhou Enlai's proposal to bring Deng back to serve as a vice-premier responsible for foreign policy, but not to his military positions. Deng made his first public appearance in seven years in late March, and in April he began to take Zhou Enlai's place at functions with foreign visitors.[104]

Mao was beginning to lose his ability to communicate orally because of congestive heart failure and what his doctors believed was amyotrophic lateral sclerosis.[105] But he still could use his remaining institutional powers to patch together a party leadership group he expected to control. The month after Deng's return, Mao convened a CCP work conference in Beijing at which he secured a resolution authorizing three regional leaders supportive of the Cultural Revolution to attend Politburo meetings: Wang Hongwen, of Shanghai "January Storm" renown; Hua Guofeng, Mao's trusted champion (and Hu Yaobang's old subordinate) from Hunan Province; and Wu De, who had been in the Beijing party apparatus since 1966.

The Tenth Party Congress, held in August 1973, was a significant advance for Mao and his leftist allies. Wang Hongwen was "helicoptered" to the post of vice-chairman of the CCP, ranking number 3 behind Zhou Enlai. Li Desheng—already head of the PLA's General Political Department and the Beijing Military Region—was added to the Politburo Standing Committee, along with Kang Sheng, Ye Jianying, and Zhang Chunqiao. Mao maintained effective control of the Standing Committee, which now numbered nine members. In the new CCP leadership announced at the First Plenum, the PLA lost many of the positions it had held on the Ninth Politburo.[106] Deng Xiaoping returned to the Central Committee but not to the Politburo. While several "old veterans" were restored to Central Committee rank, Hu Yaobang was not one of them.

Despite their political gains, the leftists squandered their opportunities in 1973–1974, which frustrated Mao. The three Shanghai leaders and Jiang Qing spent most of their time together, made little effort to work with other members of the party or State Council leadership, quarreled with Politburo rivals, disrupted meetings, and seized documents. Mao was particularly unhappy with Wang Hongwen. Handsome, vigorous, and possessed of peasant, worker, and soldier credentials, Wang was in no way prepared or qualified to fulfill his duties as party vice-chairman. When Zhou Enlai was hospitalized in June 1974, Mao entrusted "managing the work of the Center" to Wang. But Wang had no network of support in Beijing, had little knowledge of domestic or foreign affairs, didn't pay attention to briefings, and made embarrassing mistakes in front of foreign visitors. He was no match for Deng Xiaoping, who had stepped into Zhou Enlai's roles easily, with Zhou's assistance from the hospital where Deng and Ye Jianying visited him regularly.[107]

In late December, Zhou Enlai got out of his hospital bed to fly down to Changsha with Wang Hongwen to present their views to Mao on the policy and personnel arrangements for the Fourth National People's Congress. They consulted with Mao for two days, resulting in yet another change in Mao's succession plans and overall policy direction. Mao reiterated his approval for Deng to be appointed first vice-premier, but more importantly, for him to be promoted to the Politburo Standing Committee, to be vice-chairman of the party, a vice-chairman of the Central Military Commission, and chief of the PLA General Staff.[108] To retain the overall political balance within the leadership, Mao approved the appointment of Wang Hongwen to the CMC Standing Committee, and the elevation of Zhang Chunqiao to be director of the PLA General Political Department. He also approved Zhang's appointment as second vice-premier. These decisions were all approved at the Second Plenum of the Tenth CCP Congress, which met in Beijing (without Mao) in early January 1975.[109]

On January 17 the long-delayed Fourth National People's Congress was held in Beijing. Zhou Enlai himself delivered the work report, which called for a program to "comprehensively improve" China's economy by 1980, and to achieve the "four modernizations"—of agriculture, industry, military production, and science and technology—by the turn of the century. Zhou's appeal was enthusiastically welcomed. After the meeting Zhou returned to the hospital, and Deng Xiaoping took over the work of the State Council. In February the CMC Standing Committee formally resumed operation, with Ye Jianying and Deng Xiaoping in charge of military affairs. In June, Mao Zedong in Changsha approved Deng to replace Zhou in presiding over Politburo meetings, meaning that Deng was the "number one hand" (*diyi ba shou*) in all three of the PRC's major bureaucracies.[110]

In April, Mao returned to Beijing and seemed determined to play the role of factional balancer. Zhang Chunqiao and Yao Wenyuan had written articles and given speeches that were thinly disguised attacks on Deng Xiaoping and other old cadres. For his part, Deng began calling for "rectification" of the party, beginning with leadership groups in every unit. This suggested that an extensive purge might be in the offing, especially of younger cadres who came up during the Cultural Revolution.[111]

Deng wasted little time in trying to get the State Council and the party Center back onto a productive course, promoting the "four modernizations." But he had to deal with rectification of leadership groups first. "Those who cling to factionalism should be transferred to other posts, criticized or struggled against whenever necessary," he told a work conference on the steel industry in May 1975. "We should not drag things out and wait forever."[112] Deng needed theoretical and intellectual capital to withstand leftist attacks coming from Jiang Qing's propaganda apparatus, so he established a six-person Political Research Office in the State Council. It was headed by Hu Qiaomu, formerly one of Mao's *mishu* and an established writer of party documents. Deng also needed tested administrators with the toughness to stand up to political pressure.

Reenter Hu Yaobang

In late 1973 Mao Zedong had recommended that the Center establish a high-level reading class for new Central committee members, provincial and military leaders, and "liberated" veteran cadres awaiting work assignments. These four-month courses began in October 1973 under the auspices of the Central Party School and the Organization Department (both overseen by Kang Sheng and Jiang Qing). The curriculum was a combination of Marxist classics, selections of Mao's works, and articles on current ideological issues. Each class had fifty to sixty students, with Central Party School faculty leading smaller discussion groups.[113]

Hu was called to attend the fourth reading class in March 1975 and was pleased to participate. He had been busy reading Marxist classics ever since his return from the May 7 Cadre School. He enthusiastically joined in discussions and occasionally led them, helping some of the older participants understand basic principles of political philosophy. Even younger students found his remarks insightful, provocative, and sometimes humorous. Of course, all students' comments and writings were reported to the reading class supervisors in the Organization Department. At the end of the course, Hu handed in a lengthy summary of the course readings, addressed to Chairman Mao and the party Center.[114] He was given a special commendation, and his summary apparently was circulated to some senior leaders, including Ye Jianying.

Deng Xiaoping delivered a graduation address to Class 4 in the Great Hall of the People on July 4, 1975, which was attended by Ye Jianying and other senior leaders. Ye invited Hu to sit in the front row so he could hear and see better, praising his course summary. After that event, Ye recommended Hu to Deng for a position in the leadership. Deng took the advice and submitted Hu's name to Mao for approval as a State Council official.[115]

On July 17 Hu was summoned to Zhongnanhai to meet with Vice-Premier Hua Guofeng, who asked him to report immediately to the Chinese Academy of Sciences (CAS), where he was to carry out a rectification program under Deng Xiaoping's orders. His titles were "responsible person of the CAS Party Committee and Vice President of the Academy." His initial instructions were to reorganize the CCP apparatus, restore normal operations to CAS institutes, preserve "stability and unity," and resolutely combat factionalism. In the shortest possible time, Hu was to deliver to the State Council a situation report on CAS, a restoration plan, and a list of "core" members of a new leadership team.[116]

The task was formidable. During the Cultural Revolution the academy had been devastated, due to its scholarly composition, technical expertise, and numerous scholars with degrees and training from foreign universities and foreign friendships and contacts. Its president since 1949, Guo Moruo, had been humiliated by Red Guards and remained seriously ill and inactive. By 1975 only 40 of CAS's original 106 institutes were still in operation (most jointly with the PLA). According to some accounts, 229 CAS researchers had been "persecuted to death." Elderly scientists were working as manual laborers in the institutes, many were in jail. "Rebel faction" researchers or students dominated what work was being done within CAS, rejecting so-called expert credentials in favor of revolutionary experience, promoting "open door management" of research laboratories and scientific research aimed at rural villages.[117]

Hu was less than certain that he was the right person for the job. "Who am I?" he asked some CAS subordinates. "I graduated from elementary school and was in lower middle school for half a year. I am basically unsuited,

I have no foundation whatever in natural science." But he said he had determination and vowed to "shed old knowledge" to take aboard new scientific ideas.[118]

Hu showed up at CAS on July 22 along with his former Communist Youth League subordinate Li Chang. He would soon add several other former CYL staffers (including Hu Keshi) to his leadership team, assigning them tasks that would leave him time to do institute investigations. He was mindful of the "rebel faction" leaders who still oversaw much of the academy's work. But being Hu Yaobang, he could not resist the temptation to speak his mind on the issues, inserting his own brand of humor. Scoffing at the notion of "open door management" of laboratories, he asked if people thought the Beijing nuclear energy and weapons production facilities should be managed with open doors. As for running the institutes for peasant villages, Hu responded: "The Academy of Sciences is the Academy of Sciences, not the . . . vegetable institute or the potato institute; the Academy of Science does science, it does natural science."[119]

By August 1 he had drawn together a five-member team to begin drafting a summary work report for the State Council. All were staffers he brought in with him—no radical leaders were included. He gave the team one week to complete a preliminary draft, based on a six-part outline he had prepared.[120] The report would affirm that CAS's work since 1949 was basically good, and that most of its personnel were loyal. The two principal tasks were reorganizing leadership groups in the research institutes and getting them back to doing work in science and technology (S&T) instead of arguing over ideological issues. The draft also covered the use of intellectuals in S&T work, and logistical issues like providing housing and services to CAS personnel and reuniting separated families.[121]

On August 12, in a conversation between Hu and Deng on the draft document, Deng said it was "very good" but needed to focus more on solving CAS leadership problems, especially factionalism. Three days later, after Hu had submitted a revised draft, Deng circulated the document to some of his own advisors, including Hu Qiaomu. Deng said he wanted to "grind off the sharp edges" of the Outline Report draft, and appointed Hu Qiaomu to take responsibility for the writing from that point forward.[122]

Relieved of direct responsibility for the draft, Hu Yaobang continued his investigations of CAS facilities, and began giving hard-hitting speeches at each venue about the rectification process. He stressed the urgent need for putting S&T development ahead of politics, putting talented scientists back

to work, and emphasizing "expert" as being equal to "red." "If we don't succeed at science & technology, it's not just a mistake, it's a crime." "If we don't
accomplish the 'Four Modernizations,' our grandchildren and followers will
curse us!"[123] Hu's respect and support for knowledge and science were genuine, and he had never subscribed to Mao's view that intellectuals could not
be trusted, much less the more leftist perspective that advanced degrees and
foreign contacts automatically made one a class enemy. Now with an opportunity to restore the reputations of large numbers of intellectuals, Hu responded with characteristic enthusiasm and rhetorical zest.

Hu's remarks stirred controversy, and thus caused Deng some alarm. On
July 26 Deng instructed Hu Qiaomu to telephone Hu Yaobang and warn him
against making so many speeches. The elder Hu admonished Hu Yaobang
to be patient, wait until the draft Outline Report had been revised, approved
by the State Council, and reviewed by Mao, before going to the masses to
hear their views. He encouraged Hu Yaobang to talk about the principles of
the report, but not to be "too sharp."[124] Hu Yaobang ignored him, making
another provocative speech to the CAS Institute of Computing that same
afternoon. The next morning Deng summoned Hu Yaobang to his office for
what must have been a frosty meeting. Staring angrily, Deng told him, "Be
more careful, a little steadier." And he warned him severely that if he was
going to get the masses involved, he had better make sure he could control
the situation.

Hu Qiaomu continued to revise the Outline Report extensively, changing
the title and removing much of Hu Yaobang's "sharp" content. He evidently
believed the draft document would be more palatable to Mao Zedong if he
added some quotations from the Chairman, and so he interspersed several
into the text. Two more drafts and many consultations later, the "Outline Report on the Work of the Chinese Academy of Sciences" was ready for presentation to the State Council. Deng was very satisfied with it. Hu Yaobang
presented the initial briefing to the assembled vice-premiers and ministers
on September 26, during which an ebullient Deng interrupted with supportive commentary. Then he gave his own hard-hitting speech on the importance of scientific research. The State Council approved the report in
principle.

After more edits to incorporate points from Deng's speech, Hu Qiaomu
finished the fifth draft of the Outline Report and had it sent to Mao Zedong,
not in his own name or that of the Political Research Office, but in the names
of Hu Yaobang and two subordinate officials. While Hu reportedly was

pleased the report was done, he was irritated about how the drafting process had been handled and thought the inclusion of quotations from Chairman Mao was unnecessary.[125] Hu's premonition turned out to be correct. By mid-October, Deng still had not received the report back and was worried Mao might disapprove it.

On October 24 Deng summoned Hu Qiaomu and told him that Mao wanted the report changed, which Hu was willing to do. But in the few days it took him to make the corrections, Deng came under a comprehensive leftist attack, and the report was never completed. It seems one of the quotations gleaned from Mao's work was from 1963, when he approved a report saying that "science and technology are productive forces." Deng had bold-faced the quote in the report and expanded the point in his speech, saying that S&T workers and scientists were part of the working class and not targets of the dictatorship of the proletariat. Mao claimed he could not remember ever saying so and disagreed with the idea.[126]

Since May, Deng had moved very fast and pushed very hard to turn the PRC away from the disastrous course of the Cultural Revolution. He had presided over Politburo and State Council meetings at a rapid pace, to the point that Jiang Qing complained she could not keep up with the documents.[127] He made important speeches on each of the four modernizations. The capstone of his policy program was a summary of Mao's recent instructions that Deng referred to as the "Three Instructions," which were to be taken as the guiding principle, or "key link" for the work of the entire party and government. The three instructions were (1) maintain stability and unity (that is, resist factionalism), (2) boost the national economy, and (3) study the theory of the dictatorship of the proletariat to oppose and prevent revisionism. Deng used these to support his push for overall rectification of the party.[128]

Deng may have believed, after seeing the state of Mao's health at the May 1975 Politburo meeting, that the old man did not have the energy to pay careful attention to the details of Politburo power politics. At eighty-two, Mao was suffering from further deterioration of his eyesight, muscular control, and heart and lung functions. He was unable to move on his own, and his speech was so impaired by ALS that only his longtime paramour and caretaker, Zhang Yufeng, could understand him, which she did by reading his lips.[129] Mao was alert, interested in what was going on within the leadership, but access to him was strictly limited by his medical staff and his Central Guards unit, headed by Wang Dongxing.

In late September Mao's nephew Mao Yuanxin entered the scene, facilitating a crucial change in the Chairman's attitude toward Deng and his rectification program. Mao Yuanxin was the son of Mao Zedong's younger brother, Mao Zemin, who had been killed by Xinjiang warlords in 1942. Mao Yuanxin came to Beijing in 1949 to live with his uncle and aunt and became very close to both of them, calling Jiang Qing "mama." Mao Zedong treated him like a son, especially after his own son was killed in Korea. Mao Yuanxin had been a rebel faction activist in the PLA during the Cultural Revolution, moving rapidly up the ranks on his uncle's eminence, becoming deputy political commissar of the Shenyang Military Region in the early 1970s. Although his visit to Beijing was intended only as a stopover, Mao Zedong discovered not only that his nephew could still understand his speech, but that he was politically astute, and he asked his views on several issues.[130]

Mao Yuanxin used the opportunity to stir some of the doubts his uncle had long held about Deng. He told the elder Mao that he had paid careful attention to Deng's recent speeches, and found little praise for the Cultural Revolution, or class struggle, no criticism of Liu Shaoqi or revisionism. People feared a restoration of the old order, he warned. Mao Zedong changed his mind yet again. By the time Mao Yuanxin returned to Beijing en route back to Shenyang on October 10, his uncle had already made the arrangements and gotten Politburo approval for him to be officially designated as the Chairman's "liaison person" with the CCP's highest leadership.[131]

The importance of Mao Yuanxin's role became evident in mid-October, when Mao Zedong—his views of Deng hardening—instructed his nephew to help Deng "turn the corner" on the Cultural Revolution by meeting privately with him and criticizing him so he could mend his ways. Deng rejected the criticism, insisting that the policies he had pursued were in line with the Chairman's instructions.[132]

A similar meeting with a few more Politburo members received a similar rebuff from Deng, but Deng gave Mao Yuanxin a written self-criticism to take to the Chairman. Not mollified, Mao Zedong instructed that a full Politburo meeting be held, and that Mao Yuanxin be authorized to attend and speak for him—a remarkable breach of precedent. The agenda would be preparation of a Central Committee resolution on the Cultural Revolution, and Deng was to officiate. The resolution would affirm the Cultural Revolution as basically correct, but insufficient. It could be evaluated as 70 percent achievements and 30 percent mistakes. This was a bottom-line issue for Mao, and having Deng oversee a party document that affirmed the Cultural Revolution was a way of getting him to declare his allegiance to Mao and his legacy. But Deng was reluctant.[133]

Attention then turned to Deng's principal subordinates, such as Hu Yaobang and Li Chang in the CAS, Education Minister Zhou Rongxin, and Political Research Office director Hu Qiaomu. On November 13 Mao suggested (through his nephew) that these men also needed the kind of "help" that Deng was getting. He also proposed holding a special meeting to "sound an alert" for them and other returned old cadres, so they could "avoid mistakes" in their understanding of the Cultural Revolution.

The following day Deng Xiaoping convened a State Council meeting to criticize the initiatives he himself had sponsored in education and science and technology, with the targets of the alert in attendance. On November 15 Deng oversaw a full Politburo meeting to hear further criticism. The leftist faction, including Wang Hongwen, who had just returned from Shanghai, furiously denounced Hu Yaobang and the Outline Report, so much so that the meeting was continued to the next day. At that second session, Hu and the others were given an opportunity to "acknowledge their mistakes." Several did, with the kind of bowing and scraping expected. Hu Yaobang, however, was defiant. "I have some opinions," he began. "Last night, Vice Chairman Wang Hongwen said several things about me, and I hereby solemnly declare that I don't have the problems he said I have, [that] what he says I said, I did not say, and I ask the Center for verification." His unexpected boldness silenced the room and probably cost him what little chance he had of saving the CAS post he had just been confirmed in two weeks before.[134]

Deng Xiaoping's ordeals continued, although he seemed to understand he had lost the Chairman's trust and prepared himself and his followers for the consequences. He wrote a letter to Mao suggesting that Wang Hongwen take over the task of presiding over major party meetings, but Mao demurred.[135] Deng consulted other party elders, who recommended that he accede to the Chairman's demand that he supervise a resolution evaluating the Cultural Revolution. But Deng insisted it was not "appropriate."[136] He gave another written self-examination to Mao Yuanxin, and worked with the Politburo to come up with a list of 136 officials to be invited to attend the next "alert" meeting, and a set of talking points to be used. The meeting took place on November 24, attended by all the principal leaders of provinces, military regions, ministries, and CCP departments. But no one had much to say, and Deng was angry and silent after reading Mao's amendments to the talking points.[137]

Mao finally decided Deng had to be publicly criticized, as the "leftists" had been demanding for months. After hearing from his nephew about the lackluster alert meeting, Mao authorized Qinghua and Beijing Universities to begin a large-scale "big character poster" campaign to criticize Deng. Central guidance was sent out in early December and repeated a month later.[138]

Deng Xiaoping was ordered to preside over the December Politburo meetings at which he was criticized by Jiang Qing and others. He sat in stony silence. For some of the sessions, Deng was accompanied by Hu Yaobang, Zhou Rongxin, Wan Li (who oversaw the Ministry of Railways), and Zhang Aiping (from the National Defense Science & Technology Commission), who were considered strong supporters. Unlike Deng, they had been formally suspended from their positions.

Hu Yaobang was subjected to active criticism at the Chinese Academy of Sciences, but even though these sessions were stressful and humiliating, they were not like the ordeals he had suffered earlier in the Cultural Revolution. He was not incarcerated or beaten. His accusers were shrill, but sometimes found themselves unable to generate much interest among the CAS scientists and researchers. Hu was permitted to live at home and was transported to the institutes to undergo the dreary routine of interrogation, criticism, and struggle.[139] As before, Hu resisted the accusations and defended his record by insisting he was doing what the Chairman had approved. Slowly but surely, however, Hu became mildly depressed, and his health problems returned.

1976—The Last Acts of the Tragedy

On January 8, 1976, Zhou Enlai died after a long and painful struggle against his metastasizing cancers. The public announcement of his death the next day plunged the country into deep sadness, even though his death was expected. Public mourning of the esteemed premier outside of official venues was forbidden. Deng was called upon to organize the funeral arrangements, including a formal ceremony on January 15, where he read the eulogy. Mao Zedong did not attend, which Zhou's biographer, Gao Wenqian, asserts was not because of ill health—the official explanation—but because of his long-standing jealousy of and antipathy toward Zhou.[140] TV coverage of Zhou's memorial rites was limited, and even the official film of the events was suppressed for a year, due to leftist dominance of propaganda. Nonetheless, there was heavy attendance at public memorial events for Zhou, and hundreds of thousands lined the streets of Beijing to pay respects to the fallen premier on the evening of January 11, when his remains were taken by motorcade to Babaoshan Revolutionary Cemetery for cremation.[141] Hu Yaobang attended the memorial service. Hu had never worked much with Zhou, and although he was grateful for Zhou's assistance in getting him out of the May 7 Cadre School, there was no evident personal bond between them.

But the rapidity of Deng Xiaoping's (and his own) fall from grace must have been a shock to Hu. Politburo-level criticism of Deng resumed shortly after the memorial service, Deng's *jiantao* letters to Mao through Mao Yuanxin were deemed unsatisfactory, and the Chairman refused to see him. On January 20, therefore, Deng submitted his resignation from all his positions. The following day, after consulting with Mao Yuanxin, Mao Zedong directed that Hua Guofeng be appointed "acting premier" and that Deng continue supervising foreign affairs.[142] In early February, Hua Guofeng's promotion was officially announced through party channels, and Beijing Military Region commander and vice-premier Chen Xilian was placed in charge of the day-to-day affairs of the Central Military Commission, replacing Ye Jianying, who was said to be ill.[143]

Hua Guofeng was an unknown to Chinese and foreign observers alike and was considered a compromise choice. But he was Mao's choice, based upon many years of observation of Hua's steady oversight of Mao's home village and prefecture in Hunan, his firm handling of the Lin Biao investigation, and his cautious resolution of serious morale problems in the Ministry of Public Security. Hua was hardly ready, however, for the expression of public opinion on the streets of Beijing in early April 1976. As the Qingming Festival—a tradition of sweeping the tombs of ancestors and paying respects to the dead—approached, many ordinary citizens began placing poems or wreaths around the Monument to the People's Heroes in Tiananmen Square. Most honored the memory of Zhou Enlai, whose death in January had not been appropriately commemorated. Some were unhappy with the low-key ceremony; others took umbrage at leftist media articles in March that were indirectly critical of Zhou and his legacy. Many were offended by the abrupt manner of Deng Xiaoping's dismissal, and some directed their rage at the "new Empress Dowager," Jiang Qing.[144]

Public anger was seething and the crowds gathering in Tiananmen Square numbered in the hundreds of thousands when Hua Guofeng convened the

Politburo on April 4 to decide on a course of action. Ye Jianying and Li Xi-annian were absent, but Mao Yuanxin was there to hear Jiang Qing demand that the thousands of wreaths and other memorials be cleared away before daybreak. Hua concurred and instructed Beijing secretary Wu De to have the offending items removed, which was done early in the morning of April 5.[145]

Later that morning, angry crowds gathered to demand the return of their wreaths and memorabilia, and small disturbances broke out near the Great Hall of the People. Reports from other PRC cities indicated discontent was spreading and becoming more intense. Yang Jisheng claims that the demonstrations were the accumulation of discontents among virtually every segment of society—workers, peasants, intellectuals, students, cadres, even soldiers—with the politicization of everything, the inefficiencies and shortages in the economy, and the misery of everyday life. The Politburo ordered militia and Beijing Garrison units to clear Tiananmen Square in the evening of April 5. Although the troops and police prudently waited until large crowds had retreated and only a few thousand remained, there was still resistance, many arrests, and some injuries.[146]

Mao Yuanxin told his uncle it was a "counterrevolutionary mutiny" backed by Deng Xiaoping, and Jiang Qing insisted that Mao expel Deng from the party, which he refused to do. Instead Mao called on the Politburo to remove Deng from all his positions but allow him to retain party membership "to see how he behaves." Mao proposed that Hua Guofeng become premier and first vice-chairman of the CCP. Mao Yuanxin showed the Politburo the Chairman's written instructions on the morning of April 7, and it obediently voted its agreement. Not having heard or seen any of the demonstrations, Mao Zedong made the definitive judgment on their nature, intent, and political backing. Not having any leadership or power to question Mao's judgment, even delivered at second hand, the Politburo went along, setting off a new round of political turmoil.[147]

After Deng's dismissal, Hu Yaobang's troubles worsened and his health deteriorated under renewed attacks from CAS "rebels." He checked into the Peace Hospital with indications of stomach ulcers, but his detractors somehow spirited him out despite staff objections and took him to Dalian to be "struggled against" at a CAS institute there. In Dalian, Hu contracted food poisoning and had to be hospitalized again. This time staff objections and formal complaints in Beijing from Hu's wife won him a respite, and CAS rebels put him on a train back to Beijing. That train had just arrived in Shanhaiguan early in the morning on July 28 when an earthquake measuring 7.6 on the Richter scale struck the nearby city of Tangshan, devastating the city and killing more than 240,000 residents. Hu was unhurt, but the rail line was damaged, and Hu had to return to Dalian, flying home several days later.[148]

Even though Hu's home was not damaged in the earthquake, many other places in Beijing were, and the aftershocks heightened tensions in the city. Like many residents, Hu Yaobang decided to construct an "earthquake shed" adjacent to one of the bedrooms. He took great pleasure in supervising construction of the makeshift structure, particularly because it gave him some relief from the incessant struggle sessions at the CAS.

For his four months of work in rectifying the academy, Hu had been under political attack for nearly a year.[149] The CAS Outline Report had been branded a "big poisonous weed," along with other reports Deng had prepared. The version used for criticism was largely Hu Yaobang's work, as later versions contained Mao Zedong quotations, which rendered them immune to public criticism. These "poisonous weeds" were circulated to CCP branches across the country in mid-1976, which only served to popularize Deng's programs, especially when compared with leftist hyperbole used to criticize them.[150] Hu was no longer being dragged off to struggle sessions, but his home was being watched by security authorities, and he seldom received guests or went out to meet friends. His children again served as conduits of news and gossip from other sidelined leaders.

Mao Zedong had suffered a myocardial infarction in early May and by late in the month was being nourished through a feeding tube.[151] The public was not informed of any details of his condition or treatment, but his occasional meetings with prominent foreign visitors had enabled people to see his condition. At one of the last such meetings, an April 30 visit with New Zealand prime minister Robert Muldoon, Hua Guofeng had stayed behind to brief Mao on the domestic situation after the Tiananmen incident and Deng's ouster.

Even though Hua had worked many years in Hunan and had spoken often with the Chairman, Mao's speech was now so garbled that Hua could not understand him, so Mao wrote down what were to become some of his last instructions: "Take it easy, don't be anxious; do things according to past guidelines; with you in charge, I'm at ease."[152] By the end of May, Mao was no longer able to meet with foreign guests, and by early July he was no longer able to write instructions on documents.

In late August and early September, all of Beijing was on a death watch for Chairman Mao, amplified by the bad omen of the Tangshan earthquake. Although he still had moments of lucidity, Mao was mostly inert, breathing with difficulty, alone except for his medical staff and security detail. After two more heart attacks in early September, Mao Zedong died at twelve minutes past midnight on September 9, 1976, at the age of eighty-three.

The man who envisioned the need for a Cultural Revolution to maintain the purity of China's Marxist revolution, the man who incited millions of Chinese youth in Tiananmen Square to destroy both the Communist Party bureaucracy and many of China's traditions, the man who manipulated the CCP leadership and bent it to his will, who purged one successor and drove another to mutiny, the man who created irreconcilable factions within a decimated CCP and repeatedly set them against one another, the man who lived in imperial splendor while his people suffered in spiritual and physical poverty, was finally dead. The Cultural Revolution was over in one sense. In another, as Mao had wished, the Cultural Revolution continued.

Assessing the Cost

The year 2016 marked the fiftieth anniversary of the start of the Cultural Revolution. It was noted, but not celebrated. Hundreds of books and countless thousands of articles, critiques, recollections, and "scar literature" have been written since the official end of the Cultural Revolution in October 1976, when Mao's wife and her closest associates—the Gang of Four—were purged. But the Central archives and even many local ones remain closed, and officially sanitized and Central Committee–sanctioned books and articles have seldom tried to deal with it in a critical manner. As I will discuss in Chapter 7, the party negotiated with great difficulty a Central Committee resolution, approved in June 1981, that discussed the Cultural Revolution at length. Among its findings: "The 'cultural revolution,' which lasted from May 1966 to October 1976, was responsible for the most severe setback and the heaviest losses suffered by the party, the state and the people since the founding of the People's Republic. It was initiated and led by Comrade Mao Zedong." "Chief responsibility for the grave 'Left' error of the 'cultural revolution,' an error comprehensive in magnitude and protracted in duration, does indeed lie with Comrade Mao Zedong. But after all it was the error of a great proletarian revolutionary."[153]

In the introduction to his massive history of the Cultural Revolution, *Heaven and Earth Overturned,* Yang Jisheng cites a speech given by Ye Jianying at an enlarged meeting of the Politburo in early July 1981, which lists costs paid by the people of China and the Communist Party of China during the ten years of the Cultural Revolution:

(1) More than 4,300 armed events, with more than 123,700 dead;

(2) At least 2,500,000 CCP cadres subjected to struggle, more than 302,700 illegally detained, and more than 115,500 "unnatural deaths";

(3) In China's urban areas more than 4,810,000 people were labeled as some sort of "class enemy," of whom 683,000 died "unnatural deaths";

(4) In rural areas more than 5,200,000 landlords, rich and middle peasants and their families were persecuted, with 1.2 million "unnatural deaths";

(5) A total of more than 113 million people underwent some kind of political attack, and 557,000 people are "still missing."[154]

Yang acknowledges that some other estimates of Cultural Revolution mortality are higher than his, and some are lower. California State Los Angeles historian Yongyi Song reviewed several estimates between a low of around 1 million and a high of 7.7 million in a 2011 article for the Mass Violence and Resistance Research Network, coming up with an average estimate of violent deaths in the Cultural Revolution of nearly 2.95 million.[155] There are more, mostly silenced now by the CCP's unwillingness to let the Cultural Revolution issues be discussed at length.

But to return to the story of Hu Yaobang's experience at the end of Mao's life. The public mourning ended with an official ceremony for Mao at the Great Hall of the People on September 18, 1976. Unlike Zhou Enlai's funeral eight months earlier, there was full media coverage of the mourning for Mao—people in Beijing lined up to say goodbye, weeping copiously (or pretending to), bowing before Mao's body (actually a wax dummy) in a "crystal sarcophagus," while people in rural villages were filmed sobbing during the reading of his eulogy. Deng Xiaoping was not allowed to attend any of Mao's obsequies, being still under house arrest. But according to his official chronology, Deng led his family in a moment of silence before a photo of Mao on September 18. If Hu Yaobang, who also was forbidden to attend the memorial, did something comparable with his family, it is not recorded in any of his biographic materials.

We have no idea of how Hu Yaobang "really felt" about Mao—no private letters, whispered confidences, diary entries. He knew he had been beaten, humiliated, cursed, lied to, and imprisoned by people acting in Mao's name, and quite possibly with Mao's knowledge and approval. Based upon what he did in the rest of his life, the Cultural Revolution was a watershed for Hu, the point in time at which he stopped trying his best to do what Mao wanted and began trying to find ways to undo Mao's worst excesses. He stopped taking Mao's words as sacred truth and began balancing them against a pragmatic appraisal of what people really needed. He stopped being a loyal and unquestioning follower and began—cautiously and hesitantly—to be a leader in his own right.

7 Bringing Order out of Chaos

Looking back with hindsight at the political standoff in Beijing in October 1976, the last act of the drama doesn't seem all that surprising. A senile Mao Zedong—still possessed of awesome power but unable to wield it because of multiple infirmities—tinkered with his succession plans one last time, then fell silent, but still lived. Three factions within the Politburo, seemingly balanced but irreparably divided and fearful that Mao could emit one last pronouncement, circled each other warily while they marshaled their power resources and considered timing and opportunities to do away with their opponents.

After Mao's death, the Politburo was adrift and paralyzed. The Standing Committee consisted of four members—Hua Guofeng, Wang Hongwen, Zhang Chunqiao, and Ye Jianying—but even though Hua nominally was in charge, he did not call it into session.[1] Of the twenty-one full and four alternate members of the Politburo elected in 1973, five had died, and four—all PLA officers—were stationed outside Beijing. Of sixteen Politburo members resident in Beijing, one was comatose and four were "mass representatives" with little authority. Deng Xiaoping was under house arrest. Ye Jianying and Li Xiannian had both been sidelined.

There were three identifiable factions within the Politburo. First was the "leftist" faction. Led by Mao's wife, Jiang Qing, it had one party vice-chairman (Wang Hongwen), one Politburo Standing Committee member (Zhang Chunqiao), and two Politburo members (Jiang and Yao Wenyuan). Mao's nephew, Mao Yuanxin, was not a Politburo member, but acted in league with the leftists. They appeared convinced that Mao Zedong had intended for his wife to succeed him. The faction was dominant in the propaganda apparatus, the literature and art bureaucracies, and the party committees of several

Beijing universities. It dominated the Shanghai CCP committee and was said to be trying to arm enough local militia units there to present a credible counterforce to PLA units surrounding the city.[2]

The second was the "old guard" or "party veterans" faction, led by Ye Jianying and Li Xiannian. They were supported by the four military Politburo members outside of Beijing, and by navy commander and Politburo alternate Su Zhenhua. Ye and Li were sidelined after Deng Xiaoping and Zhou Enlai were off the scene. In February 1976 Ye was still a vice-chairman of the CMC, but the Politburo replaced him as the senior officer in charge of day-to-day PLA operations. Ye was not ill, but he had requested sick leave, unwilling to put up with the constant quarreling of senior leadership meetings.[3] His movements had not been restricted, and he held meetings with PLA subordinates in the General Staff department and other command positions. The old veterans were not so much a coherent faction as a group of elders who had been mistreated during the Cultural Revolution and were united only in their antipathy to Jiang Qing and her colleagues.[4]

The third faction was a group of second-tier officials, all chosen by Mao, who were beneficiaries of the Cultural Revolution. Mao chose Hua Guofeng as his successor a few months before his death, perhaps thinking that Hua could keep the other factions in line. But Hua had no support other than Mao, remained unknown to the old guard, and was harassed by Jiang Qing to relinquish his leadership positions to her. Others in this group included Ji Dengkui, whom Mao brought to the State Council and Military Commission and made political commissar of the Beijing Military Region in 1972; Wu De, assigned by Mao to the Beijing municipal committee and to the Beijing Garrison as political commissar; Wang Dongxing, Mao's personal bodyguard, whom he put in charge of the General Office in 1966 and added to the Politburo in 1969; and Chen Xilian, former Shenyang Military Region commander and Politburo member, and benefactor of Mao's nephew. Chen was transferred to the Beijing Military Region in 1973 and took charge of the CMC in early 1976 when Ye Jianying stepped back.

Mao had been obsessed with personal security, fearing both external and internal enemies. His relations with the PLA top leadership were particularly wary. Starting before the Cultural Revolution, he made sure the party Center was protected by plenty of guns in three rings around the Center under separate command authorities. After Mao died, the security structure was maintained while the factional struggle played itself out.

- The first ring was the CCP's central leadership compound and all other office, leisure, and residential facilities. It was protected by the Central Guards Unit, a bureau of the party's General Office that was trained, equipped, and commanded by the People's Liberation Army. Known at the time as Unit 8341, it was an irregular unit composed of seven regiments and thirty-six squadrons (probably about eight thousand soldiers). It was responsible not only for guarding the entrances to Zhongnanhai and other CCP facilities, but also for providing personal security guards to all senior Central leaders. In 1976 Wang Dongxing was political commissar of Unit 8341, director of the General Office, and director of the Central Security Bureau. The commander of Unit 8341 was Zhang Yaoci.[5]
- The second ring of military security was the Beijing Garrison, comprising two divisions and several regiments, totaling around thirty thousand troops deployed inside Beijing municipality. Mao Zedong and Lin Biao both had been very concerned about the Beijing Garrison and changed out commanders several times during the Cultural Revolution. During the Lin Biao incident in 1971, Mao and Zhou relied heavily on garrison commander Wu Zhong and political commissar Wu De for rounding up Lin's supporters and taking other military measures to maintain the capital's security.[6]
- The Beijing Military Region was the third component of the party's military security. It was the largest of the PRC's eleven military regions, having command of three provincial military districts and two municipal garrisons, and operational authority (with CMC approval) over several large group armies deployed along the border with Mongolia and the USSR. Its more than three hundred thousand troops were principally responsible for defense against foreign invasion but were available for domestic unrest as well. Politburo members Chen Xilian and Ji Dengkui were commander and political commissar, respectively, an indication of the importance of the troops surrounding Beijing.

With Mao dead and the Politburo at odds, control and disposition of these PLA units was bound to be a key determinant of how the political situation would be resolved. Shanghai scholar Han Gang has published extensively on the plans and complex communications involved in preparing and executing the "resolution of the Gang of Four problem." In Han's analysis, Ye Jianying had long been pondering a move against Jiang Qing and talking with other senior military leaders about it, but he was reluctant to initiate any action. It was Hua Guofeng who took the first step, on September 10, 1976, the day after Mao's death, following a Politburo meeting at which Jiang Qing demanded that Hua expel Deng Xiaoping from the party and give her custody of Mao's papers. Hua rejected her demands but evidently realized that his struggles with Jiang were only just beginning. After the meeting Hua secretly visited Li Xiannian's house and asked him to get in touch with Ye Jianying to ask his advice about dealing with the Gang of Four problem.[7]

Ye lived in the Xishan District west of Beijing, and Li took special precautions to ensure that his visit was not observed. According to one account, Ye was wary of eavesdropping, even inside his own home, and the two elders exchanged views in writing, then burned the papers. Ye specifically asked Li about the reliability of Beijing Military Region commander Chen Xilian. Li, who had served in the Red Army with Chen in the 1930s, wrote back that Chen was "completely reliable, don't worry."[8]

A series of private conversations followed, involving Hua, Ye, and Wang Dongxing. Wang, who often had suffered personal abuse from Jiang Qing, agreed that "drastic measures" were needed. Standard bureaucratic means, such as a Central Committee plenum or Politburo meeting to vote the leftists out, were considered unworkable.[9] Ye met secretly with Wang four times to work out the details of timing and operational coordination between various armed units.[10]

Plans accelerated after a stormy September 29 Politburo meeting, at which Jiang Qing demanded that Mao Yuanxin be permitted to stay in Beijing to help arrange Chairman Mao's papers and draft documents, while Wang Hongwen proposed that Jiang Qing be elected CCP chairman. Both proposals were rejected by Hua. Wang Dongxing and Hua met privately on October 2, and they agreed that the most efficient approach would be to invite the principal leftist leaders to a Politburo Standing Committee meeting in Zhongnanhai's Huairen Hall, where they would be arrested by handpicked members of Unit 8341 and "isolated for inspection" in an underground facility. Jiang Qing would be seized separately at her residence in Zhongnanhai, along with Mao Yuanxin.[11]

Plans were made to seize other leftist leaders at Tsinghua University, and to take military control of the principal media outlets in Beijing, such as

Renmin Ribao, the Central Broadcasting Service, and the Central Television Service. Because Unit 8341 was not authorized to operate outside of specified CCP locations, these moves required coordination with the Beijing Garrison, which was handled by Wu De. The use of Beijing Garrison troops in operations against civilian targets inside the city required CMC approval, which was given by Chen Xilian.[12]

After two more days of meetings, revisions, and briefings, Hua Guofeng ordered Wang Dongxing to carry out the mission on October 6. At 3:00 p.m., Hua had the General Office notify Politburo Standing Committee members of an 8:00 p.m. meeting, with an invitation sent to Yao Wenyuan. Five teams of 8341 soldiers, totaling about fifty men, were in place by early evening. Beijing Garrison commander Wu Zhong was on hand outside Zhongnanhai in case of any questions about operational authorities. Ye Jianying and Hua Guofeng arrived before 7:30 p.m. at Huairen Hall, where Wang Dongxing was already waiting with his soldiers.[13]

In the end, everything proceeded smoothly. After Wang Hongwen, Zhang Chunqiao, and Yao Wenyuan arrived separately, Hua read each the official statement that they were suspected of planning to seize power and were to be isolated for investigation, and they were marched off in manacles. Jiang Qing was arrested in her Zhongnanhai quarters by 8341 commander Zhang Yaoci and a small squad of soldiers, including one woman. The same team seized Mao Yuanxin in his room nearby. He was armed but did not resist. It was all over by 8:35 p.m.. Later that evening, future defense minister Geng Biao led Beijing Garrison teams to take control of China's central radio and televisions stations. The PRC's first military coup was complete.[14]

At 10 p.m. an expanded Politburo meeting was held in the home of Ye Jianying in western Beijing, where the CMC had several villas for its leaders. Hua Guofeng asked Ye to preside over a special meeting to consolidate the leadership in the wake of the arrests earlier that evening. Ye demurred, asking Hua to take charge. The eleven Politburo members and some Unit 8341 leaders listened as both men talked about the leftists' schemes and the necessity of taking them out by force. The meeting lasted until 6 a.m. on October 7, culminating in a unanimous vote electing Hua Guofeng as chairman of both the Central Committee and the Military Commission, a decision that required ratification by a Central Committee plenary session.[15]

Frightened and angry leaders in Shanghai, where the left was firmly in control of the CCP committee, surmised that a "counterrevolutionary coup" had occurred in Beijing, and that Shanghai needed to prepare for "decisive battle" with the Central authorities. Beijing sent a team to talk them out of extreme measures, then summoned the principal leaders of the Shanghai committee to Beijing on October 10 to explain the hopelessness of their situation. They capitulated, and a new CCP committee leadership team was sent to Shanghai two days later.[16]

In Beijing the key task was to control the distribution of the news of the arrest to the party, the society at large, and the outside world. Beijing Garrison teams had quickly imposed a complete clampdown on news of leadership events in both print and broadcast media. Meanwhile Hua and Ye convened a meeting of all members of the Central Committee in Beijing on October 7 to inform party and military officials about the significant change, and to pass along the official explanation.

The following day the Center issued a "Central Committee Notice on Smashing the Wang Hongwen, Zhang Chunqiao, Jiang Qing and Yao Wenyuan Anti-Party Clique," along with announcements of the construction of a Chairman Mao Memorial Hall and the preparation of volume 5 of *Selected Works of Chairman Mao*. On October 18 the Center put out another document passing the news to all CCP members at all levels, and the following day it issued a public announcement to the world.[17]

The reaction in Beijing was jubilation. Many party members had been informed early by the grapevine. Some heard directly from Politburo members and passed the news on to family members. Deng Xiaoping, for example, was informed by his son-in-law, who was working in one of the PLA general departments and immediately bicycled to Deng's place of confinement after he heard the news. He related the story to the whole family crowded into the bathroom with the water running—a precaution against eavesdropping. Some passed friends prearranged coded messages so as not to be accused of violating party regulations.[18]

Hu Yaobang learned the news at home on the morning of October 8 from Ye Jianying, who sent his son, Ye Xuanning, to deliver a message: "The hated leftists are in custody, you should look to your health and prepare to receive news from the Party of a new work assignment." Ye Jianying also asked Hu to consider how the new leadership should go about restoring order and rebuilding China and promised that his son would return in two days to hear Hu's opinions.[19] Hu prepared his reply carefully, probably realizing that his old friend, who had helped him several times in the past, might be able to do so again. When Ye Xuanning returned to Hu's home on October 10, Hu told him:

Since ancient times, sages have always said that after great chaos, we must conform to the people's hearts and the people's hearts are foremost. According to this reasoning, I think that there are three big things that are particularly important at present: First, stop the criticism of Deng, and the people's hearts will go along; second, once unjust cases are cleared, the people's hearts will be very happy; third, grasp production resolutely, and the people's hearts will swell with joy. Please be sure to bring these words to your father.[20]

Ye was delighted with Hu's reply, believing it was a comprehensive but concise set of recommendations for resolving the PRC's urgent political, organizational, and economic problems. He compared them to the "Three Strategies of Longzhong" presented by the renowned strategist Zhuge Liang to the first emperor of the Han Dynasty in 207 CE.[21]

The reply also summarized Hu Yaobang's view of the party's situation after the Cultural Revolution. First, the campaign to "criticize Deng and counterattack the right deviationist wind of reversing verdicts" was a Mao-approved condemnation of Deng Xiaoping's 1975 program of personnel reform in various bureaucracies. The leftists "criticize Deng" campaign cost many rehabilitated intellectuals their jobs. It had run out of steam by late 1976, but Hua Guofeng, in an early statement following his investiture, had indicated the campaign should continue because it had been authorized by Mao.[22] Hu's second suggestion reflected his recognition, going as far back as 1957, that the party had wrongly punished many of its members for ideological misdeeds that were fabricated or misguided. These errors needed to be corrected. His third suggestion was one he had made in all his regional assignments—namely, that promoting agricultural production was the essential task of every local party leader. Ye agreed with Hu but was not certain that Hua and the other beneficiaries of the Cultural Revolution on the Politburo would concur.[23]

The Importance of Being Ye

On the day after the purge of the Politburo's left wing, Ye Jianying was the most important, and potentially the most powerful, member of the CCP leadership. Of the original ten men appointed marshals when the PLA established ranks in 1955, six had died and two others were in poor health; only Ye was able to put the pieces in place for a military action. Ironically,

Ye had never held a combat command. He was always a staff officer, an organizer, networker, negotiator, problem solver. Intelligent and well-educated, Ye put people at their ease and found ways to resolve problems and disagreements.

It was those skills that Mao, Zhou Enlai, and Deng Xiaoping had valued most in Ye. Now he had done a great service for Hua Guofeng—developing the coup plans, making sure everyone understood their roles, surrounding the officers he distrusted with "insurance," setting the timing, and overseeing the completion of the mission. Hua apparently understood this and offered Ye the party chairmanship immediately afterward. But the man Hua called "the marshal of 900 million people" refused, citing his age (seventy-nine), his concern to avoid the appearance of a military takeover, and Hua's own selection by Mao.[24]

Nonetheless, Ye Jianying became the "power behind the throne" for Hua, lending his political and military prestige and skills to buttress Hua as chairman of both the party and the CMC. He probably realized that Hua was not strong, having no followers in leadership positions, little record of achievement, and no name recognition or popular reputation. Ye contributed to a nascent personality cult for Hua, suggesting the name "wise leader, Chairman Hua" to help him fit into the exalted role that Chairman Mao had created. He was also determined that the army and the old party veterans would support Hua.[25]

There was, however, a quid pro quo. Ye wanted Hua to restore Deng Xiaoping to his previous positions. This was no easy task. Deng's expulsion from office had been Mao's personal decision, approved by the Politburo. Also, there was opposition to Deng's return, on both political and ideological grounds. Some feared Deng would seek to completely repudiate the Cultural Revolution and punish those leaders who had benefited from it, while restoring many ousted CCP veterans eager to seek vengeance. Moreover, there was concern that the legacy of Mao's leadership and his ideas would be shunted aside by Deng's determination to get the economy working again. The problem of what to do about Deng was postponed in November/December, when Deng went into the hospital suffering from prostatitis. But the problems were persistent, and political battle lines were beginning to take shape between the two factions remaining after the palace coup. Hu Yaobang, although still unemployed, was about to be drawn into them.

In late October, Hua Guofeng gave a speech to propaganda workers, ostensibly on how to properly carry out criticism of the recently fallen leftists.

He made four points: Focus criticism on the Gang of Four but continue the criticism of Deng Xiaoping and the "right deviationist wind of reversing verdicts"; note that the Gang's errors were not leftism, but "extreme rightism"; do not criticize Chairman Mao; and avoid talking about the April 5 (1976) Tiananmen incident.[26] In mid-November, Wang Dongxing also spoke to a propaganda meeting in Beijing, saying that the 1976 Tiananmen incident had been designated "counterrevolutionary" by Chairman Mao, who also decided Deng was to be sacked because of his backstage support for it. Whether it was fair or not was irrelevant; Mao had decided the issue.[27] It was apparent that Hua and Wang were setting a tone for the new regime, whose key notes were "continuing the revolution under the dictatorship of the proletariat" (Mao's Cultural Revolution line), maintaining "class struggle as the key link" in the party's work, and putting off restoring Deng and other old veterans.[28]

Contrarian Comrade

Despite Ye's pledge that Hu Yaobang would soon return to work, Hu was still at home at the turn of the year. He had continued to think about why the CCP was in such a lamentable state, and what a post-Mao regime should do and look like. He shared some of his thoughts in a New Year's Day conversation with his former Communist Youth League subordinate and future biographer Yan Ruping. He got straight to the root cause of the problems: "Mao Zedong had become increasingly confused and dictatorial in his late years. He had lost touch with the people, become intolerant of other opinions, and seemed to believe the personality cult manufactured by Lin Biao and the Gang of Four." Hu said his own doubts about Mao's programs and decisions began in the mid-1950s, grew with the Great Leap Forward and its repressive aftermath, and came to a head during the Cultural Revolution. After Mao's denunciation and humiliation of Peng Dehuai at the 1959 Lushan meeting, "no one dared to open his mouth." Hu confessed, "I had to respect discipline, to raise my hand, I didn't dare think it through, didn't want to be wavering about the class struggle, or be disloyal to the old man."[29]

In another conversations with Yan the following day, Hu discussed how to evaluate Mao's thinking and policies as a guide to current problems.

Now we must still hold high the great red banner of Mao Zedong Thought, but these things the old man Chairman Mao did in his old age cannot be considered Mao Zedong Thought. . . . How should we in-herit and defend Mao Zedong Thought? . . . In the future we will al-ways need someone to take his old-age thinking and his speeches and writings and evaluate them, distinguish clearly which are correct . . . which we should raise high and continue and develop; and which are incorrect . . . but we can never say "Every sentence is truth," or "We should carry out [Mao's directives] whether we understand them or not," that is liable to kill people!

Hu complained, "[Some people want to] go along with everything Chairman Mao said, nodded his head at, drew circles around, like this is all 'carrying out the legacy of the Chairman' and continuing the revolution. . . . In those circumstances, if you want to work, you have to say things you don't believe, do things against your will. I won't do it. . . . Better for me to stay home and hold my children and grandchildren.[30]

Hu was not alone in his revulsion for what had gone before. In early January the first indications of growing sentiment for "de-Maoification" manifested themselves in big-character posters on the campuses of Beijing and Tsinghua Universities, criticizing Mao and his leftist followers. Hua warned against this, reminding people that slandering leaders, even dead ones, could be labeled as "counterrevolutionary activity," punishable by death.[31] Divisions sharpened with a front-page editorial that appeared in *Renmin Ribao* on February 7, 1977, and was circulated nationwide through Xinhua. Drafted by a writing team of "old leftists" who had worked for Kang Sheng during the Cultural Revolution and now worked for Wang Dongxing, the editorial was titled, "Study the Documents, Grasp the Key Link."

In language redolent of the Cultural Revolution, the editorial set a hard ideological line. But one sentence caught the attention of many readers and raised alarm: "We all will resolutely uphold whatever decision was made by Chairman Mao; we all will unswervingly follow whatever Chairman Mao directed, from beginning to end." Geng Biao, still nominally in charge of Central propaganda outlets, received the draft editorial from Wang Dongxing with instructions that he could not make any changes in the text. He later complained, "If we had done things according to what was demanded in this article, the smashing of the 'Gang of Four' would have been in vain." The sentence soon was known as the Two Whatevers, and became the object of a major ideological battle over Mao's legacy.[32]

In early February, Deng Xiaoping was discharged from the hospital, and Ye Jianying arranged for him and his family to be moved to a PLA villa in the Yuquan Hills. He soon began receiving old colleagues paying their respects, including a Spring Festival event attended by Hu Yaobang, Chen Yun, Wang Zhen, and others. Ye and Hua had authorized Deng to receive party documents at his residence, and he was soon up to speed on the main issues. But there had still been no decision on his return to work. Now that the Two Whatevers were a matter of public record, Hua's dilemma deepened. He had agreed to Deng's return as early as October 1976 but insisted that the process had to be gradual, to get the party to accept the Gang of Four purge before bringing back to his previous prominence the man Mao had ordered sacked. The editorial made that more difficult. Deng also understood that it made his return more problematic.[33]

Hu Yaobang, meanwhile, was being asked to come back to work, this time at the Central Party School, which had been closed since early in the Cultural Revolution. Man Mei relates that Hua Guofeng made a personal visit to Hu's home in February, and the two men talked behind closed doors. She later learned Hua had come at Ye Jianying's suggestion to invite Hu to return to work, but that Hu had refused, because he was still under attack, along with Deng, for their work in 1975.[34] On February 26 Hu was summoned to Zhongnanhai, where he met with Hua and Wang Dongxing and was asked a second time. Hu again demurred but went the following day to consult Ye Jianying at his home.[35] Although Hu still expressed misgivings, the old marshal said accepting the assignment would help him as well. He conceded that some "too important departments" would not be comfortable with Hu, but the Party School was in the western suburbs, far from Zhongnanhai, and there his talent and intelligence would enable him to restore his reputation.[36] Hu accepted appointment as the executive vice president of the school, meaning he would oversee day-to-day affairs. He formally took up his appointment on March 3, 1977.[37]

The Central Party School (CPS) is in the Haidian District of northwestern Beijing, not far from the Summer Palace. It trains senior and middle-level leading cadres, along with outstanding young and middle-aged cadres from across the country; it is also a philosophical and social sciences research institution. When Hu was appointed, classes had been suspended since 1966; the school was staffed, but it was not operating.

Hu reported for duty on March 9, bringing with him only his confidential secretary. On the same day, *Renmin Ribao* published an article by the

Chinese Academy of Science Theory Group, nullifying the 1975 Gang of Four criticism of the "Outline Report" Hu had prepared for CAS. This was seen as a vindication for Hu prior to his return to work, which was subsequently reaffirmed by the Central Committee.[38]

On March 10 Hua Guofeng convened a Central Committee work conference in Beijing to sum up the Center's work since the purge of the Gang of Four, and to take up several important policy issues. One was adjusting the 1977 national economic plan, which meant basically returning to the policies Deng had initiated in 1975. Another was resolving the 1976 Tiananmen incident that Mao had declared "counterrevolutionary" and the related issue of bringing Deng Xiaoping back to work.[39] In a speech on March 14, Hua told the conference that the overriding issue for all party members was "resolutely safeguarding Chairman Mao's great banner," which had both international and domestic implications. The former entailed avoiding the confusion that followed Nikita Khrushchev's Twentieth Party Congress "secret speech," in which he denounced Stalin. The latter involved both the demands for overturning Mao's judgment on Tiananmen and dealing with "political rumors and reactionary remarks" critical of Mao that were circulating in public. These "must be combated resolutely and not allowed to spread freely, Hua insisted."[40]

Regarding Deng's return, Hua prevaricated, asserting that all the practical problems had been resolved by reversing judgments on the 1975 rectification program, and by declaring that "the majority" of Tiananmen demonstrators in April 1976 were mourning Zhou Enlai.[41] Deng's formal reinstatement could wait until the upcoming Third Plenum of the Tenth Central Committee in July and would be finalized by the Eleventh Party Congress to follow. "Wait until the water flows into the channel, until the ripe gourd falls from the vine," Hua counseled.[42] Party elders Chen Yun and Wang Zhen had made speeches at the meeting strongly advocating Deng's prompt return to work, but they were disregarded.[43] The work conference adjourned without fanfare, but Hua's disregard for the elders' counsel was neither forgotten nor forgiven.

Hu Yaobang attended the work conference, even though he had not been restored to the Central Committee, but he was not an active participant and was disappointed with the results. He had more pressing personnel concerns at CPS. Ye Jianying provided timely assistance again, arranging for Hu's old friend and colleague Feng Wenbin to be transferred to CPS to aid with administration, and getting PLA General Staff personnel to move out of CPS housing.

Hu set about rectifying the school's leadership with a flurry of meetings, speeches, and committee formation. But he was cautious after being introduced to the school's "leading group," which had been appointed by Kang Sheng. Kang had been a major force at the school, along with his wife, Cao Yiou. Early in the Cultural Revolution they directed political attacks against several of the school's top officials and incited serious faculty infighting. Kang died in 1975, but Cao remained engaged in school politics, and some of the staff considered themselves to be "old Kang's people."[44] Had Kang lived longer, he probably would have been charged as an accomplice of Jiang Qing and her leftist associates, but no one had confronted that issue in 1977.

In these first weeks Hu held numerous meetings, trying to persuade those accused of supporting the Gang of Four to acknowledge and correct their errors, while imploring returned faculty and administrators to forswear vengeance and work together to resume classes. It was not an easy task.[45] It was rendered more difficult by Hua Guofeng's declaration in October 1976 that the Gang of Four had been not "leftists" but "extreme rightists." This enabled many of the "rebel faction" at CPS to deflect criticism by claiming their actions were inspired by calls from Chairman Mao and "old Kang" to counter rightism at the school.[46]

With the national propaganda apparatus—the Central media—firmly under the control of Wang Dongxing and what came to be called the "whatever faction" (*fanshi pai*), Hu began developing a plan for the Central Party School to play a role as an ideological change agent. Reaching back to his experience as a Youth League leader in Jiangxi and at Yan'an, Hu fastened on the idea of publishing a small-scale periodical on theoretical matters. From his very first discussions about the project in May 1977, he planned to call the publication *Theoretical Dynamics* (*lilun dongtai*), with its connotation of the openness of basic theories to dynamic evolution.[47]

Hu had ideas about the magazine's appearance and content. It was to be short, three to five pages, published every three or four days, with only one article of three to four thousand words, devoted to a specific theoretical topic. The target audience was Chairman Hua, Vice-Chairman Ye, members of the Politburo, and other Central and provincial party leaders—a total circulation of three to four hundred copies. The purpose was to help leaders understand theoretical and policy issues, to help CPS better understand and teach Marxism–Leninism–Mao Zedong Thought, and to provide resource material for lower-level party schools. Hu wanted articles to come mostly from the magazine's own small writing staff, with only occasional pieces from outside. He quipped that the publication would be like a weapon, but not heavy artillery, only a hand grenade.[48]

In early June, Hu organized a *Theoretical Dynamics* committee inside the CPS administrative office. Separately, he made sure that the publication did not require approval from the Propaganda Department or the Politburo for its articles to be printed and circulated. Then he waited for the optimal time, writer, and topic to unveil the new pamphlet. In mid-July, with the Third Plenum of the Tenth CCP Congress only days away, Hu heard a speech by Wu Jiang, head of the CPS Theoretical Research Department. Wu's topic was how to guide discussion of the forthcoming fifth volume of Mao's *Selected Works,* and specifically how to understand "Continuing the Revolution," one of Mao's primary justifications for the Cultural Revolution. Hu admired the speech and asked Wu to turn it into an article for the debut issue of *Theoretical Dynamics* on July 15 (the day before the opening of the Plenum). Hu edited Wu's "Probing the Issue of 'Continuing the Revolution'" and had it printed and circulated, sending a special copy to Deng Xiaoping.[49]

Wu discussed the issue in nonpolemical terms, examining Marxist classics to see whether a decision to call for continuing the revolution past its ostensible victory (that is, starting a Cultural Revolution after 1949) was justifiable. In his own book, Wu Jiang noted that circulation of the article was partially blocked, but many plenum delegates saw it, and reaction varied from admiration to concern at its boldness.[50] Hu did not attend the plenum, but had plenty of feedback from people who did, and said he was delighted with the controversy. "The discussion of Wu's article has been lively. . . . Theory issues need examination and argument, and that is a good thing." Hu would later tell people that he believed the theoretical process of "bringing order out of chaos" (*boluan fanzheng*)—reversing the damage wrought by the Cultural Revolution—began with the publication of Wu's article.[51]

Wu Jiang claimed the article brought Hu and Deng Xiaoping into a discussion of an ideological issue for the first time.[52] It was not a discussion between equals. Deng was no match for Hu intellectually or theoretically. He was aware of the *Theoretical Dynamics* article on "continuing the revolution" but might not have recognized the possibilities of Hu's publication. In a short period of time Hu Yaobang had put together a small but talented staff of writers—professors and Marxist intellectuals—and gave them a vehicle to address what had gone wrong during the Cultural Revolution and what needed to be done to repair the damage to the party and society. On the other hand, when it fell to Deng to make a final pronouncement on a theoretical issue, Hu was no match for him, as subsequent events would prove repeatedly.

Deng Xiaoping's Relentless Will to Power

On July 16, the day after Wu Jiang's article was published, Hua Guofeng convened the Third Plenum of the Tenth CCP Congress, which lasted five days. In his political report, Hua pledged "to uphold the great banner of Chairman Mao," "to continue the revolution under the dictatorship of the proletariat," and "to consolidate the fruits of the victory of the Great Proletarian Cultural Revolution." The meeting passed two major personnel issues: a "Resolution on the Confirmation of Comrade Hua Guofeng as Chairman of the CCP Central Committee and Chairman of the Central Military Commission," and a "Resolution on the Reinstatement of Comrade Deng Xiaoping" to all his previous positions, including Politburo Standing Committee, CCP vice-chairman, CMC vice-chairman, vice-premier, and chief of the PLA General Staff.[53]

The agreement to bring Deng back had been complex and drawn out, worked through intermediaries, avoiding direct contact, communicating through letters. It involved not repudiating Mao's decision to fire Deng but dismissing the charge that he had been behind the April 1976 Tiananmen demonstrations. Deng reiterated his opinion that the Two Whatevers were "no good" (*buxing*), and that the party would need to have "accurate and complete Mao Zedong Thought to guide our entire party, army and nation for generations."[54]

The Eleventh Congress of the CCP was convened in Beijing on August 12, 1977, right after the Third Plenum, and lasted six days. Although Deng Xiaoping's full return was much celebrated, he did not dominate the congress, and some of its decisions probably were not to his liking. The new party constitution, for example, introduced by Ye Jianying, stated that "the basic program of the Communist Party of China for the entire period of socialism is to persist in continuing the revolution under the dictatorship of the proletariat." Ye also noted that nearly half of the thirty-five million CCP members had joined since the start of the Cultural Revolution, and seven million since the Tenth Congress in 1973. That would present a huge problem for the party in trying to restore its ideological unity and sort out which members were "rebel faction" or "leftists" and had committed criminal acts during the Cultural Revolution.[55]

Deng probably was not happy with the promotion at the congress of Wang Dongxing to party vice-chairman and member of the Politburo Standing Committee. It was a recognition and reward for the central role Wang had played in toppling the Gang of Four. Hua Guofeng favored Wang's promotion, and Wang had become a stalwart supporter of the new chairman. In addition, Wang retained his position as director of the General Office, first political commissar of the Central Security Bureau, and principal overseer of the work of the Central Special Case Examination Group. He also exercised supervisory control over the party's main propaganda organs. In that capacity, Wang had been the principal promoter of the February 7 editorial that introduced the Two Whatevers. Finally, Wang had been a harsh critic of Deng personally during his period of disgrace, frequently disparaging him and resisting calls for his return.[56]

The new Central leadership that came to the fore at the Eleventh Congress was probably somewhat more to Deng's liking. Li Xiannian was added to the five-man Politburo Standing Committee (reduced from nine members), giving the veterans a three-to-two advantage over the Cultural Revolution beneficiaries. Of the twenty-three-member Politburo, eight new members were veteran cadres, and more than 60 percent of the overall body held positions in the PLA, where Deng had influence and authority through his restored positions on the CMC and General Staff.[57]

Hu on the Move

Hu Yaobang was readmitted to the Central Committee at the Eleventh Congress, after a ten-year abeyance. He continued his work of rectifying the Central Party School leadership, preparing for classes to resume in October, and publishing regular issues of *Theoretical Dynamics*. On the first task, he gave a speech in early September at CPS that confronted the residual influence of Kang Sheng, which impaired attempts to bring about leadership change. The problem was not Kang himself, who was dead, or even his wife, who had just been reelected to the Central Committee. The problem was that Kang had died with his official reputation intact, honored at his funeral as a "proletarian revolutionary" and "glorious warrior against revisionism." Everyone in the audience for Hu's speech knew Kang had done appalling things at the Central Party School. But "the lid had not been lifted" for criticizing him by name in public—that required higher authority. The nearly two hundred cadres in the audience were probably wondering whether Hu Yaobang, with his new rank of Central Committee member, now had that authority.[58]

He did not. That would have required Politburo Standing Committee approval, and everyone at that level would have known that Kang Sheng's principal backer for many years had been Mao Zedong, and Mao was still sacrosanct. But Hu Yaobang had a kind of careful courage, a willingness to take a risk. Hu first called on a CPS staffer who had suffered at Kang's hands to give a speech, which was a fiery condemnation of Kang and his wife for "ten crimes" committed at CPS, including persecution, slander, and incitement to violence. In the stunned silence that followed, Hu chose his own words carefully. "Can a Party member raise a [critical] opinion about a current leader, or a leader of the past? I think if you have an opinion, you can raise it." However, he went on, only if it is factual, at a party meeting, in a speech or written material (no big-character posters), and if the opinion-holder is willing to have the complaint sent to Chairman Hua for decision.[59] It took another three months to take that kind of risk.

By December, anger at Kang Sheng had intensified, and some staff members inquired what Hu's attitude would be if they were to put up small-character posters criticizing Kang inside one of the CPS office buildings on an upper floor, not visible to outsiders. They said they would take full responsibility and would not officially notify the school administration. Hu replied through an intermediary, "We neither advocate nor oppose [such a course]." The posters went up the following day in great numbers. When he heard about it, Hu said to his *mishu*, "Let's go see them!" "But Comrade Yaobang," the secretary replied, "you don't know about this thing!" Laughing, Hu responded, "Right, right, I don't know."[60]

In a few days, posters covered the walls of several corridors of other floors in the office building, and many people came from other units to read and discuss them. It was a sensation. Hu instructed researchers to take down details of the accusations and prepare a list of all the Party School, national, and local officials who had been persecuted by Kang Sheng. The details were compiled into a book that was sent to the Center. It contained the names of 603 senior officials, including State Council ministers, CCP department heads, provincial CCP secretaries, National People's Congress delegates, senior military officers, and others who had been falsely accused by Kang.

All these materials would be brought before the Third Plenum of the Eleventh Central Committee meeting in December 1978, which would pass proposals to revoke Kang Sheng's eulogy, remove his ashes from the Revolutionary Martyrs Cemetery at Babaoshan, and expel him from the party posthumously.[61]

The second of Hu's tasks was reopening classes at the Party School, preparations for which were complete by early October. He paired the matriculation event at the school with a Central Document laying out guidelines and encouraging provincial CCP committees to reopen party schools at every level as soon as possible.[62] More importantly, the opening of classes brought Hua Guofeng and Ye Jianying to CPS to give major speeches. Hu had drafted Ye's speech for him, and the old marshal was reportedly pleased with the text.[63] It raised issues that went beyond standard party educational issues, challenging the CPS staff to consider several problems of enduring controversy. The most significant was to compile a complete and honest history of the Chinese Communist Party, including its mistakes.[64]

Hu had been summoned to Ye Jianying's home in late September to talk about doing a definitive text of the party's history for instructional purposes, as there was no authoritative version at the time. Deng Xiaoping had joined the discussion and agreed one was needed but did not want to take the responsibility himself. He suggested that the CPS Theory Department could draft what he no doubt realized would be a difficult document. Hu suggested that the ninth, tenth, and eleventh "line struggles" (against Liu Shaoqi, Lin Biao, and the Gang of Four) should be the starting point for the work of a special research team, to be headed by Wu Jiang.[65]

Shen Baoxiang, a member of the *Theoretical Dynamics* small group at CPS and a staunch supporter of Hu Yaobang, recalled that Hu convened a drafting team within a matter of days. Hu had written the task into Ye's speech knowing it would provide political cover for what, as Shen put it, was only the first step in a "complex and difficult process of reflection and cognition," leading to the goal of having the party officially repudiate the Cultural Revolution.[66] This went to the heart of an ongoing struggle at the highest levels of the party. In his report to the party congress in August, Hua Guofeng had declared the Cultural Revolution to be over, but extolled it as "absolutely necessary, and very timely," for having "shattered the three bourgeois headquarters of Liu Shaoqi, Lin Biao and the 'Gang of Four.'" Hua favored a proposal to study the ninth, tenth, and eleventh line struggles that would reinforce the correctness of the Cultural Revolution and the brilliance of Mao Zedong Thought.[67]

Hu took an unconventional stance on the Cultural Revolution, telling *Theoretical Dynamics* staffers in the autumn of 1977, "The thinking was brilliant, but the implementation was wrong." He mocked the absurdity of "finding so many capitalist roaders" in a Communist Party, regretted the tragedy of persecuting and executing cadres on such a vast scale, and criticized the calamities it brought to China's agriculture.[68] But the CPS faculty responsible for party history and party-building courses were unprepared to tackle the job of developing teaching materials on the Cultural Revolution. There were no established texts and no one had done any research on it for years.

Hu encouraged them to form a "three line struggles study group" and prepare summary materials. Don't worry about existing documents or speeches, he chided them, find out yourselves what really happened. What were the real problems and their causes? The watchwords for the project were phrases Mao used in his earlier days: "Seek truth from facts" and "Use [actual] practice as the criterion for examining truth." Hu exhorted them to ask how the Cultural Revolution started, how it was conducted, and how it was led. He gave the group a month to prepare a new summary outline, including sections on each of the line struggles and a conclusion about the entire Cultural Revolution.[69]

The drafting of the outline continued into early 1978, and although Hu Yaobang had been given new responsibilities as director of the Central Organization Department, he retained his Party School position and continued monitoring the progress of the writing group and overseeing the publication of *Theoretical Dynamics*. As the length of the outline grew, Hu decided to have it sent for discussion to the students due to start at the Party School in April 1978, rather than sending it to the Center, where it would face certain opposition.

The 807 students matriculating at the Central Party School that session were a combination of old, middle-aged, and young cadres. Some had been recently released from Cultural Revolution disgrace; some were "model workers" who advanced during the chaos of that period; some were ideologically "emancipated"; some were doctrinaire party hacks. Hu Yaobang stressed the need for letting everyone speak freely in small group discussions, with no requirement for summing up or unanimity. He laid out strict rules for group behavior, which represented his perspective on party meetings and were Hu's philosophy against Mao's practice. They were basically a blanket prohibition against the kind of "criticism and struggle sessions" that had become nearly universal throughout the previous fifteen years. They came to be called the "Three Nos": "No grabbing pigtails" (that is, no seizing on individual shortcomings); "no putting on hats" (no political labeling); "no beating with sticks" (no violence or threats of violence). Hu also added a fourth no, considering the continuing existence of Central Special Case Groups: "No carrying dossier bags" (no bringing up unverifiable evidence).[70]

The ten-day discussion sessions in April 1978 were held in a lively atmosphere, but there was little unanimity of view on the specific issues. No grand conclusions were reached about either the Cultural Revolution in general or the specific line struggles. But Hu seemed to be satisfied with the introduction of a process and a methodology for examining difficult issues in party history.[71] It would not be long before the issues were joined again.

Reorganizing the Organization Department

Two days before the October 9, 1977, opening of classes at the Central Party School, *Renmin Ribao* published a full-page commentary by three of its professors with a rather convoluted title: "Correct the Line on Cadres That Had Been Turned Upside-Down by the Gang of Four." The article had been commissioned by Hu Yaobang in August; he had personally provided the title, and he edited the text seventeen times. He negotiated the size of the article with *Renmin Ribao* editor in chief Hu Jiwei, and chose the date for its publication—the first anniversary of the purge of the Gang of Four.[72] It was a direct critique of the Central Organization Department and its dilatory approach in addressing the countless complaints of former CCP officials punished during the Cultural Revolution.

Hu had been mulling over the topic of redressing "unjust, false, and wrong verdicts" (*yuan, jia, cuo an*) for a long time. It had been one of his prescriptions for restoring the party's leadership and prestige after the purge of the Gang of Four. He had seen or experienced the phenomenon often, especially during the Cultural Revolution. The CCP churned with paranoia, hatred, and envy that could easily be targeted at another party member, or a person who was not a party member, by a simple denunciation. All that was required was an accusation of aberrant behavior or thinking, or "emplacing a hat" by giving someone a negative label. To be a "counterrevolutionary," an "anti-party element," a "rightist," and so on—all were punishable crimes. With minimal or no due process, those accused / named by party or revolutionary committee authorities could be beaten, tortured, sent to prison or labor camps, even summarily executed or forced to commit suicide. Even when released from labor camps or prisons, many were not allowed to return home, could not find work, and were denied any political rights. Family members were subjected to discrimination and punishment.[73]

There was a political dimension to the matter of reversing these injustices in the post-Mao era. The divided Politburo differed over how they were dealt with by the Central bureaucracy. Deng Xiaoping needed to restore elder veterans to bolster his position. Those who had prospered from the purges of party veterans in the Cultural Revolution or before, including Chairman Hua Guofeng, were not enthusiastic about their return. In 1977 the Central Organization Department, the organization responsible for the management of the careers of millions of CCP officials, was overseen at the Politburo Standing Committee level by Wang Dongxing.

Wang was also responsible for the Central General Office, which handled paperwork, meetings, and security for the Central Committee, and for the Propaganda Department, which supervised the press, television, movies, and books. He had his hands on several of the key levers of power. Although the enmity between Wang and Deng was not public knowledge, it became increasingly clear, as the two men squared off over ideological and organizational issues in 1977–1978, that there would soon be a reckoning.[74] For Deng Xiaoping, moreover, the road to displacing Hua Guofeng went through Wang Dongxing.

And the road to Wang Dongxing led through the Organization Department, which in 1977 was ripe for change. Its essential personnel functions—pay and benefits, recruitment and education, appointments, transfers, promotions, appraisals—had to be performed even during the Cultural Revolution. So although many of the department's leaders had been denounced and imprisoned after the summer of 1966, Red Guards did not actually take over the Organization Department. Nor was a military control group officially assigned to run it. However, in the summer of 1967, Guo Yufeng, a political commissar of the Sixty-Fourth Army in Shenyang Military Region, was called to Beijing and assigned to work for Kang Sheng as head of an operations group inside the Organization Department.[75] Much of his work evidently was involved in Kang's obsessive search for traitors and spies, and Guo was part of the Central Special Case Group that brought terror to party cadres at all levels. When Kang's health began failing in the early 1970s, Guo moved into Wang Dongxing's orbit, and before Kang's death in 1975, he had gained formal appointment as minister of the Central Organization Department.[76]

By 1977 the bureaus of the Organization Department responsible for veteran cadres and personnel grievances were swamped with petitions and visits from former officials (or family members) who had been maltreated during the ten years of chaos. Former Public Security Ministry official Yin Shusheng estimated that roughly 75 percent of officials above the vice-minister/vice-governor level in the Center or provinces had been suspended from work on political charges. PLA officers falsely accused of political crimes numbered eighty thousand, of whom some eleven hundred had been killed. More than a million educators had been "framed" and more than fifty thousand scientists under China's Academy of Sciences had been falsely accused and suspended from work. If one added up those punished for their class background, those who spoke out on political issues, or those denounced as class enemies and sent to prison or labor reform, the total number of victims of China's ceaseless political campaigns since "Liberation" numbered more than one hundred million, according to a speech given by Ye Jianying in 1980.[77]

Within the Organization Department, however, there seemed little sense of urgency. Petitioners who traveled to Beijing to call at the Organization Department were disparaged, threatened, even expelled from the waiting area. After the Eleventh Party Congress, many staff began quietly complaining about the way the department was implementing cadre review policies. Big-character posters began appearing in the corridors of some buildings specifically criticizing Guo Yufeng for mistreating veteran cadres and mismanaging the process.[78]

The October 7 *Renmin Ribao* article added fuel to the flames. Although it did not mention names, the front-page article described the shortcomings of the Organization Department's approach to veteran cadres and the department's refusal to reconsider wrong verdicts. It also faulted "some comrades doing cadre work," for misunderstanding the bigger issues of right and wrong, and for failing to correct the mistaken cadre policies of the past.[79] The article elicited thousands of letters to the editor and telegrams from readers, mostly from veteran cadres. It also energized dissent within the Organization Department. Staffers not only wrote more big-character posters, but also began reporting them to *Renmin Ribao* for inclusion in a classified news publication for leaders called "Internal Reference."

Hu Yaobang had gained an important new ally in the attack on the Organization Department: Hu Jiwei, editor in chief of *Renmin Ribao*, crown jewel of the CCP's propaganda. The two men had met in the hospital while both were recuperating from Cultural Revolution maltreatment. A career journalist, Hu Jiwei had become disenchanted with the party's mouthpiece while the Gang of Four was running it, and preferred working in a State Council research office set up by Deng Xiaoping after 1976. But Hua Guofeng persuaded him to step back into *Renmin Ribao* to help restore it, perhaps not knowing that, as Hu put it, "I was no longer the very obedient Hu Jiwei."[80]

After the October 7 article, Hu Jiwei stoked the Politburo debate on the Organization Department by quoting critical inside commentary in the "Internal Reference" news supplement. Soon Ye Jianying and Deng Xiaoping began calling for Guo Yufeng's replacement as head of the Organization Department. Ye repeatedly recommended Hu Yaobang as the most talented official to settle unresolved grievances in the Organization Department.[81]

In late November the two Hus collaborated again on a *Renmin Ribao* front-page article that raised the stakes. Anonymously authored by a "commentator of this newspaper," it was titled, "Chairman Mao's Cadre Policy Must Be Conscientiously Implemented."[82] Although Hu Yaobang had seemed hesitant to confront Wang Dongxing directly, the commentary boldly advised organizational units to settle unresolved cases, overturn wrong verdicts, provide appropriate jobs or retirement for rehabilitated officials, and see to the needs of families of those who had died. It used Mao's authority against Guo and Wang, stating, "Chairman Mao repeatedly taught us: 'If there is opposition, it must be purged, and if there are mistakes, they must be corrected. What is truly wrong must be resolutely corrected.'"[83]

On December 10, Guo Yufeng was summoned to a meeting with Hua Guofeng and Wang Dongxing and relieved of his duties. Hu Yaobang was formally appointed minister of the Central Organization Department that same day, while continuing to serve as executive vice president of the Central Party School. He also remained the editor of *Theoretical Dynamics*, which had been growing in circulation and influence under his guidance. It remained a high priority for him, despite the heavy burden of new responsibilities at the Organization Department. In fact, up until he formally became party chairman in 1981, Hu continued to convene small group meetings every few weeks with *Theoretical Dynamics* staffers, in his various offices, and especially in his home.

Whether or not Hu had been expecting the Organization Department appointment, he was well-prepared for it, having done personnel work in the Communist Youth League, and with the Red Army's General Political Department in the 1940s. A few days after his formal appointment, he reported to the department's headquarters and set to work with zeal and efficiency. He held an all-hands meeting on his first day, setting a clear agenda of impending change. The Organization Department, he said, should "restore its fine traditions," and become every "party member's home, and the cadres home." Every visitor and petitioner should be treated respectfully, regardless of seniority, rank, or complaint. He promised to meet with any wrongly punished cadre who asked to see him, and to look at any petition that had his name on it. He admitted that there was "a mountain of accumulated cases," especially from the Cultural Revolution. He then likely shocked his audience by telling them they also had an "unshirkable responsibility" to examine the countless unjust, false, and wrong cases from the 1950s, from before 1949, and all the way back to the early days of the revolution. No matter how difficult the mountain of cases, he said, "we must have the determination to reach the summit."[84]

That same day, Hu met with each of his deputy directors, including those who had been sidelined by Guo Yufeng, and rearranged their responsibilities. He directed the establishment of a large bureau (*ju*) responsible for cadre investigations, under He Zai, who had been labeled a "rightist" and sidelined. Hu also established three large informal groups to handle immediate issues. Chen Yeping, who had been jailed for seven years during the Cultural Revolution, headed an "old cadres reception group" to ensure that veteran cadres were respectfully heard and their problems resolved. Zeng Zhi led an "unassigned cadres group," instructed to arrange appropriate assignments for the more than six thousand veteran cadres released from prison or labor reform. A "rightist correction work group" headed by Yang Shijie, also sidelined during the Cultural Revolution, focused on redressing "anti-rightist" cases that dated back to the late 1950s involving cadres and their families who suffered discrimination in housing, employment, and access to education.[85]

Hu Yaobang has received near universal acclaim for his one-year stint at the Organization Department. His personal integrity and dedication were on daily display, and his organizational skills both channeled and inspired hard work among his subordinates. He read at least twenty petition letters every day, commenting on the best means of resolving them. He met with officials who requested a face-to-face meeting, some of them at his home. He even installed a long table in his dining room to hear petitioners' cases during dinner. He regularly gave speeches to Organization Department meetings and forums, both in Beijing and elsewhere.

The results of Hu's leadership are striking. The accounts provided by Zeng Zhi and He Zai are basically in accord. From 1978 to 1982, the Organization Department reviewed and reversed verdicts on 2.9 million people. For some 547,000 people labeled rightists in the late 1950s, that label was removed, and restitution was made in many cases. More than 1.58 million cases of persecution of intellectuals were redressed, as were 1.8 million cases of persons punished by Cultural Revolution leaders for alleged crimes committed earlier. Hu personally reviewed roughly two thousand petition letters from people of all ranks and backgrounds. He attended scores of meetings and made numerous speeches, exhorting reluctant Organization Department officials to correct and implement the party's cadre policies and to undo the mistakes attributed to the Gang of Four.[86]

There was plenty of pushback. The cases that consistently were the most difficult to handle were those that had been decided or approved by Chairman Mao. The notion that Mao had been old and enfeebled, deceived by Lin Biao and the Gang of Four into making bad decisions, was flawed and unpersuasive. Thoughtful and observant party members and the tens of millions of ordinary people who had suffered through the previous decades knew that the disaster that was the Cultural Revolution was of Mao's making. So were many other ideological failures. But party members could not figure out how to acknowledge the facts and correct the wrongs without undermining a central pillar of the party's legitimacy—the leadership of Chairman Mao.

Hu Yaobang provided a way out, basing his work at the Organization Department on pragmatic Maoist tenets: "Seek truth from facts" (that is, investigate carefully), and "If you make a mistake, correct it." His response to the excuse he heard from many for not even trying to reverse miscarriages of justice—"Chairman Mao approved that case"—began in small office meetings and eventually was publicized nationally. In December 1977 he told senior Organization Department leaders: "All false words or incorrect verdicts and treatment, *no matter* at what time or under what circumstances they were done, *no matter* who at what level decided or approved them, *all* should be corrected in accordance with the facts."[87] Hu would make this "two no matters" case more clearly at a lengthy symposium on difficult cases held from February to April 1978. His tenacity, dedication, and common touch won the admiration not only of his staff, but of countless other officials and the ordinary people of China.[88]

A "Great Debate" about Truth? Or a Power Struggle?

Hu's tasks in the Organization Department were hampered by lukewarm support from Deng Xiaoping on overturning false and unjust verdicts. Deng had a well-known aversion to ideological issues, so he paid scant attention to *Theoretical Dynamics*.[89] When Hu began to seek the large-scale removal of labels such as "rightist" and "right deviationist" from those who had been punished during the 1957 campaign Deng had supervised, Deng balked. He insisted that the anti-rightist campaign was "necessary and correct" but had "expanded" too much. Deng himself had been Mao's chief coordinator of that mass repression, which Hu Yaobang knew very well. Hu Jiwei would write years later that Deng's position prevented a complete clearing of the slate, and presaged Deng's positions on other issues pertaining to Mao. But that did not reduce the significance of Hu Yaobang's efforts.[90]

As Hu Yaobang continued to press for cadre rehabilitations and for overturning judgments attributable to Mao Zedong, he made little headway. Having long favored emancipation of thinking, Hu began shifting focus to Mao's ideological authority, trying to rid party members of what he considered their unsustainable view that "every sentence of Chairman Mao's is truth," and that "one sentence of his is worth ten thousand of anyone else's." Here the opposition was deeper and more varied, but still traced back to reverence for Mao and his domination of ideological issues. And the chief guardians of orthodox Maoism in 1978 were Wang Dongxing and his supporters in the propaganda apparatus who had formulated the Two Whatevers.

Hu Yaobang had developed an effective tool for fighting ideological battles—namely, the staff and resources of *Theoretical Dynamics* at the Central Party School, which had been placed outside the editorial reach of the propaganda apparatus. They had been useful in generating the climate of opinion on unjust cases that brought down Guo Yufeng. Now they would focus on an obscure ideological question: What is truth, and how should socialist theoreticians evaluate it? The answer that Hu Yaobang had published in issue 60 of *Theoretical Dynamics* in May 1978 was that "practice is the sole criterion for judging truth." The term "practice" (*shijian*), is also translated "actual practice" or "to put into practice." The article kicked off a major ideological battle inside the party and, more importantly, a regime-changing political struggle.

It started off as two articles. One had been written by Hu Fuming of Nanjing University for *Guangming Ribao,* the CCP's official publication geared toward intellectuals. Dry and dull, it was at first rejected by the newspaper. A second article by *Theoretical Dynamics* staffer Sun Changjiang was shorter and more directly targeted at those stifling a fuller discussion of ideological concepts, preferring quotes from "sacred texts" to guide policy. "That attitude is wrong," the article declared.[91] Hu Yaobang had edited the final text of Sun's article and arranged with the editor in chief of *Guangming Ribao* to publish it. As expected, the article kicked off a fierce debate.

In fact, the "criterion of truth debate," usually portrayed by PRC historians as an ideological struggle, is better understood in the context of the political struggle between Deng Xiaoping and Wang Dongxing, each manipulating the levers of power available to him. Hu Yaobang and a small team of political theorists came to Deng's aid at a critical moment—and he to theirs—against a shared antagonist. The struggle was silent, behind closed doors, but visible to careful media watchers.

On May 10, issue 60 of *Theoretical Dynamics* was printed and circulated in Beijing, its only article being "Practice Is the Sole Criterion for Judging Truth."[92] The following day *Guangming Ribao* reprinted the article as a "special commentator" item on page one. That evening Wang Dongxing told a meeting of the editorial office for *Selected Works of Mao Zedong* that the article "points the spear at Chairman Mao."[93] On May 12 *Renmin Ribao* and the PLA's main newspaper, *Jiefangjun Bao,* both published full-text versions of the *Guangming Ribao* commentary. A former editor in chief of *Renmin Ribao* working for Wang Dongxing called Hu Jiwei to criticize him for publishing the article. The commentator article had "errors of direction, . . . was cutting down the banner of Mao Zedong Thought, . . . and was politically bad," he warned. Hu Jiwei reported the call to Hu Yaobang.[94]

As was customary, Xinhua News Agency forwarded the special commentator article to all local newspapers and broadcast stations the next day. Xiong Fu, editor of the party's theoretical journal *Hongqi* [*Red Flag*] and close associate of Wang Dongxing, telephoned the Xinhua director to tell him that Xinhua and *Renmin Ribao* had "made a mistake."[95] In the evening of May 13 Hu Yaobang met with Hu Jiwei and several members of the *Theoretical*

Dynamics group in his home, criticized the intimidation tactics of Propaganda Department leaders, and suggested the magazine move forward with an article on the "unstoppable tide of history."[96]

On May 17 Wang Dongxing convened a small group of propaganda leaders and attacked the "criterion of truth" article as being "theoretically absurd and ideologically reactionary" and anti-Mao. He instructed the Propaganda Department to investigate and prevent a recurrence. "Our Party newspaper cannot do this," he complained. "We must uphold and defend Mao Zedong Thought." The following day he summoned Propaganda Department director Zhang Pinghua and Xiong Fu, telling them that *Renmin Ribao* had been "imprudent" and should be investigated.[97]

On May 30 Deng Xiaoping summoned Hu Qiaomu—whom he had appointed to head the Chinese Academy of Social Science—to discuss his upcoming speech to the "All-PLA Conference on Political Work," at which Hua Guofeng and Ye Jianying were also speaking. Deng said he found the controversy over "the criterion of truth" to be "baffling" but intended to make it a key point in his address to PLA commissars.[98]

On June 2 Deng gave a pointed rejoinder to Wang Dongxing, although he did not mention either the "criterion of truth" debate or the Two Whatevers argument. "Some of our comrades talk about Mao Zedong Thought every day, but they often forget, abandon or even oppose Comrade Mao Zedong's fundamental Marxist viewpoint and method of seeking truth from facts, proceeding from reality, and integrating theory with practice. Some people even go further: they maintain that those who insist on seeking truth from facts, proceeding from reality, and integrating theory with practice are guilty of a heinous crime."[99] *Renmin Ribao* commented on Deng's speech the following day, calling it an "incisive elaboration of the importance of seeking truth from facts" in Mao Zedong Thought. On June 6, both *Renmin Ribao* and *Jiefangjun Bao* published the entire text of Deng's speech. Wang Dongxing reportedly was furious.[100]

Earlier in June, Hu had received an article written by *Theoretical Dynamics* leader Wu Jiang sharply critical of the Two Whatevers and supportive of the "criterion of truth" debate. In light of heavy criticism from Wang Dongxing of both him and his magazine, Hu suggested that Wu wait three months before publication. But he sent a copy of the article to Luo Ruiqing, then secretary-general of the Central Military Commission. Luo was an old friend of Hu's, rehabilitated by Mao in 1975 from early Cultural Revolution disgrace. Luo had praised the May 10 "criterion of truth" article and personally approved its inclusion in the *Jiefangjun Bao*. He suggested that if the PLA newspaper published Wu Jiang's article, the "scholars who did not agree" could not do anything about it.[101] It was essential cover for Hu, facing pressure from a vice-chairman of the CCP.

In mid-June Wang Dongxing stepped up that pressure. At a meeting of senior propaganda leaders, presided over by Hua Guofeng, Wang unleashed an apparently unscripted rant, criticizing both Hu Yaobang and Hu Jiwei by name for "serious errors" that should be investigated. Hua offered no opinion, and according to Hu's chronology, neither of the two Hus were disciplined because of Wang's outburst.[102]

On June 19, Hu Yaobang edited the final draft of Wu Jiang's article for the *Jiefangjun Bao*, "A Most Fundamental Principle of Marxism," which was scheduled for publication on June 24. Luo Ruiqing, who was then preparing to travel to West Germany to have his shattered legs (from his attempted suicide early in the Cultural Revolution) repaired by specialists there, told worried staffers, "You must boldly publish that article. There might be people who will oppose it. I am responsible. If they want to beat someone, beat me."[103] Unfortunately, Luo died on a Heidelberg operating table on August 3, depriving Hu of a valuable ally in his future party struggles.

Deng Xiaoping began showing signs of understanding the opportunity presented by the still-growing "criterion of truth" debate, however. On July 22 he summoned Hu Yaobang for a chat about the original article and its follow-on commentary. Deng admitted he had not paid much attention to the first article, but read it later, found it suitably Marxist, and approved both the debate and the *Theoretical Dynamics* participants. "This team is not bad! Don't break it up, it's a good team," Deng enthused. Later that evening Hu summoned the team to his home to tell them the good news of Deng's support. He also told them Deng had warned the Propaganda Department during this period to "not set up forbidden zones" for discussing ideological issues.[104]

Hu and Wang Dongxing crossed swords again in the summer of 1978 on another sensitive issue pertaining to rehabilitating old cadres. The "61 Traitors Group" was a case fabricated by Kang Sheng against several of Liu Shaoqi's prominent supporters in 1967. Its origins involved the 1936 arrests of several Communist Party leaders in KMT-controlled areas. Although several appeals had been made for its reversal by 1977, it remained in the Central Special Case Group's active files. Deng Xiaoping and Chen Yun had encouraged Hu Yaobang and the Organization Department to reinvestigate the case and submit a report.[105] Hu Yaobang requested a meeting with Wang Dongxing on June 9, 1978. He took with him his deputy, Chen Yeping, and Minister of Public Security Zhao Cangbi to meet with Wang and Politburo Members Ji Dengkui and Wu De for what they expected would be a handover of pertinent documents from the Central Special Case Group.[106]

Instead they received a rude lecture from Wang on why the Central Special Case Group would not turn over any of the original investigatory information, but only summaries of the verdicts. The investigations and their findings were approved by Chairman Mao and could not be reversed, Wang insisted. He added that, because they involved "contradictions with the enemy," they were classified and could not be turned over to the Organization Department. Hu refuted these arguments, but he was outranked and threatened, and left empty-handed. Returning to his office, he acknowledged the trip was a waste of time and promised to "light another oven."[107]

Hu's luck was about to change, however. *Deng Xiaoping's Chronology* notes on June 25 that Deng received some Organization Department material on the "61 Traitors Case." In his instructions, Deng wrote: "This problem must be dealt with correctly. It is a question of seeking truth from facts."[108] On July 4, Hua Guofeng invited Hu Yaobang to his home for a "chat" about the "61 Traitors" case, according to the brief notation in Hu's unofficial chronology. Hua told Hu that the case must be resolved quickly, with the Organization Department doing a reinvestigation and writing a report for the Center.[109]

Two days later Hu briefed the *Theoretical Dynamics* leading group about his talk with Hua, which he said lasted from 3 p.m. on July 4 until after 1:00 a.m. that night, including dinner. Substantively, said Hu, the talk was mostly about economic recovery, maintaining "unity and stability," and calming residual animosities from the Cultural Revolution. According to the fragmentary record Hu provided his friends, Hua "talked a lot" about several topics, and out of courtesy and convention, Hu took no notes. He was encouraged that Hua confided in him and that, despite Wang Dongxing's rebuke, reassured Hu twice of his confidence in the Organization Department.[110]

Hu called senior leaders of the Organization Department's Cadre Investigation Bureau to his office on July 10 to talk about beginning its own investigation of the "61 Traitors" case. In light of interference from the Special Case Group, he told them it would take courage and determination, as it involved "mistakes our great leader made in his late years." Hu put Chen Yeping in charge, added new staff and sent them all over the country to find original source documents and witnesses, with the goal of completing a report by September 30.[111]

In another win for Hu Yaobang's approach to correcting the party's historical errors, on September 17 the General Office distributed *Zhongfa* No. 55 of 1978, which reported that several CCP departments and State Council ministries had agreed on procedures for completely removing the "rightist hats" that had been hung on so many people in the period following 1957. Although the more than 550,000 cases of "rightist" labels still under appeal were not to be immediately overturned through reinvestigation, the individuals were to be fully restored to society, employment was to be arranged, and their family members were no longer to be stigmatized. This was a highly complex and controversial process involving numerous regional meetings and compromises. Even Deng Xiaoping had issues with it. Hu and his subordinates in the Organization Department developed a compromise formula that said, "Everyone who should not have been designated rightist but was mistakenly designated should be realistically given a correction."[112]

Hu was scheduled to deliver a major speech to personnel specialists from all over the country on September 25, concerning the handling of cadre rehabilitations. As was customary, he submitted the first draft of his address—titled "In Implementing Cadre Policy, the Key Is in Seeking Truth from Facts"—to Zhang Yaoci, Wang Dongxing's principal deputy in the General Office.[113] They disapproved of Hu's use in the speech of the "two no matters" formulation he had introduced in December 1977. Hu used it anyway, after which Zhang Yaoci deleted the offending words from the printed conference minutes because Wang had said they were "inappropriate." Hu had the full text printed in an internal Organization Department bulletin he had initiated in June. After the conference, he asked Wang Dongxing why he wanted the phrase deleted, to which Wang replied, "If the case was one Chairman Mao decided, what would you do?" Hu responded: "I believe that if the old man was still alive, he would also restore the truth from facts, as he had always advocated. Therefore, all the cases the old man decided or approved that practice has proven were unjust, false, and wrong cases should be redressed and corrected."[114]

Hu Yaobang received on schedule the first draft of the Organization Department's report on the "61 Traitors" case ordered by Hua and Deng, and began preparing it for submission to the Central Committee. Having been denied access to Special Case Group files, the Organization Department team had traveled to several provinces, reviewed hundreds of documents, and interviewed many officials in their effort to clear the case. Hu suggested to the team leaders that their next case should be that of Liu Shaoqi—the most sensitive case and controversial victim of Mao's direct persecution during the Cultural Revolution.[115]

The Renowned Third Plenum

The Third Plenary Meeting of the Eleventh Central Committee of the Communist Party of China (December 18–22, 1978) is widely acclaimed in both Chinese and foreign accounts of contemporary PRC history as a turning point, the beginning of a period of "reform and opening" (*gaige kaifang*) in Chinese economic policy, and the start of Deng Xiaoping's reign as paramount leader of the CCP. There is something premature about these judgments, however. First, the term "reform and opening" is not mentioned in the communiqué of the Third Plenum. Second, even though Deng's standing and role in the CCP were decidedly enhanced by the decisions of the plenum, Deng had not set up everything in advance, and he needed help from various other leaders, especially Ye Jianying and Hu Yaobang, in order to define and achieve his ends. Finally, the plenum itself was little more than the formal approval of decisions and arguments that took place during the thirty-six-day Central Committee work conference that preceded it.

The Central Committee work conference (November 10–December 15, 1978) that ended up gravely weakening Chairman Hua Guofeng was Hua's own idea, and its original agenda reflected his concerns. After hearing reports in late June from party and State Council delegations that had visited other countries, Hua expressed alarm that China had fallen so far behind Western and Japanese standards of economic and social progress. As he told Hu Yaobang in early July, he hoped "bigger steps" could be taken to speed up China's economic recovery.[116]

The agenda Hua suggested for a Central Committee work conference included reviewing two documents on speeding up agricultural development (which had recovered from the Cultural Revolution but was still underperforming) and approving the National Economic Plan for 1979–1980. In his opening remarks to the plenary meeting of the work conference, Hua recommended the delegates first spend some time talking about an issue the Politburo Standing Committee had discussed earlier, "shift the focus of the Party's and the country's work towards economic construction and launch reform and opening up to the outside world."[117]

This was Deng Xiaoping's issue, and it would become the headline topic of the plenum, but it got put aside while the delegates first vented their anger over historical questions.

Like Mao Zedong's favored expanded Politburo meetings, to which he invited his personal supporters, Central Committee work conferences could be packed with specially selected delegates and could exclude Central Committee members whose attendance was not desired. Unlike expanded Politburo meetings, however, work conferences could not pass resolutions or make personnel decisions for the party at large. That required a Central Committee plenum or congress, and at least early in this work conference there were no plans set for a third plenum.[118] In this case, it was decided by either the Politburo or the Standing Committee to not invite all Central Committee members (the Eleventh Congress elected 201 full members and 132 alternates), which would have brought token representatives of mass organizations and Cultural Revolution beneficiaries to the meeting, a situation that could have been unruly. It was decided to allow participation by several former Central Committee members who had been purged during the Cultural Revolution and were only recently rehabilitated. That meant the meeting was more representative of older party members. According to Wu Weifeng's quasi-official account of the meeting on *Renminwang* [People's Network], Hu Yaobang, as Organization Department director, played an important role in recommending both official and nonofficial participants in the work conference.[119]

A total of 219 participants were invited. The list included all Politburo members and principal party, government, and military leaders from provincial, ministerial, and regional military organizations—people who wielded authority that earned them the reward of Central Committee membership. The attendees were divided into six large groups, corresponding to the six CCP regional bureaus that had been disbanded early in the Cultural Revolution: Northeast, North China, Northwest, East China, Central South, and Southwest. They did not necessarily work or reside in these regions. Hu was one of the conveners of the Northwest group, which turned out to be one of the more lively and influential.[120]

After a first day of tepid discussion of Hua's opening address, former party vice-chairman and Politburo Standing Committee member Chen Yun gave a speech that upended the conference agenda and ignited long-smoldering antagonisms inside the party. Sidelined by Mao well before the Cultural Revolution and dropped from leadership roles, Chen was still widely respected for his personal integrity, and perhaps also for his principled opposition to Mao. He spoke to the Northeast regional group on November 12. He firmly supported Deng's proposed shift in the party's focus from class struggle and criticizing the Gang of Four to going all out for the modernization of China's economy. But Chen insisted that, before such a shift could take place, several problems left over from the Cultural Revolution needed to be considered by the party Center.

The so-called "61 Traitors" case—which included many who had been freed from prison but were still in political limbo—needed to be completely reversed. Party leaders who were incorrectly branded as "traitors" during the Cultural Revolution should be rehabilitated. For instance, Tao Zhu, former first secretary in Guangdong, had been brought to Beijing by Mao and installed in the Cultural Revolution Group. Purged after only a few months, he died under house arrest in 1969, having been denied proper medical care. Wang Heshou, minister of metallurgy during the Great Leap Forward, had been arrested and jailed for eight years during the Cultural Revolution and was still not free in 1978. Chen faulted the Central Special Case Group for mishandling these cases.[121] Former defense minister Peng Dehuai was purged as part of an "anti-party clique" after the Lushan meeting in 1959. During the Cultural Revolution he was savagely beaten and humiliated; he died in a Sichuan prison in 1974 and his death was kept secret. Even his burial place was unknown. Chen said Peng's body should be brought back to be interred with honors in the Babaoshan Revolutionary Cemetery.

The Tiananmen incident of 1976, a "great mass movement" to mourn Zhou Enlai and repudiate the Gang of Four, should be affirmed as "revolutionary" by the Center, and all who were arrested in connection with it should be released. Finally, Kang Sheng—who had died and was buried with full CCP honors in 1975—should be posthumously condemned by Central authorities for his many "unjust, false, and wrong cases" and other crimes.[122]

Several of these cases had it in common that they were under active investigation by the Central Organization Department under Hu Yaobang's direction. The department's draft report on the "61 Traitors" case had been delivered to the Standing Committee on November 3. Hu Yaobang brought materials from other cases to the work conference.[123] At least four other party veterans made speeches similar to Chen Yun's in other groups on November 11.[124] Hu also had played a crucial role in encouraging Central Party School faculty to document their grievances against Kang Sheng, and a joint report by the Organization Department and the International Liaison

Department was completed just prior to the work conference. Its findings, naming hundreds of Kang's victims, were widely shared at the work conference, although the report was not officially circulated.[125]

The demand to have the party Center reverse the verdict on the April 5 Tiananmen incident had built enough momentum by November 12 that Ye Jianying warned Hua Guofeng that he risked being rendered "passive" unless he took action to show that the Center supported the decision already taken by the Beijing municipal CCP committee to overturn the 1976 judgments.[126] On November 15 the *Beijing Daily* reported that the municipal committee had formally declared the Tiananmen incident to be an "entirely revolutionary act." On November 18 a book of poems commemorating the Tiananmen incident was published with Hua Guofeng's calligraphy on the cover, signifying that the Center had decided to reverse the verdict.

The speeches by Chen Yun and other elders generated a strong response among the work conference attendees. In the following days, speaker after speaker delivered remarks demanding redress for colleagues and friends who had been persecuted during the Cultural Revolution. They also raised other political and ideological questions that needed to be resolved before the party could get on with its other business. Daily briefing reports were prepared in each discussion group and delivered to the Politburo Standing Committee. They eventually totaled more than 1.5 million words.[127]

Hu Yaobang's own speech to the Northwest Group on November 14 demonstrated he had been thinking about more than just reversing verdicts on old cadres. Hu asked his audience to think more deeply. "Why were Lin Biao and the Gang of Four able to be on the stage for as long as ten years? What is the fundamental lesson?" He answered that the problem was the "abnormal life inside the party, where there existed the phenomenon of a party within the party and a law outside the law." Then he quoted Deng Xiaoping on the need for "a large number of cadres in the party who dare to think about problems, dare to speak, and dare to deal with them." In other words, the party needed to reconsider its structure, its operational guidelines, and its ideological foundations, if it was to lead China toward economic modernization.[128]

Deng Xiaoping returned from Singapore the evening of November 14 and went straight to see Ye Jianying. The old marshal told Deng about the lively nature of the group meetings, which pleased him. Deng's immediate response was to focus on Hua Guofeng, complaining that he had received excessive publicity, which Deng said was because the party, during the Cultural Revolution, had carried the post of chairman to an unduly exalted status. That, he insisted, needed to change immediately.[129]

In their biographies of Deng Xiaoping, Ezra Vogel and Alexander V. Pantsov present the November 14 meeting between Deng and Ye Jianying as a key turning point. Both portray Ye as a kingmaker, passing the baton of paramount leader from Hua to Deng, persuading Hua to accept the change, and prevailing on both men to treat each other respectfully.[130] But the power perquisites of all three men were still in play at this point. Deng would take risks in order to emerge, early in 1979, as the overall victor. In November 1978 Hua Guofeng had the titles of chairman of the Central Committee, chairman of the Military Commission, and premier of the State Council, but he was unable to fully exercise the powers of those positions. Ye supported Hua because he was Mao's choice and was supported by a slight majority in the Politburo, where there were more Cultural Revolution beneficiaries than pre–Cultural Revolution veterans. In the more important Politburo Standing Committee, the elders had a three-to-two advantage. The key instruments or pillars of power within the party were all in different hands, and were being contested.[131] The Central Committee work conference and the third plenum would change that.

Deng Xiaoping's overall approach appears to have been to weaken Hua and his supporters through intense criticism at the work conference, to take advantage of pressure for change and put himself at its forefront (particularly in the foreign media), and to get more of his supporters into the upper levels of the CCP leadership, especially the Politburo. Although he probably was not comfortable with youthful critics of the party putting up big-character posters on the Xidan Democracy Wall during the work conference, the fact that many criticized Wang Dongxing, Wu De, Chen Xilian, Ji Dengkui, and sometimes Hua Guofeng seemed to serve Deng's short-term purposes.

While the work conference meetings went on, with participants and Democracy Wall activists raising ever more controversial issues about the Cultural Revolution, the Politburo Standing Committee—whose members generally did not attend conference group meetings—met privately to hash out some of the issues being raised. The Standing Committee met on November 21 to hear briefings on the work conference.[132] The following day the regional small groups discussed the committee's instructions on how to deal with the agricultural documents that had been on the original agenda for the work conference. Hu Yaobang had addressed the problems of the agricultural documents in a speech to his group on November 16, outlining some ideas on the importance of diversifying agriculture, which he said had been too focused on grain production.[133]

On November 25, at another plenary session of the work conference, Hua Guofeng made some startling announcements. All the cases that had been raised by Chen Yun and other speakers, along with some additional unjust verdicts from the Cultural Revolution and afterward, would be overturned upon recommendations from the Standing Committee to the next plenary meeting of the Central Committee, which would follow the work conference. The original judgment of the 1976 Tiananmen incident would be set aside, and it would be recognized by the Central Committee as a "completely revolutionary activity." Peng Dehuai, Bo Yibo, Tao Zhu, Yang Shangkun, and others were to be completely rehabilitated. Local party committees were to handle similar mistaken cases at their own levels with advice from the Center. Kang Sheng and former minister of public security Xie Fuzhi had "aroused great public anger," and their crimes and mistakes were to be fully exposed and criticized. Perhaps most importantly, the Politburo Standing Committee ordered the Central Special Case Group under Wang Dongxing to discontinue its work and turn over all remaining archives to the Organization Department.[134]

It was a striking turnaround, the product of a recognition by Hua Guofeng and Wang Dongxing that they had been outmaneuvered by Deng and the old veterans who had stacked the work conference with their cohorts. Those cohorts were emboldened by Chen Yun and others who broke the silence, voicing long-stifled complaints. It was also a reproof to those who had insisted on carrying on an ideological line and a set of policies grounded in personal loyalty to Mao that many party members no longer felt. Some of those loyalists had done things to other party members that were unacceptably cruel, and now their victims were seeking justice, and in many cases, revenge.

The day after Hua's speech, delegates to the work conference began attacking Wang Dongxing by name. They had been criticizing him indirectly but had been reluctant to openly name a party vice-chairman and member of the Politburo Standing Committee, especially one who had authority over armed guards and who kept an extensive archive of secret personnel dossiers. Yu Guangyuan and another colleague made similar attacks on Wang in a regional group, and two senior journalists had done the same in other group discussions.[135] Wang was accused of trying to squelch the "criterion of truth" debate, engaging in corrupt practices in cadre housing allocation, and mishandling evidence in the Central Special Case Groups.[136]

Three other members of Hua Guofeng's support group within the Politburo—Ji Dengkui, Wu De, and Chen Xilian—also came under heavy fire during this stage of the work conference and acknowledged their errors. Wang resisted pressure to perform a public *jiantao*. Hua tried to accommodate his critics and let go of his erstwhile allies. The work conference had slipped completely out of his control, whereas Deng Xiaoping had seized a tactical advantage that he might not have planned for but was more than ready to exploit.

Not far from the Jingxi Hotel, the Xidan Democracy Wall had grown into a public gathering place for ordinary citizens to air complaints and criticisms of the CCP without fear of retribution. In light of the work conference's focus on undoing the political damage from the April 1976 crackdown in Tiananmen Square, no one wished to risk more public wrath by punishing people for exercising their constitutional right to put up big-character posters. Day after day through November, the number of critical posters grew, attracting large crowds of onlookers, including some foreign reporters. Political pamphlets—with names like Exploration, Enlightenment, and Beijing Spring—began to circulate, explicitly critical of the Communist party, Mao, and other leaders.[137]

Deng Xiaoping Takes Charge

In early December, work conference delegates turned to personnel issues, and each regional group began considering recommendations to put before a full Central Committee plenum. On December 1 the Standing Committee convened a special meeting of all provincial first secretaries and military region commanders, at which Deng Xiaoping set out guidelines for upcoming personnel decisions. He reminded all that the foreign press was watching their meetings for signs of an internal power struggle, so they would proceed carefully. The principle of "No one can go down, they can only go up" (or as other accounts put it, "Only entrances, no exits") was to be applied, and only three or four new Politburo members would be added.[138] Even those Politburo members who had been severely criticized "would not be moved." Deng was clear about who the new members would be: Chen Yun, Deng Yingchao (Zhou Enlai's wife), Hu Yaobang, and Wang Zhen, Deng's staunchest supporter.[139]

Deng's December 1 declaration set the course for concluding the work conference. The next day the six regional groups began developing policy and personnel recommendations, which corresponded with Deng's. They recommended that Wang Dongxing, Ji Dengkui, Wu De, and Chen Xilian could maintain their Central Committee ranks but their substantive responsibilities should be adjusted. Hu Yaobang's group called for Wang Dongxing to be removed as director of the party's General Office and head of the Central Guards Bureau. They even recommended that the 8341 Unit be downsized and placed under the authority of the Beijing Garrison.[140] The Politburo met on December 10 to consider the recommendations. It decided to recommend to the Third Plenum that Chen Yun be made a vice-chairman and be added to the Politburo Standing Committee; that Deng Yingchao, Hu Yaobang, and Wang Zhen be added to the Politburo; and that nine other veterans who were purged during or before the Cultural Revolution be restored to Central Committee membership.[141]

As a potent demonstration of the increased power of his position, Deng Xiaoping needed to be responsible for the most important written document of the work conference and the Third Plenum—his concluding address to the Central Committee.[142] Deng had been preparing his speech for the concluding session of the work conference even before he began his Southeast Asia tour in early November, leaving the task of drafting to Hu Qiaomu. On December 2, Deng summoned Hu Yaobang and Yu Guangyuan to his home to discuss Hu Qiaomu's draft, which was heavily freighted with class struggle references and other language that did not reflect either the modern perspective Deng desired or the energized atmosphere of the work conference. "It's no good [*buxing*]," Deng said, and he instructed the two to prepare a new draft based on a detailed outline he had written on a notepad.

Deng wanted a "forward-looking" speech, designed to "liberate thinking," generate enthusiasm, break away from old ideas and habits, and move ahead with the modernization of the economy.[143] With help from the State Council Political Research Office and oversight from Hu Yaobang, Yu Guangyuan drafted Deng's address, "Emancipate the Mind, Seek Truth from Facts, and Unite as One in Looking to the Future," which was delivered at the closing session of the Central work conference on December 13.[144] It became the "main theme" document not just for the work conference but for the Third Plenum of the Eleventh Central Committee itself, uniformly hailed in PRC publications as a "turning point" in the CCP's history.

Hu Yaobang does not generally receive much credit for the achievements of the Third Plenum, although he should. Hu had prepared the ideological groundwork for the work conference through articles in *Theoretical Dynamics* and especially the debate on the "criterion of truth," which Deng eventually found useful. In his energetic guidance of Organization Department work on redressing miscarriages of justice, Hu had provided Chen Yun and other veteran cadres with information for reversal of the verdicts on fallen colleagues. He encouraged questioning the truth of Cultural Revolution ideology and pointed out the deep flaws in the party's reverence for Mao.

Hu not only helped draft Deng's clarion call for turning away from class struggle, but he also helped draft Ye Jianying's closing speech to the work conference, which some party reformers considered more important than Deng's speech. Ye had asked for Hu's help early on, and Hu assigned the Central Party School's Wu Jiang to head the drafting team. The old marshal found Wu "too scholarly," and eventually asked his daughter and her husband to prepare the final draft, which went through Hu Yaobang.[145] Unlike Deng, Ye maintained a focus on the errors of the past, castigating the "semifeudal" and "feudal fascist" elements of the Gang of Four's thinking and practices.

Ye's speech also called for strengthening the "socialist legal system," and for more democracy, both inside and outside the party.[146] His most memorable and controversial remark, however, was deleted from subsequent versions of his speech. "This Central Work Conference embodies democracy within our Party," Ye enthused, echoing the views of many participants, "and the Xidan Democracy Wall embodies democracy in society, and these democratic spirits should be carried forward." By the time a copy of Ye's remarks was distributed to delegates at the Third Plenum itself, those comments had been removed.[147]

As the work conference morphed into the Third Plenary Session of the Communist Party of China's Eleventh Central Committee, held December 18–22, 1978, Hu Yaobang's responsibilities continued to be heavy. He was instructed to "guide" the drafting of the Plenum Communiqué in advance, which he did with inputs from Hu Qiaomu, Yu Guangyuan, and others and formal oversight by Hua, Deng, and Ye.[148]

The Politburo Standing Committee made an additional decision in early December to formally reestablish a Central Commission for Discipline Inspection (CCDI). Hu Yaobang and the Organization Department were tasked with recommending its composition. The department recommended a ninety-nine-member commission, with Chen Yun and Deng Yingchao as first and second secretaries, and several rehabilitated old cadres taking positions as secretaries, standing committee members, and commission staff. At Chen Yun's request, Hu Yaobang was appointed third secretary of the commission.[149]

Finally, as guiding editor of *Theoretical Dynamics* magazine, Hu Yaobang oversaw the publication of nine issues of the magazine during the work conference and plenum, several of them aimed specifically at questions being considered at the party conclave and timed for maximum effect. He made certain that enough copies were delivered to delegates at the Jingxi Hotel.[150] Hu also prepared important study documents for ordinary party members to review in coming to grips with the momentous changes taking place. Several commentators have observed that without Hu Yaobang's active involvement in every phase of these meetings, the Third Plenum would not have had the historic political impact it achieved as the "turning point of reform."[151]

Hu's Surprising Promotion

Hu Yaobang's significant contributions to the work conference and Third Plenum were no doubt the primary reason for his promotion at the close of the plenum on December 22, 1978, when he was elected a member of the Political Bureau and third secretary of the Central Commission for Discipline Inspection (CCDI). The first and second secretaries of the CCDI being Chen Yun (seventy-three) and Deng Yingchao (seventy-four), it was expected that much of the organizational work for the new commission would fall to Hu. Three days later, at a Politburo meeting on personnel, Hu was given additional responsibilities as secretary general (*mishuzhang*) of the Central Committee and director of the Central Propaganda Department. In both cases, Hu probably was expected to clean up bureaucratic messes left by Wang Dongxing, and he was saddled in both with the "assistance" of Hu Qiaomu.

Hu Yaobang had risen in two years from an unemployed nonperson under house arrest to be the principal executive officer of the CCP Central Committee, head of the Propaganda Department, a principal decision-maker in the CCDI, and acting president of the Central Party School. It was a remarkable rise for a man of his background and experience. The documentary evidence for the process remains locked in party archives, and the real story needs to be carefully combed out of conflicting accounts from his enemies, allies, and admirers.

Hu Yaobang was chosen not because he was a Deng Xiaoping acolyte, although Deng's support was a key factor in his success. Hu had also gained the trust of Hua Guofeng, and especially of Ye Jianying, who probably was his principal benefactor. Ye also supported Chen Yun's return to the Politburo Standing Committee, according to some accounts, because he and other elders were concerned that Deng's political instincts and drive for power were much the same as Mao Zedong's, and they were no match for him. Chen Yun, with his stubborn character, economic expertise, and party seniority, was considered likely to blunt Deng's dictatorial tendencies.[152]

Hu succeeded in 1977–1978 because he had shown himself to be capable and efficient, having overseen the complex bureaucratic process of rehabilitating thousands of officials and ordinary people purged during the Cultural Revolution. He had attracted the support of party intellectuals and guided their efforts in devising a credible ideology to replace the destructive and unworkable shambles of Mao Zedong Thought. He had the courage to seize opportunities and charge into situations where his superiors were uncertain. But his success now put him in a position where the bureaucratic terrain was different, the problems more numerous and less tractable, and the party's toxic culture more hazardous.

The post of secretary general was not a new one. Deng Xiaoping had held it in 1954, and as head of the Central Secretariat was responsible for the day-to-day administration of all the party's bureaucracies. Two years later, Deng's position was renamed "general secretary," and Deng was elected to the Politburo Standing Committee. Hu Yaobang's situation in 1978 was different, in that the Central Secretariat, abolished in the Cultural Revolution, had not yet been reestablished, so Hu had little staff and ill-defined authority. He was permitted to attend Politburo Standing Committee meetings, although only as an observer. Hu's two deputy secretaries-general, Hu Qiaomu and Yao Yilin, who were to help him manage daily CCP affairs were not his choices, but were considered key supporters of Deng Xiaoping and Chen Yun, respectively. Hu Qiaomu was Deng's principal speech and document writer, head of the Chinese Academy of Social Sciences, and had responsibility for editing Mao Zedong's selected works. Yao Yilin, formerly minister of commerce, was assigned to head the CCP General Office in place of Wang Dongxing.[153]

The three men and a small staff took over some of Wang Dongxing's office space in Zhongnanhai, much of which was used for storage of Central Special Case Group dossiers. Their first tasks involved housecleaning and staff replacement. Special case group files had been officially turned over to the Organization Department in December 1978, but it took until the end of February 1979 for the more than seventeen thousand volumes of political and personal information on more than 650 party officials to be moved and catalogued.[154] Staff replacements for those closely linked to Wang Dongxing (who at this point was only a vice-chairman of the CCP) were managed smoothly through the General Office, which had two new deputies assigned: Feng Wenbin—Hu's longtime friend and subordinate—and Deng Liqun, who would become his nemesis. Hu was able to leave much of the business of coordinating party administrative business to Yao Yilin and the General Office staff and focus on the position that would be a turning point in his career, director of the Central Propaganda Department.

In some ways Hu Yaobang was well-suited to head the Propaganda Department. From his earliest days in the Jiangxi Soviet to developing media products for the CYL, Hu had been focused on getting the party's message out. He had read the Marxist-Leninist canon repeatedly and had memorized key passages. At least until the late 1950s, Hu Yaobang would have been considered a true believer in the official ideology and a loyal student of Mao Zedong Thought. But as Deng Xiaoping noted, he was "not a blind follower," and he had developed his own ideas about Mao Zedong Thought and the decline of its patron saint. Hu's association with ideological thinkers at the Central Party School reintroduced him to the academic rigor of Marxist theoretical studies, and his guidance of the *Theoretical Dynamics* periodical enabled him to evaluate the role of ideology in a post-Mao PRC.

Hu certainly knew that the propaganda apparatus was a mess. As one of the key levers of power within the CCP system, propaganda was Mao Zedong's forte as far back as the Yan'an period. But even when his Mao's creative faculties began to decline, his prestige was such that "every sentence was truth," and people pledged to carry out his directives "even if we don't understand them." In the last years of Mao's life, people around him did not try to develop original concepts but used ideology to curry favor with him, or as a weapon to persecute adversaries in the party.

After Mao's death, Wang Dongxing tried and failed to establish authority over the propaganda system by retaining some Cultural Revolution stalwarts who had worked with Mao and the Gang of Four. But with Hu's help, Deng was able to neutralize Wang, enabling his own emergence as the dominant figure in the party. Deng, however, had interest in propaganda only as a means of maintaining the CCP's primacy, legitimizing his own position and supporting his preferences for solving China's economic problems. He had begun calling for "using a complete and accurate Mao Zedong Thought to guide our work" in 1977 but had not developed the concept much before Hu Yaobang's "criterion of truth" initiative overtook it.[155]

Hu Yaobang was probably aware that many party members were uncertain what was meant by changing the guiding direction of CCP work from continuing class struggle to supporting the Four Modernizations. Others were wary of the purpose of downgrading the importance of Mao Zedong Thought. The heart of propaganda was dissolving, but as Hu Yaobang told supporters during this period, the misapplication and abuse of propaganda was still a major problem. The Maoist idea of the existence of class struggle in a socialist society had not been rejected, nor had the godlike status of Mao Zedong himself been seriously downgraded. The practice of using ideologically based attacks to persecute others was still widespread, and party members and ordinary people alike were being punished for "erroneous thinking." Some senior propaganda officials had even begun speculating that these abuses had led to the phenomenon of "alienation" (*yihua*) of the society from the Communist Party.

That alienation was still on full display at the Xidan Democracy Wall. There students and ordinary workers awaiting buses had perused complaints about unjust treatment, housing problems, and cadre corruption. Some of these complaints were published in small-scale flyers sold to passersby for a small fee. Others were pasted up on the adjoining walls for people to read. As political disputes at the top of the leadership intensified, expressions of dissatisfaction from below also grew, and when the naming of names did not bring reprisal, the practice expanded. According to Wei Jingsheng, an early participant in the activity, it was believed Ye Jianying had instructed police authorities to photograph and transcribe some of the more trenchant commentaries and have them circulated to the attendees at the November work conference.[156]

Deng Xiaoping at first welcomed the public attacks on his adversaries, telling a visiting Japanese Socialist Party leader that it was "allowed by the Constitution of our country. We do not have the right to deny or criticize the masses for promoting democracy and posting big-character posters."[157] In early December, however, Wei Jingsheng, who was described in the

Western press as an "electrician at the Beijing Zoo" but who was actually the son of a prominent military officer, put up a poster on the Xidan Democracy Wall that shocked both Chinese and foreign observers. Wei claimed that the Four Modernizations, "which stand for everything good," could not be achieved through the same tyrannical system that had brought so much calamity. Bitterly sarcastic regarding the party's claims and demands, Wei said that democracy—"the right of the people to choose their own representatives to work according to their will and in their interests" and to "run them out of office" should they fail—was a fundamental prerequisite for achieving the Four Modernizations.[158]

A few days later Deng was still reassuring, saying, "Even if some disgruntled people want to make use of democracy to make trouble, there is nothing to be afraid of. We have to deal with it properly."[159] Ye Jianying, in his speech at the Third Plenum, praised the Xidan Wall as a "model of people's democracy." Hu Yaobang was somewhat more nuanced in his understanding, telling party media to carefully monitor the issues being raised at the Democracy Wall and report them to the senior leadership in internal publications. He noted that, unlike Cultural Revolution big-character posters, those at the Xidan Wall were not intended to persecute or do harm but represented "the voice of the peoples' hearts and a new awakening of the people."[160]

Hu Yaobang also provided guidance and support to a *Renmin Ribao* "special commentator" article published on December 21 that made a strong case for allowing the Chinese people to exercise real supervision over their leaders to forestall the emergence of another Gang of Four. As a portent of things to come, Hu Qiaomu ordered the redaction of Ye Jianying's comments about democracy from the officially circulated version of his speech, and sharply criticized Hu Jiwei for allowing the publication of the special commentator article. Hu Yaobang's effort to manage and redirect CCP propaganda was under attack before he even showed up at the Central Propaganda Department headquarters on December 29, 1978.[161]

An Obscure Ideology Conference Jars the Deng–Hu Relationship

Hu Yaobang set about his takeover of the Propaganda Department in typical fashion, first meeting with senior departmental officials to lay out his plans for change and identify new challenges in the wake of the Third Plenum and what he considered some serious shortcomings in the Department's work. He started off a major meeting on December 31 by disclosing that he thought Hu Qiaomu probably would have been a better choice to head the Department, given his long experience and expertise. But he said a party department director needed to attend to many administrative details, which was not Hu Qiaomu's strong suit, so the Politburo Standing Committee had chosen him instead, which he said was rather like taking a donkey for a horse.[162]

Hu then listed in detail what he intended to fix; namely, the many shortcomings of propaganda work in the recent past. These included cadre attitudes, work practices, training, age, education, theoretical expertise, and most of all, departmental products and output.[163] He lectured them not to use Marxism to persecute others, not to perpetuate a personality cult for anyone, and to learn from the Democracy Wall. He instructed them to break through previous "restricted zones" in literature and art and not to set up new ones. In other words, he told them to set aside many of the propaganda methods they had been using over the past several decades. He exhorted them to "emancipate their minds" and not to fear making mistakes.[164] There is no record of how Hu's listeners responded to this assessment, but many were still wedded to the Two Whatevers and orthodox Maoism, so they probably were less than enthusiastic.

Hu was far ahead of his Politburo colleagues in his ideas about repairing the party's propaganda apparatus, and certainly far ahead of Deng Xiaoping. In his speech to the Third Plenum, Deng had told people to "emancipate their minds" and seek truth from facts, but that appears to have been directed at economic management issues and permitting foreign investment rather than larger issues of ideological guidance. Deng would later make it clear: The CCP cannot do without Mao Zedong Thought, and "emancipation of the mind" needed proper guidance from the party.[165] Ye Jianying had called for a "conference on theory work principles" (*lilun gongzuo wuxu hui*) to be held after the November work conference, but that was in a speech heavily influenced by Hu Yaobang. Hua Guofeng had agreed to the idea, but probably was unsure what was in store.

The Conference on Theoretical Work Principles was scheduled to open on January 18, 1979. As planning was underway in early January, Hu Yaobang and Hu Qiaomu quarreled openly at a Propaganda Department meeting. Hu Qiaomu spoke in dire terms of the chaotic situation developing in the realm of ideology. People at the Xidan Democracy Wall, he said, were "stirring up winds to repudiate the party's leadership, the socialist system and Marxism–Leninism–Mao Zedong Thought." He charged that the situation was as bad as it had been in 1957, just before the "anti-rightist campaign" (launched by Mao with Deng Xiaoping's eager assistance). Hu Yaobang interrupted Hu Qiaomu at that point, quoting Chairman Hua on the overall good situation in the party and on the need to avoid anti-rightist rhetoric. Later Hu Yaobang summoned Hu Qiaomu to his office and told him that his characterization of the situation was incorrect, and his talk about "three winds" was inappropriate.[166]

On January 7 Hu Yaobang sent his organizational proposal for the conference and a draft of his opening speech to the Politburo for their approval, and on January 10 he had a lengthy talk with Hua Guofeng. The speech was approved a week later. Hu envisioned a two-phase meeting stretching over two to three months, with a five-day break for Spring Festival (January 26–February 1). The first phase would be attended by 150 to 200 specially invited, mostly Beijing-based intellectuals and propaganda experts, with a representative sampling of regional propaganda officials. They would meet in five small groups under the auspices of the Propaganda Department and the Chinese Academy of Social Sciences. They would hear speeches and discuss an array of topics in the ideological realm, focusing on the results of the Third Plenum. A daily briefing book covering speeches and discussions would be prepared for Central leaders and then distributed within the party. The second, larger phase would be convened by the party Center in mid-February, with four hundred to five hundred propaganda leaders from across the country being addressed by Chairman Hua or Vice-Chairman Ye. Hu expressed the hope that the conference would generate seven to ten major treatises on ideology in 1979 alone, providing the backbone for a course of study for all seventeen million CCP cadres.[167]

In his speech to the opening session of the conference on January 18, Hu Yaobang laid out its basic agenda and structure and his goals for the meetings. "First, it is necessary to sum up the basic experiences and lessons of the theoretical propaganda front. . . . [W]e can sum up two years, but we also can sum up more than ten years, or thirty years." "Second, we must study the fundamental task of theoretical propaganda work after the shift of the focus of the work of the whole party [away from class struggle and toward modernization]. These two goals are interrelated."[168] Hu's careful but rambling speech opened the door for a more open and freewheeling exchange of views. He warned of those who used propaganda to persecute people, and exhorted theory workers "to free themselves from a state of rigid or semi-rigid thinking and from all kinds of bureaucracy, to break through all 'forbidden areas,' to shatter all spiritual shackles, and to give full play to theoretical democracy, . . . to thoroughly eliminate theoretical despotism . . . and the pernicious influence of the theoretical bully work-style."[169]

Although Hu Yaobang had made an effort to include theorists of all persuasions among the 160 or so attendees at the conference, there appears to have been a preference for those with critical opinions about the past and about Mao Zedong to be the principal leaders of the five small groups chosen to carry the substantive discussion after the opening session.[170] The official records of speeches and conversations taken by group note-takers are, of course, unavailable to the public, but memoirs of some key participants suggest that the meetings quickly went off-course. Those who had suffered at the hands of Mao Zedong and considered him the principal "theoretical bully" of the previous thirty years criticized his theories, his policies and campaigns, his followers, his personal habits, and his personality cult. The Cultural Revolution was attacked on every front, from its initial phases on through to the end.[171] There was also abundant criticism of the "whatever faction" (*fanshi pai*) and their representatives, some of whom were attending the conference. Hu and others evidently felt that the battle against the Two Whatevers had not been completed at the Third Plenum, nor had the debate on the "criterion of truth" been brought to a satisfactory close, so those issues were also prominent in the remarks of several speakers.[172]

Within days Hu Qiaomu was calling on Deng Xiaoping to complain about "unacceptable" speeches being given that repudiated socialism, the dictatorship of the proletariat, the leadership of the Communist Party, Marxism–Leninism–Mao Zedong Thought, and Chairman Mao himself. Hu told Deng Liqun that Deng Xiaoping "couldn't stand to read" the daily briefing materials.[173] Deng Xiaoping left on January 28 for a much-celebrated tour of the United States and Japan, which he considered to be of utmost importance, both economically and strategically. High on his agenda, especially in Washington, was Deng's plan for a short war with Vietnam.

In Washington, Deng met privately with US president Jimmy Carter and his national security team and informed them of the PRC's plans to "teach Vietnam a lesson" by means of a one-month in-and-out attack against Vietnamese forces stationed along the Sino-Vietnamese border. Carter advised against such an action, although not publicly, which was sufficient for Deng's purposes, although he no doubt would have preferred more open support.[174]

Deng was taking a political risk by carrying out such an operation, and several senior military leaders, including Ye Jianying and Su Yu, one of China's most respected wartime commanders, considered the PLA ill-prepared to take on the battle-hardened Vietnamese army. Hua Guofeng is said to have opposed the incursion, but he had little, if any influence on military affairs, despite his title as CMC chairman.[175] Still, Deng could hardly ignore Ye's concerns, which were shared by other PLA veterans. Chen Yun allegedly supported Deng, expressing a view that the threat from the USSR could be discounted for a brief period, if the incursion was brief.[176]

On February 17 more than two hundred thousand PLA troops from the Guangzhou and Kunming Military Regions crossed the border into Vietnam, intending to capture six provincial capitals in northern Vietnam and force the Vietnamese to withdraw troops from Kampuchea to defend Hanoi. The invasion did not go smoothly. The PLA units were poorly trained and led, transportation was insufficient, reconnaissance was unreliable, communications inadequate; there was no air support and not enough artillery. As a result, only three provincial capitals had been captured when on March 6 the PRC announced that its forces had achieved their objectives and began withdrawing back across the border. Vietnamese defense forces pounded the retreating PLA units, inflicting heavy casualties in the last phases of the brief but bloody war.[177]

The historical record of this inconclusive fighting is still open to debate. Although both Beijing and Hanoi claimed victory, both also have discouraged detailed research. Most Western analyses claim that Vietnam bested China in the conflict, suffering greater relative economic damage but fewer casualties, and being able to continue its occupation of Kampuchea. Some observers claim that Deng forced the timing and objectives of the war largely as a means of gaining better operational control of the army. He certainly faced no significant challenge to his military authority afterward, and it is worth noting that Xu Shiyou, the PLA's "warlord general" whose troops performed poorly in the campaign, was retired to the Central Advisory Commission shortly afterward. Yang Dezhi's Kunming Military Region forces were said to have been more efficiently used in the incursion, and Yang was chosen to succeed Deng as chief of General Staff in 1980.[178]

Hu Yaobang had suspended all meetings of the Conference on Theoretical Work Principles during the Vietnam incursion, which was probably a prudent decision in the circumstances. He had begun to be concerned at the extreme tone of some of the conference speakers and the broad array of topics that came under critical scrutiny, including economic policy. The prompt circulation of these speeches meant that negative reaction was broad-based. Not surprisingly, Hu Yaobang himself was the target of increasing attacks. Posters appeared in Beijing criticizing him as a "revisionist" and the conference as "troublemaking."[179] Hu was trying to rein in the discussions and minimize their impact. At a late February Propaganda Conference on newspaper work, he explained, "Since so many people have spoken, it is inevitable that there will be some opinions and views that are not so per-fect. . . . Therefore, we should not regard the speeches made at the Confer-ence on Theoretical Work Principles as the opinions of the Center or as the final conclusions."[180]

But the second phase of the conference, which he had hoped to convene in mid-March, was already in doubt. The first phase had revealed so much disagreement within the party about fundamental issues and principles that organizers were having trouble putting together a coherent agenda for the larger, more formal session. Hua Guofeng and Ye Jianying—probably for dif-ferent reasons—had declined to give speeches to the conclave, leaving only a report by Deng Xiaoping as the main agenda item for the start of Phase Two. And Deng was in a towering rage. The Democracy Wall had grown and become more intense, attracting large crowds of Beijing residents and foreign journalists. Many posters focused on the need for Western-style de-mocracy and the rule of law in China. Some were critical of the attack on Vietnam, focusing on the PLA's poor preparation and high number of casualties. There was heavy criticism of the party, its leaders, and their poli-cies, and especially of Mao Zedong and the excesses of the Cultural Revolu-tion. Some of these issues were being discussed in *Renmin Ribao* and *Guangming Ribao,* two of the CCP's main newspapers.[181]

Deng called on Hu Yaobang to restore a sense of order and discipline in the party media, then began plans to place his own imprimatur on the party's ideological line. At a March 16 meeting "called by the party Center," Deng delivered an intelligence report on the war with Vietnam, then included the following on the domestic situation: "We must resolutely uphold this great banner of Chairman Mao. This is a very important issue in maintaining unity and stability and is also a very important issue for our international influ-ence. When we write articles, we must certainly pay attention to safeguarding this great banner of Chairman Mao, and we cannot use this or that method to harm this banner. To repudiate Chairman Mao is to repudiate the People's

Republic of China and to repudiate this entire period of history." He also suggested not examining the party's history in too much detail and to "temporarily put aside" questions pertaining to the Cultural Revolution.[182]

Hu Yaobang had begun backpedaling earlier, telling colleagues at the Central Party School that some of the criticism of conference speeches had merit, and that party newspapers had not been prudent in some of the articles they had published.[183] After Deng's March 16 comments, Hu retreated still further, particularly on issues concerning Mao Zedong and the Cultural Revolution. "The Center has already spoken; we cannot throw away the great banner of Chairman Mao and Mao Zedong Thought," he told CPS staffers. "Without Mao Zedong Thought, would the Chinese revolution have been victorious? Haven't we been saying in the Party since the Third Plenum that Comrade Mao Zedong had shortcomings and errors, so that sentence is enough!"[184] Hu insisted that the Conference on Theoretical Work Principles had been run well and needed to be affirmed, but he seemed uncertain of how it would proceed.

Wei Jingsheng used the uncertainty as the basis for escalating his criticism of the party and personalizing it. On March 25 he posted a blistering attack on Deng Xiaoping in a Xidan Wall poster titled "Do We Want Democracy or a New Tyranny?" Quoting Deng's supposedly secret briefing on the war, Wei faulted him for praising Mao and vowing to uphold his "great banner." He disparaged Deng's alleged commitment to democracy and freedom of speech, charging that Deng was seeking to sustain Mao's tyranny, which the people of China would not tolerate. As for Deng's modernization goals, "As long as his aim is to continue the Mao Zedong dictatorship, . . . he can only take the road of destroying the national economy and infringing upon the interests of the people." Although Deng had earned the people's trust in 1975, Wei said he was now "defrauding the people" by denying them any real voice in choosing their leaders or influencing their policies and was on the road to becoming another tyrant.[185] Wei intended the poster to alert and alarm other party elders about Deng's predilection for despotism and expected Deng to have him arrested for his effrontery. The police came for him on March 29.[186]

Hu Yaobang's comeuppance had taken place two days earlier, when Deng summoned him, Hu Qiaomu, and other members of a drafting team to his home to discuss the speech he intended to deliver on March 30 to the opening session of Phase Two of the Conference on Theoretical Work Principles. Two of Hu Yaobang's associates, Li Honglin and Wu Jiang, found themselves assigned to the drafting team, and described the scene in Deng's home in similar terms: Deng was grim, "his inner thoughts and outer appearance alike, really an 'iron and steel company', serious and calm, unsmiling. Hu Yaobang had to be respectful in front of him."[187] No one but Deng spoke, all listening carefully to his sharp criticism of "extreme democratism" in society and the "weakness of theoretical work" shown at the conference. He said he would give a speech on "upholding four fundamental principles" (*jianchi sixiang jiben yuanze*) in all propaganda and theoretical work. The principles were to uphold the socialist road, the dictatorship of the proletariat, the leadership of the Communist Party, and Marxism–Leninism—Mao Zedong Thought.[188] Hu Qiaomu would oversee the drafting of the Four Upholds. In fact, the speech would turn out to be almost entirely Hu Qiaomu's work, based on the complaints he had voiced to Deng earlier during the conference and conversations they had held more recently.

The Premature Death of Political Reform?

Although previous meetings of the Conference on Theoretical Work Principles had been held in the Friendship Hotel and the Jingxi Hotel, which had auditoriums large enough to seat the two hundred or so invited attendees comfortably, Deng's report to the opening session of Phase Two of the conference was held in the Great Hall of the People, which was packed with more than five thousand.[189] It took place on the afternoon of March 30, at a meeting presided over by Li Xiannian. Given the political intent and impact of the report, it probably should have been submitted to the Politburo for its approval, although there is no indication that it was. The drafting process was abbreviated. Hu Qiaomu assigned five individuals different sections of the speech, which they submitted on a very short deadline. Wu Jiang and Li Honglin believed their inputs were basically ignored, and the speech was mostly Hu Qiaomu's writing, with final edits by Deng himself.[190] Li Xiannian and Chen Yun reportedly approved Deng's remarks, although Ye Jianying did not, and neither Hua Guofeng's nor Wang Dongxing's views would have mattered much.[191]

"Uphold the Four Fundamental Principles" was a politically provocative speech—feisty, combative, and demanding. Its ideological lesson was a sharp turnabout. And it would set the stage and provide the ideological justification for the party's resolute stand against democracy, "liberalization," and political reform. In other words, it set the CCP on the road to June 4, 1989.

Unlike the Third Plenum's call for "emancipating the mind," and Deng's own call not to establish "forbidden zones," Deng and Hu Qiaomu established an easy-to-remember set of ideological premises that would operate as boundaries, even shackles, for the party's ideological development. If an idea or program did not uphold the Four Fundamental Principles, it was forbidden territory, subject to party discipline. Small wonder the Four Upholds were immediately dubbed the Four Whatevers by some intellectuals.

Blatantly pulling back from any previous commitments to democracy or freedom of expression, Deng lashed out at people like Wei Jingsheng who put up big-character posters criticizing the party or its leaders or its principles. He belittled "some Party comrades [who] have not yet freed themselves from the . . . ultra-Left ideology of Lin Biao and the Gang of Four." But he saved his most pointed criticism for "a handful of people in society at large" who oppose or cast doubt on the Four Fundamental Principles, and "individual Party comrades, [who,] instead of recognizing the danger of such ideas, have given them a certain degree of direct or indirect support." Whereas Hu Yaobang and others at the conference had focused their criticism on the prevalence of "leftist" thinking and practices, Deng claimed that the most worrisome trend of thought facing them was "a trend of thought which is skeptical of, or opposed to, our Four Cardinal Principles, . . . which comes from the Right."[192]

The speech was filled with Hu Qiaomu's Marxist boilerplate about capitalism versus socialism, class struggle and economic determinism. "While we will import advanced technology and other things useful to us from the capitalist countries," Deng intoned, "we will never learn from or import the capitalist system itself, nor anything repellent or decadent."[193] He insisted that, while the idea of "continuing the revolution under the dictatorship of the proletariat" may have ceased to be appropriate, it was essential to maintain all the tools of that dictatorship, such as the army, the public security apparatus, courts and prisons. "In our socialist society there are still counterrevolutionaries, enemy agents, criminals and other bad elements of all kinds who undermine socialist public order, as well as new exploiters who engage in corruption, embezzlement, speculation and profiteering. . . . It is still necessary to exercise dictatorship over all these antisocialist elements, and socialist democracy is impossible without it."[194]

Perhaps most importantly, Deng revived the ghost of Chairman Mao, calling for a moratorium on the kinds of personal, political, and ideological criticism of him that had permeated much of the conference. "While conducting our modernization program in the present international environment, we cannot help recalling Comrade Mao's contributions. Comrade Mao, like any other man, had his defects and made errors. But how can these errors in his illustrious life be put on a par with his immortal contributions to the people? . . . Mao Zedong Thought has been the banner of the Chinese revolution. It is and always will be the banner of China's socialist cause and of the anti-hegemonist cause. In our forward march we will always hold the banner of Mao Zedong Thought high."[195]

As a warning to the Propaganda apparatus and especially its new director, Deng fulminated: "The Central Committee considers that we must now repeatedly emphasize the necessity of upholding these four cardinal principles, because certain people . . . are attempting to undermine them. In no way can such attempts be tolerated. No Party member and, needless to say, no Party ideological or theoretical worker, must ever waver in the slightest on this basic stand. To undermine any of the four cardinal principles is to undermine the whole cause of socialism in China, the whole cause of modernization."[196]

Hu Yaobang was surprised at some aspects of Deng's speech, even though he had participated in a preliminary drafting meeting only days before. No one other than Deng and Hu Qiaomu had seen the final draft, which had both theoretical and practical inconsistencies with the Third Plenum, and with what Deng had said earlier about the conference itself.[197] Hu summoned a few subordinates to his home that evening to discuss how and whether the conference should proceed, given early indications that some participants were unhappy with Deng's remarks. Hu was scheduled to give a keynote speech after attendees had a chance to discuss Deng's address in small group sessions, and his guests were talking about what he should say to reassure them in the wake of Deng's diatribe. Hu paced back and forth for a time, smoking furiously, then announced suddenly, "The meeting will not open, I will not make a speech."[198]

But that was too abrupt, and he ended up giving a short closing address on April 3. He began: "Well, how was our meeting? The safest way is to let history test it. Have we not been saying that practice is the only criterion for testing truth! So let the vast number of cadres and the broad masses of the people test it and look back at it after a period of time, so that history can test it." He thanked Deng for his "important speech representing the Center," and for raising the four principles, "which the vast majority of cadres and party members and the vast majority of the people of our nation have long

believed and supported." He acknowledged that some aspects of the conference had been criticized, which was all right, but admonished his audience
not to think there was a major political change impending, such as a new
anti-rightist campaign, although he probably knew there would be pressure
in that direction, especially from Hu Qiaomu. He concluded his remarks
with a repetition of the Three Nos: No beating with sticks, no putting on
hats, and no pulling pigtails just because you don't agree with what someone
else has to say.[199]

Hu had clearly suffered a personal and political setback at the hands of
Deng Xiaoping and Hu Qiaomu. His words and activities in the ensuing days
and weeks reflected his disquiet. His speeches were fewer and more carefully worded, he edited more heavily *Theoretical Dynamics* articles submitted
to him for approval, recommending some be withheld from broader circulation. He advised liberal journalists like Wang Ruoshui and Hu Jiwei to be
more prudent in putting controversial articles into party newspapers.[200] He
actively promoted more education and the Propaganda Department giving
more attention to the Four Modernizations and to economic policy support
work in general.

But Hu's independent cast of mind and contrarian nature persisted. He
quietly encouraged Li Honglin to write a series of articles about each of the
four fundamental principles Deng had enunciated. Li cleverly twisted each
interpretation so that it supported greater openness and democracy. The articles, some published in *Renmin Ribao,* attracted both praise and criticism,
but Li eventually was disciplined and reassigned.[201]

At Deng's order, the Xidan Democracy Wall was officially closed in
April 1979, though it lingered on a few months in diminished form until the
National People's Congress (NPC) banned it in the autumn. Later the NPC
rescinded the constitutionally guaranteed right to put up big-character
posters (which dated to 1975). According to Hu Jiwei's recollection, Hu Yaobang briefly supported setting up a "democracy park" in a less public venue
of Beijing, but the idea never took off.[202]

Although Wei Jingsheng's trial and conviction took place in October 1979,
his fate had been decided at a Politburo meeting in May or June, and Hu
discussed it during the April NPC meetings. He acknowledged he had been
heavily criticized for "supporting the so-called democratization movement
that violated the 'four fundamental principles' and encouraged anarchism,"
but he stuck to his own opinion. He also advised against arresting people for
expressing their opinions in public. "Those who dare to raise these questions

boldly may not care about being in jail," Hu warned. "Wei Jingsheng has been arrested for more than three months, and once he dies, he will be a martyr among the masses, a martyr in everyone's heart."[203] Wei was sentenced to fifteen years in prison, and served the full term.

Deng and Hu's relationship was not permanently damaged by Deng's quashing of Hu's effort to liberate thinking about the PRC's guiding ideology, to disperse the remains of Mao's personality cult, and to repair the ruinous effect of Mao's policies on China's economy. The two men had worked together over many years, always in a superior-subordinate, although not patron-protégé, relationship. Hu acquiesced in Deng's authority and retreated from a position that had already exposed him to much criticism within the party. Ideologically, Hu had always been more liberal in his views than Deng, less controlling and peremptory in his actions, more grounded in Marxist theory, more inclined to credit scholars and intellectuals.

When Hu Yaobang was both physically beaten and sent to a labor reform camp for two years during the Cultural Revolution, Deng and Hu Qiaomu had been protected by Mao—Deng in a quiet military facility in rural Jiangxi, Hu Qiaomu in sheltered quarters in Beijing. Deng had been Mao's general secretary and Hu Qiaomu his personal secretary, giving both a personal interest in preventing "de-Maoification" after his death. Deng even resisted Hu Yaobang's work in correcting Mao's anti-rightist campaign and some specific rehabilitations of senior officials sacked by Mao, including Liu Shaoqi.[204]

But even though Hu Yaobang lost some influence with Deng during the period following the Conference on Theory Work Principles, Deng still needed the talents and enthusiasm that Hu brought to his work—superior organizational skills, propaganda resources, a reputation for probity. He probably understood the value of Hu's familiarity with Youth League leaders who were still relatively young, but whose loyalty and experience predated the Cultural Revolution. For Deng faced a shortage of capable officials to do the hard work of modernizing China's agriculture, industry, science and technology, and military. Many younger officials who rose during the Cultural Revolution were poorly trained and disposed to be hostile toward the kinds of policy changes Deng was proposing. Moreover, the veteran cadres being rehabilitated from political exile (a process still under Hu's aegis as secretary general) were mostly in their sixties or seventies, and lacked experience in economic development, especially with learning foreign techniques and technology.

Notwithstanding the claims of some historians and Western journalists that Deng had achieved the position of paramount leader of the PRC, Deng probably was not satisfied with the configuration of the CCP leadership as it prepared to celebrate its thirtieth anniversary in power in October 1979. Hua Guofeng was still CCP chairman, chairman of the Central Military Commission, and premier of the State Council, positions that gave him significant potential power. Deng was in actual charge of the PLA through his position as chief of the General Staff and had consolidated his authority through the war with Vietnam. The security apparatus probably was still in some disarray from the dissolution of the party's Investigation Department in the Cultural Revolution and the abuse of political investigative authority by the Central Special Cases Group under Wang Dongxing. The key bureaucracies of the CCP's Central apparatus (the Organization Department and the General Office) were still being recovered from Wang Dongxing's control. The propaganda apparatus, long under leftist control, was under Hu Yaobang and Hu Qiaomu—both loyal enough to Deng but feuding with each other over ideological issues. The foreign policy portfolio was firmly in Deng's hands, but control of economic policy and direction was more in the hands of Chen Yun and Li Xiannian in the State Council.

At age seventy-five, Deng faced monumental and complex policy problems, and his own energies and political resources were reduced. He would focus first on his political power problems, and Hu Yaobang was a key member of his team. For his part, Hu Yaobang must have known that he had been disciplined and his powers circumscribed, but he was still in a position to influence important policies. Hu disagreed strongly enough with Deng over the evaluation of Mao Zedong that he would imperil their relationship and risk his own career to revisit the issue. Deng's intransigence could not prevent the issue from continuing to bubble to the surface, with or without Hu Yaobang's encouragement. But to the degree that meaningful political reform needed to shed Maoist dogmatism and its oppressive side effects, Deng's Four Upholds would prove to be an overwhelming hindrance to that process.

8 The Making of a Reformer

Three years after the death of Mao Zedong, his successors were still struggling not only with his ideological legacy, but with the consequences of the economic, social, and political structure his long domination of the CCP had engendered. In late 1976 the country had been near economic collapse. Hua Guofeng said as much in his report to the National People's Congress in February 1978, and he was eager to find ways to restore both agricultural and industrial productivity to pre–Cultural Revolution levels.[1]

In fact, most senior leaders were similarly inclined, but there was little agreement on how to proceed. China's centrally planned economy—with state-owned enterprises dominating the heavy-industry sector—had declined during the Cultural Revolution. Work stoppages, transportation interruptions, factory factionalism, and general urban turmoil prevented many enterprises from reaching production quotas of earlier years. In 1978 it was estimated that output of many industrial commodities fell below levels achieved in the 1950s. Stagnant production led to money-losing enterprises, which brought down state revenues and caused Central budget shortfalls.[2]

Beginning in the 1960s, Mao had exhorted industrial labor to "learn from Daqing," China's premier oil field in Heilongjiang Province, which he saw as a model of hard work, class struggle, and improvisation. Given that Daqing was a naturally large oilfield that enabled China to ease dependence on foreign oil imports, it was perhaps not an appropriate model for the PRC's often resource-poor industrial growth, but it was Mao's choice, and in 1978, "In industry, learn from Daqing" was still used as an exhortative slogan.

Believing perhaps that restoring industrial production was mostly a matter of willpower, adjusting quotas, and increasing capital construction, Hua, Deng, Vice-Premier Li Xiannian, and others adopted in early 1978 a ten-year economic plan that rivaled some from the Great Leap Forward in terms of unrealistic planning and industrial overreach. It included "ten new oil bases, ten new steel bases and eight coal bases" planned for completion by 1985. When investment—both domestic and some from outside China—began to be diverted to finance them, the national budget became noticeably strained, with huge deficits in both 1978 and 1979.[3]

The agricultural situation in 1978–1979 was far worse. Despite twenty years of forced compliance with the commune system, China's agriculture in 1978 was neither meeting its productivity goals nor, more importantly, enabling many rural inhabitants to have enough to eat. There was no mass starvation, but grain output per capita was lower than it had been in 1957, as were grain rations. More than one hundred million farmers were malnourished, and in some of the poorer regions, annual per capita grain consumption was below subsistence level, leaving many peasants whose income was below one hundred yuan per year resorting to begging for food or borrowing from their work brigades.[4]

Compounding the problems were Maoist ideological shibboleths from the 1950s and 1960s that discouraged efforts at any level to develop improvements. "Take grain as the key link" became the dominant instruction for agriculture after the famine years, entailing labor-wasting efforts to grow rice, wheat, or other food grains on land unsuited for them, with predictable low crop yields and shortages. "In agriculture, learn from Dazhai" began in the 1950s and was continued even when many knew it had become fraudulent. Dazhai was a commune in Shanxi Province famous for terracing barren hillsides and building reservoirs in mountainous areas so grain could be grown. It also was also a model for class struggle in the rural areas and for intensive labor mobilization.

The commune's principal secretary, Chen Yonggui, was "helicopter promoted" by Mao to the Politburo in 1973. He was the State Council vice-premier in charge of agriculture after Mao's death. Mao also had firmly insisted that the "small producer mentality" typical of peasant farmers led to "feudal" enslavement and eventually to "capitalist" thinking, so he enjoined all rural cadres to "cut off the tail of capitalism" wherever they found it. This led to widespread abuses by local officials, including eliminating the small private plots many peasants used for essential sideline production, cutting down fruit trees, barring small-scale handicrafts, prohibiting the cultivation of tobacco, garlic, or peppers to be sold in markets, and banning the private raising of female pigs. Such measures were widely resented in the impoverished countryside.[5]

One burdensome legacy of Mao's agricultural policies in 1978–1979 was the absolute official prohibition against contracting production of agricultural goods to individual farm families, the so-called *bao chan dao hu*. Mao had called it "dividing the land and going it alone," and banned it even after it helped many survive the Great Leap Forward. But the commune system was a failure, and everyone knew it. The two agricultural resolutions discussed and heavily criticized at the November-December 1978 work conference acknowledged the failure but still specifically forbade *bao chan dao hu*.

By early 1979, however, it was being experimentally practiced in two areas of Anhui Province under the careful supervision of newly appointed provincial secretary Wan Li, who made sure it got no publicity while he awaited approvals from Beijing. The idea of tinkering with Mao's commune system was resisted by those who clung to his ideological dogmas; those more disposed to changing agricultural policy—including Hu Yaobang—were preoccupied with other issues and wary of the complex problems of altering such a fundamental aspect of rural life and production.[6]

But by far the heaviest weight of Mao's legacy was the dysfunctional, disorganized, and quarrelsome political system he left for his party heirs to sort out. Not only did his death leave an ideologically divided Politburo, but also, even two years after the Gang of Four purge, his successors were confronted with personnel gaps and shortages that hampered their ability to agree on, justify, or implement any of their plans.

The basic problem was a disparity between formal positions and actual power, evident in the immediate aftermath of the Third Plenum in late 1978. Following the palace coup of 1976, Hua Guofeng had been unanimously chosen as party and CMC chairman by the reduced Politburo, but after what some called "two years of dithering" and a full year after Deng Xiaoping's return to his previous positions, little was being accomplished. Hua at first had acted prudently to hold on to his positions and expand his base in the party. Within the Politburo Standing Committee, he relied for support on Ye Jianying, who referred to him as "the wise leader" and encouraged his efforts to build a Mao-like personality cult.[7]

Li Xiannian provided continuity but little else as ranking vice-premier of the State Council. Wang Dongxing had controlled the Central CCP apparatus, but lost these positions after the Third Plenum, although he was still nominally a party vice-chairman. Within the Politburo, Hua's putative supporters—Ji Dengkui, Chen Xilian, and Wu De—had all been obligated to submit *jiantao* during the work conference and were suspended from substantive duties but not formally purged, in accordance with Deng's (temporary) personnel principle of "only entries, no exits" for Politburo members.[8]

Hua had suffered a political setback at Deng Xiaoping's hands, but his position was far from hopeless. He still held the top positions in the party, government, and armed forces. But he was unable to capitalize on them, lacking personal supporters in key positions. As chairman and Mao's chosen successor, Hua may have had one other possibility for fending off Deng Xiaoping's quest for predominant power—seeking the favor of other CCP veterans wary enough of Deng to want to keep him in check. Foremost among them would have been Chen Yun—former party vice-chairman and seasoned economic planner—who held a higher CCP rank than Deng and was favored by other veterans. Chen had been recommended for membership in the Politburo at the Eleventh Congress in August 1977, but Hua and Wang Dongxing rejected him because of Mao's antipathy toward him.[9] It was a mistake that would cost both men their jobs.

Chen Yun and "Twin Peaks Politics"

Many accounts of the Third Plenum have focused on Deng Xiaoping's emergence as the "preeminent leader" of the CCP, with "de facto supreme power over the party and state."[10] Indeed, Deng began to be called the "core" (*hexin*) of the "second generation" of the party's collective leadership at that time.[11] Chen Yun's rise from mere Central Committee member to party vice-chairman, Politburo Standing Committee member, and head of the Central Commission for Discipline Inspection (CCDI) marked a return to power as noteworthy as Deng's; but it has been less reported, for several reasons. Deng was much better known to Western observers and officials because of his responsibility for Beijing's foreign policy and his successful management of normalizing US-PRC relations during this period. Deng was confident and decisive and knew how to use the Western press. Chen Yun, by contrast, was self-effacing, avoided meeting with foreigners, and preferred working behind the scenes, often outside Beijing. Chen had support within the CCP's old guard, and most importantly was willing to become a political counterweight to Deng, if perhaps not an active rival for political dominance.[12] His sudden appearance at the topmost level of decision-making in Beijing—the Politburo Standing Committee—would have a major effect on both power and policy for the next several years, and would affect the fate of reform and reformers, including Hu Yaobang.

The Standing Committee at the end of 1979 consisted of six members: Hua Guofeng, Ye Jianying, Li Xiannian, Deng Xiaoping, Chen Yun, and Wang Dongxing. Ye was eighty-two and in failing health, but he was still supportive of Hua. Li Xiannian and Chen Yun had worked together on economic issues for many years. Wang Dongxing was in state of suspension and probably played little role in decision-making. Despite Deng's being known as the "core" of the new leadership, his effectiveness would depend on maintaining good relations with Chen Yun, and on edging out and replacing the two Standing Committee members he could not trust, Hua and Wang Dongxing. As Yang Jisheng aptly put it, "Deng Xiaoping and Chen Yun were evenly matched, checked and balanced, neither could push the other out, neither could do without the other. On some major issues, they . . . had to agree before it would work. Therefore, in China's reform era, there was a condition of twin peaks. Since Deng Xiaoping was actually the number one hand, that peak was slightly higher."[13]

Chen Yun was a year younger than Deng (born in 1905 to a Shanghai working-class family) but was senior to Deng in rank, having become a Politburo member in 1934 and a Standing Committee member just before the Long March. After study in the Soviet Union, Chen arrived in Yan'an in 1937 and resumed work at the top of the CCP hierarchy, becoming a member of the Politburo and the Central Secretariat in 1945. Chen was director of the party's Organization Department for several years in Yan'an and maintained a lifelong interest in personnel matters. After the Japanese surrender in 1945, he was sent to the Northeast, where he headed up the Northeast Bureau's Finance and Economic Commission, restoring the infrastructure of China's main industrial region.[14]

After the PRC was established, Chen directed the Central Finance and Economic Commission and was responsible for the successful first five-year plan. By 1956 he had become a party vice-chairman, fifth-ranking member of the Politburo Standing Committee (Deng was ranked seventh), and vice-premier of the State Council. He was at the apogee of his power.[15] But he fell afoul of Mao Zedong in the 1950s over economic policy issues. After sitting out the Great Leap Forward, Chen returned briefly to Beijing to advise Liu Shaoqi on recovery policies, but retired to a villa in Hangzhou when Mao rejected his advice about contracting agricultural production to households.

During the Cultural Revolution, Chen was exiled to a remote part of Jiangxi, then allowed to reside in Shanghai and Hangzhou to recover his perennially poor health.[16] He returned to some political activity after Lin Biao's death, but he did not work with Deng during the latter's 1973–1976 return to Beijing. After Mao's death and the fall of the Gang of Four, Chen pressed Hua and Wang Dongxing to allow Deng Xiaoping's return to work, but without success. They even blocked Chen's speech from being published in the official record of the March 1977 work conference.[17]

At the November 1978 Central Committee work conference, however, Chen's speech proved to be a critical turning point. The boldness of his proposals resonated with other veteran cadres and generated a consensus in favor of Chen being restored to the Politburo Standing Committee and to a party vice-chairmanship ranking above Wang Dongxing. This was accomplished at the Third Plenum, which also approved the reestablishment of the Central Commission for Discipline Inspection (CCDI), responsible for enforcing CCP rules and cracking down on corruption. Chen was named to head it.

At Chen Yun's request, Hu Yaobang was appointed third secretary of the CCDI, even though he demurred at first. Some observers expected that Hu would play an important role in the day-to-day management of CCDI business, given Chen's and second secretary Deng Yingchao's advanced ages, but it did not work out that way. Chen's recommendations for many of the other members of the Commission, made through the Organization Department, were quickly accepted by the Politburo by mid-December. The message was clear—as a member of the Standing Committee and head of the CCDI, Chen Yun would play a key role in decisions on high-level personnel issues.[18]

Chen Yun was restored to his previous positions because of his party rank, prestige among other veterans, perceived knowledge of economics and personnel, and a broad recognition that he had been wronged by Mao Zedong and his leftist colleagues. According to some accounts, Ye Jianying supported Chen Yun's return to the Politburo Standing Committee because he and other elders were concerned that Deng's political instincts and drive for power were much the same as Mao's, and they were no match for him. Chen Yun, with his stubborn character and party seniority, was considered likely to blunt Deng's dictatorial tendencies.[19]

Chen Yun had two political assets Deng Xiaoping needed: historical expertise in managing a socialist planned economy; and a circle of senior economic officials or former officials who were capable and loyal, having worked for Chen in the war or in the finance and economic bureaucracy in the 1950s. Chen also had policy ideas that had been ignored for a long time. Deng had ambitions and misconceptions about economic development, and evidently was willing to cooperate with Chen to see them progress. Chen wasted little time in moving to the fore.

In early 1979, after he had supported Deng's military incursion into Vietnam and gave his tacit support for the Four Upholds dogma Deng laid down in late March, Chen Yun moved quickly back into a leadership role in national economic planning. In January he wrote a letter to all members of the Politburo Standing Committee saying that the already approved 1979–1980 economic plan was unsustainable—production quotas were too high and financial resources allocated to infrastructure development would leave major gaps elsewhere. In March, Chen and Li Xiannian followed up with a joint letter proposing a work conference to unify thinking on economic planning and to reestablish the State Council Finance and Economic Commission.[20]

At an expanded Politburo meeting in mid-March, Chen was appointed to head the State Council commission, with Li Xiannian as his deputy and Yao Yilin as secretary general—clearly Chen's choices. The rest of the twelve members of the commission were people who had worked with Chen or Li in the financial apparatus.[21] Chen was emerging as a powerful figure in economic policy early in 1979 with his high-profile State Council commission.

Chen dominated the Central Committee work conference of April 5–28, 1979—which was devoted to planning and economic issues and developed a new direction for China's overall economic policy very much in line with Chen's disciplined and balanced approach: "readjustment, reform, rectification, and advance." The key, Chen insisted, was readjustment, which required restoring macroeconomic balances between industry and agriculture, between government expenditure and income, and between foreign investment and debt. He was very critical of plans approved in 1977–1978 to jumpstart China's economic modernization by importing foreign technology and paying for it through loans, compensation trade, or deferred payments. Because China's own foreign exchange reserves at the time were only about US$1.5 billion, the Politburo proposed significantly increasing exports of crude oil, coal, nonferrous metals, and other processed goods. But in the end, it accepted the need to use foreign loans to finance the ambitious economic plans.[22]

During his October 1978 visit to Japan, Deng Xiaoping had signed an agreement for the Nippon Steel Corporation to build a modern steel production plant at Baoshan, north of Shanghai near the mouth of the Yangzi River. The state-of-the-art facility was to be financed by selling to Japan crude oil from the Daqing oilfield to pay the cost of equipment, site construction, and management expertise. By early 1979, however, it became clear that the expected boost in PRC oil production was not taking place, risking a default and great embarrassment for Deng. In his role as head of the State Council Finance and Economic Commission, Chen Yun stepped in to restructure the agreement to allow for a longer and later repayment period.[23]

Chen worked personally with the Shanghai CCP committee, several State Council ministries, and Chinese banks, and indirectly with Japanese corporate executives, to come up with a satisfactory agreement by mid-July 1979. But the many meetings, negotiations, and briefings, and the travel between Beijing and Shanghai, took a heavy toll on Chen's frail health. He fell ill with pneumonia in June and was hospitalized. On October 1 he briefly left the hospital to observe the thirtieth anniversary of the founding of the People's Republic of China; but he told colleagues, "My health is just no good. . . . I can only work about two hours a day, and in the evening, I can't see out of my right eye."[24] Four days later, Chen was diagnosed with colon cancer and entered a Beijing hospital for extended treatment, including surgery, which sidelined him for the next few months.[25]

By the time Chen was healthy enough to return to the political fray, Deng had made significant changes to the power structure, including replacing Chen in two "power" positions—head of the State Council Finance and Economic Commission and Standing Committee overseer of political/legal affairs. Deng had arranged for Chen's replacements at the Fourth Plenum of the Eleventh CCP Congress, held September 25–28, 1979. At the meeting two additions were made to the Politburo, both of which strengthened Deng's position: Peng Zhen and Zhao Ziyang.[26]

Peng Zhen was older than Deng and had joined the Politburo before him, but Deng had eclipsed him at the Eighth Congress in 1956. Peng had served with Chen Yun in the Northeast during the civil war, when the two had developed an acrimonious feud that lasted for decades.[27] Peng also had been Deng's principal deputy on the Central Secretariat in the 1950s. Garrulous and tough-minded, Peng headed the Central Political Legal Commission in the 1950s. His split with Mao was bitter and deeply personal, and he spent eight years in solitary confinement in Qincheng Prison after Mao purged him during the Cultural Revolution. Peng's restoration after Mao's death was difficult. Hu Yaobang had to take personal charge of the process in late 1978, and wasn't able to secure Peng's full rehabilitation until January 1979, just before Peng was appointed vice-chairman of the National People's Congress Standing Committee.[28]

Zhao Ziyang, who turned sixty not long after his promotion to full Politburo membership, was the kind of successor party elders were eager to find in the aftermath of the Cultural Revolution. Smooth, prudent, affable, and good-looking, Zhao had missed the Long March and most of the civil war, then spent his early party career in Guangdong, where he came to Zhou Enlai's attention. Sidelined briefly during the Cultural Revolution, Zhao returned to Guangzhou and was promoted to the Tenth Central Committee in 1973. In 1975 Deng Xiaoping had him transferred to Sichuan, where Zhao earned a reputation as an innovative administrator who succeeded in restoring the province's agricultural productivity. "Want to eat grain, look for Ziyang" (*Yao chi liang, zhao ziyang*) ran a popular ditty that enhanced his reputation in Beijing. At Deng's behest, Zhao had been named an alternate member of the Politburo in 1977, so his promotion to the next rung of the power ladder was not a surprise. Zhao was also assigned the position of vice-premier of the State Council.[29]

The Fifth Plenum and Leadership Change

Slowly but surely, the reconfiguration of the central leadership was taking place. Chen Yun's cancer surgery had been successful, so he was again a factor in personnel adjustments. He and Deng were in full agreement on some of the most important issues. First, new blood was needed in the Politburo, especially in its Standing Committee, four of its five active members being over seventy-five. Second, the Central Secretariat (*zhongyang shujichu*), which had been under Deng's management in the 1950s, needed to be reestablished. Third, it was "not appropriate" for Hua Guofeng to hold the three positions of party chairman, Military Commission chairman, and premier of the State Council. Finally, Mao's lingering influence on the CCP, its practices and history, needed to be officially redefined.[30] That reconfiguration began early in 1980, with a series of party and government meetings that made important procedural and personnel changes to the leadership.

On January 4–17, Hu Yaobang presided over a plenary meeting of the Central Commission for Discipline Inspection, which approved a twelve-

point draft, "Guidelines on Political Life in the Party." Circumspect and ob-
viously weakened in the drafting process, the guidelines were a preliminary
effort to restore regulations on inner-party behavior that had been shattered
during the Cultural Revolution. Included were prohibitions against factionalism, "personal arbitrariness," and the silencing of dissenting opinions,
and standard calls for obeying directions from the party Center.[31] The
meeting also finalized a "Report on the Reinvestigation and Rehabilitation
of Comrades Liu Shaoqi and Qu Qiubai" (Qu was a CCP general secretary
in the 1920s) for submission to the next full party meeting.[32]

On January 24 the Central Committee announced the reestablishment of
the Central Political and Legal Commission, responsible for overseeing
courts, prosecutors, and police departments at all levels and for guiding
people's congresses in carrying out the party's policies in these areas. The
commission was tasked with restoring and repairing the CCP's security
apparatus, which was badly damaged on Mao's orders during the Cultural
Revolution. Peng Zhen was named secretary of this reestablished commission, with eight senior officials from the court system and the Ministry of
Public Security as deputies.[33]

On January 29 a Central Party History Committee was established,
composed of the five active members of the Politburo Standing Committee
plus PLA marshal Nie Rongzhen, Deng Yingchao, and Hu Yaobang. The
idea of writing a comprehensive assessment of the party's post-1949 history, which Hu had actively championed during his assignment to the
Central Party School, was a sensitive issue within the leadership. Hu had
encouraged a structured discussion, allowing party members damaged by
the Cultural Revolution to examine who had initiated it, why it had lasted
ten years, and how Lin Biao and the Gang of Four had been able to wreak
such havoc.

Everyone knew the answers pointed directly at Mao Zedong and those
who served him. They had seen the barely contained rage of party intellectuals at the 1979 Conference on Theoretical Work Principles, which led to
Deng's Four Upholds speech. But Deng had approved the inclusion of CCP
history in Ye Jianying's October 1 PRC founding anniversary speech. At the
Fourth Plenum, the Politburo Standing Committee approved the preparation of a Central Committee resolution—"On Certain Questions in the
History of Our Party since the Founding of the Nation"—to be completed
before 1981. The January 29 announcement included a party History Editing and Screening Committee and a Historical Research Office headed by

Hu Qiaomu, to whom Deng had assigned the task of principal drafter of the resolution.[34]

The Fifth Plenary Session of the Eleventh Central Committee was held in Beijing on February 23–29; its principal item of business was "strengthening and improving the Party's leadership."[35] Although less ballyhooed in PRC history than the Third Plenum of 1978, the Fifth Plenum was more significant politically. Most importantly, it approved the elevation of Hu Yaobang and Zhao Ziyang to the Politburo Standing Committee. Both were younger and healthier than most of the other members, and both were considered close to Deng Xiaoping.

Hu Yaobang was chosen to head the newly reestablished eleven-member Central Committee Secretariat as general secretary (*zongshuji*). Chen Yun and Li Xiannian were said to be unhappy with the choice but were unable to prevent the appointment.[36] Aside from Hu Yaobang, the ten other members of the Secretariat seemed equally divided between supporters of Chen Yun and supporters of Deng Xiaoping. The Secretariat's purpose was to be the administrative "first line" under the guidance of the Politburo and its Standing Committee, seeing to the day-to-day business of the party and enabling the older generation of decision-makers to focus their attention on larger policy issues.[37] But in fact the Secretariat would be pulled and turned by the two patriarchs, between whom were many substantive and personal disagreements.

The Fifth Plenum also approved the requests to resign from all party and State Council positions of the four Politburo members who had been Hua Guofeng's principal supporters following the coup against the Gang of Four: Wang Dongxing, Chen Xilian, Ji Dengkui, and Wu De. This left Hua with little political support even for remaining in the top leadership, much less influencing substantive decision-making. But the stoic and tenacious Hua would stay on, probably believing that Mao's backing legitimized him in the eyes of the party faithful and that Deng was reluctant to convey the impression of yet another "palace coup."

In addition to approving the CCDI Report "Certain Guidelines for Political Life in the Party," the Fifth Plenum revised the CCP charter, permitting some structural changes. It also adopted the Politburo's draft resolution (based on the CCDI report) on "completely rehabilitating and exonerating Comrade Liu Shaoqi" and revoking the 1968 Central Committee resolution "forever expelling him from the party."[38]

Equally symbolic of the scope of Deng's political dominance and his distrust of public participation, the Fifth Plenum approved a resolution to formally propose to the National People's Congress the abolition of Article 45 of the PRC State Constitution. Article 45 guaranteed citizens' rights to express their political views through the use of "big blooming, big contending [big public arguments], big debates, and big-character posters." Inserted into the Constitution in 1975, the Four Bigs were beloved by Mao, a staple of political discourse during and after the Cultural Revolution, and were even considered a fundamental right of citizens as late as 1978. The Xidan Democracy Wall, however, with its cluster of foreign reporters, brought public criticism to bear directly on Deng Xiaoping, and he ordered it closed in 1979, then mandated the constitutional guarantees be abolished.[39] That did not diminish the interest of students and intellectuals in the ideals and structures of democratic systems, but it did indicate the regime's intolerance of public expression of that interest.

The overall leadership picture in early 1980 was mixed for Deng. He had restored the Central Secretariat and established Hu Yaobang as general secretary, but he was probably concerned that Hu's agenda for party change and reform was different from his own. Deng doubtless understood that some of his old comrades returning to leadership in Beijing were not confident that the voluble general secretary was the right man for the job.

Finally, as Deng knew well from his own experience under Chairman Mao, the general secretary position was subordinate to the chairman, who now was Hua Guofeng. Zhao Ziyang, although head of the party's Finance and Economic Leading Group, was subordinate to Premier Hua in the State Council, where most economic work was carried out. And Deng himself was technically subject to Hua's authority as chairman of the Central Military Commission, although Hua certainly knew better than to try to exercise that authority. The bottom line, about which Deng and Chen Yun reportedly agreed, was that Hua had to go.

Hu Yaobang and the Central Secretariat

After several organizational meetings to establish the substantive responsibilities of each secretary, the Central Secretariat announced on March 27 that Hu Yaobang had overall responsibility for the Secretariat's work. But he was not in charge of its composition. From the outset, Hu had little influence on the personnel chosen for the Secretariat. Some of the ten members had career associations with Deng: Wan Li, in charge of agriculture; Fang Yi, overseeing science and technology; Song Renqiong, new head of the Organization Department; Yang Dezhi, the PLA representative; and Hu Qiaomu, Deng's long-time preferred "scribe" (*biganzi*). Others had closer ties to Chen Yun: Wang Renzhong, in charge of Propaganda; Yao Yilin, head of the party's General Office and the State Council's Planning Commission; Gu Mu, responsible for trade and, later, the special economic zones; and Peng Chong, involved in the political-legal apparatus. Yu Qiuli had military ties to Deng and planning commission relationships with Chen and Li Xiannian. Some of these men would shift allegiance from Deng to Chen in the next few years, while others crossed the other way or tried to act as bridges between the two patriarchs.

Hu and the Central Secretariat began regularly scheduled meetings every two to three days in early March in the newly rebuilt *Qinzheng Dian* (Hall of Diligent Governance), formerly one of Zhongnanhai's choice reception and office buildings, where Mao had received foreign dignitaries. It was a particularly apt workplace for Hu, a workaholic who usually slept in his office and only returned home for family dinners on Saturday.[40] Hu refused to move his family into Zhongnanhai, preferring the homier atmosphere of No. 6 Fuqiang Hutong, where he had lived for many years. After the combined pressure of Deng Xiaoping and Chen Yun in 1984 induced him to move his home closer to his office, he relocated to a house backed up onto the east wall of Zhongnanhai. There the General Office installed a gate from the house into the official compound, enabling Hu to walk to his office in about ten minutes.[41]

Hu's workload was broad and demanding. Judging by the selective chronologies published by former staffers, in his first month as general secretary he had to deal with: overseeing Politburo Standing Committee meetings; Secretariat forums and national CCP conferences on Tibet policy; propaganda; organization and science and technology; getting the special economic zones organized in Guangdong and Fujian; the rehabilitation of Liu Shaoqi and the trial of the Gang of Four; Youth League commemorations; Central Party School events; officiating at funerals for rehabilitated party leaders; approvals of articles in various publications; and meeting with foreign dignitaries. Hu still found time to continue his hands-on guidance of *Theoretical Dynamics*, the ideological magazine he had started at the Central Party School in 1977.[42]

Hu's style of managing meetings was informal and inclusive, allowing for more discussion and the airing of dissenting views, of which there were plenty among the mostly elderly veterans who made up the Secretariat.[43] No records of Secretariat meetings are available to outside researchers, but there are enough examples of Hu having to settle for Secretariat decisions he did not like to make it clear that he was neither willing nor able to run it as an *yiyan tang*—a "place where one man has the final say."

For example, one of his first missions as Secretariat chief was to try to improve the situation in Tibet, where ethnic discontent and hostility brought on by China's military invasion and occupation in 1959 were exacerbated by Red Guard depredations during the Cultural Revolution. In mid-March Hu convened a full Secretariat meeting that approved a series of policies intended to improve economic, political, ethnic, and religious conditions in the Tibet region. The Secretariat's report led in April to a Central directive that called for significant loosening of controls over agriculture for ethnic Tibetans, a two-year moratorium on agricultural taxes, and a proposal for two-thirds of the cadres in Tibet to consist of ethnic Tibetans within two years. The new policy acknowledged ongoing discussions between regime representatives and the older brother of the Dalai Lama in Hong Kong to try to arrange conditions for Tibet's spiritual leader to return to China.[44]

Hu and Secretariat member Wan Li traveled in late May 1980 to Lhasa, where they met with Tibetan and Han cadres for a week, explaining the proposals for change and soliciting support. Hu gave a speech before a large gathering at which he suggested "six big things" that needed to be done, most of which entailed providing more flexibility, direct financial support and incentives to Tibetan cadres and agricultural producers, and a reduction in the number of resident Han cadres. Hu conceded that many of the cadres were ill-prepared to serve in the Xizang Autonomous Region (Tibet) and should be permitted to return home.[45]

Hu and Wan were warmly welcomed by Tibetans, but they received a negative response from the Han cadres, and little was done to implement the policies they recommended.[46] Part of the problem was that both the hard-handed approach to minorities and the insistence on collective agriculture were deemed Chairman Mao's policies, untouchable and unchangeable. Three years later the Secretariat held another symposium on Tibet, admitting that little progress had been made since the Hu-Wan trip.[47] The intractability of the problems in Tibet—the limited flexibility on both sides—frustrated Hu and Wan's efforts to resolve them, and they remain unresolved to this day.

Hu and Wan Li also teamed up to get agricultural policy moving in a positive direction. Wan, fresh from his experience managing partial implementation of the "household responsibility system" in Anhui, was trying to win Central approval so that farmers who dared to experiment with it would not be punished for being more productive. But because the issue was tied directly to the agricultural collectivization system Mao had created and repeatedly defended, it was still controversial. Mao had anathematized small family farming as a direct path to "capitalism," so even though it repeatedly had been shown to be more productive than communal agriculture, the label "surnamed 'capitalist'" ("*xing 'zi,*'") prevented most cadres from allowing it to be practiced.

In fact, after Wan Li transferred to Beijing, his successor as first secretary in Anhui tried to roll back the household responsibility system in the counties where it was practiced.[48] The Politburo Standing Committee in mid-1980 appeared undecided on whether and how to support it. Hua Guofeng opposed it, considering it disloyal to Mao Zedong. Li Xiannian was indecisive, seldom expressing a strong opinion one way or the other until knowing what Deng and Chen Yun thought. Chen told Wan Li he supported it, as he had in the 1960s, but did not express his view openly. Hu Yaobang strongly supported it, while Zhao Ziyang cautiously supported it.[49]

Deng Xiaoping's viewpoint was considered most important. He appeared ambivalent, knowing that the places where the practice was allowed had increased agricultural production significantly. But he was wary of attacks equating it with "capitalism"—still a troubling label for one who had been purged for being an "unrepentant capitalist roader." When he did speak more directly to the issue on May 31, 1980, his remarks were careful and brief.[50] He focused on the positive results in Anhui and reassured "some people" that it would not affect the collective economy. The collective economy, he said, would still dominate agricultural production.[51]

Deng's remarks, while somewhat supportive of the household responsibility system, did not resolve the ideological dispute. The fiercest opposition came from secretaries in several provinces of central China where commune farming was somewhat successful. In June, Zhao Ziyang wrote a letter to Hu Yaobang and Wan Li, proposing a compromise. Poorer and more remote regions could contract production to households; more advanced collectives would continue the three-level (commune / production brigade / production team) system. They could allow experiments with contracting to households or to "professional groups" to cultivate special crops or raise animals, with results to be carefully studied by the Center.[52]

Hu Yaobang took a more direct approach, trying to correct ideological problems at their core, hoping to improve the lives of hundreds of millions of farmers. On July 12, 1980, he gave a speech to a National Propaganda Work Conference in Beijing in which he laid out a carefully argued Marxist theoretical justification for *bao chan dao hu* . After saying the party needed to look carefully not only at Chairman Mao's contributions, but also at his "serious mistakes," Hu said: "The Center does not object to contracting production to households. We should not mix up contracting production to households with every household going it alone, and even if it is working alone, we should not equate [that] with capitalism. . . . To say that working alone is tantamount to taking the capitalist road is theoretically wrong. . . . It cannot develop into capitalism. Don't scare yourselves."[53]

Despite their best efforts, in 1980 Wan Li and Hu Yaobang made little progress on pushing ahead with contracting agricultural production to households. After another contentious national conference on agricultural work in September, they settled for a complex and confusing policy that permitted different production responsibility systems for different regions and did not expressly prohibit the household responsibility system.[54] Wan was disheartened by the outcome, but Hu promised continued support and pressure going forward step by step.[55]

He made good on that promise, pushing agriculture to the primary position on the Secretariat's agenda every following year, traveling extensively in rural China and endorsing efforts to experiment with contracting agricultural production to households. The disagreement and uncertainty at the top, in fact, facilitated experimentation in rural areas, nullifying local leaders' ability to oppose local experiments. It began to be seen as an idea that originated with the peasants—which was true—and it gained support year by year as agricultural output continued to grow and diversify.[56]

By the time Central Document No. 1 (1984) came out, the people's communes and their subsidiary collective organizations were already being dismantled. Townships and villages were organized to replace the commune system, preserving CCP authority and public services. More importantly, millions of eager farmers set about farming as their families had practiced it for generations before Mao's collectivization impoverished and starved them.

Rural reform became the showcase for the PRC's overall reform effort in the early 1980s by focusing on undoing Mao's mistakes and bringing the greatest benefit to the largest numbers of ordinary Chinese. Like the removal of political labels from scholars and intellectuals going back to the 1950s and the rehabilitation of hundreds of thousands of party officials who had been punished during the Cultural Revolution, Hu Yaobang's rural reform proposals focused on correcting the CCP's mistakes for people harmed by them. Later, rural reform was credited to Deng Xiaoping as the "chief architect of reform." But it was Hu Yaobang and Wan Li who did the heavy lifting, politically and ideologically.[57] Deng appeared more interested in consolidating his personal power in the face of potential challenges from Chen Yun and Hua Guofeng.

A Controversial History Resolution

At the Fourth Plenum of the Eleventh Central Committee in late September 1979, the Politburo Standing Committee approved the idea of drafting a formal CCP history resolution, called "Resolution on Certain Questions in the History of Our Party since the Founding of the People's Republic of China."[58] The title was not accidental, being nearly identical to a party history resolution carefully overseen by Mao Zedong in 1943–1945 that he used to solidify his domination of both ideological and personnel issues prior to the Seventh Congress. Also not coincidentally, Hu Qiaomu, who had played a key role as Mao's *mishu* in researching, drafting, and editing the earlier document, was named principal drafter of the new resolution in January 1980.

As early as October 1979, Hu Qiaomu called together a small group to discuss how to proceed with the resolution and to begin preparing an outline for the draft. He told his team they needed to answer two questions in particular: Why did the Cultural Revolution happen? and What was the essence of Mao Zedong Thought?[59] Deng Xiaoping had been reluctant to do a resolution, but probably saw it as a way to burnish his ideological credentials, quelling doubts and anger about Mao and the Cultural Revolution, and uniting the party to move ahead on economic modernization. Equally importantly, perhaps, Deng Xiaoping would use the resolution as a means of weakening Hua Guofeng. Comments he made in late 1979 suggested that he believed the process could be completed by the end of 1980.[60] That expectation was optimistic. The resolution would take twenty months and what one participant described as "countless" drafts.[61] Deng himself frequently met with the drafting team or its leaders and made sixteen "important" speeches on the history resolution.[62]

Hu Yaobang, designated one of the leaders of the history resolution project, was both enthusiastic and well-prepared. Having suffered through violence, intimidation, privation, and forced labor during the Cultural Revolution, he knew firsthand the damage it had done to the party. His attitude toward the resolution was relatively straightforward and mirrored his attitude toward reform in general: "If you make a mistake, acknowledge it and correct it." As for the Cultural Revolution and a "comprehensive evaluation" of Mao Zedong, Hu had said in 1978, "This is something that we cannot avoid even though we may want to avoid it."[63] Although Deng had quashed criticism of Mao at the Conference on Theoretical Work Principles in early 1979, Hu seemed determined to press ahead.

In late February 1980 the drafting group delivered its first proposed outline to Deng and Hu. It consisted of five parts, including one on the Cultural Revolution and one on Mao. Deng summoned Hu Yaobang, Hu Qiaomu, and others to his office on March 19 to discuss the outline. He conveyed three "principles" he said must be incorporated into the Resolution:

1) Establish the historical status of Comrade Mao Zedong as the core principle, ensuring adherence to Mao Zedong Thought.
2) Conduct a realistic analysis of the great events in the thirty years since the founding of the PRC, determine what had been correct and what had been wrong, making a fair evaluation of the merits and demerits of its leaders.
3) Make a basic summary of the past, general and not detailed, enabling the party to unite and look forward, unify thinking, and put historical controversies to rest.[64]

That perspective may have been persuasive to Hu Qiaomu, who was protective of Mao and reluctant to reopen old quarrels. But the first draft, delivered in late June, infuriated Deng, who rejected it as overly focused on the mistakes of Mao's later years, not consistent with Deng's instructions, and boring.[65] After doing a self-criticism at a Central Secretariat meeting in early July, Hu Qiaomu put his own hand to writing the segments on the Cultural Revolution and accounting for Mao's malign decisions in his later years. He devised the novel explanation that Mao Zedong's launching of the Cultural

Revolution and other erroneous ideas were the result of Mao "departing from the 'scientific system' of Mao Zedong Thought."[66]

During the summer of 1980, as more revisions were done in coordination with comments from Deng and members of the Secretariat, a rumor started in Beijing that the resolution would be scrapped and a full-fledged de-Maoification campaign would follow. Deng called in Hu Yaobang to discuss the issue and decided to be interviewed by Italian journalist Oriana Fallaci in late August, which helped quell the rumor campaign.[67] Deng had occasionally used interviews with foreign journalists to get his opinions out through Xinhua's daily selections from foreign media, bypassing the more cumbersome process of going through formal propaganda channels. On this occasion he added the unusual additional step of sharing the interview contents with members of the Central Guards, who expressed approval.[68] Fallaci had asked if the portrait of Mao would soon be taken down from Tiananmen Gate, to which Deng replied firmly that it would stay there "forever." "Mao was, after all, a principal founder of the Chinese Communist Party and the People's Republic of China. . . . What he did for the Chinese people can never be erased."[69]

The draft resolution seemed to be shaping up as Deng and Hu Qiaomu had planned by mid-September, when it was discussed in a forum of provincial first secretaries in Beijing. Not long afterward, the Politburo decided that in October the latest draft would be sent out for discussion to four thousand senior party and government cadres, PLA officers, and provincial leaders. This meeting would turn out to be like the November 1978 Central work conference and the January–March 1979 Conference on Political Work Principles—freewheeling discussions in which criticisms of individuals and policies were permitted. Eventually fifty-six hundred officials—including an entire class of Central Party School students—participated.

Just before the meetings, Hu Qiaomu drafted a new section assessing the party's record in the four years after the fall of the Gang of Four; that is, evaluating the chairmanship of Hua Guofeng. When the addition was sent to the Politburo Standing Committee for approval in early October, Hua objected, and Hu Yaobang withheld the added language until after the four-thousand-person discussion. Evidently a brief description of the section was included in the materials sent out for discussion, asking participants for opinions as to whether it should be written more fully.[70]

The discussions took place from mid-October to the end of November. Party, State Council, and military officials were divided into groups of thirty to forty individuals, and each group would summarize its discussions and send briefing reports to the Center.[71] The meetings were lively, and many welcomed the "democratic" atmosphere. Over a thousand briefing reports were sent back to Beijing. Some participants have published memoirs recalling that the discussions were heated and the draft resolution roundly criticized. Guo Daohui's article, for example, said the draft's description of the first seven years after 1949 was faulted for being too cautious and protective of Mao. The Great Leap Forward, described as having "caused serious losses to our country and people," was denounced in one meeting as "in fact, a great famine, in which tens of millions of people died."[72] Hu Qiaomu's proposal of separating Mao Zedong Thought from "Mao Zedong's Thinking" was ridiculed, and some suggested the resolution be rewritten to include a comprehensive accounting of Mao's "leftist errors."[73]

Deng Xiaoping, however, was not receptive to major changes. Hu Qiaomu wrote him a long letter examining the various critiques, and they decided to take note of the continuing controversy but to push ahead. Deng was adamant about limiting the criticism of Mao Zedong. On October 25, even before the cadres had completed their review of the draft, he told Hu Yaobang and Hu Qiaomu: "On no account can we discard the banner of Mao Zedong Thought. To do so would, in fact, be to repudiate the glorious history of our Party. . . . When we write about [Mao's] mistakes, we should not exaggerate, for otherwise we shall be discrediting Comrade Mao Zedong, and this would mean discrediting our Party and state. Any exaggeration of his mistakes would be at variance with the historical facts." Deng had decided that criticism of Hua Guofeng, however, would be included in the resolution. "Many discussion groups want a section in the draft to be devoted to the period following the smashing of the Gang of Four. It seems we shall have to write one."[74]

The Inglorious End of Hua Guofeng

Although Deng probably intended the history resolution to be the culmination of his effort to gradually remove Hua Guofeng from power, the continuing controversy made it necessary for him to advance his plans. Hua had been proceeding slowly on a path to irrelevance since the Fifth Plenum in February. By summer, some official media were beginning to criticize leadership practices, such as the "personality cult," that could be attributed to either Mao or Hua. At a three-day Politburo Standing Committee meeting in mid-August, Deng Xiaoping delivered a strongly worded address about the need for reforms in party and state leadership practices. The speech, later celebrated by some in the party as evidence of Deng's support for serious political reform, drew little attention at the time. Hu Yaobang may not even have been in attendance.[75] Hu Qiaomu even restricted its circulation and downplayed its significance.[76]

Deng's speech called for reducing the concentration of power in individuals and eliminating the practice of leaders holding several concurrent posts in different bureaucracies. He also recommended separation of party and state bureaucracies, and more urgent attention to the issue of succession.[77] Deng Liqun, who drafted the speech along with Hu Qiaomu, claimed in his autobiography that Deng Xiaoping proposed and outlined the speech himself, and that its principal purpose was "exerting pressure on Hua Guofeng" to step down as premier.[78]

Shortly afterward, the National People's Congress met in a full plenary session. Hua Guofeng delivered a work report as premier of the State Council, then later in the ten-day meeting resigned from that position "in accordance with the proposal of the CCP Center." He was replaced as premier by Deng's handpicked successor, Zhao Ziyang. To demonstrate commitment to the principles of reducing multiple party and state positions, and of elders giving way to younger officials, Deng, Chen Yun, Li Xiannian, Wang Zhen, and three other CCP elders stepped down from their positions as vice-premiers of the State Council at the same NPC session.[79]

The meeting of four thousand senior cadres ended with sharp disagreements about the draft history resolution and its evaluation of Mao Zedong, but there apparently was support for including a judgment about Hua Guofeng's performance in four years as party chairman. The regional sessions may still have been going on when a "continuous" series of nine expanded Politburo meetings convened in Beijing on a single topic: whether Hua Guofeng should continue to serve as chairman of the CCP and its Military Commission. These meetings were not publicized at the time.[80] Beijing issued a "Notification" a month later, accompanied by the admonition to all party members to maintain secrecy. The removal of Hua Guofeng as chairman of the party and the Central Military Commission, and his replacement by Hu Yaobang and Deng Xiaoping, respectively, would not be formalized until June 1981.

The secrecy has been maintained. More than forty years later, many of the key details of those meetings remain hidden or contradictory. The meetings began on November 10, 1980, and continued on November 11, 13, 14, 17, 18, 19, and 29, and December 5, when the issues were finalized. Altogether, twenty-two members or alternate members of the Political Bureau and seven members of the Central Secretariat attended at least some of the sessions.[81] On November 10, Hua Guofeng apparently delivered a *jiantao,* along with an explanation of what he considered to be the principal charges against him: engaging in excessive self-promotion; continuing the 1976–1977 criticism of Deng and impeding his return to work; slowing down the work of rehabilitating veteran cadres purged in the Cultural Revolution; supporting the "two whatevers" and other leftist ideological platitudes and resisting a review of Mao Zedong Thought; and championing unrealistic economic growth policies in 1977–1978.[82]

Most of the accounts of that first meeting omit a crucial fact: Hua Guofeng asked the Politburo accept his resignation from both positions.[83] But the ritual, the political exorcism, had to continue, just as it did with Mao Zedong and Peng Dehuai in 1959, and with Mao and Luo Ruiqing in 1966. The loser in the political struggle had to be humiliated. The political winners intoned solemn critiques, while the second-tier players all listened intently and expressed approval by making speeches critical of the victim or submissive to the victors. All twenty-nine attendees at the Politburo meetings made speeches. Only a few records of those speeches, however, have leaked out.

On the second day of the meetings, November 11, Li Xiannian, Chen Yun, Zhao Ziyang, and Deng Xiaoping all spoke. It was a foregone conclusion that they would not support Hua. Chen made three succinct points. First, Hua had done a good deed in organizing the arrest of the Gang of Four, and the party correctly credited him for it, but he disappointed the party for the ensuing four years. Second, it was "unsuitable" for Hua to continue serving as chairman, and he should have understood that he risked his reputation by staying on longer. Third, this decision should not be put off any longer and could not wait until the Twelfth Congress (in 1982).[84]

According to some versions of the meetings, Chen also made other comments aimed at Deng and Hu Yaobang. "It is the hope of many that Comrade Xiaoping serve as [party] Chairman. However, I believe Comrade Xiaoping does not want to do it, and he is trying his very best to push Comrade Yaobang to come do it, and I say good, Comrade Yaobang can come do it." "This Comrade Hu Yaobang, you [Deng] say he has no shortcomings, I think that's hard to say, we are old friends, but we can still have faith he will not do anything crooked or corrupt." Deng's brief remarks make him seem peevish, observing that Hua should have offered him the premiership in January 1977, even though Deng would not have accepted it. Zhao Ziyang also spoke, indicating to Hua that four of the seven members of the Politburo Standing Committee were aligned against him.[85]

Hu Yaobang's role in the drama was to present the evidence against Hua and enumerate for the assembled Politburo and Secretariat members the errors justifying Hua's removal. Hu did so on November 19, and his remarks were included in the *Chronicle of Hu Yaobang's Thought*, appearing in several online sites outside the PRC under the byline Shi Yijun. Hu presented the case without rancor or sarcasm, going out of his way to defend Hua against invidious accusations that he had been a "rebel" during the Cultural Revolution. But he went into detail about decisions made and policy courses pursued since 1976 that were incorrect, for which he asserted that Hua bore the main responsibility. He focused on five issues: Hua exaggerated his own role in the purge of the Gang of Four; slowed down Deng Xiaoping's return to work; resisted the rehabilitation of veteran cadres; maintained allegiance to Mao Zedong's incorrect ideas and resisted new approaches to ideology; and built a personality cult around himself.[86]

Subsequent analysis by PRC historians has provided a plausible case that the evidence against Hua provided at the nine Politburo meetings and the subsequent Central Committee report citing his "errors" was not accurate.[87] But this was not a jury trial, and Hua was not going to be let off the hook. This was a political purge, a power play carefully planned and organized by Deng Xiaoping, with the cooperation and approval of other senior leaders. Hu Yaobang had his assigned role, and he played it well. In his debut as a key member of the new leadership team, he made sure to remind his listeners that he understood his responsibilities:

> I think it is good for Comrade [Hua] Guofeng himself to resign. . . .
> I agree with Comrade [Zhao] Ziyang that this is good for the Party
> and for Comrade Guofeng himself. . . . I think it is only appropriate
> for Comrade Xiaoping to serve as Chairman of the Central Military
> Commission. The army is a pillar of our country, and if this pillar is
> not handled well, that won't do. . . . No matter who is in charge, as
> long as a few veteran comrades are alive, especially Comrade Xiaoping,
> they are the core figures in the core of our party's leadership. . . . On
> this point, I propose that we should make it clear to the whole Party in

a formal document, so that those who serve as Chairmen in the future will have a more secure mind. Comrade Xiaoping is at the helm, and other veteran comrades are also the core figures.[88]

Hu Yaobang's son, Hu Deping, and others have claimed that Hu's relationship with Hua Guofeng was quite amicable, and that Hu did not want to replace him or become chairman himself. He quoted Zhao Ziyang as saying that Hu Yaobang's main consideration was that he was afraid of having to replace Hua. He wanted the Politburo to consider instituting a sort of rotating CCP chairmanship or presidium, with each member of the Politburo Standing Committee—including Hua—serving six months.[89] The idea was discussed by the Standing Committee but was dismissed.

The November 29 Politburo meeting was dramatic but apparently played out calmly. According to unofficial accounts, Ye Jianying—Hua's main support ever since the arrest of the Gang of Four—finally declared his position. In a long, tearful self-criticism, the eighty-three-year-old marshal told his Politburo colleagues that he had thought he was fulfilling an unspoken entreaty from Mao on his deathbed to help Hua be successful. He admitted that he overpraised Hua and didn't help him correct what Ye knew were poor decisions. "This was blind loyalty and foolish chivalry," he said, and he deserved to be blamed for Hua's mistakes. Ye offered his resignation and asked to be allowed to retire.[90]

With no support remaining at all, Hua asked again to resign, and suggested Ye be named chairman in his stead, a notion Ye immediately refused. For his part, Ye nominated Deng Xiaoping as chairman, but Deng demurred, saying he would only consent to be chairman of the Military Commission. Deng recommended Hu Yaobang replace Hua as CCP chairman, preempting his objections by advising him "not to yield to others in doing right."[91] According to Hu's daughter, her father had turned down the idea of being chairman no fewer than ten times, but Deng had finally told him the party had decided the matter, and Hu was duty-bound to obey.[92]

At the last of the nine Politburo meetings on December 5, 1980, the final act of the charade played out. With obeisance to the CCP charter, which stipulates that the party chairman may only be removed by a full plenary session of the Central Committee, the expanded Politburo meeting decided to propose to the Sixth Plenum of the Eleventh Central Committee (tentatively scheduled for June 1981) that it approve Hua's resignation as party and Military Commission chairman. The meeting proposed to the next plenum that

Shortly after ousting Hua Guofeng as Party and Central Military Commission chairman in late 1980, Deng Xiaoping and Hu Yaobang reviewed a PLA parade in 1981, Deng wearing a People's Liberation Army uniform, Hu in civilian attire. (AP Photo / Xinhua via Kyodo, FILE)

it elect Hu Yaobang CCP chairman and Deng Xiaoping chairman of the Central Military Commission. It decided that, prior to the plenum, Hu Yaobang "will temporarily preside over the work of the Political Bureau and Central Standing Committee [of the CCP], and Deng Xiaoping will preside over the work of the Central Military Commission, all without using the formal titles."[93]

The meeting expressed the hope that Hua Guofeng would continue to serve as titular chairman, to attend ceremonial functions or meetings with foreigners; it did not act on Ye Jianying's request to resign from his positions. Hua, however, refused to attend any meetings other than Central Committee congresses for the rest of his life (he died in 2008). Ye Jianying, who retired to his native Guangdong to recover his health, rarely returned to Beijing.

Hu Yaobang decided to absent himself from the last of the nine meetings, possibly because he did not wish to be seen as voting for his own promotion to CCP chairman. Or possibly he was unhappy with the way the meetings had played out. He departed Beijing on December 3 and spent ten days in Hunan and Jiangxi inspecting rural areas and expounding on the need for agricultural and political reform. He decried the "extremely abnormal" political life within the Politburo over the previous decade, focusing particularly on the absence of "true collective leadership" and of "normal criticism and self-criticism."[94]

The Deng–Chen Contest Goes On

In mid-1980 Deng was faced with a seven-member Politburo Standing Committee (Hua, Ye, himself, Li Xiannian, Chen Yun, Hu Yaobang, and Zhao Ziyang), of whom only Hu and Zhao could be counted on to support his effort to oust Hua, while Ye was strongly opposed. Both Li Xiannian and Chen Yun had supported Deng's return in early 1977 and the steps he had taken to whittle away Hua's power. Support for the final push, however, was not automatic. The backstage negotiations to secure their support can only be imagined, but in November both men agreed that Hua staying on as chairman was "unsuitable."

If there was a quid pro quo, it appeared to be in economic policy and leadership. During an expanded Politburo meeting on November 28, Chen Yun and Yao Yilin warned about the dangers of an overheating economy. Yao, a longtime Chen ally in charge of the State Planning Commission, laid out a case for slowing down the overall growth rate of the economy. Despite the 1979 Central call for "adjustment," local areas had continued investment in infrastructure, and the Central planners were saying that the economic "retreat" had not gone far enough. Yao suggested lowering the overall growth rate to 3.7 percent and reducing infrastructure spending by 40 percent.[95]

Deng Xiaoping, along with Hu Yaobang, had talked with local officials in July about "quadrupling" the value of China's industrial and agricultural output by the year 2000—which would have necessitated an annual growth rate of just over 7 percent.[96] But after Chen Yun aided in Hua's ouster, Deng seemed eager to go along with Chen's austerity program. He suggested, in fact, that a short Central work conference be scheduled at which Chen could deliver a keynote speech on the need for the economy to "retreat enough."[97]

Economic studies were flourishing at Beijing universities and academies during this period, with special attention devoted to how to introduce more market measures into the PRC's still heavily controlled system. Zhao Ziyang had attracted a group of progressive economists to advise him on the structural and policy changes needed to modernize the economy. Chen Yun and Li Xiannian were inclined to consider small market experiments, but as a

"supplement" to the planned economy, and then only after the economic balance had been brought under control.

This approach was dominant at the CCP work conference held in Beijing on December 16, 1980. Hu Yaobang presided over the meeting, but it
was Chen Yun's conference, and he set the tone on the first day with a
fourteen-point speech stressing the importance of state planning, state in-
tervention, discipline, balance, and subordinating economic reform to
"adjustment." His prescription for the next two years of economic work
was to "suppress demand and stabilize prices; give up development and
seek stability; defer reform and emphasize readjustment; more centraliza-
tion, less decentralization."[98]

Zhao Ziyang and Li Xiannian supported Chen's recommendations, which
Deng praised extravagantly in his closing speech on December 25: "I fully
agree with Comrade Chen Yun's speech. He correctly summarized our experience in . . . economic work over the past thirty-one years and the lessons we have drawn from it. His statement will serve as our guide in this
field for a long time. . . . [We] should make readjustment our main job, with
reform subordinate to readjustment so as to serve it and not impede it. The
pace of reform should be slowed a little, but that doesn't mean a change of
direction."[99]

Hu Yaobang was not invited to do anything but supervise the proceed-
ings. He gave no speech that has been made public. He did, however, make
some remarks that had an impact, largely negative, on himself. In a group
discussion of some early speeches, Hu said he agreed that readjustment was
necessary in the case of serious economic imbalance. But he cautioned that
readjustment should by no means be allowed to cause reform and development to be set aside. This kind of "cold wind" could have a very bad influence, he said, and he warned against allowing the growth rate to sink below
4 percent. "We can't hang onto the old tricks and old conventions and not
let go," he concluded.[100] Hu would later tell a confidant that he had "lost his
temper," and Chen Yun was unhappy with his remarks, thinking them directed at him.[101]

They probably were. Deng had repaid Chen Yun's cooperation in the purge
of Hua Guofeng with support for Chen's leadership selections and economic
policies, even though he probably had reservations about both. Hu Yaobang
perhaps was not quite so willing to cede the initiative in economic policy to
Chen Yun. In a private conversation with Wang Zhongfang, the *mishu* of his
old friend Luo Ruiqing on March 1, 1980, Hu had explained his boldness and

impatience: "If you want to make a contribution, you have to dare to charge. What do I have? It's that I dare to charge. Comrade Xiaoping understands me. My coming out to work this time, I have at least three things: First, although I don't have his [Deng's] strategic vision, when he raises an idea, I can understand and follow it; Second, I can carry out various organizational work to realize his strategic arrangements; Third, he knows I am decent, and won't go in for anything dishonest."[102]

It seems that, from the start of 1981, Acting Chairman Hu Yaobang had decided to charge ahead and take the initiative to counter a return to "leftist" thinking. In January he gave two speeches to an All-Army Political Work Conference, leveling a sharp attack at the long-standing prevalence of "leftist" thinking in economics and military political work.[103] In March, Hu spoke to a Central Secretariat meeting about the need to press further in agricultural reform, including fully permitting contracted farming to households and allowing farmers to diversify their crops.[104] A week later he gave a long speech to the Secretariat about the need for change in PRC foreign policy, especially toward the USSR. He advocated no longer referring to the Soviet Union as "social imperialist" and no longer "allying with America to oppose the USSR," remarks Premier Zhao called "too bold" and recommended against adopting.[105]

If there was an overarching theme to Hu's forays into controversy, it was perhaps a call to reconsider some of Mao Zedong's less successful ideas and policies. Thus, on February 11, 1981, when the "History Resolution" drafting team—led by Deng Liqun due to Hu Qiaomu's exhaustion—delivered a new draft incorporating some of the recommendations from the four-thousand-person meeting, Hu Yaobang got involved. He called the drafting team together on February 17 and suggested making an entirely new start, retitling the resolution, and focusing more on current and future tasks and responsibilities. He even prepared a new outline, although its content is unknown.[106]

Hu had talked about the resolution in a speech at the Central Party School, and his positions on major issues did not seem fundamentally different from those Deng had expressed repeatedly. But this was less about specific issues, and more about power. Deng Xiaoping needed to keep control of the process of writing the historical resolution, on which he had expended much effort. On March 7, 1981, Deng summoned Deng Liqun to his home and told him to disregard Hu Yaobang's idea of starting a new approach to the resolution. On March 9 he saw Deng Liqun again and blasted the most recent draft for being too critical of Mao and not sufficiently laudatory of his contributions to the revolution.

By March 18, in yet another meeting with Deng Liqun, Deng Xiaoping continued moving the draft toward his preferred outcomes.[107] But there were still major differences within the drafting team and in senior CCP ranks about how to evaluate Mao's contributions to the party since 1949. In his eagerness to find a solution, Deng went to see Chen Yun in the hospital on March 24, asking for advice on finding the right balance in judging Mao. Chen suggested expanding the historical scope of the resolution all the way back to the party's founding in 1921, to include Mao's leadership of the party and his contributions to its ideological foundations in the 1930s and 1940s. That would balance out the more negative evaluation of Mao for the period after 1949.[108] Deng welcomed the suggestion, and on March 26 he invited Deng Liqun and several others to his home. He told them he liked Chen Yun's suggestions and the writing team should incorporate them into the next draft. Hu Yaobang evidently did not attend the meeting.[109]

On March 30 Hu Yaobang presided over a Central Secretariat meeting to discuss the history resolution. At the meeting, he conceded defeat, acknowledging Hu Qiaomu as leader of the drafting team and directing him to deliver a revised draft to the Politburo by mid-April. Deng Xiaoping had earlier agreed with Hu Yaobang's suggestion to circulate the draft to about forty veteran cadres for discussion, along with its consideration again by the Politburo and Secretariat.[110] But Hu Yaobang had suffered a major setback when he was removed from a project he had spearheaded and replaced by his nemesis, shortly after taking over as acting chairman of the party and after he expected to oversee a new draft. But worse was to come.

More than a month later, Hu revealed to an audience in Shandong Province that in late March he had been ordered by the Politburo Standing Committee to take a month of "forced rest." The order was described as a "decision," which means there could have been a vote, but not necessarily, if the outcome was known in advance. With Standing Committee members Hua Guofeng, Ye Jianying, and Chen Yun not participating in decision-making in early 1981, Hu probably knew better than to call for a vote. Hu tried to take his rest in Beijing, but it didn't work out, so he left on April 12 for Zhejiang and Shandong, where he climbed Mount Tai—one of China's most scenic and iconic mountains—finally returning to Beijing in mid-May.[111] Deng had essentially kicked Hu Yaobang off the drafting team for the history resolution.

While Hu was out of the picture in mid-April, Hu Qiaomu and Deng Liqun continued working on the resolution, consulting with Chen Yun and Deng Xiaoping. Hu Qiaomu came out of recuperation to edit the seventh draft for ten days. Chen Yun's suggestions resulted in the addition of a lengthy preamble about the twenty-eight years prior to 1949. Deng had accepted Hu Yaobang's suggestion that the draft be given to forty or so veteran party leaders for discussion and further changes before being finalized for the Sixth Plenum. But even though Deng "packed" the meeting with trusted old veterans, it grew highly contentious, with accusations against Mao and insistence on radical changes in the draft. Deng rejected most of the critiques, but sent the resolution back for more changes, insisting that the drafters stay true to his original instructions from a year earlier. One of his goals, he said, was to "stop arguing" and unite to move forward.[112]

When Hu Yaobang returned to Beijing in mid-May, he sat in on another discussion meeting about the resolution at Deng's home with several of the older ideologues who had helped Hu Qiaomu write the latest draft. Hu raised ten objections to the current version, but accepted Deng's proposal that an expanded Politburo Standing Committee meeting should move it forward.[113] The expanded meeting convened on May 19, attended by seventy-four persons, not including Hu, who disengaged from the process. Deng gave a strong speech, saying the document could not be delayed any longer, that it was a good resolution. He also ended with the line that Mao Zedong may have made mistakes, "but after all, they are the mistakes of a great revolutionary, a great Marxist."[114] The delegates evidently were not persuaded by Deng's rhetoric but continued to call for change in the document over the next eight days.

Hu Yaobang was not involved. He finally reengaged in the history resolution process on June 13, when he presided over another expanded Politburo meeting that approved "in principle" the latest resolution draft, which it decided to submit to the Sixth Plenum for deliberation. The preparatory meeting for the plenum began on June 15 and went on for ten days. It was attended by more than a thousand Central Committee members, retired veteran cadres, and even some non-party leaders. Deng Xiaoping made another major speech on June 22. "This 'Resolution' is a good resolution," he insisted, because it was "written on the basis of the three basic requirements [that I] put forward at the outset." He defended the decision to include criticism of Hua Guofeng in the Resolution: "Comrade Hua Guofeng's name had to be mentioned because that is in keeping with reality.

If he were not mentioned by name, there could be no apparent reason for changing his post."[115]

After Deng's speech, there was little further discussion and only a few editorial changes to the resolution before it was presented to the Sixth Plenum of the Eleventh Central Committee, which met June 25–27, 1981. The Central Committee unanimously approved the "Resolution on Certain Questions in the History of Our Party since the Founding of the People's Republic of China."[116] It also unanimously approved personnel changes from June 27, although many members of the Central Committee, including Hu Yaobang, did so with serious reservations.[117] But Deng had the final say. He had worn down the opposition. It was not a logical or ideological argument. It was not about history. It was not even about Mao. It was about power. The document was distributed publicly through *Renmin Ribao* on July 1, 1981, the sixtieth anniversary of the founding of the Communist Party of China.

Hu's speech at the close of the plenum was short, unpretentious, and blunt. Without saying so directly, he made it clear that he did not seek the position to which he had been "elected" and did not expect to hold it for long. He made three points. First, he said it was the CCP's good fortune to have Deng Xiaoping, Ye Jianying, Li Xiannian, and Chen Yun still able to provide leadership and guidance—especially Deng Xiaoping, whom he called the "core" of the leadership, the principal decider, and the "chief architect." Second, in self-effacing terms, Hu declared that his own abilities remained modest, but he would put them to work on implementing policies of the collective leadership, guided by the veterans of the older generation. Third, he told the delegates that a great deal of time and effort had been expended on resolving difficult historical issues, and he was certain most party members would welcome the resolution. However, bringing order out of the chaos of the previous decade would take another three to five years. Work should focus on economic modernization and building a "socialist spiritual civilization."[118]

Although Deng and others called the history resolution a great achievement and a unifying element, Hu's praise was faint at best for a process that had ignored his input and produced a resolution that had little to do with real history. It was both a symbol of a compromise between Deng and Chen Yun and a propaganda document—not expected to be accurate so much as to be official and final. Subsequently, historians have done careful studies of some of the issues mentioned briefly in the resolution, such as the Great Leap

Hu and members of the Politburo Standing Committee, June 29, 1981. After passing the landmark History Resolution at the Sixth Plenum of the Eleventh Central Committee, Chairman Hu Yaobang meets with the active members of the Politburo Standing Committee. From left: Chen Yun, Deng Xiaoping, Hu Yaobang, Li Xiannian, and Zhao Ziyang. (AP Photo)

Forward, the 1957 anti-rightist campaign, and the Cultural Revolution. They have acknowledged that it did not go far enough, especially with respect to the Cultural Revolution.[119] Even Deng himself admitted to the Politburo in 1993 that some of the facts in the resolution were "not accurate," and that the harsher judgments of Mao made by other senior leaders were correct. He recommended that another resolution might do a better job.[120]

Deng Xiaoping had wanted the resolution to settle the party's judgment on Mao, to preserve Mao Zedong Thought as a sterilized ideological foundation for his own pragmatic policies, and to put an end to ideological splits and quarrels. That didn't really work. Although Deng had clearly emerged from the process as the strongest leader in the party, he was not unchallenged, and certainly did not command the policy agenda. His consultations with Chen Yun had given Chen and his anti-reformist associates an economic policy platform that was regressive and conventional, similar in form and content to the first five-year plan adopted in 1952. Deng's harsh treatment of Hua Guofeng had offended his old "friend" and supporter, Ye Jianying, and driven him from the capital.[121] There are even some observers who suggest that Deng lost some of his support from Hu Qiaomu, Deng Liqun, and Wang Zhen during this period, when they gravitated to Chen Yun, particularly on the issue of support for Hu Yaobang.[122]

The "Deng-Hu-Zhao System"

Despite Deng's rough treatment Hu Yaobang during the last months of the history resolution process, the relationship between the two men suffered no obvious damage as Hu took his position at the nominal apex of the CCP's hierarchy, chairman of the Central Committee and head of the Central Secretariat. Deng praised Hu's brief closing remarks to the Sixth Plenum, saying it proved the Central Committee had "made the right choice" in electing him chairman.[123]

It took another fourteen months for the Twelfth National Congress of the CCP to be cobbled together, primarily because of the Deng-Chen disagreements on both policy and personnel issues. The two elders, of course, did not meet privately to work out their differences, nor were they inclined to attend Politburo Standing Committee meetings called by Hu Yaobang. They are believed to have communicated through intermediaries such as Wang Zhen and Bo Yibo, their *mishu,* and letters addressed to others, along with the *pishi* (approval / comment) process of official paper circulation.

The main business of the Twelfth Congress (September 1–11, 1982) was the political report to be delivered by Hu Yaobang. It set out not only the party's achievements for the previous five years, but more importantly its aspirations for the next few years. Hu was responsible for the report and had begun meeting with the drafting team in January 1982. Unfortunately, the principal drafter—appointed by Deng and Chen—was Hu Qiaomu, with whom Hu Yaobang had growing ideological and personal differences.[124] They quarreled over several important ideological and even economic policy issues in the report, which went for final review to the Standing Committee, but it chose not to resolve them. Thus, as longtime CCP observer Laszlo LaDany noted, "The Congress was the triumph of a Deng [Xiaoping] who had had to yield to his opponents on almost every point. The economic policy outlined by Hu Yaobang in his Congress report is not that of the Third

Plenum of Deng; it is the economic policy . . . and . . . the economic program of Li Xiannian and Chen Yun."[125]

In the wake of the party's stern judgment of Mao Zedong in the history resolution, it might have been expected that Mao would be somewhat de-emphasized at the congress. But he continued to be extolled and praised. Hu Yaobang mentioned him more than twenty times in his report. Moreover, the report included the need for the entire party to continue "the great task of building socialist spiritual civilization in the whole society under the guidance of communism."[126] The words were written by Hu Qiaomu and Deng Liqun, representing a position with which Hu disagreed, and it would take him until 1986 to get them corrected.[127]

On the personnel front, Hu and Deng fared somewhat better. The new Central Committee "elected" a twenty-five-member Politburo, a slight increase in overall size with quite a few holdovers from the Eleventh Congress group. The Politburo Standing Committee was virtually unchanged at six members, formally rank-ordered as Hu Yaobang, Ye Jianying, Deng Xiaoping, Zhao Ziyang, Li Xiannian, and Chen Yun, although the actual power ranking probably would have been Deng Xiaoping, Chen Yun, Ye Jianying, Li Xiannian, Hu Yaobang, Zhao Ziyang.

The most important personnel change from Hu Yaobang's perspective was the turnover in the Central Secretariat, bringing in six new members, including some with stronger ties to Deng Xiaoping and even to Hu Yaobang. Xi Zhongxun, Yang Yong (Hu's cousin), and Chen Pixian (Hu's old friend) were generational peers brought in to replace some older Secretariat members who had retired or moved up to the Politburo. Younger members brought in included two who had come out of the Communist Youth League: Hu Qili (who took over the General Office) and Qiao Shi (Organization Department). Balancing them were Chen Yun's evident choices, Deng Liqun (Propaganda) and Yao Yilin (vice-premier, Finance and Economics).

In addition to eliminating the posts of party chairman and vice-chairman, the revised CCP charter adopted at the Twelfth Congress formally created a Central Advisory Commission. It was composed of 172 superannuated cadres—many recently rehabilitated from Cultural Revolution disgrace and some unable to perform regular official duties—as a means of providing them an honorable retirement. Deng Xiaoping was elected chairman. Certain members of its standing committee received special privileges, such as being able to attend Politburo and Secretariat meetings, where they were not allowed to vote but did have the right to speak. Although its members were directed not to impede the work of the Center or any party or state organizations, some did not heed these instructions, with unfortunate results for Hu Yaobang.

The Twelfth Congress marked the beginning of what Deng Xiaoping himself called the "Hu-Zhao system" (*Hu-Zhao tixi*); later observers more accurately called it the "Deng-Hu-Zhao system" (*Deng-Hu-Zhao tizhi*).[128] Former *Renmin Ribao* editor in chief and Hu Yaobang confidant Hu Jiwei referred to the ten-year period from 1979 to 1989 as the "Hu-Zhao New Deal" (*Hu-Zhao xin zheng*), while historian Gao Gao called the Deng-Hu-Zhao linkup from 1982 to 1987 a "troika" (*santou mache*).[129] All agreed in retrospect that the structure was unsustainable, given the political issues and personalities involved, particularly the policy and power disputes between Deng and Chen Yun. As these splits deepened, Hu and Zhao became the main targets of attack by Chen's subordinates.

The "Hu-Zhao system" seems off to a good start at the Twelfth Congress of the Chinese Communist Party in September 1982. (AP Photo / Xinhua News Agency)

The Comprehensive Reform Speech

On January 20, 1983, Hu Yaobang attended the National Staff Workers' Ideological and Political Work Conference and delivered a speech titled "Construction of the Four Modernizations and the Issue of Reform." It was one of the most important speeches he ever gave, and almost one of the last. Although the meeting was intended "to convey the spirit of the Twelfth Congress" to a gathering of state-owned enterprise cadres, this was no standard boilerplate propaganda talk.

Hu chose the occasion to carefully address a very controversial issue: how to translate into action Deng Xiaoping's goal—affirmed by the Twelfth Congress over the evident objections of Hu Qiaomu and Chen Yun—of "doubling and redoubling" the gross value of China's industrial and agricultural output (essentially its gross national product) between 1980 and 2000.[130] This was more than a question of annual growth rates and setting production quotas, although it certainly was that. It involved generating interest and enthusiasm for the complex task of reforming the PRC's massively inefficient state planning and production mechanisms. The first task was piecing together a set of policies to bring about in urban industrial areas the kind of rapid growth and progress seen in rural areas since the implementation of agricultural reform.[131]

Hu prepared for the speech with unusual care, drafting a nine-thousand-word outline he discussed with seven members of the Central Secretariat and, more importantly, with Deng Xiaoping at his home. He even sent a copy of the outline to Hu Qiaomu, who was recuperating in Yunnan. All expressed varying degrees of satisfaction with the speech, especially Deng.[132] This was Hu's first policy speech as general secretary before a large audience.

Hu traced the important, hard-won ideological changes that had brought them to that point, insisting that the spirit of the Twelfth Congress was "building socialism with Chinese characteristics" through reform. The Four Modernizations (agriculture, industry, science and technology, and national defense) would not succeed unless the entire party and people embraced the need for "comprehensive reform" (*quanmian de gaige*). By this, Hu meant changes in ideology, organizations, attitudes, procedures, economic goals and management, political leadership, education, foreign policy, political and legal work, and other areas. Even though the need for change was urgent, the work had to be carefully planned and carried out gradually, he cautioned.

Only the party could lead this effort, which would be filled with controversy and differing views.

The standard by which Hu said the policies should be judged would be whether the results were "beneficial to productivity, comprehensive national strength, and the improvement in the people's standard of living." To accomplish the Four Modernizations, he insisted, "a series of reforms must be carried out, and reform should run through the entire process of the Four Modernizations. . . . All fronts, all regions, all departments, and all units have the responsibility of reform. We must get rid of old frameworks, old clichés, and old workstyles that hinder our progress."[133] The terms Hu used for "old frameworks, old clichés, and old workstyles" (*lao kuangkuang, lao taotao, lao zuofeng*) were ones he had used to describe the party's economic policies in the 1950s (under Chen Yun).[134]

It was a bravura performance and generated enthusiasm in his audience. *Renmin Ribao* highlighted the speech on its front page the following day and ran supportive editorials on three occasions in early February.[135] That took the issue from the confines of intra-party briefings to a matter of public opinion. *Renmin Ribao* had a circulation of several million, and the Xinhua News Agency routinely republished and broadcast its editorials throughout the country. The Propaganda Department, headed by Deng Liqun and under Politburo supervision by Hu Qiaomu, took notice after the fact.

On February 17, Hu Qiaomu summoned *Renmin Ribao* editor Qin Chuan and one of his deputies to reprimand them. Speaking elliptically, he said that "at a certain meeting, a particular leader made a certain speech, but don't be in a rush to publicize it. It cannot be a center of propaganda." When the two editors expressed bewilderment, Hu clarified: "Comrade Yaobang's speech at the Staff Workers' Ideological and Political Work Conference has nothing to do with the spirit of the Twelfth Party Congress and is inconsistent with the spirit of the Twelfth Congress." Qin Chuan was shocked. Criticism of the general secretary by an ordinary Politburo member was a violation of discipline and protocol. He surmised Hu Yaobang was in for trouble.[136]

In early February, Hu Yaobang went on an eighteen-day inspection tour of Guangdong, Hainan, Hunan, and Hubei. He visited the Shenzhen special economic zone (SEZ) for the first time, accompanied by Guangdong party leaders. Shenzhen was having problems with smuggling, land management, development financing, and limited cooperation from Beijing ministries. Its leaders were frightened of being criticized by economic conservatives in

Beijing, who were attacking the experiment on financial and ideological grounds. Both Chen Yun and Li Xiannian were known to be opposed to SEZ development, considering the zones to be only a small step away from pre-revolutionary "foreign concession areas." But Hu was impressed with the SEZ and provided support and encouragement for its innovations and experimentation. He even ordered a ministry in Beijing to increase Shenzhen's limited supply of telecommunications equipment.[137]

On his travels Hu also encouraged local party committees to increase the pace of economic development in support of Deng's "redoubling" goal, and he dispensed instructions to allow rural areas to open small-scale mining enterprises, which then made requests for central financial support. Hu probably was overstepping his boundaries as general secretary, and his actions were seen to be creating "pressure." In early March, Yao Yilin, head of the State Planning Commission, wrote a letter to Deng Xiaoping and the Politburo Standing Committee detailing Hu's errors. Zhao Ziyang also was concerned that Hu's advocacy of transferring into urban industrial plants the rural area practice of using contracts to promote production would create too much pressure for change and excessive government expenditure.[138]

In mid-March, Deng met separately at his home first with Chen Yun, then with Hu Yaobang, Zhao Ziyang, and Hu Qiaomu, after which he convened a joint Politburo and Central Secretariat meeting on March 17 to hear a report on the economy from the State Planning Commission and the Party's Finance and Economic Small Group.[139] Partway into the meeting, Chen Yun delivered a prepared speech, with mounting rancor. It was directed at Hu Yaobang, along with Hu Qili, whom Chen considered a Hu protégé. Chen charged Hu with knowing nothing about economics, misunderstanding policy, and disrupting orderly planning. But as Chen continued a ten-point harangue, it occurred to some that it was actually aimed at Deng Xiaoping's economic policies and at Deng himself for promoting and supporting Hu. Deng, unhappy with the direction of the conversation, finally said, "That's gone far enough" (*zhici weizhi*). Hu Yaobang, meanwhile, sat uncomfortably, apparently unable to defend himself.[140]

Hu Qiaomu promptly proposed that Chen Yun's important speech be circulated to all party members, which Deng Xiaoping deferred. But Deng Liqun, who attended the meeting, relayed the content of its discussions at a Xinhua staff meeting the same day. His remarks were widely reported in Xinhua channels, and rumors of high-level dissension soon spread nationwide, much to Deng Xiaoping's chagrin. He had evidently intended the meeting to clarify bureaucratic responsibility for economic policymaking, removing the Central Secretariat from the decision chain and placing it in Zhao Ziyang's hands in the party's Economic and Finance Small Group and the State Council's Planning Commission.[141]

According to some accounts, Hu Qiaomu called for a Central Committee work conference to be convened to consider the issue of whether Hu Yaobang should be relieved of his post as general secretary and replaced by Deng Liqun.[142] Hu Qiaomu told Deng Xiaoping he thought Hu Yaobang's faith in socialism was "wavering," which angered Deng. Hu Qiaomu even went to Hu Yaobang's home in tears to urge him to step down. Hu Yaobang later told Li Rui: "Qiaomu suddenly came over weeping and said: 'If you are not general secretary, you can do other things. Our friendship will last forever.' I was astonished at the time; I didn't understand his reasons. After [that], he burst into laughter and talked about other things."[143] Deng Liqun, meanwhile, began gathering "materials" to decide Hu's fate.

On March 19 a special meeting was held to hear reports from the Central Secretariat on the rumors among lower levels about divisions in the leadership. The *Chronicle of Hu Yaobang's Thought* reported that Ye Jianying was present at this meeting, along with Deng, but doesn't name other attendees. Deng ordered that all materials sent out in advance of the proposed work conference be recovered and sealed. He spoke clearly to those in attendance: "The Hu-Zhao arrangement cannot be changed!" (*Hu-Zhao geju buneng bian*).[144] As Hu would put the whole episode to Li Rui in 1989: "At that meeting in 1983, when they were preparing to change horses, it was Deng who protected me."[145] The first serious challenge to Hu's standing as general secretary had been surmounted. It would not be the last.

"Spiritual Pollution" and Its Consequences

Despite the ambiguous outcome of the political confrontation of March 17, political wrangling intensified in the weeks that followed. Deng and Chen Yun's dispute over the pace of economic development became more open, the ideological divide between Hu Yaobang and Hu Qiaomu widened, and fights over personnel began to cause casualties. The next confrontation was already in motion.

In honor of the hundredth anniversary of Karl Marx's death, on March 8, 1993, the CCP leadership held two commemorations. One was a formal party ceremony at the Great Hall of the People, at which Hu Yaobang gave a lengthy report, "The Light of the Great Truth of Marxism Illuminates Our Way Forward." In view of the simmering controversy over his January 20 speech, Hu appears to have used the draft prepared by the Propaganda Department and delivered a standard CCP boilerplate address. The other meeting was an academic forum sponsored by the Propaganda Department and the Central Party School, to be addressed by Zhou Yang, a former vice-minister of culture who was purged and jailed during the Cultural Revolution. His report, "Theoretical Issues of Marxism," focused on the issues of socialist "humanism" and "alienation" in a Communist Party state and was well-received by the audience of intellectuals and writers.

The problem was not so much an issue of philosophy as of power: Zhou had not cleared his report with the Propaganda Department and he ignored Hu Qiaomu's complaints afterward. *Renmin Ribao* published the report in full on March 16 but evidently did not clear it with Propaganda Department chief Deng Liqun.[146] Under its editor in chief, Hu Jiwei, *Renmin Ribao* was very helpful to Hu Yaobang, prominently posting articles he sponsored, often without going through Propaganda Department channels. Wresting the party's propaganda crown jewel from Hu Yaobang's hands was a key goal for his opponents.

On March 20, Hu Qiaomu ordered Deng Liqun to prepare a report for the Central Secretariat assessing blame and punishment for the publication of Zhou Yang's report. Deng's report recommended requiring Zhou Yang to do a *jiantao* and dismissing the responsible Deputy Editor, Wang Ruoshui. The following day, Hu Qiaomu convened a meeting to present the Propaganda Department report to Zhou Yang. The two men quarreled violently, and Zhou appealed his case to Hu Yaobang. Hu left the matter with *Renmin Ribao*, instructing it to revise Zhou's report and let the matter drop.[147] Zhou subsequently had to do repeated self-confessions, which broke his health, sidelining him until his death in 1989. Wang Ruoshui, a popular liberal thinker and critic of Hu Qiaomu, was sacked and eventually left the PRC.

Having won another round on an ideological issue, Hu Qiaomu and Deng Liqun increased the pressure. At an April–May Propaganda Conference, Hu presented the recent proliferation of heterodox theories and "scar literature" about Cultural Revolution abuses from a new perspective, stressing their divergence from Deng's Four Fundamental Principles, which had become an ideological touchstone. In several meetings with Deng Xiaoping that summer, both Hu Qiaomu and Deng Liqun highlighted that divergence, arousing Deng's anger especially toward Hu Yaobang, whom

Deng considered responsible for literary and art matters.[148] In June, Deng Liqun had given the phenomenon a catchy name, "spiritual pollution" (*jingshen wuran*), and encouraged the Central Propaganda Department to publicize the issue broadly.[149]

Deng Xiaoping and Chen Yun were both scheduled to address, in October, the party's Second Plenum, which would take up a resolution on party rectification. Three months before, Deng Xiaoping had chosen Deng Liqun to head the drafting team for his speech. They met several times to focus on two points: the planned "party rectification plan" could not be done in a half-hearted way; and "people working on the ideological front must not engage in spiritual pollution." With Deng Liqun's encouragement, Deng Xiaoping chose to focus on spiritual pollution, leaving Chen Yun to discuss rectification.[150]

Chen Yun had always paid attention to personnel issues and had a specific focus for the party consolidation program. With an eye on younger party members who had prospered during the Cultural Revolution, he insisted that the primary goal of the rectification effort must be to "get rid of 'three types of people'" (*qingchu "sanzhongren"*): those who got their start with the rebel factions (*zaofanpai*) in the Cultural Revolution; those who still engaged in serious factional quarrels from that period; and those who engaged in "beating, smashing, and looting" at any point and had not been called to account. Even though the most violent part of the Cultural Revolution had been fifteen years earlier, and investigations at every level had filtered out many bad elements, Chen was vehement: "Not one of these 'three kinds of people' can be promoted. Those who have been promoted must be resolutely removed from leadership teams."[151]

Deng Xiaoping's October 12, 1983, plenum speech would deal with both rectification and spiritual pollution. Drafted by Deng Liqun, it came down on the conservative (leftist) side of the discussion on both issues. Hu Yaobang had clashed with Hu Qiaomu and Deng Liqun at a Secretariat meeting just prior to the plenum, insisting that party rectification efforts should focus on opposing residual leftism from the Cultural Revolution. Hu Qiaomu, claiming to represent Deng Xiaoping, said there must be equal attention paid to opposing rightist ideas. The Secretariat itself was split, with Hu Yaobang gaining support from Wan Li, Hu Qili, Chen Pixian, and Xi Zhongxun.[152] Deng Xiaoping settled the left-right issue, chiding "a few comrades" who "are only interested in combating 'left' mistakes and not right ones . . . people have tended in recent years to be a little too tolerant, hesitant, tenderhearted and ready to gloss things over to avoid trouble. Consequently, party disci-

pline has been [so] lax that some bad people have been shielded."[153] Hu Yaobang apparently was not concerned about rectification issues. He knew the
plenum would appoint a Central Steering Committee on Party Consolidation (Rectification), and he would head it, assisted by group carefully balanced between Deng and Chen supporters.[154] He had done similar work in
the Organization Department, and likely believed he could control it.

Hu was probably more concerned by Deng's statements—again, written
by Deng Liqun—about combating spiritual pollution. Deng had described
the situation as "confusion among our theorists, writers, and artists," who
instead of acting as "engineers of the soul" were "polluting people's minds
with unwholesome ideas, works, and performances. In essence, spiritual
pollution means the spread of the corrupt and decadent ideas of the bourgeoisie and other exploiting classes and the spread of distrust of socialism,
communism and leadership by the Communist Party."[155] Reminiscent of the
class struggle arguments that were so common during the Cultural Revolution, Deng's speech opened the door for the Propaganda Department to use
ideology as a weapon to attack opponents at any level. When trouble would
start was only a matter of time.

At a Central Secretariat meeting not long after the plenum, Hu Yaobang
urged careful handling of Deng's and Chen's speeches, discouraging local
party committees from distributing them without Central instructions, or
without recognizing the "boundaries" of the spiritual pollution issue. He
reprimanded Hu Qiaomu for ordering certain controversial authors to
write confessions of their spiritual pollution errors requiring party committee approval.[156] And he was adamant that the CCP not return to Cultural
Revolution practices of labeling, public shaming, and punishing people for
listening to or singing popular music, wearing colorful clothing, or styling
their hair.[157]

But that is exactly what happened. Deng's tough speech emboldened those
at lower levels offended by the rapid infiltration of foreign ideas, fashions,
music, and dress to take action against mostly youthful offenders. Excesses
began almost immediately. While Deng Xiaoping had said party members
in literary and art domain should not "engage in" (*gao*) spiritual pollution,
Deng Liqun ordered the Propaganda Department and local party committees to "eliminate" (*chingchu*) spiritual pollution. It became the "campaign
that was not a campaign," and so-called leftists at all levels took charge of it.
Young factory workers' bellbottom trousers had to be cut off before the
workers were allowed to enter factories, young women's curly hairdos were

cut off, dancing was forbidden, and PLA soldiers turned in pictures of girl-friends for fear the images would be considered pornographic.[158]

Soon Hu's Secretariat colleagues were calling for boundaries to be drawn around their areas of responsibility. Wan Li insisted there was no spiritual pollution in rural reforms, Fang Yi claimed there was no need for eliminating spiritual pollution in science and technology, and Zhao Ziyang belatedly insisted that urban economic reforms should not be interrupted by eliminating spiritual pollution. Zhao also observed that the issue had created a bad impression among foreign leaders that China was moving back toward Cultural Revolution–style campaigns.[159]

On November 21, Hu convened another Secretariat meeting to discuss spiritual pollution. He instructed the Propaganda Department to send out guidance immediately to local CCP committees to clarify the definition of the term and set its boundaries, instructing them to not carry spiritual pollution issues into people's lifestyles or economic policy implementation. Hu directed provincial secretaries and *Renmin Ribao* to suspend further spiritual pollution measures during his impending trip to Japan (November 23–28).[160] That brought things to a standstill. Hu and others referred to the period from just after the Second Plenum to the November 21 Secretariat meeting as the "twenty-eight-day little Cultural Revolution" and considered their actions to have stopped it.[161] But the larger and more salient issue (for Deng Xiaoping) of "bourgeois liberalization" had not gone away and would return to haunt Hu. Moreover, in the course of the fight over terminology that was more a matter of personnel, Hu Yaobang had lost Hu Jiwei and Wang Ruoshui, both sacked from *Renmin Ribao* in October, and barely held off an effort by Deng Liqun to replace them on the editorial board with two of his Propaganda Department theorists.[162]

Deng Xiaoping was frustrated and angry at both Deng Liqun and Hu Yaobang, but since both sides were using his Second Plenum speech to justify their actions, resulting in the "fizzling out" of the spiritual pollution effort, there was little he could say or do.[163] He railed at Deng Liqun for his persistent efforts to pull the party leftward, but his anger at Hu Yaobang seemed deeper. In his memoir, Zhao Ziyang observed: "I feel that the way Hu Yaobang handled this matter aggravated the conflict between them a great deal. This ultimately played a key role in the final rift between the two."[164]

Having worked under Deng for more than thirty years, Hu no doubt was accustomed to his mercurial approach to ideological issues, his dictatorial impulses, and his desire to have the final say. He may also have seen in both

Deng and Chen Yun the infirmities of old men with power that he had witnessed with Mao: confusion, stubbornness, jealousy, failing memory.

Although Hu had done more than any other leader to bring about the rehabilitation of many party elders purged in the Cultural Revolution, he also wanted them to make way for talented younger leaders. He had led efforts to eliminate "lifetime tenure" and establish retirement guidelines for CCP cadres. Deng and Chen both paid lip service to the concepts, but their reluctance to leave the stage was increasingly obvious. In his January 1983 speech on comprehensive reform, Hu had pointed out: "Our old comrades, especially old comrades over age sixty-five, must understand, it is difficult for us to work into our nineties. So old comrades must earnestly and sincerely support younger people rising to power, and moreover should regard as their most important historical mission to let go and allow them to develop their own talent and intelligence."[165]

Troika Charging Ahead?

In early 1984 Deng Xiaoping made his first visit to the Shenzhen special economic zone in Guangdong Province, and like Hu Yaobang the year before, he was impressed with the vitality and growing prosperity of the experiment the party had approved in 1979. He instructed Hu to prepare a "guiding ideology" document that would facilitate further reform and opening and the revision of "some outdated concepts" in PRC economic policy. In light of the ongoing dispute between Deng and Chen Yun over the very nature of China's economy and the policies that should be pursued to modernize it, it was a tall order.

By May, Deng and Chen had agreed to the formation of a drafting group to prepare a resolution on economic structural reform for the Third Plenum in the fall. It consisted of Hu Yaobang, Zhao Ziyang, Hu Qili, Hu Qiaomu, Yao Yilin, and Tian Jiyun—an unusually high-powered group. Hu Yaobang took charge of it quickly, speaking to the drafting team, even preparing an eight-point outline of the resolution. Zhao Ziyang seemed to have his own idea of what the process should look like and requested prominent economists from the recently organized State Structural Reform Commission (*guojia tigaiwei*) to present insights on what should be included in the resolution.[166]

But both Hu and Zhao appear to have had the same goal of changing the theoretical premise of Chen Yun, Li Xiannian, and Hu Qiaomu for economic development, which was "The planned economy is the mainstay, and market regulation is the supplement." The definition in the 1984 decision was a "planned commodity economy based on public ownership," which danced carefully around the still strongly held views of Chen Yun and others that a "planned economy" and a "commodity economy" were theoretically incompatible.[167] In his autobiography Deng Liqun observes that Hu Qiaomu was not allowed to participate in the drafting of the decision, and his own participation was only sporadic.[168]

Despite the absence of the two ideologues, the drafting process was contentious and drawn out, going through eight drafts before being submitted in early October to the Politburo and Secretariat, where it underwent further change. In content, it reflected more the views of Zhao Ziyang and his economic experts than those of Hu Yaobang, although Hu played an important role by adding economic "liberals," including his *mishu,* Zheng Bijian, to the drafting team in July.[169]

In late August, Hu gave encouragement to the drafting team and specifically deferred to Zhao Ziyang as the one to whom they should listen on economic policy issues. Zhao wrote a long, very detailed letter in early September, which seemed to ease the objections of Chen Yun and Li Xiannian, at least temporarily, and won Deng's strong approval.[170] Although the final "Decision of the CCP Central Committee on Reform of the Economic System," passed on October 20, 1984, was only a partial win for the "troika," it was enough to impart a kind of momentum to reform, enabling progress to be made on important personnel issues. Most importantly, the resolution marked the second instance (after smothering "spiritual pollution") of successful cooperation between Hu Yaobang and Zhao Ziyang on a major policy initiative.

9 Deng's Wrath and Hu's Fall

Looking back at the mid-1980s and the complex interactions between leaders at the top of the CCP hierarchies, relatively little attention has been paid to the relationship between General Secretary Hu Yaobang and Premier Zhao Ziyang. It could have been a key to a different political outcome, had they joined forces against Deng and the combined influence of leftist conservatism and elder obstinacy. But they did not, and probably could not do so, for structural, political, and personal reasons.

There was a four-year age difference between Hu and Zhao. They were born in different provinces, spoke different dialects, and had completely different experiences in the anti-Japanese and civil wars. Hu was in much more political trouble during the Cultural Revolution, and served a longer term in labor reform than Zhao did. Both were affiliated with Deng Xiaoping in the mid-1970s, but Zhao was working in Sichuan Province, while Hu was at the center of left-right controversies in Beijing. Like Deng, Hu noticed Zhao's successful management of economic recovery in Sichuan, and especially agriculture. Hu probably understood when he and Zhao were both assigned to the Politburo Standing Committee in 1980 that they were meant to work together to support Deng's policies on modernizing China's economy. They both understood the hostility of residual leftist elements like Deng Liqun and Hu Qiaomu. Zhao even told one of Hu's Youth League supporters that he and Hu were "both in the same boat" in 1984, which Hu Yaobang found very encouraging.[1] But Zhao's own book and interviews with other historians after his own ouster are self-serving and not entirely consistent.

Hu Flexes His Muscles

In early 1985 a case of criminal activity by the son of a Politburo member was brought to Hu Yaobang's attention. Local police suspected Hu Shiying—son of Hu Qiaomu—of engaging in corrupt practices and hiding a large amount of cash inside his Zhongnanhai home. Hu approved a plan to escort police officers to the house for a search while Hu Qiaomu was at a meeting and to make an arrest if sufficient evidence was found.[2] The youth was tried and convicted of fraud, given a short sentence, which was soon reduced, and sent home.[3] The case created a sensation inside Zhongnanhai, although it remained unreported for several years, even in the Chinese diaspora press. Its effects on leadership dynamics were to increase the antipathy of Hu Qiaomu toward the general secretary, but also reduce his influence with Deng Xiaoping. It also resulted in a growing sense of alarm and resentment among party elders toward Hu Yaobang, who seemed unnecessarily eager to persuade—or force—them to retire.

In June, Deng Liqun suddenly asked Hu Yaobang and Hu Qili (now executive secretary of the Secretariat) for permission to resign as head of the Propaganda Department. Deng offered no rationale for his decision, and he retained his position on the Secretariat and as head of its Research Office. With no indication of whether Deng Xiaoping or Chen Yun was consulted, the Central Organization Department in less than a month chose a successor: Zhu Houze, previously secretary of the Guizhou CCP committee. Deng Liqun claimed that Hu Yaobang was intent on controlling propaganda work, with the help of Secretariat members Xi Zhongxun and Qiao Shi. Hu took the unusual step of inviting Zhu to the leadership's summer retreat in Beidaihe, where he met with him privately, advising him on how to handle problems in the department.[4]

Also in 1985, Hu agreed to do a rare private interview with a Hong Kong political news editor named Lu Keng, whose *Pai Hsing* (*Baixing*) magazine was popular in Hong Kong but did not circulate in the PRC. A former Kuomintang newspaper editor, Lu was arrested as a rightist in 1957. He spent more than twenty years in jail, was released in 1978 under Hu's auspices, and moved to Taiwan and then the United States. The interview took nearly a year to arrange through United Front channels, assisted by PRC officials in Hong Kong, who attested to Lu's favorable opinion of "reform and opening." It took place on May 10, and although a transcript was sent back through channels for Hu's edits and corrections, they were returned too late to be incorporated into the published version, which came out June 1, 1985.[5]

The interview was blunt, full of probing questions of the sort that would not have been asked of Deng Xiaoping. Hu, unaccustomed to dealing with foreign press, seemed thrown off balance by Lu's amiable but overbearing manner. Lu asked a lot of questions about internal PRC politics and personalities, to which Hu responded sometimes with nervous laughter or weak denials. Lu asked about rumors, factions, and ideological disputes. He asked about Taiwan policy and the Military Commission. He probed relations between Chen Yun and Deng Xiaoping, even raising the question of when Deng Xiaoping would retire. Some of Hu's answers alluded to frictions in the leadership between elders and younger successors. It made for fascinating reading, but was not helpful for Hu.

Because *Pai Hsing* was not widely read on the mainland, the interview did not cause immediate controversy. But Deng Liqun passed a copy of the transcript to Deng Xiaoping, who was not pleased. Even a year later, reminded of the interview by Yang Shangkun, Deng reportedly exclaimed, "Lu Keng was attacking us under the guise of flattering Yaobang! If I've made any mistakes in the past few years, it's that I misread Hu Yaobang."[6]

In September 1985 Hu Yaobang presided over three separate meetings of the Central Committee devoted to personnel issues, one of which was a "national representatives meeting" (*quanguo daibiao huiyi*) sandwiched between the Fourth and Fifth Plenums. There had been only one similar Central Committee meeting before, in May 1958 when Mao engineered sweeping changes in CCP policies and personnel to carry out his radical collectivization plans.

The 1985 meeting had been agreed to by the party leadership well in advance. It evolved from a collective consensus that the post–Cultural Revolution CCP leadership was old, not well-educated or professionally skilled, and overrepresented the PLA and "mass organizations" while underrepresenting the intelligentsia. Repairing that situation required an arduous process of clearing out unfit leaders, rehabilitating those unfairly removed during the Cultural Revolution, recruiting and training younger leaders, and arranging for elderly leaders to leave their positions in an orderly manner. Hu Yaobang played a leading role at every phase of the process, with explicit approval from Deng Xiaoping, Ye Jianying, and Chen Yun.

At the Fourth Plenum in mid-September, proposed changes were approved for presentation to the National Delegates Meeting. Ten Politburo

members and fifty-four members and alternate members of the Central
Committee would no longer serve. Thirty-seven members of the Central Ad-
visory Commission and thirty members of the Central Discipline Inspection
Commission also requested retirement from their duties. The Central
Committee retirees included Ye Jianying, Deng Yingchao, Wang Zhen, and
many of the PLA representatives on the Central Committee.[7]

The National Delegates Meeting was held September 18–23, 1985. Hu Yaobang presided and gave a congratulatory opening speech, and Zhao Ziyang
explained the seventh five-year plan (in draft). Deng and Chen Yun both
gave brief addresses, and Li Xiannian spoke at the closing ceremony. The delegates approved the decisions of the Fourth Plenum and commended Ye
Jianying and others for their service and leadership in stepping down. They
then approved 56 full and 35 alternate members joining the Central Committee to replace the retirees, 56 new members of the CAC, and 31 new additions to the CCDI.[8]

On September 24 the Fifth Plenum of the Twelfth Central Committee met
to approve partial "adjustments" to the Politburo and Central Secretariat. Six
new members were added to the Politburo: Tian Jiyun, Qiao Shi, Li Peng,
Wu Xueqian, Hu Qili, and Yao Yilin. Four of them have been considered
"reformers," three had served in the Youth League. Hu Qili, Tian Jiyun, Qiao
Shi, and Wang Zhaoguo (CYL background) also were added to the Secretariat, Hu Qili as executive secretary. Even though Hu Yaobang would always rebuff later charges that he was forming a "Youth League faction," it is
not difficult to see how the suspicion arose. After the plenum, of the ten
members of the Central Secretariat, Hu probably had hopes of working effectively with seven of them.

He was soon disabused of that idea. According to the *Chronology of Hu
Yaobang's Thought*, Hu chaired a meeting of the Secretariat the day after the
plenum, at which he proposed that, in an effort to practice "youthification,"
newly elected member Wang Zhaoguo should replace Deng Liqun as director of the Secretariat Research Office. The Research Office had long been
a nuisance to reform efforts, being independently guided by Deng Liqun
and Hu Qiaomu to write articles critical of reforms. Deng Liqun reported
to the Secretariat that Hu Yaobang had not informed him of the change,
and he had some opinions about it.[9] He wrote a letter of complaint and self-
defense to the Politburo Standing Committee. When the Secretariat posted
its official notice of the personnel change, Chen Yun ordered all copies of it
withdrawn immediately.[10]

1986: Accumulating Grievances

After the Fifth Plenum in 1985 had approved important personnel changes in the Secretariat, Hu focused intently on the lengthy process of drafting and gaining Central Committee approval for a "Resolution on Construction of Socialist Spiritual Civilization," an arcane ideological topic that had been hanging fire since the abortive campaign against "spiritual pollution" in 1983, and even since the 12th Congress and its insistence on "communism." In December Hu appointed the drafting group, which included Zheng Bijian and several other reform supporters but not Deng Liqun. Over the next several months, he held a number of meetings with the drafting team, and by the time senior leadership gathered at Beidaihe in August, the resolution had won broad approval, even among some of the elders.[11]

The resolution had been partly the product of party ideological workers' confusion about how to deal with the contradictory side effects of "reform and opening" and the "four fundamental principles." Party elders had difficulty agreeing to the "capitalist" practices like markets, material incentives, and production contracts they had vilified under Mao Zedong. There was also the question of "bourgeois liberalization," the label the party's remaining

General Secretary Hu Yaobang and Premier Zhao Ziyang meet at the Beijing airport after Hu's return from his first trip to western Europe, 1986. (AP Photo / Neal Ulevich)

leftist ideologues wanted to use against writers and artists who leaned toward Western ideas and attitudes. But Hu and Zheng Bijian had carefully controlled the drafting process, consulting frequently with party leaders and fending off ideological assaults from Hu Qiaomu and Deng Liqun.

The most serious challenge came in a letter Deng Liqun wrote to the Politburo Standing Committee in September, in which he tried to shift the focus to the question of whether a "capitalist restoration" was endangering the CCP. Chen Yun and Li Xiannian seemed to agree with him, but Deng Xiaoping did not, accusing Deng Liqun of trying to widen his disagreements with Chen Yun. Hu and Zhao Ziyang wrote a joint letter defending the resolution, particularly on the issue of whether "communism was the core of socialist spiritual civilization," which they said still divided the party and could not be forced. Deng Xiaoping told them to disregard Deng Liqun.[12]

With Deng's support seemingly set, the "Spiritual Civilization" resolution was easily passed at the Sixth Plenum on September 28. But at the closing session, Hu Yaobang asked if anyone had additional comments. Former propaganda department director Lu Dingyi—one of the first victims of the Cultural Revolution—said he thought the term "bourgeois liberalization" should be deleted from the resolution, as it had been used by the Gang of Four to persecute many old comrades, including himself. Lu's remarks were heavily applauded, but a *biaotai* (attitude declaration) exercise followed in which various leaders spoke in favor of what they assumed would be Deng Xiaoping's position—maintaining the attack on "bourgeois liberalization." Deng's unscripted remarks would make the problem worse:

> With regard to the question of opposing bourgeois liberalization, I am the one who has talked about it most often and most insistently. Why? First, because there is now a trend of thought among the masses, especially among the young people, in favor of liberalization. Second, because . . . there have been some comments from people in Hong Kong and Taiwan who . . . think we should introduce the capitalist system [entirely], as if that were the only genuine modernization. What is this liberalization? It is an attempt to turn China's present policies in the direction of capitalism. . . . Liberalization by itself means antagonism to our current policies and systems and a wish to revise them. In fact, exponents of liberalization want to lead us down the road to capitalism. . . . It doesn't matter if the term has been used elsewhere in other

contexts, for our current politics demands that we use it in the resolution, and I am in favor of it.[13]

All those referred to as the "Eight Elders" (*ba lao*)—Deng Xiaoping,
Chen Yun, Li Xiannian, Yang Shangkun, Bo Yibo, Peng Zhen, Wang Zhen,
and Deng Yingchao—spoke in favor of keeping "bourgeois liberalization" in
the resolution.[14] Among younger leaders, only Wan Li spoke up in support
of Lu Dingyi's proposal. Zhao Ziyang and all the members of the Central
Secretariat—including Hu Yaobang—voted with the majority.

Despite his vote, Hu Yaobang expressed understanding of Lu's position
and a concern that the term could be used as a political "hat," or label, to
demonize those who did not have the same opinions as party leaders on
freedom of expression and belief. His concern would soon prove justified.
Hu probably worsened the situation, however, by approving the spiritual
civilization resolution for distribution within the party but embargoing distribution of the debate record, which included Deng's impromptu speech.
Wang Zhen and Bo Yibo objected to this, although Deng did not seem
concerned.[15]

Zhao Ziyang recognized much later that Deng's diatribe at the Sixth
Plenum was directed at Hu Yaobang, although it did not name him, and he
believed it signified that Deng had decided to "bring Yaobang down." Para-
doxically, Zhao observed that the Deng-Hu relationship was still sound despite growing evidence of Deng's displeasure.[16]

It is difficult to determine exactly what issues or events in the fall of 1986
were most crucial in pushing Deng to oust his presumed successor and longtime subordinate. The official version is that Hu's inattention to the issue of
"bourgeois liberalization" led him to be overly lenient toward dissatisfied intellectuals and protesting students, who threatened to overthrow the regime. A plausible alternative explanation takes more account of the personal
power considerations in play at the time—Deng's aspirations, Chen Yun's
hindering actions, competition among potential successors, and "old man
politics."

Social grievances began to pile up in 1986, and the party seemed unable
to resolve them. There were too many officials at every level, with rehabilitated veterans refusing to step back and allow younger cadres to work. Little
was being accomplished, though regulations and documents proliferated.
Promotions were slow, and opportunities for graft plentiful. The public

stepped up pressure for political reform. Increased access to foreign products, investment, and ideas led to more dissatisfaction with the CCP and its methods. University students flocked to lectures by dissident intellectuals like Fang Lizhi and Liu Binyan, who advocated more democracy and study of Western forms of governance.[17] Deng faulted Hu Yaobang for not controlling them better or kicking them out of the party.

Relations between Hu and Deng had edged further downward in early 1986. Hu seemed to spend more time on inspections of rural counties far from Beijing in the first half of the year. He had made more inspection trips to the grassroots level than any other senior leader, visiting some 1,600 of the more than 2,200 counties and all but ten of 331 districts between 1980 and 1987. Chen Yun and Li Xiannian—who spent much of their time in plush official villas in their later years—disparaged such activity, but Hu reveled in it. He was a genuine "man of the people" who had a natural feel for peasant farmers. Hu also advocated policies that empowered rural communities, such as "diversified agriculture" and "village industries."

He also appeared to enjoy the relative freedom of being away from Beijing's bureaucratic atmosphere, sometimes speaking candidly or sarcastically about problems he was trying to resolve. On May 22, 1986, in Sichuan, for example, he called for a radical personnel restructuring of the Central Committee at the Thirteenth Congress in 1987, removing a third of all remaining old cadres and replacing them with more than a hundred younger party members in their thirties and forties. He added, "Now, I'm almost seventy years old, and I'm about to retire. Those veteran comrades over the age of 80 even more should step down. Whether there is a concept of the overall situation should be reflected in this issue."[18]

The *Deng Xiaoping Chronology* notes that after Hu returned to Beijing, a "chat" (*tanhua*) was held in Zhongnanhai's Huairen Hall that included Hu Yaobang, Zhao Ziyang, Chen Yun, and Li Xiannian. With Ye Jianying gravely ill, this gathering was essentially a Politburo Standing Committee meeting, although it was not called such, and its agenda remains unknown.[19] Earlier in May, Chen Yun had vetoed the nomination of Hu Yaobang's principal deputy in the Central Secretariat, Hu Qili, to replace Wang Zhen as president of the Central Party School.[20]

The "twin peaks" phenomenon cited by Yang Jisheng, which ultimately proved insuperable for both Hu and Zhao Ziyang, was worsening. In many ways the Deng Xiaoping–Chen Yun relationship was a dialogue of indirect communications and tacit understandings. They each seemed to know the boundaries and protocols. Deng said he and Chen Yun could not reach an agreement by talking, so Deng resisted efforts to call a Politburo Standing Committee meeting.[21] The two elders both had said openly that the older generation needed to step back, but neither seemed willing to take the lead or risk allowing the other's protégés to dominate the party. The other elders seemed to understand that once Deng and Chen stepped aside, they would have no choice but to do likewise. Hu Yaobang had often expressed his hope that Deng Xiaoping and Chen Yun would lead the process. But because his relationship with Chen Yun was frosty, it was not a topic he could raise with him. Various sources indicate that Hu did meet with Deng to discuss the leadership issue, but they differ on the details of the meeting.[22]

The Humiliation of Hu Yaobang

Deng Xiaoping had spoken both publicly and privately about wanting to retire but was deliberately vague about details. In early September 1986, in an interview with Mike Wallace for the CBS *60 Minutes* program, he said, "Personally, I should like to retire soon. However, this is a rather difficult question. It is very hard to persuade the Party rank and file and the Chinese people to accept that . . . I need to work harder to talk people around. . . . To be quite frank, I am trying to persuade people to let me retire at the Party's Thirteenth National Congress next year. But so far, all I have heard is dissenting voices on all sides."[23]

Although Deng did not say so, the opposition to his retirement most likely was coming from his strongest support base, the elderly veterans Hu Yaobang had done so much to return to power in the late 1970s. Most of them were not in the front line of party or government administration. But they remained a political force—attending meetings as Central Advisory Commission representatives, speaking out on various controversial issues, plotting and gossiping among themselves, and resisting the forward movement of reform in general and political reform in particular. They were increasingly distrustful of Hu and his zeal to not just restore the old CCP, but to repair and reform its personnel practices, regulations and procedures, accountability to the people, ideology, and work style.

Not long after Deng's CBS interview but before the Sixth Plenum, Hu met with Katharine Graham, owner of the *Washington Post,* who asked him about Deng and the succession problem. His answer, which was not included in the US account of the interview, was noticed in Beijing. Hu told her:

First, we have clearly stipulated that the lifelong tenure system of leadership is abolished and no one can have the right to hold leadership positions for life. Second, we have also clearly defined the system of collective leadership of the Party and the State in order to avoid giving undue prominence to the authority of one person. Third, not long ago our party agreed to work out a political system reform program within a year. With the above three items, I believe that at the 13th National Congress of our Party next year, the issue of succession of the Party and State leaders can be resolved in a more complete manner.[24]

In October 1986 a showdown of some kind took place within the leadership over the retirement / succession issue. There are several versions of the story, not all consistent. Most agree it was at a Politburo meeting, but none provide the date—just sometime in October. Hu spoke directly and frankly:

If you say in the past that I showed some confusion on this issue, was not too clear, and easily led people to create misunderstanding, then I want to speak specifically and frankly today. I approve of (*zancheng*) Comrade Xiaoping taking the lead in stepping back, this is a very good example. So long as Comrade Xiaoping retires, the work of the other old comrades can be done well. My term as general secretary is coming to an end, and I will also step down, completely making way for a younger comrade.[25]

A more controversial account of this meeting has Deng stating his intention to retire, which was met with near-unanimous opposition from the attending Politburo members. The sole exception was Hu Yaobang, who reportedly said, "I raise two hands in support." Both Hu and Zhao Ziyang later denied the "two hands" description, but not the fact of the meeting or its outcome.[26] On October 21, *Shenzhen Youth Daily*—a tabloid-style newspaper set up in the special economic zone under loosened ideological oversight—published a front-page commentary, "I Approve of Comrade Xiaoping's Retirement," using the same phraseology (*zancheng*) Hu Yaobang had employed. The article aroused a strong reaction among readers and was picked up by the Xinhua News Agency in its daily summary of news articles from around China.[27]

On October 22 Ye Jianying died in Beijing at the age of eighty-nine. His death was not a surprise, as he had been under medical care for neurological and pulmonary disorders for several years. Hu had ordered the establishment of a special medical team to care for Ye in his Xishan residence, and also had prearranged official publicity and funeral arrangements for his death.[28] Ye's passing did not directly affect party leadership, as he had dropped out of politics a few years before officially retiring in September 1985, but it enabled an important change in the personality-driven "old-man politics" at the top of the CCP.

Ye's death mattered particularly for Hu Yaobang. Ye had been an old friend and patron for more than fifty years and had come to Hu's rescue on several important occasions, most recently in 1983. Now that constant source of support was gone. As general secretary, Hu Yaobang delivered the party's official judgment on Ye, reading the eulogy at the funeral on October 29. Written by a committee and approved well in advance, Hu's speech had no personal content about his long friendship with the man everyone called *Ye Shuai*, Marshal Ye. As for Hu's personal appraisal of his old comrade, there is little in the public record, apart from one brief note that Hu said if Ye had lived longer, "many things perhaps may not have become so terrible."[29]

On the day of Ye's funeral, when all the key leaders of the party and army were gathered in the Great Hall of the People, Deng Xiaoping suggested to Chen Yun and Li Xiannian that they get together for a chat the next day. Although Chen expected the discussion to take place at Deng's home, Deng insisted he would come to Chen's residence, perhaps an indication that he wanted a favor. The three gathered there the next morning, and after some photographs were taken, all staffers, including *mishu* and security guards, were asked to depart, leaving the three men alone with no note-takers.[30] While it is likely they told their respective private secretaries about the meeting afterward, none of the three included details of the meeting in their published records.

The unusual nature of the meeting, its hour-and-a-half duration, the exclusion of staff, and reports of Li and Chen fussing over ensuring Deng had a full supply of cigarettes have generated some speculation about the meeting being a "secret plot" (*mimou*) to decide Hu Yaobang's fate. The official explanation was that the three men chatted calmly about all of them retiring together.[31] There is ample room for speculation, given how quickly subsequent events unfolded to Hu's detriment.

In early November, after news of the *Shenzhen Youth Daily* article reached Beijing, the other elders roared to Deng's aid, while Hu Yaobang went on the defensive. Meeting with the writing team drafting the 13th Congress political report on November 11, Hu seemed to Wu Jiaxiang to be pensive, resentful that his record of success since 1982 had not been better recognized. And perhaps insecure. He probably knew that he and Zhao Ziyang were expected to give major reports to the congress, and that Zhao's—on "development"— would be more important than Hu's political work report.[32] He also knew that Deng had ordered the formation of a five-person small group to study political structural reform, with Zhao Ziyang in charge.[33] Hu nonetheless stressed to the drafters that Deng's political reforms should be highlighted in his report. He then doubled down on his suggestion that the preeminent elders should step down at the Thirteenth Congress:

> We must absolutely get rid of lifetime tenure, talk about the significance of a large group of older revolutionaries taking the lead in stepping down. . . . We must especially talk sufficiently about the significance of Comrade Xiaoping and Comrade Chen Yun taking the lead in retiring, one or two hundred words is not clear enough, otherwise the *Shenzhen Youth Daily* will talk, and take the credit, damn them![34]

Shortly after these remarks, Hu began to be referred to as the "pushing for retirement faction" (*cutui pai*), which only heightened the anger building against him among the elders. Bo Yibo demanded that the *Shenzhen Youth Daily* be closed (which eventually was done). Wang Zhen thundered at the Central Party School that "Comrade Xiaoping is our emperor, he cannot retire, and [I] would oppose whoever wants Xiaoping to give way."[35]

The Student Unrest Factor

The proximate (official) cause of Hu Yaobang's sudden ouster began on December 1, 1986, in Anhui Province, at the University of Science and Technology of China (USTC), where students and faculty were beginning to consider their own interpretations of the party's call for "political structural reform." The university's vice president, an astrophysicist named Fang Lizhi, had made critical comments, both inside and outside the country, about the party's leaders, powers, and procedures. Branded a "rightist" in 1957, Fang's CCP membership had been restored, but he had developed independent notions about education, science and technology, governance, and leadership.

As a proponent of "Westernization" and democracy, Fang's reputation grew among students both at USTC and other universities, and his speeches on contemporary issues drew large, enthusiastic crowds. Top party leaders, however, viewed him with distaste, and Deng Xiaoping developed a particular hostility toward him. On December 1, students already dissatisfied with poor housing and food at one of China's elite universities took on local electoral issues as well, putting up posters calling for people to "struggle for real democracy" in resolving problems. Three days later, at a large public meeting in the school auditorium, Fang declared that democracy "is not a gift from above but relies on our own struggle to obtain it."[36]

In the following few days, about four thousand students from local universities took to the streets of Hefei, demonstrating at municipal party headquarters and the *Anhui Daily* in support of greater democracy, civic rights, and an end to "feudal dictatorship." Demonstrations also spread to other major education hubs in Central China, including Shanghai, Wuhan, Nanjing, Changsha, Xi'an, and Hangzhou. By December 10, students at Beijing's major universities were considering comparable activities, although blustery winter weather inhibited participation.[37]

On December 8, Hu Yaobang chaired a Secretariat meeting to discuss the growing unrest. Available accounts of the meeting indicate the Secretariat agreed on "cool handling" of the disturbances, with "dialogue" (*duihua*) as the best way to ensure the protests did not become violent. Hu Yaobang observed that the overall situation in China was the best it had been since 1949. He warned, however, that some would try to stir up the students to cause bigger problems, naming Fang Lizhi and Liu Binyan. A Youth League journalist sacked in 1957 as a "rightist," Liu had made a joint appearance with Fang at a Shanghai university in November, extolling the superiority of Western democracy and multiparty systems, which had further irritated Deng Xiaoping.[38]

By mid-December, student activism had spread to more cities—eventually twenty-nine would report disturbances—but the scale was still relatively small and mostly on campuses. Speakers and posters demanded that universities improve living and study conditions, and called for more democracy, freedom of speech, and accountability from government. Shanghai became the hot spot on December 18, when Mayor Jiang Zemin went to Jiaotong University (his alma mater) to talk the students out of a large demonstration planned for the following day. Jiang was treated rudely, but he continued talking with student leaders, listening to their complaints.

The next day, however, thousands of students from several universities descended on Shanghai's main thoroughfares—Nanjing Road and the area along the Huangpu River known as "The Bund"—demanding the punishment of corrupt officials and greater press freedom. They ignored Jiang's efforts to persuade them to return to campus, and eventually had to be forcibly dispersed by police, causing some property damage. Smaller demonstrations continued over the next few days.[39] None of the municipal governments or universities involved solicited help from Beijing in handling the issues.

Official Beijing, however, was beginning to fracture. The tenuous stalemates between the Chen and Deng camps, between Deng Liqun and Zhu Houze factions within the Propaganda Department, and between restored elders and younger leaders were causing political immobility. Wu Jiaxiang observed that there seemed to be no guidance for the work he was doing on preparing Thirteenth Congress documents. The team was instructed to keep working on the drafts, but not to become involved in the political infighting. They could see that Hu Yaobang was besieged but could do nothing to help him.[40]

The city was awash in rumors about what was happening in the provinces, which Deng's old cronies used to stoke his anger at Hu and his concern about mob violence. At Secretariat meetings on December 8 and 22, Hu continued to insist the student unrest was "no big deal" and just needed some editorials to provide guidance. But the propaganda apparatus was paralyzed. And the students weren't listening anyway.[41]

On December 19, demonstrations in Shanghai grew, involving "tens of thousands" of students from more than twenty Shanghai schools and more than two thousand police. Again, Jiang Zemin and his deputies met with the students and tried to persuade them to return to their campuses, then relied on public security units to truck them back, none too gently. There were some arrests and injuries, but the students failed to garner much public support. After the Shanghai events, Wuhan, Hangzhou, Nanjing, Chengdu, Xi'an, Tianjin, and Changsha reported "student demonstrations of varying sizes," although Shanghai itself remained relatively calm.[42]

It is difficult to judge how impactful the demonstrations of December 1986 were, except insofar as they provided the impetus to a group of angry old men to push out a successful, even popular, general secretary. Hu's Central Secretariat devoted at least three sessions to preparing guidance on how to handle the students. On December 27, Hu Yaobang presided over a national conference of regional party secretaries to discuss Central guidance on how to handle the growing tide of demonstrations and public criticism. As at all these meetings, Hu continued to counsel "cool handling," patience, and per-suasion, rather than brute force, to deal with protestors.

That same evening, according to unconfirmed accounts from Sheng Ping and Chen Liming, Deng invited to his home some of Hu Yaobang's fiercest critics for an emergency meeting to discuss what needed to be done about the unrest, and who should be blamed. Participants included Peng Zhen, Bo Yibo, Yang Shangkun, and Wang Zhen, and perhaps others (name lists vary). Sheng Ping's description of the meeting was understated, indicating they analyzed "the serious nature of the student demonstrations, unanimously agreeing that they were the result of Hu Yaobang's overly conciliatory and weak leadership, and that he should be held responsible for the current sit-uation."[43] The absence of Chen Yun and Li Xiannian can be attributed to health reasons, although Deng may have reached agreement with them at their late October private meeting.

A Party "Life" Meeting Brings Political Death

With the assurance of elder support, Deng called another group of party leaders to his home on December 30: Hu Yaobang, Zhao Ziyang, Wan Li, Hu Qili, Li Peng, and Education Minister He Dongchang. They were once Deng's chosen successor generation, and his intent likely was to shake them up and impel them to take firm—even violent—action against demonstra-tors who broke the law. But even though Deng did not mention Hu Yaobang by name, the general subject matter and the examples he used made clear his speech was directed at him:

> A rumor is going around Shanghai to the effect that there is disagree-ment in the Central Committee as to whether we should uphold the Four Cardinal Principles and oppose liberalization, and that there is therefore a layer of protection. . . . Originally, at the Sixth Plenary Session . . . I felt I had to intervene . . . on the necessity of combating bourgeois liberalization. Apparently, my remarks on that occasion had no great effect. I understand they were never disseminated throughout the Party.[44]

In a thirdhand account of Deng's comments, Wu Jiaxiang wrote that Deng told his audience that if any students tried to enter Tiananmen Square, they were to be arrested without exception, using all necessary force. "If one goes, arrest one, if a thousand go, arrest a thousand." "Don't be afraid of blood-shed." Zhao Ziyang expressed his agreement, in ways that left many subsequent observers convinced he not only knew about Deng's plans to bring down Hu Yaobang but was in on them.[45]

Hu Yaobang was shocked by Deng's anger, according to Sheng Ping's conjectural notes in his *Chronology of Hu Yaobang's Thought*. Not citing Hu directly, a parenthetical observation reads:

> Hu Yaobang pondered over and over and felt that he had never real-ized before how great the differences [with Deng] were: to consider the development of socialist democracy to be "bourgeois liberalization," and their views and policies toward the student demonstrations, ide-ology and intellectuals to be so completely different. Now, if one had to . . . use dictatorial methods to [deal with] the students and "oppose bourgeois liberalization," these were things he could not do, no matter what. Thinking that the student movement would be suppressed, and a large number of intellectuals and good cadres would be affected, he could not sleep all night. But . . . even if he asked for discussion, he would only be besieged at the meeting to defend himself, which did not help. So he determined to take all responsibilities on himself, to take into account the overall situation, and to resign and step down, calming everything down.[46]

New Year's Day 1987 was cold, with sleet and snow, but several hundred Beida and other university students set out from their campuses before noon, heading toward Tiananmen Square. When they arrived, they discovered the area around the Martyrs' Monument at the center of the square was occupied by several thousand Young Pioneers and Communist Youth League students in close-order formation, surrounded by hundreds of uniformed police. They had been there since early morning, ordered to block the Martyr's Monument from being used by protestors.

The university students, unable to proceed into the square, gathered at its north edge near the National History Museum, where they were easily broken up or distracted by police and university officials. There was some slogan shouting and pushing and shoving, but fewer than a hundred were arrested. By 3 p.m. the square was nearly deserted, and the students had returned to their dorms. Small demonstrations popped up on campuses for the next several days, but the larger demonstrations had been thwarted, and they stopped altogether less than a week later.[47]

Some observers credit Hu Yaobang with this outcome, as he had reached out to Minister of Public Security Ruan Chongwu, a former CYL subordinate, and asked that the students be given a "soft landing" (*ruan zhuolu*). Ruan, brother of Hu's Central Party School researcher and stalwart reformer Ruan Ming, had only been appointed to the post in 1985. Whether because he foiled Deng's desire to "arrest a thousand" on January 1 or because he was Hu Yaobang's choice, Ruan was transferred to a less significant post after Hu's ouster.[48]

On January 2, Hu Yaobang submitted his resignation directly to Deng Xiaoping in the form of a personal letter he titled "Opening My Heart To Comrade Xiaoping." Prior to sending the letter, Hu had heard from Zhao Ziyang, who advised him to seek a meeting with Deng to try to resolve their differences, and to do a *jiantao* to account for his errors.[49] The story from that point forward becomes rather murky, as Hu's fate marks the collapse of the Deng-Hu-Zhao "troika," and memoirists recounting the events have different recollections of dates and details, depending upon which of the three leaders they supported.

Chen Liming's earlier biography has what purports to be the text of Hu's letter. Hu acknowledged he had made several mistakes, including that he had not been cautious in handling party and state matters, causing some loss of prestige, and that he had failed to guard sufficiently against "bourgeois liberalization" as Deng had charged, enabling some bad elements to lead the youth astray and damage the country's "unity and stability." These were serious errors that showed his incompetence as general secretary. Why did he make such errors? He mismanaged his time, spending too much time on economic issues, especially reform and opening up, and not enough time on "grasping politics," the proper duty of the party secretary.

Hu acknowledged he did not go deeply enough into resolving the "contradictions" that emerged between reform and the "four fundamental principles." Finally, he did not properly evaluate himself, recognize his own limitations and restrain his self-confidence. He denied accusations that he was putting together a "circle" (faction) and challenged Deng to examine the personnel appointments he had made to verify this was so. He concluded by requesting, in light of these serious errors, that he be allowed to step down, in order to clarify his own thinking and "make an accounting to the Party."[50]

In response, Deng Xiaoping made several decisions that were not in his ambit of authority, but that probably only he had the wherewithal and audacity to make. They were the decisions of a man who believed "what I say decides it" (*wo shuole suan*). On the morning of January 4, Deng convened what his official chronology claims was a "Politburo Standing Committee" meeting in his home.[51] Zhao Ziyang's memoirs only refer to it as a "meeting," realizing that only the general secretary was authorized to convene a Standing Committee meeting; not only did Hu Yaobang not call the meeting, he was not even included. Chen Yun was the only other Standing Committee member attending. Deng had sent CMC Secretary General Yang Shangkun to Shanghai the previous day to bring Li Xiannian back to Beijing, but Li refused, for reasons that are obscure.[52] The other participants appear to be representative of the principal party and government organizations: Bo Yibo (CAC), Yang Shangkun (CMC), Peng Zhen (NPC), and Wang Zhen, who appeared to be there only as a crony of both Deng and Chen Yun. All shared a disdain for Hu Yaobang and a desire for his immediate removal. Deng shared Hu's letter with them and proposed they approve his request to resign. No one objected.[53]

Deng then made a startling decision, although it evidently passed without much discussion or objection. He proposed that the work of the Politburo Standing Committee, the highest decision-making level in the party, be taken over by a five-man small group before the Thirteenth Congress met in October. That group would be headed by Zhao Ziyang, replacing Hu as general secretary, Bo Yibo, Yang Shangkun, Wan Li, and Hu Qili. There was little reported discussion of what the political impact would be or whether a process more in keeping with the party's actual organizational charter should be adopted. Chen Yun gave a lengthy speech on how propaganda surrounding Hu's resignation should be focused on its "legality." Zhao later speculated that both Chen and Deng were concerned about possible negative public reaction to Hu's ouster.[54]

Deng then moved on to the specifics of ousting Hu Yaobang. He said there should be a "soft handling" (*ruan chuli*), allowing Hu to retain a position on the Politburo Standing Committee (which Deng had just declared would be suspended). This would avoid the perception, inside and outside of China, that this was some kind of coup—although that's precisely what it was. Deng called for a "life meeting" (*shenghuo hui*) to be held soon for Hu by his party committee, to carry out criticism of his errors and help him correct them. Deng proposed that the Central Advisory Commission be authorized to convene this meeting, even though Hu was not a member. Deng certainly knew Hu had plenty of enemies among the elders there, and Chen Yun was in charge.[55]

The practice of holding so-called democratic life meetings dates back to the Yan'an era and the party rectification movement of the early 1940s. Although such meetings were intended to promote "inner party democracy" and trust within individual CCP units by normalizing criticism and self-criticism as means of administering discipline, they did not work well in practice, particularly at the upper levels of the party. As interpersonal competition and ideological dissension fed power disputes, such meetings tended to become opportunities for attacking opponents or subjecting them to humiliation by the group. The *jiantao*, or "self-confession," became a particularly disliked practice.

Deng had mapped the process out in advance. After the "life meeting" was completed, an "expanded" Politburo meeting would be held to approve a resolution on the outcome, followed by a controlled release of supporting information to the party at large. The final step would be for the Thirteenth Party Congress to pass a resolution approving the process by which Hu was removed and to formally install his replacement.

On January 6, Hu Yaobang finally got his "chat" with Deng Xiaoping at his home. It is mentioned in both Hu Yaobang chronologies, but not in Deng's. In neither of Hu's chronicles is there any significant account of the substance of their conversation. Deng appears to have recounted Hu's "errors" and informed him of the upcoming "life meeting," though not its schedule. Hu responded with an explanation of some of the factual misstatements in the charges against him. Deng went on to set restrictions on the subjects that could be raised in criticism of Hu at the life meeting: no discussion of "line problems" (that is, no Cultural Revolution-style branding of Hu as ideologically apostate); no discussion of Hu's character or moral fiber; no raising the issue of a "Youth League Faction"; and no talk of a "sectarian" nature. Deng apparently did not make clear to Hu what kind of treatment he was about to receive.[56]

On January 7 the five-man small group convened to discuss the life meeting. It would begin the morning of January 10 in the Huairen Hall of Zhongnanhai, and invitations were to be sent out to all members and alternate members of the Politburo and Secretariat, seventeen members of the Central Advisory Commission, and two members of the Central Commission for Discipline Inspection. Bo Yibo would chair the meeting; he and

Yang Shangkun made arrangements for the first few speakers: Yu Qiuli, Deng Liqun, Hu Qiaomu, Yao Yilin, and Wang Heshou, some of whom Hu Yaobang knew were opponents, some of whom he considered friends. Zhao Ziyang was tasked with informing Hu of the meeting time and place, but only got around to doing so the evening before, January 9, when he visited Hu at his home and gave him some suggestions of issues to include in his *jiantao*.[57]

There are several versions of what followed, although no official records are publicly available. Memoirs of two of the actual participants, Zhao Ziyang and Deng Liqun, tilt their accounts somewhat to exculpate themselves. Other perspectives are found in secondhand or thirdhand accounts, mostly by friends or supporters of Hu who portray him as the perhaps naive victim of a "palace coup" planned and orchestrated by Deng Xiaoping and Chen Yun. There is even a play written by Sha Yexin in 2015, informed by conversations with Hu Yaobang's son, Hu Dehua, which the playwright claimed accurately depicted the actual dialogue from the life meeting.[58] Historian Chen Xiaoya presents a credible timeline of the personalities and attacks on Hu from the five-day meeting (actually five half-days) that ran from January 10 to January 15.[59]

At 10 a.m. on January 10, Hu Yaobang took his place in a Huairen Hall meeting room occupied by more than fifty people. He may have noticed immediately the absence of Deng Xiaoping, Chen Yun, and Li Xiannian, sitting out what they knew would be an unpleasant meeting. The person in charge was Bo Yibo, a vice-chairman of the Central Advisory Commission but not a member of the Political Bureau, which would have been more correct for a life meeting at Hu's level. Bo had been one of the first beneficiaries of Hu's diligence when he was reversing "unjust, false, and wrong cases" in 1978. But Bo's assignment was to shame and humiliate Hu on behalf of Chen Yun and the other elders. He was brusque to the point of rudeness, instructing Hu to get on with his *jiantao*.

Hu took up most of Saturday morning with his lengthy presentation. It is impossible to know what his thinking was when he prepared his self-confession for this audience of mostly elder cadres. He would later say he chose to take responsibility for all the problems in order to protect a group of others, in light of the need to preserve stability and unity within the leadership. But he also said that, had he known the intentions of this group were to "humiliate me and criticize me until I stank," he would not have submitted his resignation or written this kind of *jiantao*.[60]

Perhaps Hu thought he could shorten the ordeal by agreeing with some but not all of the charges. By "going against his conscience" and admitting fault, throwing himself on the mercy of this court of unfriendly but respected elders, he could persuade them of his good intentions, and his resignation could be accepted without further ado. It was a serious misjudgment of both the individuals involved and the nature of the process. Hu acknowledged nearly all the charges against him, attempting to explain his actions rather than to rebut the charges:

On failing to adhere to Deng's "four fundamental principles": "I did say some things and grasped some things, but I did not strictly grasp these basic principles."

On "bourgeois liberalization": "I didn't think this issue was serious. I thought that as long as I did my job well, the problem would naturally be solved."

On "spiritual pollution": "After Comrade Xiaoping spoke about it, I did not take correct measures in time to stop some wrong words and deeds."

On the training of cadres and successors: "The Party Center, especially some old revolutionaries, repeatedly asked me to train good successors and boldly promote comrades with both political integrity and experience. I firmly supported this. I have never taken myself as the center in promoting and assigning cadres. I have always discussed them in groups and have never promoted people with personal ties or supported small circles. But I also made some mistakes."

On foreign affairs activities: "The department in charge of receiving foreign guests asked me to see Lu Keng. I did not refuse. This was a mistake. When I talked with him, I did not categorically deny some of his statements."

On the "ideological roots" of his mistakes: ". . . after the Cultural Revolution, I always wanted to maintain stability during the ideological struggle, and I was worried about disorder. I used my energy mainly to guard against the left, not against the right . . . After a long term in office, I became too excited and irritable to listen to other people's opinions."

On "promising too much to lower levels": "I have never approved anything beyond the scope of my powers."

Finally, Hu repeated his request to resign as general secretary.[61]

This was all red meat for his antagonists, and they started in on him the next day. First was Vice-Premier Yu Qiuli. Hu had considered Yu a friend and often solicited his views on economic issues in the Secretariat. Yu, however, had gathered some of Hu's public statements on economics, and attacked him sharply, asking him directly why he had said such things.

Next was archrival Deng Liqun, who was asked by Yang Shangkun and Bo Yibo to stand in for Hu Qiaomu to blast Hu Yaobang on a long list of ideological shortcomings. In fact, Deng's diatribe was so protracted (more than six hours) that he used up the allotted time for January 12 and had to continue the following morning. He focused heavily on the "spiritual pollution" campaign of 1983, and on the "bourgeois liberalization" question, all issues on which he had attacked Hu many times before.[62]

The barrage of criticism continued at high intensity over the next three days. Everyone was expected to say or write something. It didn't matter if it was fair or even true. The elders routinely violated Deng's restrictions on subject matter, accusing Hu of factional activity, abuse of power, ideological distortion, and personal ambition. They falsified or distorted information, such as Bo Yibo dismissing Hu's inspections of remote and impoverished areas as "tourism." Some close to Hu on the Secretariat criticized his inattention to warnings and guidance from Deng or Chen Yun.[63] Even his old friend from Yan'an days, Wang Heshou, with whom he had sworn an oath of friendship and loyalty, turned on him, reporting Hu's private feelings about the life meeting first to Chen Yun, then the full session.[64]

But probably the most damaging blow of the entire travesty was delivered by Zhao Ziyang on the last full day. Although Hu and Zhao were not considered close, they had worked together successfully as part of the troika that had promoted economic reform and, more recently, political reform as well. Zhao had told Hu they were "in the same boat" in 1983, when Hu was under heavy attack from Chen Yun and Deng Liqun.[65] But Zhao had also written a private letter to Deng and Chen Yun in May 1984, asking the two elders to "formulate the necessary leadership system for our party, and personally supervise and implement it."[66] Zhao's speech to the life meeting was more direct, and referred to the earlier letter:

At that time, I felt that Hu Yaobang did not abide by [party] discipline. To wait until the situation changed, when Xiaoping and Chen Yun were gone, and the party elders were gone, then the two of us would be unable to work together, and [I would] have to resign. . . . Now it is not possible for him to act freely; with Comrades Xiaoping and Chen Yun here, and especially Xiaoping, he cannot help but consider them. Once the situation changes, and he can move freely, there will be no constraint.[67]

In the afternoon, the bullying continued, with Yao Yilin attacking Hu on economic issues, Bo Yibo faulting his inspection trips, and Yang Shangkun accusing him of trying to seize military power by replacing Deng on the CMC.[68] Wang Zhen, Peng Zhen, Song Renqiong, and other elders piled on, as was expected. Finally, Xi Zhongxun had seen enough. Jumping to his feet, he shouted at his elderly colleagues, "What are you doing?! A replay of 'Forcing the Emperor to Abdicate' [a classical Peking opera]? This is not normal! A 'party life' meeting cannot discuss the issue of dismissing or retaining the Party General Secretary. It's against Party principles! I resolutely oppose this method . . ." But Hu Yaobang stood up, not letting Xi continue. "Comrade Zhongxun, I have already considered this well. [They are] not allowing me to do it, so I will resign."[69] After the meeting adjourned, Hu walked into the hallway outside the meeting room, sat down heavily on the stairs, and sobbed loudly and bitterly. Wan Li and Tian Jiyun stood by to comfort him, but Hu Yaobang was a broken man—as had been intended.

The next morning, January 16, Deng Xiaoping convened and chaired an expanded meeting of the Politburo in the same room, with mostly the same participants. Chen Yun also attended, but Li Xiannian remained in Shanghai, although he made enough disparaging remarks about Hu subsequently to show he was not opposed to the outcome. Deng started by setting his own rules for the event. "It's inappropriate for Yaobang to preside over today's meeting, so I will preside. The meeting is to approve this communiqué, there will be no talk of anything else. Comrades from the Advisory Commission may raise your hands [to vote—ordinarily not permitted for attendees who are not members of the Politburo]."[70]

Bo Yibo reviewed the meeting in harsh terms, leveling critiques of Hu that eventually became a document circulated to the entire party. The meeting then heard a speech by Chen Yun in which he insisted that the process of sacking Hu was entirely consistent with the party charter and should be affirmed as such. He criticized the activities of the Central Secretariat under Hu's leadership and Hu's style of running meetings. According to one observer, Deng kept his eyes resolutely ahead while Chen was speaking, as if ignoring him. Bo Yibo had to wave his hands in front of Deng's face when Chen was finished, after which Deng called for a show of hands on the resolution before the Politburo, declared it passed, and adjourned the session.[71] The resolution, broadcast to the public that same evening, unanimously approved Hu's request to resign; unanimously approved the election of Zhao Ziyang as general secretary; agreed to submit those two decisions to the next plenary meeting of the Central Committee; and agreed to retain Hu Yaobang as a member of the Politburo and its Standing Committee.

Hu Yaobang was obligated to do another self-criticism, this one also abject but mercifully brief, titled only "My Declaration of Attitude" (*wo de biaotai*). Declaring one's attitude is one of the CCP's loyalty rituals, in which all members are expected to agree publicly with a position or decision handed down from a higher level. In Hu's case, everyone would have understood that it was "against his will" (*weixin*), but he was in no political or emotional condition to do otherwise. Finally, Hu returned to his office in the QinzhengDian building in Zhongnanhai and had his secretary send word to his family that no one should come to see him. Exhausted in body and spirit, he stayed there for two weeks before walking home alone on a cold and blustery winter night, carrying only a few books and papers.[72]

On January 19 the party Center issued Central Document No. 3 (1987), which directed that the preparation of a "concise" briefing of the life meeting for distribution to the entire party be assigned to Bo Yibo, with assistance from Hu Qiaomu, based on Deng Liqun's notes. Not surprisingly, the document accentuated the negative, criticizing virtually every aspect of Hu Yaobang's work. Deng Liqun wrote that there was some pushback from party members at different levels, who questioned the legitimacy of the process and the accuracy of the points raised. Deng prepared "supplemental materials," which, in the style of the Cultural Revolution, were entirely derogatory. In his eagerness to discredit a leader who was still popular within the rank and file, however, Deng Liqun made some serious errors.[73]

Aftereffects and Collateral Damage

Before the life meeting was even underway, a major intraparty struggle was beginning to take shape. Although it was shrouded in an ideological fogbank of renewed attention to "bourgeois liberalization," the real targets were people on various lists prepared by Hu Yaobang's adversaries. The first and easiest targets, of course, were those singled out by Deng Xiaoping himself. Fang Lizhi was relieved of his position as vice president of the University of Science and Technology of China on January 12, as was university president Guan Weiyan. Fang was expelled from the CCP a week later. Shanghai writer Wang Ruowang was expelled from the Shanghai party committee on January 19, while former reporter Liu Binyan lost his party card on January 25.[74] Hu's close associates—prominent scholars and speechwriters like Shen Baoxiang, Sun Changjiang, Ruan Ming, Li Honglin, and others—were also blacklisted and faced various punishments and official inquiries.

Deng Xiaoping had made it known in early January that he wanted Zhao Ziyang to put together a list of the people most active in spreading "bourgeois liberalization," so they could be examined and punished. Zhao sought to minimize the numbers of people investigated, both to maintain morale among those who supported "reform and opening" and to prevent another persecution campaign that would remind both Chinese and foreign observers of the Cultural Revolution. Deng Liqun's Political Research Office drew up a preliminary list of twelve names, headed by Yu Guangyuan, director of the Marxism-Leninism Institute of the Chinese Academy of Social Sciences, several other leaders of which also were on the list. Working through his *mishu*, Bao Tong, Zhao sent the list to Deng, Chen Yun, and other elders, with a recommendation that Yu Guangyuan's name be removed. When Deng agreed, others had to go along. Some on the list were persuaded to withdraw from the party rather than go through the indignity of being expelled or undergoing a life meeting of their own.[75]

Chen Yun and other elders were rumored to be focused on Zhao, Tian Jiyun, Hu Qili, and Wang Zhaoguo, but Zhao moved deftly to keep the younger reform leaders under Deng's protection. Hu Qili was particularly important, because he was executive secretary of the Central Secretariat. In late January, despite pressure from Bo Yibo and Deng Liqun, the Secretariat agreed to protect economic and science and technology work from ideological reprisals. On January 28 the Center issued Central Document No. 4 (1987), which restricted "bourgeois liberalization" investigations to the realm of propaganda, art, and ideology work within the CCP.[76]

But the personnel issue, as always, weighed more heavily than the policy documents. And the activity of what has been called the "conservative faction" (*baoshoupai*) took the form of both writing articles and attacking specific members of the "reform faction" (*gaige pai*), which was equated with "bourgeois liberalizers." On the same day as Central Document No. 4 was issued, Deng Liqun personally led Hu Yaobang's Propaganda Department director Zhu Houze before a large assembly of departmental cadres and announced his removal and replacement by Wang Renzhi.[77]

Deng Liqun and his Political Research Office had begun preparing materials on both Hu Yaobang's staff and supporters and some of Zhao's staff (such as Chen Yizi and Bao Tong, both of whom were involved in Zhao's "political structural reform small group"). Rumor had it that at a March 10 Politburo Standing Committee meeting (the five-person group established by Deng Xiaoping in early January), Deng Liqun charged Zhao's staffer Chen Yizi with "carrying out bourgeois liberalization," a charge Zhao rejected. With Deng Liqun continuing to add his people to senior Propaganda Department posts, Chen Yun crony Song Ping newly in charge of the Organization Department, and Yao Yilin having (unofficially) taken over Zhao's role as premier, Zhao risked being seen as a "decoration."[78]

Less than two months after dumping Hu Yaobang, Deng Xiaoping seemed in fact to have lost political ground, both in policy and in personnel. Deng was still CMC chairman, but Executive Vice-Chairman Yang Shangkun, now more in charge of day-to-day military affairs, was pushing his own agenda. Chen Yun had strengthened his hold on the Organization and Propaganda Departments, and had several allies on the seven-person group Deng Xiaoping had set up to do "personnel work for the Thirteenth Congress."[79] As political commentator Li Jie put it in 2020: "The power in Chen Yun's hands can be said to have been consolidated and strengthened step by step by extraordinary means similar to palace coups. Every coup ended with Deng Xiaoping's defeat and Chen Yun's gain."[80]

The Struggle to Recover

Hu returned home just before the Spring Festival (Lunar New Year) in 1987 in very low spirits. He had been subjected to six days of merciless, deceitful attacks on his character, integrity, and performance of duty by people he respected and even considered friends. A record of his ordeal was being prepared to send out to every party committee in the country. Adding insult to injury, as a member of the Politburo Standing Committee, Hu was expected to perform some ritual duties, like paying Spring Festival calls on superiors in their homes. Sometime during the customary period of family and friend visitations after January 29, Hu and Li Zhao made a brief courtesy call on Deng Xiaoping and his family. Deng told Hu there might still be work he could do, but then grumbled to him about his attitude during the purge of Hua Guofeng. Hu did not respond and left after about fifteen minutes.[81]

After the first three batches of Deng Liqun's materials on Hu Yaobang were circulated in March, Hu asked one of his secretaries to gather up from his personal office and from General Office archives all his speeches, articles, reports, remarks, and approvals from the last ten years—comprising millions of words. He then asked his oldest son, Hu Deping, to assist him in going through all the records to find out if the errors he was accused of making were verifiable. When they finished in June, they found no support for the accusations already sent to the party.[82]

Hu happily boasted to a former subordinate and future biographer, Zhang Liqun, "[I am] worthy of the Party's and the people's confidence and trust."[83] But probably knowing how difficult it would be to convince any party leaders of this finding, Hu set himself another task, to read the complete works of Karl Marx and Friedrich Engels to find out if his own words and actions were consistent with the canonical works of his faith. He had done this near the end of the Cultural Revolution and had also read them often before that. This time he took copious notes.[84] There is no record of his devoting the same kind of attention to the works of Lenin, Stalin, or Mao. It was exhausting work, and although he kept up a modest schedule of exercise, reading, and meetings with friends, Hu's health was fragile.

Hu was probably aware that his life meeting was an object of dispute within the party's upper ranks. Rather than diminish the bitter struggle for power that had precipitated his fall, his ouster had intensified it. Of the first three batches of materials on Hu's errors Deng Liqun sent out in March, the first had covered Hu's ideological flaws—all issues cribbed directly from Deng Liqun's own speech at the life meeting. The second batch concerned Hu's foreign affairs mistakes, while the third was selected quotations from the Lu Keng interview of May 1985.[85]

But perhaps in rushing to get out a fourth batch of materials in mid-May Deng Liqun's Political Research Office staff confused some dates and documents, rendering anachronous some of the accusations against Hu. The errors were picked up by document handlers in the General Office and reported on June 2 to Hu Qili, who sent Zhao Ziyang the report immediately. Zhao ordered an investigation the same day.[86] Errors also were found in the fifth batch of materials, which included a transcription of Hu's resignation letter to Deng Xiaoping, his *jiantao* from the life meeting, and his *biaotai* from the January 16 Politburo meeting. Word of the errors was leaked to Hong Kong media, and headlines blared that Deng Liqun had "falsified" Hu's statements before circulating them.[87] Deng denied personal fault, but took responsibility, then complained he was not notified that the problem was under investigation until afterward.[88]

Zhao Ziyang had immediately forwarded Hu Qili's July 2 report to Deng Xiaoping, Chen Yun, and Li Xiannian with a recommendation that Deng Liqun should no longer oversee propaganda work. He included a letter from Li Rui, who still held a vice-ministerial post in the Organization Department, recounting issues of Deng Liqun's personal immorality from Yan'an days. Deng Xiaoping immediately suspended Deng Liqun's authority for propaganda, over the objections of Chen and Li. With important negotiations for power and position for the Thirteenth Congress still ongoing, neither man wanted to get on the wrong side of Deng Xiaoping.

On July 7, Deng Xiaoping convened a meeting of the five-man Politburo Standing Committee group and ordered the Secretariat Research Office disbanded and its staff transferred to other units. The staff members who lost positions included the wives of Chen Yun and Song Ping and the children of several other important elders. Hu Qili was appointed to oversee propaganda matters from his position as executive secretary of the Central Secretariat.[89]

Zhao Ziyang followed up in August by suspending the publication of *Red Flag* magazine, long a bastion of leftist ideology, and demoting its editor in chief. These moves temporarily muted the nearly public ideological quarreling between "reformers" and "conservatives," but did not suspend the more important struggle between Deng Xiaoping and Chen Yun. Chen summoned Zhao for a chat after the Secretariat research office dustup, advising him to remember that many thousands of party members had died for the cause, which he said Hu Yaobang had forgotten. Zhao seemed to understand this was vaguely threatening.[90]

At the July 7 meeting, Deng had broken precedent and announced many of the Thirteenth Congress key personnel appointments, including the Politburo Standing Committee, which comprised two Deng choices (Zhao Ziyang and Hu Qili), two Chen choices (Li Peng and Yao Yilin), and Qiao Shi, who evidently was satisfactory to both. Deng also announced the choice for the state chairmanship (Yang Shangkun), Zhao's replacement as premier of the State Council (Li Peng), and the chairman of the NPC Standing Committee (Wan Li). In his account of the meeting, Zhao noted that Deng had preferred a seven-person Standing Committee, but having received negative feedback from Yao Yilin (speaking for Chen Yun) on reform advocates Wan Li and Tian Jiyun, Deng immediately dropped them both from the list.[91] In other words, he had made his compromises with Chen Yun. Zhao Ziyang complained afterward to Yang Jisheng: "People on the front desk [i.e., the general secretary] had no say in the personnel affairs of the top leadership. The ones who really had a say were those two elderly people (Deng and Chen). The third one (Li Xiannian) had influence but not decisive effect. As long as the two old men reached an agreement, it was done."[92]

The Thirteenth Congress (October 25 to November 1, 1987) was billed as a "congress of reform," and indeed several new changes were introduced. Zhao and his political reform research team explored many ideas intensively, and proposed two major changes. The first was "differential elections" of Central Committee members (*cha'e xuanju*), meaning more candidates would be presented for election than the number of seats to be filled. The measure was implemented at the Thirteenth Congress, with 185 candidates standing for 175 Central Committee positions. Although Deng Liqun had expected to be chosen for the Politburo, he failed to win enough of the 1,936 delegates votes even to qualify for the Central Committee, making him ineligible for the Politburo.[93]

The second "reform" was separation of party and state. This was the most controversial and sweeping set of changes proposed at the Thirteenth Congress. Zhao and the Political Reform Office developed a series of structural adjustments to the CCP, including eliminating "party groups" from government offices at all levels, streamlining party committees, and limiting their decision powers. These proposals were stoutly resisted by many elder veterans and middle-level cadres, who foresaw a weakening of their powers and a reduction in available party posts. Disputes about implementation began almost immediately after the congress adjourned. After extensive redrafting and repeated consultation, the final report was passed easily by the Thirteenth Congress.[94] But within two years, most of the "reforms" adopted by the congress had been abandoned.

As usual, the personnel changes mattered most, both in the short and long term. They also were key to why the reforms failed. First and foremost, the three elders who had dominated the Politburo Standing Committee in the previous congress all "retired" from the Politburo Standing Committee, but did not give up their influence, remaining "national rank" (*guojiaji*) leaders. Deng Xiaoping was "elected" by the congress to retain his Central Military Commission chairmanship, so by giving up his chairmanship of the Central

Advisory Commission, he was "half-retiring." Chen Yun stepped down as head of the Central Commission for Discipline Inspection and replaced Deng as head of the CAC. Li Xiannian, who had held the powerless position of state chairman since 1983, resigned that role and took over as chairman of the Chinese People's Political Consultative Conference (CPPCC), another powerless but prestigious position. Li was careful to maintain correct relations with both Deng and Chen, but was reported to be very unhappy and demonstrated his anger by making Zhao Ziyang's life difficult.[95]

Aside from maintaining control of the Central Military Commission, the other aspect of power Deng often boasted about was "final decision-making authority on major issues." That also had been settled at the July 7 meeting, according to Zhao Ziyang, and was revealed at the First Plenum of the Thirteenth Central Committee on November 1, 1987, when Zhao secretly told the new Politburo and its Standing Committee that all important issues would be submitted to Deng Xiaoping for his instructions and decision.[96] Deng reportedly passed on a message to Chen Yun and Li Xiannian that the Politburo Standing Committee "can only have one mother-in-law" (*zhi neng you yige popo*).[97] But this arrangement was not made public. When Zhao disclosed the fact to visiting Soviet general secretary Mikhail Gorbachev in April 1989, he was heavily criticized for violating CCP security regulations. But it made Zhao's situation nearly identical to Hu Yaobang's. He had no real decision-making authority. In a later interview with Yang Jisheng, he referred to himself as "just a big chief administrator," or a servant with two masters.[98]

Zhao radiated confidence, however, when the Thirteenth Congress opened on October 25, after a six-day final plenum of the Twelfth Congress approved Hu Yaobang's resignation and Zhao's selection as general secretary. The congress went smoothly enough—Zhao delivered his report, "Advance along the Road of Socialism with Chinese Characteristics," and set out his version of Deng Xiaoping's policy preferences as "one central task [economic development] and two basic points [the four cardinal principles and reform / opening up policies]." Foreign journalists observing the new leadership noted that they all dressed in Western suits and carried glasses of wine to greet them. Zhao seemed especially comfortable in the spotlight, conveying an air of optimism and openness.[99]

The new leadership groups announced on November 1 were smaller in numbers and younger. The seventeen-member Politburo had nine new members; three new members were added to a much-reduced six-man

Secretariat. With a younger and healthier Politburo Standing Committee, Zhao was able to convene meetings more often—sometimes twice per week—and other major bureaucracies such as the State Council and National People's Congress could submit issues to the Standing Committee directly, without going through the Secretariat.[100] One of the new Politburo members, Jiang Zemin, had earned a reputation in Shanghai for deft handling of student protestors in 1986 and was promoted to party secretary of the Shanghai municipal committee. He was considered close to Chen Yun and Li Xiannian, both of whom often retreated to Hangzhou and Shanghai to recover their health or get away from Beijing. Deng's regional favorite, Li Ruihuan, also was added to the Politburo.

Hu Yaobang was elected to the Thirteenth Congress Politburo, although he did not wish to be. He had asked Zhao Ziyang to be left off the ballot, on grounds of being too old at seventy-two, preventing a younger person from taking the position, and focusing too much attention on persons who "cannot retire" (that is, Deng, Chen, and Li). Besides, he argued, he would have nothing to do except attend meetings and nod his head; he would have no supervisory responsibility. Zhao said he would not have any specific work obligations but could "support the Party's unity."[101] Hu's reelection to the Politburo was approved by 166 of the 173 Central Committee members chosen at the Thirteenth Congress.

After the first organizational Politburo meeting on November 14, Hu attended only a few official meetings for the next year. He showed up for funerals of old friends and party leaders, but mostly he stayed at home. Not long after the Thirteenth Congress adjourned, Deng Xiaoping began to invite Hu Yaobang to join him for an evening of bridge. The two men had been playing bridge since the early 1950s and had attended a tournament together only days before Deng purged Hu in late 1986. Hu had declined the invitations, citing health reasons, but finally relented on December 30, 1987, when he agreed to play at Deng's house. It was a difficult experience for him, according to brief accounts, probably saved only by Deng's long-standing prohibition against discussing politics, work, or family at the bridge table. Hu never went again.[102]

Man Mei described her father's condition in somber terms. After eight months of reviewing his records and Marxist classics, Hu Yaobang spent most of his time at home in silence, seeing few visitors and seldom even playing with his grandchildren. "Silence was not his character," she explained. "However, at this time it became a necessity . . . , a way of existence that left no choice . . . I knew that . . . silence was his loyalty to the party, his consideration of the overall situation, and his contribution to stability and unity." She noted, "He could not explain the facts to people, nor could he confide in his loved ones. He had to use discipline and will to close his heart, and sometimes even had to close himself entirely."[103]

In February 1988 Hu checked into the PLA No. 305 hospital in Beijing for treatment of pneumonia and probably depression. Visitors told of his anxiety, resentment, fear, anger, sadness, self-reproach, and bitterness over the way he had been treated. His visitors were mostly former secretaries, speechwriters, and subordinates; some of them would write—two decades later—about their impressions and concerns. None of his Politburo peers are recorded as having called on him or inquired about his health. Hu was careful and deliberate, telling visitors that his overall attitude was "obey the Party's decision, uphold the Party's unity." He probably was aware his visitors would be contacted by security personnel to report on his moods and plans, so he reassured them that he represented no threat: "I will not make trouble. I have a wife and sons and daughters I could not be separated from, and besides, I never did bad things or created scandals." He also told them he did not feel free to speak out about his own issue, much less about current political matters, was not comfortable moving around among ordinary citizens, and was not ready to write his memoirs.[104]

In mid-May 1988 Hu left Beijing for the first time in more than a year, traveling to Yixian in Hebei, about 130 kilometers to the southwest. While there, he inspected some novel experiments in developing rural industry that integrated animal husbandry and forestry. He traveled to Tianjin in late May and met with principal secretary Li Ruihuan, now a Politburo member. When Hu suggested he could write up a report for the Politburo on what he learned, Li Ruihuan replied bluntly, telling him his political utility was finished and he should talk less: "Small matters are not worth talking about, and on large issues, there won't necessarily be anyone listening." Li told Hu he should turn his attention to "spiritual sustenance" and restoring his health. Hu returned to Beijing in low spirits.[105]

While Hu was out of Beijing, Deng Xiaoping used his prerogative as the party's "core" leader to push forward a controversial plan to "sort out commodity prices" as a way of jump-starting the reform process. Wages and prices had been tightly controlled for many years under the planned economy, leading to a welter of inequities and discontents and no small amount of corruption. Deng and Zhao agreed it was urgent to show resolve and planning. Choosing perhaps a somewhat incongruous image from the Romance of the Three Kingdoms, Deng invoked the spirit of China's equivalent of the god of war, Guan Gong (or Guan Yu), saying the party would have to "cross five passes and slay six generals" to accomplish the task of wage and price reform.[106]

On May 31, Zhao Ziyang convened a two-day Politburo meeting—which Hu Yaobang attended—to discuss how to implement price reform without causing undue economic or political disorder. The meeting approved further study on how to bring this about within five years, starting in 1989. Chen Xiaoya called it "Zhao's Waterloo."[107] But there is no indication that Hu was expected to play a role in the process; he had in any case decided he would "rest and recuperate, spending his twilight years in peace."[108]

While party leaders traveled to Beidaihe in August to hammer out details of the now widely anticipated wage and price adjustments, Hu Yaobang was relaxing at the Shandong seaside resort of Yantai, exchanging poems in classical style with friends, practicing calligraphy, and reading the memoirs of Chinese civil war leaders. While economic conservatives like Li Peng and Yao Yilin took dominant roles in the planning for price reform, leaving Zhao Ziyang somewhat on the sidelines, Hu was visiting and corresponding with friends. He was no doubt aware that public mistrust of price and wage reform plans had led to hoarding and panic-buying, soaring prices for meat and vegetables, and even bank runs during August.[109] In September, while the Politburo held a Central Work Conference to decide how to "manage the economic environment, consolidate the economic order and deepen the reforms," Hu Yaobang was climbing Shandong's Mount Tai for a second time.[110]

Hu Yaobang loved poetry all his life and had written countless poems in both classical and contemporary styles, from political doggerel for educating peasant soldiers to odes for friends to memories of scenic vistas. He had a love of language built up over years of diligent reading that infused his own writing with a recognizable elegance and depth. His much-practiced calligraphy was an outgrowth of his literary flair. Hu's friends treasured his work, not only for its style and originality, but because his poems and writings reflected his lively personality. But in 1988 Hu measured his writings against historically renowned poets and scholars and judged himself inadequate, so he gave it up.

Hu returned to Beijing for the Third Plenum of the Thirteenth Central Committee in late September, and doubtless observed that the political situation had deteriorated. Splits within the leadership were as bad as ever, and the separation of party and government had worsened them. Zhao was less able to affect economic policy as general secretary than he had been as premier. Most of the important bureaucracies working economic issues were now under Li Peng and the State Council.[111] Public confidence in the entire political structure had declined, and college campuses were boiling with pro-democratic sentiment and antigovernment anger. For his part, Deng seemed determined to force through wage and price reforms regardless of opposition or consequences. Hu told unnamed colleagues he did not agree with the slogans being used to promote economic and political reform at the meeting, nor was he very impressed with Zhao Ziyang's work report.[112]

It seems that Deng bought his "core" position rather dearly by agreeing to Chen Yun and Li Xiannian's recommendations of Li Peng and Yao Yilin to be members of the Standing Committee and the principal economic policy decision-makers on the State Council. They greatly hindered Zhao's management of economic policy, especially critical issues of structural reform. Zhao's dislike and distrust of both men is clear from his memoirs, but he trusted his own relationship with Deng and other reformists in the leadership to continue his ambitious reform plans. After the Third Plenum, the opposition to Zhao among several elders—including Li Xiannian, Wang Zhen, Hu Qiaomu, and Deng Liqun—was out in the open. Zhao was being referred to as "Hu Yaobang the Second."[113]

For his part, Hu Yaobang the First saw fit to get out of Beijing again. In early November he told friends that he had been advised to talk less and not expect people to listen, so he was heading south to visit his home province of Hunan. The trip had an impromptu air about it, with Hu's wife and primary security guard unable to travel along. Hu made it clear he wanted no official escort in Hunan, no receptions, no propaganda or news coverage, no banquets, and especially no official briefings or requests for his opinion.[114] His primary goals were tourism and family history research.

With only his fifty-five-year-old niece Hu Suzhen and a substitute security detail, Hu took a special train from Beijing to Changsha, arriving on November 11, 1988. After a day's rest, he took an overnight train to the newly developed tourist resort of Zhangjiajie, whose quartzite and limestone topography now attracts thousands of tourists.[115] Hu had stopped there briefly on one of his earlier inspection tours and was charmed by the rugged scenery. He spent two days walking around its forests, limestone caves, and mountain lakes and streams.

There were plenty of tourists at the National Forest Park, and many recognized the former general secretary immediately. They crowded around him, asking him to pose for photos and chatting happily with this "man of the people" they remembered so well. When security personnel tried to move the crowds aside, Hu checked them, saying "the masses won't kill me." Later he told his niece that there were two things about his career that surprised him: first, that he had risen to such a high position, and second, that after he had stepped down, ordinary people would still treat him so well.[116] No doubt suspicious people in Beijing noticed his popularity with local crowds.

Hu would spend the next two months in and around Changsha, meeting relatives (even reconciling with his long-suffering older brother) and old friends and touring scenic areas and parks. He carefully skirted current politics in talks with visitors, intoning politically neutral opinions when necessary. He spoke more bluntly about his views of Mao, "old man politics," and his own downfall. But while he endeavored to steer clear of Beijing politics, Beijing politicians began coming to him. In late November, a symposium was held in Changsha to discuss Liu Shaoqi's ideology. Several of Hu's old associates, including Yu Guangyuan and Hu Jiwei, called on him. Both had been roughly treated in the political battles of the previous few years, but were still free to travel, and they met briefly with him outside his quarters.[117]

Then Deng Liqun showed up at the symposium and had his secretary request a meeting with Hu. The meeting details are vague, even though both Hu's biographers and Deng Liqun himself wrote about it several years later. Sheng Ping's *Chronology of Hu Yaobang's Thought* records that in "late November" Deng Liqun called on Hu Yaobang at the provincial guesthouse and they talked for more than three hours. Deng proposed that they "join hands to oppose Zhao Ziyang, which received a stern refusal" from Hu.[118] Deng's own account of the meeting is more nuanced and detailed, specifically denying he made, or even considered making, any offer about opposing Zhao Ziyang. Deng observes that Hu "did not mind" the role Deng had played in his ouster and claims Hu did most of the talking.[119]

After Deng left, Hu was in a foul mood, pacing back and forth anxiously, his face drawn with anxiety, refusing even his wife's pleas to eat dinner. When he finally told his *mishu* about Deng's idea of teaming up to "bring down Zhao" and the secretary approved of getting some revenge for Zhao's role in Hu's downfall, Hu reproved him at length. "You've been with me so many years and your thinking is still so narrow-minded! Just because I have suffered a wrong, we cannot bear a grudge against another person. Zhao has

been affirmed by the Central Committee, and we must support him and uphold him, not overthrow him. If we continue repeating that, our Party and
country will have no hope!"[120] Hu's anxiety seemed to increase, and his health
continued to decline. His appetite was poor, his teeth were giving him pain,
and he was losing weight.

In mid-December, he suffered some chest pain that Changsha doctors
thought might be a heart ailment, but Hu dismissed it as a cold. He was hospitalized for about a week.[121] He secured the assistance of a political secretary named Liu Chongwen, who had worked for him previously, to help go
through some of the issues that continued to plague him. But he was caught
between apprehension that if he wrote or spoke too directly, he would come
under criticism again and worry that if he remained silent, his side of the
story would never be told.

Above all, Hu wanted the 1987 "verdict" on him to be reviewed, but the
people responsible for his downfall were still in power and would not admit
their actions were wrong. He had time and incentive to write his memoirs
but didn't want to risk offending others. Liu Chongwen wrote that Hu seemed
depressed and fearful, concerned that his quarters were under surveillance
by people loyal to both Deng Xiaoping and Chen Yun. Hu did not mention
directly his worries about surveillance, but pointed to his ears instead of
speaking the names of Deng Xiaoping or Chen Yun, and related a well-
known story about Ye Jianying's concern about electronic eavesdropping in
his own house.[122]

In early January 1989, Hu moved to Nanning, in Guangxi, ostensibly to
get away from Hunan's colder winter temperatures, but possibly just to get
farther away from Beijing. He stayed at the West Garden State Guesthouse,
a sprawling hotel and luxury residence compound built in the 1920s and
taken over by the PRC after 1949. In late February, when Liu Chongwen
returned from Beijing, he had a long conversation with Hu about his situation and plans. Liu found Hu in somewhat worse health, anxious and undecided. On the one hand, he was still distraught about his own status, believing
he had been incorrectly treated in 1987, yet unable to find anyone to support his complaint or review his case. On the other hand, he received internal situation reports from Xinhua, saw the worsening political crisis in
Beijing, and considered whether he could be helpful.[123]

Fierce political infighting continued within the leadership—Li Peng and
Yao Yilin had organized a life meeting in early January to criticize Zhao
Ziyang for the price reform fiasco, but it accomplished little, since Deng

Xiaoping didn't support it. Some of the other elders, including Li Xiannian and Wang Zhen, were telling Deng that Zhao was not up to the job and should step down. Intellectuals and college students were very active, arguing about cadre corruption, party policies and ideological issues. And the economic situation was still "rather serious."[124] Liu Chongwen told Hu that if he returned to Beijing, he should be prepared for Zhao to ask him for his opinions on these matters. Hu debated aloud with himself, finally deciding he would "learn from Comrade Chen Yun and not speak at all."[125]

Sometime in mid-March, Hu left the quiet and warmth of Nanning and returned to Beijing for a National People's Congress meeting and a Politburo session to discuss education. He had always promoted education and thought the topic needed top-level attention and decisions, but told Liu Chongwen it was uncontroversial and therefore suitable for his reentry into Politburo politics. He didn't wish to remain in Beijing long, however, and talked about other places he could go and get started on putting his papers in order.[126]

Hu attended a session of the Seventh National People's Congress on March 20 in the Great Hall of the People, looking "extremely thin." He exchanged greetings with several leaders, including Zhao Ziyang, but made no substantive contributions to the meeting.[127] A week later, he met with Zhang Liqun to discuss education issues. Aware of growing student dissatisfaction, Hu counseled patience and forbearance: "If youth are on the streets and saying strange things, it's not something to make a big fuss about. We must be good at guiding and educating, we must not suppress or imprison them . . . Chairman Mao said suppressing students will not end well . . . As a progressive party, we absolutely cannot treat youth as our enemies."[128] Hu's biographers have noted several prophetic comments he made in his final weeks of life. These certainly are among the most poignant.

Hu's most consequential visitor in Beijing that April was Li Rui—former senior official, political chronicler, and careful critic of the CCP and its leaders. He had interviewed Hu Yaobang twice in the previous five years and counted himself an admirer and fellow reformer. He would write the foreword for the first collection of essays about Hu, published in Hong Kong, along with articles praising Hu in *Yanhuang Chunqiu* and other intellectual magazines and websites. His last conversation with Hu took place on April 5 and lasted seven hours. The account was not formally published until 2001.

Li observed that Hu was in good spirits, clearheaded, did not seem tired or dispirited, and ate a good dinner. Their discussion ranged across many topics, and Hu held forth as if speaking for the record rather than to an old friend. He focused on ten issues about which he and Deng Xiaoping were not in agreement—from the treatment of Hua Guofeng and the trial of the Gang of Four to spiritual pollution, economic policy, foreign policy, and "bourgeois liberalization," which he thought was most significant in relation to his own fall from grace.[129] Toward the end of the discussion, Hu grew more philosophical: "There is bitterness, but it's not a personal issue, it is that the history is unfair, and [they] should return to the original face of history. I hope there's a new verdict that fits the original facts. If not, I can't force it, if I go to see Marx [the CCP's euphemism for dying], I am at peace. It doesn't matter." He added, "It is impossible for me to come out to work again. I am an old man. And even if you work for another two or three years, what can you do? Old man politics are no good."[130]

The evening of April 7, Hu Yaobang began feeling some pain in his chest and shoulders, and his wife recommended he not attend the Politburo meeting the following morning. But he signed the notification indicating he would attend. As his house was only a few minutes away from the meeting site at Huairen Hall, he probably walked to the meeting, as was his custom, the morning of April 8. He arrived just before the session came to order at 9:00 a.m., sitting in the back row next to Tian Jiyun and Qin Jiwei. The meeting, chaired by Zhao Ziyang, began with a reading of the draft resolution on improving education, during which Hu appeared to be in increasing discomfort. Suddenly, he lurched to his feet to ask permission to leave the meeting but staggered and had to be helped back into his chair. Hu Qili told attendants to summon the medical staff, who arrived in about ten minutes.

Beijing Hospital emergency personnel arrived shortly afterward and set up treatment equipment in the conference room. They kept Hu under observation until about 3:00 p.m., then transported him to the hospital, where he was treated in intensive care. The head of his care team even ordered construction work on the hospital stopped to limit the noise and enable Hu to rest more comfortably. But while he recovered somewhat over the next six days, Hu Yaobang had another heart attack and died suddenly on the morning of April 15, with only a staff doctor and his third son, Hu Dehua, by his side.[131]

10 Hu Yaobang and the Fate of Reform

Hu Yaobang's daughter, Man Mei, wrote that several hundred thousand people visited her father's gravesite every year after his interment in 1990.[1] But as far as the party was concerned, Hu Yaobang was a nonperson. The political climate in the wake of the catastrophe of June Fourth was not conducive to celebrating Hu's virtues, and his name disappeared completely from the media. He was not banned, but was a taboo topic, subject to a "sealed lips" embargo by the official media, based on unspoken political sensitivity about the events of 1989.[2] Moreover, as long as Deng Xiaoping and the other elders who purged Hu were alive, there was no possibility for Hu's name to be restored without an explanation of why and how he was ousted. Jiang Zemin, the former Shanghai mayor and party secretary chosen to replace Zhao Ziyang in 1989, resisted any calls for a review of what happened at Tiananmen.

The Road to Rehabilitation

In July 1991, several elderly intellectuals, with political backing from retired but still influential military officials, established a magazine of historical analysis called *Yanhuang Chunqiu* (炎黄春秋), which published articles that shed light on contemporary issues.[3] Although it had no official financial support, the journal became popular among intellectuals and overseas Chinese readers and began to attract articles by noted scholars. Politically, its prospects were probably improved by its open support for Deng Xiaoping's economic reforms, then in the midst of a revival in Guangdong Province.[4]

Yanhuang Chunqiu had additional advantages. Its funding source was a private foundation called the "China Yanhuang Cultural Research Association," and its circulation—less than fifty thousand—was mostly by subscription. It had a small but highly dedicated staff, headed by veteran Xinhua editor Du Daozheng and historical researcher Yang Jisheng. And most importantly, it had a powerful benefactor, a former senior general in the PLA named Xiao Ke. A full general in 1955, Xiao fell afoul of Mao and Peng Dehuai in the mid-1950s and was suspended from all military duties, only returning to the PLA in the early 1970s. He was a renowned calligrapher, editor of a multivolume general history, and writer of numerous short stories and an award-winning novel. He had served in the Red Army with Hu Yaobang, and reportedly was unhappy with the way Hu had been forced out of office and with the armed crackdown on demonstrators in 1989. Xiao was adamant about putting historical truth above philosophy or politics in *Yanhuang Chunqiu*.[5]

In 1994, before the fifth anniversary of Hu Yaobang's death, Du Daozheng decided to publish a photograph of Hu on the inside cover of the April edition, along with a short commemorative poem. Du did not notify party authorities to obtain content approval, because he wanted to break the silence on Hu Yaobang—which he considered an "unscientific" attitude toward a man who had made great contributions to reform. But knew he had to tread cautiously.[6]

The issue was well-received by readers, but not by the censors, who demanded that all copies of the magazine be destroyed. When informed of official displeasure with the photograph of Hu in the magazine, Xiao told the staff, "Don't panic . . . [S]ay it was Xiao Ke's idea. Give them my telephone number and have them give me a call."[7] Higher-level officials decided not to pursue the matter, effectively breaking the embargo on the public usage of Hu's name.

Du wanted to follow up with more articles about Hu's work in the Central Organization Department—where he had organized a massive campaign in 1978 to release from prison hundreds of thousands of victims of China's political campaigns—but the department director would not allow access to departmental files. So Du persuaded one of Hu's former subordinates, Dai Huang, to write a retrospective on his experience. Dai's book was published in November 1998, and gradually Hu's reputation began to be restored. In an article in 2001, Du Daozheng noted that they had "actively and systematically organized a series of articles on Hu Yaobang's performance," to support a fair judgment of his achievements by the party.[8]

Although Dai Huang's book had to be published in Hong Kong because of political obstacles in Beijing, its success prompted others who had been close to Hu Yaobang to publish memoirs. Wu Jiang, who worked with Hu at the Central Party School in 1977, published *Ten Year Road—Days Together with Hu Yaobang* in 1995. In 1997 Zeng Zhi, who worked with Hu in the Organization Department in 1978, published *Hu Yaobang Outside the Red Walls.* Wang Ruoshui, deputy editor in chief of *Renmin Ribao* in the late 1970s, brought out *Background of the Fall of Hu Yaobang* that same year. In 1998 respected economist and philosopher Yu Guangyuan, who played a major role in developing reform policies under Hu and Deng, wrote *The 1978 Turning Point: Behind the Scenes at the 3rd Plenum of the 11th Central Committee,* published by the Central Compilation and Translation Press in Beijing.

The timetable for Hu Yaobang's rehabilitation was partly dictated by the passing of his tormentors from the political scene. Between 1992 and the turn of the twenty-first century, most of the key participants in the "party life meeting" and Hu's forced resignation in January 1987 succumbed to old age and infirmity. Those most actively involved in the late 1986 plots to bring down Hu—including Hu Qiaomu, Li Xiannian, Wang Zhen, Chen Yun, Deng Xiaoping, Peng Zhen, Yang Shangkun, and Yu Qiuli—had all died by 1999. Jiang Zemin finally stepped down from all his positions in 2004, which likely reduced the degree of opposition to a reconsideration of Hu's standing within the party.

Moreover, in 2005 growing support for Hu's rehabilitation among intellectuals and others belonging to the "reform" element of the CCP was probably a factor. Major studies of Hu were begun in both the PRC and Hong Kong after his death. Five of Hu's former subordinates in the Communist Youth League and the Central Party School had begun to collect speeches and publications pertaining to Hu as early as the summer of 1989, and they subsequently organized a study group, traveling around the country to acquire materials. It took over ten years before their labors bore fruit with the publication in Hong Kong of *Remembering Yaobang,* which included articles and reminiscences of Hu from more than a hundred contributors.[9]

The five principal authors—Zhang Liqun, Zhang Ding, Yan Ruping, Tang Fei and Li Gongtian—continued working with the Central Party History Research Office, which must approve all published work on CCP history. Despite other articles and books about Hu, they had no idea whether party censors would permit them to publish their work, which had grown to nearly one million characters. By late 2004 they were losing hope.[10] Man Mei, who had spent six years researching and writing a biography of her father, was in similar straits—by 2005 no one in an official position would respond to her queries about whether her work could be approved for publication.[11] It was still an issue of great political sensitivity, requiring Politburo consideration.

Hu Jintao, who succeeded Jiang Zemin as general secretary of the CCP in 2002, got off to a rocky start when Jiang arranged to stay on in the most important power position—chairman of the Central Military Commission—for an additional two years. The "skip generation" succession that Deng Xiaoping had agreed to after 1989 was already under challenge. Although Jiang was eventually induced to step back in 2004, Hu was still saddled with a nine-member Politburo Standing Committee on which no fewer than four members were considered associates of Jiang and two others were seen as opponents of political reform.[12]

When Jiang finally let go of the CMC, Hu Jintao only had partial control over one of the four pillars of power noted earlier, the others being under the supervisory ambit of former members of Jiang's Standing Committee.[13] Hu Jintao had been a protégé of Hu Yaobang, appointed by him to senior positions in the Communist Youth League. But it was probably Deng's approval of Hu Jintao's tough-minded approach to dissent in Tibet in 1989 that secured Hu Jintao's rise to the Politburo Standing Committee in 1992. It is likely that Hu Jintao's appreciation of Hu Yaobang's support was a factor in his decision to restore partially the older man's reputation in 2005.

In January 2005 the death of Zhao Ziyang—whose stubborn refusal to apologize or atone for his mistakes during the run-up to June 4 kept him under house arrest for nearly sixteen years—created additional pressures to reconsider Hu Yaobang's case. According to a respected China watcher writing in *The China Brief,* Hu Jintao was balancing hopes of gaining support from party reformers and intellectuals by rehabilitating Hu Yaobang against criticism from former Jiang allies for building a "CYL faction." Security specialists were said to be concerned about the prospects for unrest and confusion if Hu Yaobang's case were reconsidered.[14]

Hu Yaobang's family and friends still wanted the official judgment on him—the Central Document of January 1987—rescinded. They also wanted the protocol "specifications" for a rehabilitation ceremony to reflect Hu's position as general secretary, rather than the lower rank he held at the time of his death. There was dissatisfaction that Hu had not been referred to as a "great Marxist" in his 1989 eulogy, a title either Deng Xiaoping or Chen Yun, or both, evidently had refused to confer on him.[15]

The negotiations between the Politburo and the family continued until just prior to the ninetieth anniversary of Hu Yaobang's birth on November 20, 2005. The result, in the form of a Central Committee meeting to commemorate the occasion, was an important lifting of the taboo on mentioning Hu Yaobang's name or writing about him in party media, but otherwise was a compromise in the party's favor. The event, held in the Great Hall of the People, honored Hu's birthday and lavishly praised his contributions. But the ceremony was a smaller event than the family had requested, and the presiding official was a member of the Politburo Standing Committee, not Hu Jintao. The new eulogy was longer and more detailed than Zhao Ziyang's 1989 eulogy, but there was no change in the honorifics used to describe Hu, nor any improvement in his grade as a "Marxist."[16] Neither was there any mention of the circumstances under which he had resigned, or a reversal of the 1987 verdict.[17]

The four living authors of Hu's biography (principal organizer Zhang Liqun had died in 2003) were authorized to publish volume 1, covering Hu's life from his birth in 1915 to the end of the Cultural Revolution in 1976. However, volumes 2 and 3, though they were completed, were held by party authorities for "revisions." The authors were warned not to try to have any of the work published in Hong Kong. Party officials told them that "your speech has freedom, your publication has discipline."[18] Discussion of official publication of *The Selected Works of Hu Yaobang* by the party's Literature Research Institute was suspended.

A Wave of Nostalgia and Hope

Arguably as important as the ninetieth birthday ceremony was the publication of the November 2005 issue of *Yanhuang Chunqiu,* containing two lead articles about Hu Yaobang. Although the magazine had published several articles about him since 1994, this issue went well beyond the regime's carefully negotiated perspective on Hu, extolling him in terms like those used by students and activists after Hu's death in 1989. Its authors were senior party and government officials who had worked with Hu Yaobang and wanted both to pay homage to his character and to rebut some of the charges made after his ouster.

Hao Huaiming's article on Hu's leadership of the all-important Central document drafting process traced how Hu carefully guided the writing of the 1986 Central Committee resolution on "Spiritual Civilization."[19] The article described Hu pulling together divergent views on "bourgeois liberalization," crafting an important party document that was approved at the Sixth Plenum. Even more remarkable was the article titled "The Hu Yaobang in Our Hearts," a collection of short essays by former vice-premier Tian Jiyun and thirteen other prominent reformist officials associated with Hu Yaobang, some of whom fell after his ouster.[20] Tian lauded Hu as the "conscience of Chinese Communists" (*zhongguo gongchandangren de liangxin*)—unselfish, courageous, honest, and intelligent, a proponent of both economic and political reform, modest, a public servant and "dedicated Communist Party member."[21] The collection was filled with warm respect for a man they believed had not received the appraisal he deserved. And equally importantly, they supported the comprehensive (political, legal, and economic) reform Hu Yaobang had espoused.

Shortly after the November issue came out and before the official ceremony, the editors of *Yanhuang Chunqiu* received a telephone call from the Central Propaganda Department ordering them to cease circulation of the issue, which had "violated the rules." When informed that most of the fifty thousand copies printed had already been mailed to subscribers or purchased, the authorities ordered the remaining copies sequestered. The editors ignored the order, which was moot when plans for the official celebration of Hu's life became known a few days afterward.[22] In the December issue of *Yanhuang Chunqiu,* former Communist Youth League leader, Central Secretariat member, and Hu Yaobang protégé Hu Qili presented another encomium to his mentor's unique and inspiring style of leadership.[23]

In the ensuing months, nearly every issue of *Yanhuang Chunqiu* had at least one article about Hu Yaobang's life. There were not many articles about him in other publications, however. Burgeoning internet news and commentary sites, moreover, were under a voluntary "pledge of self-discipline," which obligated internet sites "to refrain from spreading information that might jeopardize state security and to remove harmful information promptly." Numerous websites were closed down by authorities during this period, and few seemed willing to test whether the taboo was really broken.

But in May 2006 Hu Deping informed Hong Kong's *Ta Kung Pao* newspaper that a commemorative website for his father had been approved by the authorities and was up and running. Privately financed and managed, the Hu Yaobang Historical Materials Information Web (胡耀邦史料信息网) started out small, with little PRC media attention and a very cautious approach to historical materials. It included some photographs of Hu, and letters from former subordinates, friends, and appreciative general readers, but organizers said they were still collecting materials.[24] Over time the site added a chronology of Hu's early life, some of his poems and calligraphy, photographs, biographies of other leaders, a rich historical materials section, and many other attractions for casual readers and historical researchers.[25]

More books and articles about his life were published, some in Hong Kong, such as Chen Liming's massive *Biography of Hu Yaobang,* some in Beijing, including books by three of Hu's four children, his staffers, subordinates from the CYL and the Central Party School, the Propaganda Department, and some prominent party historians. As the laudatory articles about Hu Yaobang accumulated, there was a gradual shift in focus, from fond recollections of his personality toward his role as one of the earliest proponents of reform, even comprehensive reform. Hu Yaobang was becoming an icon for political reform, and to the degree that successive leaders paid at least lip service to reform, he remained an important national symbol.

The Seventeenth Party Congress in 2007 seemingly sharpened the factional contest between Hu Jintao and his "Youth League faction" (*tuanpai*) and the Jiang Zemin / Zeng Qinghong "Shanghai gang" (*Shanghai bang*). Increasingly obvious corruption at all party levels led to a resurgence of both "leftist" sentiment and an effort to rekindle genuine political reform. As old disputes about the direction and speed of economic reform and the need for political reform continued to constrain any bold decisions, some of the retrospectives on Hu Yaobang took on a wistful tone, recalling his tolerance, integrity, and concern for ordinary people, qualities that seemed to be lacking in his successors.

In 2009 Hu Deping published a book on his father's life, a combination of cherished memories and lessons learned. He placed his father at the forefront of economic reform in the early 1980s, including the abolition of communes, the adoption of contract agricultural production, and acceptance of special economic zones where Western economic management methods would be permitted. He also discussed his father's views on ideological reform, the broadening of democratic rights, and the need for the rule of law.[26]

The March 2009 issue of *Yanhuang Chunqiu* made another step forward on perceptions of Hu Yaobang. Feng Lanrui's article praised Hu's management of the 1986 CCP resolution on "spiritual civilization," crediting him with extolling "democracy, freedom, equality, and fraternity," which he said were the "advanced cultural heritage of mankind and modern politics." Feng praised Hu's emphasis on economic reform, political reform, and the cultivation of socialist values, but faulted the Communist Party, which "only grasped tightly the reform of the economy and ignored the reform of other aspects." And he disparaged the party for "forcing Hu's resignation" after the "spiritual civilization" resolution was passed.[27]

The following month, nonagenarian Li Rui took the gloves off in a retrospective on Hu Yaobang published in *Yanhuang Chunqiu*. Starting with his opinion that Hu Yaobang would eventually be seen as the CCP's most popular leader, Li praised Hu's respect for knowledge and intellectuals and his appreciation of those who promoted human rights, democracy, and freedom. Li named those who had thwarted Hu's efforts at reform—especially Hu Qiaomu and Deng Liqun—and those who supported them, including Zhao Ziyang. Without mentioning June 4, he credited those who came out to honor Hu after his death not only for "mourning an elderly bosom friend," but also in support of "comprehensive reform." Li concluded, "It is hoped that the reform of the political structure will be realized . . . and that the democratization, rule of law and modernization of the country will come at an early date."[28]

The magazine's authorization to publish some of the articles had to have come from the Center. Some have surmised that Hu Jintao was using Hu Yaobang's virtues as justification for promoting his own former subordinates in the Communist Youth League to important positions in the party Center and the provinces. The Youth League, as the second largest and second most important party organization, was a natural place to turn for younger leaders to bring forward. That, after all, had been its purpose from its inception early in the revolution. Between 2007 and 2012, Hu Jintao was able to bring at least nine former CYL leaders into the Politburo, with several poised to enter the Politburo Standing Committee at the Nineteenth Congress in 2017.[29]

Red Sons Rising

The power game in Beijing is personal and persistent, and as Hu Jintao's tenure drew to a close, his reputation and perceived authority were declining. His power had been weakened by an informal mechanism known as "skip generation succession," which Deng had instituted after June 4 as a way to avoid the chronic succession crises that had beset the CCP, now faced its most serious challenge. Deng did not choose Jiang Zemin as his successor, but designated Jiang's successor, Hu Jintao.[30] Jiang was not able to name his own successor but was apparently able (with help from his close associate Zeng Qinghong) to pick Xi Jinping as Hu's successor, and packed enough of his own supporters around Hu Jintao to prevent him from upsetting the plan. There were rumors that Hu Jintao wanted to extend his own tenure as head of the Central Military Commission in 2012, as Jiang had done ten years before, but they proved to be unfounded.[31]

In early 2012 Bo Xilai, Politburo member and principal party secretary in Chongqing, who was expected to become a member of the Politburo Standing Committee at the Eighteenth Congress, was arrested in Beijing. In the ensuing weeks, Bo was removed from all his positions, expelled from the party, put on trial for corruption and abuse of power, and jailed for life. Bo's wife and an accomplice were tried and convicted that summer for the 2011 murder in Chongqing of a British businessman with whom she had conducted illicit business deals.[32]

Bo Xilai was a son of Bo Yibo, one of the party's most prominent economic officials in the 1950s and tormentor of Hu Yaobang in 1987. His son had gained prominence for leading a resurgence of Maoist-style mobilization campaigns in Chongqing, complete with the singing of Cultural Revolution songs, and for a fierce crackdown on criminal gangs there. He was one of the most celebrated exemplars of a growing force in CCP politics in the early twenty-first century, the "Red Second Generation" (*hong er dai*), also known as the "princelings party" (*taizi dang*). These children of China's first-generation revolutionaries—especially those who had led the People's Liberation Army—were born in difficult circumstances during the anti-Japanese and civil wars. But after 1949 they became a favored elite—living in special compounds, going to exclusive schools, forming circles of friends who viewed themselves as chosen ones. They were not hesitant to flaunt their privileges. The Cultural Revolution disrupted their educational plans, but they threw themselves into the revolution, becoming the first Red Guards, the first sent down to the countryside en masse, and the first to return to the cities. Many were able to take advantage of their special status to enter reopening universities in the late 1970s.

As they began to enter the workforce, they found their pedigrees often opened doors for them, whether in party politics, where they were expected to maintain the reputations of their famous parents, or in China's rapidly growing business arena, where they were handsomely paid based on their anticipated influence. By the beginning of the second decade of the twenty-first century, the Red Second Generation was reaching the apogee of its influence in China's increasingly corrupt economy, in its heavily bureaucratized political system, and in the People's Liberation Army, where old-boy networks dominated at nearly every level.

Xi Jinping, who took over as general secretary of the CCP in late November 2012, was a princeling by pedigree. His father, Xi Zhongxun, was recruited early by Communist revolutionaries in his home province of Shaanxi and was already active in Yan'an when Mao Zedong and his Long Marchers arrived in 1935. Xi stayed in northwest China throughout the civil war. He moved to Beijing in 1952, became a vice-premier, but fell victim to the toxic politics of Mao Zedong, spending many years in political limbo or in prison until after Mao's death. Xi returned to play a lead role in Guangdong, and became a Politburo member in 1982, then retired from public life in 1988, at the age of seventy-five. He died in 2002, just as his son was coming to national attention as CCP secretary in Zhejiang and a Central Committee member. In the comparative ranking of "princelings" based upon their fathers' positions (a popular pastime of PRC observers), Xi Jinping was considered rather low on the list, and some believe it was his relationship to Jiang Zemin that earned him rapid promotion to the Politburo Standing Committee in 2007. Others considered it likely that Xi would turn to putative "princeling" allies in order to put together his own team within the CCP's power structure.[33]

There was a conjunction of family ties and "princeling" relationships in 2012 involving Hu Yaobang. It was Hu Yaobang in his role as head of the Organization Department in 1977–1978 that "reversed the verdict" on Xi Jinping's father and Bo Xilai's father, both imprisoned during the Cultural Revolution. In 1987 it was Bo Yibo who presided over the party life meeting that humiliated Hu Yaobang at Deng's order. Only Xi Zhongxun stood up to defend Hu Yaobang and deplore the process as a "palace coup," at great cost to his own career.

In July 2012, as Xi Jinping was awaiting his promotion to be general secretary, he summoned Hu Deping to his home for a two-hour conversation. Xi was eleven years younger than Hu Deping, so even though they had known each other in Beijing in the early 1960s, they had little interaction as youths. Hu Deping had been only a modestly successful bureaucrat in the PRC system. Diffident and scholarly, he had served as a deputy director of the CCP's United Front Work Department and was a member of the Tenth National People's Congress and its legal affairs committee. He also was a Standing Committee member of the Chinese People's Political Consultative

Congress and vice-chairman of its economic committee. He was an ardent defender of constitutional reform, democratization of the party, and promotion of private enterprise, but was not a power player at the Central level.

It probably was Hu Deping's status as one of the more outspoken of the Red Second Generation reformers in the CCP that made him of interest to Xi Jinping. Xi was coming into the position of general secretary with few of his own people around him and with the party in internal disarray and suffering from declining public support.[34] He perhaps needed some evidence of approval from the reform wing of the party, and the family connection with Hu Yaobang's son presumably was sufficient for his needs. There was no mention of the meeting in the PRC press at the time, and only when both sides began leaking vague details to the overseas press two months later did China-watchers begin to speculate on its significance.

Some observers saw the meeting as a harbinger of a return to some of the reform ideas and policies that had been considered earlier—such as expanding competition in the state-owned enterprise sector, and even political structure reform. For his part, Xi may have wanted Hu's support on dealing with the Bo Xilai and other party corruption cases. The two reportedly agreed to let CCP discipline and the legal system deal with Bo.[35] There was also a hint that a reversal of the party's official verdict on Hu Yaobang might be in the offing.[36]

After the Eighteenth Congress in November 2012, however, Xi and Liu Yunshan, the former Propaganda Department chief elevated to the Politburo Standing Committee, wasted little time in demonstrating their intolerance for any kind of political reform that involved expanding press freedoms. *Yanhuang Chunqiu* again became a battleground when its January 2013 issue led off with an editorial board article entitled "The Constitution Is the Consensus of Political Structural Reform." The article was probably a response to a very tough speech Xi had delivered in early December on the thirtieth anniversary of the PRC constitution, in which he took a hard line on the party's dominant position in all legal matters, reminding citizens that it was their responsibility to understand their obligations and their rights.[37]

The *Yanhuang Chunqiu* article, in blunt and sarcastic language, pointed out that political reform had been lagging behind economic reform for thirty years, with unsatisfactory consequences. It suggested that rather than trying to craft a new structure for political reform, the regime should begin by properly employing the existing state constitution. It proposed specific articles that could be better implemented, such as clauses guaranteeing property rights, human rights, freedom of speech and the press, and an independent judiciary. "The reform of the political system," it claimed, "is to establish a system of checks and balances on power, that is, to effectively guarantee the rights of citizens. The Constitution contains a wealth of guarantees of human rights and restrictions on the power of the state. If we compare the Constitution with reality [however], we will find that . . . our Constitution is largely empty."[38]

The regime's response was quick: on December 31 the *Yanhuang Chunqiu* office and website were closed down by order of the Ministry of Industry and Information Technology, even before the article appeared in the magazine.[39] Normal operation was restored some time later, but the noose was beginning to tighten.

Backlash and Retrogression

Xi Jinping's counterstroke probably reflected a deeper dissatisfaction with the party's overall condition, as well as his conviction that China should not proceed any further along a path toward Western values and practices. It should instead return to the strict discipline and ideological orthodoxy of the Maoist past. His most obvious and highly publicized measure was a fierce campaign against rampant corruption in the party, under the aegis of the Central Commission for Discipline Inspection. In its early phases, the campaign brought down some "tigers"—former Politburo members and senior PLA officials—and was considered a success. However, it soon became a tool for power manipulation. By early summer the internet was buzzing with rumors that all of Hu Yaobang's children were under suspicion for financial improprieties. Under their father's serious admonitions, all four had been careful about even the appearance of illicit activity, so the charges were quickly rebutted, but they no doubt served as a warning that Xi did not welcome opposition.[40]

Xi then used his powers as general secretary to energize both the propaganda apparatus and the party's bureaucratic control mechanisms to establish his personal authority and undermine erstwhile party "reformers" like Hu Deping. In mid-April 2013 the General Office began circulating to party organizations at local levels a document titled "Notice on the Current Situation in the Ideological Domain." The General Office imprimatur suggests that the imperative to get party committees to "tightly grasp" ideological work was more important than the content of the message. It demanded the party apparatus become involved in controlling discussion of dangerous Western values and practices in university classrooms, public and private publications, the internet, and social media. "We must uphold strict and clear discipline, maintaining a high-level unity with the party Central Committee under the leadership of General Secretary Xi Jinping. . . . We must not permit the dissemination of opinions that oppose the party's theory or political line, the publication of views contrary to decisions that represent the central leadership's views, or the spread of political rumors that defame the image of the party or the nation."[41]

The party's General Office was able to keep what became known as Document No. 9 out of electronic circulation and out of the hands of foreign journalists for several months. Eventually parts leaked to the foreign press in August. It gained instant notoriety as the "Seven Do Not Mentions" (*qi bujiang*) for specifying seven topics on which public discussion was considered inimical to the party's and the country's interests, and that therefore were proscribed: constitutional democracy, universal values, civil society, neoliberalism, the Western idea of journalism, historical nihilism, and questioning reform and opening and socialism with Chinese characteristics.[42]

Hu Deping chose to make a stand in the face of Xi's growing power and pressure, writing articles in defense of constitutional democracy.[43] His article in the *Economic Observer* (an "independent" news magazine published in Beijing) on August 8, 2013, was ostensibly a review of Alexis de Tocqueville's classic *L'Ancien Régime et la Révolution*. Its point was unmistakable: the Chinese Communist Party needed to put into practice a constitutional form of governance or it could suffer the fate of the Old Regime in France, overthrown by revolution. "The power of the Communist Party is entrusted to it by the people. The Communist Party's grasp of political power is not once and for all. Holding power today does not equal holding it forever."[44]

On August 19–21, the Central Propaganda Department held a National Conference on Propaganda and Ideology Work in Beijing. Xi Jinping delivered a powerful rebuttal that doubled down on Document No. 9. Scornfully xenophobic and pugnacious, Xi's address exhorted propaganda workers from all over the country to understand that "Western countries regard China's development and growth as a challenge to their values and institutional models and intensify the ideological and cultural penetration of China. . . . Hostile forces are doing their utmost to propagate so-called 'universal values.' . . . The purpose is to compete with us for positions, compete for people, compete for the masses, and eventually overthrow the leadership of the Communist Party of China and the Chinese socialist system." Xi insisted that all party workers must "resolutely maintain a high degree of consistency with the party Center, and resolutely maintain the Center's authority." The internet, he asserted, "has become the main battlefield of the public opinion struggle. . . . Western anti-China forces have been trying vainly to use the internet to 'pull down China.' . . . On this battlefield of the internet, whether we can stand up and gain victory directly relates to our country's ideological security and regime security."[45]

The slow death of *Yanhuang Chunqiu* probably was inevitable after Xi energized the party apparatus to get control of propaganda issues. The journal had always been a target of disaffection—from conservative party elders and propaganda apparatchiks to "Mao-leftist" websites. After General Xiao Ke died in 2008, its influential defenders were mostly gone, and its survival depended upon its popularity and the wily maneuvering of Du Daozheng. The magazine editors negotiated with propaganda authorities, agreeing not to publish articles on sensitive topics like the Tiananmen incident, current leaders' families, separation of powers, and so forth. But it still "violated regulations" in every issue, and authorities looked for excuses to crack down, removing editorial personnel and threatening closure.

In 2014 the State Administration of Radio, Film and Television (SARFT) informed Du Daozheng that the magazine needed a better supervisory organization than the "China Yanhuang Cultural Research Association" to ensure its accountability to content regulations. It assigned that task to China Academy of Art, which was subordinate to the Ministry of Culture. Looking for a politically influential patron to avoid this fate, Du Daozheng asked Hu Deping in October to take over as the magazine's nominal publisher. Hu evidently was not comfortable with the idea, and hesitated.[46] Yang Jisheng took over as editor in chief while the magazine hired a noted human rights defense lawyer to appeal its case to the authorities. SARFT rejected the appeal, and Yang asked Ding Dong to take charge as executive editor. Two representatives of the Chinese Academy of Art began attending editorial board meetings in February 2015.[47]

The magazine had not paid enough heed to the pressure from authorities, which had been increasing since 2010. Of the articles submitted to the authorities for advance approval, the percentage denied or ignored rose from 62 percent in 2010 to 90 percent in 2014. In April 2015 SARFT issued a written warning that 36 of the 87 articles published in the first four issues of the year "violated regulations" on content and demanded that all articles for the next issue be submitted for prior review. The editorial board balked.[48]

In early 2015 Hu Dehua was named a deputy editor. Yang Jisheng was forced to retire or forfeit his Xinhua pension. The plan for the May 2016 issue, to highlight the fiftieth anniversary of the Cultural Revolution with five articles, was rejected outright by the China Academy of Art, backed up by closure of the printing plant. After Du Daozheng and Hu Dehua agreed to remove four of the articles and heavily edit the other one, the magazine was finally printed two weeks late.[49]

The end came abruptly on July 13, 2016, when unidentified security personnel descended on the *Yanhuang Chunqiu* office carrying mattresses and blankets, expelled staffers, then changed the locks and computer passwords to make it impossible for the original staff to do any work. The Chinese Academy of Art announced that Du Daozheng, recovering in hospital, was removed from his post as editor. The rest of the editorial staff resigned.[50] On July 17, Du Daozheng issued a "Notice of Suspension of Publication," accusing the Academy of Art of violating its agreement with Yanhuang Chunqiu Publishing, and of violating the PRC Constitution's guarantee of freedom of publication. He declared that the Academy of Art was no longer recognized as the supervisory unit of the magazine, and that any further publication using the name *Yanhuang Chunqiu* was not legally authorized.[51] In August, all forty-eight members and advisors of the editorial board signed a public document supporting Du's statement and threatening legal action. But nothing came of it.

Legal challenges were dismissed by local courts, and the new editors of *Yanhuang Chunqiu* continued to publish with the same format, even using the same website. But now rather than having articles that challenged the party's orthodox view of its own history, it published tepid pieces supportive of regime goals. Observers noted that writers invited to contribute to the "new" magazine were "Mao-leftists," repugnant to the remaining "reform faction" of the CCP.[52]

Some observers inside and outside the PRC saw the closure of *Yanhuang Chunqiu* as a death knell for reform in general. Not long afterward, several other websites and publications that supported reformist ideas were closed down by the authorities. The Hu Yaobang Historical Materials Information Web, however, remained open, along with its archive of controversial articles deleted from other sites. Its new items, however, have generally focused on less sensitive topics. And some special articles previously posted about controversial figures or issues gradually began to be taken off the site.

The Party Reclaims Its Own

Prior to the *Yanhuang Chunqiu* imbroglio, Hu Yaobang's family suffered another setback on the occasion of the party's commemoration of his hundredth birthday in 2015. It is customary for the Central Committee to hold a commemorative forum for deceased party officials above a certain rank on or about their hundredth birthdays. These are formal, impersonal events, strictly controlled in terms of venue, size, attendees, and speeches, depending on the rank and political favor of the departed.[53]

Hu Yaobang's hundredth birthday fell on November 20, 2015, and while there were no expectations that there would be deviations from protocol, there were some "loose ends" left over from earlier commemorations: Would there be a reassessment of the official "verdict"? Would Hu be accorded the title "great Marxist"? Would the remaining two volumes of Hu's biography be published? Would his *Selected Works* be brought out?

In April, Hu Deping and Hu Dehua had given conflicting assessments of what they expected. Hu Deping, speaking to *China Youth Daily* reporters, said he thought the Center was making "earnest preparations" to commemorate the event, and expected that, as per the official guidelines, the "main leading comrade" would make a speech.[54] Hu Dehua took a different tone. "The entire family is very appreciative of the decision to commemorate my father's hundredth birthday," he told the Voice of America. "[But] again, there is a Central Document that says he made organizational and ideological and some serious political errors, but what specific errors have not been made clear; from start to finish, they have not stated them clearly. We hope there is a resolution, but this resolution has always left a bitter taste." Hu also complained that Deng Xiaoping had received credit for some of the reforms Hu Yaobang had initiated.[55]

As the date neared, both overseas and internal media focused on Hu Yaobang and his reputation. Central Party School historian and *Yanhuang Chunqiu* editorial board member Wang Haiguang observed that China and the CCP were in a new era with numerous contradictions, such as abuse of power and "unimaginable corruption" at high levels. Society has "already lost the consensus on reform," Wang lamented, but hoped that, through unsentimental and serious research on Hu Yaobang, people could "revive the original intentions of reform, and reconstruct the consensus on reform."[56]

Two days before the ceremony, the *Global Times* (*Huanqiu Shibao*), a tabloid newspaper published by *Renmin Ribao,* reflected an "informed, but not official" judgment of Hu Yaobang in an editorial. It acknowledged that the criticisms of Hu Yaobang's mistakes in 1987 had been "watered down by history since that time." But it recognized that the issue was still a matter of dispute "in a few circles." Dismissing the arguments over Hu as "gimmicks" to push one or another side of an argument, the editorial expected the formal CCP commemoration would enable Hu's "brilliant achievements and glorious personality" to "become an incentive for the entire Party and society." Hu's "lifetime of loyalty will serve to actively bring about the consolidation of consensus throughout the whole society."[57] It is ironic, but hardly surprising, that this tiny olive branch has been removed from the *Global Times* website.

The actual commemorative event was attended by about 200 to 250 people, with all seven Politburo Standing Committee members present. All four of Hu's children were shown in the official film of the occasion, seated in the middle of the audience with some of his secretaries and staff. Hu's wife, Li Zhao, was not present due to old age and illness.[58] Xi Jinping gave a speech longer than Zeng Qinghong's 2005 address, summarizing Hu Yaobang's career in almost exactly the same terms as in the two previous commemorations. Hu still was not called a "great Marxist." Xi directed all party members to learn from

> Hu's noble character of "dedication to beliefs and devotion to ideals," his loyalty to the people . . . his "probing spirit of seeking truth from facts and courageously blazing new trails," . . . and his "lofty air of impartial honesty and incorruptible self-discipline." He concluded that the betterment of the Party required the commitment of all members to "unite as one, forge ahead, and strive to create new achievements worthy of the times, worthy of the people, worthy of our predecessors. This is our best commemoration of the older generation of revolutionaries."[59]

Other events on Hu's hundredth birthday included a symposium at the Central Party School and another in his hometown, both attended by family members. *The Selected Works of Hu Yaobang,* a curated collection of some of his speeches and writings, was published, and a five-part television documentary was aired on national television. Volumes 2 and 3 of the *Biography of Hu Yaobang* were finally published. Three more of its five authors had died, and it appears that major gaps in the story, especially in volume 3, can only be explained by significant text deletions demanded by censors. As far as the party was concerned, the manufactured Hu Yaobang of 2015 was now more important than the Hu Yaobang of 1987.

Who Was the Real Hu Yaobang?

Thus was Hu Yaobang gathered back into the party's embrace. Twenty-six years after his death, he became an emulation model for the party that had purged and humiliated him. "Arranged" and redacted, his colorful prose was packaged for party loyalists to study diligently. Some but not all of his life was presented on screen to help people remember those parts the party approved. His legacy was trimmed and reshaped by the propaganda apparatus.

But what about the Hu Yaobang his followers and admirers remembered? His "democratic spirit," the "outstanding humanist," the "conscience of Chinese Communist Party members," the "great liberator," a "pioneer of reform," who inspired so many during his life and after his death? What were his particular talents, and how did he rise to the top of a political party so focused on personal political power, yet so absolutist in its demands of its adherents and subjects? What was his relationship to Mao Zedong, Deng Xiaoping, and other "great" PRC leaders? What were Hu's views on the party's excesses and errors? When did the "conscience of the party" discover his conscience? What was his reform agenda? What were his goals, his policies? And why did he fail?

In 1989 the ordinary people who admired and respected him turned his funeral into an occasion for pent-up fury at a corrupt, tyrannical Communist regime, which then lashed out at his supporters in ways Hu himself could never have imagined or condoned. That party, broken and cynical, bereft of anything more than empty ideology and overwhelming police power to maintain its legitimacy, has restored pieces of Hu Yaobang's history and carefully selected parts of his reputation, though it never seemed to understand what made him so popular and revered, even now more than thirty years after his death.

It is tempting but pointless to speculate whether Hu Yaobang would have been able to handle more successfully than Deng and Zhao the strains that were rending the post-Mao CCP and weakening its public support. Unlike Deng, who enjoined his supporters in both 1986 and again in 1989 not to eschew bloodshed in dealing with crowds of protestors, Hu took a more patient and tolerant attitude. In fact, he appears to have submitted his resignation to Deng partly in hopes of forestalling a violent confrontation between police and students. And he took steps to secure a "soft landing" for those demonstrators looking for trouble in early January 1987.

But it is appropriate to ask whether Hu Yaobang's ideas about systemic reform in its larger sense might have made a difference. One could make the case that Hu's ideas about "comprehensive reform" were better than those belatedly adopted by Deng Xiaoping and Zhao Ziyang and subsequently abandoned. But Hu never really got the chance to develop them in detail. Less than two months after he delivered his 1983 "comprehensive reform" speech, it was embargoed. Hu was censured at a high-level meeting by none other than Chen Yun, and plans were hatched to have him denounced at a Central Committee work conference and removed from office. Deng Xiaoping and Ye Jianying evidently thwarted those plans, but the pressure of the campaign to "eliminate spiritual pollution" never really let up for long. Eventually enemies of the man and his ideas brought him down.

Why Hu Yaobang Succeeded

Hu Yaobang did not strike people as a born leader. Short and slight, he was no doubt teased, bullied, and disregarded by many of his peers. Deng Xiaoping was also short, but stocky and robust, and he cultivated an air of stern resolve. Hu by contrast was often animated, full of nervous energy. He was also tough and wiry. As a child he had walked twenty kilometers to and from school every day. He survived the Long March, multiple illnesses, beatings during the Cultural Revolution, and a harsh labor camp.

"Comrade Yaobang," as he preferred to be called, was honest and incorruptible. He didn't put on "official airs" of expecting special privileges or treatment. He didn't abuse power or position to enrich himself or his family. He was proud of that uprightness, as it distinguished him from many of his party colleagues. Even his fiercest critics agreed he embodied very high standards of rectitude in his personal life and professional deportment.

Hu's most prominent characteristic, his gift, was a prodigious intellect and a determination to develop it to the fullest. He left school at age fourteen, but he never abandoned his appreciation for education and educated people.

Hu Yaobang read avidly anytime he had a few idle minutes and a book at hand. He became an intellectual and enjoyed the company of intellectuals.

Hu's bureaucratic skills were formidable, and he continued to hone them with every new position. He was organized, task-oriented, and hardworking, putting in long hours at every job, often sleeping in his office. He got to know his chain of command, both up and down. He reorganized staffs, made sure his people knew what he was doing and why, and what roles he expected them to play. In each new bureaucracy, he quickly scheduled large-audience speeches, addressing his subordinates in a down-to-earth way that clarified his mission and inspired those who heard him.

Hu worked well when his bureaucratic "reins" were loose and he had a degree of independence. As Deng put it, Hu did not "follow blindly." He did his most celebrated work from 1977 to 1979, when Hua Guofeng and Ye Jianying held sway over decision-making. Once the Deng Xiaoping–Chen Yun contest for power began in late 1978, Hu was whipsawed between their changing views and under increasing attack from Chen's supporters.

Although relatively unschooled, Hu developed strong writing skills, particularly during his tenure in the Youth League, where he actively developed its daily and weekly publications. He often drafted his own speeches instead of using party hack writers. For important documents, like Central Committee resolutions, he worked well with assigned drafting teams, proofreading drafts and editing final versions. While he was running the Central Party School's ideology publication, *Theoretical Dynamics,* Hu assigned topics, edited articles, and prepared them for publication in the national media.

CCP politics are dominated by interpersonal relationships (*guanxi*). Hu's most important relationships by far were with Mao Zedong, Ye Jianying, and Deng Xiaoping. Mao spotted Hu as a talented fellow-Hunanese at the end of the Long March and as an eager student at Kang Da in Yan'an. He placed Hu in sensitive personnel positions in the Red Army, but later seemed to sour on him when Hu rebuffed Mao's and Kang Sheng's efforts to root out "spies" in the Military Intelligence Department. Mao was behind Hu's assignment to North Sichuan in 1949 and to the Communist Youth League in 1952. He authorized Hu's 1962 assignment to Xiangtan, Hunan, then both his transfer to and withdrawal from Shaanxi in 1964–1965. Mao was willing to let Hu undergo brutal beatings at the hands of Red Guards early in the Cultural Revolution, then let him attend Central Committee meetings to support the expulsion of Liu Shaoqi from the party. But Hu did not return to the Chairman's good graces, and was sent to a labor reform camp for the next three years. Mao endorsed Hu's short-term appointment in 1975 to help clean up the China Academy of Science, but also his ouster from that position after only 120 days. When Mao finally died in September 1976, Hu Yaobang was unforgiven and unforgiving. He never actively supported de-Maoification, but he didn't suppress it, either.

Ye Jianying was Hu's supervisor in the Military Commission in Yan'an and appears to have established a strong bond with his fellow Hakka-speaker. During the civil war, Hu served mostly in North China. There Ye saved him several times from life-threatening illnesses and persecution. Ye recommended Hu to Hua Guofeng and Deng Xiaoping in 1975, and again in 1976 after the fall of the Gang of Four. Ye was the power behind the throne for Hua, but Deng humiliated the old marshal in his eagerness to bring Hua down in 1980. Although Ye fully supported Hu's promotion to chairman / general secretary and remained the second-ranking member of the Politburo Standing Committee, he was mostly in hospital or in Guangzhou recuperating during Hu's term. Ye's death in 1986 may have enabled Chen, Deng, and Li Xiannian to set in motion the plan to end Hu's tenure as general secretary.

Hu Yaobang's most consequential and complex relationship was with Deng Xiaoping. There are some misconceptions about that relationship among both Western and Chinese observers of elite politics in the PRC. First, Hu was Deng's subordinate, but not his protégé. Second, they were not united in their views on what reforms were needed and how to go about them. Third, Hu's fall was not the result of his failure to deal with "bourgeois liberalization," as Deng charged. It was in fact, the consequence of Deng's failure to support him against attacks from party elders.

Hu's first professional encounter with Deng was in February 1950, when Deng convened all the provincial party chiefs, administrators, and military commanders in Chongqing, headquarters of the CCP's Southwest Region. Deng ruled the Southwest with an iron fist, and carried out successive campaigns of bandit suppression, anticorruption, and land reform with high casualties. Hu was uncomfortable with the harshness of some of the policies coming out of both Beijing and Chongqing. But he was never insubordinate or inattentive, and he got the work done to both Mao's and Deng's satisfaction.

Deng and Hu were both under Mao Zedong's wing after they transferred to Beijing in 1952, Hu to head the Communist Youth League and Deng to join the Central Secretariat, which oversaw the CYL. Deng became a diligent enforcer of Mao's anti-rightist decrees, forcing Hu's hand by sending CYL staffers off to labor reform in 1957. As Mao's economic and social programs wreaked havoc on the countryside, Deng edged closer to Liu Shaoqi politically while Hu sought to escape Beijing politics altogether, taking temporary posts in Hunan and Shaanxi. Hu was heavily persecuted in Shaanxi by leaders associated with Deng's Secretariat, causing his health to collapse. Mao sent Ye Jianying to rescue him, while Deng declined to help Hu resolve his problems. Hu was still recuperating in Beijing when Mao unleashed the Cultural Revolution in 1966.

The Cultural Revolution was a turning point for Hu Yaobang, a ten-year stretch of pain, humiliation, isolation, and estrangement. He needed all his inner resources to survive physical abuse, emotional torture, and crushing loneliness. And they seemed to be sufficient—he did not break, beg, betray, or confess, nor did he provide evidence against Deng. Although Mao gave him a temporary reprieve in 1968, Hu refused to abase himself enough to qualify for the Ninth Central Committee in 1969, and rejected Mao's Cultural Revolution, and so was sent to a cadre school in remote Henan Province, where he spent three years at hard labor. In 1972 he was finally allowed to return home to recover his health, though not his freedom, after the Lin Biao incident had derailed the Cultural Revolution. Hu spent three years under house arrest, mostly alone with his thoughts, with interrogators still badgering him to confess. He was aware of the desperate condition the CCP was in—Mao gravely ill and unable to speak but still terrorizing the leadership.

Deng and Hu worked together again in 1975 when Mao brought them both back into the Central government to begin repairing the institutional damage done by the Cultural Revolution. But their somewhat strained work was cut short when factional infighting and Mao's declining health caused Mao to sideline Deng again, and Hu along with him. After the death of Mao and the purge of the Gang of Four in 1976, Hu Yaobang was rehabilitated before Deng, thanks to his ties with both Hua Guofeng and Ye Jianying.

Hu's energy and organizational skills served him well in the ensuing two years. As executive president of the Central Party School, he reopened classes, established an influential theoretical magazine and began the process of restoring purged faculty. As head of the party's Organization Department, he oversaw a massive program of reviewing mistaken judgments imposed on hundreds of thousands of cadres and ordinary citizens going back to the

1950s, even some that had been approved by Deng. His work was welcomed by many and cleared a path for Deng to return to primacy in the CCP in late 1978. Hu was rewarded with promotion to the Politburo and an appointment to head the troubled Propaganda Department, and with being named secretary general, a position Deng had held in the early 1950s.

Why Hu Failed

Hu's rapid promotion to key administrative positions in the party, Deng's perceived elevation to "core" status as the CCP's "architect of reform," and Chen Yun's unexpected return to the apex of political power set in motion the processes and personalities that would bring about Hu's eventual downfall.

Hu Yaobang's rise from political unemployment in 1977 to the nominal top position in the party by 1979 was a remarkable story brought about by the broken political succession system that followed Mao's death, and the anomalous and inherently unstable relations between Hua Guofeng, Ye Jianying, Deng Xiaoping, and Chen Yun. Hu was a known quantity to three of them, having worked with them earlier in his career. He was very favorably regarded by all of them due to his exceptional bureaucratic abilities, excelling at "bringing order out of chaos." Working behind the scenes, he made the Third Plenum of the Eleventh Central Committee a success.

But he was in some ways the victim of his own success and the enthusiastic support he got from the delegates to the November 1978 Central Committee work conference. At the Third Plenum, he was rewarded with the titles secretary general of the Central Committee, minister of the Central Propaganda Department, and third secretary of the Central Commission for Discipline Inspection, and he maintained his post as executive president of the Central Party School. He was put into the secretary general position with a temporary office, almost no staff, and two unsupportive deputies. And although he was familiar with its work, the Central Propaganda Department was a badly divided organization full of quarrelsome bureaucrats and a penchant for using ideology as a bludgeon.

Hu must have considered that his work at the Central Party School, and particularly his management of *Theoretical Dynamics*, prepared him better for the Propaganda Department than for the ill-defined position of party secretary general. So he initially focused his efforts there. His decision, with support from Ye Jianying, to put together in early 1979 a Conference on

Theoretical Work Principles, at which he hoped to clarify issues and unify the party's line on Mao and the Cultural Revolution, was probably premature. Attended by several hundred intellectuals, the lively three-month conference allowed a greater degree of criticism of Mao and his ideology than Hu expected and more than Deng and other elders were willing to tolerate. Added to increased public criticism of Deng on the Xidan Democracy Wall and tales of PLA ineptitude during the Vietnam incursion, he did not welcome the prospect of de-Maoification raised by some of the participants in the Conference. Deng scuttled the conference on March 30 with a tough speech on "upholding the four fundamental principles." Abashed, Hu shut down the second half of the conference and retreated into bureaucracy-building work and trying to reset the party's guiding ideals through the completion of the party history resolution. And now he was working directly for two "masters" of great skill and experience: Deng Xiaoping and Chen Yun.

The pragmatic Deng Xiaoping was principally concerned with the PRC's economic performance and achievement of international prestige, espousing a classic "wealth and power" agenda for modernization. To him, reform was a willingness to allow an opening of the PRC's autarkic trade and investment structure and relaxation of the Communist Party's monopolization of all economic decisions in order to hasten its recovery from decades of internal chaos. Deng also shared Mao's and many other CCP veterans' disdain for Western culture and values, which he called "opposing bourgeois liberalism" but which might also be termed xenophobia. Deng vacillated during the early 1980s between promoting "reform and opening," which tended to foster innovation and some Western practices, and "maintaining the four cardinal principles," which took aim at increasingly popular Western concepts of freedom and democracy. Reform and opening gained popularity among intellectuals, while the four principles were more familiar to elder CCP veterans and residual "leftists."

Since returning after two dismissals from all positions by Mao, Deng had behaved as if his political skills and career trajectory—interrupted by the Cultural Revolution and Mao's decline into senescence—destined him to be the "core" of the CCP's leadership. Mao, in fact, had told him so in the 1950s. Moreover, the destruction of the pre–Cultural Revolution political structure worked to Deng's advantage by taking out so many of the political "stars" of his generation. Deng viewed Hua Guofeng as an unqualified upstart who needed to be briskly ushered off the political stage so the work of repairing the country's economy and the party's reputation could proceed. Deng was pushy and overconfident, skilled at power maneuvering and giving orders. And his desire for predominant political power was relentless. He eagerly accepted the popular moniker of "chief architect of reform," although he initially did not seem to have a well-defined sense of what that meant.

Chen Yun had been sidelined for several years, but was not dismissed or discarded, and became a key player quickly in 1977, despite his poor health. His seniority (a Politburo member before Deng), knowledge of personnel issues, and accredited experience at managing a planned economy put him in a strong position within the post-Mao Politburo Standing Committee. Chen did not at first have supporters in the power bureaucracies (military, security, central administration, and propaganda), but he did favors for Deng and others in return for primacy in economic policymaking and equality in key personnel appointments. Acutely sensitive to his own prestige and perquisites, Chen was dismissive of both Hu Yaobang and Hua Guofeng as economic lightweights who didn't know their own limitations. Chen himself spent a great deal of time in Shanghai and Hangzhou, where he resided in luxurious villas, recuperating from his numerous ailments. Chen had a reputation as a firm believer in Soviet-style economic planning, and he was unfailingly skeptical of reformist notions of market economics and openness to foreign participation in Chinese economic development.

Hu Yaobang's approach to reform was different, reflecting his more populist roots and his deeper alienation from Mao Zedong. For him, reform entailed a recognition that something had gone wrong and needed to be changed. For Hu, that was more than simply economic performance and competitiveness. He recognized that the Communist Party of China, under the misguided leadership of Mao, had done enormous damage to the people of China. Of the six members of the Politburo Standing Committee in 1980, Hu Yaobang had suffered by far the most physical and spiritual harm—closer to that suffered by millions of ordinary citizens. To repair that damage required a frank acknowledgment of the mistakes, an inquiry into their causes, and a determination to fix them. If the problems were caused by incorrect or misused ideology, the party should investigate and correct the ideology, no matter who originated or promoted the thinking. That guided Hu's early work in the Central Party School to desensitize ideological inquiry and break the barriers posed by Mao's personality cult.

Once he became general secretary in 1980 and had a fully staffed Central Secretariat, Hu teamed up with Wan Li to bring about decollectivization of the countryside, thereby improving the lives and the productivity of hundreds of millions of peasant farmers. By dint of repeated review and alteration of policies on the agricultural system over several years, Hu and Wan were finally able to bring about the return of family farming and the dissolution of the much-hated and inefficient commune system. It took four years, until 1984. Agricultural reform was the key change that benefited the largest number of Chinese people and provided the impetus for the adoption of other economic reform measures.

Hu and Deng again were at odds on the issue of evaluating Mao and the history of the CCP. Deng wanted personal control of the process and its outcome and used his "core" powers to dictate the terms and participants in the drafting of the history resolution, which began in October 1979 and continued until mid-1981. Hu wanted more critical voices to be heard, organizing large meetings of senior CCP officials to consider the draft resolution at various stages. When their differences over Mao became obvious, Deng ordered Hu to take a vacation, allowing Hu Qiaomu and Deng Liqun to finish the resolution. The result was a whitewash of Mao's errors and a downplaying of the causes and costs of the Cultural Revolution.

Deng and Hu also differed strongly regarding Hua Guofeng and his role in the post-Mao leadership. Deng was uncompromising that it was "not appropriate" for Hua to hold the posts of party chairman, CMC chairman, and premier of the State Council, and he pressed for the Politburo Standing Committee to remove him. Hu tried to set up a system that would rotate Standing Committee members into the chairman's position, but Deng rejected it out of hand, considering Hu's approach obstructive. Accepting his fate, Hu played a key role in enumerating Hua's faults and errors and demoting him in late 1980. The first of Deng's three "palace coups" also humiliated Ye Jianying and in effect forced him into retirement.

Hu's approach to inner party politics, particularly the conduct of political struggle, represented a major change from the CCP's political culture, which had validated violence and persecution from the beginning of the revolution and maintained it even after the revolution had triumphed. "Contradictions between the enemy and ourselves," "suppress counterrevolutionaries," "you-die-I-live," forced confessions, "destroy the four olds," "reform through labor," "strike hard" campaigns against crime, and many more party-authorized activities emphasized a culture of violence emanating from the very top. Beating or killing someone for being from a different class background or thinking different thoughts or holding a certain office reached a high point in the Cultural Revolution, and Hu Yaobang was an early victim. Afterward he advocated "four nos" in resolving contradictions within the party: No seizing on individual shortcomings ("pulling pigtails"), no political labeling ("putting on hats"), no violence or threats of violence ("beating with sticks"), and no bringing up unverifiable evidence ("packing bags of materials.") It was a hard sell with hardboiled party elders, who used these methods against both Hua Guofeng and Hu Yaobang himself.

Deng and Hu also differed substantially on the question of "lifetime tenure" for senior leaders. Both recognized and agreed on the need to prevent another "cult of personality," such as Mao and Lin Biao created around the chairman during the Cultural Revolution. The lifetime tenure issue was linked to Mao, who wouldn't have had the cult had he not been guaranteed the lifetime position. But it was also needed in the post-Mao era due to the return of so many septuagenarians from Cultural Revolution disgrace who wanted to enjoy the benefits of being senior cadres for a few more years and secure appropriate comforts for their families after they stepped down. The result was a surfeit of senior cadres in general and blocked promotions for younger officials who needed experience to qualify for advancement. Hu was conflicted because he had been responsible for so many of the elders being restored to office in 1978–1980 and soon wanted to establish appropriate procedures for them to retire.

Hu's relationship with Deng Xiaoping was affected by Deng's relationship with Chen Yun, which began to deteriorate almost immediately after the Twelfth Congress. The two men seldom spoke to each other, and Deng resisted Hu even trying to convene Politburo Standing Committee meetings because he and Chen "could not agree." Neither Hu nor Zhao Ziyang could get the two elders to see eye to eye on major issues, such as the basic definition of China's economy or whether special economic zones—approved in 1980—were worth preserving. As prominent historian Yang Jisheng put it:

> In this type of leadership system, people with nominal power had no actual power, people with actual power had no nominal power, and contradictions between the first line and the second line were hard to avoid. Once there was a contradiction between the first line and the second line, it was bound to be the second line with real power overwhelming the first line without real power. . . . [W]hen Deng Xiaoping and Chen Yun in the second line were "not able to agree," it was even more difficult for the leaders in the front line. Therefore, the 'Deng-Hu-Zhao system' was a system that could not be stable for very long.[60]

The problem was compounded by the emergence of the "Eight Elders," under the aegis of the Central Advisory Commission: Deng Xiaoping, Chen Yun, Li Xiannian, Yang Shangkun, Bo Yibo, Peng Zhen, Wang Zhen, and Deng Yingchao.[61] They were sought out by both Deng and Chen for support and communication, and eventually were involved informally in key decision-making issues. Hu Yaobang's own relationship to Chen was distant, at best. The two had no career associations nor much mutual regard. Chen impugned Hu's knowledge of economics and used his shortcomings to get at Deng. Hu was not above referring to Chen's economic ideas as "that old stuff." His ties with the other elders were not much better, and their propensity to spread gossip had a ripple effect, damaging to Hu's reputation in several important bureaucracies, such as the propaganda apparatus, the State Council, and the PLA.

As Hu grew more confident of his position in 1985–1986, he accomplished a significant personnel gain at the "national representatives meeting" and two Central Committee plenums in September 1985, thinning the ranks of elders in all the representative bodies. At the Sixth Plenum in 1986, he demonstrated his mastery of the documentary process with the completion of the "Resolution on Spiritual Civilization." At a meeting with PLA cadres in Qinghai on August 19, 1986, Hu detailed some of his plans for political reform. It must have startled many with its scope, which included: separation of party and government; abolishing lifetime tenure; adjusting the "entire cadre ranks" to make them younger, more knowledgeable, professional and institutionalized; strengthening the political and legal apparatus; reestablishing rural villages; streamlining military units; decreasing propaganda about individuals; "developing socialist democracy"; clarifying the roles of local legislatures; and ensuring party and government workers "receive the people's supervision" if they were corrupt.[62]

On October 30, 1986, Chen Yun hosted a meeting with Deng and Li Xiannian, which probably started the process that led to Hu's resignation in early 1987. But it was Deng who took the lead, calling several of the Eight Elders to his home on December 27 and rousing them into expressing support for removing Hu Yaobang as general secretary for "ineffective" action against student demonstrators. It was Deng to whom Hu submitted his resignation and Deng who set him up for the life meeting that crushed his spirit. Deng set the parameters for the meeting, the convening authority (the Central Advisory Commission), and probably approved the speakers. Deng called for a "soft landing" for Hu, including his retention on the Politburo

Standing Committee, and set restrictions on topics of criticism at the party life meeting—such as factionalism—which were largely ignored by zealous older participants. In early January 1987 Deng rendered the Standing Committee useless by replacing it with a "five-man small group" to handle CCP affairs until the Thirteenth Congress. After the preordained verdict against Hu was announced in mid-January, Deng again usurped the Central Committee's authority to announce outcomes of the Thirteenth CCP Congress in July, several months ahead of schedule.

But it was Chen Yun and his allies who gained most from the ouster of Hu Yaobang, reclaiming the Organization Department, the propaganda apparatus, and the premiership with its influence over the economic planning bureaucracies. They would use those positions, according to Zhao Ziyang, to weaken his ability to carry out any kind of reform after he replaced Hu as general secretary. Less than two years after bringing down Hu Yaobang, Deng Liqun was planning the ouster of Zhao Ziyang, with the collaboration of Chen Yun and Li Xiannian.[63]

Deng Xiaoping was probably unhappy about these events, but had his own problems with Zhao, and more problems after Hu Yaobang's death, when public protests changed everyone's political calculations and plans. It would not be farfetched to say that the CCP leadership facing massive demonstrations in April 1989 was the group selected mostly by Deng Xiaoping and Chen Yun. Through their domination of the personnel selection processes, Deng and Chen balanced each other out through joint control of the power of appointments from about 1979 to 1989. And under pressure, their chosen successors failed to coordinate a response, but focused on mutual recriminations.

Chen Yun and Li Xiannian came to Deng's assistance after the fragmented political leadership in April-May 1989 could not cope with the challenge of massive demonstrations in Tiananmen. They recommended that Jiang Zemin—then secretary of the Shanghai CCP committee—replace Zhao Ziyang as general secretary. The "skip-generation" succession framework came into formal existence at this point in 1989. Deng's choice of Hu Jintao to succeed Jiang held even after Deng's death in 1997, while Jiang Zemin's chosen successor for Hu Jintao turned out to be Xi Jinping. Xi prevented Hu Jintao's successor from emerging and has decided against specifying a successor at all.

In the wake of the Tiananmen events, the CCP leadership reverted to its old ways. At a meeting to congratulate the PLA on June 9, surrounded by several of the "Eight Elders," Deng praised the "veteran comrades" who came to his aid. Once the crackdown on demonstrators passed from the military to public and state security forces, the CCP held a plenary meeting June 23–24 and stripped Zhao Ziyang and Hu Qili of their positions on the Standing Committee. Zhao refused adamantly to admit his mistakes and spent the rest of his life under house arrest. Hu Qili, the principal perceived supporter of Hu Yaobang, was removed from the Politburo Standing Committee and Secretariat but returned to a degree of political favor in 1991 at a level far below his former prominence. Jiang Zemin, Li Ruihuan, and Song Ping joined the Standing Committee, now more tilted toward Chen Yun supporters, virtually guaranteeing a stall in economic reform and a complete stoppage of political reform efforts.

For two years after June 4, the PRC economy stagnated, due to a combination of foreign sanctions, the Chen Yun-Li Xiannian-Li Peng focus on "readjustment," and concerns about the future of the Special Economic Zones. Deng eventually recovered the political and economic policy initiative, making a heavily publicized trip to Shenzhen in early 1992. The so-called "southern tour" (*nanxun*) was his swan song, to which he added a direct threat to Jiang Zemin: he had to support the SEZs or lose his job as general secretary.[64]

Deng won the "longevity contest" with Li Xiannian and Chen Yun, both of whom died in the following two years. Deng lasted until 1997, having secured the succession to Jiang Zemin by Hu Jintao. Hu had been first secretary of the Communist Youth League in the 1980s, he was often accused of trying to promote a Youth League faction in his own political struggle with Jiang Zemin. The competition for power between Jiang Zemin and Hu Jintao was intense, behind-the-scenes, and very personal, with the ultimate victors being Jiang, his crony Zeng Qinghong, and their chosen successor, Xi Jinping.[65]

Did Hu Yaobang Fail or Did the CCP Fail Him?

The Chinese Communist Party, which had brought so much damage and suffering to the Chinese people, proved itself incapable of self-reform, or of being reformed from outside by its own citizens. At the outset of this book, I noted that Hu Yaobang was a failure as a reformer and we should ask why. On review, the question is somewhat unfair. Despite being the only leader in

PRC history to have held the titles of both chairman and general secretary, Hu Yaobang never held the power sufficient to direct party or government policies on political, ideological, economic, or foreign affairs. His influence derived from his ability to persuade the real power players above him to adopt his ideas for changing the status quo. The return of Deng Xiaoping in 1977 and promotion of Chen Yun in 1978 created a power competition at the top that made Hu's role far more difficult—a servant of two masters.

Within the established structure of the Chinese Communist Party—Central Committee/Political Bureau/Standing Committee—competition for power among the top leaders involves acquiring the ability to put subordinates or cronies into the leading positions of the most important bureaucracies for preserving the party's power and ruling the country: the military, the civilian security apparatus, the administrative and personnel centers of the CCP, and the propaganda organs, along with the economic planning system. Hu Yaobang's power to appoint was constrained by Deng and Chen. The successes he had as general secretary were in part the result of having a large and capable Central Secretariat (eleven secretaries) operating under his leadership. After he was ousted, the Secretariat was downsized under Zhao, and while still important to the day-to-day management of Central Committee business, it has remained at six or seven members ever since. The first- and second-line leadership structure and the Central Advisory Commission were both abandoned by 1992.

Given that desire for political power—which is a near-universal solvent of ideologies, structures, relationships, and ideals in autocracies—is not well-constrained in the CCP, competition has usually been a factor in relationships among members of this highest leading group, and those who aspire to join it. And because the winners of political struggles get to write the histories, it is generally only when one individual prevails that the term "core" (*hexin*) is used to describe his role. It is a term with a positive connotation. Of those who have been named chairman or general secretary in the post-1949 era, Mao Zedong, Deng Xiaoping, Jiang Zemin and Xi Jinping all have been called "core" leaders. Hua Guofeng, Hu Yaobang, Zhao Ziyang, and Hu Jintao have not. Three of these latter were removed from office, and Hu Jintao was considered weak and ineffective. The CCP system, in other words, tends to value more highly the emergence of one-man rule than it does the practice of "collective leadership" enshrined in its ideology.

In 2014 Hu Yaobang's youngest and most outspoken son, Hu Dehua, spoke with a Hong Kong reporter about the "lost opportunity" for reform in the 1980s:

> There was a window for reform then [in the 1980s] but it was missed, and I don't know when the next one will come. When you have no law to protect these rights, everything is in the hands of the officials. . . . Today, corruption among officials is impossible to rein in and ethnic tension is intense. . . . Although we have a constitution which guarantees freedoms in speech and assembly . . . in fact, there are hardly any freedoms. We have no right to supervise [the government].[66]

Xi Jinping, in a private speech acquired by Hong Kong's avowedly anti-Communist *Outpost* 前哨月刊 magazine in April 2013, made it clear that political reform was not on his agenda. Speaking apparently to an audience of princelings in late 2012, Xi complained that there were too many vested interests inside the party, too many local and international problems, and that he was only a "big manager" trying to keep everyone satisfied:

> Once the reform of the political system is begun, it will be very diffi-cult to go back and control it. When the time comes, whether this General Secretary can do it or not, and whether the leading position of the Party can still be maintained, it will be very difficult to say. There-fore, it is not that we do not change, but it is actually that we cannot change, and dare not change lightly. Who dares to shoulder this re-sponsibility? At the time of Deng Xiaoping, the attempt to reform turned out to be a major problem.[67]

In the years Xi Jinping has been in power, he and the Communist Party have moved determinedly away from anything that could be described as political or comprehensive reform. Even initiatives that were initially de-scribed as economic reforms have foundered in the face of the party's need for control. Most of the reforms Hu Yaobang made or was considering in the mid-1980s have been abandoned or even reversed. Ideologically, the CCP has beaten Marxism-Leninism into a lengthy series of slogans bereft of any moral content, mostly words and numbers to be memorized, the principal message being to obey or be punished. Far from separating party and gov-ernment, Xi and his associates have strengthened CCP control of nearly all aspects of social and political activity. What was aspirational under Mao's dictatorship of the proletariat has come closer to being realized under "Xi Jinping Thought on Socialism with Chinese Characteristics for a New Era"—an effectively functioning police state.

Xi has moved contrary to Hu Yaobang's reformist ideas with respect to concentration of power, party-government relations, lifetime tenure (for himself, at least), and even creation of a personality cult. And while the PRC's economic productivity over the last forty years has been remarkable, lifting China to a world-leading position in many areas, Hu Yaobang's aspiration to let ordinary people (the *laobaixing*) prosper first has not been achieved. According to figures disclosed by Premier Li Keqiang in 2020, more than six hundred million of China's 1.4 billion people—mostly in poor rural areas—were subsisting on less than a thousand yuan (about US$154) per month.[68]

After his ouster, Hu Yaobang agreed to occasional visits by old friends and subordinates, although he did not do so often, possibly for fear of being suspected of trying to make a comeback. On March 19, 1989, less than a month before his death, Hu met with Wang Zhongfang, who had been the *mishu* of Hu's friend Luo Ruiqing, the secretary general of the CMC whose death in 1978 deprived Hu of an important military ally. In a cheerful mood, Hu noted the two things he had not expected about his career: that he had risen to such a high position, which he attributed to "unique historical circumstances" rather than his own abilities; and that after he stepped down, his prestige among the people had not diminished and his reputation had increased. Wang replied that the biggest loss of Hu's 1987 ouster was not to Hu himself, but the damage to the party's image and repute, which he had helped restore after the Cultural Revolution. "The shadow of abnormal political life within the party seems to have reappeared," he observed.[69] A month later, Hu was dead, and the "abnormal" political life of the CCP became a permanent fixture.

The story of Hu Yaobang, in the end, is a tragedy. Hu was a classic tragic hero, whose efforts to do the right thing brought about his own downfall. But the fact of his downfall and death also precipitated events that led the Communist Party, which Hu had sought to change, to return to its violent ways, dictatorial reign, and corrupt practices. Xi Jinping, the man who eagerly occupies the position Hu Yaobang reluctantly held, has made structural and personnel changes that strengthen the concentration of power, the cult of personality, and the lifetime tenure that Hu strongly opposed. He has controlled the key levers of power more effectively than many expected, although he does not appear to be without enemies or anxieties about them. The progression of leaders from the Deng-Hu-Zhao troika to Xi Jinping as "number one hand" has been a tragedy for many Chinese people as well. Those who looked on the mid-1980s as "the most democratic era of CCP politics" have been especially aggrieved by the steady erosion of citizens' rights and constitutional freedoms under Xi. But they seem increasingly powerless.

NOTE ON ARCHIVAL SOURCE

Much of the research for this book was done online, using Internet services located in the People's Republic of China. The website that was most consistently helpful for biographic information, and for other historical content for which it was an aggregator, was the Hu Yaobang Historical Materials Information Network (in Chinese, 胡耀邦史料信息网) at http://hybsl.cn. Like all websites in the PRC, it is subject to official supervision and sometimes suspension. Late in 2023, hybsl.cn went offline without explanation. Several weeks later it came back up, with a note citing technical difficulties, but all articles had their URLs (uniform resource locators) changed. The new addresses were found at that point for most materials used in this book. In March 2024, however, the website went down again, and new addresses for the many articles sourced from it could not be found. The author has retained hard copies of all articles cited and can make them available to interested readers.

NOTES

Introduction

1. For further reading on what happened at Tiananmen and after, see among others, Geremie Barmé and Linda Jaivin, eds., *New Ghosts, Old Dreams* (Crown, 1992); Chen Xiaoya 陈小雅, 八九民运史 [The history of the 1989 democracy movement] (Citizens Press, 2019); Eddie Cheng, *Standoff at Tiananmen* (Sensys, 2009); Lee Feigon, *China Rising: The Meaning of Tiananmen* (Dee, 1990); Julian Gewirtz, *Never Turn Back: China and the Forbidden History of the 1980s* (Belknap Press of Harvard University Press, 2022); Adi Ignatius, *Prisoner of the State: The Secret Journal of Premier Zhao Ziyang* (Simon and Schuster, 2009); Louisa Lim, *The People's Republic of Amnesia: Tiananmen Revisited* (Oxford University Press, 2014); Richard Madsen, *China and the American Dream: A Moral Inquiry* (University of California Press, 1995); Tony Saich, *The Chinese People's Movement: Perspectives on Spring 1989* (M. E. Sharpe 1990); Scott Savitt, *Crashing the Party: An American Reporter in China* (Soft Skull, 2015); Robert L. Suettinger, *Beyond Tiananmen: The Politics of US-China Relations, 1989–2000* (Brookings Institution, 2003); Zhang Liang, comp., *The Tiananmen Papers*, ed. Andrew J. Nathan and Perry Link (Public Affairs, 2001).

2. Man Mei 满妹, 思念依然无尽：回忆父亲胡耀邦 [Still endless yearning—Remembering father, Hu Yaobang] (Beijing chubanshe, 2005), 18–21. Man Mei is Hu Yaobang's daughter.

3. Zhang Liang, *The Tiananmen Papers*, 19–23. There is controversy over the book's authenticity, but its general chronology of facts and events seems reliable.

4. Zhang Liang, 中国六四真相 [China's June 4th] (Mirror Books, 2001), Chinese-language version of *The Tiananmen Papers*, also online at http://beijingspring.com/big5bjs/bjs/ls/4.txt.

5. Tian Jiyun 田纪云, "我们心中的胡耀邦" [The Hu Yaobang in our hearts], *Yanhuang Chunqiu*, November 2005.

6. Yang Jisheng 杨继盛, 中国改革年代的政治斗争 [The political struggles of China's reform era] (Cosmos Books, 2010), 7–8.

7. Former *Renmin Ribao* editor in chief Hu Jiwei 胡绩伟 makes this argument in 胡赵新政齐示录 [The beginnings of reform under Hu Yaobang and Zhao Ziyang] (New Century Press, 2012), 104–108.

8. Anon., "中共中央政治局扩大会议公报" [Communiqué of the enlarged meeting of the Political Bureau of the Chinese Communist Party], January 16, 1987, http://www.reformdata.org/1987/0116/2918.shtml.

9. Li Rui 李锐, "耀邦去世前的谈话" [A talk with Yaobang before his death], excerpted from the fourth collection of "Remembering Yaobang: Essays" (Asia-Pacific International Publishing, 2001), July 13, 2014, https://www.aisixiang.com/data/20900.html.

1. Born to the Revolution

1. Man Mei 满妹, 思念依然无尽: 回忆父亲胡耀邦 [Still endless yearning: Remembering father, Hu Yaobang] (Beijing chubanshe, 2005) (hereafter cited as Man Mei, *Endless Yearning*), 37; Zhang Liqun 张黎群, Zhang Ding 张定, Yan Ruping 严如平, Tang Fei 唐非, and Li Songtian 李松天, 胡耀邦传 [Biography of Hu Yaobang], vol. 1, *1915–1976* (Renmin chubanshe, 2005) (hereafter cited as Zhang et al., *Biography of Hu Yaobang*), 3; Qian Jiang 钱江, "胡耀邦的家世和童年" [Hu Yaobang's family background and childhood], *Nanfang Zhoumo*, November 18, 2005, www.aisixiang.com/data/8973.html. (hereafter cited as Qian, "Family Background").

2. Mary S. Erbaugh, "The Secret History of the Hakkas: The Chinese Revolution as a Hakka Enterprise," *China Quarterly* 132 (December 1992): 937–968. See also "浏阳市胡耀邦故里" [Hu Yaobang's home village in Liuyang], Hakka Online, March 18, 2012, http://www.hakkaonline.com/thread-87341-1-1.html.

3. Yang Zhongmei, *Hu Yaobang: A Chinese Biography*, trans. William A. Wycoff (M. E. Sharpe, 1988), 162–163. Also Yang Zongzheng 杨宗铮, "胡耀邦的客家身世和客家精" [Hu Yaobang's Hakka history and Hakka spirit], Hakka Online, July 13, 2009, http://www.hakkaonline.com/article-3118-1.html.

4. Erbaugh, "Secret History." Erbaugh emphasizes the difficulty of tracing Hakka roots for Sun Yat-sen and Deng, who did not clearly acknowledge them. But the Hu family has spoken with pride of their Hakka heritage.

5. Mao Zedong, "Report on an Investigation of the Peasant Movement in Hunan," in *The Selected Works of Mao Zedong*, vol. 1 (Foreign Language Press, 1971). English version at https://www.marxists.org/reference/archive/mao/selected-works.

6. Zhang et al., *Biography of Hu Yaobang*, 1:5.

7. Yang Zhongmei, *Hu Yaobang*, 5.

8. Qian, "Family Background."

9. Qian, "Family Background"; Chen Liming 陈利明, 从小红鬼到总书记 [From little red devil to general secretary], vol. 1 (Renmin Ribao chubanshe, 2013), 6–8 (hereafter cited as Chen Liming, *Little Red Devil*).

10. Chen Liming, *Little Red Devil,* 1: 9.

11. Qian, "Family Background."

12. Yu Zhenkui 余振魁,"胡耀邦和他的老师们" [Hu Yaobang and his teachers], *Hunan Tide,* September 2012, http://www.xzbu.com/1/view-3614267.htm; Zhang et al., *Biography of Hu Yaobang,* 1:8–9.

13. Yang Zhongmei, *Hu Yaobang,* 12.

14. Zhang et al., *Biography of Hu Yaobang,* 1:10–11.

15. Xiaobing Li, *China at War: An Encyclopedia* (ABC Clio, 2012), 308–309.

16. Li, *China at War,* 492–493; Zhang et al., *Biography of Hu Yaobang,* 1:11.

17. Li, *China at War,* 296–297.

18. Chen Liming, *Little Red Devil,* 1: 11; Zhang et al., *Biography of Hu Yaobang,* 1:12–14.

19. Yang Zhongmei, *Hu Yaobang,* 12–14.

20. Chen Liming, *Little Red Devil,* 1: 18–19; Man Mei, *Endless Yearning,* 44–45.

21. Yang Zhongmei, *Hu Yaobang,* 17.

22. The Chinese term *suweiai* (苏维埃), a transliteration of the Russian term *soviet,* meaning council, denoted a quasi-representative governing body (consisting of peasants, workers, and Red Army soldiers) under the control of the Communist Party. These councils provided defense, law and order, social services, banking and currency, trade policies, and land reform.

23. Zheng Zhongbing 郑仲兵, ed., 胡耀邦年谱资料长编 [Hu Yaobang chronological materials, long form] (International Times, 2005), entries for 1930–1932 (hereafter cited as Zheng, *Hu Yaobang Chronological Materials,* followed by entry date).

24. Yang Zhongmei, *Hu Yaobang,* 21.

25. Zhang et al., *Biography of Hu Yaobang,* 1:21–22.

26. Yang Zhongmei, *Hu Yaobang,* 25; Zhang et al., *Biography of Hu Yaobang,* 1:24.

27. Mao Zedong, "A Single Spark Can Start a Prairie Fire," letter to the Central Committee, January 5, 1930, in *Selected Military Writings of Mao Tse-tung* (Foreign Languages Press, 1964).

28. Zhang et al., *Biography of Hu Yaobang,* 1:29.

29. Dai Xiangqing 戴向青, "论 AB 团和富田事变" [On the AB League and the Futian incident], Hu Yaobang Historical Materials Information Network (hereafter HYBSL), January 6, 2014, http://w.hybsl.cn/article/13/44100 (hereafter cited as Dai, "Lun AB tuan"). Dai's account is not without critics, but more than sixty years later there are still suspicions about the Futian incident and its aftermath. See also Joseph Fewsmith, *Forging Leninism in China: Mao and the Remaking of the Chinese Communist Party, 1927–1934* (Cambridge University Press, 2022), 131–134.

30. Dai, "Lun AB tuan." See also Li Weimin 李维民,"从共产国际档案看反'AB团' 斗争" [The struggle against the "AB League" from the archives of the Communist

International], *Yanhuang Chunqiu,* July 2009 (hereafter cited as Li Weimin, "The Struggle").

31. Li Weimin, "The Struggle."

32. Gao Hua 高华, "'肃 AB 团'事件的历史考察" [Historical examination of the "purge of the AB League"], HYBSL, July 2, 2007, http://w.hybsl.cn/article/13/38316.

33. Dai, "Lun AB tuan."

34. Dai, "Lun AB tuan."

35. Fewsmith, *Forging Leninism,* 134.

36. Yao Jianfu 姚监复, "徐向前回忆 30 年代的苏区'大肃反'" [Xu Xiangqian recalls the 'great purge of counterrevolutionaries' in the soviet areas in the 1930s, HYBSL, September 26, 2007, http://w.hybsl.cn/article/13/3798.

37. Yang Kuisong 杨奎松, "毛泽东谈肃反" [Mao Zedong talks about the purges], from Yang's book, 中间地带"的革命 [Revolution in the Middle Zone] (Guangxi, 2010), HYBSL, June 5, 2015, http://w.hybsl.cn/article/13/52602.

38. Chen Liming, *Little Red Devil,* 1: 37.

39. Tan Qilong 谭启龙, "莫逆之交六十春" [Great friends for sixty years], HYBSL, April 2, 2009, http://w.hybsl.cn/article/10/104/13366 (hereafter cited as Tan Qilong, "Great Friends").

40. Zhang et al., *Biography of Hu Yaobang,* 1:28–30.

41. Tan Qilong, "Great Friends"; Shui Xinying 水新营, "张爱萍两救胡耀邦" [Zhang Aiping's two rescues of Hu Yaobang], HYBSL, December 29, 2016, http://w.hybsl.cn/article/11/109/63928 (hereafter cited as Shui, "Zhang Aiping's Two Rescues").

42. Anon., "胡耀邦与苏区青年团的工作" [Hu Yaobang and Youth League work in the soviet areas], HYBSL, March 18, 2007, http://w.hybsl.cn/article/11/110/851.

43. Zheng, *Hu Yaobang Chronological Materials,* "Early Spring, 1934."

44. Suyun Sun, *The Long March: The True History of Communist China's Founding Myth* (Knopf Doubleday, 2010), 16–17.

45. Sun, *The Long March,* 33.

46. Chen Tiejian 陈铁健, "红军撤离中央苏区原因新探" [A new inquiry into the reasons for the evacuation of the Red Army from the Central Soviet area], HYBSL, April 15, 2015, http://w.hybsl.cn/article/13/51712.

47. Sun, *The Long March,* 27; Anon., "红军历史上罕见的败仗：广昌保卫战" [A rare defeat in the Red Army's history: The Guangchang defensive battle], *Party History World,* October 28, 2014, https://m.sohu.com/n/473962166/.

48. Tang Jingtao 汤静涛, "共产国际与红军长征决策" [The Comintern and Red Army decisions about the Long March], HYBSL, December 16, 2014, http://w.hybsl.cn/article/13/49920.

49. Edgar Snow's *Red Star over China* (1937) and the newspaper reporting of Agnes Smedley were some of the earliest works to mythologize the Long March, but

Mao had decided well before that to collect the stories of Long March veterans and publish them for their propaganda value. See Yu Jizeng 于继增, "原始文献 红军长征记 揭秘了什么?" [What does the "True Record of the Long March" reveal?], HYBSL, January 29, 2015, http://w.hybsl.cn/article/13/50623.

50. Zhang et al., *Biography of Hu Yaobang,* 1:39; Tang Bofan 唐伯藩, "胡耀邦在长征途中" [Hu Yaobang on the Long March], HYBSL, August 14, 2012, http://w.hybsl.cn/article/11/109/30543 (hereafter cited as Tang, "Long March").

51. Zhang et al., *Biography of Hu Yaobang,* 1:39.

52. Sun, *The Long March,* 65–66.

53. Sun, *The Long March,* 78.

54. Zhang et al., *Biography of Hu Yaobang,* 1:44–45.

55. Anon., "中央红军长征落脚点的七次变化" [The Red Army changed its destination seven times on the Long March], *Jiefangjunbao,* April 3, 2015, http://dangshi.people.com.cn/n/2015/0401/c85037-26784595.html.

56. Li Yubo 李宇博, "长征中确立巩固毛泽东领导地位" [During the Long March, Mao Zedong's leadership position was established and consolidated], Renminwang, March 10, 2015, http://dangshi.people.com.cn/n/2015/0309/c85037-26660677.html.

57. Tang, "Long March."

58. Shui, "Zhang Aiping's Two Rescues"; Zheng, *Hu Yaobang Chronological Materials,* February 27, 1935.

59. Tang, "Long March."

60. Zhang et al., *Biography of Hu Yaobang,* 1:57, 60.

61. Zheng Zhongbing, "胡耀邦长征记略" [A record of Hu Yaobang's Long March], HYBSL, March 16, 2007, http://w.hybsl.cn/article/10/104/570.

2. Basking in the Light of Mao Zedong

1. Mao Zedong, "On Tactics against Japanese Imperialism," December 27, 1935, in *Selected Works of Mao Zedong,* vol. 1 (Foreign Languages Press, 1951).

2. Xiaobing Li, ed., *China at War: An Encyclopedia* (ABC Clio, 2012), 183. See also Yang Kuisong 杨奎松, 西安事变新探 [New exploration of the Xi'an Incident] (Jiangsu chubanshe, 2006) (hereafter cited as Yang, *Xintan*), chap. 2.

3. Yang Kuisong, "西安事变是中国历史的转折点" [The Xi'an Incident was a turning point in Chinese history], Hu Yaobang Historical Materials Information Network (hereafter HYBSL), December 29, 2014, http://w.hybsl.cn/article/13/50140 (hereafter cited as Yang, "Turning Point").

4. Yang, "Turning Point."

5. Zheng Zhongbing, ed., 胡耀邦年谱资料长编 [Hu Yaobang chronological materials, long form] (International Times, 2005), January 31, 1936 (hereafter cited as

Zheng, *Hu Yaobang Chronological Materials,* followed by date of entry). See also Li Zhu 李柱,"东征路上抢救胡耀邦" [Rescuing Hu Yaobang on the Eastern Expedition], Jiangnan Capital Times, 江南都市报, HYBSL, April 12, 2013, http://w.hybsl.cn /article/11/109/36094 (hereafter cited as Li, "Dongzheng").

6. Zhang Liqun, Zhang Ding, Yan Ruping, Tang Fei, and Li Songtian, 胡耀邦传 [Biography of Hu Yaobang], vol. 1, *1915–1976* (People's Publishing House, 2005) (hereafter cited as Zhang et al., *Biography of Hu Yaobang*), 1:65–66.

7. Li, "Dongzheng."

8. Yang, *Xintan,* 82–83.

9. Zhang et al., *Biography of Hu Yaobang,* 1:68.

10. Yang, "Turning Point"; Zhang Youkun 张友坤, "张学良在物资、财政上对陕 北红军的援" [Zhang Xueliang's material and financial assistance to the Northwest Shaanxi Red Army], *Yanhuang Chunqiu,* June 2011.

11. Yang, *Xintan,* 235.

12. Yang, *Xintan,* 282. See also Steve Tsang, "Chiang Kai-shek's 'Secret Deal' at Xian and the Start of the Sino-Japanese War," *Palgrave Communications* 1, no. 1 (January 20, 2015): Article 14003.

13. Yang, *Xintan,* 282; Tsang, "Chiang Kai-shek's 'Secret Deal.'"

14. Yang, *Xintan,* 288–289.

15. Zhan Shanqin 占善钦, "从审判到保蒋" [From judging to saving Chiang], HYBSL, October 27, 2010, http://w.hybsl.cn/article/13/23144 (hereafter cited as Zhan, "From Judging to Saving").

16. Yang, *Xintan,* 322–323.

17. Zhan, "From Judging to Saving."

18. Yang, *Xintan,* 333; Tsang, "Chiang Kai-shek's 'Secret Deal.'"

19. Zhan, "From Judging to Saving."

20. Yang, *Xintan,* 358–360, 366; Tsang, "Chiang Kai-shek's 'Secret Deal.'"

21. Yang, *Xintan,* 371–373.

22. Ma Shuangyou, 马双有, "张学良和杨虎城的结局为何不同?" [Why did Zhang Xueliang and Yang Hucheng end up differently?], HYBSL, October 21, 2015, http://w .hybsl.cn/article/13/54920.

23. Ma Shuangyou, "对'逼蒋抗日说'的质疑" [Questioning the 'Forcing Chiang to Resist the Japanese' theory], HYBSL, September 8, 2015, http://w.hybsl.cn/article/13 /54202.

24. Tsang, "Chiang Kai-shek's 'Secret Deal.'"

25. Yang Zhongmei, *Hu Yaobang: A Chinese Biography,* trans. William A. Wycoff (M. E. Sharpe, 1988), 40.

26. Zhang et al., *Biography of Hu Yaobang,* 1:71–72; Zheng, *Hu Yaobang Chronological Materials,* April 14–17, 1934.

27. Zhang et al., *Biography of Hu Yaobang,* 1:74.

28. Shu Yun 舒云, "毛泽东写给抗大的十九件手迹" [Nineteen of Mao Zedong's handwritten items for Kang Da], *Party History Overview,* July 2015, http://www .yancloud.red/Education/News/info/id/2673.

29. Chen Wensheng 陈文胜, "胡耀邦在'抗大'的岁月" [Hu Yaobang's years at Kang Da], HYBSL, March 10, 2010, http://w.hybsl.cn/article/10/104/19523.

30. Shui Xinying 水新营, "胡耀邦第一次见到毛泽东因何事" [What was the reason Hu Yaobang met Mao Zedong for the first time?], HYBSL, November 2, 2015, http://w.hybsl.cn/article/11/110/55123.

31. Zhang et al., *Biography of Hu Yaobang,* 1:79.

32. Zhang et al., *Biography of Hu Yaobang,* 1:79–80.

33. Zhang et al., *Biography of Hu Yaobang,* 1:81–82.

34. Zhang et al., *Biography of Hu Yaobang,* 1:88.

35. Gao Hua, *How the Red Sun Rose: The Origins and Development of the Yan'an Rectification Movement, 1930–1945,* trans. Stacy Mosher and Jian Guo (Chinese University of Hong Kong Press, 2018), originally published as Gao Hua 高华, 红太阳是怎样升起的— 延安整风运动的来龙去脉 (Chinese University of Hong Kong Press, 2011).

36. Gao, *How the Red Sun Rose,* 138–139, 143–144.

37. Gao Hua, "抗战前夕延安发生的的一场争论" [The debate that took place in Yan'an on the eve of the War of Resistance], HYBSL, January 4, 1011, http://w.hybsl .cn/article/13/24571.

38. Tetsuya Kataoka, *Resistance and Revolution in China: The Communists and the Second United Front* (University of California Press, 1974), 145. Gao Hua puts the number of Communist troops at more than 250,000. Gao, *How the Red Sun Rose,* 163.

39. Gao, *How the Red Sun Rose,* 248–255.

40. Gao, *How the Red Sun Rose,* 161–186.

41. Zhang Chengjie 张成洁, "延安话语系统是怎样形成的" [How the Yan'an discourse system was developed], *Yanhuang Chunqiu,* December 2015 (hereafter cited as Zhang, "Yan'an Discourse System").

42. Yu Jizeng 于继增, "康生在延安" [Kang Sheng in Yan'an], HYBSL, February 5, 2015, http://w.hybsl.cn/article/13/50729 (hereafter cited as Yu, "Kang Sheng in Yan'an"). See also Matthew Brazil's study of the early days of the CCP intelligence services: Matthew Brazil, "The Darkest Red Corner" (PhD diss., University of Sydney, 2012), 134–138.

43. Yu, "Kang Sheng in Yan'an."

44. Gao, *How the Red Sun Rose,* 227–230; Brazil, "Darkest Red Corner," 141; Wang Jun 王珺, "康生在中央社会部" [Kang Sheng in the Central Social Department], HYBSL, January 21, 2015, http://w.hybsl.cn/article/13/50503 (hereafter cited as Wang, "Kang Sheng in CSD").

45. Brazil, "Darkest Red Corner," 145.

46. Gao, *How the Red Sun Rose,* 227.

47. Brazil, "Darkest Red Corner," 151.

48. Chi Zaijin 郝在今, "1940 年代的 "审干" 与 "锄奸" ["Examining cadres" and "weeding out traitors" in the 1940s], HYBSL, January 7, 2016, http://w.hybsl.cn/article/13/56343.

49. Wang, "Kang Sheng in CSD."

50. Brazil, "Darkest Red Corner," 153–165.

51. Man Mei 满妹, 思念依然无尽: 回忆父亲胡耀邦 [Still endless yearning—Remembering father, Hu Yaobang] (Beijing chubanshe, 2005), 64; Xiao Zushi 肖祖石, "一个不平凡的女性— 记胡耀邦夫人李昭 (之二) " [An extraordinary woman: A record of Hu Yaobang's wife, Li Zhao, part 2], HYBSL, March 17, 2007, http://w.hybsl.cn/article/10/104/743 (hereafter cited as Xiao, "Record of Li Zhao").

52. Xiao, "Record of Li Zhao," part 2.

53. Xiao, "Record of Li Zhao," part 3, http://w.hybsl.cn/article/10/104/742.

54. Xiao, "Record of Li Zhao," part 5, http://w.hybsl.cn/article/10/104/740.

55. Xiao, "Record of Li Zhao," part 5. See also Chen Liming 陳利明, 胡耀邦傳 [Biography of Hu Yaobang] (Swindon Books, 2005) (hereafter cited as Chen Liming, *Biography of Hu Yaobang* [2005]), 1:149–150. The 2005 edition is the original version of Chen's biography and has more detail than the abridged version published in Beijing in 2013.

56. Xiao, "Record of Li Zhao," part 5.

57. CCP Central Party Research Office 中共中央党史研究室, 中国共产党简史 [A brief history of the Communist Party of China], rev. 2021, http://fuwu.12371.cn/ddzs/zggcdjs/.

58. Frederick C. Teiwes, *Politics and Purges in China: Rectification and the Decline of Party Norms, 1950–1965* (M. E. Sharpe, 1979), 64–78.

59. Gao, *How the Red Sun Rose,* chap. 11.

60. Gao, *How the Red Sun Rose,* chap. 11; Yang Kuisong 杨奎松, "毛泽东发动延安整风的台前幕后" [Behind the scenes of Mao's launching of the Yan'an Rectification], HYBSL, October 14, 2017, http://w.hybsl.cn/article/13/48740 (hereafter cited as Yang, "Behind the Scenes").

61. Yang, "Behind the Scenes."

62. Zhang, "Yan'an Discourse System."

63. Gao, *How the Red Sun Rose,* 305, 306–308.

64. Gao, *How the Red Sun Rose,* 422–424.

65. Chen Yong-fa 陳永發, 延安的陰影 [Yan'an shadows] (Academica Sinica Institute of Modern History, 2015) (hereafter cited as Chen Yong-fa, *Yan'an Shadows*). The chapter on Hu, at 229–243, is titled "胡耀邦在軍委會二局" [Hu Yaobang in the CMC 2nd Bureau].

66. Qian Jiang 钱江, "胡耀邦与苏进将军" [Hu Yaobang and General Su Jin], HYBSL, July 29, 2010, http://w.hybsl.cn/article/11/109/21516 (hereafter cited as Qian, "Hu and Su Jin").

67. Chen Yong-fa, *Yan'an Shadows,* 229.

68. Chen Liming, *Biography of Hu Yaobang* (2005), 1:145; Xiao, "Record of Li Zhao," part 5.

69. Chen Yong-fa, *Yan'an Shadows,* 230.

70. Cao Ying 曹瑛, "親歷者: 整風時毛澤東為搶救運動深鞠躬道歉" [Eye-witness: During Rectification, Mao Zedong bowed deeply and apologized for the Rescue Movement], May 5, 2015, CCP History Web, https://read01.com/e50Ezm.html.

71. Zhang et al., *Biography of Hu Yaobang,* 1:92–93.

72. Xiao, "Record of Li Zhao," part 5; Chen Liming, *Biography of Hu* (2005), 1:151.

73. Fang Shi 方实, "我在延安被'抢救'" [I was 'rescued' in Yan'an], *Yanhuang Chunqiu,* October 2003; Du Hui 杜惠, "亲历延安抢救运动" [Personal experience of the Yan'an rescue campaign], *Yanhuang Chunqiu,* October 2015.

74. Wang Yugui 王玉贵, "康生延安整风标准: 长这么漂亮定是特务" [Kang Sheng's rectification standard: One who grew up this pretty must be a spy], HYBSL, January 28, 2015, http://w.hybsl.cn/article/13/50598.

75. Gao, *How the Red Sun Rose,* 486.

76. Chen Yong-fa, *Yan'an Shadows,* 234–238; Qian, "Hu and Su Jin."

77. Chen Yong-fa, *Yan'an Shadows,* 240; Zhang et al., *Biography of Hu Yaobang,* 1:94; Qian, "Hu and Su Jin."

78. Tang Fei, "胡耀邦在陕北10 年" [Hu Yaobang's ten years in North Shaanxi], HYBSL, February 14, 2007, http://w.hybsl.cn/article/11/109/1328 (hereafter cited as Tang, "Hu in North Shaanxi").

79. Qian, "Hu and Su Jin."

80. Gao, *How the Red Sun Rose,* 580–588.

81. Mao Zedong, "关于审干的九条方针和在敌后的八项政策" [Nine-clause direction on cadre examination and eight-point policy on enemy rear areas], July 30, 1943, http://db.cssn.cn/sjxz/xsjdk/mkszyjd/mzdsx/840204/84020402/201311/t20131124 _878367.shtm.

82. Gao, *How the Red Sun Rose,* 593, 595.

83. Zheng, *Hu Yaobang Chronological Materials,* April 23–June 11, 1945 (7th CCP Congress).

84. Gao Hua, "毛主席万岁"— 延安整风的完成" ["Long live Chairman Mao": The completion of Yan'an Rectification], excerpted from his book 红太阳是怎样升起的 [How the Red Sun arose] (Chinese University of Hong Kong Press, 2011), HYBSL, September 13, 2011, http://w.hybsl.cn/article/13/26823.

85. Zhang et al., *Biography of Hu Yaobang,* 1:91–93.

86. The three pledged that they would be eternally loyal to Chairman Mao, that they would not betray the CCP, and that they would not be boastful, according to Meng Fei 梦菲, "陶铸、胡耀邦、王鹤寿的 '约法三章'" [Tao Zhu, Hu Yaobang and Wang Heshou's "Three Part Covenant"], HYBSL, March 24, 2015, http://w.hybsl.cn /article/11/109/51348.

3. Winning the Wars, Securing Power

1. A. J. Baime, "Harry Truman and Hiroshima: Inside His Tense A-Bomb Vigil," History Channel, October 11, 2017.

2. David Rees, *The Defeat of Japan* (Praeger, 1997), 157–159.

3. Rees, *Defeat of Japan,* 159–160; Alex Wellerstein, "Nagasaki: The Last Bomb," *New Yorker,* August 7, 2015.

4. Tsuyoshi Hasegawa, "The Atomic Bombs and the Soviet Invasion: What Drove Japan's Decision to Surrender?," *Asia-Pacific Journal—Japan Focus* 5, no. 8 (August 2007).

5. Dieter Heinzig, *The Soviet Union and Communist China, 1945–1950: The Arduous Road to the Alliance* (M. E. Sharpe, 1998; repr., Routledge, 2015), 59–71.

6. Rana Mitter, *Forgotten Ally: China's World War II, 1937–1945* (Houghton Mifflin Harcourt, 2013), 345.

7. Mitter, *Forgotten Ally,* 347.

8. Heinzig, *Soviet Union,* 73.

9. Mitter, *Forgotten Ally,* 364; Heinzig, *Soviet Union,* 76.

10. Undated "Baidu-Baike" Chinese encyclopedia reference, "双十协定" [The Double Ten Agreement], http://baike.baidu.com/view/69735.htm.

11. Mao Zedong cable to CCP representatives in Chongqing on October 29, 1945, "同国民党谈判的补充意见" [Additional views on negotiations with the Kuomintang], https://marxistphilosophy.org/maozedong/mx4/018.htm. Mao's cable instructed CCP military forces to avoid conflict while moving toward strategic rail corridors.

12. Rees, *Defeat of Japan,* 170; Charlie Chi, "The Surrender of Japanese Forces in China, Indochina, and Formosa," Taiwan Documents Project, 2002.

13. Wang Qisheng 王奇生, "评蒋永敬 '蒋介石、毛泽东的谈打与决战,' 金冲及 '转折年代— 中国的1947年' 及 '决战— 毛泽东、蒋介石是如何应对三大战役的" [Reviews of Jiang Yongjing's "Chiang and Mao's Talking while Fighting," and Jin Chongji's "Decisive Battles of 1947" and "How Chiang and Mao Handled Three Battles"], Hu Yaobang Historical Materials Information Network (hereafter HYBSL), March 11, 2016, http://w.hybsl.cn/article/13/57536 (hereafter cited as Wang Qisheng, "Critique of Jiang and Jin").

14. Richard Bernstein, *China 1945: Mao's Revolution and America's Fateful Choice* (Knopf, 2014), 299.

15. Qian Jiang 钱江, "胡耀邦逆风千里上战场" [Hu Yaobang battled the winds for a thousand *li* to get to the battlefield], HYBSL, March 12, 2013, http://w.hybsl.cn/article/11/109/35072 (hereafter cited as Qian, "Hu Yaobang battled the winds").

16. Man Mei 满妹, 思念依然无尽： 回忆父亲胡耀邦 [Still endless yearning— Remembering father, Hu Yaobang] (Beijing chubanshe, 2005), 68.

17. Man Mei, *Remembering Father, Hu Yaobang* (Cosmos Books, 2016), 1:111. See Xiao Zushi 肖祖石, "一个不平凡的女性— 记胡耀邦夫人李昭" [An extraordinary

woman—A record of Yaobang's wife, Li Zhao], pt. 6, HYBSL, March 17, 2007, http://w.hybsl.cn/article/10/104/739.

18. Zheng Zhongbing, ed., *Hu Yaobang Chronological Materials, Long Form* (International Era, 2005), October 14, 1945. Also Qian, "Hu Yaobang battled the winds."

19. Xiaobing Li, *A History of the Modern Chinese Army* (Kentucky University Press, 2007), 70. KMT ground forces numbered two million men in eighty-six divisions; other military organizations numbered over one million and about 740,000 irregulars. Twenty-two of Chiang's divisions were American-equipped.

20. Li, *A History,* 65.

21. Li, *A History,* 71. See also "Comparing the Reality to the Rumored Number of 8 Million KMT Soldiers in the Civil War," Sina.com military blog post, November 19, 2015, http://mil.news.sina.com.cn/2015-11-19/1429844316.html. Hereafter cited as Sina.com, "Comparing Reality to Rumor."

22. Zheng, *Hu Yaobang Chronological Materials,* October 10, 1945.

23. Zhang Liqun, Zhang Ding, Yan Ruping, Tang Fei, and Li Songtian, 胡耀邦传 [Biography of Hu Yaobang], vol. 1, *1915–1976* (Renmin chubanshe, 2005), 1: 98–99 (hereafter cited as Zhang et al., *Biography of Hu Yaobang*).

24. Ambassador in China (Hurley) to President Truman, doc. 530, November 26, 1945, *Foreign Relations of the United States, Diplomatic Papers, 1945,* vol. 7: *The Far East, China,* ed. Ralph Goodwin et al. (US Government Printing Office, 1969).

25. "General Marshall's Appointment and Instructions," in *United States Relations with China: With Special Reference to the Period 1944–1949,* Department of State Publication 3573 (US Government Printing Office, 1949), pt. 1, chap. 5, "The Mission of General George C. Marshall," 132.

26. "The Cease-Fire Agreement of January 10, 1946," in *United States Relations with China,* pt. 2, chap. 5, 137; Zhang et al., *Biography of Hu Yaobang,* 1:99.

27. Zhang et al., *Biography of Hu Yaobang,* 1:99, 100.

28. Zhang et al., *Biography of Hu Yaobang,* 1:101–102.

29. I am grateful to Dennis Blasko for clarifying the roles of political commissars and heads of political departments.

30. Chen Liming, *Biography of Hu Yaobang* (Swindon Books, 2005), 1: 98.

31. He Renxue 何仁学 and Yang Feng 杨峰, "大同集宁战役：华北解放军被傅作义部重创" [The battle of Datong-Jining: North China Liberation Army hit hard by Fu Zuoyi troops], posted April 3, 2013, http://www.jianglishi.cn/zhanshi/196949.html, accessed July 4, 2021, URL no longer valid (hereafter cited as He and Yang, "Battle of Datong").

32. He and Yang, "Battle of Datong"; Zhang et al., *Biography of Hu Yaobang,* 1:102–103.

33. He and Yang, "Battle of Datong." See also "聂荣臻最耻辱一战" [Nie Rongzhen's most humiliating battle], Sina.com History, November 5, 2015, http://mil.news.sina.com.cn/2015-11-05/1727843142.html.

34. "Nie Rongzhen's Most Humiliating Battle."

35. Zhang et al., *Biography of Hu Yaobang,* 1:104.

36. Battle statistics from different KMT or CCP accounts cannot be considered accurate measures of battle outcomes. The inaccuracy results from such factors as an inability to count corpses accurately, an unwillingness to admit high casualties, and commanders' inability to determine who was wounded and evacuated and who had fled. The use of the terms "*jianmie*" or "*xiaomie,*" both of which translate as "annihilate," adds to the uncertainty. Notwithstanding, the accounts of Datong-Jining casualties being as high as twelve thousand on the KMT side and as many as a hundred thousand killed and wounded on the CCP side should not be taken lightly. Chinese civil war battles were bloody affairs, with machine guns, artillery, and occasionally aircraft taking enormous tolls on poorly equipped and poorly trained infantry attacking across open ground.

37. "The Drift toward All-Out Strife," in *United States Relations with China,* pt. 7, chap. 5, 184–195.

38. Zhang et al., *Biography of Hu Yaobang,* 1:104. See also Central Documents Research Office, "聂荣臻传 从大同集宁之战到撤离张家口" [Biography of Nie Rongzhen, from the battle of Datong-Jining to the evacuation of Zhangjiakou], http://www.quanxue.cn/ls_gonghe/niyz/NiYZ48.html (hereafter cited as "Biography of Nie Rongzhen").

39. "Biography of Nie Rongzhen."

40. Bo Yu 伯玉, "傅作义经典战役之二— 张家口" [Fu Zuoyi's second classic battle—Zhangjiakou], http://tieba.baidu.com/p/91149418 (hereafter cited as Bo, "Fu Zuoyi's Second Classic Battle").

41. Bo, "Fu Zuoyi's Second Classic Battle."

42. He and Yang, "Battle of Datong."

43. Wang Qisheng, "Critique of Jiang and Jin."

44. "The End of the Marshall Mission," in *United States Relations with China,* pt. 8, chap. 5, 217.

45. Qian Jiang 钱江, "胡耀邦在冀中战场" [Hu Yaobang in central Hebei battlefields], HYBSL, September 6, 2012, http://w.hybsl.cn/article/11/109/30803 (hereafter cited as Qian, "Hu Yaobang in Central Hebei Battlefields").

46. Qian, "Hu Yaobang in Central Hebei Battlefields"; "正太路战役" [Battle of the Zhengding-Taiyuan Line], Baidu-Baike Online Encyclopedia, http://baike.baidu.com/view/3079921.htm.

47. Zhang et al., *Biography of Hu Yaobang,* 1:112–115.

48. Christopher Lew, *The Third Chinese Revolutionary Civil War, 1945–49: An Analysis of Communist Strategy and Leadership* (Routledge, 2011), 92.

49. Zhang et al., *Biography of Hu Yaobang,* 1:117.

50. Zhang et al., *Biography of Hu Yaobang,* 1:117; Lew, *Third Chinese Revolutionary Civil War,* 93.

51. Wang Qisheng, "Critique of Jiang and Jin."

52. Mao Zedong, "Manifesto of the Chinese People's Liberation Army," October 1947, in *Selected Works of Mao Zedong*, vol. 4 (Foreign Languages Press, 1967).

53. Jiang Linping 江林平, "解放战争解放军为何越打越多" [Why the Liberation Army grew as it fought in the Liberation War], *Sina History*, February 22, 2016, https://mil.sina.cn/ls/2016-02-22/detail-ifxprucu3079190.d.html (hereafter cited as Jiang Linping, "Why the Liberation Army Grew"). See also Wang Qisheng, "Critique of Jiang and Jin."

54. Sina.com, "Comparing Reality to Rumor."

55. Wang Qisheng, "Critique of Jiang and Jin"; Jiang Linping, "Why the Liberation Army Grew."

56. Jiang Linping, "Why the Liberation Army Grew."

57. Mao Zedong, "The Present Situation and Our Tasks," report to Central Committee meeting, December 25, 1947, in *Selected Works*, vol. 4.

58. Zhang et al., *Biography of Hu Yaobang*, 1:119–126.

59. Dominic Meng-Hsuan Yang, "Noble Ghosts, Empty Graves, and Suppressed Traumas: The Heroic Tale of 'Taiyuan's Five Hundred Martyrs' in the Chinese Civil War," *Historical Reflections* 41, no. 3 (2015): 109–124. See also Chen Liming, *Biography of Hu Yaobang*, 1: 203.

60. Peng Hai 彭海, "沧桑阅尽话太原" [The vicissitudes of Taiyuan], chap. 30, "The Battle of Taiyuan," pt. 1, "Soldiers at the Gate"], http://www.tydao.com/tycs/cs30 -jiefang/cs30-1.htm (hereafter cited as Peng Hai, *Vicissitudes*).

61. Chen Liming, *Biography of Hu Yaobang*, 1: 202–203; Zhang et al., *Biography of Hu Yaobang*, 1:128–129.

62. Wang Wendong 王文栋 and Bai Meiyue 白梅月, "太原战役为何成为解放军付出代价最大的城市攻坚战?" [Why did the Battle of Taiyuan become the costliest urban assault for the PLA?], February 27, 2018, https://kknews.cc/zh-my/history /93lk525.html (hereafter cited as Wang and Bai, "Battle of Taiyuan").

63. Yang, "Noble Ghosts."

64. Wang and Bai, "Battle of Taiyuan."

65. Zheng, *Hu Yaobang Chronological Materials*, October 10 and 23, 1948.

66. Peng Hai, *Vicissitudes*, pt. 1.

67. Peng Hai, *Vicissitudes*, pt. 1.

68. Yang Yunlong 杨云龙, "闪耀着人文精神光芒的太原战役" [The Taiyuan battle that sparkled with human spirit], HYBSL, September 11, 2009, http://w.hybsl.cn /article/13/16018.

69. Zheng, *Hu Yaobang Chronological Materials*, November 29, 1948.

70. Peng Hai, *Vicissitudes*, pt. 2; Yang, "Noble Ghosts."

71. Zhang et al., *Biography of Hu Yaobang*, 1:137.

72. Mao Zedong, "Carry the Revolution through to the End," December 30, 1948, in *Selected Works*, vol. 4.

73. Peng Hai, *Vicissitudes,* pt. 3. Other accounts put the number of Yan's troops as high as 89,000.

74. Peng Hai, *Vicissitudes,* pt. 3; Zheng, *Hu Yaobang Chronological Materials,* March 17, 1949.

75. Zhang et al., *Biography of Hu Yaobang,* 1:145–146.

76. Zhang et al., *Biography of Hu Yaobang,* 1:149. See detailed account in "The Battle of Taiyuan," Wikipedia, undated, https://zh.wikipedia.org/wiki/太原戰役.

77. Yang, "Noble Ghosts." Beginning in 1951 the Nationalist government on Taiwan began an annual commemoration of the "five hundred martyrs of Taiyuan," even though investigations showed that most of the five hundred potassium cyanide pills Yan intended for his supporters were never consumed.

78. Zhang et al., *Biography of Hu Yaobang,* 1:150.

79. Zheng, *Hu Yaobang Chronological Materials,* May 4, 1949; Chen Liming 陈利明, 从小红鬼到总书记 [From little red devil to general secretary], vol. 1 (Renmin Ribao chubanshe, 2013) (hereafter cited as Chen, *Little Red Devil*), 1: 125–127.

80. Zhang et al., *Biography of Hu Yaobang,* 1:163–167.

81. Zhang et al., *Biography of Hu Yaobang,* 1:167; Mao Zedong, "The Chinese People Have Stood Up!," September 21, 1949, in *Selected Works,* vol. 4.

82. Anon. writing group, 编写组, 贺龙传 [Biography of He Long], chap. 15, part 6, 进军四川 [Advancing into Sichuan], National Cultural Information Resources Sharing Project, Shaanxi Provincial Branch, Copyright 1998, https://www.sxlib.org.cn/dfzy/rwk/bqjsldr/hl/qwts/hlz/201707/t20170719_821707.html (hereafter cited as *Biography of He Long*).

83. *Biography of He Long,* chap. 15, part 6.

84. Zhang et al., *Biography of Hu Yaobang,* 1:171–172.

85. *Biography of He Long,* chap. 15, part 6.

86. Qian Jiang 钱江, "胡耀邦和起义将领裴昌会," [Hu Yaobang and the Uprising of General Pei Changhui], HYBSL, September 7, 2007, http://w.hybsl.cn/article/103/1010/12070.

87. Chen Xianqing 陈贤庆, 民国军阀派系 [Warlord factions of the Republic of China], chap. 12, "Sichuan and Xikang," (Unity Publishing, 2007), http://www.2499cn.com/jf/junfamulu.htm.

88. Wang Rui 王锐, "主政川北的胡耀邦" [Hu Yaobang in charge of North Sichuan], HYBSL, September 16, 2009, http://w.hybsl.cn/article/10/104/16124 (hereafter cited as Wang Rui, "Hu Yaobang in Charge"). See also Zheng, *Hu Yaobang Chronological Materials,* December 18, 1949.

89. Ma Kemin 马克敏, "建国初期党的民族政策在川北区的实践" [The practice of the party's ethnic policy in North Sichuan in the early days of the founding of the country], selections from *Party History,* July 2014, http://www.dsbczzs.cn/zzshow.asp?nid=4160.

90. Pang Song 庞松, "邓小平与西南区征粮剿匪及经济恢复" [Deng Xiaoping and the southwest region's grain requisition, bandit destruction and economic recovery], Xinhuanet, April 26, 2011, http://news.qq.com/a/20110426/001046.htm, accessed June 11, 2016, URL no longer valid (hereafter cited as Pang Song, "Deng and Grain Requisition").

91. *Biography of He Long*, chap. 16, pt. 2, "土匪一定要剿灭," [The bandits will certainly be destroyed], https://www.sxlib.org.cn/dfzy/rwk/bqjsldr/hl/qwts/hlz/201707/t20170719_821705.html.

92. Anon., "胡耀邦在川北大事辑录" [A compilation of major events for Hu Yaobang in North Sichuan], HYBSL, September 18, 2009, http://w.hybsl.cn/article/10/104/16023.

93. Wang Rui, "Hu Yaobing in Charge"; Chen Jun 陈钧, "胡耀邦在川北" [Hu Yaobang in North Sichuan], HYBSL, September 17, 2009, http://w.hybsl.cn/article/10/104/16131.

94. Yang Kuisong 杨奎松, "新中国'镇压反革命'运动研究" [Research on new China's campaign to "suppress counterrevolutionaries"], Aisixiang Network, December 13, 2011, http://www.aisixiang.com/data/48152.

95. Wang Haiguang 王海光, "中共对新区的接管：从军事占领、政治占领到社会占领" [The CCP takeover of new regions: From military to political to social occupation], March 30, 2010, http://www.aisixiang.com/data/32718 (hereafter cited as Wang Haiguang, "CCP Takeover of New Regions").

96. Wang Rui, "Hu Yaobang in Charge"; Zhang et al., *Biography of Hu Yaobang*, 1:198.

97. Zhang et al., *Biography of Hu Yaobang*, 1:198.

98. There is terminological vagueness in PRC descriptions of actions against "enemies" (*diren*), including "class enemies" (*jieji diren*), in nonbattlefield situations. But given the levels of violence in the pacification of the southwest in 1950–1952, "annihilate" probably means "kill."

99. Yang Kuisong, "新中国'镇压反革命运动'研究" [Researching new China's "suppress counterrevolutionaries campaign"], *History Monthly,* January 2006 (hereafter cited as Yang Kuisong, "Zhenfan 2006"); republished as Yang Kuisong, "Reconsidering the Campaign to Suppress Counterrevolutionaries," *China Quarterly* 193 (2008): 102–121.

100. Pang Song, "Deng and Grain Requisition."

101. See, for example, Baidu-Baike encyclopedic reference, "西南剿匪," [Bandit annihilation in the Southwest], June 13, 2016, http://baike.baidu.com/view/1153880.htm.

102. Yang Kuisong, "新中国镇反运动始末" [New China's suppression of counterrevolutionaries from start to finish], June 22, 2012, https://club.6parkbbs.com/chan1/index.php?app=forum&act=threadview&tid=12094298, (hereafter cited as Yang

Kuisong, "Zhenfan 2011"). See also Yin Shusheng 尹曙生, "毛泽东与第三次全国公安会议" [Mao Zedong and the third National Public Security Congress], HYBSL, May 21, 2014, http://w.hybsl.cn/article/13/46378 (hereafter cited as Yin, "Third Public Security Congress").

103. Pang Song, "Deng and Grain Requisition."

104. Yang Kuisong, "Zhenfan 2006"; Frank Dikötter, *The Tragedy of Liberation: A History of the Chinese Revolution, 1945–1957* (Bloomsbury, 2013), 86–88; Huang Zhong 黄钟, "第一次镇反运动考察" [Examination of the first Zhenfan campaign], HYBSL, December 29, 2014, http://w.hybsl.cn/article/13/50141 (hereafter cited as Huang Zhong, "Examination").

105. Huang Zhong, "Examination."

106. Hu Deping 胡德平, "父亲读 三国演义 的几个片断— 修改名联" [Father revised several couplets from *Romance of the Three Kingdoms*], HYBSL, September 9, 2011, http://w.hybsl.cn/article/11/110/26783.

107. Zheng, *Hu Yaobang Chronological Materials*, August 1950 speech to North Sichuan Military District, HYBSL, August 22, 2007, http://w.hybsl.cn/article/11/109/2195.

108. Yin, "Third Public Security Congress."

109. Pan Jiazhao 潘嘉钊, "邓小平曾因何事批评重庆'镇压不够不及时'" [Why did Deng Xiaoping criticize Chongqing's "suppression is too little and too late?"], China Police Web, December 30, 2015, https://read01.com/zh-sg/5zRG2E.html, accessed July 8, 2021, URL no longer valid; Wang Haiguang, "CCP Takeover of New Regions."

110. "第三次全国公安会议决议" [Resolution of the Third National Conference on Public Security], May 12, 2012, http://www.zhzky.com/news/?5193.html.

111. Yang, "Zhenfan 2011."

112. Yang Kuisong, "暴力土改及其原因" [Violent land reform and its causes], September 12, 2018, *Memories of the Five Black Classes,* https://botanwang.com/articles/201809/暴力土改及其原因.html (hereafter cited as Yang Kuisong, "Violent Land Reform").

113. Wang Anping 王安平, Han Liang 韩亮, and Zhu Hua 朱华, "胡耀邦与川北土地改革" [Hu Yaobang and North Sichuan land reform], *CCP Historical Research* 1 (January 2010): 97–107, http://www.nssd.org/articles/article_detail.aspx?id=33147609, accessed June 24, URL no longer valid (hereafter cited as Wang et al., "North Sichuan Land Reform").

114. Luo Pinghan 罗平汉, "地改革运动是动员农民参加革命的有效方式" [The land reform movement effectively mobilized peasants to join the revolution], HYBSL, June 20, 2016, http://w.hybsl.cn/article/13/59648.

115. Wang et al., "North Sichuan Land Reform."

116. Yang, "Violent Land Reform."

117. Zhang et al., *Biography of Hu Yaobang*, 1:205; Qian Jiang, "胡耀邦是怎样进入邓小平视野的" [How did Hu Yaobang come into Deng Xiaoping's field of view?], Renminwang, December 14, 2015, http://dangshi.people.com.cn/n1/2015/1214/c85037 -27923929.html (hereafter cited as Qian Jiang, "Field of View").

118. Wang et al., "North Sichuan Land Reform"; Zhang et al., *Biography of Hu Yaobang*, 1:206.

119. Tian Jiyun 田纪云, "近距离感受胡耀邦" [Experiencing Hu Yaobang at close range], *Yanhuang Chunqiu,* October 2004, https://www.aisixiang.com/data/4455 .html.

120. Qian Jiang, "Field of View"; Wang Daming 王大明, "邓小平打桥牌与胡耀邦争冠军" [Deng Xiaoping competed with Hu Yaobang for the bridge championship], Duowei news, August 19, 2014, http://www.wenxuecity.com/news/2014/08/19 /3529921.html.

121. Yang Kuisong, "毛泽东与三反运动" [Mao Zedong and the Three Antis campaign], *Shi Lin,* April 2006, http://w.hybsl.cn/article/13/1858.

122. Zhang Ming 张鸣, "三反"成了一"反," ["Three antis" became one "anti"], HYBSL, August 30, 2013, http://w.hybsl.cn/article/13/40160 (hereafter cited as Zhang Ming, "'Three Antis'").

123. Zhou Zhen 周震, "反腐倡廉的大会战" [The great battle to fight corruption and advocate probity], HYBSL, March 4, 2014, http://w.hybsl.cn/article/13/45043 (hereafter cited as Zhou Zhen, "Great Battle").

124. Zhou Zhen, "Great Battle."

125. Zhang Ming, "'Three Antis.'" See Alexander V. Pantsov, with Steven I. Levine, *Deng Xiaoping: A Revolutionary Life* (Oxford University Press, 2015), 148.

126. Chen Liming, *Little Red Devil*, 1: 157–158; Zheng, *Hu Yaobang Chronological Materials,* various entries for 1952.

127. Zhou Zhen, "Great Battle." North Sichuan reported that only 17 percent of its party cadres were involved in corrupt activities, a significantly lower percentage than reported for the other provinces of the Southwest Bureau.

128. Yang Zhizhao 杨治钊, "胡耀邦情牵拆迁户" [Hu Yaobang's emotions about housing destruction], HYBSL, May 27, 2016, http://w.hybsl.cn/article/11/109/59152. Zhang cites only "has strong views, doesn't blindly follow" from Deng's appraisal. Zhang et al., *Biography of Hu Yaobang*, 1:230.

129. Deng Xiaoping, "三反五反运动应当防止'左'的偏向" [The Three Anti / Five Anti campaigns should guard against a "left" bias], May 11, 1952, https://wenku.baidu .com/view/d4527353ad02de80d4d84019.html.

130. Zhang et al., *Biography of Hu Yaobang*, 1:228.

131. Zheng, *Hu Yaobang Chronological Materials,* late June 1952.

132. Huang Tianxiang 黄天祥, "胡耀邦在川北" [Hu Yaobang in North Sichuan], HYBSL, September 18, 2009, http://w.hybsl.cn/article/10/104/16120.

4. Growing Doubts

1. Man Mei 满妹, 思念依然无尽：回忆父亲胡耀邦 [Still endless yearning: Remembering father, Hu Yaobang] (Beijing chubanshe, 2005) (hereafter cited as Man Mei, *Endless Yearning*), 68–69; Zhang Liqun, Zhang Ding, Yan Ruping, Tang Fei, and Li Gongtian, *Biography of Hu Yaobang* (Renmin chubanshe, 2005) (hereafter cited as Zhang et al., *Biography of Hu Yaobang*), 1:231–232. See also Gao Yong, *I Was Hu Yaobang's Secretary* (Joint Publishing, 2014), 3 (hereafter cited as Gao, *Secretary*).

2. Zheng Zhongbing, ed., *Hu Yaobang Chronological Materials, Long Form* (International Era, 2005), August 1, 1952.

3. Gao, *Secretary*, 3–4; Zheng, *Hu Yaobang Chronological Materials*, August 1952.

4. Man Mei, *Endless Yearning*, 99; Zhang et al., *Biography of Hu Yaobang*, 1:231.

5. Gao, *Secretary*, 4.

6. Chen Liming, *Hu Yaobang: From Little Red Devil to General Secretary* (Renmin Ribao, 2013), 1:165.

7. See, for example: Frederick Teiwes, *Politics and Purges in China: Rectification and the Decline of Party Norms, 1950–1965* (M. E. Sharpe, 1979), chap. 4; Andrew G. Walder, *China under Mao: A Revolution Derailed* (Harvard University Press, 2015), chap. 6; Yuan Xi 袁晞, "毛泽东时代的常委和常委会" [The Standing Committee and its meetings in the Mao era], Hu Yaobang Historical Materials Information Network (hereafter HYBSL), March 26, 2016, http://w.hybsl.cn/article/13/57831.

8. Pang Song 庞松, "高岗、饶漱石问题研究述评" [A review of research on the Gao Gang–Rao Shushi problem], HYBSL, July 11, 2014, http://w.hybsl.cn/article/13/47200 (hereafter cited as Pang, "Review of Research.")

9. The details of Mao Anying's death remain secret, but rumors abound. Li Rui, formerly one of Mao's *mishu*, claimed that Mao became distraught over the death of his son and possible heir, which was a factor in Mao's later harsh treatment of Peng. See Wang Shubai 汪澍白, "彭德怀的厄运是如何注定的" [How Peng Dehuai's doom was decided], *Yanhuang Chunqiu*, October 2002 (hereafter cited as Wang Shubai, "Peng Dehuai's Doom").

10. The term *zhongyang* (中央) is used in CCP parlance both as an adjective—as in Central Committee—and as a noun, usually translated as "the Center." It refers to an entity—the Central authority—which may be a collective leadership, meaning the Central Committee or the Politburo or the Politburo Standing Committee, or the chairman.

11. Zheng, *Hu Yaobang Chronological Materials*, August 14 and 16, 1952.

12. Central Leadership Database, "中国共青团大事记 (1919–2005)" [China Communist Youth League record of major events], vol. 1: 1919–2005, HYBSL, February 14, 2007, http://w.hybsl.cn/article/13/346.

13. Zhang et al., *Biography of Hu Yaobang,* 1:233; Zheng, *Hu Yaobang Chronological Materials,* August 23 and 30, 1952.

14. Central Leadership Database, "中国新民主主义青年团第一次全国代表大会" [The First National Congress of the China New Democratic Youth League], http://m.cyol.com/content/2017-04/25/content_15990078.htm.

15. Zheng, *Hu Yaobang Chronological Materials,* September 1952.

16. Hu Yaobang 胡耀邦, "在毛主席的亲切教导下把青年工作更加推向前进" [Under the kind guidance of Chairman Mao, press youth work forward more], September 14, 1952, HYBSL, http://w.hybsl.cn/article/11/107/1425.

17. Zhang et al., *Biography of Hu Yaobang,* 1:250.

18. Zhang et al., *Biography of Hu Yaobang,* 1:238; Yang Zhongmei, *Hu Yaobang: A Chinese Biography* (M. E. Sharpe, 1988), 86.

19. Yang Zhongmei, *Hu Yaobang,* 87; Sheng Yujiu 盛禹九, "胡耀邦和'中国青年'" [Hu Yaobang and *Zhongguo Qingnian*], *Tongzhou gongjin,* November 23, 2015, https://cul.sina.cn/zl/2015-11-23/hiszl-ifxkwuxx1725193.d.html (hereafter cited as Sheng, "Hu Yaobang and China Youth").

20. Zhong Peizhang 钟沛璋, "我和张黎群办'中国青年报'遭难记" [A record of problems Zhang Liqun and I had managing *China Youth News*], *Yanhuang Chunqiu,* August 2003.

21. Cao Zhixiong 曹治雄, "我给胡耀邦当秘书" [I was a *mishu* for Hu Yaobang], *Yanhuang Chunqiu,* March 2004 (hereafter cited as Cao Zhixiong, "*Mishu*").

22. Sheng Yujiu, "Hu Yaobang and China Youth."

23. Zhong Peizhang, "Record of Problems."

24. Cao Zhixiong, "*Mishu*"; Zhang et al., *Biography of Hu Yaobang,* 1:240–241.

25. Jiang Zhongping 蒋仲平, "耀邦与我们共青人" [Hu Yaobang and our Communist Youth," *Yanhuang Chunqiu,* May 2006, http://w.hybsl.cn/article/10/104/1442.

26. Hu Yaobang, "把我国青年引向最伟大的目标" [Lead our youth toward the greatest goals], Report to the Eighth CCP Congress, September 25, 1956, http://w.hybsl.cn/article/11/107/1805.

27. Zheng, *Hu Yaobang Chronological Materials,* September 27, 1954.

28. Wang Haiguang 王海光, "高饶事件的再解读" [Reinterpretation of the Gao Rao incident], HYBSL, May 25, 2015, http://w.hybsl.cn/article/13/52383 (hereafter cited as Wang Haiguang, "Reinterpretation"). Also Lin Yunhui 林蕴晖, "无中生有的"高饶联盟" [The "something out of nothing" Gao-Rao alliance], HYBSL, June 27, 2011, http://w.hybsl.cn/article/13/26186 (hereafter cited as Lin, "Something out of Nothing").

29. Pang, "Review of Research"; Lin, "Something out of Nothing"; Frank Dikötter, *The Tragedy of Liberation: A History of the Chinese Revolution, 1945–1957* (Bloomsbury Press, 2013), 231–233.

30. Wang Haiguang, "Reinterpretation."

31. Lin, "Something out of Nothing."

32. Wang Haiguang, "Reinterpretation"; Hu Fuchen 胡甫臣, "高岗和毛泽东" [Gao Gang and Mao Zedong], Aisixiang Network, January 1, 2007, http://www.aisixiang.com/data/12716.html.

33. Andrew Walder, *China under Mao,* chap. 5, "The Socialist Economy."

34. Luo Pinghan 罗平汉, "1956年的冒进与反冒进" [Rash advance and opposing rash advance in 1956], HYBSL, November 4, 2014, http://w.hybsl.cn/article/13/49105 (hereafter cited as Luo Pinghan, "1956 Rash Advance"); Shen Zhihua 沈志华, "周恩来与1956年的反冒进" [Zhou Enlai and opposing rash advance in 1956], *Shi Lin,* January 2009, http://www.71.cn/2012/0814/685617.shtml (hereafter cited as Shen Zhihua, "Zhou Enlai in 1956."

35. Ma Shuangyou 马双有, "刘周为何要反冒进" [Why Liu and Zhou wanted to oppose rash advance], HYBSL, April 26, 2016, http://w.hybsl.cn/article/13/58471.

36. Luo Pinghan, "1956 Rash Advance"; Gao Huamin 高化民, "1955 年'砍社风波'真相" [The truth about the "co-op busting" disturbances in 1955], *Yanhuang Chunqiu,* August 2002 (hereafter cited as Gao Huamin, "The Truth"); Yang Mingwei 杨明伟, "50 年代中后期的毛泽东与周恩来" [Mao Zedong and Zhou Enlai in the mid-to-late 1950s], in several issues of *Yanhuang Chunqiu,* 1999–2002, aggregated at http://www.yhcw.net/famine/Reports/zhou_mao_00.html (hereafter cited as Yang Mingwei, "Mao and Zhou").

37. Mao Zedong, "On the Cooperative Transformation of Agriculture," July 31, 1955, in *Selected Works of Mao Zedong,* vol. 5 (Foreign Languages Press, 1977. Online at https://www.marxists.org/reference/archive/mao/selected-works/volume-5/mswv5_44.htm.

38. Mao Zedong, "On the Cooperative Transformation."

39. Guoguang Wu, *The Anatomy of Political Power in China* (Marshall Cavendish, 2005), chap. 5, 99–115.

40. Mao Zedong, "Prefaces to Socialist Upsurge in the Countryside," in *Selected Works,* vol. 5, September and December 1955, https://www.marxists.org/reference/archive/mao/selected-works/volume-5/mswv5_47.htm.

41. Shen Zhihua, "Zhou Enlai in 1956"; Liu Wusheng 刘武生, "周恩来与冒进、反冒进、反反冒进" [Zhou Enlai and rash advance, opposing rash advance, and opposing opposition to rash advance], HYBSL, November 21, 2011, http://w.hybsl.cn/article/13/27600.

42. Yang Mingwei, "Mao and Zhou"; Shen Zhihua, "Zhou Enlai in 1956."

43. Zhang et al., *Biography of Hu Yaobang,* 1:284–286; Man Mei, *Endless Yearning,* 236–237.

44. Yang Kuisong 杨奎松, 毛泽东与莫斯科的恩恩怨怨 [Mao Zedong and Moscow grudges] (Jiangxi, 1999), 387; Alexander V. Pantsov, with Steven I. Levine, *Deng Xiaoping: A Revolutionary Life* (Oxford University Press, 2015), 165–166.

45. Pantsov and Levine, *Deng Xiaoping*, 169.

46. Pantsov and Levine, *Deng Xiaoping*, 172–173.

47. Liu Shaoqi, "The Political Report of the Central Committee of the Communist Party of China to the Eighth National Congress of the Communist Party of China," September 15, 1956, https://www.marxists.org/subject/china/documents/cpc/8th_congress.htm.

48. Liu Shaoqi, "The Political Report."

49. "The 8th National Congress of the Communist Party of China," available at http://www.chinatoday.com/org/cpc/cpc_8th_congress_standing_polibureau.htm.

50. Anonymous, "刘源谈刘少奇与毛泽东: 毛刘分裂革命一败涂地" [Liu Yuan on Liu Shaoqi and Mao Zedong: When Mao and Liu split the revolution was a failure], HYBSL, December 2, 2016, http://w.hybsl.cn/article/13/63357.

51. Zhu Zuoxun 朱佐勋, "毛泽东与'大鸣大放" [Mao Zedong and "great blooming and contending"], *Yanhuang Chunqiu,* July 2010.

52. Zhu Zheng 朱正, "中国现代知识份子的消失" [1957: The disappearance of China's modern intellectuals], HYBSL, November 21, 2012, http://w.hybsl.cn/article/13/32286 (hereafter cited as Zhu Zheng, "Disappearance."

53. Mao Zedong, "Things Are Beginning to Change," May 15, 1957, in *Selected Works,* vol. 5, https://www.marxists.org/reference/archive/mao/selected-works/volume-5/mswv5_61.htm.

54. Mao Zedong, "Muster Our Forces to Repulse the Rightists' Wild Attacks," June 8, 1957, online English version at https://www.marxists.org/reference/archive/mao/selected-works/volume-5/mswv5_63.htm.

55. "Education through labor" was generally distinguished from "labor reform" (*laogai*), which was for petty criminals; but due to the large influx of political prisoners in the mid-1950s the Ministry of Public Security often assigned them to the same facilities. See Yin Shusheng 尹曙生, "劳动教养和反右派斗争" [Education through labor and the anti-rightist struggle], *Yanhuang Chunqiu,* April 2010.

56. Guo Daohui 郭道晖, "毛泽东发动整风的初衷" [Mao Zedong's original intention for launching the rectification], *Yanhuang Chunqiu,* February 2009 (hereafter cited as Guo Daohui, "Mao Zedong's Original Intention."

57. Guo Daohui, "Mao Zedong's Original Intention."

58. Zhu Zheng, "Disappearance."

59. Mao Zedong, "The Situation in the Summer of 1957," in *Selected Works,* vol. 5, July 1957.

60. Li Honglin 李洪林, 中國思想運動史 [A history of Chinese ideological movements] (Cosmos, 1999), 102–103.

61. Hu Yaobang, "团结全国青年建设社会主义的新中国" [Unite the youth of the country to build a new socialist China], Opening address to CYL Congress, April 15, 1957, HYBSL, August 28, 2007, http://w.hybsl.cn/article/11/109/2661.

62. Mao, "Things Are Beginning to Change."

63. Zhang et al., *Biography of Hu Yaobang,* 1:290.

64. Zheng, *Hu Yaobang Chronological Materials,* September 1957.

65. Zhong Peizhang, "Record of Problems."

66. Dai Huang 戴煌, 胡耀邦与平反冤假错案 [Hu Yaobang and the redress of unjust, false and wrong cases] (Xinhua, 1998), 8; Man Mei, *Endless Yearning,* 244.

67. Zheng, *Hu Yaobang Chronological Materials,* February 1958.

68. Deng Xiaoping, "关于整风运动的报告" [Report on the rectification campaign], September 23, 1957, https://banned-historical-archives.github.io/articles/5269ce2c8f/.

69. Central Leadership Database, "胡耀邦同志在中共八届三中全会上的发言" [Comrade Hu Yaobang's speech at the Third Plenary Session of the Eighth CCP Central Committee], October 9, 1957, in *Compilation of League Documents: 1957* (China New Democratic League Central General Office, 1959), Chinese University of Hong Kong archival research, October 2015.

70. Man Mei, *Endless Yearning,* 246–247.

71. Zheng, *Hu Yaobang Chronological Materials,* July 12, 1958.

72. Yan Ruping 严如平, "吾爱吾师，吾尤爱真理" [I love my teacher, but I especially love the truth], *Yanhuang Chunqiu,* April 2002.

73. Pantsov and Levine, *Deng Xiaoping,* 186.

74. Pantsov and Levine, *Deng Xiaoping,* 189; Ye Yonglie 叶永烈, "毛泽东批周恩来和陈云：离右派50米远" [Mao Zedong criticizes Zhou Enlai and Chen Yun: "50 meters away from the right wing"], HYBSL, January 4, 2009, http://w.hybsl.cn/article/13/11741 (hereafter cited as Ye Yonglie, "50 Meters Away").

75. Jiang Changqing 姜长青, "'大跃进'前周恩来的三次检讨" [Zhou Enlai's three confessions before the Great Leap Forward], HYBSL, February 17, 2009, http://w.hybsl.cn/article/13/12614 (hereafter cited as Jiang, "Zhou Enlai's Three Confessions."

76. Luo Pinghan, "发动'大跃进'的1958年南宁会议" [The 1958 Nanning Conference that launched the "Great Leap Forward"], Xinhua News, December 15, 2014, http://dangshi.people.com.cn/n/2014/1215/c85037-26210862.html.

77. Ye Yonglie, "50 Meters Away."

78. Ma Shuangyou, "毛泽东四批'反冒进'" Mao Zedong's four criticisms of "Opposing Rash Advance"], HYBSL, April 28, 2016, http://w.hybsl.cn/article/13/58526.

79. Central Leadership Database, "中国共产党第八次全国代表大会第二次会议 (1958年5月5–23日)" [The CCP's Eighth Central Committee, Second session (May 5–23, 1958)], http://dangshi.people.com.cn/GB/151935/176588/176596/10556148.html, accessed March 30, 2017, URL no longer valid.

80. Jiang, "Zhou Enlai's Three Confessions."

81. Lin Yunhui, "20世纪50年代的个人崇拜" [The cult of personality in the 1950s], HYBSL, January 4, 2015, http://w.hybsl.cn/article/13/50216.

82. Lin Yunhui, "毛泽东1958年压制反对声音：与其你独裁，不如我独裁" [Mao Zedong suppressed opposing voices in 1958: Your dictatorship is not as good as my dictatorship], HYBSL, February 26, 2013, http://w.hybsl.cn/article/13/34761 (hereafter cited as Lin Yunhui, "Your Dictatorship").

83. Lin Yunhui, "Your Dictatorship."

84. Zheng, *Hu Yaobang Chronological Materials,* May 5–23, 1958.

85. Zheng, *Hu Yaobang Chronological Materials,* July 1, 1958.

86. Wu Xinfeng 吴欣峰, "1958年军委扩大会议真相" [The truth about the 1958 enlarged military committee meeting," *Yanhuang Chunqiu,* January 2008.

87. Playwright and political commentator Sha Yexin 沙叶新 wrote that the *jiantao* was a useful tool Mao used to maintain his dominance over other party leaders. See Sha Yexin, "'检讨'文化" [The culture of "self-confession"], Aisixiang Network, September 5, 2005, http://www.aisixiang.com/data/8557.html.

88. Chung Yen-lin 鍾延麟, "1958 年鄧小平在解放軍 「反教條主義」 運動中之角色與活動" [The role and activities of Deng Xiaoping in the PLA's "anti-dogmatism" campaign in 1958], *Mainland China Research* 49, no. 4 (December 2006): 77–103.

89. Lin Yunhui, "1958年中央军委扩大会议纪实" [A record of the 1958 CMC expanded meeting], *Party History Expo,* March 2005, http://www.aisixiang.com/data/65991.html.

90. Central Party History Research Office, 中国共产党历史, 第二卷 (1949–1978), *History of the Chinese Communist Party, vol. 2, 1949–1978* (CCP Party History Publishing House, 2011).

91. Wang Quanbao 王全宝 and Wang Di 王迪, "中共党史二卷：三年自然灾害死亡人口1000多万" [History of the CCP, vol. 2: More than 10 million people died in three years of natural disasters], China News Network, January 14, 2011, http://w.hybsl.cn/article/13/24703.

92. Yang Jisheng 杨继绳, "1958–1962中国大饥荒" [1958–1962: China's great famine], September 5, 2010, http://www.ywpw.com/forums/history/p0/html/830.html#google_vignette (hereafter cited as Yang, "China's Great Famine").

93. Yang Jisheng, *Tombstone: The Great Chinese Famine, 1958–1962,* trans. Stacy Mosher and Guo Jian (Farrar, Straus and Giroux, 2013), 429–430.

94. Frank Dikötter, "Mao's Great Leap to Famine," *New York Times,* December 15, 2010.

95. Even the 1981 "Resolution on Certain Questions in the History of Our Party since the Founding of the People's Republic of China" continued to perpetrate the myth that external forces were at least partly responsible. The English-language version of the resolution is available at https://www.marxists.org/subject/china/documents/cpc/history/01.htm.

96. Yang, "China's Great Famine."

97. Jia Yanmin 贾艳敏 and Zhu Jin 朱进, "国内学者'大饥荒'问题研究述评" [A review of domestic scholars' research on the "Great Famine"], *Jiangsu University*

Journal of Social Science 17, no. 2 (March 2015), Aisixiang Network, August 23, 2016, https://www.aisixiang.com/data/101083.

98. Li Rui 李锐, "'大跃进'的高潮北戴河会议" [The Beidaihe meeting, high tide of the "Great Leap Forward"], HYBSL, July 10, 2012, http://w.hybsl.cn/article/13/30201 (hereafter cited as Li Rui, "High Tide"); also Xie Chuntao 谢春涛, "1958年北戴河会议述评" [The story of the 1958 Beidaihe meeting], http://www.yhcw.net/famine/Reports/r020121a.html (hereafter cited as Xie Chuntao, "Story of Beidaihe").

99. Yang Jisheng, *Tombstone,* 165–166.

100. See Central Party History and Documentation Institute, "第一次郑州会议 (1958年11月2–10日" [The first Zhengzhou meeting (November 2–10, 1958)], http://www.dswxyjy.org.cn/n/2012/1129/c244520-19738174.html.

101. Yang, *Tombstone,* 169.

102. Li Rui, "High Tide"; Xie Chuntao, "Story of Beidaihe."

103. Luo Pinghan, "一九五八年全民大炼钢" [In 1958, the whole nation made steel], HYBSL, August 1, 2014, http://w.hybsl.cn/article/13/47542.

104. Shi Lianzhi 师连枝, "大跃进工作方法归谬" [Great Leap Forward work methods were absurd], *Socialist Studies,* September 2009, http://w.hybsl.cn/article/13/3074.

105. Luo Pinghan, "1958年的神话：'跑步进入共产主义'" [The magic incantation of 1958: "Running into Communism"], HYBSL, October 27, 2014, http://w.hybsl.cn/article/13/48909.

106. Luo Pinghan, "毛泽东与庐山会议前人民公社的整顿" [Mao Zedong and adjustment of communes before the Lushan meeting], HYBSL, March 20, 2015, http://w.hybsl.cn/article/13/51303.

107. Xiao Donglian 萧冬连, "滑向大饥荒的 '大跃进'" [The "Great Leap Forward" slides into the Great Famine], HYBSL, December 27, 2013, http://w.hybsl.cn/article/13/43971.

108. Zhang Beigen 张北根, "'大跃进'运动的决策问题研究" [Research on decision-making problems in the "Great Leap Forward" campaign], *Journal of Yunnan Administrative College,* December 2012, http://www.aisixiang.com/data/60170.html.

109. See Li Rui 李锐, 庐山会议实录 [True record of the Lushan meeting] (Henan People's Publishing House, 1996) (hereafter cited as Li Rui, *True Record*).

110. Wang Shubai, "Peng Dehuai's doom."

111. Li Rui, *True Record,* 99.

112. Peng Dehuai 彭德怀, "我的一点意见 (1959年给毛泽东的信)" [My small complaint (letter to Mao Zedong, 1959)], HYBSL, October 14, 2009, http://w.hybsl.cn/article/13/16643.

113. Huang Kecheng 黄克诚, "我所知道的庐山会议" [What I know about the Lushan meeting], October 22, 2014, http://www.aisixiang.com/data/79148.html.

114. Wen Ji 闻集, "张闻天在庐山会议上的抗争" [Zhang Wentian's opposition at the Lushan meeting], *Yanhuang Chunqiu,* December 2000.

115. Mao Zedong, "Speech at the Lushan Conference," July 23, 1959, in *Selected Works,* vol. 8, (Kranti Publications, Secunderabad, India, 1994), https://www.marxists.org/reference/archive/mao/selected-works/volume-8/mswv8_34.htm.

116. Zhang Sheng 张胜, "康生庐山评彭德怀万言书：他是想要换掉主席!" [Kang Sheng criticized Peng Dehuai's manifesto at Lushan: He wants to replace the chairman!], HYBSL, January 12, 2012, http://w.hybsl.cn/article/13/28285.

117. Gao, *Secretary,* 50–51; Man Mei, *Endless Yearning,* 250–251.

118. For a discussion of "declaring one's position" as a method the CCP uses to exert political pressure and enforce uniformity, see Sha Yexin 沙叶新, "'表态'文化" ["Biaotai" culture], Aisixiang Network, September 5, 2005, http://www.aisixiang.com/data/8555.html.

119. Zheng, *Hu Yaobang Chronological Materials,* August 2, 1959.

120. Zhang et al., *Biography of Hu Yaobang,* 1:304–305.

121. Eighth Plenum of the Eighth Central Committee, "关于以彭德怀同志为首的反党集团 的错误的决议" [Resolution on the errors of the anti-party group headed by Comrade Peng Dehuai], dated August 16, 1959, http://www.yhcw.net/famine/Documents/d020202n.html.

122. Central Leadership Database, "中央军委扩大会议(1959年8月18日—9月12日)" [Central Military Commission Expanded Meeting (8/18 —9/12/1959)] has been deleted from PRC official websites, although it is still available unofficially at http://www.yhcw.net/famine/Documents/d020202n.html. Eventually all the decisions of the expanded CMC meeting of August 1959 were rescinded.

123. Zhang et al., *Biography of Hu Yaobang,* 1:305.

5. Into the Maelstrom

1. Zheng Zhongbing, ed., *Hu Yaobang Chronological Materials, Long Version* (International Era 2005), entries for September 1960.

2. Zhang Liqun, Zhang Ding, Yan Ruping, Tang Fei, and Li Gongtian, *Biography of Hu Yaobang,* 1:310–311.

3. Zheng, *Hu Yaobang Chronological Materials,* March 5, 1960, and April 8, 1960.

4. Yin Shusheng 尹曙生, "公安工作 '大跃进'" [The "Great Leap Forward" in public security work], *Yanhuang Chunqiu,* January 2010.

5. Anon., "大饥荒年代的北京 '特需'" [Beijing's "special supplies" during the famine era], *Shi Hai,* July 1, 2021, https://www.secretchina.com/news/gb/2021/07/01/975235.html.

6. Gao Hua 高华, "大饥荒与四清运动的起源" [The Great Famine and the origins of the Four Clean-Ups campaign], Hu Yaobang Historical Materials Information Network (hereafter HYBSL), September 9, 2008, http://w.hybsl.cn/article/13/9664 (hereafter cited as Gao Hua, "Great Famine"); Yang Jisheng, *Tombstone: The*

Great Chinese Famine, 1958–1962, trans. Stacy Mosher and Guo Jian (Farrar, Straus and Giroux, 2013), 23–31.

7. Yang Jisheng, *Tombstone,* 61–63; Zhang Qianfan 张千帆, "从 '信阳事件' 看央地关系" [Looking at Central-local relations from the "Xinyang incident"], HYBSL, September 14, 2009, http://w.hybsl.cn/article/13/16069.

8. Yin Shusheng 尹曙生, "曾希圣是如何掩盖严重灾荒的" [How Zeng Xisheng covered up a serious famine], *Yanhuang Chunqiu,* December 2015.

9. Yang Jisheng, "打捞大饥荒记忆" [Salvaging memories of the Great Famine], HYBSL, May 15, 2012, http://w.hybsl.cn/article/13/29700.

10. Yang Jisheng, "公共食堂的历史记忆" [The historical record of the public mess halls], HYBSL, May 7, 2010, http://w.hybsl.cn/article/13/20211.

11. Chen Yiran 陈一然, "毛已知亩产造假 1959年经济计划继续"跃进" [Mao already knew per mu yields were falsified, and continued the Great Leap in 1959], excerpted from his book, 亲历共和国60年 [Sixty Years of the Republic] (Renmin chubanshe, Beijing, 2009), HYBSL, October 12, 2012, http://w.hybsl.cn/article/13/31437; Gao Hua, "Great Famine."

12. Xiao Xiang 萧象, "毛泽东对于人的生命态度与大饥荒的悲剧发生" [Mao Zedong's attitude toward human life and the tragedy of the Great Famine], Aisixiang Network, December 25, 2015, https://chinadigitaltimes.net/chinese/275860.html.

13. Yang Jisheng, *Tombstone,* 317.

14. Gao Hua, "Great Famine."

15. Yang Kuisong 杨奎松, "毛泽东是如何发现大饥荒的" [How Mao Zedong discovered the Great Famine], Aisixiang Network, April 17, 2015, https://www.aisixiang.com/data/81435.html.

16. Liu Yuan 刘源 and He Jiadong 何家栋, "毛泽东为什么要打倒刘少奇" [Why Mao Zedong wanted to overthrow Liu Shaoqi], HYBSL, April 6, 2010, http://w.hybsl.cn/article/13/19576 (hereafter cited as Liu and He, "Why Mao Wanted Liu Out").

17. Li Zhisui, *The Private Life of Chairman Mao,* trans. Tai Hung-chao (Random House, 1994), 400.

18. Wang Haiguang 王海光, "林彪私密日记：毛泽东善用捏造打倒对手" [Lin Biao's private diary: Mao uses fabrications to defeat his opponents], December 14, 2014, http://www.aboluowang.com/2014/1214/485956.html.

19. Zheng, *Hu Yaobang Chronological Materials,* September 4–29, 1961.

20. Qian Jiang 钱江, "胡耀邦和'包产到户'的初次接触" [Hu Yaobang's initial contact with the "household responsibility system" in the famine era], HYBSL, April 28, 2016, http://w.hybsl.cn/article/11/110/58558 (hereafter cited as Qian, "Famine Era").

21. Qian, "Famine Era."

22. Gao Yong 高勇, 我给胡耀邦当秘书 [I was Hu Yaobang's secretary] (Joint Publishing Hong Kong, 2014), 73–74 (hereafter cited as Gao, *Secretary*).

23. Qian, "Famine Era."

24. Tang Zhengmang 唐正芒, "1962年中央解决粮食问题内幕: 七千人大会吃饭 . . ." [The inside story of the Center's 1962 solution to a food problem: Feeding the seven-thousand-person meeting], HYBSL, March 21, 2012, http://w.hybsl.cn/article/13/29048.

25. Wang Jianmin 王聿文, "'七千人大会'五十周年的思考" [Thoughts on the fiftieth anniversary of the "seven-thousand-person meeting"], HYBSL, April 11, 2012, http://w.hybsl.cn/article/13/29323.

26. Zhang Suhua 张素华, "七千人大会打下毛刘分歧的楔子" [The seven-thousand-person meeting drove a wedge into the Mao-Liu disagreement], HYBSL, September 26, 2013, http://w.hybsl.cn/article/13/40081.

27. Zhang Suhua, "毛泽东究竟对刘少奇和邓小平的报告怎么看?" [What did Mao Zedong finally think of Liu Shaoqi's and Deng Xiaoping's reports?], HYBSL, April 20, 2012, http://w.hybsl.cn/article/13/29447.

28. Zhang Suhua, "1962年林彪如何让毛泽东感觉 "患难逢知己" [In 1962, how did Lin Biao make Mao Zedong feel he had a "friend in adversity"?], HYBSL, January 12, 2012, http://w.hybsl.cn/article/13/28303.

29. Mao Zedong, "Talk at an Enlarged Working Conference Convened by the Central Committee of the Communist Party of China," January 30, 1962, in *Selected Works of Mao Zedong,* vol. 8 (Kranti Publications, Secunderabad, India, 1994); https://www.marxists.org/reference/archive/mao/selected-works/volume-8/mswv8_62.htm.

30. Zhang Suhua, "七千人大会上从省委书记到部长的检讨," [The *jiantao* from provincial secretaries to ministers at the seven-thousand-person meeting], HYBSL, July 12, 2010, http://w.hybsl.cn/article/13/21229.

31. Li Zhisui, *Private Life of Chairman Mao,* 386–387.

32. Han Fudong 韩福东, "亲历七千人大会" [My experience of the seven-thousand-person meeting], HYBSL, February 16, 2012, http://w.hybsl.cn/article/13/28612.

33. Anon., "陈云'西楼会议'长篇发言出台幕后" [Behind the scenes of Chen Yun's long speech at the West Tower meeting], HYBSL, November 28, 2011, http://w.hybsl.cn/article/13/27687 (hereafter cited as Anon., "West Tower Meeting").

34. Anon., "West Tower Meeting"; Feng Laigang 冯来刚, "大跃进后刘少奇批示: 这样搞下去难道不会亡国吗?" [After the Great Leap Forward, Liu Shaoqi instructed: Wouldn't the country perish if this continued?], Excerpted from Lu Tong 鲁彤, Feng Laigang冯来刚, 刘少奇在建国后的 [20年 [Liu Shaoqi 20 Years after the founding of the PRC] (Liaoning renmin chubanshe, 2001), HYBSL, April 2, 2011, http://w.hybsl.cn/article/13/25486.

35. Liu and He, "Why Mao Wanted Liu Out."

36. Luo Zhenzhi 罗贞治, "1962年包产到户始末" [The whole story of contracting production to households in 1962], HYBSL, August 27, 2009, http://w.hybsl.cn/article/13/15710.

37. CCP Central Documentary Research Office, ed., 毛泽东年谱，第五卷 [Mao Zedong chronology, vol. 5], May 16, 1962, 5:102–103 , 110–111, (hereafter cited as *Mao Zedong Chronology*). (Searchable online e-book at https://ebook.dswxyjy.org.cn /storage/files/20220616/ddcdf1b3887dbedd06965f2619a3727d77188/mobile/index .html)

38. *Mao Zedong Chronology,* July 8, 1962, 5:111–112.

39. Liu and He, "Why Mao Wanted Liu Out."

40. *Mao Zedong Chronology,* August 4 and 6, 1962, 5:125–127.

41. *Mao Zedong Chronology,* notations for August and September 1962, 5:127–160.

42. Mao Zedong, "Speech at the Tenth Plenum of the Eighth Central Committee," September 24, 1962, in *Selected Works,* vol. 8.

43. CCP Historical Assessment, "八届十中全会(1962年9月24–27日)" [The Tenth Plenary meeting of the Eighth Central Committee], May 5, 2012, https://blog .wenxuecity.com/myblog/37995/201205/3275.html.

44. Jia Juchuan 贾巨川, "习仲勋冤案始末" [The whole story of Xi Zhongxun's unjust case], *Yanhuang Chunqiu,* January 2011.

45. Zhang et al., *Biography of Hu Yaobang,* 1:317–318.

46. Zheng, *Hu Yaobang Chronological Materials,* May 1962, July 18, 1962.

47. Man Mei, *Remembering Father, Hu Yaobang* (Cosmos Books, 2016), 1:264–265. This is Man Mei's second biography of her father, published in two volumes in Hong Kong. It is hereafter cited as Man Mei, *Remembering Father.*

48. Tang Fei 唐非, "耀邦同志在湘潭专区" [Comrade Yaobang in Xiangtan District], HYBSL, March 16, 2007, http://w.hybsl.cn/article/10/104/555.

49. Zheng, *Hu Yaobang Chronological Materials,* November 16, 1962.

50. Zhang et al., *Biography of Hu Yaobang,* 1:266–272.

51. Chen Liming, *Hu Yaobang: From Little Red Devil to General Secretary* vol. 1, (Renmin Ribao, 2013), 1:110–114 (hereafter cited as Chen Liming, *Little Red Devil*).

52. *Mao Zedong Chronology,* February 20, 1963, 5:193–194.

53. *Mao Zedong Chronology,* May 7–11, 1963, 5:216–227. See also "杭州小型会议 (1963年5月2–12日)" [The Hangzhou small-scale meetings (May 2–12, 1963)], Party History, http://www.chinavalue.net/Wiki/杭州小型会议.aspx.

54. Ma Shuangyou 马双有, "刘少奇和毛泽东在'四清'中的矛盾" [Liu and Mao's contradictions in the "Four Clean-Ups"], Gongshiwang (Consensus Network), September 19, 2014, https://blog.creaders.net/u/8311/201409/192061.html (hereafter cited as Ma Shuangyou, "Liu-Mao Dispute."

55. Zheng, *Hu Yaobang Chronological Materials,* several entries for May 2–12, 1963; Man Mei, *Remembering Father,* 1:278.

56. Suggested by Chung Yen-lin 鍾延麟, author of 文革前的鄧小平 [*Deng Xiaoping before the Cultural Revolution*] (Hong Kong Chinese University Press, 2013) in a conversation on November 21, 2017.

57. Zheng, *Hu Yaobang Chronological Materials,* late May 1963.

58. Man Mei, *Remembering Father,* 1:278.

59. Zhang et al., *Biography of Hu Yaobang,* 1:336–339, 342, 346.

60. Zhang et al., *Biography of Hu Yaobang,* 1:355–356.

61. Zhang et al., *Biography of Hu Yaobang,* 1:358.

62. Man Mei, *Remembering Father,* 1:280–281.

63. Ma Yongmei 马永梅 and Zhang Guoxin 张国新, "刘少奇指导四清运动思想与实践" [Liu Shaoqi directed the Four Clean-Ups campaign in ideology and practice], HYBSL, June 2, 2011, http://w.hybsl.cn/article/13/25995 (hereafter cited as Ma and Zhang "Liu Shaoqi Directed"); also Ma Shuangyou, "Liu-Mao Dispute."

64. *Mao Zedong Chronology,* October 31, November 3, and November 14, 1963, 5:273, 277, 280.

65. Han Gang 韩钢, "中共历史研究的若干难点热点问题" [Certain hot and difficult issues in the study of CCP history], Aisixiang Network, November 26, 2015, https://www.aisixiang.com/data/7247.html.

66. Ma and Zhang "Liu Shaoqi Directed."

67. *Mao Zedong Chronology,* August 31, 1964, 5:402.

68. Luo Pinghan 罗平汉, "'四清' 性质的高层分歧" [High-level differences over the nature of the "Four Clean-Ups"], HYBSL, October 7, 2008, http://w.hybsl.cn/article/13/10084 (hereafter cited as Luo Pinghan, "High-Level Differences."

69. Chen Liming, *Little Red Devil,* 1:280.

70. Man Mei, *Remembering Father,* 1:281.

71. Zhang et al., *Biography of Hu Yaobang,* 1:359–360.

72. Bai Lei 白磊, "1965年胡耀邦 电话通讯 产生前后" [Before and after the production of Hu Yaobang's "Telephone Communication" in 1965], *Yanhuang Chunqiu,* January 2016, https://difangwenge.org/archiver/?tid-19006.html (hereafter cited as Bai Lei, "Telephone Communication").

73. Gao Hua, "在贵州 '四清运动' 的背后" [Behind the "Four Clean-Ups" campaign in Guizhou], HYBSL, May 29, 2015, http://w.hybsl.cn/article/13/37497.

74. Chen Liming, *Biography of Hu Yaobang* (Swindon Books, 2005), 1:466.

75. Lin Xiaobo 林小波, "'四清'运动中的毛泽东与刘少奇" [Mao Zedong and Liu Shaoqi in the "Four Clean-Ups" campaign], Aisixiang Network, November 15, 2013, http://www.aisixiang.com/data/69584.html (hereafter cited as Lin Xiaobo, "Four Clean-Ups").

76. Luo Pinghan, "1964年毛泽东对刘少奇说：我骂娘没有用，你厉害" [In 1964, Mao told Liu: I curse their mothers, it's no use, but you are formidable], excerpted from Luo's book "文革"前夜的中国" [China on the eve of the Cultural Revolution] (People's Publishing House, 2007), HYBSL, April 15, 2010, http://w.hybsl.cn/article/13/19837 (hereafter cited as Luo, "Mao Told Liu").

77. Zhang et al., *Biography of Hu Yaobang,* 1:367.

78. Quoted in Xiao Donglian 萧冬连, "'一线'与'二线'— 毛刘关系与文革发起" ["First line" and "second line"—Mao-Liu relations and the start of the Cultural Revolution], HYBSL, December 19, 2011, http://w.hybsl.cn/article/13/27952. See also Luo, "Mao Told Liu."

79. Luo, "Mao Told Liu."

80. Luo Pinghan, "High-Level Differences."

81. Xiao Xiang 萧象, "刘少奇是什么时候感到自己要挨整的" [When did Liu Shaoqi feel he would be persecuted?], Aisixiang Network, May 14, 2013, http://www.aisixiang.com/data/63932.html.

82. *Mao Zedong Chronology,* December 17, 1964, 5:449–450.

83. Man Mei, *Remembering Father,* 1:284.

84. Anon., "杨尚昆谈'四清'" [Yang Shangkun talks about the "Four Clean-Ups"], HYBSL, July 24, 2015, http://w.hybsl.cn/article/13/53426 (hereafter cited as Anon., "Yang Shangkun Talks."

85. Zhang et al., *Biography of Hu Yaobang,* 1:369–371.

86. Chen Liming, *Little Red Devil,* 1:290–291; Hu Deping, "耀邦同志的安康" [Comrade Yaobang's Ankang], Aisixiang Network, August 31, 2014, www.aisixiang.com/data/77434.html (hereafter cited as Hu Deping, "Comrade Yaobang's Ankang").

87. The full text of Hu's message is in Bai Lei, "Telephone Communication."

88. Bai Lei, "Telephone Communication"; Hu Deping, "Comrade Yaobang's Ankang."

89. Zheng, *Hu Yaobang Chronological Materials,* February 18, 1965.

90. Lü Kejun 吕克军, "胡耀邦在陕西的新政及其结局" [Hu Yaobang's New Deal in Shaanxi and its consequences], *Yanhuang Chunqiu,* June 2015 (hereafter cited as Lü, "New Deal").

91. Lü, "New Deal."

92. Chen Liming, *Little Red Devil,* 1:297.

93. See Sha Yexin, "'检讨'文化" [The culture of "self-confession"], Aisixiang Network, May 28, 2008, http://www.aisixiang.com/data/8557.html.

94. Bai Lei, "1965年胡耀邦陕西检讨始末" [The whole story of Hu Yaobang's 1965 *Jiantao* in Shaanxi], *Yanhuang Chunqiu,* June 2016, http://w.hybsl.cn/article/11/110/59848 (hereafter cited as Bai, "The Whole Story").

95. Zheng, *Hu Yaobang Chronological Materials,* March 6 and 7, 1965.

96. Anon., "Yang Shangkun Talks."

97. Lü, "New Deal."

98. Zheng, *Hu Yaobang Chronological Materials,* March 11–14, 1965.

99. Bai, "The Whole Story"; Zheng, *Hu Yaobang Chronological Materials,* March 18–19, 1965.

100. Anon., "Yang Shangkun Talks."

101. Zheng, *Hu Yaobang Chronological Materials,* March 31, May 1965; Lü, "New Deal."

102. Man Mei, *Remembering Father,* 1:295–296.

103. Anon., "陕西主政两百天," [Governing in Shaanxi for 200 days], Renminwang, January 6, 2014, http://dangshi.people.com.cn/n/2014/0106/c85037-24031859.html.

104. Zhang et al., *Biography of Hu Yaobang,* 1:386; Chen Liming *Little Red Devil,* 1:303.

105. Chen Liming, *Little Red Devil,* 1:303.

106. Luo Pinghan, "High-Level Differences."

107. Man Mei, *Remembering Father,* 1:300–301.

108. Zheng, *Hu Yaobang Chronological Materials,* August 28, 1985.

109. Zhang et al., *Biography of Hu Yaobang,* 1:389; Chen Liming, *Biography of Hu Yaobang,* 1:533.

110. Man Mei, *Remembering Father,* 1:298.

111. Lü, "New Deal."

112. Dimon Liu, "The Chinese Communist Party's Four Instruments of Power," from "China 2030," unclassified paper written for the US Department of Defense, Office of Net Assessment, in 2017, cited by permission.

113. Li Zhisui, *Private Life of Chairman Mao,* 291–293.

114. Qiao Yu 乔雨, ". . . 谈文革初期毛泽东对党内高层的批判" [Talking about Mao Zedong's criticisms of the party upper level in the early Cultural Revolution], HYBSL, June 2, 2010, http://w.hybsl.cn/article/13/20703.

115. Ding Kaiwen 丁凯文, "文革前军内的一场大搏斗" [A big struggle within the army before the Cultural Revolution], HYBSL, November 27, 2015, http://w.hybsl.cn/article/13/55638 (hereafter cited as Ding Kaiwen, "A Big Struggle").

116. Roderick MacFarquhar and Michael Schoenhals, *Mao's Last Revolution* (Belknap Press of Harvard University Press, 2006), 20–26.

117. Ding Kaiwen, "A Big Struggle."

118. Xiao Xiang 萧象, "罗瑞卿悲剧的历史原因" [The historical reasons for the Luo Ruiqing tragedy], Aisixiang Network, November 21, 2012, http://www.aisixiang.com/data/59302.html.

119. Yang Jisheng 杨继绳, 翻天覆地—— 中国文化大革命历史 [Heaven and earth turned upside down: A history of the China's Cultural Revolution] (Cosmos Books, 2016), 146–149 (hereafter cited as Yang Jisheng, *Heaven and Earth*).

120. MacFarquhar and Schoenhals, *Mao's Last Revolution,* 34–35.

121. Yang Jisheng, *Heaven and Earth,* 115.

122. Yang Jisheng, *Heaven and Earth,* 109; MacFarquhar and Schoenhals, *Mao's Last Revolution,* 27–28.

123. Xiao Xiang 萧象, "毛泽东发动文革新探" [A new exploration of Mao Zedong launching the Cultural Revolution], HYBSL, September 23, 2015, http://w.hybsl.cn/article/13/54493 (hereafter cited as Xiao, "New Exploration").

124. Yang Jisheng, *Heaven and Earth,* 118.

125. MacFarquhar and Schoenhals, *Mao's Last Revolution,* 29–30; Yang Jisheng, *Heaven and Earth,* 120–121.

126. Xiao, "New Exploration." Xiao maintains that this speech contains Mao's first formal use of the term "Great Cultural Revolution" (文化大革命).

127. Yang Jisheng, *Heaven and Earth,* 124–125.

128. MacFarquhar and Schoenhals, *Mao's Last Revolution,* 33.

129. Yang Jisheng, *Heaven and Earth,* 131.

130. Yang Jisheng, *Heaven and Earth,* 131, 170–171.

131. Hu Yaobang probably would have been eligible to attend expanded Politburo meetings, but his biographers seem to obfuscate whether he attended. They list the important Central Committee meetings that passed the resolutions bringing on the Cultural Revolution, but they don't use the Chinese term *chuxi* 出席, meaning "participated in."

132. 五● 一六通知全文 [The May16 Notification] (full text), *Renmin Ribao,* May 17, 1966, http://www.maoflag.cc/portal.php?mod=view&aid=6042.

133. MacFarquhar and Schoenhals, *Mao's Last Revolution,* 38.

134. Yang Jisheng, *Heaven and Earth,* 175.

135. Chen Xiaojin 陈小津, "文革前夕, 胡耀邦与陈丕显关起门来'密谋'什么?" [On the eve of the Cultural Revolution, what were Hu Yaobang and Chen Pixian "secretly plotting" behind closed doors?], HYBSL, January 30, 2012, http://w.hybsl.cn/article/11/109/28410. Chen Xiaojin was Chen Pixian's son.

136. Zheng, *Hu Yaobang Chronological Materials,* April 1–20, 1966.

6. Cultural Revolutions

1. Principal sources used here are Roderick MacFarquar and Michael Schoenhals, *Mao's Last Revolution* (Belknap Press of Harvard University Press, 2006); Frank Dikötter, *The Cultural Revolution: A People's History, 1962–1976* (Bloomsbury Press, 2017); Yang Jisheng 杨继绳, 翻天覆地— 中国文化大革命历史 [Heaven and earth turned upside down: A history of the China's Cultural Revolution] (Cosmos Books, 2016) (hereafter cited as Yang Jisheng, *Heaven and Earth*).

2. MacFarquhar and Schoenhals, *Mao's Last Revolution,* 55–58; Yang Jisheng, *Heaven and Earth,* 181.

3. Chen Boda, "横扫一切牛鬼蛇神" [Sweep away all monsters], editorial, *Renmin Ribao,* June 1, 1966, English translation at https://www.marxists.org/subject/china/peking-review/1966/PR1966-23c.htm.

4. MacFarquhar and Schoenhals, *Mao's Last Revolution,* 64–65.

5. Miao Weidong 苗伟东, "文革岁月中的胡耀邦" [Hu Yaobang in the Cultural Revolution years], Hu Yaobang Historical Materials Information Network (hereafter HYBSL), November 22, 2010, http://w.hybsl.cn/article/11/109/23647 (hereafter cited as Miao, "Revolution Years").

6. Zhang Liqun, Zhang Ding, Yan Ruping, Tang Fei, and Li Songtian, *Biography of Hu Yaobang,* vol. 1: *1915–1976* (People's Publishing, 2005), 392–393.

7. Man Mei, *Remembering Father, Hu Yaobang* (Cosmos Books, 2016), 1:302–303.

8. Yin Hongbiao 印红标 (pseud.), "红卫兵运动的兴起与流派" [The emergence and divisions of the Red Guard movement], HYBSL, January 5, 2016, http://w.hybsl .cn/article/13/56296. Students at these exclusive Beijing middle schools were mostly children of senior officials of the CCP, government, and military.

9. Yang Jisheng 杨继绳, "从清华大学看文革" [Looking at the Cultural Revolution from Qinghua University], HYBSL, January 15, 2013, http://w.hybsl.cn/article /13/33895.

10. MacFarquhar and Schoenhals, *Mao's Last Revolution,* 72–74.

11. Yang Jisheng, *Heaven and Earth,* 196–197, 222.

12. Yang Zongli 杨宗丽 and Ming Wei 明伟, "毛泽东如何掀起'文革'高潮" [How Mao Zedong set off the high tide of the Cultural Revolution], excerpted from their book 周恩来26年总理风云 [Turbulence in Zhou Enlai's 26 years as Premier] (Liaoning renmin chubanshe, 2001) March 16, 2012, http://w.hybsl.cn/article/13/28991; MacFarquhar and Schoenhals, *Mao's Last Revolution,* 88–89.

13. Zheng Zhongbing, ed., *Hu Yaobang Chronological Materials: Long Version* (Times International, 2005), July 29, 1966. Also Miao, "Revolution Years."

14. Lu Tong 鲁彤 and Feng Laigang 冯来刚, "刘少奇下台序幕" [Prologue to Liu Shaoqi's ouster], excerpted from their book 刘少奇在建国后的20年 [Liu Shaoqi in the twenty years after the founding of the nation] (Liaoning renmin chubanshe, 2001), January 5, 2012, http://w.hybsl.cn/article/13/28176.

15. Zhang et al., *Biography of Hu Yaobang,* 1:395; Zheng, *Hu Yaobang Chronological Materials,* August 1–12, 1966.

16. Yang Jisheng, *Heaven and Earth,* 12. Jiang made this statement at her trial in 1981.

17. Man Mei, *Remembering Father,* 1:305.

18. Mao Zedong, "Bombard the headquarters: My first big-character poster," August 5, 1966, English translation at https://www.marxists.org/reference/archive /mao/selected-works/volume-9/mswv9_63.htm.

19. Yang Jisheng, *Heaven and Earth,* 228–229.

20. MacFarquhar and Schoenhals, *Mao's Last Revolution,* 94–95; Yuan Xi 袁晞, "毛泽东时代的常委和常委会" [The Standing Committee and Standing Committee meetings in the Mao era], HYBSL, March 26, 2016, http://w.hybsl.cn/article/13/57831.

21. Man Mei, *Remembering Father,* 1:306–307.

22. Man Mei, *Remembering Father,* 1:307, 309–310.

23. Zhang et al., *Biography of Hu Yaobang,* 1:398.

24. Gao Yong, 我给胡耀邦当秘书 [I was Hu Yaobang's secretary] (Joint Publishing Hong Kong, 2014) (hereafter cited as Gao, *Secretary*), 107–109.

25. Man Mei, *Remembering Father,* 1:311.

26. Zheng, *Hu Yaobang Chronological Materials,* August 1966; Man Mei, *Remembering Father,* 1:316.

27. Ye Yonglie 叶永烈, "胡克实自述: '文革'中的团中央" [Hu Keshi in his own words: The League Central Committee in the Cultural Revolution], *Yanhuang Chunqiu,* August 2005 (hereafter cited as Ye, "Hu Keshi").

28. Ye, "Hu Keshi." See also Guobin Yang, *The Red Guard Generation and Political Activism in China* (Columbia University Press, 2016), 83.

29. Ye, "Hu Keshi."

30. Man Mei, *Remembering Father,* 1:319–321.

31. MacFarquhar and Schoenhals, *Mao's Last Revolution,* 162–169.

32. Gao, *Secretary,* 110–111.

33. Yin Jiamin 尹家民, "毛泽东关于军队介入'文革'的思想变化过程" [Mao Zedong's changing thought process about the army intervening in the "Cultural Revolution"], HYBSL, April 22, 2014, http://w.hybsl.cn/article/13/45870.

34. MacFarquhar and Schoenhals, *Mao's Last Revolution,* 175–177; Yang Jisheng, *Heaven and Earth,* 431–435.

35. Yang Jisheng, *Heaven and Earth,* 386–394; Dikötter, *The Cultural Revolution,* 137–138.

36. Hu Deping 胡德平, "我见到父亲唯一一次痛哭失态" [The only time I saw my father cry uncontrollably], excerpted from Zhou Haibin 周海滨, 失落的巅峰 [Lost pinnacles] (Renmin chubanshe, 2012), July 10, 2012, http://w.hybsl.cn/article/11/109/30162; Man Mei, *Remembering Father,* 1:324–325.

37. Zhang et al., *Biography of Hu Yaobang,* 1:402–403.

38. Zheng, *Hu Yaobang Chronological Materials,* July 1967; Man Mei, *Remembering Father,* 1:323.

39. Zhang et al., *Biography of Hu Yaobang,* 1:403–404.

40. Gu Baozi 顾保孜, "野心家康生如何用阴谋敲开权力之门?" [How did the careerist Kang Sheng use conspiracy to open the door to power?] Renminwang, June 14, 2011, https://read01.com/xKgOD.html.

41. Huang Jinsheng 黄金生, "令人谈虎色变的'文革'专案组" [The terrifying "Cultural Revolution" special case groups], HYBSL, September 22, 2014, http://w.hybsl.cn/article/13/48361 (hereafter cited as Huang Jinsheng, "Special Case Groups").

42. Michael Schoenhals, "The Central Case Examination Group, 1966–79," *China Quarterly* 87 (1996): 87–111 (hereafter cited as Schoenhals, "Central Case").

43. Huang Zheng 黄峥, "江青等人为迫害刘少奇如何制造伪证" [How Jiang Qing and others created false evidence to persecute Liu Shaoqi], HYBSL, January 3, 2014, http://w.hybsl.cn/article/13/44037 (hereafter cited as Huang Zheng, "False Evidence"). See also Wu Faxian 吴法宪, "我所知道的十四个中央专案组" [The fourteen central case groups I knew], HYBSL, February 8, 2014, http://w.hybsl.cn/article/13/44615.

44. Schoenhals, "Central Case," 103; Huang Jinsheng, "Special Case Groups."

45. Huang Zheng, "False Evidence."

46. Zhang et al., *Biography of Hu Yaobang*, 1:405.

47. Zheng, *Hu Yaobang Chronological Materials*, May 1968 and July 21, 1968.

48. Gao, *Secretary*, 120–123.

49. Zhang et al., *Biography of Hu Yaobang*, 1:405–406.

50. Man Mei, *Remembering Father*, 1: 328; Ye, "Hu Keshi."

51. MacFarquhar and Schoenhals, *Mao's Last Revolution*, 273–274; Yang Jisheng, *Heaven and Earth*, 688–691.

52. Miao, "Revolution Years"; Man Mei, *Remembering Father*, 1:328.

53. MacFarquhar and Schoenhals, *Mao's Last Revolution*, 273–274.

54. MacFarquhar and Schoenhals, *Mao's Last Revolution*, 279.

55. Work Report of the Twelfth Plenum of the Eighth Central Committee, https://baike.baidu.com/item/中国共产党第八届中央委员会第十二次全体会议.

56. Man Mei, *Remembering Father*, 1:328–330; Miao, "Revolutionary Years."

57. Hu Deping, "耀邦文革给毛泽东的'万言书'里写了什么?" [What did Yaobang write in his '10,000 word letter' to Mao Zedong during the Cultural Revolution?], HYBSL, November 6, 2015, http://w.hybsl.cn/article/11/109/55219.

58. Zheng, *Hu Yaobang Chronological Materials*, April 1–24, 1969.

59. "Resolution on Certain Questions in the History of Our Party since the Founding of the People's Republic of China," adopted by the Sixth Plenary Session of the Eleventh Central Committee on June 27, 1981, English version at http://www.marxists.org/subject/china/documents/cpc/history/01.htm (hereafter cited as "1981 CCP History Resolution").

60. MacFarquhar and Schoenhals, *Mao's Last Revolution*, 245–246.

61. Gao Hua 高华, "'林彪事件'的再考察" [A reexamination of the "Lin Biao affair"], *21st Century*, October 2006, https://www.cuhk.edu.hk/ics/21c/media/articles/c097-200608073.pdf (hereafter cited as Gao Hua, "A Reexamination"). See also Yang Jisheng, *Heaven and Earth*, 414–420.

62. Yang Jisheng, *Heaven and Earth*, 433–434. See also Dong Fu 东夫, "造反派才是文革最大的受害者" [The rebel faction was the biggest victim of the Cultural Revolution], HYBSL, January 22, 2016, http://w.hybsl.cn/article/13/56640.

63. Yang Jisheng, *Heaven and Earth*, 432–433.

64. Michel Bonnin, *The Lost Generation: The Rustication of China's Educated Youth (1968–1980)* (Chinese University of Hong Kong Press, 2013).

65. "The 'May 7' Directive," https://baike.baidu.com/item/五·七指示/5331499.

66. Yang Jisheng, *Heaven and Earth*, 360.

67. Zhang Shaochun 张绍春, "五七干校的历史脉络与特点研究" [Study of the historical lineage and characteristics of the May 7 cadre schools], Sina.com, May 20, 2017, https://bbs.wenxuecity.om/memory/1131384.html.

68. Cheng Min 程敏, "胡耀邦在黄湖农场" [Hu Yaobang at Huanghu Farm], HYBSL, February 13, 2007, http://w.hybsl.cn/article/14/114/155; Man Mei, *Remembering Father*, 1:332–333.

69. Gao, *Secretary*, 127–129.

70. Yang Chunxiang 杨春祥, "胡耀邦在黄湖干校" [Hu Yaobang at the Huanghu cadre school], January 9, 2016, https://www.sohu.com/a/53531739_115854 (hereafter cited as Yang Chunxiang, "Hu at Huanghu").

71. Man Mei, *Remembering Father*, 1:335.

72. Zhang et al., *Biography of Hu Yaobang*, 1:414–415.

73. Gao, *Secretary*, 129–130; Man Mei, *Remembering Father*, 1:334.

74. Man Mei, *Remembering Father*, 1:344–345.

75. Yang Chunxiang, "Hu at Huanghu."

76. Dikötter, *The Cultural Revolution*, 241–242; Gao Hua, "A Reexamination."

77. Yang Jisheng, *Heaven and Earth*, 764–765.

78. Cao Ying 曹英, "毛泽东在林彪事件前的关键决策" [Mao's key decisions before the Lin Biao incident], HYBSL, February 3, 2010, http://w.hybsl.cn/article/13/18616.

79. Yu Yunshen 于运深, "口述：我给林彪当秘书的最后一年" [Oral interview: The last year I was Lin Biao's secretary], HYBSL, September 14, 2015, http://w.hybsl.cn/article/13/54312.

80. Han Gang, "'九一三'事件考疑" [Checking doubts about the '9–13' incident], *Tongzhou gongjin*, October 21, 2013, http://w.hybsl.cn/article/13/41922 (hereafter cited as Han Gang, "Checking Doubts").

81. Wang Haiguang 王海光, "'九.一三事件'谜团解析" ['September 13 incident' riddles explained], HYBSL, December 9, 2013, http://w.hybsl.cn/article/13/43447.

82. Han Gang, "Checking Doubts."

83. The purported full text of "Outline of Project 571" is online at https://chinadigitaltimes.net/space/林立果 "五七一工程"纪要全文; see also Qiu Huizuo 邱会作, 邱会作回忆录 [Memoirs of Qiu Huizuo] (New Century Press, 2011), 861.

84. Hong Yuzhai 红雨斋, "'九.一三事件'后的清洗" [The purge after the "9-13 incident"], HYBSL, June 25, 2009, http://w.hybsl.cn/article/13/14764 (hereafter cited as Hong Yuzhai, "The Purge").

85. Wang Nianyi 王年一, "关于'军委办事组'的一些资料" [A few materials pertaining to the 'CMC Administrative Group'], HYBSL, April 28, 2014, http://w.hybsl.cn/article/13/45976.

86. Gao Hua, "A Reexamination."

87. Yu Ruxin 余汝信 "蒙古官方调查报告中的'九一三事件'" [Mongolian official investigation report on the "9-13 incident"], HYBSL, April 8, 2016, http://w.hybsl.cn/article/13/58093; and 最"新解密的蒙古官方对于林彪专机坠毁原因的调查报告" [newly declassified official Mongolian investigation report on the cause of the crash of Lin Biao's plane], HYBSL, April 11, 2016, http://w.hybsl.cn/article/13/58130.

88. MacFarquhar and Schoenhals, *Mao's Last Revolution*, 337–339; Dikötter, *The Cultural Revolution*, 255–256.

89. Gao Wenqian, *Zhou Enlai, the Last Perfect Revolutionary: A Biography*, trans. Peter Rand and Lawrence R. Sullivan (Public Affairs Press, 2007), 236. Also Li Zhisui, *The Private Life of Chairman Mao*, trans. Tai Hung-chao (Random House, 1994), 572–573.

90. Li Zhisui, *Private Life of Chairman Mao*, 542–543.

91. MacFarquhar and Schoenhals, *Mao's Last Revolution*, 340; Qin Jiufeng 秦九凤, "1973年毛泽东稳定中国政局的愿望为何落空?" [Why did Mao Zedong's wish to stabilize the political situation in China in 1973 fall through?], HYBSL, November 8, 2011, http://w.hybsl.cn/article/13/27458.

92. Alexander Pantsov, with Steven I. Levine, *Deng Xiaoping: A Revolutionary Life* (Oxford University Press, 2015), 262.

93. Pantsov and Levine, *Deng Xiaoping*, 268–269.

94. Hong Yuzhai, "The Purge."

95. Yin Shusheng 尹曙生, "毛泽东与砸烂公, 检, 法" [Mao Zedong and the smashing of public security, prosecutors, and the courts], *Yanhuang Chunqiu*, October 2013.

96. Yu Ruxin 余汝信 and Zeng Ming 曾鸣, "也谈中央文革小组的结束时间问题" [Also on the issue of when the Central Cultural Revolution Group ended], Aisixiang, December 12, 2013, http://www.aisixiang.com/data/70376.html

97. Man Mei, *Remembering Father*, 1:346–349.

98. Hu Deping, "在王灵书出版座谈会上的发言" [Speech at the symposium on the publication of *Wang Lingshu*], HYBSL, July 4, 2015, http://w.hybsl.cn/article/13/53054 (hereafter cited as Hu Deping, "Speech").

99. Zheng, *Hu Yaobang Chronological Materials*, October 1971.

100. Zhang et al., *Biography of Hu Yaobang*, 1:421.

101. Gao, *Secretary*, 148–157.

102. Zhang et al., *Biography of Hu Yaobang*, 1:421–422. All five of the authors of *The Biography of Hu Yaobang* were Hu's subordinates in the Communist Youth League or the Central Party School and would have had opportunities to talk to him about his thoughts during this phase of his life, although they did not quote him directly.

103. Hu Deping, "Speech."

104. Pantsov and Levine, *Deng Xiaoping*, 275–277.

105. Li Zhisui, *Private Life of Chairman Mao*, 581.

106. Yang Jisheng, *Heaven and Earth*, 852; MacFarquhar and Schoenhals, *Mao's Last Revolution*, 360–365.

107. Li Xun 李逊, "王洪文的升沉" [The rise and fall of Wang Hongwen], *Yanhuang Chunqiu*, October 2015.

108. Pantsov and Levine, *Deng Xiaoping*, 287–288; Yang Jisheng, *Heaven and Earth*, 894.

109. Yang Jisheng, *Heaven and Earth,* 895.

110. MacFarquhar and Schoenhals, *Mao's Last Revolution,* 381.

111. Yang Jisheng, *Heaven and Earth,* 896–902.

112. Deng Xiaoping, *The Selected Works of Deng Xiaoping,* vol. 2 (Beijing Foreign Languages Press, 1984), 10.

113. Liu Yan 刘岩, "我在'中央读书班'的见闻" [What I saw and heard in the 'Central Reading Class'], *Party History Expo,* February 20, 2009, http://w.hybsl.cn/article /13/12744.

114. Qian Jiang 钱江, "胡耀邦在第四期中央读书班" [Hu Yaobang at the fourth Central reading class], HYBSL, July 5, 2016, http://w.hybsl.cn/article/11/110 /60000.

115. Qian Jiang, "胡耀邦是怎样进入邓小平视野的?" [How did Hu Yaobang come into Deng Xiaoping's field of vision?], 湘潮[Hunan Tide magazine], December 14, 2015, http://w.hybsl.cn/article/11/109/55933.

116. Zhang et al., *Biography of Hu Yaobang,* 1:425–426.

117. Li Chang 李昌, "我与耀邦共事" [I worked together with Yaobang], *Yanhuang Chunqiu,* January 2006.

118. Wu Mingyu 吴明瑜, "难忘的一百二十天" [Unforgettable 120 days], HYBSL, September 21, 2015, http://w.hybsl.cn/article/11/110/54446, (hereafter cited as Wu Mingyu, "Unforgettable").

119. Zhang et al., *Biography of Hu Yaobang,* 1:426.

120. Zheng, *Hu Yaobang Chronological Materials,* August 1, 1975.

121. Wu Weifeng 吴伟锋, "1975年胡耀邦整顿中国科学院始末" [The whole story of Hu Yaobang's rectification of the CAS in 1975], *Party History Collection,* June 2017, http://www.hybsl.cn/ybsxyj/shengpingyusixiang/2018-06-11/67766.html, last accessed June 12, 2018, URL no longer valid. Condensed version at https://www .csibaskets.com/show-54-44263-1.html.

122. Wu Mingyu, "Unforgettable."

123. *Selected Works of Hu Yaobang* (People's Publishing House, 2015), 61–71.

124. Zheng, *Hu Yaobang Chronological Materials,* August 26, 1975.

125. Zhang et al., *Biography of Hu Yaobang,* 1:440.

126. Zhang et al., *Biography of Hu Yaobang,* 1:443. See also Central Documentary Research Office, ed., 毛泽东年谱，第五卷 [Mao Zedong chronology], http://mks .bucm.edu.cn/kckz/lnmzddxpwx/43228.htm (hereafter cited as *Mao Zedong Chronology*), 6:612–613.

127. MacFarquhar and Schoenhals, *Mao's Last Revolution,* 382.

128. Yang Jisheng, *Heaven and Earth,* 908–909.

129. Li Zhisui, *Private Life of Chairman Mao,* 596.

130. Yang Jisheng, *Heaven and Earth,* 917; Jiang Yiran 姜毅然 and Xia Fei 霞飞, "1975年邓小平进入中央领导核心后的整顿风云" [The rectification situation after Deng Xiaoping entered the Central leadership core in 1975], CCP Newsnet,

November 30, 2010, http://www.ce.cn/xwzx//dang/fc/200708/03/t20070803_12416837 .shtml (hereafter cited as Jiang and Xia, "Rectification Situation").

131. Jiang and Xia, "Rectification Situation." Also *Mao Zedong Chronology,* 6:613.

132. Jiang and Xia, "Rectification Situation." Also MacFarquhar and Schoenhals, *Mao's Last Revolution,* 408–409.

133. Zhao Shukai, "纪登奎与高层派系" [Ji Dengkui and high-level factions], Gongshiwang, April 16, 2016, https://read01.com/7Kd2Om.html.

134. Man Mei, *Remembering Father,* 1:383; Zhang et al., *Biography of Hu Yaobang,* 1:444–445.

135. *Mao Zedong Chronology,* 6:624

136. Ezra F. Vogel, *Deng Xiaoping and the Transformation of Modern China* (Belknap Press of Harvard University Press, 2010), 148–149.

137. Jiang and Xia, "Rectification Situation."

138. Jiang and Xia, "Rectification Situation"; MacFarquhar and Schoenhals, *Mao,* 411.

139. Man Mei, *Remembering Father,* 1:385, 386.

140. Gao Wenqian, *Zhou Enlai,* 305–307.

141. Vogel, *Deng Xiaoping,* 158–159.

142. Pantsov and Levine, *Deng Xiaoping,* 161.

143. Yang Jisheng, *Heaven and Earth,* 933–934.

144. Dikötter, *The Cultural Revolution,* 310.

145. Vogel, *Deng Xiaoping,* 168.

146. Yang Jisheng, *Heaven and Earth,* 956–958.

147. Yang Jisheng, *Heaven and Earth,* 956–958; Vogel, *Deng Xiaoping,* 168–169; Pantsov and Levine, *Deng Xiaoping,* 199.

148. Man Mei, *Remembering Father,* 1:389.

149. Man Mei, *Remembering Father,* 1:390.

150. Zhang et al., *Biography of Hu Yaobang,* 1:446.

151. Li Zhisui, *Private Life of Chairman Mao,* 614.

152. Yan Changgui 阎长贵, "毛远新再谈毛泽东1976年状况" [Mao Yuanxin talked again about the condition of Mao Zedong in 1976], *Yanhuang Chunqiu,* October 2011.

153. "1981 CCP History Resolution."

154. Yang Jisheng, *Heaven and Earth,* 36–38. At the Stanford Center at Beijing University on October 25, 2013, Yang also presented an oral version of this "introduction": "Road—Theory—System: My Thoughts on the Cultural Revolution", which was on the Boxun network in Chinese but has been taken down. A version is available on China News Digest at http://hx.cnd.org/?p=133984.

155. Song Yongyi, "Chronology of Mass Killings during the Chinese Cultural Revolution (1966–1976)," August 25, 2011, https://www.sciencespo.fr/mass-violence -war-massacre-resistance/en/document/chronology-mass-killings-during-chinese -cultural-revolution-1966-1976.html.

7. Bringing Order out of Chaos

1. Han Gang 韩钢, "还原华国锋" [Restoring Hua Guofeng—Certain historical facts about Hua Guofeng], November 18, 2008, http://m.aisixiang.com/data/22330 .html (hereafter cited as Han, "Restoring Hua"). See also Yuan Xi 袁晞, "毛泽东时代 的常委和常委会" [The Politburo Standing Committee and its meetings in the Mao Zedong era], Hu Yaobang Historical Materials Information Network (hereafter HYBSL), March 25, 2016, http://w.hybsl.cn/article/13/57831.

2. Ji Xizhen 纪希晨, "粉碎'四人帮'全景写真" [Panoramic portrait of smashing the "Gang of Four"], *Yanhuang Chunqiu*, October 2000 (hereafter cited as Ji Xizhen, "Smashing the Gang").

3. Xiong Lei 熊蕾, "1976年, 华国锋和叶剑英怎样联手的" [How Hua Guofeng and Ye Jianying joined forces in 1976], *Yanhuang Chunqiu*, October 2008 (hereafter cited as Xiong Lei, "Hua and Ye").

4. Ding Dong 丁东, "毛泽东选谁接班?" [Who did Mao Zedong choose to suc-ceed him?], in *The Continuing Revolution That Was Hard to Continue*, vol. 8 of *His-tory of the People's Republic of China* (Chinese University of Hong Kong Press, 2008), http://club.6parkbbs.com/chan1/index.php?app=forum&act=threadview&tid =10475102. Also Chu Fang (Zhu Fang), *Gun Barrel Politics: Party-Army Relations in Mao's China* (Westview Press, 1998), 221–223.

5. Feng Lizhong 冯立忠, "我所知道的8341部队" [The Unit 8341 I knew], *Renmin Ribao*, February 7, 2006, http://www.bangtai.us/jt/news/view.asp?id=1356.

6. Li Weisai, "李维赛, "吴德、吴忠与林彪、江青集团的覆灭" [Wu De, Wu Zhong, and the destruction of the Lin Biao and Jiang Qing groups], 军史历史 [*Mili-tary History*], 2004, no. 3: 45–48.

7. Han Gang 韩钢, "粉碎'四人帮'细节考证" [Detailed research into smashing the "Gang of Four"], June 1, 2015, http://www.aisixiang.com/data/51074.html; Wu De 吴德, "粉碎四人帮绝密档案" [Top secret files on crushing the Gang of Four], *Huaxia Wenzhai*, October 2, 2005, http://hx.cnd.org/2005/10/02/吴德: 粉碎四人帮绝密 档案: 北京卫戍区的斗争/ (hereafter cited as Wu De, "Top Secret Files").

8. Xu Yan 徐焰, "1976年李先念密会叶剑英" [Li Xiannian's secret meeting with Ye Jianying in 1976], May 5, 2005, http://news.ifeng.com/a/20160505/48686618_0 .shtml.

9. Ji Xizhen, "Smashing the Gang." Also Zhang Gensheng 张根生, "华国锋谈粉 碎'四人帮'" [Hua Guofeng talks about smashing the "Gang of Four"], *Yanhuang Chunqiu*, July 2004.

10. Wu Jianhua 武健华, "叶剑英汪东兴密谈处置四人帮" [Ye Jianying and Wang Dongxing secret talks about disposing of the Gang of Four], *Yanhuang Chunqiu*, February 2013 (hereafter cited as Wu Jianhua "Ye-Wang Talks"). Wu was the political commissar of Unit 8341 in 1976.

11. Ji Xizhen, "Smashing the Gang."

12. Ji Xizhen, "Smashing the Gang"; Wu De, "Top Secret Files"; Wu Jianhua, "Ye-Wang Talks."

13. Ji Xizhen, "Smashing the Gang"; Wu De, "Top Secret Files"; Wu Jianhua, "Ye-Wang Talks."

14. Ji Xizhen, "Smashing the Gang."

15. See Ye Xuanji 叶选基, "叶帅在十一届三中全会前后" [Marshal Ye before and after the Third Plenum of the Eleventh Central Committee], October 30, 2008, http://www.aisixiang.com/data/21785.html (hereafter cited as Ye Xuanji, "Marshal Ye"). Ye Xuanji was a nephew of Ye Jianying.

16. Li Haiwen 李海文, "中央八人小组瓦解四人帮余党武装叛乱" [An eight-member Central small group dismantled the armed rebellion of remnants of the Gang of Four], HYBSL, December 18, 2012, http://w.hybsl.cn/article/13/32913.

17. Anon., "揭密'四人帮'垮台全过程" [Disclosing the whole process of the fall of the "Gang of Four"], HYBSL, September 25, 2009, http://w.hybsl.cn/article/13/16303 (hereafter cited as "Disclosing the Whole Process").

18. "Disclosing the Whole Process"

19. Man Mei, *Remembering Father, Hu Yaobang* , vol. 1, (Cosmos Books, 2016), 1:396. See Miao Tijun 苗体君 and Dou Chunfang 窦春芳, "叶剑英与胡耀邦的友谊" [The friendship of Ye Jianying and Hu Yaobang], HYBSL, February 13, 2012, http://w.hybsl.cn/article/11/109/28573.

20. Man Mei, *Remembering Father,* 1:396.

21. Yan Ruping 严如平, "叶剑英在逆境中扶助胡耀邦" [Ye Jianying supported Hu Yaobang in adversity], *Yanhuang Chunqiu,* November 2003 (hereafter cited as Yan Ruping, "Ye Supported Hu").

22. Anon., "如何从毛泽东、邓小平之间看叶剑英的特殊功勋" [How Mao Ze-dong and Deng Xiaoping both saw the special merit of Ye Jianying], HYBSL, April 22, 2010, http://w.hybsl.cn/article/13/19996.

23. Yan Ruping, "Ye Supported Hu."

24. Yan Ruping, "Ye Supported Hu." Also Zhang Gensheng 张根生, "张根生谈华国锋：他曾提议叶帅当主席" [Hua Guofeng . . . once proposed Marshal Ye as chairman], HYBSL, September 2, 2014, http://w.hybsl.cn/article/13/48050.

25. Xiong Lei, "Hua and Ye"; Han, "Restoring Hua."

26. Ma Licheng 马立诚, "'两个凡是'的兴起和落败" [The rise and fall of the "Two Whatevers"], HYBSL, July 19, 2010, http://w.hybsl.cn/article/13/21317 (hereafter cited as Ma Licheng, "Rise and Fall").

27. Sheng Ping 盛平, ed., 胡耀邦思想年谱 [A chronology of Hu Yaobang's thought], (Taide Shidai, 2007) (hereafter cited as Sheng Ping, *Chronology of Hu Yaobang's Thought,* followed by entry date and page no.), vol. 1, November 18, 1976, 32.

28. Ling Zhijun 凌志军 and Ma Licheng马立诚, "邓小平并非公开反对华国锋'两个凡是'的第一人" [Deng Xiaoping was not the first person to openly oppose Hua Guofeng's "Two Whatevers"], excerpted from their book 呼喊— 当今中国的五种声音 [Shouts—Five kinds of voices in Contemporary China] (Renmin Ribao chubanshe, 2011), HYBSL, December 21, 2011, http://w.hybsl.cn/article/13/27984 (hereafter cited as Ling and Ma, "Deng and Two Whatevers").

29. Sheng Ping, *Chronology of Hu Yaobang's Thought,* January 1, 1977, 1:36. Yan Ruping summarized these conversations in a two-part *Yanhuang Chunqiu* article in 2002 as part of an effort to restore Hu's reputation. The article appeared on HYBSL March 19, 2007. Yan Ruping 严如平, "'吾爱吾师，吾尤爱真理'; 胡耀邦关于毛主席晚年的一席谈" [I love my teacher and I especially love the truth; Hu Yaobang talks about Chairman Mao's later years (part 1)], HYBSL, March 19, 2007, http://w.hybsl.cn/article/11/110/911, (hereafter cited as Yan Ruping, "Love the Truth").

30. Sheng Ping, *Chronology of Hu Yaobang's Thought,* January 2, 1977, 1:37–38; Yan Ruping, "Love the Truth."

31. Ma Licheng, "Rise and Fall."

32. Ma Licheng, "Rise and Fall."

33. Alexander V. Pantsov with Steven I. Levine, *Deng Xiaoping: A Revolutionary Life* (Oxford University Press, 2015), 326.

34. Man Mei, *Remembering Father,* 1:401.

35. Zheng Zhongbing, ed., *Hu Yaobang Chronological Materials, Long Version* (International Era, 2005), entry for February 26, 1977.

36. Sheng Ping, *Chronology of Hu Yaobang's Thought,* February 27, 1977, 1:38.

37. Zheng, *Hu Yaobang Chronological Materials,* March 3, 1977.

38. Sheng Ping, *Chronology of Hu Yaobang's Thought,* March 9, 1977, 1:39.

39. Huang Yibing 黄一兵, "一九七七年中央工作会议研究" [Study of the Central work conference of 1977], August 15, 2013, https://difangwenge.org/forum.php?mod=viewthread&tid=8830 (hereafter Huang, "The 1977 Work Conference").

40. Huang, "The 1977 Work Conference."

41. Huang, "The 1977 Work Conference."

42. Ling and Ma, "Deng and Two Whatevers."

43. Yang Jisheng 杨继盛, 中國改革年代政治鬥爭 [*The Political Struggles of China's Reform Era*], (Cosmos Books, 2010), 78–79 (hereafter cited as Yang Jisheng, *Political Struggles*).

44. Ye Kuangzheng 叶匡政, "'四人帮'覆灭后, 胡耀邦如何巧妙揭发康生?" [After the destruction of the "Gang of Four," how did Hu Yaobang subtly expose Kang Sheng?], excerpted from Ye's book 大往事: 纵横历史解密档案 [The great past: Declassified historical archives] (Zhongguo wenshi chubanshe, 2006), HYBSL, July 29, 2015, http://w.hybsl.cn/article/11/110/53499.

45. Sheng Ping, *Chronology of Hu Yaobang's Thought,* April–May 1977, 1:43–54.

46. Zhang Liqun, Zhang Ding, Yan Ruping, Tang Fei, and Li Songtian, *Biography of Hu Yaobang,* vol. 2 (Beijing United, 2015), 2:457.

47. Sheng Ping, *Chronology of Hu Yaobang's Thought,* "mid-May" 1977, 1:55.

48. Sheng Ping, *Chronology of Hu Yaobang's Thought,* 1:55. Also Shen Baoxiang 沈宝祥, "胡耀邦组建的理论动态组" [The theoretical dynamics group formed by Hu Yaobang], HYBSL, January 16, 2008, http://w.hybsl.cn/article/10/104/6943 (hereafter cited as Shen, "Theoretical Dynamics Group").

49. Shen, "Theoretical Dynamics Group"; Sheng Ping, *Chronology of Hu Yaobang's Thought,* July 12, 1977, 1:74–75.

50. Wu Jiang 吴江, 十年的路：和胡耀邦相处的日子 [Ten year road: Days together with Hu Yaobang] (Mirror Cultural Enterprises, 1995), 20.

51. Sheng Ping, *Chronology of Hu Yaobang's Thought,* July 19, 1977, 1:76.

52. Wu Jiang, "胡耀邦与邓小平在理论问题上的'第一次接触'" [Hu Yaobang and Deng Xiaoping's "first contact" on theoretical issues] Sina.com, August 12, 2003, https://news.sina.com.cn/c/2003-08-12/09241526271.shtml.

53. "Communique of the 3rd Plenary Meeting of the 10th CCP Congress," July 22, 1977, http://cpc.people.com.cn/GB/64162/64168/64562/65368/4429440 .html.

54. Ling and Ma, "Deng and Two Whatevers."

55. "The Eleventh Party Congress," *China News Analysis,* October 7, 1977.

56. Yu Guangyuan 于光远, "1978年为何要点名批评汪东兴" [Why Wang Dongxing was criticized by name in 1978], excerpted from Yu's book 大转折— 十一届三中全会的台前幕后 [The great turning point of 1978: Behind the scenes at the 3rd plenum of the 11th congress] (Central Compilation and Translation Press, Beijing, 1998), HYBSL, December 27, 2010, http://w.hybsl.cn/article/13/24345 (hereafter cited as Yu Guangyuan, "Criticizing Wang Dongxing"). See also Ma Licheng, "Rise and Fall."

57. "Communique of the 1st Plenum of the 11th Congress of the Communist Party of China," August 19, 1977, http://cpc.people.com.cn/GB/64162/64168/64563 /65369/4441892.html.

58. Xia Fei 霞飞, "胡耀邦'揭'康生问题" [Hu Yaobang "exposed" the Kang Sheng problem], HYBSL, January 12, 2016, http://w.hybsl.cn/article/11/109/56427. Also Sheng Ping, *Chronology of Hu Yaobang's Thought,* September 3, 1977, 1:92–94.

59. Shen Baoxiang, "胡耀邦关于支持揭露康生的讲话," [Hu Yaobang's speech on supporting the exposure of Kang Sheng], HYBSL, July 8, 2013, http://w.hybsl.cn /article/13/38926.

60. Cheng Guanjun 程冠军, "康生问题被揭露始末" [The entire story of exposing Kang Sheng], HYBSL, January 4, 2011, http://w.hybsl.cn/article/13/24572 (hereafter cited as Cheng, "Exposing Kang Sheng").

61. Cheng, "Exposing Kang Sheng."

62. Zheng, *Hu Yaobang Chronological Materials,* October 5, 1977.

63. Sheng Ping, *Chronology of Hu Yaobang's Thought,* "early October" 1977, 1:101.

64. Ye Jianying, "叶剑英在中共中央党校开学典礼上的讲话" [Speech at the opening of classes ceremony for the Central Party School] October 10, 1977, https://banned-historical-archives.github.io/articles/a05697e5c4/.

65. Sheng Ping, *Chronology of Hu Yaobang's Thought,* September 21–22, 1977, 1:96–97. The concept of "line struggles" (路线斗争) was adapted by Mao from Stalin's practice of "life and death struggles" against his adversaries in the CPSU. It was a way of elevating personal power struggles into ideological battles of right vs. wrong and justifying their outcomes. Mao rewrote CCP history each time he vanquished a political foe, eventually identifying eleven villains and naming their erroneous political "lines." See Baike-Baidu on "Ten Line Struggles," 十次路线斗争, undated, https://baike.baidu.com/item/十次路线斗争/195846.

66. Wang Haiguang 王海光, "中央党校1977年的800人大讨论" [The Central Party School's 1977 800-person big debate], September 1, 2011, http://www.reformdata.org/2011/0901/2318.shtml.

67. Wang Haiguang, "胡耀邦与党内第一次集体反思文革的大讨论" [Hu Yaobang and the big debate over the first collective review of the Cultural Revolution], HYBSL, August 13, 2010, http://w.hybsl.cn/article/13/21798 (hereafter cited as Wang Haiguang, "Hu and CR Debate").

68. Sheng Ping, *Chronology of Hu Yaobang's Thought,* "Autumn" 1977, 1:91; Wang Haiguang, "Hu and CR Debate."

69. Wang Haiguang, "Hu and CR Debate."

70. Sheng Ping, *Chronology of Hu Yaobang's Thought,* September 1977, 1:100.

71. Wang Haiguang, "Hu and CR Debate."

72. Yu Huanchun 余焕椿, "胡耀邦与拨乱反正中的人民日报" [Hu Yaobang and *Renmin Ribao* bringing order out of chaos], *Yanhuang Chunqiu,* June 2015 (hereafter cited as Yu Huanchun, "HYB and *Renmin Ribao*").

73. Yin Shusheng 尹曙生, "冤案是怎样酿成的" [How unjust cases came about], *Yanhuang Chunqiu,* April 2015, http://w.hybsl.cn/article/13/52292 (hereafter cited as Yin, "Unjust Cases").

74. Yu Guangyuan, "Criticizing Wang Dongxing."

75. Gao Tianding 高天鼎, "中组部冤案平反始末" [The whole process of redressing unjust cases in the Central Organization Department], HYBSL, March 26, 2015, http://w.hybsl.cn/article/13/51383 (hereafter cited as Gao Tianding, "Redressing Unjust Cases").

76. Gao Tianding, "Redressing Unjust Cases."

77. Yin, "Unjust Cases."

78. Gao Tianding, "Redressing Unjust Cases."

79. Zeng Zhi 曾志, 红墙外的胡耀邦 [Hu Yaobang outside the red walls] (Hong Kong China Children's Publishing, 1999) (hereafter cited as Zeng Zhi, *Red Walls*), 38–39.

80. Yu Huanchun, "Hu Yaobang and *Renmin Ribao.*"

81. Yan Ruping, "Ye Supported Hu."

82. Renmin Ribao Commentator, 本报评论员 "毛主席的干部政策必须认真落实" [Chairman Mao's cadre policy must be conscientiously implemented], *Renmin Ribao,* November 27, 1977, http://www.reformdata.org/1977/1127/14018.shtml (hereafter cited as "Chairman Mao's Cadre Policy").

83. "Chairman Mao's Cadre Policy."

84. Sheng Ping, *Chronology of Hu Yaobang's Thought,* December 19, 1977, 1:124–126.

85. Zeng Zhi, *Red Walls,* 54–55; He Zai 何载, "耀邦同志平反冤假错案" [Comrade Yaobang overturned unjust, false, and wrong cases], Aisixiang Network, November 23, 2018, http://www.aisixiang.com/data/113574.html (hereafter cited as He Zai, "Hu Overturned").

86. He Zai, "Hu Overturned."

87. Dai Huang 戴煌, 胡耀邦与平反冤假错案 [Hu Yaobang and redressing unjust, false, and wrong cases], (Xinhua, 2006) (hereafter cited as Dai Huang, *Hu Yaobang and Unjust Cases*), 110, emphasis added.

88. He Zai, "Hu Overturned."

89. Pantsov and Levine, *Deng Xiaoping,* 330–331.

90. Hu Jiwei 胡绩伟, "邓小平曾阻碍平反冤案" [Deng Xiaoping once blocked the reversal of unjust cases], *China News Digest,* October 4, 2015, http://hx.cnd.org/?p =115891.

91. The article was published anonymously in *Theoretical Dynamics.* See "实践是检验真理的唯一标准" [Practice is the sole criterion for judging truth], text available at http://www.chinadaily.com.cn/dfpd/jiandang90nian/2011-04/20/content _12364302.htm.

92. Jiang Shuping 姜淑萍, Zhang Mingjie 张明杰, and Zhang Shu 张曙, 实践是检验真理的唯一标准》文章播发始末" [The whole story of broadcasting the article "'Practice Is the Sole Criterion for Testing Truth,"], October 10, 2014, http://www .ccpph.com.cn/ywrd/syxw/201005/t20100512_70549.htm, accessed April 11, 2019, URL no longer valid (hereafter cited as Jiang Shuping et al., "Broadcasting the Article").

93. Sheng Ping, *Chronology of Hu Yaobang's Thought,* May 11, 1978, 1:179.

94. Ling Zhijun 凌志军 and Ma Licheng 马立诚, "胡耀邦 '文章救国'" [Hu Yaobang and the "article to save the country"]," Aisixiang Network, March 22, 2011, http://www.aisixiang.com/data/39530.html (hereafter cited as Ling and Ma, "Save the Country"). See also Sheng Ping, *Chronology of Hu Yaobang's Thought,* May 12, 1978, 1:180.

95. Jiang Shuping et al., "Broadcasting the Article."

96. Sheng Ping, *Chronology of Hu Yaobang's Thought,* May 13, 1978, 1:181.

97. Ling and Ma, "Save the Country"; Jiang Shuping et al., "Broadcasting the Article."

98. Ma Licheng, "Rise and Fall."

99. Deng Xiaoping, "Speech at the All-Army Conference on Political Work," June 2, 1978, https://dengxiaopingworks.wordpress.com/2013/02/25/speech-at-the -all-army-conference-on-political-work/.

100. Jiang Shuping et al., "Broadcasting the Article."

101. Sheng Ping, *Chronology of Hu Yaobang's Thought*, "early June," 1978, 1:191– 192. See also Yu Huanchun, "罗瑞卿与'克思主义的一个最基本的原则'" [Luo Ruiqing and "One of Marxism's Most Fundamental Principles"], *Beijing Ribao*, July 7, 2008, http://www.reformdata.org/2008/0707/2265.shtml.

102. Sheng Ping, *Chronology of Hu Yaobang's Thought*, June 15, 1978, 1:192–193.

103. Yu Huanchun, "罗瑞卿与真理标准大讨论" [Luo Ruiqing and the great debate on the criterion of truth], HYBSL, February 12, 2009, http://w.hybsl.cn/article/13 /12548.

104. Sheng Ping, *Chronology of Hu Yaobang's Thought*, July 22, 23, 1978, 1:203– 205; also Ma Licheng, "Rise and Fall."

105. Anon., "40年前胡耀邦与中央专案组的一场斗争" [Forty years ago, Hu Yao-bang's battle with the Central Special Case Group], HYBSL, June 21, 2018, http://www .hybsl.cn/ybsxyj/shengpingyusixiang/2018-06-21/67818.html, accessed June 26, 2018. URL no longer valid.

106. Sheng Ping, *Chronology of Hu Yaobang's Thought*, June 10, 1978, 1:190; Zheng, *Hu Yaobang Chronological Materials*, June 9, 1978.

107. Sheng Ping, *Chronology of Hu Yaobang's Thought*, 1:191.

108. Leng Rong 冷溶 and Wang Zuoling 汪作玲, eds., 邓小平年谱 *Deng Xiaoping Chronology* (Central Literature Publishing House, Beijing, 2004), Vol. 1, June 25, 1978, 1:332. Hereafter cited as *Chronology of Deng Xiaoping*, date, volume: page.

109. Zheng, *Hu Yaobang Chronological Materials*, July 4, 1978.

110. Sheng Ping, *Chronology of Hu Yaobang's Thought*, July 6, 1978, 1:195–198; Shen Baoxiang, "沈宝祥：胡耀邦与华国锋" [Hu Yaobang and Hua Guofeng], *Tongzhou gong jin*, November 2009.

111. Sheng Ping, *Chronology of Hu Yaobang's Thought*, entries for July 10, 1977 and "early July" 1977, 1:200–201.

112. Hu Zhian 胡治安, "回忆'摘帽办：'解决55万人的问题" [Remembering the "Hat Removal Office": Solving the problems of 555,000 people], 壹讀*Yidu*, September 8, 2017 https://read01.com/zh-my/Rng0JLO.html.

113. Hu Yaobang, "落实干部政策，关键在于实事求是" [In implementing policy, the key is seeking truth from facts], September 25, 1978, in *Selected Works of Hu Yao-bang* (Renmin Chubanshe, 2015), 95–101 (excerpts). Also Sheng Ping, *Chronology of Hu Yaobang's Thought*, September 25, 1978, 1:224–228.

114. Dai Huang 戴煌, "胡耀邦怀仁堂讲话被删内幕" [The inside story of deletions from Hu Yaobang's Huairentang speech], Aisixiang Network, January 5, 2015, https://www.aisixiang.com/data/48842.html.

115. Sheng Ping, *Chronology of Hu Yaobang's Thought*, September 30, 1978, 1:229. See Zhang Hongbo 张宏波 and Zheng Zhiyong 郑志勇, "胡耀邦主政中组部" [Hu Yaobang in charge of the Central Organization Department], HYBSL, May 12, 2014, http://w.hybsl.cn/article/11/110/46232.

116. Han Gang 韩钢, "权力的转移：关于十一届三中全会" [Transferring power: On the Third Plenum of the 11th Central Committee], HYBSL, March 11, 2009, http://w.hybsl.cn/article/13/13022 (hereafter cited as Han, "Transferring Power").

117. Introduction to "3rd Plenary Session of the 11th CPC Central Committee," December 18–22, 1978, April 25, 2021, https://en.theorychina.org.cn/c/2021-04-25/1438324.shtml.

118. Han, "Transferring Power."

119. Wu Weifeng 吴伟锋, "胡耀邦出席1978年中央工作会议始末" [The full story of Hu Yaobang attending the 1978 Central work conference], *Renminwang*, January 5, 2018, http://dangshi.people.com.cn/n1/2018/0105/c85037-29747419.html (hereafter cited as Wu, "1978 Work Conference").

120. Wu, "1978 Work Conference"; Han, "Transferring Power."

121. Tao Zhu and Wang Heshou were close friends of Hu Yaobang dating back to Yan'an days.

122. The general content of Chen Yun's speech is cited in many works, including Yang Mingwei 杨明伟, 晚年陈云 [Chen Yun in his later years] (Xiandai, 2015), 11–15; Zhang et al., *Biography of Hu Yaobang*, 2:564; Wu, "1978 Work Conference"; Han, "Transferring Power."

123. Wu, "1978 Work Conference."

124. Han, "Transferring Power."

125. Sheng Ping, *Chronology of Hu Yaobang's Thought*, November 13, 1978, 1:239–241.

126. Ye Xuanji, "Marshal Ye."

127. Anon., "十一届三中全会回顾：邓小平春天里的'宣言书'" [Looking back at the 3rd Plenum of the 11th Central Committee: Deng Xiaoping's springtime "manifesto"], *Beijing Daily*, June 21, 2011, http://www.chinanews.com/gn/2011/06-21/3125186.shtml.

128. Wu, "1978 Work Conference"; Sheng Ping, *Chronology of Hu Yaobang's Thought*, November 13, 1978, 1:239–241.

129. Ye Xuanji, "Marshal Ye."

130. Ezra F. Vogel, *Deng Xiaoping and the Transformation of China* (Belknap Press of Harvard University Press, 2011), 240–241; Pantsov and Levine, *Deng Xiaoping*, 339. Both books draw heavily on Ye Xuanji, "Marshal Ye."

131. Dimon Liu, "The Chinese Communist Party's Four Instruments of Power," from "China 2030," unclassified paper written for the Department of Defense, Office of Net Assessment, in 2017, cited by permission.

132. *Chronology of Deng Xiaoping*, November 21, 1978, 1:433.

133. Sheng Ping, *Chronology of Hu Yaobang's Thought,* November 16, 1978, 1:242–244.

134. Yu Guangyuan 于光远, 1978 大转折— 十一届三中全会的台前幕后 [The great turning point of 1978: Behind the scenes at the 3rd Plenum of the 11th Congress] (hereafter cited as Yu Guangyuan, *Turning Point*), 128–129. Also Han Gang, "Transferring Power"; Wu, "1978 Work Conference."

135. Yu, *Turning Point,* 96–97.

136. Han, "Transferring Power."

137. Hu Jiwei 胡绩伟, "胡耀邦与西单民主墙" [Hu Yaobang and the Xidan Democracy Wall], April 17, 2004, *China News Digest,* http://hx.cnd.org/2004/04/17/胡绩伟:胡耀邦与西单民主墙/ (hereafter cited as Hu Jiwei, "Xidan Democracy Wall").

138. *Chronology of Deng Xiaoping,* December 1, 1978, 1:445; Wu, "1978 Work Conference"; Yu, *Turning Point,* 151–154.

139. Wu, "1978 Work Conference."

140. Wu, "1978 Work Conference." Although the 8341 Unit would remain under the control of the General Office, Wang's longtime subordinates Zhang Yaoci and Wu Jianhua were transferred to PLA units far from Beijing in early 1979.

141. Wu Weifeng, "Hu at Work Conference."

142. Wu Guoguang, in his insightful book *Anatomy of Political Power in China* (Marshall Cavendish, 2005), devotes an entire chapter to "documentary politics," a facet of CCP decision-making that gets little attention. In the CCP's highly bureaucratized structure, "the only way leaders have to establish legitimacy . . . remains the transfer of their own personal preferences into collective decisions," and "the major symbol of collective approval is the formulation of a [Central] document," which may include "resolutions, directives, reports, and even key leadership speeches." Wu, 99–102.

143. Sheng Ping, *Chronology of Hu Yaobang's Thought,* December 1, 1978, 1:255; Yu, *Turning Point,* 161–167.

144. Deng Xiaoping, "Emancipate the Mind, Seek Truth from Facts, and Unite as One in Looking to the Future," December 13, 1978, English version at https://dengxiaopingworks.wordpress.com/2013/02/25/emancipate-the-mind-seek-truth-from-facts-and-unite-as-one-in-looking-to-the-future/.

145. Cheng Guanjun 程冠军, "叶剑英1978年中央工作会议讲话稿起草内幕" [The inside story of drafting Ye Jianying's speech to the 1978 Central work conference], *Tongzhou gongjin,* September 6, 2016, https://pinglun.youth.cn/ll/201609/t20160906_8629109.htm.

146. Ye Jianying, "Speech to the Closing Meeting of the Central Work Conference," December 13, 1978, Aisixiang Network, http://www.aisixiang.com/data/23237.html.

147. Sheng Ping, the compiler of the *Chronology of Hu Yaobang's Thought,* and Hu Jiwei later claimed that Hu Qiaomu deleted from the official transcript Ye's remarks on the Democracy Wall, but they offer no evidence. See Sheng Ping, *Chronology of Hu Yaobang's Thought,* December 13, 1978, 1:257; Hu Jiwei, "Xidan Democracy Wall."

148. Zhang et al., *Biography of Hu Yaobang,* 2:578–580.

149. Zhang et al., *Biography of Hu Yaobang,* 2:581.

150. Shen Baoxiang, "胡耀邦与十一届三中全会前后的 理论动态" [Hu Yaobang and *Theoretical Dynamics* before and after the Third Plenum], HYBSL, May 3, 2017, http://w.hybsl.cn/article/10/104/64413.

151. Issue 69 of the e-magazine *Yaobang Studies* contains twenty-three articles by former party officials and historians about the Third Plenum and Hu Yaobang's contributions to its success. See "胡耀邦与十一届三中全会" [Hu Yaobang and the Third Plenary Session of the 11th Central Committee], May 3, 2017, http://w.hybsl.cn/sjournal/104/69.

152. An account of Ye's wariness about Deng—"a grasper of power and the guest who usurps the host"—has been quoted in overseas Chinese publications. See "叶剑英联手华国锋也斗不过邓小平" [Even Ye Jianying joining hands with Hua Guofeng could not overcome Deng Xiaoping], *Aboluowang News,* May 19, 2017, https://www.aboluowang.com/2017/0519/931799.html.

153. Su Weimin 苏维民, "胡耀邦与中南海" [Hu Yaobang in Zhongnanhai], HYBSL, May 3, 2017, http://w.hybsl.cn/article/10/104/64415 (hereafter cited as Su Weimin, "Hu Yaobang in Zhongnanhai").

154. Su Weimin, "Hu Yaobang in Zhongnanhai."

155. Shen Baoxiang, "胡耀邦发动和推进真理标准问题讨论纪实" [The record of how Hu Yaobang launched and promoted the debate on the criterion of truth], from 百年潮 [Centennial tide], issue 4, March 15, 2007, http://w.hybsl.cn/article/11/109/1574.

156. Author interview with Wei Jingsheng 魏京生, June 16, 2019.

157. Hu Jiwei, "Xidan Democracy Wall."

158. Wei Jingsheng, "The Fifth Modernization," December 5, 1978, English translation at https://weijingsheng.org/doc/en/THE%20FIFTH%20MODERNIZATION.html.

159. Hu Jiwei, "Xidan Democracy Wall."

160. Hu Jiwei, "Xidan Democracy Wall."

161. Hu Jiwei, "Xidan Democracy Wall"; Sheng Ping, *Chronology of Hu Yaobang's Thought,* December 21, 1978, 1:263.

162. Sheng Ping, *Chronology of Hu Yaobang's Thought,* December 31, 1978, 1:268. Also Li Ping 李平, "胡耀邦就职中宣部的三次讲话" [Hu Yaobang's three speeches upon taking office in the Propaganda Department], *Yanhuang Chunqiu,* August 2015.

163. Sheng Ping, *Chronology of Hu Yaobang's Thought,* notes on Hu's speech to senior Propaganda Department officials, December 31, 1978, 1:267–274.

164. Sheng Ping, *Chronology of Hu Yaobang's Thought,* December 31, 1978, 1:267–270.

165. Anon., "邓小平为何不满1979年理论工作务虚会" [Why Deng Xiaoping was unhappy with the Conference on Theoretical Work Principles in 1979], *Renminwang,* September 20, 2014, http://view.news.qq.com/a/20140920/000823.htm.

166. Sheng Ping, *Chronology of Hu Yaobang's Thought,* January 3, 1979, 1:283. Also Zheng Zhongbing, "胡耀邦与胡乔木— 在历史转折的十字路口" [Hu Yaobang and Hu Qiaomu—at the crossroads of history], Aisixiang Network, July 27, 2013, http://www.aisixiang.com/data/22487.html.

167. Sheng Ping, *Chronology of Hu Yaobang's Thought,* January 10, 1979, Hu Yaobang speech to propaganda officials, 1:285–292.

168. Hu Yaobang, "Introduction to the Conference on Theoretical Work Principles," in *The Selected Works of Hu Yaobang* (People's Publishing House, 2015), 109–122

169. Hu, "Introduction."

170. Zhang Xianyang 张显扬, "邓小平突令理论务虚会转向" [Deng Xiaoping suddenly ordered the Conference on Theoretical Principles to change direction], Mirror History, July 22, 2012, http://www.mingjinglishi.com/2012/07/blog-post_22.html; also Merle Goldman, "Hu Yaobang's Intellectual Network and the Theory Conference of 1979," *China Quarterly* 126 (June 1991): 219–242.

171. Wang Tao 王涛, "1979年理论工作务虚会" [The 1979 Conference on Theoretical Principles], HYBSL, August 28, 2014, http://w.hybsl.cn/article/13/47973.

172. Shen Baoxiang, "胡耀邦主持的理论工作务虚会(一)" [The Conference on Theoretical Principles that Hu Yaobang led (part 1)], HYBSL, January 16, 2019, http://www.hybsl.cn/beijingcankao/beijingfenxi/2019-01-16/69069.html, accessed March 18, 2019, URL no longer valid, (hereafter cited as Shen Baoxiang, "The Conference Hu Led").

173. Deng Liqun 邓力群, 邓力群自述: 十二个春秋 [Deng Liqun autobiography: Twelve seasons] (Dafeng Chubanshe, 2006), 137. Given Hu Qiaomu's and Deng Liqun's central roles in attacking Hu Yaobang, the veracity of this story is at least questionable.

174. Vogel, *Deng Xiaoping,* 339; Pantsov and Levine, *Deng Xiaoping,* 348–349.

175. Shi Yijun 史义军, "关于华国锋下台的几个细节" [Several details about Hua Guofeng's downfall], HYBSL, April 20, 2015, http://w.hybsl.cn/article/13/51780.

176. "邓小平打越南阻力重重 陈云一句话扭转乾坤" [Deng Xiaoping faced heavy obstacles in attacking Vietnam, one sentence from Chen Yun turned the tide], *Wenxuecity,* April 26, 2015, https://www.wenxuecity.com/news/2015/04/26/4220671.html (hereafter cited as *Wenxuecity,* "Chen Yun Support").

177. Anon., "揭秘：1978年对越自卫反击战始末," [Revealed: The 1978 attack in self-defense against Vietnam from beginning to end], *Phoenix News,* August 3, 2008, http://news.ifeng.com/history/1/midang/200808/0803_2664_692237.shtml; Shen Tingxue 沈听雪, "军史揭秘：开国上将杨勇与对越自卫反击战" [Military history revealed: Senior general Yang Yong and the self-defensive counterattack on Vietnam], May 22, 2017, https://m.sohu.com/n/493932722/.

178. Xiaoming Zhang, *Deng Xiaoping's Long War: The Military Conflict between China and Vietnam, 1979–1991* (University of North Carolina Press, 2015), chap. 2, "Deng Xiaoping's War Decision." Also *Wenxuecity,* "Chen Yun support."

179. Yang Jisheng, *Political Struggles,* 107.

180. Sheng Ping, *Chronology of Hu Yaobang's Thought,* February 28, 1979, 322–324.

181. Hu Jiwei, "Xidan Democracy Wall."

182. *Chronology of Deng Xiaoping,* March 16, 1979, 1:493.

183. Sheng Ping, *Chronology of Hu Yaobang's Thought,* speech to a national forum on newspaper work, March 10, 1979, 1:326–332.

184. Sheng Ping, *Chronology of Hu Yaobang's Thought,* speech to Central Party School, March 17, 1979, 1:333–336.

185. Wei Jingsheng, "Do We Want Democracy or a New Dictatorship?," posted March 25, 1979, on the Xidan Democracy Wall in Beijing, http://weijingsheng.org /doc/cn/23.htm.

186. Author interview with Wei Jingsheng.

187. Li Honglin 李洪林, "我的'理论工作者'经历" [My experience as a "theory worker"], HYBSL, April 6, 2011, http://w.hybsl.cn/article/13/25499 (hereafter cited as, Li Honglin, "My Experience"). See also Wu Jiang 吴江, "1979年理论工作务虚会追记" [Memoir of the 1979 Theory Work Principles conference], *Yanhuang Chunqiu,* November 2001 (hereafter cited as Wu Jiang, "1979 Memoir").

188. Deng Xiaoping, "Uphold the Four Cardinal Principles," speech delivered March 30, 1979, English translation at http://en.people.cn/dengxp/vol2/text/b1290 .html (hereafter cited as Deng, "Uphold").

189. Shen Baoxiang, "The Conference Hu Led."

190. Li Honglin, "My Experience"; Wu Jiang, "1979 Memoir."

191. Pantsov and Levine, *Deng Xiaoping,* 355.

192. Deng, "Uphold."

193. Deng, "Uphold."

194. Deng, "Uphold."

195. Deng, "Uphold."

196. Deng, "Uphold."

197. Sheng Ping, *Chronology of Hu Yaobang's Thought,* March 30, 1979, 1:345–346.

198. Wu Jiang, "1979 Memoir."

199. Sheng Ping, *Chronology of Hu Yaobang's Thought,* April 3, 1979, 1:345–347.

200. Sheng Ping, *Chronology of Hu Yaobang's Thought,* April 3, 1979, 1:345–347.

201. Hu Jiwei, "论胡赵十年新政／胡绩伟口述 姚监复整理" [On the Hu-Zhao new administration, narrated to and arranged by Yao Jianfu], Wordpress.com, January 6, 2010, https://wlcp.wordpress.com/2010/01/06/论胡赵十年新政胡绩伟口述-姚监复整理/.

202. Hu Jiwei, "Xidan Democracy Wall."

203. Hu Jiwei, "Xidan Democracy Wall"; author interview with Wei Jingsheng. Wei was sentenced to fifteen years for "selling intelligence to a foreign journalist" during the Vietnam incursion. He admitted the charge, he said, not because it was true but because it did not entail a death sentence. Wei had been told by family friends that, in a long Politburo meeting, Deng had demanded his death, while Chen Yun insisted he be released and Ye Jianying suggested he undergo reeducation because Wei was "one of us." Other elders, and Hu Yaobang, also opposed Deng's evident assumption that he could arbitrarily impose a death sentence.

204. Hu Jiwei, "On the Hu-Zhao New Administration."

8. The Making of a Reformer

1. See Xiao Donglian 萧冬连, "中国改革开放的缘起" [The origins of China's reform and opening], Aisixiang Network, September 24, 2019, http://www.aisixiang .com/data/117851.html (hereafter cited as Xiao, "Origins").

2. Xiao Donglian, "1978–1984年中国经济体制改革思路的演进— 决策与实施" [The 1978–84 evolution of thinking about China's economic structural reform: Decision-making and implementation], Hu Yaobang Historical Materials Information Network (hereafter HYBSL), August 30, 2013, http://w.hybsl.cn/article/13/40161 (hereafter cited as Xiao, "1978–84 Evolution").

3. Wu Xiaobo 吴晓波, "1979: '调整'与'改革'之争" [1979: The battle between 'adjustment' and 'reform'], HYBSL, January 11, 2010, http://w.hybsl.cn/article/13/18302.

4. Han Gang 韩钢, "艰难的转型：一九七八年中央工作会议的农业议题" [Difficult transition: The agricultural question at the 1978 CCP Work Conference], HYBSL, October 26, 2011, http://w.hybsl.cn/article/13/27298.

5. Li Kejun 李克军, "千万不要忘记'割资本主义尾巴'的历史教训" [Never forget the historical lessons of "Cutting Off Capitalist Tails"], Aisixiang Network, December 13, 2017, http://www.aisixiang.com/data/107304.html.

6. Ling Zhijun 凌志军 and Ma Licheng 马立诚, 呼喊— 当今中国的五种声音 [Shouts: Five kinds of voices in today's China] (Hubei People's Publishing House, 2008), 103–105.

7. Yu Guangyuan 于光远, "华国锋太胆小怯弱" [Hua Guofeng was too timid], Aisixiang Network, July 20, 2012, https://www.aisixiang.com/data/55610.html.

8. Leng Rong 冷溶 and Wang Zuoling 汪作玲, eds., 邓小平年谱 *Deng Xiaoping Chronology* (Central Literature Publishing House, Beijing, 2004), Vol. 1, December 1, 1978, 1:445. Hereafter cited as *Chronology of Deng Xiaoping*, date, volume: page.

9. Huang Wei 黄卫, "谁提出要坚决拥护以邓小平为'头子'的党中央?" [Who proposed firmly supporting the party Center with Deng Xiaoping as the 'boss'?], *China Newsweek,* October 13, 2015, http://w.hybsl.cn/article/13/54767.

10. See, for example, Ezra F. Vogel, *Deng Xiaoping and the Transformation of China* (Belknap Press of Harvard University Press, 2011), 238. Also Alexander V. Pantsov with Steven I. Levine, *Deng Xiaoping: A Revolutionary Life* (Oxford University Press, 2015), 343.

11. See Song Yijun 宋毅军, "邓小平为核心的中央领导集体形成始末" [The full story of how the Central leadership collective with Deng Xiaoping as the core came into being], *CCP News Network,* June 8, 2013, http://dangshi.people.com.cn/n/2013/0608/c85037-21793779.html; also Han Gang 韩钢, "权力的转移: 关于十一届三中全会" [Transferring power: On the 3rd Plenum of the 11th Central Committee], HYBSL, March 11, 2009, http://w.hybsl.cn/article/13/13022.

12. Yang Guang 杨光, "华国锋、邓小平、陈云之间的派系之争" [Factional struggle between Hua Guofeng, Deng Xiaoping, and Chen Yun], Independent Chinese Pen Center (US-based), January 16, 2017, https://www.chinesepen.org/blog/archives/75916 (hereafter cited as Yang Guang, "Factional Struggle").

13. Yang Jisheng 杨继绳, 中国改革年代的政治斗争 [The political battles of China's reform era] (Cosmos Books, 2010) (hereafter cited as Yang Jisheng, *Political Battles*), 6–7.

14. Zhang Jincai 张金才, "陈云与中央财经工作领导机构的变迁" [Chen Yun and changes in the leadership organs of Central finance and economic work], HYBSL, February 3, 2015, http://w.hybsl.cn/article/13/50689.

15. Yang Mingwei 杨明伟, 晚年陈云 [Chen Yun in his later years] (Modern Publishing House, 2015) (hereafter cited as Yang Mingwei, *Chen Yun*), 1–3.

16. Zhu Jiamu 朱佳木, "改革开放初期的陈云与邓小平" [Chen Yun and Deng Xiaoping in the early period of reform and opening], *Contemporary China History Studies* 17, no. 3 (May 2010) (hereafter cited as Zhu Jiamu, "Chen Yun"), 4–15.

17. Yang Jisheng, *Political Battles,* 78–79; Cai Rupeng 蔡如鹏, "求实者陈云" [Chen Yun the realist], *China Newsweek,* July 23, 2015, http://w.hybsl.cn/article/13/53398.

18. Anon., "陈云力荐胡耀邦任中纪委书记" [Chen Yun strongly recommended Hu Yaobang to be CCDI secretary"], 山西晚报 [Shanxi Evening News], June 2, 2013, https://groups.google.com/g/axth518/c/Sb6f3aF4TkA?pli=1.

19. Yang Guang, "Factional Struggle."

20. Yang Mingwei, *Chen Yun,* 28–33; Xiao Donglian, "1978–84 Evolution."

21. Yang Mingwei, *Chen Yun,* 39.

22. Xiao, "Origins."

23. Yang Mingwei, *Chen Yun,* 27–28, 43–56.

24. Yang Mingwei, *Chen Yun,* 58.

25. Wang Gang 王刚, "陈云在哪三次重要历史关头成关键人物" [In which three historical moments did Chen Yun become a key figure?], *CCP News Network,* June 30, 2015, http://w.hybsl.cn/article/13/52984.

26. "Major Events in the Chinese Communist Party: 1979," http://cpc.people.com.cn/GB/64162/64164/4416113.html.

27. Chung Yen-lin 鐘延麟, "彭真和中共東北局爭論: 兼論其於高崗，林彪，陳雲之關係" [Peng Zhen and the debate in the CCP Northeast Bureau: Also his relationships to Gao Gang, Lin Biao and Chen Yun], *Academica Sinica, Contemporary History Collection* 91 (2016): 99–151.

28. Gao Tianding 高天鼎, "彭真蒙冤及平反始末" [The whole story of the injustice done to Peng Zhen and its resolution], HYBSL, July 8, 2015, http://w.hybsl.cn/article/13/53123.

29. Yang Jisheng, *Political Battles,* 130–131; Xu Qingquan 徐庆全, "'八老'与1980年代政治格局" [The 'eight elders' and the political situation in the 1980s], Aisixiang Network, December 23, 2014, http://www.aisixiang.com/data/81722.html (hereafter cited as Xu, "Eight Elders").

30. Zhang Liqun, Zhang Ding, Yan Ruping, Tang Fei, and Li Gongtian, *Biography of Hu Yaobang,* vol. 2 (Beijing United Press, 2015), 2:582–583; Zhu Jiamu, "Chen Yun"; Yang Mingwei, *Chen Yun,* 161–163.

31. "关于党内政治生活的若干准则" [Concerning certain norms of internal party political life], text and analysis at https://baike.baidu.com/item/关于党内政治生活的若干准则.

32. "中国共产党大事记 (1980年)" [Record of Chinese Communist Party major events (1980)], undated, http://www.gov.cn/test/2007-09/04/content_736395.htm (hereafter cited as "Record of CCP Major Events (1980)").

33. "Record of CCP Major Events (1980)."

34. "Record of CCP Major Events (1980)."

35. "Record of CCP Major Events (1980)."

36. Yang Guang, "Factional Struggle."

37. Li Lin 李林, "中共中央书记处组织沿革与功能变迁" [The organizational evolution and functional changes of the CCP Central Secretariat], *CCP News Network,* October 22, 2012, http://news.sohu.com/20121022/n355444622.shtml.

38. "中国共产党第十一届中央委员会第五次全体会议公报" [Communiqué of the Fifth Plenary Session of the Eleventh Central Committee of the Communist Party of China], adopted February 29, 1980, text online at http://cpc.people.com.cn/GB/64162/64168/64563/65373/4441915.html.

39. "Communiqué of the Fifth Plenary Session."

40. Su Weimin, "Zhongnanhai after the 3rd Plenum," HYBSL, May 3, 2017, http://w.hybsl.cn/article/10/104/64415 (hereafter cited as Su Weimin, "Hu in Zhongnanhai").

41. Man Mei, *Remembering Father, Hu Yaobang* (Cosmos Books, 2016), 2:534–536.

42. See Zheng Zhongbing, ed., *Hu Yaobang Chronological Materials, Long Form* (International Era, 2005), March 25, 1979. See also Sheng Ping, ed., *A Chronology of Hu Yaobang's Thought* (Taide Shidai, 2007), 1:484–496.

43. Zhang et al., *Biography of Hu Yaobang*, 2:586–588

44. Chen Weiren 陈维仁, "胡耀邦与西藏" [Hu Yaobang and Tibet], HYBSL, November 28, 2012, http://w.hybsl.cn/article/10/104/32430.

45. Wang Yao 王尧, "我陪耀邦书记进藏侧记" [Sidelights of my accompanying Secretary Yaobang into Tibet], HYBSL, November 28, 2012, http://w.hybsl.cn/article/10/104/32429 (hereafter cited as Wang, "Sidelights").

46. Wang, "Sidelights."

47. "中共中央关于印发 西藏工作座谈会纪要的通知(一九八四年四月一日)" [Central Committee circular on issuing the "Summary of the Symposium on Tibet Work" (April 1, 1984)], HYBSL, July 15, 2007, http://w.hybsl.cn/article/15/38928.

48. Zhao Shukai 赵树凯, "胡耀邦与'包产到户'政策突破" [Hu Yaobang and the breakthrough on the "bao chan dao hu" policy], *China's Reform*, February 2018, https://www.aisixiang.com/data/110007.html (hereafter cited as Zhao, "Hu and Breakthrough").

49. Xu Qingquan 徐庆全 and Du Mingming 杜明明, "包产到户提出过程中的高层争论 . . ." [High-level disputes in the process of raising bao chan dao hu . . .], *Yanhuang Chunqiu*, November 2008, https://bbs.wenxuecity.com/memory/512163 .html; Vogel, *Deng Xiaoping*, 439.

50. *Deng Xiaoping Chronology*, 1:641–642.

51. Zhao, "Hu and Breakthrough."

52. Zhao, "Hu and Breakthrough."

53. Sheng Ping, *Chronology of Hu Yaobang's Thought*, Hu Yaobang speech to National Propaganda Work Conference, July 12–13, 1980, 1:526–527.

54. Wu Xiang, 吴象, "胡耀邦与万里在农村改革中" [Hu Yaobang and Wan Li in the rural reforms], 财新 [*Caixin Magazine*], May 26, 2021, https://shengping.blog .caixin.com/archives/246266.

55. Zhao, "Hu and Breakthrough"; Zheng, *Hu Yaobang Chronological Materials*, September 27, 1980.

56. Zhao Shukai 赵树凯, "农村改革的政治逻辑" [The political logic of rural reform], *Journal of Central China Normal University* (February 2020), https://www .aisixiang.com/data/120604.html.

57. Hu Jiwei 胡绩伟, in his autobiographical and often polemical works, argues that Deng Xiaoping should not receive credit for Hu Yaobang's and Zhao Ziyang's reformist initiatives. See Hu Jiwei, 胡绩伟自选集 餘絲集 [Hu Jiwei's self-selected works—residual selections] (Zhuoyue Wenhua, 2013), 70–76.

58. Zhen Shi 甄实, "胡耀邦与关于建国以来党的若干历史问题的决议" [Hu Yaobang and the "Resolution on Certain Questions in the History of Our Party . . ."],

HYBSL, September 4, 2012, http://w.hybsl.cn/article/11/110/30794 (hereafter cited as Zhen, "HYB and the History Resolution").

59. Huang Li 黄黎, ". . . 历史问题的决议》起草的台前幕后" [The full story behind the drafting of the "Resolution on Party History"], *CCP News Network,* April 2, 2009, http://www.reformdata.org/2009/0420/3623.shtml (hereafter cited as Huang, "Full Story").

60. Chen Donglin 陈东林, "邓小平与'关于 . . . 历史问题的决议'的形成'" [Deng Xiaoping and the shaping of the'[history] resolution'], Party History Expo, June 2013, https://www.dswxyjy.org.cn/n1/2019/0228/c423730-30915972.html (hereafter cited as Chen, "Shaping the Resolution").

61. Song Yuehong 宋月红, "起草党的第二个历史决议的思想史料整理与研究" [Organizing and considering historical material for drafting the second party history resolution], *CCP Historical Research,* April 2014, https://www.reileurope.com /dsdj/dsdj_ggkfsq/201910/t20191031_5024247.shtml.

62. See "Remarks on Successive Drafts of the 'Resolution on Certain Questions in the History of Our Party since the Founding of the People's Republic of China'" (March 1980–June 1981), in *Selected Works of Deng Xiaoping (1975–1982)* (Foreign Languages Press, 1983), 276–296.

63. Zhen, "HYB and the History Resolution."

64. *Deng Xiaoping Chronology,* 1:609–611; Huang, "Full Story."

65. Jiang Yongqing 将永清, "邓小平主持起草'历史决议' . . ." [Deng Xiaoping oversaw the drafting of the 'history resolution' . . ."], CCP News Network, March 17, 2014, http://cpc.people.com.cn/n/2014/0317/c69113-24656794.html (hereafter cited as Jiang Yongqing, "Deng Xiaoping Oversaw").

66. Jiang Yongqing, "Deng Xiaoping Oversaw."

67. Jiang Yongqing, "Deng Xiaoping Oversaw"; Huang, "Full Story"; Chen Donglin, "Shaping the Resolution."

68. Jiang Yongqing, "Deng Xiaoping Oversaw."

69. Deng, *Selected Works,* "Answers to the Italian Journalist Oriana Fallaci," August 21 and 23, 1980, 326–334.

70. Sheng Ping, *Chronology of Hu Yaobang's Thought,* October 10, 1980, 1:542.

71. Guo Daohui 郭道晖, "问四千老干部对党史的一次民主评议" [Asked four thousand old cadres for a democratic appraisal of the party's history], March 25, 2010, https://www.aisixiang.com/data/32590.html (hereafter cited as Guo, "Appraisal").

72. Guo, "Appraisal."

73. Guo, "Appraisal."

74. Deng, "On History Resolution," in *Selected Works,* 282–287.

75. Both Zheng's *Hu Yaobang Chronological Materials* (August 17–19, 1980) and Sheng Ping's *Chronology of Hu Yaobang's Thought* (1:534–537) place Hu in remote

Ningxia Province during the three-day Politburo meeting, although both also note Deng's August 18 speech, and Zheng claims Hu "attended" (*chuxi*).

76. See Wu Wei 吴伟, "邓小平与 '党和国家领导制度的改革'" [Deng Xiaoping and "reform of the party and state leadership system"], HYBSL, October 11, 2014, http://w.hybsl.cn/article/13/48626.

77. Deng, "On the Reform of the System of Party and State Leadership," in *Selected Works,* August 18, 1980, 302–325.

78. Deng Liqun 邓力群, 邓力群自述: 十二个春秋 [Deng Liqun autobiography: Twelve seasons] (Dafeng, 2006) (hereafter cited as Deng Liqun, *Autobiography*), 183.

79. "Record of CCP Major Events (1980)."

80. "Record of CCP Major Events (1980)."

81. I am indebted to Warren Sun of Monash University for sharing via email his extensive notes on the process of Hua Guofeng's ouster in late 1980. Hereafter cited as Warren Sun material. Other important sources include: Shi Yijun 史义军, "关于华国锋下台的几个细节" [Several details about Hua Guofeng's fall], HYBSL, April 20, 2015, http://w.hybsl.cn/article/13/51780; Han Gang 韩钢, "对华国锋的争议从何而来" [Where the opposition to Hua Guofeng came from], HYBSL, August 26, 2011, http://w.hybsl.cn/article/13/26654 (hereafter cited as Han, "Opposition to Hua").

82. Han "Opposition to Hua"; Warren Sun material.

83. Sheng Ping, *Chronology of Hu Yaobang's Thought,* November 19, 1980, 1:558.

84. Warren Sun material; news aggregator Sina.com quoted extensively from the meetings in a January 9, 2015 story: "华国锋辞去中央主席：陈云建议其'让贤,'" ["Hua Guofeng resigned as CCP chairman: Chen Yun proposed he give way to 'one more worthy'], https://cul.sina.cn/sh/2015-01-09/detail-iavxeafr9793894.d.html?from=wap (hereafter cited as "Chen Yun Suggested").

85. Warren Sun material.

86. Sheng Ping, *Chronology of Hu Yaobang's Thought,* October 19, 1980, 1:551–559; Shi Yijun, "胡耀邦狠批华国锋'五宗罪'" [Hu Yaobang ruthlessly criticized Hua Guofeng's 'five mortal sins'], https://www.aboluowang.com/2015/0427/548066.html.

87. Wu Wei 吴伟, "很多扣给华国锋的罪名是子虚乌" [Many of the charges made against Hua Guofeng were false], Phoenix Information, September 2, 2014, https://news.creaders.net/china/2014/09/02/1425945.html; Han Gang 韩钢, "Opposition to Hua." .

88. Shi Yijun, "胡耀邦崛起的垫脚石" [The stepping stones of Hu Yaobang's rise], Gongshiwang, April 21, 2015, https://bbs.wenxuecity.com/huyaobang/737961.html.

89. Hu Deping, "胡德平,"为何"耀邦不愿动华国锋?" [Why was Hu Yaobang unwilling to displace Hua Guofeng?], *Yanhuang Chunqiu,* July, 2010.

90. "Chen Yun Suggested"

91. "Chen Yun Suggested."

92. Man Mei 满妹, "胡耀邦十次拒任中共中央主席 邓小平出招应对" [Hu Yao-bang refused ten times to be named CCP chairman; Deng Xiaoping moved to deal with it], *Sohu News,* August 20, 2015, http://news.sohu.com/20150820/n419337166 .shtml.

93. "Record of CCP Major Events (1980)."

94. Sheng Ping, *Chronology of Hu Yaobang's Thought,* December 3–12, 1980, 1:568–571.

95. Jiang Yongqing 蒋永清, "简述1977年至1982年国民经济调整的两次决策" [A brief description of the two decisions on adjustment of the national economy from 1977 to 1982], CCP History and Literature Institute, December 16, 2015, http://www .dswxyjy.org.cn/n1/2019/0228/c423964-30930048.html (hereafter cited as Jiang Yongqing, "Two Decisions"); Xiao Donglian, "1978–84 Evolution."

96. Hu Fuchen 胡甫臣, "胡耀邦鲜为人知的两大贡献" [Two of Hu Yaobang's little-known contributions], *Yanhuang Chunqiu,* September 2010, https://www .aisixiang.com/data/36465.html.

97. Jiang Yongqing, "Two Decisions."

98. Xiao Donglian, "1978–84 Evolution."

99. Deng Xiaoping, "Implement the Policy of Readjustment, Ensure Stability and Unity," in *Selected Works,* December 25, 1980, 335, 343.

100. Sheng Ping, *Chronology of Hu Yaobang's Thought,* December 16, 1980, 1:573.

101. Li Rui 李锐, "耀邦去世前的谈话" [A talk with Yaobang before his death], *Modern China Studies,* April 2001, https://www.aisixiang.com/data/20900.html, pre-sents a detailed discussion, held on April 8, 1989, of Hu's experiences as general secretary. Hereafter cited as Li Rui, "Last Talk."

102. Wang Zhongfang 王仲方, "耀邦与我的两次谈心" [Two heart-to-heart talks between Yaobang and me], HYBSL, December 22, 2012, http://w.hybsl.cn/article/11 /109/24271.

103. Sheng Ping, *Chronology of Hu Yaobang's Thought,* January 29–30, 1981, 1:591–602

104. Sheng Ping, *Chronology of Hu Yaobang's Thought,* March 2, 1981, 1:606.

105. Sheng Ping, *Chronology of Hu Yaobang's Thought,* March 9, 1981, 1:609–614.

106. Sheng Ping, *Chronology of Hu Yaobang's Thought,* February 17, 1981, 1:604; Deng Liqun, *Autobiography,* 173–174.

107. *Deng Xiaoping Chronology,* March 7, 9, and 13, 1981, 2:718–721. See also Jiang Yongqing, "Two Decisions."

108. *Deng Xiaoping Chronology,* 2:725–726; Chen Donglin, "Shaping the Resolu-tion." Deng's seeking help from Chen Yun, paying a call on him, was an indication of his impatience to finish the resolution.

109. *Deng Xiaoping Chronology,* March 26, 1981, 2:726; Sheng Ping, *Chronology of Hu Yaobang's Thought,* 1:617–618.

110. Zhang et al., *Biography of Hu Yaobang,* 2:651.

111. Sheng Ping, *Chronology of Hu Yaobang's Thought,* May 4, 1981, 1:622–623.

112. Zhen, "HYB and the History Resolution"; Chen Donglin, "Shaping the Resolution."

113. Sheng Ping, *Chronology of Hu Yaobang's Thought,* May 15, 1981, 1:627.

114. Deng Xiaoping, "Speech to an Enlarged Session of the Political Bureau," in *Selected Works,* May 19, 1981, 293.

115. Deng Xiaoping, "Speech during the Preparatory Meeting for the Sixth Plenary Session of the Eleventh Central Committee, June 22, 1981," in *Selected Works,* 293–296.

116. An English-language version of the full text can be found at https://www.marxists.org/subject/china/documents/cpc/history/01.htm. As of August 26, 2021, the Chinese-language version, on the CCP's official website at http://cpc.people.com.cn/GB/64162/64168/64563/65374/4526448.html, is not publicly available.

117. Chen Donglin, "Shaping the Resolution"; see also Sheng Ping, *Chronology of Hu Yaobang's Thought,* vol. 1, editorial comments by Sheng Ping at 1:635, 636.

118. Hu Yaobang, "在党的十一届六中全会闭幕会上的讲话" [Speech at the closing ceremony for the 6th Plenum of the 11th CCP Congress], June 29, 1981, in 胡耀邦文选 [The selected works of Hu Yaobang] (Renmin Ribao Publishing House, 2015), 261–265.

119. See, for example, "Stick to the Bottom Line, Push for Change: Commemorating the 30th Anniversary of the Publication of 'The Resolution on Certain Questions . . . ," *China Reform,* August 27, 2011, https://magazine.caixin.com/2011-09-28/100310283.html (*Caixin* subscribers only).

120. Huang Jiayang 黄家杨, "邓小平:'历史决议'起草受时局所限" [Deng Xiaoping—The 'history resolution' drafting was limited by the situation at the time], HYBSL, March 15, 2012, http://w.hybsl.cn/article/13/28976.

121. Pantsov and Levine, *Deng Xiaoping,* 376.

122. Yang Guang, "Factional Struggle."

123. Chen Liming 陈利明, 从小红鬼到总书记 [From little red devil to general secretary] (Renmin Ribao chubanshe, 2013), 2:465.

124. Sheng Ping, *Chronology of Hu Yaobang's Thought,* vol. 2, September 1, 1982, 2:765–781. Text and interpretative notes by Sheng Ping.

125. *China News Analysis,* "The 12th Party Congress (September 1–11, 1982)," no. 1243, October 8, 1982, 1–8. LaDany, a Jesuit priest resident in Hong Kong, based his analysis and commentary on listening to Radio Peking in Chinese for hours every day.

126. "胡耀邦在中共十二大上的报告" [Hu Yaobang's report to the 12th Congress of the Chinese Communist Party], delivered September 1, 1982, in *Selected Works of Hu Yaobang,* 435ff. More-recent online versions of Hu's speech have excised the

references to "communism." See, for example, http://cpc.people.com.cn/GB/64162
/64168/64565/65448/4526430.html.

127. Xu Qingquan 徐庆全, "胡耀邦对十二大报告的一个修正" [Hu Yaobang's revi-
sion of the 12th Congress report], HYBSL, November 5, 2008, http://w.hybsl.cn
/article/11/110/10515.

128. Yang Jisheng, *Political Battles,* 8.

129. Hu Jiwei 胡绩伟, "论胡赵十年新政" [On the Hu-Zhao New Deal], Wordpress,
January 6, 2010, https://wlcp.wordpress.com/2010/01/06/. Gao Gao 高皋, 三頭馬車
時代— 鄧小平 – 胡耀邦 – 趙紫陽 [Troika era: Deng Xiaoping—Hu Yaobang—Zhao
Ziyang] (Mirror Books, 2009), 116.

130. Sheng Ping, *Chronology of Hu Yaobang's Thought,* September 1, 1982,
2:768–769.

131. The officially approved text of Hu's January 20, 1983, speech, "四化建设和改
革问题" [Construction of the Four Modernizations and the question of reform], is
in his *Selected Works,* 474–493. Hereafter cited as Hu Yaobang, "Modernization and
Reform."

132. Shen Baoxiang 沈宝祥, "历史新时期最早的改革宣言书—— 重读胡耀邦 '四化
建设和改革问题'重要讲话" [The earliest reform manifesto in the new historical
period: Rereading Hu Yaobang's important speech on "Construction of the Four
Modernizations and the Issue of Reform"], HYBSL, July 24, 2014, http://w.hybsl.cn
/article/11/110/47398 (hereafter cited as Shen Baoxiang, "Reform Manifesto").

133. Hu Yaobang, "Modernization and Reform."

134. Hu Yaobang, "Modernization and Reform."

135. Qin Chuan 秦川, "一九八三年初风云中的胡耀邦" [Hu Yaobang amid turmoil
in early 1983], HYBSL, December 10, 2013, http://w.hybsl.cn/article/10/104/43459
(hereafter cited as Qin, "Hu amid Turmoil").

136. Qin, "Hu amid Turmoil." Also Sheng Ping, *Chronology of Hu Yaobang's
Thought,* 2:832–833, 839–840.

137. He Yunhua 何云华, "1983，总书记胡耀邦在深圳" [General Secretary Hu Yao-
bang in Shenzhen in 1983], HYBSL, August 28, 2010, w.hybsl.cn/article/10/104/22023.

138. Chen Xiaoya 陈小雅, 八九民运史 [The history of the '89 people's movement],
pt. 1 (Citizen Publishing, 2019) (hereafter cited as Chen Xiaoya, *People's Movement*),
1:112–113. See also Yang Jisheng, *Political Battles,* 237–239.

139. Yang Jisheng, *Political Battles,* 237–239; *Deng Xiaoping Chronology,*
2:895–896.

140. Yang Jisheng, *Political Battles,* 237–239; Sheng Ping, *Chronology of Hu Yaobang's Thought,* March 17, 1983, 2:853–856.

141. *Deng Xiaoping Chronology,* 2:895–896.

142. Deng Liqun, *Autobiography,* 261. There were several different apparent
agendas in play at this meeting. Hu Qiaomu, abetted by Deng Liqun and with Chen
Yun's tacit support, wanted to get rid of Hu Yaobang. Deng Xiaoping seemed to want

to move ahead with his "quadrupling" agenda with Zhao Ziyang, and was nonplussed by Chen's diatribe. Hu Yaobang understood he was under attack and needed support from Ye Jianying. Man Mei claims Ye played a key role in stopping an attempt to replace her father. See Man Mei, *Remembering Father,* 2:731.

143. Li Rui, "Last Talk"; Sheng Ping, *Chronology of Hu Yaobang's Thought,* March 18, 1983, 2:857.

144. Sheng Ping, *Chronology of Hu Yaobang's Thought,* March 19, 1983, 2:857–858. Qin, "Hu amid Turmoil."

145. Li Rui, "Last Talk."

146. Sheng Xia 盛夏, "中共两支笔的争斗" [The battle of two CCP scribes], Sina .com, October 10, 2014, https://xifeizaixian.com/shcg/2352.

147. Yang Jisheng, *Political Battles,* 206–215.

148. Chen Xiaoya, *People's Movement,* 1:96–97.

149. Qin Chuan 秦川 and Xu Qingchuan 徐庆全, "1983年'清除精神污染'" [Purging 'spiritual pollution' in 1983], HYBSL, May 20, 2015, http://w.hybsl.cn/article/13 /52285.

150. Lin Mu 林牧, "习仲勋在胡耀邦下台前后" [Xi Zhongxun before and after Hu Yaobang stepped down], HYBSL, February 16, 2013, http://w.hybsl.cn/article/13 /34498 (hereafter cited as Lin Mu, "Hu Yaobang and Xi Zhongxun").

151. Zhang Shu 张曙, "陈云力主清理'三种人'" [Chen Yun strongly advocated getting rid of "three kinds of people"], CCP News Network, June 30, 2015, http:// dangshi.people.com.cn/n/2015/0630/c85037-27228518-3.html.

152. Sheng Ping, *Chronology of Hu Yaobang's Thought,* October 11, 1983, 2:922–923.

153. Deng Xiaoping, "The Party's Urgent Tasks on the Organizational and Ideological Fronts," speech to the Second Plenary Session of the Twelfth CCP Congress, October 12, 1983, https://www.marxists.org/reference/archive/deng-xiaoping/1983 /161.htm (hereafter cited as Deng Xiaoping, "Urgent Tasks").

154. See "中共中央整党工作指导委员会名单" [Central Party consolidation guidance commission name list], http://www.gov.cn/test/2008-06/26/content_1028086 .htm.

155. Deng Xiaoping, "Urgent Tasks."

156. Li Rui, "Last Talk."

157. Li Rui, "Last Talk"; also Wei Jiuming 魏久明, "胡耀邦谈'反对精神污染'" [Hu Yaobang chats about opposing 'spiritual pollution'], *Yanhuang Chunqiu,* June 2008.

158. "Spiritual Ecology," *China News Analysis,* no. 1254, February 12, 1984, 1–8.

159. Zhao Ziyang 赵紫阳, 改革歴史 [History of reform] (New Century Press, 2009) (hereafter cited as Zhao, *History of Reform*), 182.

160. Sheng Ping, *Chronology of Hu Yaobang's Thought,* November 21, 1983, 2:931.

161. Lin Mu, "Hu Yaobang and Xi Zhongxun."

162. Yang Jisheng, *Political Battles,* 224–225.

163. Chen Xiaoya, *People's Movement,* 1:119.

164. Zhao, *Reform History,* 181–182.

165. Hu Yaobang, *Selected Works,* 480.

166. Gao Shangquan 高尚全, "胡耀邦主持起草'中共中央关于经济体制改革的决定'" [Hu Yaobang was in charge of drafting the "Central Committee Decision on Economic Structural Reform"], *Yanhuang Chunqiu,* December 2015; also Shi Binhai 施滨海 and Shi Yijun 史义军, "关于'经济体制改革的决定'起草过程" [On the drafting process for "Decision on Economic Structural Reform"], *Yanhuang Chunqiu,* July 2015 (hereafter cited as Shi and Shi, "Drafting Process").

167. Gao Shangquan, "80年代的国家改委" [The State Structural Reform Commission in the 1980s], Aisixiang Network, July 2, 2020, http://www.aisixiang.com/data/121922.html.

168. Deng Liqun, *Autobiography,* 346.

169. Ma Licheng 马立诚, "胡耀邦的'光彩讲话'" [Hu Yaobang's "Guangcai speech"], HYBSL, June 14, 2016, http://w.hybsl.cn/article/11/109/59534.

170. Shi and Shi, "Drafting Process."

9. Deng's Wrath and Hu's Fall

1. Zhao Ziyang 赵紫阳, 改革历程 [The secret journal of Zhao Ziyang] (New Century Press, 2009) (hereafter cited as Zhao Ziyang, *Secret Journal*), 178.

2. Man Mei 满妹, 思念依然无尽：回忆父亲胡耀邦 [Still endless yearning: Remembering father, Hu Yaobang] (Beijing chubanshe, 2005) (hereafter cited as Man Mei, *Endless Yearning*), 458, 459.

3. See Gao Xin 高新, "胡耀邦犯了中南海大忌" [Hu Yaobang broke a taboo in Zhongnanhai], *ApolloNet,* January 27, 2013, https://tw.aboluowang.com/2013/0127/280721.html.

4. Deng Liqun, 邓力群, 邓力群自述：十二个春秋 [Autobiography: Twelve seasons] (Dafeng, 2006) (hereafter cited as Deng Liqun, *Autobiography*), 356–357.

5. Lu Keng 陸鏗, 回憶與懺悔錄 [A record of memories and regrets] (China Times, 1997), 445–446. The transcript of the interview, 胡耀邦访问记 [A record of the visit to Hu Yaobang], can be found at https://blog.creaders.net/u/3843/201511/240988.html.

6. Ezra F. Vogel, *Deng Xiaoping and the Transformation of China* (Belknap Press of Harvard University Press, 2011), 569, as translated. Sheng Ping 盛平, ed., 胡耀邦思想年谱 [A chronology of Hu Yaobang's thought] (Taide shidai, 2007), 2:1110–1116, 1121 (hereafter cited as Sheng Ping, *Chronology of Hu Yaobang's Thought,* followed by entry date, page number).

7. "中共第十二届历次中央全会" [Plenary meetings of the 12th Congress of the Chinese Communist Party], http://www.gov.cn/test/2007-08/28/content_729805.htm.

8. "Plenary Meetings of the 12th Congress."

9. Sheng Ping, *Chronology of Hu Yaobang's Thought,* September 25, 1985, 2:1144; Deng Liqun, *Autobiography,* 365

10. Sheng Ping, *Chronology of Hu Yaobang's Thought,* September 28, 1985, 2:1146–1147; Deng Liqun, *Autobiography,* 366.

11. Hao Huaiming 郝怀明, "耀邦指导我们起草中央文件" [Hu Yaobang led us in drafting Central documents], *Yanhuang Chunqiu,* November 2005. Also Zheng Bijian 郑必坚, "在胡耀邦同志身边工作的回顾和感言" [Retrospective and testimonial of working beside Comrade Hu Yaobang], *Study Times,* January 25, 2011, https://www.aisixiang.com/data/38603.html.

12. Deng Liqun, *Autobiography,* 399–400; Leng Rong 冷溶 and Wang Zuoling 汪作玲, eds., 邓小平年谱 *Deng Xiaoping Chronology* (Central Literature Publishing House, Beijing, 2004), Vol. 2, September 15, 1986, 2:1138-1139 (hereafter cited as *Chronology of Deng Xiaoping,* date, volume: page); Sheng Ping, *Chronology of Hu Yaobang's Thought,* September 14, 1986, 2:1259–1264.

13. Deng Xiaoping, "Remarks at the Sixth Plenary Session of the Twelfth Central Committee," September 28, 1986, https://dengxiaopingworks.wordpress.com/2013/03/18/remarks-at-the-sixth-plenary-session-of-the-partys-twelfth-central-committee/.

14. Xu Qingquan 徐庆全, "'八老'与1980 年代政治格局" [The 'eight elders' and the political situation in the 1980s], Aisixiang Network, December 23, 2014, http://www.aisixiang.com/data/81722.html.

15. Yang Jisheng 杨继绳, 中国改革年代的政治斗争 [The political battles of China's reform era] (Cosmos Books, 2010) (hereafter cited as Yang Jisheng, *Political Battles*), 316–317.

16. Zhao Ziyang, *Secret Journal,* 187–189. Zhao's role in Hu's downfall is the subject of continuing debate, and his contradictory recollections of key events during the period are not entirely convincing.

17. Chen Xiaoya 陈小雅, 八九民运史 [The history of the '89 people's movement], pt. 1, (Citizen Publishing, 2019) (hereafter cited as Chen Xiaoya, *People's Movement*), 1:130.

18. Sheng Ping, *Chronology of Hu Yaobang's Thought,* May 22, 1986, 2:1211.

19. *Chronology of Deng Xiaoping,* May 25, 1986, 2:1119.

20. Wu Jiaxiang 吴稼祥, 中南海日記 [Zhongnanhai diary] (Mirror Books, 2002) (hereafter cited as Wu Jiaxiang, *Zhongnanhai Diary*), 64.

21. Li Rui 李锐, "冲在改革开放第一线的先锋人物是谁?" [Who stood on the front line of reform?], *Yanhuang Chunqiu,* November 2008.

22. Two versions involve Hu meeting with Deng in his home in 1986, ostensibly to talk about the issue of Deng stepping down at the Thirteenth Congress. However, these versions are dated six months apart and differ on whether Deng raised the issue of Hu succeeding him as chairman of the Central Military Commission or the Central Advisory Commission. Neither is referenced in the *Deng Xiaoping Chronology.*

Sheng Ping's *Chronology of Hu Yaobang's Thought* ("May 1986," 2:1212–1213) dates the meeting sometime in May 1986. Zhao Ziyang (*Secret Journal*, 191) places the conversation in October. Chen Xiaoya (*People's Movement*, 1:124–126) sifts through the details of these accounts but also finds problems with the ambiguity of sources.

23. From *60 Minutes* interview with Deng Xiaoping, September 2, 1986, English transcript at https://china.usc.edu/deng-xiaoping-interview-mike-wallace-60 -minutes-sept-2-1986.

24. Hu Yaobang interview with Katharine Graham, CEO of the *Washington Post*, September 23, 1986, cited in Man Mei, *Remembering Father, Hu Yaobang* vol. 2, (Cosmos Books, 2016), 2:754.

25. Sheng Ping, *Chronology of Hu Yaobang's Thought*, "October," 1986, 2:1286.

26. Gao Yong 高勇, "从来历史非钦定 自有实践验伪真" [Gao Yong: Never in recorded history has practice so proven truth and falsehood], Hu Yaobang Historical Materials Information Network (hereafter HYBSL), April 20, 2010, http:// w.hybsl.cn/article/11/109/19886 (hereafter cited as Gao, "Truth and Falsehood"). Also Sun Changjiang 孙长江, "赵紫阳口述其与胡耀邦的关系" [Zhao Ziyang describes his relations with Hu Yaobang], *Dong Xiang* magazine, May 2006, https://www .secretchina.com/news/gb/2006/05/19/151790.html (hereafter cited as Sun, "On Zhao and Hu").

27. Wu Jiaxiang, "胡耀邦与邓小平矛盾的起因" [The Cause of the Contradiction between Hu Yaobang and Deng Xiaoping], excerpted from *Zhongnanhai Diary*, chapter 12, at https://www.epochtimes.com/gb/2/3/1/n173706.htm; Chen Xiaoya, *People's Movement*, 1:138.

28. Miao Tijun 苗体君 and Dou Chunfang 窦春芳, "叶剑英与胡耀邦的友谊" [The friendship of Ye Jianying and Hu Yaobang], HYBSL, February 13, 2012, http://w.hybsl .cn/article/11/109/28573.

29. Sheng Ping, *Chronology of Hu Yaobang's Thought*, October 29, 1986, 2:1284–1286.

30. Cai Rupeng 蔡如鹏, "求实者陈云" [Chen Yun the realist], *China Newsweek*, July 23, 2015, http://w.hybsl.cn/article/13/53398.

31. Yang Mingwei 杨明伟, "邓小平与李先念陈云 密商'交班'揭胡耀邦辞职内幕" [Deng Xiaoping, Li Xiannian, and Chen Yun secretly discussed a 'handover'; background to Hu Yaobang's resignation], Phoenix Network, December 20, 2012, https://book.ifeng.com/gundong/detail_2012_12/20/20360325_1.shtml, accessed September 26, 2020, URL no longer valid.

32. Chen Xiaoya, *People's Movement*, 1:135.

33. Chen Xiaoya, *People's Movement*, 1:135–136. The five people in the group were Zhao, Hu Qili (representing the Central Secretariat), Tian Jiyun (State Council), Bo Yibo (Central Advisory Commission), and Peng Chong (National People's Congress). Zhao's mishu, Bao Tong, headed the group's administrative staff.

34. Wu, *Zhongnanhai Diary*, 159–160.

35. Wu, *Zhongnanhai Diary*, 190.

36. Yang Jisheng, *Political Battles*, 265.

37. Anon., "'八六学潮'始末" [The whole story of the '86 student demonstrations], anonymous US-based Chinese-language weblog, September 7, 2011, http://program -think.blogspot.com/2011/09/june-fourth-incident-6.html.

38. Wu, *Zhongnanhai Diary*, 198–199.

39. Wu, *Zhongnanhai Diary*, 198–199; Chinese Wikipedia, "八六学潮" [The '86 student demonstrations], https://zh.wikipedia.org/zh-hans/八六学潮.

40. Wu, *Zhongnanhai Diary*, 211–215.

41. Sheng Ping, *Chronology of Hu Yaobang's Thought*, "mid-December," 1986, 2:1296–1297

42. Chen Xiaoya, *People's Movement*, 1:146–153; Yang Jisheng, *Political Battles*, 266–268.

43. Sheng Ping, *Chronology of Hu Yaobang's Thought*, December 27, 1986, 2:1297. Chen Liming, *Biography of Hu Yaobang* (Swindon, 2005), vol. 2, mentions the meeting (2:414), but omits it in the later Beijing-published version. Deng Xiaoping's chronology does not mention it.

44. Deng Xiaoping, "Take a Clear-Cut Stand against Bourgeois Liberalization," December 30, 1986, https://dengxiaopingworks.wordpress.com/2013/03/18/take-a -clear-cut-stand-against-bourgeois-liberalization/.

45. Wu, *Zhongnanhai Diary*, 226–227; Chen Liming, *Biography of Hu Yaobang*, 2:410–411.

46. Sheng Ping, *Chronology of Hu Yaobang's Thought*, December 30, 1986, 2:1297– 1299 (author translation). Also Gao, "Truth and Falsehood."

47. Chen Xiaoya, *People's Movement*, 1:166–167.

48. Chen Xiaoya, *People's Movement*, 1:168–169.

49. Chen, Xiaoya *People's Movement*, 1:169. See also Sheng Ping, *Chronology of Hu Yaobang's Thought*, January 2, 1987, 2:1302.

50. Chen Liming, *Biography of Hu Yaobang*, 2:414–416.

51. *Deng Xiaoping Chronology*, January 4, 1987, 2:1163. Attendees not listed.

52. Zhao Ziyang, *Secret Journal*, 194; Chen Xiaoya, *People's Movement*, 1:174.

53. Chen Xiaoya, *People's Movement*, 1:174–175.

54. Zhao Ziyang, *Secret Journal*, 194.

55. Chen Xiaoya, *People's Movement*, 1:174.

56. Sheng Ping, *Chronology of Hu Yaobang's Thought*, January 6, 1987, 2:1302; Deng Liqun, *Autobiography*, 415.

57. Zhao Ziyang, *Secret Journal*, 195.

58. Sha Yexin 沙叶新, 良心胡耀邦 [The conscience Hu Yaobang] (Eastern Era, 2015).

59. Chen Xiaoya, "'倒胡'生活会" [The 'down with Hu' life meeting], *People's Movement*, 1:174–190.

60. Li Rui 李锐, "耀邦去世前的谈话" [A talk with Yaobang before his death], Aisixiang Network, July 13, 2014, https://www.aisixiang.com/data/20900.html (hereafter cited as Li Rui, "Last Talk").

61. Chen Liming, *Biography of Hu Yaobang,* 2:419–425; Chen Xiaoya, *People's Movement,* 1:175.

62. Deng's text of his long diatribe is highlighted in Deng Liqun, *Autobiography,* 417–443.

63. Chen Xiaoya, *People's Movement,* 1:177.

64. Gao, "Truth and Falsehood."

65. Sun, "On Zhao and Hu."

66. Zhao Ziyang, *Secret Journal,* 198–199.

67. Ruan Ming 阮铭, "邓小平政变 赵紫阳发言尖锐 . . ." [Deng Xiaoping's coup—Zhao Ziyang's sharp remarks . . .], *Aboluowang,* January 15, 2009, http://www.aboluowang.com/2009/0115/116493.html; Deng Liqun *Autobiography,* 445.

68. Chen Xiaoya, *People's Movement,* 1:181–182. Yang, who some said had his eyes set on the Military Commission, circulated his speech to senior PLA officers, but it was so venomous that Deng ordered him to withdraw the document.

69. Chen Xiaoya, *People's Movement,* 1:186.

70. Sheng Ping, *Chronology of Hu Yaobang's Thought,* January 16, 1987, 2:1307.

71. Yang Jisheng 杨继绳, "追忆朱厚泽" [In memory of Zhu Houze], HYBSL, May 10, 2012, http://w.hybsl.cn/article/13/29679 (hereafter cited as Yang Jisheng, "Recalling Zhu Houze").

72. Man Mei, *Endless Yearning,* 473.

73. Deng Liqun, *Autobiography,* 446; Sheng Ping, *Chronology of Hu Yaobang's Thought,* January 1987, 2:1914; Chen Liming, *Biography of Hu Yaobang,* 2:433.

74. Yang Jisheng, "Recalling Zhu Houze."

75. Chen Xiaoya, *People's Movement,* 2:209–211; Zhao Ziyang, *Secret Journal,* 216–217.

76. Wu Jiaxiang, *Zhongnanhai Diary,* 242.

77. Yang Jisheng, "Recalling Zhu Houze."

78. Wu Jiaxiang, *Zhongnanhai Diary,* 301–303.

79. The seven members were all "old cadres": Yang Shangkun, Bo Yibo, Yao Yilin, Wang Zhen, Song Renqiong, Wu Xiuquan, and Gao Yang, most of them closer to Chen than to Deng. See *Deng Xiaoping Chronology,* February 4, 1987, 2:1167.

80. Li Jie 李劼, "论八十年代改革悲剧" [On the tragedy of reform in the 1980s], May 27, 2020, https://yibaochina.com/?p=238621. "Li Jie" is a pseudonym.

81. Sheng Ping, *Chronology of Hu Yaobang's Thought,* "early February" 1987, 2:1317.

82. Sheng Ping, *Chronology of Hu Yaobang's Thought,* "年初" [beginning of the year], 1987, 2:1317; Zhang Liqun, Zhang Ding, Yan Ruping, Tang Fei, and Li Gongtian, *Biography of Hu Yaobang,* vol. 3 (Beijing United Press, 2015), 3:958.

83. Zhang Liqun 张黎群, "胡耀邦最后的二十七个月" [Hu Yaobang's last 27 months], Aisixiang Network, February 27, 2013, www.aisixiang.com/data/61598 .html.

84. Sheng Ping, *Chronology of Hu Yaobang's Thought,* January–February 1987, 2:1316–1317.

85. Deng Liqun, *Autobiography,* 447.

86. Chen Xiaoya, *People's Movement,* 2:215–216.

87. Chen Xiaoya, *People's Movement,* 2:215.

88. Deng Liqun, *Autobiography,* 446–454.

89. Zhao Ziyang, *Secret Journal,* 221–222.

90. Chen Xiaoya, *People's Movement,* 2:217.

91. Zhao Ziyang, *Secret Journal,* 234.

92. Yang Jisheng, *Political Struggles,* 317.

93. Chen Xiaoya, *People's Movement,* 2:218

94. Wu Wei 吴伟, "中共十三大报告起草过程述实" [Relating the facts about the process of drafting the 13th Congress Report], HYBSL, April 28, 2014, http://w.hybsl .cn/article/13/45980.

95. Chen Xiaoya, *People's Movement,* 2:221.

96. Chen Xiaoya, *People's Movement,* 2:219–220.

97. Zhao Ziyang, *Secret Journal,* 233.

98. Yang Jisheng, *Political Struggles,* 287.

99. Jaime FlorCruz, "What Would China Look Like Today Had Zhao Ziyang Survived?," *ChinaFile,* August 18, 2016, https://www.chinafile.com/conversation/what -would-china-look-today-had-zhao-ziyang-survived.

100. Wu Wei, "中共十三大前后的政治体制改革" [China's political system reform before and after the 13th Congress"], *Leader,* December 2011, https://www.aisixiang .com/data/49946.html.

101. Sheng Ping, *Chronology of Hu Yaobang's Thought,* "October 1987," 2:1326.

102. Li Rui, "Last Talk." Also Wang Daming 王大明, "邓小平打桥牌与胡耀邦争冠军" [Deng Xiaoping competed with Hu Yaobang for the bridge championship], *Duowei News,* August 19, 2014, http://wap.sinoca.com/news/china/2014-08-20/357071 .html.

103. Man Mei, *Endless Yearning,* 3–4.

104. Sheng Ping, *Chronology of Hu Yaobang's Thought,* January–February 1988, 2:1335–1337; Liu Chongwen 刘崇文, "胡耀邦和我谈下台前后" [Hu Yaobang and I talked about before and after his ouster], Aisixiang Network, July 2, 2014, https://www.aisixiang.com/data/75989.html (hereafter cited as Liu, "Talks about Ouster").

105. Sheng Ping, *Chronology of Hu Yaobang's Thought,* May 15–19, 1988; "late May" 1988, 2:1338–1339.

106. Gao Gao, *Troika Era,* 280.

107. Chen Xiaoya, *People's Movement,* 2:228–232; Sheng Ping, *Chronology of Hu Yaobang's Thought,* May 19, 1988, 2:1339.

108. Sheng Ping, *Chronology of Hu Yaobang's Thought,* June 1988, 2:1340.

109. Central Leadership Database, "中国共产党大事记" [Major events of the Communist Party of China, 1988], entries for late September, http://cpc.people .com.cn/GB/64162/64164/4416138.html.

110. Sheng Ping, *Chronology of Hu Yaobang's Thought,* September 12, 1988, 2:1346.

111. Chen Xiaoya, *People's Movement,* 2:228–230.

112. Sheng Ping, *Chronology of Hu Yaobang's Thought,* September 26–30, 1988, 2:1348.

113. Zhao Ziyang, *Secret Journal,* 257–261.

114. Sheng Ping, *Chronology of Hu Yaobang's Thought,* November 10–11, 1988, 2:1349.

115. Qian Jiang 钱江, "青山绿水总关情— 胡耀邦游览张家界" [Always caring about the green hills and clear waters: Hu Yaobang goes sightseeing in Zhangjiajie], HYBSL, February 13, 2014, http://w.hybsl.cn/article/11/109/44703, (hereafter cited as Qian, "Sightseeing").

116. Qian, "Sightseeing."

117. Liu, "Talks about Ouster."

118. Sheng Ping, *Chronology of Hu Yaobang's Thought,* "late November," 1988, 2:1356.

119. Deng Liqun, *Autobiography,* 482–484.

120. Sheng Ping, *Chronology of Hu Yaobang's Thought,* "late November," 1988, 2:1356.

121. Sheng Ping, *Chronology of Hu Yaobang's Thought,* "mid-December," 1988, 2:1358.

122. Liu Chongwen, "胡耀邦逝世前半年的心态" [Hu Yaobang's mindset in the half year prior to his death], HYBSL, September 23, 2009, http://w.hybsl.cn/article /11/110/16329, (hereafter cited as Liu Chongwen, "Mindset").

123. Liu Chongwen, "Mindset."

124. Chen Xiaoya, *People's Movement,* 2:238–240.

125. Liu Chongwen, "Mindset."

126. Liu Chongwen, "Mindset."

127. Zheng Zhongbing, ed., *Hu Yaobang Chronological Materials, Long Form* (International Era, 2005), March 20, 1989.

128. Sheng Ping, *Chronology of Hu Yaobang's Thought,* March 26, 1989, 2:1367.

129. Li Rui, "Last Talk." Sheng Ping's *Chronology of Hu Yaobang's Thought* summarizes the key points of Li's article with explanatory notes; see 2:1369–1371.

130. Li Rui, "Last Talk."

131. Man Mei, "My Father Hu Yaobang's Last Seven Days," excerpted from *Endless Yearning,* https://www.sohu.com/a/271037500_100123653.

10. Hu Yaobang and the Fate of Reform

1. Man Mei 满妹, 思念依然无尽: 回忆父亲胡耀邦 [Still endless yearning—Remembering father, Hu Yaobang] (Beijing chubanshe, 2005) (hereafter cited as Man Mei, *Endless Yearning*), 485.

2. Xu Qingquan 徐庆全, "耀邦'脱敏'过程" [The Hu Yaobang 'desensitization' process], Aisixiang Network, September 16, 2014, http://www.aisixiang.com/data/77976.html (hereafter cited as Xu Qingquan, "Desensitizing Hu Yaobang").

3. Anon., "25年前，炎黄春秋 这样诞生在地下室" [25 years ago, *Yanhuang Chunqiu* was born this way in an underground room], *China News Digest,* July 26, 2017, http://hx.cnd.org/2016/07/26/25年前，炎黄春秋》这样诞生在地下室/.

4. Wei Yi 卫毅, "Du Daozheng's Yanhuang: 'True at Both Ends,'" *Southern People Weekly,* November 2, 2011, https://grjs770237233.wordpress.com/2021/11/02/杜导正：两头真的春秋/.

5. Du Daozheng 杜导正, "炎黄春秋的春秋" [The spring and autumn of *Yanhuang Chunqiu*], *Yanhuang Chunqiu,* July 2001.

6. Xu Qingquan, "Desensitizing Hu Yaobang."

7. Xu Qingquan 徐庆全, "文人将军萧克" [The scholar General Xiao Ke], Hu Yaobang Historical Materials Information Network (hereafter HYBSL), November 21, 2013, http://w.hybsl.cn/article/13/42751.

8. Du, "Spring and Autumn."

9. Two volumes of the four-volume set came out in 1999, the other two in 2001. See Zhang Wanjia 张宛佳, "胡耀邦传写作经过" [The process of writing *The Biography of Hu Yaobang*], March 23, 2016, https://www.sinovision.net/home/space/do/blog/uid/31319/id/280831.html (hereafter cited as Zhang Wanjia, "Process of Writing").

10. Zhang Wanjia, "Process of Writing."

11. Man Mei, *Endless Yearning,* 525–526.

12. Joseph Fewsmith, "The Succession That Didn't Happen," *China Quarterly* 173 (March 2003): 1–16.

13. Dimon Liu, "The Chinese Communist Party's Four Instruments of Power," unclassified chapter from "China: The Year 2030," paper written for the Department of Defence, Office of Net Assessment, in 2015, 250–277, cited with permission from the author. Luo Gan and Zhou Yongkang controlled the Political and Legal Commission, Liu Yunshan supervised propaganda, Wang Gang headed the General Office, and He Guoqiang headed the Organization Department.

14. Willy Wo-lap Lam, "Hu Boosts Power as He Scrambles to Maintain Social Stability," *China Brief* 5, no. 19 (September 13, 2005), https://jamestown.org/program/hu-boosts-power-as-he-scrambles-tomaintain-social-stability.

15. Yu Guangyuan 于光远, "揭秘: 周恩来与胡耀邦讣告都少了什么评语?" [Revealing a secret: What honors did Zhou Enlai's and Hu Yaobang's obituaries lack?], *Ta Kung Pao* (Hong Kong), May 29, 2014, http://sinofo.com/m/view.php?aid=12880.

16. Xinhua News Service, "中共中央举行座谈会纪念胡耀邦诞辰90周年" [The CCP Central Committee Holds a Symposium to Commemorate the 90th Anniversary of the Birth of Comrade Hu Yaobang], November 18, 2005, http://news.sina.com .cn/c/2005-11-18/18207477868s.shtml.

17. Xinhua News Service, "曾庆红在纪念胡耀邦诞辰90周年座谈会上的讲话" [Zeng Qinghong Speech at the Forum Commemorating the 90th Anniversary of the Birth of Hu Yaobang], November 18, 2005, http://dangshi.people.com.cn/n/2013 /0412/c85037-21118362.html.

18. Zhang Wanjia, "Process of Writing."

19. Hao Huaiming 郝怀明, "耀邦指导我们起草中央文件" [Yaobang Led Us in Drafting Central Documents], *Yanhuang Chunqiu,* November 2005.

20. Tian Jiyun et al. 田纪云 等, "我们心中的胡耀邦— 纪念胡耀邦同志九十诞辰" [The Hu Yaobang in our hearts—Remembering Comrade Hu Yaobang on his 90th birthday], *Yanhuang Chunqiu,* November 2005, http://w.hybsl.cn/article/11/109 /10277 (hereafter cited as *Yanhuang Chunqiu,* November 2005).

21. Tian Jiyun, "胡耀邦是共产党人的良心" [Hu Yaobang is the conscience of the communists], *Yanhuang Chunqiu,* November 2005.

22. Xu Qingquan, "Desensitizing Hu Yaobang."

23. Hu Qili 胡启立, "我心中的耀邦" [The Yaobang in my heart], *Yanhuang Chunqiu,* December 2005.

24. Ding Xiao 丁小, "胡耀邦纪念网站开通" [Hu Yaobang memorial website opens], Radio Free Asia report, May 17, 2006, https://www.rfa.org/mandarin /yataibaodao/huyaobang-20060517.html.

25. The site's "background and analysis" section, which aggregates historical articles from many mainland magazines and websites, has been particularly valuable as a resource and bellwether for the political climate in China. See HYBSL, http://www .hybsl.cn/.

26. Hu Deping 胡德平, 中國為什麼要改革— 回憶父親胡耀邦 [Why China must reform—Remembering my father Hu Yaobang] (Open Page, 2009).

27. Feng Lanrui 冯兰瑞, "精神文明决议：擦肩而过的遗憾 . . ." [The resolution on spiritual civilization: Regret that it was lightly passed over], *Yanhuang Chunqiu,* March 2009.

28. Li Rui 李锐, "向胡耀邦学习— 胡耀邦传序言," [Learn from Hu Yaobang, preface to *Biography of Hu Yaobang*], *Yanhuang Chunqiu,* April 2009.

29. Willy Wo-lap Lam, "Hu Jintao Picks Core Sixth-Generation Leaders," *China Brief,* May 15, 2009, https://jamestown.org/program/hu-jintao-picks-core-sixth -generation-leaders/; Willy Wo-lap Lam, "Communist Youth League Clique Maintains Clout Despite Congress Setback," *China Brief,* November 30, 2012, https:// jamestown.org/program/communist-youth-league-clique-maintains-clout-despite -congress-setback/.

30. Joseph Fewsmith, "Authoritarian Resilience Revisited," *Journal of Contemporary China* (September 23, 2018): 167–179.

31. Benjamin Kang Lim (Reuters), "Analysis: China's Mission Impossible: A Date for Hu's Military Handover," November 5, 2012, https://www.reuters.com/article/us-china-military/analysis-chinas-mission-impossible-a-date-for-hus-military-handover-idUSBRE8A407020121105. Also Peter Mattis, "Hu Jintao's Doubtful Future on the Central Military Commission," *China Brief,* August 17, 2012, https://jamestown.org/program/hu-jintaos-doubtful-future-on-the-central-military-commission/.

32. "Bo Xilai Scandal: Timeline," *BBC News,* November 11, 2013, https://www.bbc.com/news/world-asia-china-17673505.

33. Cheng Li, "Rule of the Princelings," August 2013, https://www.brookings.edu/articles/rule-of-the-princelings/.

34. Chris Buckley, "Exclusive: China President-in-Waiting Signals Quicker Reform: Sources," Reuters, September 7, 2012, https://www.reuters.com/article/us-china-politics-xi/exclusive-china-president-in-waiting-signals-quicker-reform-sources-idUSBRE8860BI20120907.

35. Edward Wong and Jonathan Ansfield, "Many Urge Next Leader of China to Liberalize," *New York Times,* October 21, 2012, https://www.nytimes.com/2012/10/22/world/asia/many-urge-chinas-next-leader-to-enact-reform.html.

36. Anon., "习近平胡德平政改谈话内幕曝光 18大后或平反胡耀邦" [Xi Jinping–Hu Deping Reform Talks Content Revealed: After 18th Congress He Might Rehabilitate Hu Yaobang], *Epoch Times,* September 26, 2012, http://www.epochtimes.com/gb/12/9/26/n3691507.htm.

37. Xi Jinping 习近平, "恪守宪法原则弘扬宪法精神履行宪法使命 . . ." [Adhere to constitutional principles, carry forward the spirit of the constitution, carry out the constitutional mission . . .], speech delivered December 4, 2012, summarized on Xinhuanet, http://jhsjk.people.cn/article/19791897.

38. *Yanhuang Chunqiu* editorial board, "宪法是政治体制改革的共识" [The Constitution is the consensus of political system reform], *Yanhuang Chunqiu,* January 2, 2013, https://www.bbc.com/zhongwen/simp/chinese_news/2013/01/130104_yanhuang_editorial.

39. Deutsche Welle (Chinese service), "*Yanhuang Chunqiu* Network Closed, the Xi-Li [Keqiang] 'New Deal' Is Being Tested," January 4, 2013, www.dw.de/炎黄春秋网被关闭-习李新政受考验/a-16498907, accessed November 12, 2014, URL no longer valid.

40. Su Renyan 蘇仁彥, "胡耀邦子女與習近平決裂" [Hu Yaobang's Children Break with Xi Jinping], Open Network (Hong Kong), August 10, 2013, https://botanwang.com/node/13284.

41. "Document 9: A *ChinaFile* Translation: How Much Is a Hardline Party Directive Shaping China's Current Political Climate?" November 8, 2013, http://www.chinafile.com/document-9-chinafile-translation.

42. Anon, "关于当前意识形态领域情况的通报" [Briefing on the current situation in the ideological field], https://chinadigitaltimes.net/chinese/2013/08/自由微博-网传9号文件原文/.

43. Luo Ya 骆亚,"胡德平'拼了' 三代常委遭'大革命'警告" [Hu Deping 'Fought' Three Generations of the Standing Committee to Warn of a 'Great Revolution'"], *Epoch Times,* August 12, 2013, http://www.epochtimes.com/gb/13/8/11/n3938662.htm.

44. Hu Deping 胡德平, "破解 旧制度与大革命 之问" [Explaining the question of the old regime and the revolution], http://w.hybsl.cn/article/10/102/39485.

45. Xi Jinping, "言论方面要敢抓敢管敢于亮剑" [On matters of speech, we must dare to grasp, dare to manage, dare to show our swords], delivered August 19, 2013, *China Digital Times,* November 4, 2013, https://chinadigitaltimes.net/chinese/321001 .html.

46. Qiao Long 乔龙,"炎黄春秋 高层掀辞职风波 胡德平尚未承诺任社长" [*Yan-huang Chunqiu* high-level resignation turmoil, Hu Deping has not yet committed to be director], Radio Free Asia exclusive report, November 7, 2014, https://www .rfa.org/mandarin/yataibaodao/meiti/ql2-11072014102954.html.

47. Ding Dong 丁东, "我在 炎黄春秋 的最后一程" [My last journey at *Yanhuang Chunqiu*], *Ming Pao Monthly,* http://hx.cnd.org/2017/01/02/丁东：我在 炎黄春秋 的最后一程/(hereafter cited as Ding, "Last Journey").

48. Ding, "Last Journey."

49. Ding, "Last Journey."

50. Ding, "Last Journey."

51. Yang Yifan 杨一帆, "杜导正发公告 正式宣布 炎黄春秋 停刊" [Du Daozheng issues an announcement formally declaring that *Yanhuang Chunqiu* has ceased publication], *Epoch Times,* July 18, 2016, http://www.epochtimes.com/gb/16/7/18 /n8112434.htm.

52. Jun Mai, "'Leftist Takeover' at Chinese Liberal Leading Light *Yanhuang Chunqiu,*" *South China Morning Post,* August 16, 2016, https://www.scmp.com/news /china/policies-politics/article/2004292/leftist-takeover-chinese-liberal-leading -light-yanhuang.

53. Zhu Honglei 朱洪蕾, "揭秘官方如何纪念已故国家领导人" [Demystifying how officialdom commemorates a deceased national leader], *China News Network,* August 17, 2017, http://news.ifeng.com/a/20170817/51662762_0.shtml.

54. Anon., " 胡德平: 中央对胡耀邦百年诞辰活动已有郑重安排" [Hu Deping: The Center has already made earnest arrangements for Hu Yaobang's 100th birthday activities], *China Youth Online* 中青在线, April 16, 2015, http://news.sina.com.cn/c/2015 -04-16/083731724078.shtml.

55. Anon., "前中共總書記胡耀邦親屬要求'公平結論'" [Former general secretary Hu Yaobang's family demands a 'fair verdict'], Voice of America, April 15, 2015, https://www.voacantonese.com/a/hu-yaobang-will-be-honored-by-the-party -20150415/2719745.html.

56. Wang Haiguang 王海光, "如何研究胡耀邦" [How to study Hu Yaobang], *Yan-huang Chunqiu,* November 2015, https://www.aisixiang.com/data/94126.html.

57. *Global Times* editorial, "历史沉淀之后 留下对胡耀邦敬意" [After history settles, it leaves behind respect for Hu Yaobang], November 18, 2015, http://opinion .huanqiu.com/editorial/2015-11/8000273.html?agt=61, accessed accessed February 28, 2019, URL no longer valid.

58. Video of the ceremony is at http://news.sina.com.cn/c/nd/2015-11-20/doc -ifxkwuwx0254335.shtml.

59. Anon., "习近平在纪念胡耀邦同志诞辰100周年座谈会上的讲话" [Xi Jinping Speaks at the Ceremony Commemorating the 100th Anniversary of Comrade Hu Yaobang's Birth], Xinhuanet, November 20, 2015, http://www.xinhuanet.com/politics /2015-11/20/c_1117214229.htm.

60. Yang Jisheng 杨继绳, "邓胡赵体制自相矛盾注定失败" [Internal contradictions in the Deng-Hu-Zhao system guaranteed its failure], Aboluowang News, March 16, 2015, https://www.aboluowang.com/2015/0316/528630.html.

61. Xu Qingquan 徐庆全, "The 'Eight Elders' and the Political Situation in the 1980s," *Yanhuang Chunqiu,* October 2015.

62. Zheng Zhongbing 郑仲兵, ed., 胡耀邦年谱资料长编 [Hu Yaobang chronological materials, long form] (International Times, 2005), entries for August 18, 19, 1986.

63. Zhao Ziyang 赵紫阳, 赵紫阳, 改革历程 [The secret journal of Zhao Ziyang] (New Century Press, 2009), 257–265.

64. See Robert Suettinger, *Beyond Tiananmen: The Politics of US-China Relations* (Brookings Institution, 2003), chap. 4.

65. Joseph Fewsmith, "The 16th Party Congress: Implications for Understanding Chinese Politics," *China Leadership Monitor* 5 (Winter 2003), https://www .hoover.org/research/16th-party-congress-implications-understanding-chinese -politics.

66. Verna Yu, "Son of Reformer Hu Yaobang Rues Lost Chance for Change, 25 Years after His Father's Death," *South China Morning Post,* April 14, 2014, https://www.scmp.com/news/china/article/1482513/son-reformer-hu-yaobang -rues-lost-chance-change-25-years-after-his-death.

67. Xi Jinping, "習近平「我還能怎麼樣？」的內部談話" [Xi Jinping's 'What Else Can I Do?' Internal Speech], 前哨月刊 [Outpost Monthly], Hong Kong, April 2013, posted online by Aboluowang News, April 25, 2013, http://tw.aboluowang .com/2013/0425/301625.html. *Outpost* was a popular observer of mainland political affairs, but has been discontinued. The Xi speech cannot be verified from other sources but has several indicators of verisimilitude.

68. Jack Goodman, "Has China Lifted 100 Million People out of Poverty?," BBC News, February 28, 2021, https://www.bbc.com/news/56213271.

69. Wang Zhongfang 王仲方, "耀邦与我的两次谈心" [Two heart-to-heart talks between Yaobang and me], *Yanhuang Chunqiu,* July 2005.

ACKNOWLEDGMENTS

This book is the product of a nine-year process of research and drafting and redrafting, much longer than I had anticipated, but satisfying as a learning experience. I am grateful for the assistance I have received from special teachers in my life. To Chong-Do Hah, emeritus professor at Lawrence University, for introducing me to Asian politics and recommending I learn Chinese. To Michel Oksenberg, who introduced me to the importance of researching domestic politics in the PRC. To Roderick MacFarquhar and Ezra Vogel of Harvard University, who encouraged me to write a biography of Hu Yaobang using Chinese-language sources.

I would like to note some things about the sources. As a former employee of the U.S. Intelligence Community and a National Security Council China specialist, I have found my access to archives, publications, and people in the People's Republic of China to be limited, even closed. On research visits to China and Hong Kong, I sought no interviews with family members, friends, or associates of Hu Yaobang, whom I believed would be subjected to unfriendly scrutiny, even harassment, by security authorities because of meeting with me. I relied instead on books, magazines, and most importantly, the flourishing internet in China to obtain firsthand information, memoirs, and in-depth analyses of contemporary historical issues. I was fortunate that the time frame of my inquiry corresponded with a period of unusual openness on the part of several websites and courageous historians. Their work, widely circulated online, provided me with anecdotes, hard facts, and controversial analyses of many of the people and events relevant to my research. And then, beginning in 2016 with the closure of *Yanhuang Chunqiu* magazine and other reformist websites and publications, those sources began to dry up. I found that a large number of online articles from the early phases of my research had been taken offline.

The crackdown on democratic activism in Hong Kong in 2019 likewise caused the closing of several independent publishing houses that were an important source of historical data, relatively free of official PRC interference. The Chinese University of Hong Kong and its affiliated Universities Service Center—long a key resource for contemporary social science research on China—is in the process of being "restructured," which many fear will further reduce access to Chinese-language materials available to outside scholarship.

I wish to thank Allan Song, of the Smith Richardson Foundation, who approved my research project and patiently extended it. Peter Bernstein, my agent, assisted in refining my book proposal and finding suitable publishers. Kathleen McDermott, of Harvard University Press, as well as Aaron Wistar and Stephanie Vyce, skillfully guided me through the unfamiliar territory of bringing a manuscript to publication. Mary Ribesky brought the work to its final form.

Several people read portions of the manuscript and provided invaluable advice on improving it and making it relevant. Of special note are Paul Monk, Shaomin Li, Steven I. Levine, David Shambaugh, Richard MacGregor, and Volker Stanzel. Many have discussed PRC elite politics in general and Hu Yaobang in particular with me, including Wei Jingsheng, Huang Ciping, James Mulvenon, Peter Mattis, Jeffrey Bader, Willy Wo-lap Lam, Ching Cheong, Christopher Buckley, Jamil Anderlini, Demetri Sevastopulo, Mike Forsythe, Dennis Kwok, Andrew Nathan, Joseph Fewsmith, Maochun Yu, Alice Miller, Wu Guoguang, and Minxin Pei.

Notwithstanding the manifold assistance I have received from these people and others, I am aware there are mistakes of many sorts in this work, translation and analysis being chief among them. I alone am responsible for these errors and welcome correction and criticism. As a former US Government employee, I freely make the following statement: "All statements of fact, opinion, or analysis expressed are those of the author and do not reflect the official positions or views of the U.S. Government. Nothing in the contents should be construed as asserting or implying U.S. Government authentication of information or endorsement of the author's views."

One person stands out above all others in supporting this project, from beginning to end. To Dimon Liu—inspiration and muse, collaborator, critic, facilitator, interpreter, friend, devoted spouse, fellow-traveler and celebrated chef—I gratefully dedicate this book, which could not have been done without her.

INDEX